Slasher Films

*An International Filmography,
1960 through 2001*

by KENT BYRON ARMSTRONG

McFarland & Company, Inc., Publishers
Jefferson, North Carolina, and London

The present work is a reprint of the illustrated case bound edition of Slasher Films: An International Filmography, 1960 through 2001, *first published in 2003 by McFarland.*

LIBRARY OF CONGRESS CATALOGUING-IN-PUBLICATION DATA

Armstrong, Kent Byron, 1977–
Slasher films : an international filmography,
1960 through 2001
p.   cm.
Includes index.

ISBN 978-0-7864-4231-7
softcover : 50# alkaline paper ∞

1. Slasher films—Catalogs.   2. Slasher films—History and criticism.
I. Title.
PN1995.9.S554A76   2009   791.43'655—dc21   2003007620

British Library cataloguing data are available

©2003 Kent Byron Armstrong. All rights reserved

No part of this book may be reproduced or transmitted in any form or by any means, electronic or mechanical, including photocopying or recording, or by any information storage and retrieval system, without permission in writing from the publisher.

Manufactured in the United States of America

*McFarland & Company, Inc., Publishers
Box 611, Jefferson, North Carolina 28640
www.mcfarlandpub.com*

To Mary and Rick,
for sharing their love of cinema

Acknowledgments

This book could not have been completed without the tremendous help from Jerry Ohlinger's Movie Material Store, for the wonderful photo stills; and an astounding online supplier of horror films and the like, Shocking Images, for providing me with some terrific, hard-to-find slasher films.

The author would like to offer special thanks to the following people: Jackie, for her kindness and impressive selection of horror films; Ginger, Jeff and Amy, for making a day at work seem like a get-together with friends; Myndie, for graciously letting me use her laptop computer; Justin, the other punk of Punx, for being a great friend throughout the years; my movie-loving aunt and uncle, for helping me put my thoughts and writings into a comprehensible order; Emily, for her support and genuine interest in slashers via thoughtful purchases of cheap DVDs; Mark, still my favorite movie-watching pal, for his brotherly love and uncanny ability to recite obscure bits of cinematic dialogue; and finally to Robin and Mom, both of who have suffered endless hours of listening to one-sided discussions of slasher movies, and both of whose love and harmony are unparalleled.

Contents

Introduction 1

The Films 21

Appendix A: Slasher Directors 353

Appendix B: Slasher Actors and Actresses 355

Appendix C: Slasher Writers 359

Appendix D: Slasher Composers 361

Index 363

Introduction

How is a slasher film defined? The obvious solution is to create a formula for neatly categorizing slasher films; but formulas are uncompromising and too precise — they eliminate too many movies and unwittingly include films that do not fit into the specified genre. Take a look at a couple of the more popular slasher film formulas. One idea deals with a maniac who slashes people to death utilizing a knife or similar weaponry. The problem with this formula is that numerous slasher film killers find countless other ways to exterminate characters. Then there is a formula concerning victims who are all oversexed and salacious teenage females murdered in explicit fashion. This formula is likewise diluted by the fact that many slasher film killers dispose of men and women of all ages using various execution methods.

It is impossible to look at a group of films and define them all by a single list of conditions. One must examine each film and define it on its own terms. Once the idea of formula is jettisoned, it becomes easier to identify the defining characteristics of slasher films. A prototypical slasher film will exhibit a combination of the following: (1) an introductory murder or an event that evokes future murders; (2) a setting that does not inspire terror, but which may be confined; (3) visualized killings and killers; (4) a human or human-like killer; (5) the systematic killing of characters; (6) a theme that connects the murders; and (7) an unhappy, often unresolved, ending.

THE OPENING SCENE

Some slasher films introduce the film (and the killer) with a murder. An apparently insignificant character may be killed simply to provide the audience with an accurate display of the murderer's lethal abilities. Dario Argento's *Phenomena* (1984) begins with the slashing of a tourist. *Hide and Go Shriek* (1987) and George Mihalka's *My Bloody Valentine* (1981) also open with the murders of unknown women. Other films, such as John Carpenter's *Halloween* (1978), Michael A. Simpson's *Sleepaway Camp III: Teenage Wasteland* (1988) and *Edge of the Axe* (1988), commence with a character's death. In *Cutting Class* (1989), the introductory killing turns out to not be a killing at all, as a man is perforated with an arrow but manages to survive in the swamps for an entire week with only a single biscuit. Wes Craven's *Scream* (1996) and many subsequent slashers turned the introductory bloodshed into a gimmick by casting established actors as the characters in the preliminary killings.

Other films begin with a scene that

will eventually incite a slashing revenge. The accidental deaths of young girls in the opening scenes of *Graduation Day* (1981) and *Prom Night* (1980) lead to many homicides throughout the films, much like the incidental shooting of the mother in *The Mutilator* (1983). Argento's *Deep Red* (1975) provides the audience with a teaser of the pre-revenge murder spree during the opening credits. *Slaughter High* (1986) and *Terror Train* (1980) open with elaborate practical jokes played on the unpopular Marty and Kenny, who eventually vent their frustrations in the form of murder. In *The Burning* (1981), people are being killed by a gardener who is still upset over the prefatory fiery prank. At the beginning of Robert Fuest's *The Abominable Dr. Phibes* (1971), Dr. Phibes plays eerie music on his organ before traveling to a victim's house for the preliminary killing. As the film progresses, the viewers learn that not only was this murder actually the second murder committed by Phibes, but it is also the result of a slashing revenge.

Whether it is an introductory killing or a scene establishing the succeeding murderous vengeance, the beginnings of many slasher films undertake the task of letting the audience know they are watching a slasher film. Some movies attempt to do this on title alone, by including words such as "blood" or "massacre" in the titles. Other films employ more creative means, such as the disclaimer at the start of Tobe Hooper's 1974 *The Texas Chainsaw Massacre* (as well as all the sequels) or Saul Bass' splendid slashing credit sequence, along with Bernard Herrmann's famous score, at the beginning of Alfred Hitchcock's *Psycho* (1960).

THIS PLACE DOESN'T SEEM SO BAD

The setting of a slasher film differs from other horror films that rely on terror-inducing locales like haunted houses and rat-infested castles. Attempting to prove that the setting of a particular film is a source of horrific feelings detracts from the centralization of slasher movies, which direct their focus on the people being murdered. The fear and apprehension — the absolute dread and horror — of slasher films lies in the dutiful hands of the murderer, not in the characters' surroundings. No matter where the characters or would-be victims of a slasher film are, the place will seem terrifying for the simple reason that it boasts the presence of a vicious psychopath who thrives on eliminating excessive amounts of people. In other words, slasher films do not focus on the setting, but instead highlight the slashing: The murders, the murderer(s) and the victims.

Most slasher films feature one or more confined settings. These confined areas often function to produce a general sense of claustrophobia or a feeling of not being able to escape from a homicidal deviant. For example, in *My Bloody Valentine* the principal characters are isolated in a mine with a killer in murderous pursuit. However, the murderer dispatches characters before entering the mine, in places such as a kitchen and a laundromat. It is not the settings that are frightening, but the killer, who finds his victims wherever they are. Likewise, in *Intruder* (1988), the murders seem to be contained within the market. But the killer is after all the people on the night crew, and when one worker goes outside to get in her car and drive home, she is stopped and killed.

A confined setting does not necessarily mean that the characters are all trapped inside a minuscule area, like an elevator or an icebox. In some cases, the setting can be as spacious as a camp, which happens to be a very popular resort for slasher film victims, as evidenced by films like *Cheerleader Camp* (1987), *Sleepaway Camp* (1983) and its sequels, Sean S. Cunningham's classic

Michael Myers places a dead Annie (Nancy Loomis) near his sister's headstone in John Carpenter's *Halloween* (1978).

Friday the 13th (1980) and *Bloody Murder* (2000). In *Halloween*, Laurie (Jamie Lee Curtis) escapes from her friend's house after discovering the killer's victims. But even in the open area of her neighborhood, she cannot find safety. Her neighbors ignore her pleas for help, and because she is unable to enter her own house, it seems that Laurie cannot elude Michael, no matter how slowly he walks. In this case, the whole neighborhood is a confined setting. Some slasher films shift the killings from one confined setting to another, as in *Pieces* (1981) and Lamberto Bava's *Body Puzzle* (1991).

Some filmmakers have employed "safe" or joyous settings to inject a touch of irony into their slasher films. Nice, quiet hospitals served as the locales for bloody murders in *Hospital Massacre* (1981) and *Halloween II* (1981), while exercising in a gym in *Killer Workout* (1986) is certainly not good for a person's health. *The Initiation* (1984) shows that malls do not always provide a pleasurable shopping experience, while Tobe Hooper's *The Funhouse* (1981) is anything but fun. Partying evolved into killing in *Slumber Party Massacre* (1982) and *Prom Night*, and a Thanksgiving get-together turns deadly in *Home Sweet Home* (1981).

Visualized Killings and Killers

Rather than simply implying the murders, slasher films often visualize the killings, even as far back as 1960 when Alfred Hitchcock embedded a fear of shower-curtain silhouettes into the cultural mind with *Psycho*; that same year, Mark of Michael Powell's *Peeping Tom* attempted to capture on film the fear generated at the precise moment a person is being murdered. In slasher films, the murders are usually included for the murder itself, and the visualization of the murders is similar to spotlighting the main performer onstage.

The idea of visualization is a very important factor in slasher films. For instance, if a person cannot clearly see the murderer, then the lack of visualization will often result in murder. In *Just Before Dawn* (1980), one of the victims-to-be is a photographer who in one scene is snapping photos of a female friend playfully modeling for him. However, earlier in the film, he had lost his glasses and can now only see a blurry image when someone approaches. He mistakenly believes the person to be his friend, but realizes it is someone else when he is stabbed in the stomach with a machete. The female friend flees into a nearby church (another apparently safe setting). She keeps an eye on the killer, but fails to see the killer's brother standing behind her, now sporting the recently deceased man's glasses. The brother murders her while the other killer snaps a few pictures. In this case, the male victim's ways of visualizing, his camera and his glasses, are both used by the two killers. But he failed to "see" the killer even when he was standing right in front of him.

If the victims-to-be are not inflicted with a deficiency in visualization, then some slasher killers will "de-visualize" the victims. In the film-within-the-film in *Anguish* (1986), the killer is an optometrist who cuts out the eyes of his victims. His first victim is a woman who had earlier visited his office and complained about painful contact lenses. In movies like Umberto Lenzi's *Eyeball* (1974), and for one of the homicides in *Body Puzzle* and *Crawlspace* (1986), the murders take the victims' eyes. In *Eyeball*, the killer is traveling on a sightseeing tour bus. In *Body Puzzle*, the victim is teaching a class for the blind; the killer decides to cut out the eyes of an apparent peeping tom in *Crawlspace*. Similarly, one of the patients in Jess Franco's *Faceless* (1989), Mrs. Sherman, claims to know of the doctor's criminal deeds, and for her knowledge, she receives a syringe in her eye. A victim in Dario Argento's *Four Flies on Grey Velvet* (1971) is not de-visualized; after her death, the authorities get a picture of the last thing she saw by shooting a laser through her detached eyeball, and the picture eventually leads to the killer's identity.

In Brian De Palma's *Body Double* (1984), Jake Scully uses a telescope on a nightly basis to watch his female neighbor Gloria dance seductively. But he literally sees Gloria only a few times. During the multiple dance sequences that Jake finds so enticing, he is unknowingly watching Holly, a hired body double, do her nightly routine. Additionally, Jake sees three different people for what is truly one person. It is not until the end of the film, when Jake is struggling with the killer and the mask is torn off, that he realizes his friend Sam, Gloria's husband, and the evil "Indian" are all the same person. Jake's inability to "see" prevents him from stopping a murder and later nearly causes his own death.

There are many instances in which not recognizing the killer results in murder. Chucky and Jason are frequently mistaken for, respectively, an innocent doll and a joker in a hockey mask. In *Child's Play* (1988), Andy's aunt sends her nephew back to bed in a fit when he is walking around the apartment past bedtime. She impertinently carries Chucky by one arm and puts him in bed with Andy. Later, when the aunt hears noises, she believes it is Andy again, and soon a hammer is thrown, striking her in the face (very close to her eye, in fact). In some of the *Friday the 13th* movies, such as *Part 3* (1982) and

Part VIII: Jason Takes Manhattan (1989), Jason is mistaken for someone else. Ironically, in *Friday the 13th: A New Beginning* (1985), when the man in the hockey mask really *is* someone else, people think he is the bloodthirsty Jason.

In other slasher films, the killer's identity is unknown (to both the audience and the characters within the film) until the movie's conclusion. Often, the murderer turns out to be someone involved with the central characters, leading them and the audience to believe that the killer, like everyone else, was a potential victim. In films like *Happy Birthday to Me* (1981), *School's Out* (2000) and *Urban Legend* (1998), the killer is revealed to be a close friend of the protagonist. The murderer might even be a family member to many of the victims, whether by blood, as in Francis Ford Coppola's *Dementia 13* (1963), or foster care, as in *Mikey* (1991). In these films, the murderer is often right in front of the victims' eyes, but they still cannot see that the person is responsible for the slayings.

The killer's identity may also be hidden behind physical objects that prevent or impair others from recognizing him. For instance, some slasher movies present murderers who wear masks (Michael Myers, Jason Voorhees and Leatherface). For the majority of such masks, the only open part are the eyes, which makes them imperceptible or nearly so, and frequently gives them the appearance of having no eyes, as in Michele Soavi's *Stage Fright* (1987), *My Bloody Valentine*, *Torso* (1973) and Mario Bava's *Blood and Black Lace* (1964). The razor-welding killer in Brian De Palma's *Dressed to Kill* (1980) and the power-drill toting killer in *Body Double* wear dark sunglasses to cover their eyes, while in *Night School* (1981) and *Welcome to Spring Break* (1988), the murderers don motorcycle helmets. In Bob Clark's *Black Christmas* (1974), the only part of the murderer shown is a hand rocking a chair, and shots of a single eye behind the door or in the closet. In Simon Hunter's *Dead of Night* (1999) and William Lustig's *Maniac Cop* (1988), the killers' eyes are only shown in glimpses. In Lucio Fulci's *Murder Rock* (1984), a young girl snaps a few photos of her babysitter, Jill, and manages to get a photograph of the killer, but captures no part of the killer's face. In films like *Don't Open Till Christmas* (1984) and Jess Franco's *Bloody Moon* (1980), victims who have survived an attack from the killer remember, over anything else, the killer's eyes. For good measure, Laurie's defense in *Halloween II* was shooting Michael in his eyes, and Henry stabbed the eyes of Otis.

While the slasher film killer may be hard to recognize, the killings themselves are often relentless visualizations of the victims. In Dario Argento's *The Bird with the Crystal Plumage* (1969), the killer photographs the victims before the murders occur. In another Argento movie, *Tenebrae* (1982), the victims are photographed after the murders. The killer videotapes his work in progress in *Video Murders* (1987); the murderer in *The Slasher* (1972) photographs the corpses. The killer in *Peeping Tom* photographs his victims at the moment of their demise. A character in *Cheerleader Camp* incessantly carries a video camera, and when jokingly videotaping himself during a call of nature, he inadvertently records his own murder. In *Cutting Class*, a victim's head is repeatedly slammed into a copy machine, which photocopies the killing, much like in *Psycho Cop 2* (1994), in which the crazed police officer faxes copies of a recently deceased person. In *Henry: Portrait of a Serial Killer*, the audience watches with Henry and Otis as they view a videotape of the murder of a family. After the videotape ends, Otis rewinds the tape and tells Henry: "I wanna see it again."

The visualizations of murder are consistently present throughout slasher films. In *Eyes of Laura Mars* (1978), the title character is a photographer plagued with visions of murder. These visions are of actual murders from the perspective of the killer, and in one intriguing scene, the killer pursues Laura — allowing her to watch herself flee for her life (almost as if she were looking through the viewfinder of a camera and photographing herself). In Argento's *Opera* (1987), the killer tapes pins under the protagonist's eyes, which prevents her from shutting her eyelids, and forces her to witness the killings.

In other slasher films, this endless cycle of visualization acquaints itself in a semi-parodic manner by showing films-within-films. *Anguish* is set almost entirely within a movie theater, packed with an audience watching a slasher film. And even in the film-within-the-film, *The Mommy*, the killer goes to a movie theater. Similarly, in Lamberto Bava's *A Blade in the Dark* (1983), Bruno is residing in a villa, composing a score for a horror film. The homicidal character in this film-within-the-film is based in part upon the same woman who once stayed at the villa and is killing all of Bruno's visitors (people who know her secret).

The murders of *Drive-In Massacre* (1976) take place at a drive-in theater, while the killer in *New Year's Evil* (1981) takes refuge at a drive-in when eluding a biker gang (in the background, a trailer for Herschell Gordon Lewis' 1963 *Blood Feast* is being shown on the big screen). In *Scream 2* (1997), the film-within-the-film, *Stab*, is a dramatization of the incidents from the first film, and by *Scream 3* (2000), the third installment of the *Stab* series is being filmed. The yuppie killer Patrick Bateman (Christian Bale) of *American Psycho* (2000) does his daily workout in front of a television, which at one time is shown playing *The Texas Chainsaw Massacre*, a film that apparently gives him the idea to employ a chainsaw later in the film. *The Last Horror Film* (1984) deals with murders occurring during the Cannes Film Festival, and *Urban Legends: Final Cut* (2000) is about slayings among a group of aspiring film students. Ed, of *Evil Ed* (1995), is an editor of horror films, and is eventually driven into a murderous rampage.

The visualized killing is such a well-established slasher film characteristic that often filmmakers play with the idea of witnessing the murder. In Dario Argento films *The Bird with the Crystal Plumage*, *Tenebrae* and *Trauma* (1992), a character witnesses a murder presented in full view. But in each film, there is something unique about that murder that will eventually lead to the identity of the murderer. In other films, characters are shown as dead (or being "killed") but turn up later as killers (*Scream* and *Scream 3*, *House of Death* [1983] and Mario Bava's *Bay of Blood* [1971].)

VISUALIZED KILLINGS THAT ARE NOT SHOWN

There are instances where implying murder substitutes for actually showing it. In Hitchcock's *Frenzy* (1972), one of the two murders is not visualized. A man (whom the audience knows is a homicidal maniac) leads a woman into his room. The door is shut, and the camera travels backwards to the outside of the apartment complex, leading the viewer to merely speculate as to the circumstances inside. But what the audience sees later is just as vicious and horrifying as a visualized murder would have been, as the murderer must retrieve the cadaver from a potato sack and pry open the gangrene fingers in order to obtain an incriminating broach.

Similarly, the majority of murders in *The Abominable Dr. Phibes* are not visualized at the precise moment of the murder. In one particular scene, Dr. Phibes releases a number of bats (flesh-eating killer bats, apparently) into a man's room. The audience watches as the bats slowly approach the man, but then the camera cuts away and the man is not seen again until after his demise. Dr. Phibes was not even present during the killing and the viewer does not witness the character's death. But later seeing the expression on the dead victim's bloody face is just as horrifying as seeing the murder. What we see is not the visualized murder, but the result of murder, in a thoroughly visualized manner. Although the bats killed the victim, the audience knows that the one truly responsible is the man with a penchant for playing organ music.

In *Phenomena*, a detective who has been beaten and chained to the wall restrains the murderous mother and allows Jennifer to climb out of the pit of dirty water and maggots and flee for her life. But the mother resurfaces at the film's end for one more chance to kill Jennifer. Although what happens to the detective remains unknown, it can be inferred that he was murdered, most likely by the mother. The detective's poor condition when chained to the wall (he even breaks his thumb trying to free himself) functions effectively as a pre-murder visualization. Likewise, in *Friday the 13th: The Final Chapter* (1984), a woman turns, looks at something or someone (presumably Jason), screams in terror and is apparently murdered. But the audience never sees her murdered, and never even sees the result of her murder; the eyes and face of sheer terror are adequate enough. The protagonist in *Stripped to Kill II* (1989) dreams of slicing and killing people, and various bodies (without having witnessed the actual murder) are turning up. In *Henry: Portrait of a Serial Killer*, some past murders committed by Henry are relayed to the audience via the screams of the victims (screams which seem to play in Henry's mind).

Another memorable "unseen visualization" of murder occurs in *The Hitcher* (1986), in which Jim (the driver) is eating French fries and one of the fries turns out to be a severed finger. It is evident that the finger belongs to a recently deceased person, and that the evil hitchhiker is responsible for both the corpse and the detached finger. Without knowing the victim, what the victim looked like or even which finger was taken from which hand, the audience has witnessed a visualized murder via a bloody finger. *Friday the 13th: A New Beginning, Sleepaway Camp II: Unhappy Campers* (1988), *Urban Legend* and *I Still Know What You Did Last Summer* (1998) present bloody and lifeless dead bodies that are discovered without the audience having witnessed the death.

CHOOSE A WEAPON

An essential part of the visualization of the murder is the killer's weapon of choice. It is not unusual for slasher film killers to employ unusual weapons in gruesome ways. People have been killed with boiling water in *My Bloody Valentine* and *Deep Red*. A ball bearing propelled by a slingshot was more than adequate for the boy in *Mikey*. Norman Bates used a shovel in *Psycho II* (1983), and the title killer in *The Stepfather* (1987) bludgeoned a man to death with a piece of plywood. Jason used many weapons aside from the popular machete: a spear in *Friday the 13th, Part 2* (1981), a sleeping bag (he zips a girl inside and slams her against a tree) in *Friday the 13th, Part VII: The New Blood* (1988) and his own hands in *Friday the 13th, Part 3*, in which he squeezed a man's head until the eyes popped out of the sockets. A character was squashed to death in a garage door in *Scream*, while another victim was crushed with a van in *Cheerleader Camp*. The killer used a vise in *Silent Madness* (1984), and a running motorbike wheel (along with a scarf) was a big help for the murderer in *Happy Birthday to Me*. Nearly every victim in *Trauma* was beheaded, and even the killer fell victim to decapitation.

Some slasher film killers pride themselves on the application of a sundry variety of weapons. Chucky is a very efficient killer, using a hammer in *Child's Play* and an assortment of nails in *Bride of Chucky* (1998), and even by simply causing a man to have a heart attack in *Child's Play 3* (1991). If ever there was an award given to the most productive and creative killer, it might go to Angela of the *Sleepaway Camp* movies. Few slasher film killers have committed murders in such a large number of ways. She bludgeoned, burned, mowed, drowned, axed and shot her victims. In the first *Sleepaway Camp*, she penetrated one victim with an arrow, and in the third film, she pulled someone up on a rope and then let the victim drop. In *Sleepaway Camp III*, when Angela's true identity is finally revealed to a police officer, he asks her how she is going to kill him by inquiring about her weapon of choice. Angela, being the polite, soft-spoken serial killer she is, tells him she is going to use a gun and then proceeds to shoot him.

Killings do not always have to involve close interaction between the killer and victim. In Argento's *Phenomena*, the murderer employs a long metal toothpick which enables him to kill standing a few feet away. A car separates the killer and the victim in *Torso*, and the killer shoots someone through a door in *Opera*. In *The Hitcher*, the sanguinary hitchhiker binds a woman's feet to a parked truck, ties her hands to another truck, and drives one of the trucks away (a murder which the murderer obviously cannot even see). Likewise, a victim is kicked into a river in *Just Before Dawn* and kicked from a tall building in Alfred Sole's *Alice, Sweet Alice* (1976). In *Black Christmas*, the killer swings a large hook from across the room to finish off one of the victims. The maniac in James Mallon's *Blood Hook* (1986) hardly had to go anywhere to collect his victims, utilizing a fishing line to hook his prey and simply reel them in.

THE HUMAN (OR HUMAN-LIKE) KILLER

The murderer of a slasher film must be human or at least seem human. This automatically eliminates science fiction and fantasy movies such as *Alien* (1979) and *Predator* (1987), which are both structured like slasher films but with alien creatures responsible for the systematic and visualized killings. This criterion also eliminates vampire films, some of which are also structured like slasher films (*From Dusk Till Dawn* [1995], *The Brides of Dracula* [1960]). Additionally, one must disqualify movies like Lamberto Bava's *Demons* (1985) and Michele Soavi's *The Church* (1989), in which seemingly crazy people are possessed by something supernatural.

Wes Craven's classic *A Nightmare on Elm Street* (1984) cannot be classified as a slasher film because Freddy Krueger has an unfair advantage over slasher killers. His supernatural powers enable him to murder characters without even being visible; in one scene, one character witnesses another forced up the wall and ceiling while claws are digging into her body. In many other aspects, *A Nightmare on Elm Street* is a prototypical slasher film.

In "seeming human," a killer might appear to have supernatural qualities but still murder his victims like a human being. Michael Myers in the *Halloween* movies appears virtually indestructible. Through all of the plotlines of the *Halloween* series, it seems that Michael cannot be killed, leading Dr. Loomis to claim

Michael "is not human." But Michael certainly appears human, and he murders people like a human being, employing various stabbings and strangulations. Therefore, the *Halloween* films are slasher films, with the exception of the installment, *Halloween III: Season of the Witch* (1983) in which Michael Myers does not appear. Naturally, Chucky from the *Child's Play* movies is supernatural since he is a living doll with the soul of a serial killer. But Chucky, like Michael, must kill like a human. While Chucky does have an advantage over other slasher killers with his ability to pose as an actual doll and trick people who do not believe in animated dolls that murder people, the fact that he is shorter than a young child is disadvantageous. Additionally, his sole supernatural power is his ability to transport his soul into other things, which he has up to this point only achieved successfully with the Good Guy doll Chucky.

There are some killers who, although human, seem limited in characteristics that many humans have. And the fact that a number of slasher film killers are disguised in masks or don't speak makes them seem even less human. But it could be stated that the more human the killer, the more frightening — a concept that is frequently associated with slasher films. While Michael Myers seems like an inhuman killing machine, he is indeed a human being. His apparent rejection of human emotion makes him seem all the more malicious.

Other slasher films, however, present murderers who seem as human as the victims. In *The Abominable Dr. Phibes*, the doctor exits a room and, just before leaving, returns to gaze upon a hanging picture. He then turns and offers the picture's owner a look of aversion. Of course, the owner is a fresh and pasty white corpse, who only moments before had been completely drained of blood by Phibes (and whose blood was carefully packaged in jars sitting directly under the very picture that the doctor finds so detestable). It is an effective scene that humanizes Phibes while reminding the viewer how disturbed he is. In *Scream*, both of the killers seem very human. They are two ordinary high school students, and considering that many of the one-dimensional characters are interchangeable, the killers are just as obnoxious and irritating as the people they are systematically eliminating. The two *Just Before Dawn* killers seem to be nothing more than emotionless animals, until it is discovered that they are brothers who have a family willing to protect them.

But Who Is the Killer?

The killer of a slasher film can be anyone. People often wrongly assume that slasher film murderers are sexually disturbed and wickedly demented deviants, much like Norman from *Psycho*, or members of a completely twisted family, like the familial household of *The Texas Chainsaw Massacre*. But slasher films have offered an array of vicious, homicidal maniacs who feed on mayhem and flourish by spilling the blood of others. There are weird men who kill in *Open House* (1987) and *The Mutilator* and weird women who kill in *The Final Terror* (1983) and *Deep Red*. Age is not a factor, as evidenced by the elderly male murderers in *Blood Hook* and *Silent Night, Bloody Night* (1973) and the elderly female murderer in *Alice, Sweet Alice*. There are even pre-adolescent killers, like the youngsters in *Bloody Birthday* (1981) and the boy in *Mikey*, in which Brian Bonsall of the TV series *Family Ties* killed other families. Then there are yuppie killers, like the murderers of *April Fool's Day* (1986), *Blood Rage* (1983) and *American Psycho*. Even priests have become murderous, as shown in *Welcome to Spring Break*. At the conclusion of the first *Sleepaway*

Camp, the murderer is discovered to be not only a young child, but both male and female.

Not all slasher films feature only one murderer. In movies like *Scream* and *Scream 2*, there are two killers, but throughout the film, it is made to look like a single murderer. Furthermore, there is one murderer who has instigated the killings, while the other murderer is a second-hand man, only present for the novelty of having two killers. In *Tenebrae*, there are two killers, but they do not cooperate with one another. In fact, one begins his own murder spree by murdering the preliminary killer. Likewise, there are two conflicting murderers in Duccio Tessari's *Bloodstained Butterfly* (1971). Mario Bava's *Bay of Blood* contains several murderers, each killing for different reasons and eventually killing one another. In *The Texas Chainsaw Massacre*, the family could be amalgamated and considered a single killer, although Leatherface actually does commit the murders alone.

The idea that the murderer is an outcast or a pariah of society is not always true. Patrick Bateman of *American Psycho* is a good example of a yuppie killer who is very well-connected in society. But in a number of slasher films, the identity of the killer remains a mystery until the end, which is why the pariah is generally not the killer; it is someone within the film's character clique. In films like *The Dorm That Dripped Blood* (1981), *Urban Legend* and *Sisters of Death* (1978), the murders are at one point made to look as if they have been committed by an outcast, when the real killer is one of the peers.

Despite the occasional argument to the contrary, viewers need not identify with the malevolent murderer of a slasher film. The killers in slasher pictures are simply the people performing the slayings in the film. The killer may be female or male, old or young, moronic (*The Slumber Party Massacre*) or highly intelligent (*Tenebrae*), mute (*Silent Madness*) or even a killer that sounds like a duck (Lucio Fulci's 1982 offering, *The New York Ripper*). Every killer signifies the same thing: the person responsible for the murder(s).

Of course, a number of slasher films do manipulate the camera's point of view, coercing the audience in sharing the perspective with the murderer. But because the viewers are pushed to the front row in seeing a character's death, it does not mean that they must also co-exist with the killer. The audience witnesses a murder in full view, as close as the killer, but without the ability to stop it and with no control. If anything, this witnessing of murder distances the audience from the killer, rather than forcing people to associate themselves with a homicidal maniac. This seems especially true when dealing with unemotional, seemingly inhuman killers like Michael Myers and the unknown maniac in *The Town That Dreaded Sundown* (1976), and killers that are uncomfortably erratic, like the hog-loving Buddy of *Slaughterhouse* (1987).

Who Are the Victims?

Any character who makes an appearance in a slasher film is a potential victim. The only qualification is to be present when the killer is around. Victims often function as suspects initially. In *Slumber Party Massacre III* (1990), an eerie man sits and watches the female friends during the pre-terrorization exposition scenes and even manages to weasel his way into the basement, only to turn up much later in the film as a victim of the maniac. There is a weird janitor in *Prom Night* and a peculiar man in *The Dorm That Dripped Blood* who are both, at least at one point in the film, suspected of the murders due to their overly suspicious behavior. At one point in *Drive-In Massacre*, the cops are staking out the drive-in, keeping an eye on a suspicious man they'd questioned earlier. The killer decides that night to murder not only a fresh victim, but the police officers' only suspect.

A surprising number of slasher films feature victims that are students and/or yuppies. *Black Christmas*, *Sorority House Massacre* (1986) and *Rush Week* (1989) focus on sorority and fraternity houses, while in *The Initiation* and *Sisters of Death*, the protagonists are being initiated into a sorority. The characters of *Scream 2* all seem to live in a fraternity or sorority, while *The Dorm That Dripped Blood*, *Final Exam* (1981) and *Urban Legend* are also set on campuses. In these campus-set slasher films, the characters are often shown partying or having a get-together, which makes it very easy for the killer to clear out some victims, like the effortless bathroom murder in *Urban Legend*. Other slasher pictures have been set at schools (*Cutting Class*, *Slaughter High*, *Prom Night* and *Graduation Day*), and these films frequently concentrate on the more popular, yuppie students. In *Cutting Class*, two of the characters (one is a cheerleader) are killed during a basketball game (right under the bleachers). In *Prom Night*, all five of the people murdered are killed during the prom, and in the final death, a bloody head rolls down the walkway while a crowd of students awaits the prom king and queen.

April Fool's Day is about a group of yuppie college students who are invited to a remote island to spend their spring break weekend. They are frequently shown acting feeblemindedly and playing pranks on one another, which, in addition to establishing the April Fool's theme, makes each character look like a spoiled rich kid. In fact, one of the characters, Arch, describes many slasher films when he states, with a smirk on his face: "Here we are — privileged, independent, the hope for the future right at this table. Not one of us knows what we're gonna do with the rest of our lives." Such a carefree attitude from "independent" and "privileged" yuppies is generally what slasher films are against.

When Bret Easton Ellis' novel *American Psycho* was published in 1991, it sparked much controversy over its violent context and apparent misogynistic undertone. But many critics, whether a supporter or adversary, cited the book as a social satire, lampooning the role of the yuppie in the 1980s since the murderer, Patrick Bateman, was a seemingly normal, rich, upper-class white-collar businessman. Film critics picked up on this and recycled the argument when Mary Harron's terrific adaptation was released in 2000.

It is interesting to note that while many *American Psycho* film reviews focused on the satirical angle, they often failed to even mention the film's violent murder sequences (some even complimented the film for being less violent than the book). A number of slasher films involve what can be considered the murder of yuppies, in the same vein of satire as both the movie *American Psycho* and its source text. However, some critics have focused solely on the violent murder sequences and failed to recognize the yuppie parody.

Another common slasher film misconception is that the victim's sexual promiscuity is related to the killer's motive. *Black Christmas* is set predominantly within a sorority house loaded with promiscuous teenagers. In fact, the protagonist, Jess, is pregnant, and her suspiciously demonic boyfriend is the soon-to-be father. However, the six people murdered in the course of the film are not all promiscuous teenagers: victim #1, who is murdered by asphyxiation, is the sorority house's solitary virgin (according to one of the sisters); victim #2 is the sorority's housemother, a foul-mouthed, booze-chugging woman, killed when accidentally coming upon the body of the aforementioned victim in the attic; victim #3 is the only established promiscuous sorority girl, murdered while sleeping; victim #5 is a policeman, apparently killed while sitting in his car, and whose murder is not visualized; victim #4 is another seemingly innocent sorority girl, killed after discovering victim #3, and whose murder is also not shown; victim #6 is Jess' questionably evil-eyed boyfriend and is killed by Jess herself, who incorrectly believes him to be the obscene phone caller and killer of her two friends victim #3 and victim #4.

As these descriptions show, the mysterious killer murdered five of the six people, apparently because they discovered other corpses. The first girl killed was murdered while in her room, completely dressed and not even preparing to change her clothes or take an early evening shower or anything that can be considered sexualized. The only victim presented in any sort of sexual manner is #3, who was killed in her bed (although she was sleeping).

In slasher films, sexuality is present because humans are sexual; it does not present itself through the murders. This is why killers are both male and female, and it explains why sexuality is present throughout, both preceding the killings and afterwards. Furthermore, it is why, despite the misconceptions, the murders are not restricted to the sexually liberated.

In *Cutting Class*, there are only two females killed: a cheerleader and the principal. The others killed are a basketball coach, a math teacher, an art teacher, a male student and the killer himself. (There is also an attempt on the life of the protagonist's father near the film's beginning.) The only characters shown as being sexually liberated are the cheerleader and her male friend, who sneak under the bleachers during a basketball game, presumably to make out. The three teachers and principal are killed because they angered the killer, and the killer himself is murdered with a hammer in the forehead due to his homicidal deeds.

Nice, "un–sexually liberated" people are constantly killed in slasher pictures like *Black Christmas, Cheerleader Camp*, the first two *Friday the 13th* installments and *Tenebrae*. In the latter film, a girl rejects the advances of a jerk and is subsequently chased by a vicious dog and eventually murdered by the killer for entering his home while trying to escape the angry canine. In addition to *Black Christmas*, established virgins are slain in *Friday the 13th, Part 3, The Burning* and *Prom Night*. And in *Friday the 13th, Part 2* and *The Texas Chainsaw Massacre*, wheelchair-bound males join the list of victims. *Scream* even intentionally plays with the vacuous assumptions of virginal safety in slasher films by presenting a female who has sex and is not murdered, clearly breaking the moronic "rules" of slasher films. Geoffrey Wright's *Cherry Falls* (2000) furthers this with a murderer who concentrates his homicidal urges on virgins.

Just as sexual promiscuity has been overstated as the killer's motive, the same can be said of the victims' guilt. Certainly, there are slasher films like *The Abominable Dr. Phibes* where the victims are guilty (directly or indirectly) of harming the killer. However, there are also numerous slasher films which present victims who, as far as the audience knows, harbor no guilt. Apparently innocent victims include the tourist abandoned by the tour bus in *Phenomena*, a store owner in *Body Puzzle*, a moviegoer kind enough to look for someone in the bathroom in *Anguish* and an abundance of homeless men on the street in *The Driller Killer* (1979). Often, these victims appear only briefly and with minimal character development. Their lack of characterization may contribute to why they seem completely free of guilt.

Even when the victims are connected by guilt, they may share no other characteristics. In *Prom Night*, the killer targets the four students responsible for the death of a young girl years earlier. The potential victims are three females and one male, each with differing personalities and each with different responses to the phone calls from the murderer (although the male does not answer his phone).

The first victim is Kelly, a sexually repressed girl who worries constantly about having sex for the first time with her horny boyfriend. Out of the three who answered the killer's call, she is the only one who is visibly upset by the eerie voice. On the night of the prom, she is alone with her boyfriend, kissing and cuddling and evidently preparing to engage in a sexual liaison. Kelly resists the advances, even though her boyfriend tries to convince her to go further. He then crudely informs Kelly he will find another partner for sex. Left by herself, Kelly's confidence is shattered and she begins to cry. Afterwards, the killer approaches and murders Kelly.

The next victim is Jude. When she answers the phone and hears the killer's voice, Jude remains quite composed, believing the call to be an anonymous obscene caller. On prom night, she and her new boyfriend Slick, head to his van to have sex. Later, when they are smoking a joint in the van, Jude tells Slick: "I'll remember this night for the rest of my life." Suddenly, the van door swings open, Jude falls back and the killer stabs her in the neck with a shard of glass.

Essentially, the victims Kelly and Jude are the opposite of each another in terms of both situation and character. At the time of her murder, Kelly is teary-eyed, very sad, still a virgin and has just had any remaining pride stripped away from her. At the time of her murder, Jude is getting high, very happy, and certainly not a virgin. This example reinforces the point that a character's background and current situation are often of no consequence in a slasher film. If characters stay in the path of the murderer, whether literally or figuratively, then the killer will kill them.

The Systematic Killing of Characters

One of the most notable and perhaps most popular traits of a slasher film is the systematic elimination of characters. In *Halloween*, Michael escapes from the mental institution and spends the next day stalking Laurie and her friends. He murders three of Laurie's pals and a dog before finally going after Laurie. In Michael's case, there was no pattern to his killings. He just killed whoever happened to be alone at the time, and apparently killed whenever it was convenient for him (although *Halloween II* elaborates on his killing pattern to explain that he had targeted Laurie due to an inexplicable sibling rivalry).

This convenience of murder seems to hold true in other slasher films as well. Characters are often killed just to be killed; there appears to be no specific reason for a particular character to be murdered (other than the person just happens to be alone). In certain instances, for example as if the majority of the characters live near one another, the killings might be aimed at a group of people. In *My Bloody Valentine* and *Graduation Day*, the murderers are angry at entire towns, and in *Cheerleader Camp*, the killer is upset with nearly all the cheerleaders at the camp. In other slasher films, the murderers attack gatherings, as in *Scream*, *April Fool's Day* and *Slaughter High*. In all the movies, anyone is up for grabs as a potential victim, and random murders ostensibly result. Any campers in a film like *Friday the 13th* might as well sign their own death warrants. The same is true for dressing like Santa Claus in *Don't Open Till Christmas*, living in a certain apartment complex in *The Toolbox Murders* (1977), playing loud music in *Blood Hook*, being a patient at a particular hospital in *The Surgeon* (1994) or preparing to be a bride in Mario Bava's *Hatchet for the Honeymoon* (1969).

In other cases, the killer specifically selects victims. In *Mommy* (1995), anyone who has crossed Mommy or her daughter (or anyone who might have gathered too much information) is a potential victim. Similarly, in both *The Abominable Dr. Phibes* and *Trauma*, the killers are after a certain group of doctors whom they blame for horrible occurrences. The difference between these two films and a film like *Mommy* in terms of selective victimization is that Dr. Phibes and the murderer in *Trauma* appear to be randomly dispatching characters until the protagonists learn of the murderous rationalizations.

Sometimes, the reasons for even the most inexplicable slasher murders are obvious. In *Alice, Sweet Alice*, innocent little Alice is suspected of killing her little sister and brutally stabbing her aunt. However, the ending reveals that the actual murderer is an elderly woman, who additionally beats Alice's father and tosses him off a building. But why did the old woman commit the murders and vicious stabbings? Well, she was *insane*.

In *Final Exam*, why did the mysterious man drive his van around campus during the day and then, as night fell, proceeded to selectively annihilate all the students he could find? It seems very likely that the man was *insane*.

Many times, the reasons for a murderer's actions are inconsequential and not at all important to the story. Insanity, revenge or a combination of both are the most popular foundations for the killings, and even if such reasoning is determined within the course of the film, it often means nothing. It is similar to what Randy (Jamie Kennedy) says in *Scream*: "Motives are incidental."

With respect to the systematic murder of characters, it is not mandatory for slasher films to be comprised of such a proliferation of murders that it guarantees double digits. In *Body Double*, there is only one murder (aside from the killer's death, which is the result of the killer's dog inadvertently pushing the both of them into a reservoir). Yet, this single murder can still be perceived as systematic because it is the central point of the film. All the events in the first half of the film — Jake finding a place to stay after his wife has had an affair, the invitation to stay at Sam's place, Jake spying on his neighbor — lead to Jake witnessing his neighbor's murder. Likewise, the events in the second half focus on Jake's attempts to solve the mysterious crime by locating a body double that proves he had been set up as the witness. Essentially, the action and structure of the film, both before and after the murder, revolve around the solitary slaying.

Much like *Body Double*, Hitchcock's *Psycho* presents only two murders for the audience: The murder of Marion Crane and the murder of the detective, Milton Arbogast. But there are 30 or 40 minutes of screen time before the first murder of Marion. Again, the scenes without murder act as a preamble to the murder and mayhem that will ostensibly follow. Marion's flight to escape the consequences of her embezzlement results in a much more virulent judgment by the hands of Norman Bates and "his mother." Similarly, Kate Miller of *Dressed to Kill* is murdered after having an extra-marital affair with a complete stranger, an affair that takes place following the establishment of a insecure marriage and with a mysterious encounter in an art museum.

Whether the systematic killings result in one corpse or a dozen, it is the location of the dead bodies that often determines whether other characters know a killer is on the loose. The killer essentially leaves his calling card if he leaves corpses lying all over the place or poses his victims for others to see, like the killer in *Stage Fright*, who literally poses all of his victims on stage. However, some of the brighter murderers hide their victims so well that the corpses are never discovered during the course of the movie.

In Brian De Palma's *Sisters* (1973), the first man murdered, Phil, is hidden inside a foldaway couch near the beginning, and his body is never recovered from the couch (although a private investigator knows where it is). Phil's undiscovered corpse, however, is effective in terms of the film's theme. Grace Collier (Jennifer Salt) witnesses Phil's murder from her apartment, but she and two police officers enter the apartment where Phil was murdered, and they cannot find his corpse. Without a body, of course, there is no murder, which allows the killer to kill *more* people.

The first two people murdered in *Black Christmas* are hidden in the attic, where the killer continually hides out, and they are never found. In fact, during the entire film, no character even knows they are dead: One is considered missing, while the other is thought to be gone for the holidays. Because the corpses are undiscovered, it allows for the employment of the classic suspense tactic of letting the audience know something that the film's characters do not. Consequently, Jess believes she is safe inside the sorority house, when the audience knows that it might be best for her to be anywhere else.

In *Sleepaway Camp III*, the camp is split into three parties. Angela, the evil killer, goes from campsite to campsite, killing each and every camper, without a single person aware of her actions. The final two campers, who have been wrapped up in their innocent romance, learn of their dead fellow campers when the film is nearly over. Likewise, Natalie, of *Urban Legend*, is present during the second and third murders of the movie. However, the other characters ignore her and persist in believing one is gone for the weekend and the other committed suicide. The former's corpse is not discovered until the film's end (although Natalie saw it when it landed on a car that she was trying to escape in).

Interestingly, in some slasher films, the actual discovery of the corpse is not an issue because no one ever mentions the victim following the murder. In *My Bloody Valentine*, a character is murdered at the beginning but is never spoken of by other characters, and as far as the audience knows, the body remains undiscovered. Similarly, in *The Burning* and *Hide and Go Shriek*, characters are murdered in the initial scenes of the film and are never referred to by anyone for the remainder of the movie.

THEMATIC MURDERS

A unique characteristic of slasher films is that the murders may be tied to a theme. This "theme" may be a weapon(s), use of a disguise, a locale or, most notably, a holiday. For example, the killer in *The Texas Chainsaw Massacre* employed a chainsaw as his weapon of choice. Other "thematic" weapons include the tools in *The Toolbox Murders*, the fishing line in *Blood Hook*, the hook in *I Know What You Did Last Summer* (1997), the movie theater props in *Popcorn* (1991), the drill in *The Driller Killer*, the lawnmower in *Wacko* (1981) and track-and-field–related weapons (e.g., a football with an attached blade) in *Graduation Day*. Some slasher films even have titles that describe the murderer's choice weapon, like *Nail Gun Massacre* (1985) and *Edge of the Axe*. Of course, titles can be misleading. In *Hatchet for the Honeymoon*, a cleaver is most often employed (as the killer himself says, "I must go on wielding the cleaver. It's most annoying!"). Sometimes, the choice of weapon contributes a little thematic irony. In *Wacko*, the lawnmower mows down people instead of grass, and the fishing lure from *Blood Hook* is used to hook people instead of fish.

Another slasher film theme is the employment of a disguise to hide the murderer's face. The intent may be to shield the killer's identity, as in *Scream*, or it may be a stylistic preference, such as the spray-painted Captain Kirk mask worn by Michael in *Halloween*. Some films add an ironic touch by having murderous people dress as lovable characters. A jester costume was employed in *Slaughter High*, the young Michael Myers wore a clown mask in *Halloween* and the killer dressed up like jolly St. Nicholas in *Silent Night, Deadly Night* (1984). In the *Scream* movies, the killers wears a "screaming mask," when it is the victim who is often screaming.

The locale of the murders may also be the "theme" that connects them. Examples include the camps in *The Burning*, *Cheerleader Camp* and *Friday the 13th*, the movie theater in *Popcorn*, the theater in *Stage Fright*, the train in *Terror Train* and the hospitals in *Hospital Massacre* and *Slaughter Hotel* (1971)—which takes place in a mental institution, not a hotel.

A number of slasher films have featured slayings set during, or thematically induced by, holidays. In some instances, the setting may be used solely as a gimmick. *My Bloody Valentine* takes place near Valentine's Day, and the killer sends bloody hearts packaged within heart-shaped boxes. However, the majority of the film is set within a mine shaft. The murderer is upset with the town over a horrible incident involving his father that occurred on Valentine's Day only as a happenstance. Similarly, the killings in *Hospital Massacre* were set around Valentine's Day for no particular reason. The holiday's theme is not incorporated into the plot.

Christmas has been treated as both a gimmick and as a setting relevant to storyline. *Silent Night, Deadly Night* gained notoriety by having its killer dress as Santa Claus. While the idea of Santa Claus murdering people is eerie, it is difficult to get past the fact that the killer is only a weird guy dressed as Santa. Likewise, *Don't Open 'Till Christmas* employs the holiday as a gimmick with its premise of a maniac who only kills people wearing Santa Claus outfits. On the other hand, both *Black Christmas* and *The Dorm That Dripped Blood* incorporate the Yuletide season into their plots. In both films, the killers attack while many students are leaving for the holidays (in the latter film, the victims are students who were kind enough to give up their Christmas vacations to help clean the dormitories).

April Fool's Day cleverly integrated its "holiday" into its homicidal plot. Not only is the film set on April 1, but the would-be victims do not know whether the killings are real or just a series of April Fool's jokes. It is not until the film's conclusion that the surviving characters learn the truth.

John Carpenter made the most successful use of a holiday in *Halloween*. In the spirit of the holiday, Carpenter's film asked the audience: Do you *really* want to be scared? *Halloween* then proceeded to offer the personification of Halloween: a really scary killer who hides behind a creepy mask, never speaks, kills without an agenda and appears to be indestructible. When Laurie refers to Michael Myers as "The Boogey Man," she is equating him with imaginary monsters that haunt the dark closets of childhood.

THE KILLER'S DEMISE ... OR MAYBE NOT

There really is no formula for the fate of the killer in a slasher film. The murderer can be killed in plain sight and actually die, such as in *Tenebrae*. He can apparently die, yet mysteriously disappear at the film's end (possibly with the hopes of appearing in a sequel), like Michael in *Halloween*. The guilty party can avoid detection altogether, such as in *Black Christmas*, *The Town That Dreaded Sundown* and *Drive-In Massacre*, in which the killers' identities or reasons for killing are never known. The killer may even simply be led away by the authorities, as in *The Bird with the Crystal Plumage*. There are also bizarre endings, such as the conclusion to *Maniac* (1980) in which the killer dreams that his victims come back to life and tear him to pieces (as it turns out, he has actually killed himself).

From the murderer's perspective, a very effective conclusion is for him to make other characters believe someone else is responsible for the slayings. By the end of *Cheerleader Camp*, the killer has murdered a number of people and is still able to successfully pin the massacre on someone else. The culprits in *Graduation Day* and *The Dorm That Dripped Blood* convince police officers that other parties are guilty. In both cases, the innocent characters are subsequently shot to death. In *Tenebrae*, the initial killer is murdered so that the new killer can murder whoever he wants and avoid suspicion by leading people to believe the original killer is still killing (the substitute killer has a sound alibi for the first murder, and the initial killer phoned him once when the police were present). And in *Psycho II*, several policemen mistake Meg Tilly as the murderer, and she is killed.

Slasher films rarely have happy endings for two reasons. First, as previously discussed, it is not unusual for the killer to get away with murder. At the end of *Deep Red*, the "killer" is fired upon by the police, chased down, sideswiped by a truck, inadvertently and mercilessly dragged down several streets when his foot gets caught on the vehicle, and dies when a tire crushes his skull. This horrendous death seems even more catastrophic when Argento reveals that the dead man was not the killer. The second reason that for the lack of happy slasher film endings is also an obvious one. How can the surviving characters be happy when several friends, relatives or acquaintances have been brutally murdered? Granted, there may be some happiness in just living through the ordeal, but often the survivors are left with gaping emotional scars. In the conclusion to *Tenebrae*, the killer dies a gruesome death courtesy of a sharp, well-placed piece of metal and survivor Daria Nicolodi is left to close the movie with hysterical screaming.

A Prototypical Slasher Film

When defining a film genre, it may be helpful to compare two films that exhibit most of the genre's characteristics. For the slasher genre, John Carpenter's *Halloween* and Bob Clark's *Black Christmas* serve as excellent prototypes, or best examples.

Halloween opens with a flashback of little Michael's murder of his sister. This scene informs viewers from the beginning that they are watching a slasher film. Both the murder and the murderer are visualized because Carpenter shoots the scene in first-person so that we can see the knife enter the victim's flesh from Michael's perspective. *Black Christmas* also begins with the killer's perspective. The murderer scales the wall of the sorority house, enters through a window in the attic and eventually comes down for the introductory killing.

The setting of *Halloween*, a quiet suburban Illinois town, elicits no apprehension. Laurie and her friends live in a nice, safe neighborhood. In fact, when Laurie temporarily escapes Michael by fleeing from the house, we think she has reached

The killer's first victim, Clare (Lynn Griffin), gazes out the sorority's attic window in Bob Clark's *Black Christmas* (1974).

safety. In *Black Christmas*, the longer Jess stays inside the sorority house, the more terrifying the film becomes. But it is not the sorority house the audience fears; it is the killer residing in the attic. If the audience needs a reminder to fear the murderer and not the confined setting, a police officer, outside of the sorority house and in his car, is slashed to death.

Michael is a human killer, although he seems difficult to kill and Laurie compares him to "The Boogey Man." His motives remain unknown (although that changes in the sequels). He shows no specific interest in murdering characters who are sexually promiscuous (in fact, he pursues the virginal Laurie with more zeal than the sexually active Lynda). By all accounts Michael is an emotionless killing machine who systematically attempts to exterminate Laurie and her friends. The only method to Michael's madness is that he kills exclusively on Halloween. Neither the identity nor the motives of the killer in *Black Christmas* are made known. The victims were a motley assortment, from the sorority housemother to the film's established virgin. Like *Halloween*, the killings can only be connected via the holiday as the murderous backdrop. In the end, the murderer seems inhuman simply because he (or she) had only been shown in glimpses, while speaking and singing in a scratchy, indistinct voice.

At the end of *Halloween*, Laurie appears to have escaped from Michael, but his "dead" body is nowhere to be found. And one has to wonder about her emotional state after being terrorized by a madman with a big knife and experiencing the death of several close friends. *Black Christmas* concludes with Jess killing her boyfriend Peter, believing that he was the murderer. Emotionally distraught, she is left alone to rest. However, the killer is alive and well, still inhabiting the attic, and now the only person in the sorority house with Jess, dismantling any hope for a happy ending.

Halloween and *Black Christmas* are rare examples that exhibit nearly all the characteristics of a slasher film. However, as stated in the beginning of this introduction, there is no set formula for a slasher film. Any film that displays one or more of the characteristics described (without dismantling or neglecting other attributes) may belong in the slasher film genre. The determination must be made on a film-by-film basis.

CATALOGING SLASHER FILMS

This book will present a list of slasher films, complete with major credits, a synopsis and critical opinion for each entry. I selected the films using the slasher film criteria set forth in this introduction. Therefore, you will not find entries for any of the *Nightmare on Elm Street* films, any films with zombies or any film dealing with some kind of supernatural force that drives the murderous developments (which will explain the absence of films from certain series, such as the *Prom Night* movies and the *Slumber Party Massacre* movies). You will find entries for famous slasher films (*Friday the 13th*), cult slasher films (*Faceless*) and foreign slasher films (*Deep Red*). To all the slashers who have slipped through my grasping hands and are consequently absent from the slasher list, I offer my sincerest apologies. Someday, somehow, I will find you.

I have no doubt that some readers will disagree with the films I have chosen or with the content of some of the entries. I welcome all feedback. Please send corrections and recommendations to me in care of my publisher.

Kent Byron Armstrong
March 2003

THE FILMS

The Abominable Dr. Phibes (aka *The Curse of Dr. Phibes*) (1971)

Written by James Whiton and William Goldstein; Directed by Robert Fuest; American International Pictures; 95 min.

Cast: Vincent Price (Doctor Phibes); Joseph Cotten (Doctor Vesalius); Virginia North (Vulnavia); Hugh Griffith (Rabbi); Terry-Thomas (Doctor Longstreet); Peter Jeffrey (Trout); Derek Godfrey (Crow); Norman Jones (Schenley); John Cater (Waverley); Aubrey Woods (Goldsmith); John Laurie (Darrow); Maurice Kaufmann (Doctor Whitecombe); Susan Travers (Nurse Allen); David Hutcheson (Doctor Hedgepath); Edward Burnham (Doctor Dunwoody); Alex Scott (Doctor Hargreaves); Peter Gilmore (Doctor Kitaj); Barbara Keogh (Mrs. Frawley); Sean Bury (Lem); Charles Farrell (Chauffeur); Alan Zipson, Dallas Adams (Police Officials); James Grout (Sergeant); Alister Williamson, Thomas Heathcote, Ian Marter, Julian Frant (Policemen); John Franklyn (Graveyard Attendant); Walter Horsbrugh (Butler)

Crew: Samuel Z. Arkoff, James H. Nicholson (Executive Producers); Basil Kirchin, Jack Nathan (Composers); Norman Warwick (Director of Photography); Tristam Cones (Editor)

A man plays some organ music, and then conducts a clockwork band. A mysterious woman and the man dance, and then head out to the car with a bird cage. They drive to a house and lower the cage into a room from the roof. Inside, a sleeping man awakes to the noise of fluttering wings and passing shadows on the walls. Suddenly there are bats surrounding him, crawling on him and biting his flesh.

The next day, after the butler has discovered the dead man, Inspector Trout is at the crime scene. The man, Doctor Dunwoody, was "literally shredded to death," and it reminds an officer of the death of another surgeon, Doctor Thorton, who had been stung to death by bees and ended up with boils all over his face.

Later, the man in black is at a costume party, speaking with Doctor Hargreaves. The man has constructed a frog mask for Hargreaves, and he places it on and tightens it for the doctor. But unbeknownst to Hargreaves, the mask continues to tighten on its own, and soon he is killed, falling down a flight of stairs in front of the other party guests.

Trout sees a connection with the three murders, since the victims are all doctors, but his boss disagrees. Doctor Longstreet receives a package of a film with dancing ladies, and while watching the movie, the mysterious woman appears. Longstreet is mesmerized while she sits him down, and he hardly notices when the man in black enters and stabs him with a needle. The man drains Longstreet's blood into jars and sits them on a mantle, while his beautiful assistant is outside playing the violin. Meanwhile, Trout visits Doctor Vesalius to tell him about the three murdered doctors who all, at one point or another, worked for the doctor.

At the scene of Longstreet's death, the

police find a necklace which the killer had been placing on wax figures and burning after each death. Trout sees the jeweler who made the necklace, and he tells the inspector it is from a set of ten that he sold to a woman ("She didn't speak much, but she was fashionable!"). He says he believes the inscribed symbol is Hebrew. A rabbi tells Trout the symbol is Hebrew for "blood." He then tells about the ten curses of the pharaohs, including boils, bats, frogs and blood.

Doctor Vesalius finds only one case study in which he and the four doctors worked together. It involved the failed surgery of Victoria Regina Phibes. Her husband Anton Phibes had raced over to see his wife, but his car had gone over a cliff and he was burned to death. Doctor Phibes, the man in black, sits and speaks to a picture of his wife: "Nine killed you. Nine shall die! Nine eternities in doom!"

Doctor Hedgepath is out driving, and he asks his driver to pull over and help a lady at the side of the road. Vulnavia, Phibes' assistant, feigns car trouble, and when the driver steps out of the car, Phibes knocks him out. The doctor then places a machine inside Hedgepath's car. After the doctor is discovered frozen to death, Vesalius' son mentions organist "greats," and says the name Phibes. Upon investigation, Vesalius suspects that Doctor Phibes is not dead. He and Trout go to where Phibes and his wife are buried, and while the ashes inside Phibes' coffin proves nothing, they find Victoria Phibes' coffin empty. Doctor Kitaj is out flying his plane when he is suddenly attacked by rats and subsequently crashes and dies.

The police find Doctor Whitecombe, another doctor who assisted in the infamous surgery, but when leaving Whitecombe's hotel, a brass unicorn head is catapulted through the hotel door, killing Whitecombe. The last remaining members of the surgery team, Vesalius and Nurse Allen, are sealed inside the hospital, surrounded by police officers. However, Phibes has gotten inside dressed as a chef transporting giant pots. He heads to the floor above Nurse Allen's room and drills a hole through the floor. Gooey vegetable substitute is sent through a tube to cover Allen's face, followed by locusts, which consume all the food and manage to chew off all the skin on the woman's face as well. When discovering that Vesalius has a son (the death of the first-born son is one of the curses), Trout quickly sends cops to Vesalius' home, but his son has already been taken.

Doctor Phibes calls Vesalius and tells him where he and the boy are. Vesalius eludes Trout and goes alone, to find his son locked onto an operating table. Phibes tells him a key has been placed inside the boy's chest, and he must retrieve the key within six minutes, or acid will be released unto the boy's face. Phibes pulls off his mask and shows Vesalius' his distorted features. Vesalius manages to free his son in time, and when Vulnavia is running from the officers, the acid spills unto her face. Vesalius and the cops go after Doctor Phibes, but he has gone to sleep with the body of his wife.

Vincent Price gives a wonderful performance as Doctor Phibes, as does Virginia North as his never-speaking assistant. *The Abominable Dr. Phibes* is a gratifying movie experience, with colorful and grotesque murders. Although appearing only in photographs and as a corpse, an uncredited Caroline Munro portrays the deceased Victoria Phibes. Director Fuest also directed episodes for the cult television series *The Avengers* (as well as *The New Avengers*). Virginia North appeared in the Bond film *On Her Majesty's Secret Service* (1969), along with *Avengers* star Diana Rigg.

Alice, Sweet Alice (aka *Communion*; *Holy Terror*) (1976)

Written by Rosemary Ritvo and Alfred Sole; Directed by Alfred Sole; 106 min.
   Cast: Linda Miller (Catherine Spages); Mildred Clinton (Mrs. Tredoni); Paula Sheppard (Alice); Niles McMaster (Dom); Jane Lowry (Aunt Annie Delorenzo); Louisa Horton

(Doctor Whitman); Rudolf Willrich (Father Tom); Michael Hardstark (Detective Spino); Alphonso De Noble (Mr. Alphonso); Gary Allen (Jim Delorenzo); Brooke Shields (Karen Spages); Tom Signorelli (Detective Brennan); Antonino Rocca (Funeral Director); Lillian Roth (Pathologist); Patrick Gorman (Father Pat); Kathy Rich (Angela Delorenzo); Ted Tinling (Detective Cranston); Mary Boylan (Mother Superior); Peter Boschi (Monsignor); Joseph Rossi (Father Joe); Marco Quazzo (Robert Delorenzo); Dick Boccelli (Hotel Clerk); Ronald Willoughby (Funeral Director); Sally Anne Golden (Policewoman); Lucy Hale (Church Soloist); Libby Tennelly (Nun); Maurice Yonowsky, Beth Carlton (Attendants); Drew Roman (Policeman); Antonino Rocca, Michael Weil (Funeral Attendants); Leslie Feigen, M.D. (Doctor)

Crew: Richard K. Rosenberg, Alfred Sole (Producers); Stephen Lawrence (Composer); Edward Salier (Editor)

Catherine Spages and her two young daughters Alice and Karen arrive at the home of Father Tom. While there, Alice asks to go the bathroom, and instead decides to use a mask to spook Mrs. Tredoni, who is cleaning the floors. Father Tom gives Karen a crucifix as a gift, and Alice seems envious.

Later, Karen shows up at the home to tell her mother that Alice has taken her doll. Karen looks for her, and Alice frightens her sister with the mask and threatens to never return her doll if she tells their mother. Back at home, Karen is preparing for her first communion. Alice takes Karen's veil and tries it on, upsetting Karen and agitating her mother. Alice leaves and heads to the basement of the apartment complex, passing by sleazy landlord Mr. Alphonso, who tries to get Alice to go to the store for him.

At the church, before the communion, Alice has not arrived, and Angela, her cousin, is sent to look for her. While alone, Karen is attacked by a figure wearing a yellow raincoat (similar to one worn by both Karen and Alice) and a mask that resembles the one Alice wore. Karen's body is placed inside a box, her crucifix is taken and she is set afire. Alice suddenly appears in the front of the church wearing her sister's veil, and she is ready to take communion. Just as the communion wafer nears Alice, a nun screams at the discovery of Karen. When asked where she was and where she got Karen's veil, Alice says she wanted a communion and she found the veil on the floor. Catherine is told Karen is dead, and as she cries, Alice slips the veil into her pocket.

The cops initially suspect Angela of the murder. Alice's estranged father Dom arrives for Karen's funeral, and it is evident that Annie, Catherine's sister, does not like him. During a discussion in the kitchen, Dom becomes upset when Annie implies that Alice has killed her sister. Dom goes to the police station, where the cops request to speak with Alice, which only agitates Dom further. He telephones Father Tom so that they can talk about his daughter.

At home, Catherine tries to rest, but Annie and Alice have an argument when Alice accidentally knocks over a bottle of milk. "She hates me!" Alice says about her irate aunt. Catherine calms her daughter, and tells her to take the rent money to Mr. Alphonso. Inside the landlord's apartment, Mr. Alphonso tries to force himself on Alice, and she clutches one of his cats by the neck ("You never do that again!"). She heads downstairs with Mr. Alphonso crying for his feline friend, whom Alice has just killed (or so the landlord claims). In the basement, Alice puts on her mask. The figure in the raincoat and mask is creeping near the staircase when Annie is walking down the stairs. Annie is brutally stabbed, and the figure disappears. Alice's aunt manages to crawl outside in the rain, and Catherine quickly runs to her side. Dom and Father Tom arrive, and they speed off to the hospital. Dom stays behind to find Alice, who is in the basement, frightened and saying that she saw Karen.

Annie had cried out Alice's name during the attack, and so the cops believe the girl is the assailant, which Annie confirms, much to the dismay of her sister ("You hate her!" screams Catherine). Alice is given a lie detector test, and when pressed about whether or not she knows who attacked her aunt, she

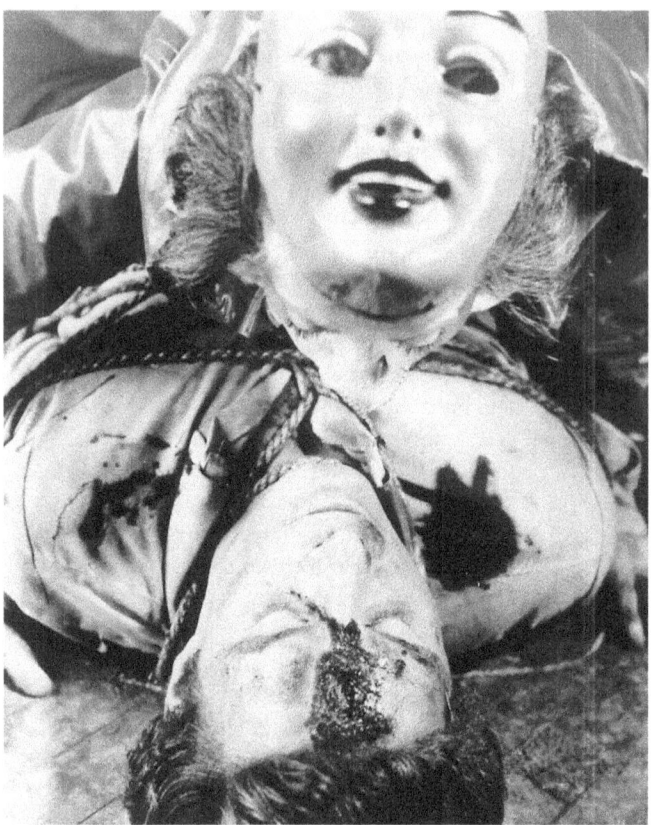

Mrs. Tredoni (Mildred Clinton) lies over Alice's beaten father Dom (Niles McMaster), ready to push him off the building at any moment, in Alfred Sole's *Alice, Sweet Alice* (1976).

says it was Karen. According to the man who gave Alice the test, Alice was not lying about believing her dead sister was accountable. Alice is placed in the Sara Reed Children's Shelter for psychiatric evaluation.

Dom now suspects Angela is the killer. While at the hotel, he receives a call from Angela, telling him to meet her somewhere. He goes there and spots the masked, raincoat-sporting figure, who runs inside a building. He follows the person up a flight of stairs and is stabbed in the shoulder. Still in pursuit, he approaches the figure again and is additionally hit with a brick. After being tied up with rope, Dom is rolled to the edge of a large window. The killer strips off the mask, and Dom sees that Mrs. Tredoni is the murderer. The wounded Dom manages to grasp Karen's crucifix (which Mrs. Tredoni is wearing) with his teeth. In order to retrieve the crucifix, the killer pummels his teeth but is unsuccessful. In frustration, Mrs. Tredoni kicks Dom to his death. She then goes to the church for confession.

Later, Catherine goes to Father Tom's place in search of Dom. Mrs. Tredoni is there, and she eventually tells Catherine that her daughter had been "taken from her," and (while pointing a knife at Catherine) that Mrs. Tredoni, not Catherine, had been sent to watch Father Tom. Alice, in a raincoat and mask, sneaks into the landlord's room while he is sleeping and releases cockroaches inside. Mrs. Tredoni, in her murderous garb, bangs on Catherine's door, but Alice and her mother are gone. Mr. Alphonso awakes and cries when seeing the roaches. He runs out, believes Mrs. Tredoni is Alice, and is stabbed when trying to grab her. Mrs. Tredoni heads to the church, where police officers are waiting, and where Alice hopes to get her first communion.

Father Tom tells the policeman to wait outside, saying of Mrs. Tredoni, "I can handle her. She won't do anything to me." While Mrs. Tredoni and Alice await their communion, Alice is skipped, and Father Tom tells Mrs. Tredoni he cannot give her communion. She pulls a knife from her paper bag and stabs the priest in the neck. As blood pours from the dying Father Tom, Mrs. Tredoni lovingly embraces him. The people are ranting and raving, and Alice, still without her communion, quietly takes Mrs. Tredoni's paper bag and walks away.

Alice, Sweet Alice is a superb film, with a spooky and eerie atmosphere and some brutal and frightening attacks and murders. Actress Linda Miller is the daughter of actor-comedian Jackie Gleason and the mother of actor Jason Patric. Although portraying a 12-year-old, Paula Sheppard, who also appeared in the cult sci-fi film, *Liquid Sky* (1982), was in actuality 19 when the movie was filmed. *Alice, Sweet Alice* was originally released as *Communion* in 1976, and then re-released in 1978 with the *Alice* title when Brooke Shields was becoming popular with *Pretty Baby* (1978). In 1981, it was released again, in an edited form, as *Holy Terror*, when Shields was becoming even more popular with *The Blue Lagoon* (1980) and other films.

Alone in the Dark (1982)

Written and Directed by Jack Sholder; Masada Productions/New Line Cinema; 93 min.

Cast: Jack Palance (Frank Hawkes); Donald Pleasence (Doctor Leo Bain); Martin Landau (Byron "Preacher" Sutcliff); Dwight Schultz (Dan Potter); Erland Van Lidth (Ronald "Fatty" Elster); Deborah Hedwall (Nell Porter); Lee Taylor-Allan (Toni Potter); Phillip Clark (Tom Smith/Skagg); Elizabeth Ward (Lyla Potter); Brent Jennings (Ray Curtis); Gordon Watkins (Detective Barnett); Carol Levy (Bunky); Keith Reddin (Billy); Annie Korzen (Marissa Hall); Lin Shaye (Receptionist at Haven); Dorothy Dorian James (Mom); John Weissman (Bicycle Messenger); Jana Schneider (Spaced-out Girl at Club); Robert Pastner (Customer at Diner); Larry Pine (Doctor Harry Merton); Frederick Coffin (Jim Gable); Mallory Jones (Anchorwoman); Laura Esterman (Woman Voyager); Earl Michael Reid (Cursing Voyager); Paula Raflo (Voyager); Steven Daskawisz (Doctor); Michael Medieros (Club Manager); E.D. Phillips (Jailer); Norman Beim (Cop at Haven); Webster Whinery (Cop at House); Ralph Carrado, Jr. (Looter); The Sic F*cks (Themselves)

Crew: Benni Korzen (Executive Producer); Robert Shaye (Producer); Sara Risher (Associate Producer); Renato Serio (Composer); Joseph Mangine (Director of Photography); Arline Garson (Editor).

Preacher walks into Mom's Diner on a snowy evening, sits and orders his usual. An unattractive fish on a platter is brought to him, and Leo Bain, the chef, comes out from the back and begins talking to him. It starts to rain in the diner, Preacher is hoisted up on chains and Bain swings a blade as Preacher sits up in bed and screams. Doctor Dan Potter arrives at the hospital to see Doctor Leo Bain, and Bain hugs him (although they have never met before). Dan is moving things into his house with his wife Nell and daughter Lyla.

In the hospital at night, Frank Hawkes places his hands near a window, causing a gate to shut and an alarm to go off. The next day, Bain introduces Dan to the patients (Bain calls them "voyagers") from the third floor, including Hawkes, Preacher, Ronald and, not wanting to show his face, John (a.k.a. "The Bleeder"). Dan tells the group that the previous doctor, Harry Merton, had to leave, but that night, Hawkes tells the others that Dan has killed Merton and that, to counterattack his desire to murder them, they will have to kill Dan. Later, Ray tells Dan that the voyagers want to kill him and says that they are "intense." He pushes a button that shuts a steel door to his office, and Ray tells the doctor that electricity is the only thing that separates him from the voyagers.

Outside, Preacher asks Bain for a match and subsequently sets his shirt on fire and swings it at people. Bain whispers to Preacher and calms him, and he tells Dan he threatened to hoist Preacher up and "cut him in half." Ronald finds a letter addressed to Dan and a framed picture of Nell and Lyla. Dan goes to speak with Hawkes about Merton, and Hawkes says he knows the doctor is somewhere in Philadelphia. Dan is with Nell and his visiting sister Toni, on their way to a concert, and Nell lets Toni know why John is named "The Bleeder" (he would get nose bleeds after strangling people). While the Sic F*cks (a band that Dan certainly does not enjoy) are on stage, the electricity goes out, and outside they realize that it is a blackout.

In the hospital, Preacher sits up in bed ("I made the lights go out"). Hawkes puts his hands near the window, and neither the gate nor the alarm are active, and so the four voyagers walk out of their room. Preacher and

Ronald find Ray hiding in a closet, and after Preacher kicks him a couple of times, Ronald picks Ray up and breaks his back. The group walks outside, and Ronald punches through a window, and throws a doctor out. They drive away in his car. Dan finds out about the escaped voyagers and the people they have killed, and the group walk into a store (already packed with looters). They arm themselves. Outside, "The Bleeder," now adorned in a hockey mask, swipes a man with a gardening fork, an act which apparently disturbs the other voyagers so much that they get in the dead man's van and leave "The Bleeder" behind.

The next day, the voyagers torment a bicycle messenger, and when the man mouths off, Hawkes throws the van in reverse and plows into him. Preacher goes to Dan's house (wearing the bicycle messenger's hat), and he tells Nell that he has a telegram for the doctor. Nell offers to take it, but Preacher says he will come back later. Lyla comes home to a vacant house (Nell and Toni have gone to a demonstration against nuclear power), and Ronald is there, claiming to be the babysitter. He suggests going to Lyla's room (it was made clear earlier that Ronald has perverse intentions towards young girls). Nell and Toni are in jail, and Tom lets Nell use his turn at the phone. Dan telephones Bunky the babysitter to check on Lyla, and after Bunky sees Lyla sleeping in her bed, she calls her boyfriend Billy. He arrives, they kiss on the bed for a little bit, and Billy goes to check the closet (Bunky heard a noise). He is pulled under the bed, and a knife is stabbed through the bed several times until Bunky jumps off and to the door (Preacher was under the bed). Ronald grabs her neck and lifts her up.

Nell and Toni return home with Tom and see cops around the house. Lyla is fine but the police do not know about the dead Bunky and Billy. Tom is staying for dinner, and Dan invites Detective Barnett to stay as well. Bain is trying to get hold of Dan on the phone but he is getting no response. Barnett goes outside to investigate a noise, and as the family and Tom watch from a window, a crossbow is fired and Barnett is hit. The group quickly begins making sure all the windows and doors are shut, and they learn that the phone is dead. Toni is too scared to go upstairs (she once had a "breakdown"), and Tom goes instead. Dan looks outside and sees that Barnett's body is gone.

After an arrow is shot into the house, Tom and Dan barricade a door with furniture. Bain is told that Dan's phone line is "out of order." The group hears a car approaching, and they see Bain exit his vehicle. Bain tries to let the family know there is something wrong with their phone, but they yell from the window to get back in his car. Bain decides it is best to talk with the voyagers, and he calls them out. Preacher comes out and cuts Bain, and the doctor runs to his car. Preacher is by the vehicle with an axe ("Vengeance is mine, saith the Lord!"). Tom looks out of the window, and no one is inside Bain's car. Dan tries to scream to the men and let them know that he did not kill Merton, but he receives no reply. Barnett's body is thrown through the window, and the group stacks furniture against it. Toni thinks she sees a window open and a bloody body jump at her, but she has only imagined it ("I'm getting sick again").

There is a fire in the basement, and Nell goes for the fire extinguisher and finds Bunky and Billy in the closet. Dan runs down, knocks out Preacher with the extinguisher and puts the fire out. Upstairs, Ronald appears and runs for the group. Lyla cuts his leg with a knife, and Tom swings a cleaver into his back. Tom then picks up Ronald's baseball bat and beats the cleaver in further, and Roland falls over dead. Dan runs out to get the car, and as Tom embraces Toni inside, blood begins to pour from his nose. Nell realizes who Tom really is, and Tom wraps his hands around Toni's neck. Dan, back inside, grabs Tom, and Lyla hands her mother a knife, which she uses to stab Tom in the stomach. When Preacher comes out from the basement, Dan struggles with him, gets his knife and stabs him and throws him in the basement. As the family gather together for comfort, they notice Hawkes standing there with his crossbow pointed at them ("It's not just us crazy ones who kill"). Suddenly the electricity comes back on, and Hawkes sees Merton interviewed in a news report on television. Evidently upset, he breaks the TV and leaves. Hawkes goes to the club, and a girl whacked out on something talks to him. He points his gun at her, she laughs, and so does Hawkes.

Alone in the Dark is a fun movie with a nice blend of humor and horror. Pleasence is great as the quirky Doctor Bain. Actor Schultz is perhaps best known as the insane Murdock from the hit television series *The A-Team*. Sholder also directed the cult sci-fi film *The Hidden* (1987).

American Psycho (2000)

Written by Guinevere Turner and Mary Harron (from the novel by Bret Easton Ellis); Directed by Mary Harron; Edward R. Pressman Film Corporation/Muse Productions/P.P.S. Films/Quadra Entertainment; 102 min.

Cast: Christian Bale (Patrick Bateman); Justin Theroux (Timothy Bryce); Josh Lucas (Craig McDermott); Bill Sage (David Van Patten); Chloe Sevigny (Jean); Reese Witherspoon (Evelyn Williams); Samantha Mathis (Courtney Rawlinson); Matt Ross (Luis Carruthers); Jared Leto (Paul Allen); Willem Dafoe (Donald Kimball); Cara Seymour (Christie); Guinevere Turner (Elizabeth); Stephen Bogaert (Harold Carnes); Monika Meier (Daisy); Reg. E. Cathey (Homeless Man); Blair Williams, Christina McKay (Waiters); Marie Dame (Victoria); Kelley Harron (Bargirl); Patricia Gage (Mrs. Wolfe); Krista Sutton (Sabrina); Landy Cannon (Man at Pierce & Pierce); Park Bench (Stash); Catherine Black (Vanden); Margaret Ma (Dry Cleaner Woman); Tufford Kennedy (Hamilton); Mark Pawson (Humphrey Rhineback); Jessica Lau (Facialist); Lilette Wiens (Maitre Dí); Glen Marc Silot (Waiter); Charlotte Hunter (Libby); Kiki Buttingnol (Caron); Joyce Korbin (Woman at ATM); Rueben Thompson (Waiter #2); Bryan Renfro (Night Watchman); Ross Gibby (Man Outside Store); Allan McCullough (Man in Stall); Anthony Lemke (Marcus Halberstram); Connie Chen (Gwendolyn Ichiban)

Crew: Michael Paseornek, Jeff Sackman, Joseph Drake (Executive Producers); Edward R. Pressman, Chris Hanley, Christian Halsey Solomon (Producers); Ernie Barbarash, Clifford Streit, Rob Weiss (Co-Producers); John Cale (Composer); Andrzej Sekula (Director of Photography); Andrew Marcus (Editor)

Patrick Bateman and his yuppie pals are dining in an extravagant restaurant. They discuss Paul Allen handling the Fisher account and throw in their platinum credit cards when the check arrives ("Only $570"). Later, at a nightclub, a mildly discourteous bartender tells Patrick he must pay for his drinks with cash, and when she turns her back, Patrick's smile fades and he verbally abuses her and threatens her (which she cannot hear over the loud music).

The next morning, Patrick awakes and, via a voice-over, he discusses his "balanced diet" and "rigorous exercise routine." He describes in great detail all the different lotions and creams he uses to wash and clean himself every day. He heads to work, talks with his secretary Jean and watches TV in his office. Later, Patrick is with his "supposed fiancée" Evelyn in a taxi. Evelyn mentions that Patrick's father owns the company and that she does not understand why Patrick does not quit, and he tells her he "wants to fit in." At the restaurant Espace, the voice-over suggests that Timothy Bryce and Evelyn are having an affair, and Patrick is having an affair with Courtney, who is engaged to Luis.

A woman passes Patrick when he is at a cash machine. He follows the woman to the crosswalk and says hello. The next day, Patrick is arguing with a woman in a laundry about his sheets, which are soaked in red. Patrick invites Courtney to dinner and, unable to make a reservation at Dorsia, the couple go to Barcadia, which Patrick tells the drugged Courtney is Dorsia. In the office, Patrick talks to Paul Allen, who mistakes him for Marcus Halberstram, although Patrick has a "slightly better haircut." Patrick brings out his new business card, and his office pals compare cards. They look at Paul's card ("Oh my God, it even has a watermark"), and Patrick is visibly disturbed.

In a dark alley, Patrick encounters a homeless man. He introduces himself and offers him money, and then he decides instead to stab him and kick his dog a couple of times. At a Christmas party, Patrick talks to Paul about having dinner. Later, they meet at a not-quite-as-popular-as-Dorsia restaurant, Texarkana, and Paul, still believing Patrick is Marcus, mocks Evelyn's boyfriend ("What a dork!"). Patrick and Paul are at Patrick's place, and Patrick puts on a raincoat and brings out an axe. He plays Huey Lewis and the News' "Hip to Be Square" for an inebriated Paul, and finally says, "Hey, Paul!" and swings the axe in his face ("Try making a reservation at Dorsia now!"). He sits, smokes a cigar and heads to Paul's apartment to make it look as if he has taken a trip.

The next day, Detective Donald Kimble visits Patrick in his office. He is investigating Paul's disappearance, and after he asks some questions, Patrick finally gets rid of him by saying he has a lunch meeting with Cliff Huxtable. Patrick picks up a blonde prostitute ("You're Christie") and then calls an escort service. He calls the other woman Sabrina, and he videotapes the three of them having sex while listening to Phil Collins. Later, they ask if they can leave, and Patrick gets a hanger out of his bureau drawer. Afterwards, he sends the bloody and beaten women away.

Luis shows his new business card to Patrick, Van Patten and McDermott as the men are sitting at a table together. Patrick follows him to the bathroom, puts on his leather gloves and wraps his hands around Luis' neck. Luis mistakes the murderous impulse as a sexual advance. Patrick is very upset, and he washes his hands (with his gloves still on) and heads for the door. When Luis asks him where he is going, he responds, "I've got to return some videotapes."

Kimble visits Patrick's office again and asks him if he remembers where he was on the night of Paul's disappearance ("I guess I was probably returning videotapes"). Patrick says he was on a date, which conflicts with Kimble's information. He manages to talk his way out of any more questions, and they agree to meet at a dinner on a later date. Patrick sees Courtney again, and then he goes to a club and does some cocaine with Bryce. He tells a blonde model that he is into murders and executions (Mergers & Acquisitions), and he leaves with her in a taxi. The next day, Patrick is in his office fingering a lock of golden hair, and he invites Jean to dinner when she enters the room. He feigns getting a reservation at Dorsia. That night, Jean is sitting in the living room while Patrick walks around his kitchen and looks at his various weapons. He decides on a nailgun, and he points it at the back of Jean's head, but the telephone rings before he does anything. He finally suggests that Jean leave ("I think if you stay, something bad will happen.... I think I might hurt you").

Patrick is with Kimble at a restaurant. Kimble finally tells them that Paul was not with Marcus that night, because Marcus has an alibi. He was with several of his friends from the office, including Patrick ("Oh right, yeah, of course"). Patrick convinces Christie to spend some more time with him, and they go to Paul's apartment and are joined by Elizabeth. In bed later, Patrick ferociously bites Elizabeth. Wearing nothing but a chainsaw, he chases Christie down the hallway, drops the chainsaw down the spiral staircase and hits her. The next day, in a restaurant, he breaks up with Evelyn by telling her nicely, "You're not terribly important to me." When he stands to leave, and Evelyn asks him where he is going, he says, "I have to return some videotapes."

At night, Patrick passes by a cash machine whose screen reads: "Feed me a stray cat." He gets out his gun and is ready to oblige, when a nearby woman reacts, and Patrick shoots her. Soon Patrick is running from cops, blowing up cop cars and shooting multiple people. He finally makes it to his office, calls his lawyer Harold and confesses to as many murders as he can remember. The next day he goes to Paul's apartment, but it is goes back to his friends and sits at the table. He decides that, even after admitting he wishes to inflict pain upon others, he gains no insight of himself. "This confession has meant nothing."

Mary Harron's *American Psycho* is a sensational adaptation of Bret Easton Ellis' potent and captivating novel. Many of the best lines from the novel appear in the movie due to a thoughtful and intelligent screenplay adaptation from Harron and Guinevere Turner (who appears in the film as Elizabeth), and Bale is absolutely superb in the title role of Patrick Bateman. Harron was originally set to direct the film, and she wanted Bale for the lead role. The studio disagreed and pushed for Leonardo DiCaprio, so Harron left and Oliver Stone took the directing reins. Fortunately, DiCaprio fled from the controversial script and novel, and Stone quickly followed. Harron returned, and she was able to cast Bale.

Patrick Bateman (Christian Bale), the suave serial killer, carries a nail gun to complement his attractive suit and stylish haircut in Mary Harron's *American Psycho* (2000).

completely empty and white-washed, and is being shown to potential renters. He goes to have a drink with his yuppie friends, spots Harold and runs over to talk to him. Harold thinks Patrick's message was a joke, and he keeps calling him Davis. Patrick tells him he is Patrick Bateman and that he killed Paul Allen. Harold says he had dinner with Paul twice in London ten days before. Patrick

Anguish (aka *Angustia*) (1986)

Written and directed by Bigas Lunas; Luna/Pepon Coromina/Samba P.C.; 84 min.

Cast: Zelda Rubinstein (Mother); Michael Lerner (John); Talia Paul (Patty); Angel Jove (Killer); Clara Pastor (Linda); Isabel Garcia Lorca (Caroline); CAST OLD MOVIE *(see synopsis):* Nat Baker (Teaching Doctor); Edward Ledden (Doctor); Gustavo Gili, Antonio Reguerio, Joaquin Ribas (Students); Janet Porter (Laboratory Nurse); Patricia Manget, Merche Gascon

(Nurses at Clinic); Jose M. Chucarro (Boyfriend); Antonella Murgia (Ticket Girl); Josephine Borchaca (Concession Girl); George Pinkley (Laura); Françesc Rabella (Dan); Diane Pinkley (Popcorn Woman); Benito Pocino (Popcorn Husband); Victor Guillen (Sleepy); Evelyn Rosenka (Bathroom Woman); Michael Chandler (Projectionist); Vincente Gil (Taxi Driver); Michael Heat (Inspector); Pedro Vidal, Robert Long, Jaume Ros, Miguel Montfort, Jordi Estivill, Alberto Merelles, Javier Moya, John Garcia (Policemen); CAST NEW MOVIE *(see synopsis)*: Kit Kincannon (Salesman); Tatianna Thauven (Ticket Girl); Joy Blackburn (Concession Girl); Marc Maloney (Elderly Man); Jasmine Parker (Elderly Woman); Jean Paul Soto (Manny); Javier Duran (Moe); Marc Auba (Jack); Randall Stewart (First Murder); Eva Heald (Granny); Rose Sherpac (Granny's Friend); Emi Matias (Hairy Woman); Elisa Crehuet (Ann); Mingo Rafols (Chicano); Maribel Martinez (Hysterical Woman); Gustavo Guarino (Hysterical Husband); Frank Craven (Sleepy); Mario Fernandez (Black Boy); May Vives (Bland Girl); Craig Hill (Doctor at Hospital); Anita Shemanski (Nurse at Hospital); Fiacre O'Rafferty (Projectionist); Maria Richard (Patty's Mother); John Shelly (Patty's Father); Ricardo Azulay (Police Captain); Joe Wolberg (Swat Commander); Steven Brown, Fabia Matas, Mark Parker (Swat); Philip Rodgers, Joan Lloveras, Ignacio Garcia (Medics); Jose Luis Amposta, Eric Pier, Claus Braun, Jorge Ferrer, Jorge Torras, Pep Cuxart, Tito Alvarez, John Heald, Dinky (Policemen); Angelika Thibiant, Elvira Salles, Tatianna Gari, Margarita Borchaca, Julia Carrasco, Maria Guerin (Nurses in Street)

Crew: Andres Coromina, George Ayoub (Executive Producers); Pepon Coromina (Producer); J.M. Pagan (Composer); J.M. Civit (Director of Photography); Tom Sabin (Editor)

John is at home with his mother. While he is playing with the birds in their cages, a bird flies up and around the room, until he manages to catch it and give the bird to his mother. After a doctor shows John and a group of students a collection of eyeballs in jars, John is with a patient, Caroline, trying to put contact lenses in her eyes. John leaves after Caroline makes a comment about his eyes, and a nurse tells her he is sensitive to such comments because John is diabetic and is losing his vision. Caroline continues her complaints, and John's mother seems to "listen" to her through a shell ("You'll be sorry!"). Later John is eating dinner, and Mother plays a spiral on the turntable, takes off John's glasses and relaxes him ("Now you are with Mommy as one"). John visits Caroline's place, telling her he has the correct prescription for her eyes, and they try out the lenses. Caroline seems content, so John apologizes about that morning and slits Caroline's throat. When Caroline's husband sees his dead wife, John throws his scalpel at him and then stabs his stomach. At home, his mother gets a phone call from the hospital. She says that John is not coming back (a conversation which John "hears"). Mother thinks the entire hospital is against John, and John cuts out the husband's eyes.

An audience is shown in a movie theater, watching John and his mother on the big screen in a slasher film called *The Mommy*. Patty is disgusted and frightened by the film, and her friend Linda tells her "it's only a movie." John is called home by Mother, and she comforts him ("All the eyes of the city will be ours"). Patty's eyes are irritated from her contact lenses, and she sees a man who is also rubbing his eyes. Mother begins an eerie trance for John involving spirals, and many people in the theater audience seem dazed by the movie. Patty tells Linda she feels dizzy, and her breathing gets heavier, until finally the trance is over and John stands to leave ("They're going to be very sorry, Mother"). John goes to a movie theater, sits behind a man, stabs him with a screwdriver and cuts out his eyeballs. Patty finally leaves Linda to watch the film alone.

Mother tells John to go for more people in the theater. John sits behind a couple as the woman goes for more popcorn, and he kills the unaccompanied husband. In a bathroom stall, Patty sees a pair of shoes outside the door, and when they are gone, she runs back to the theater and tells Linda the weird man was in the bathroom. Linda points him out, still sitting in his seat. But Patty is convinced a man was in the bathroom and she persuades Linda to go and check. Linda finally agrees and tells Patty to stay to tell her what happens. The woman returns and offers popcorn to her dead husband (which John accepts), and John puts a cloth around her face.

Patty, continually eying the weird man, becomes even more uneasy when he stands up and leaves. Mother tells John to come home, but he says he can "do it alone," and he goes to the bathroom and counts his eyeballs. In the theater lobby, the girl at the concession stand and the girl at the ticket booth are shot and killed, and Linda comes out of the bathroom to see the bodies being dragged away. Linda takes cover in the men's bathroom, where the killer hides the corpses in the stall next to Linda. A woman confronts John (he is in the ladies' room), and he chokes her and loses his glasses in the struggle. Mother continues to plead with John to return home. The killer reloads his gun. The ticket lady enters the bathroom, screams when she sees John hanging over the stall and is swiped with a blade. A boy sitting behind a very anxious Patty asks her if she is okay, and she tells him that her friend has been gone a long time. John goes to the lobby for some popcorn.

The boy asks Patty what her friend's name is, saying that he will go find her. He heads to the bathroom ("Excuse me?") and is shot in the neck as soon as he enters. Linda slips out, passes the dead people and gets outside. The killer and John secure the theater doors, and the killer says, "Don't worry, Mother, I won't leave." Linda stops a man on the sidewalk and tells him there is a murderer in the theater. The woman who was with the helpful boy tells Patty she will be back right, and she is grabbed and killed when she walks past a curtain. The killer grabs Patty and puts the gun to her neck. A little girl finds the results of John's killings, and soon people are screaming in the theater. The man walks with Linda to the theater doors and he goes inside, where he sees secured doors and blood. He runs back out, and the two go to call the police. John grabs a girl hostage, and the killer yells at the onscreen John. A man in the audience stands to confront him, the killer shoots him.

The killer, still holding Patty, stands in front of the screen, shooting members of the panicking audience. The police get inside, cut the movie's sound and tell the killer to let Patty go. He says he has to wait until his mother comes to get him. He shoots at the screen (and lets go of Patty), and is shot and killed. When Patty looks at John on the screen, he addresses her, saying, "I want your eyes, too!" He throws a scalpel out the screen and hits Patty's eye. The police find her screaming hysterically (with no scalpel in her eye), and they get her outside. In the hospital, Linda and Patty's parents are with the girl. Linda tells Patty she will be back tomorrow. In the elevator, Linda is grabbed, and a scalpel is aimed at her throat. John walks into Patty's room with a tray, and she tries to scream. "Like the doctor said, it's all in your imagination. I really don't exist." Patty finally manages to scream.

Anguish has a terrific premise, with real-life events interacting and "playing along" with what is happening onscreen, but the film is not fully realized, with the real-life killer far less interesting than the eyeball-hungry John in *The Mommy*. The closing credits are played on a screen within the film, as the theater audience clears out.

April Fool's Day (1986)

Written by Danilo Bach; Directed by Fred Walton; Paramount Pictures/Hometown Films; 89 min.

Cast: Amy Steel (Kit); Deborah Foreman (Muffy/Buffy); Ken Olandt (Rob); Jay Baker (Harvey); Deborah Goodrich (Nikki); Tom Heaton (Constable Potter/Uncle Frank); Mike Nomad (Buck); Griffin O'Neal (Skip); Leah King Pinsent (Nan); Clayton Rohner (Chaz); Thomas F. Wilson (Arch)

Crew: Frank Mancuso, Jr. (Producer); Charles Bernstein (Composer); Charles Minsky (Director of Photography); Bruce Green (Editor)

In a cellar, Muffy picks up a jack-in-the-box, and thinks back to when she received the birthday gift as a little girl (a tiny alien jumped out and scared her, making others laugh).

A group waits to be picked up by a ferry and transported to Muffy's island for the weekend. Kit, Rob, Nikki, Chaz and Arch are all friends; the rest of the group includes Nan, Harvey/Hal and Muffy's cousin Skip. On the ferry, Skip and Arch play "Stretch" (throwing a switchblade and both trying to stretch for it) until an irritated Arch throws the blade at Skip and hits him in the stomach. Skip falls into the water, and Buck and Rob jump in and see Skip with a trick knife-belt. Skip and Arch laugh at their April Fool's joke. Buck stays in the water and tries to hook the ferry as it comes in, and as the group argues, Buck is hit. He jumps out of the water with a chopped face, and Buck is taken away in a boat, screaming, "They did it!"

Muffy takes the group to the house. That night, the group sits around the dinner table as Skip, still upset over the Buck wounding, stays outside and drinks. Nan sits on a whoopie cushion, and Arch leans back in a breakaway chair. They talk about what they are doing after graduation, and they drink to a toast, each spilling champagne on themselves as Muffy laughs. They retire to their rooms, where Hal finds snipped newspaper articles about people dying in a fog and a fire, Arch finds drug paraphernalia in the bathroom cabinet, and Nikki finds a studded collar with chain. Nan comes out of the shower and, hearing a baby cry, finds a tape recorder playing. A drunken Skip enters the boathouse and is grabbed by someone.

The next day, Kit and Rob find Muffy in the kitchen with her hair astray and acting strangely. The group enjoys the backyard, and Nan tries to chase down Muffy. Rob is still upset (his counselor informed him that he was not serious enough to go to med school); he and Kit head to the boathouse to kiss. Kit sees Skip float by, and the two run out and tell the others. Chaz finds Skip's bloody and broken switchblade, and Arch suggests that it is Buck. Nan finds Muffy and is angry about the cassette-tape joke, and Muffy says she does not know what Nan is talking about. Arch, caught in a trap, hangs upside down while a snake tries to bite him. A person kicks away the snake and stands over Arch. Now no one can find Arch. Rob tries the telephone but is unable get a call to go through.

They cannot get water in the house, so Hal and Nikki go to the well. Hal drops the bucket and does not want to go down. Nikki falls into the well when a rung breaks. As Hal climbs down to help her, Nikki finds the head of Arch and the body of Nan. Back at the house, Constable Potter calls and says that he is at the hospital with Buck, and he tells Rob that he will send a flare later at the dock. The group goes around and locks the doors and windows of the house. In the study, Kit finds an old photograph of twins. Nikki says that Muffy has been acting peculiarly and mentions her "nurse's shoes." Hal says he heard Muffy and Nan arguing earlier about something in Nan's room, referencing an abortion. They talk about the things they found in their rooms. Muffy returns and says that she is going to bed. Chaz and Nikki go upstairs as Rob heads for the attic to keep an eye out for the constable. Kit goes with Rob, and Hal stays to watch downstairs.

As Nikki packs her bags to leave, Chaz tries to calm her down by putting on leather masks. She pushes him to the bed and leaves. Nikki returns to see Chaz still lying on the bed. He does not respond to her, and she moves his hands and sees some blood. She is approached by someone at the door. In the attic, Rob tells Kit that the constable said that no one was to be left alone with Muffy. They find a collection of dolls, apparently representing the dead people, and a flare goes off outside. They run out and call everyone, but they cannot find the others. The two open Nikki's door and find a bloody room. Kit runs to Muffy's room and discovers a hanging Hal. They run to the dock, pull in a boat and find a letter to Constable Potter which talks of "Miss St. John," a dangerous patient.

Kit says that Muffy was at Vassar all that time. Rob says that the key to the boat is in the house. They enter through the cellar window, see a blood trail and find Muffy's clothes in the furnace. Height measurements for Muffy and Buffy are on the wall. Kit, recalling the photograph, says that Buffy must be Muffy's twin.

Kit and Rob see eyes behind a painting, and they discover the head of Muffy. They run to the kitchen for the key and see Muffy/Buffy at the door, trying to get inside. Rob is locked in a closet, and Buffy chases Kit to the dining room and lifts the knife. Kit runs to the adjacent room and finds all of the dead people, alive and well, having a get-together. Buffy walks in, pushes in the fake blade and the group of people laugh ("April Fool's!"). Buck appears in the closet with Rob, pulls off his prosthetic, slaps it on Rob's face and unlocks the door for him. Rob runs to the room, and the people laugh some more. Muffy thanks everyone, tells of her idea of a country inn and "whodunit weekend," and she says she needed a "rehearsal" (once a person was "killed," they were let in on the joke). Muffy's twin is actually Skip, and Buck is a make-up artist. Muffy apologizes for some of the more personal jokes, and the group drinks and has a good time. Later, an inebriated Muffy returns to her room, opens a gift on the bed and sees a jack-in-the-box. As the jack jumps out, Nan grabs Muffy's head, slices her throat and Muffy screams. Nan smiles, shows Muffy the fake knife and playfully kisses her.

Although the ending is perhaps a bit predictable, *April Fool's Day* is still a fun film. The performances are enjoyable, especially from Steel and Wilson, and actress Foreman is excellent in the dual role of Muffy and Buffy.

Bay of Blood (aka *Reazione a catena; Twitch of the Death Nerve; Carnage; New House on the Left*) (1971)

Written by Joseph McLee, Filippo Ottoni and Mario Bava; Directed by Mario Bava; Nuova Linea Cinematografica; 84 min.

Cast: Claudine Auger (Renata); Luigi Pistilli (Albert); Claudio Volonté (Simon); Anna M. Rosatti (Laura); Chris Avram (Frank Ventura); Leopoldo Trieste (Paolo Fosatti); Laura Betti (Mrs. Fosatti); Brigitte Skay (Brunhilda); Isa Miranda (Countess Federica Donati); Roberto Bonanni (Bob); Giovanni Nuvoletti (Filippo Donati); Paola Rubens; Guido Boccaccini

Crew: Giuseppe Zaccariello (Producer); Stelvio Cipriani (Composer); Mario Bava (Director of Photography); Carlo Reali (Editor)

Near a bay at night, a woman in a wheelchair moves to a window and looks outside. As she turns off a lamp, someone strings her up and kicks the wheelchair away, and she hangs to her death. The killer, an older gentleman, removes his gloves and, after investigating a noise, plants a suicide note on the table in the bedroom. He takes off his coat and is suddenly stabbed twice in the back by an unseen murderer.

Frank Ventura is lying in bed with his secretary Laura. He is heading out to the bay early due to the recent death of the Countess. He tells Laura that the police initially suspected that the Countess' husband had murdered her, but the husband has disappeared, leading the police to accept the suicide account. Before he leaves, Frank says, "All I need is that signature." Simon the fisherman is being watched via binoculars by Albert and his wife Renata. Paolo passes by Simon, trying to catch an insect for "study," which disgusts Simon. "If you kill for killing's sake, you become a monster," says the fisherman, having just caught a squid. Frank is on the phone with "your honor," assuring him that the rightful heir will sign the bay to him.

Four young adults, Brunhilda, Denise, Duke and Bobby, are driving around. They come across an abandoned building that was evidently once a nightclub. Someone is watching from the woods. Anna, Paolo's wife, laying out tarot cards, tells her apparently uninterested husband that she is predicting death in the future ("Can't you sense the rattled breathing of death?").

Back at the "club," Brunhilda heads to the bay while Duke manages to get inside a house, letting Denise and Bobby inside. Duke does not want Bobby around with Denise, and he threatens Bobby with a spear in an uncomfortable place. Inside, Denise finds a bedroom with a framed picture of Frank by the bed. Down by the bay, a nude Brunhilda discovers a corpse in the water, and she quickly jumps out, puts her clothes on and runs to the club ("There's a dead man in the bay!"). She sees someone following her, is grabbed and her throat slit open. While Duke and Denise are enjoying an intimate time in the bedroom, Bobby is by himself in the living room. He opens the door when he hears a noise, and a blade is swung into his face. For the two lovers, the killer shoves a spear through the couple and out the bed.

Albert and Renata leave their children alone in a camper and head for the bay, passing by Frank as he stands by the door to his home. Renata visits Paolo's place to talk about her father, Filippo, the Countess' husband and his disappearance. Anna suggests that the Countess might leave everything to her illegimate son Simon, "the offspring of her secret affair." Renata goes to talk to Simon, and Anna advises her to speak with Frank and points her towards a path. As Albert and Renata approach Simon's place, he is speaking with Frank, who leaves. Renata asks about her father, and then pulls a cover aside from Simon's boat and finds her father's corpse covered in squids. Simon says he found him in the sea. The couple head to Frank's place and, in the bathroom, Renata finds the bodies of the four dead friends. Frank appears with an axe, but Renata quickly stabs him with a pair of scissors when he runs towards her.

Albert gets to Frank's place and sees Paolo running out. Albert finds his wife and tells her about a stabbed Frank. She says she did it and that Albert must stop Paolo before he manages to call the police. As Paolo frantically dials the police, Albert wraps the phone cord around Paolo's neck and chokes him. Laura calls Frank's place from a gas station, but there is no response. Anna discovers Frank and the bloody scissors, and she is rewarded with an axe beheading. Renata finds Albert, says she killed Anna, and now they must "get rid of Simon" for the bay to be theirs. Laura finds a wounded Frank crawling on the floor, and he tell her to go get Simon. Laura goes to Simon's place, where he accuses her of convincing Filippo to kill the Countess. Laura says it was all Frank's idea. The Countess refused to sell the bay, and Frank and Laura, having taken the Countess' diary, discovered an entry that sounded like a suicide note. Frank then told Laura to persuade Filippo to murder his wife. Laura tries to get away from Simon, but he stops her and chokes her.

Simon picks up his scythe and walks outside. A flashback explains that he killed the four young adults. He tells Frank what has happened, and he says he does not have money to disappear. Frank says if Simon signs over the property he inherits to Frank, he can get a loan from the bank. Simon is angry, but before he can take out his frustration on anyone else, he is stabbed with the spear by Albert, with Renata standing behind her husband. As the couple look for documents in Frank's place, the lights suddenly go out. Frank and Albert begin struggling in the darkness, and one of them is stabbed. Someone approaches Renata in the dark. Later, the young happy couple burn a signed document ("We'll come back and the whole bay will be ours") The children call them, fire a shotgun twice, and Albert and Renata are dead. "Gee, they're good at playing dead, aren't they?" The two kids run to the bay to spend a merry time in the sun.

Mario Bava's *Bay of Blood* is a slashing treat and a wonderfully gory film, with everyone killing everyone else in creative ways. The movie is also very influential; watch it along with Steve Miner's *Friday the 13th, Part 2* (1981). *Bay of Blood* was at one point sold in America as a sequel to Wes Craven's *The Last House on the Left* (1972), although Bava's film had been released first.

The Bird with the Crystal Plumage
(aka *L'uccello dalle piume di cristallo*; Bird With the Glass Feathers; The Gallery Murders; Phantom of Terror)
(1969)

Written and Directed by Dario Argento; CCC Filmkunst GmbH/Glazier/Seda Spettacoli; 98 min.

Cast: Tony Musante (Sam Dalmas); Suzy Kendall (Julia); Enrico Maria Salerno (Inspector Morosini); Eva Renzi (Monica Ranieri); Umberto Raho (Alberto Ranieri); Renato Romano (Carlo); Gianni Di Benedetto (Professor Renaldi); Omar Bonaro (Other Agent); Werner Peters (Antique Dealer); Reggie Nalder (Assassin); Giuseppe Castellano (Agent); Mario Adorf (Berto Consalvi); Raf Valenti; Pino Patti; Rosa Toros; Fulvio Mingozzi; Karen Valenti; Gildo Di Marco

Crew: Salvatore Argento (Producer); Ennio Morricone (Composer); Vittorio Storano (Director of Photography); Franco Fraticelli (Editor)

Sam Dalmas, an American writer, is living in Italy because an acquaintance told him he might find "inspiration." After two years of hardly writing anything, he is nearly broke. After receiving a check for his most recent gig (which his friend Carlo found for him), he plans to head back to the United States. On the way home that night, Sam passes an art gallery. Through the glass doors, he sees a woman struggling with a man in black. The woman is stabbed and the man runs away. Sam, locked between the glass doors, is unable to help the wounded woman.

Eventually the police arrive, and Sam discusses the situation with Inspector Morosini. Sam says that he knows there was something odd about the scene, but he cannot place what was wrong about it. The police take Sam to the station, and he is questioned all night. Before he leaves, Morosini takes his passport, since Sam is considered an important witness and must not leave Italy. As Morosini tells him, there have already been three unsolved murders, and it is apparent that a "dangerous maniac" is on the loose. Sam cancels his flight reservation and heads home to his girlfriend, Julia. On the way, someone swings a cleaver aimed at his head. He narrowly escapes the attack.

The next day at the police station, Sam is told that a glove, discovered at the crime scene, has been analyzed. Apparently the attacker was left-handed and a smoker. Later, when visiting Monica (the woman attacked in the art gallery), Sam tosses a nearby pack of cigarettes to Monica's husband Alberto, who catches it with his left hand. While the killer seeks out additional people to kill, Sam and Julia research previous victims. Sam visits an antique shop (where the first victim worked), and the owner mentions a painting sold on the night of the woman's disappearance. The owner lets Sam borrow a black-and-white copy of the painting, which consists of a woman being attacked in the snow.

Morosini visits Sam at home, tells him about the most recent murder and takes him to the police station. There, Morosini returns Sam's passport. By now, Sam has decided to stay and investigate the killings. Morosini tells him that he has a police officer following the writer for protection. After seeing Alberto again, this time with Monica present (she thanks the writer), Sam goes to see the second victim's pimp, residing in prison, for information about the woman. Later, when Sam and Julia are out walking, the police officer following them is crushed by a car. The passenger, a strange man in a yellow jacket, jumps out and pursues the couple with a gun. Julia gets away, Sam reaches the street with many witnesses around, and soon becomes the pursuer. He loses the shooter in a room full of yellow jackets.

Sam goes again to see the pimp, who tells him he knows someone who can help. A man arrives at Sam's place, is given money and says he will contact Sam later. The killer telephones Sam and threatens Julia and the writer. In the recorded phone call, Sam and Morosini hear a mysterious creaking sound in the background. The hired man calls Sam and gives him the name and address of the yellow-jacketed shooter. Sam goes to see him but finds the man dead. Later, Sam and Morosini are told that Sam's recorded call and an earlier menacing telephone call placed to Morosini were made by two separate people. Carlo hears the call and believes the background noise sounds familiar. He takes the tape to listen to it some more.

Before his plane leaves, Sam decides to see the painter of the eerie painting. He leaves Julia alone, but while he is gone, the killer pays Julia a frightening visit. Sam returns in time and Julia is saved, but the killer is nowhere to be found. The next day, Carlo says he finally realizes that the mysterious sound is the call of a rare bird that can only live in Nothern Siberia, and that one resides at the local zoo. Sam and the police arrive at the zoo and realize that it is near the apartment of Alberto and Monica. When bursting into the place, the couple are struggling with a knife. When the police intervene, Alberto falls out of the window. As he is dying, he admits to being the murderer.

Sam now cannot find Julia, who had run out of Alberto's apartment with Carlo and Monica. When the writer finally tracks them down, he discovers a dead Carlo and a snickering Monica dressed in black. Sam finally realizes that what he saw at the art gallery that night was not Monica being attacked by her husband, but her husband trying to stop an attack from Monica. A chase leads to the art gallery, where Monica drops a heavy sculpture that pins Sam down. Before she can utilize her knife, Monica is stopped and arrested by the police. Sam and Julia can now return to the United States.

Director Argento was a screenwriter for some years (including co-writing Sergio Leone's 1969 classic western *Once Upon a Time in the West* and Don Taylor's 1970 western *Five Man Army*) before making his directorial debut with *The Bird With the Crystal Plumage*. With his debut, Argento proved adept at combining scenes of suspense with many humorous moments.

Black Christmas (aka *Silent Night, Evil Night; Stranger in the House*) (1974)

Written by Roy Moore; Directed by Bob Clark; Canadian Film Development Corporation/Famous Players; 98 min.

Cast: Olivia Hussey (Jess Bradford); Margot Kidder (Barb); Keir Dullea (Peter); John Saxon (Lieutenant Fuller); Andrea Martin (Phyl); Marion Waldman (Mrs. Mac); James Edmond (Mr. Harrison); Douglas McGrath (Sergeant Nash); Art Hindle (Chris); Michael Rapport (Patrick); Les Carlson (Graham); Lynne Griffin (Clare Harrison); Martha Gibson (Mrs. Quaife); John Rutter (Laughing Detective); Robert Warner (Doctor); Syd Brown (Farmer); Jack Van Evera, Les Rubie (Search Party); Marcia Diamond (Woman); Pam Barney (Jean); Robert Hawkins (Wes); Dave Clement (Cogan); Julian Reed (Jennings); Dave Mann, John Stoneham, Danny Gain, Tom Foreman (Cops)

Crew: Findlay Quinn (Executive Producer); Bob Clark (Producer); Richard Schouten (Associate Producer); Gerry Arbeid (Co-Producer); Carl Zittrer (Composer); Reg Morris (Director of Photography); Stan Cole (Editor)

The girls of Pi Kappa Sigma are having a Christmas party to celebrate the upcoming holiday. Unbeknownst to any of the party goers, a prowler scales the side of the sorority house and enters through the attic window. Soon the telephone rings, and Jess answers to a somewhat familiar voice ("It's him again! The Moaner!"). The clearly upset Clare Harrison verbalizes her trepidation, and after being mocked by the crude and frequently inebriated Barb, she heads to her room for some packing. Unfortunately, the prowler is already there, hiding in the closet, and he asphyxiates Clare with plastic. As the party continues, the killer takes Clare's body up to the attic with him to rock in a rocking chair.

The next day, Mr. Harrison is looking for his daughter. He and Clare had intended to meet so that he could take her back home for the holiday break. Jess goes to see her boyfriend Peter to let him know that she is now an expectant mother, and that she has decided to abort the child. Peter does not want her to have the abortion. Mr. Harrison, Phyl and Barb file a missing persons report at the police station, while Jess receives another call from the Moaner. During this call, rather than uttering random obscenities, the caller says peculiar but specific things, such as the recurring names of Billy and Agnes. The agitated Peter's piano recital is unsatisfactory, and he destroys the piano afterwards.

Mrs. Mac, the housemother who is always searching the house for hidden bottles of booze, is preparing to leave for the holidays when she hears her cat meowing in the attic. She looks through the attic door and comes upon Clare's body, but she is murdered before she can let anyone know. When Jess returns from the search party (looking for Clare but instead finding the body of a missing high school girl), she receives another Moaner call, and finally telephones the police about the recurring episodes. Peter is already inside the house, and he pleads with Jess to marry him. Jess declines the proposal and Peter departs, angry about her decision to go through with the abortion.

Lieutenant Fuller and Graham arrive at the sorority to tap the telephone. Graham informs Jess that the police phone tap is a mechanical device that requires her to keep the caller on the line for some time. Peter is outside after the cops leave, and Phyl is upset, believing that Clare is dead. As Jess awaits another phone call, the killer enters Barb's room. Jess runs up to the room when she hears Barb, but the girl is only having an asthma attack. Barb says she was having a nightmare of a stranger coming into her room. Jess goes to the door for carolers, and the killer goes back to Barb's room, stands over the slumbering girl ("It's me — Billy") and stabs her to death with a glass unicorn.

After the carolers leave, the Moaner phones again, and this time says something about "having a wart removed," a metaphor earlier used by Peter in reference to Jess' abortion. Fuller calls and says the caller was not on line long enough, and he asks about Peter, who was leaving when the police arrived. Jess talks to Phyl about believing the caller is her perturbed boyfriend. Peter calls, unsettled and crying about the baby, and Graham keeps tracing the call. Fuller calls afterwards and asks about Peter's behavior. He then asks if Peter was with her when she received a call, and she recalls Peter being in the house during a Moaner incident; her suspicions momentarily subside. Phyl is scared by a couple of men from the search party who ask if they noticed "anything suspicious" that night. The lieutenant asks Sergeant Nash to get records on Peter. Jess and Phyl lock the windows and doors, and Phyl goes to check on Barb. The killer closes the door behind her.

After the Moaner places another call, Graham and the cops discover that the calls have been coming from inside the sorority house. Fuller calls Jennings, the officer keeping an watch on the house, and the cop is dead behind the wheel with a slit throat. Jess calls for Phyl, and Nash telephones. The officer attempts to calmly suggest that Jess get out of the house, and finally tells her that the caller is inside the house with her. Jess arms herself with a firepoker and goes upstairs looking for the others. When she throws open the door to Barb's room, she sees the bodies of her sorority sisters. Standing behind the door is the killer. She takes refuge in the cellar and locks the door, and the killer bangs and screams. There are sounds of the killer apparently walking away, and then the slam of a door.

Lieutenant Fuller and the cops race to the sorority house. As Jess hides in the cellar, Peter appears outside, breaks a window and gets inside. As her seemingly concerned boyfriend approaches, Jess braces herself, unsure as to whether he is the killer. The cops arrive, see the dead Jennings and hear Jess scream. They burst inside, run to the cellar and find Jess with her dead boyfriend lying in her lap. Jess lies on a bed sleeping, and the cops leave her alone for some peace and quiet. Up in the attic, the killer continues to talk and sing to the corpses of Clare and Mrs. Mac, and soon the phone is ringing again.

Bob Clark's *Black Christmas* is a superior slasher, with a very spooky atmosphere and some truly terrifying scenes; it is, quite simply, one of the best. Kidder is a treat as the unparalleled Barb, and Hussey is outstanding as the tormented Jess. The versatile Clark also helmed *Children Shouldn't Play With Dead Things* (1972), *Porky's* (1982) and *A Christmas Story* (1983). Hindle and Carlson have appeared in films from David Cronenberg and additional films from Clark: Hindle in Cronenberg's *The Brood* (1979) and Clark's *Porky's* and *Porky's II: The Next Day* (1983), Carlson in Cronenberg's *Videodrome* (1982), *The Dead Zone* (1984) and *The Fly* (1986) and Clark's *A Christmas Story* (as the tough, negotiating Christmas tree salesman).

A Blade in the Dark (aka *La casa con la scala nel buio*) (1983)

Written by Dardano Sacchetti and Elisa Briganti; Directed by Lamberto Bava; National Cinematografica/Nuova Dania Cinematografica; 108 min.

Cast: Andrea Occhipinti (Bruno); Anny Papa (Sandra); Fabiola Toledo (Angela); Michele Soavi (Tony); Valeria Cavalli (Katia); Stanko Molnar (Giovanni); Lara Naszinski (Julia); Giovanni Frezza (Boy in Film)
Crew: Michele Soavi (Assistant Director); Guido De Angelis, Maurizio De Angelis (Composers); Gianlorenzo Battaglia (Director of Photography); Lamberto Bava (Editor)

Three boys walk into a house and toss a ball down a dark stairway. One boy is told to retrieve the ball or he will be considered a girl ("You are a female!"). He cries and walks down, and, after a scream, a bloody ball is thrown back up, and the other two boys run away.

Giovanni, a caretaker, trims the hedges as Tony shows Bruno the villa. Bruno is staying there as he composes a score for a thriller film. Sandra, the film's director, shows Bruno the stairway scene, and the composer discusses her "secret" final reel. Sandra says she is having Bruno stay in a large, isolated villa to get him in the proper mood for the film. At the villa, a person walks inside and slices a magazine photo with a cutter. Bruno arrives, turns on his tape recorder and records some piano music. A person nearby whispers, and Bruno hears the voice and the sound of the cutter's blade being pushed out. High-heeled feet are near, and as Bruno looks around, a woman jumps out of a closet (a spider scared her). The woman, Katia, asks if Bruno is a friend of Linda, and adds that she lives nearby. When Tony calls and Bruno asks him about the lights, he is told that the last tenant, Linda, liked the dark. Katia had asked where the bathroom was, but she is gone, and Bruno finds her diary in the closet. He reads, and it mentions Linda's secret. Outside, Katia is chased by a cutter-wielding person ("I didn't say anything!"), and she runs inside and hides. She is later found, stabbed in the stomach and cut on the throat.

Bruno rewinds the tape and plays it, and hears the recorded whispering. He plays it again and hears something about a "secret," the name Linda and "No one must know." Bruno goes out for a smoke as a dead Katia is being dragged by the bushes. He approaches the killer, and the cutter is prepared, but Bruno returns to the house for the ringing phone. The phone only crackles; he hangs up and sees blood on his pants. He returns to the bushes and finds blood. At Giovanni's place in back, he finds blood on the steps. The music is turned off, and Bruno returns to the house to find diary pages torn out. Giovanni's light comes on, and Bruno walks over and helps him with a trash bag (Giovanni says it has old papers and magazines). Bruno asks about Linda, and Giovanni says he does not know her well. Julia arrives and tells Bruno that her rehearsal was canceled and she called earlier but something was wrong with the line.

The next day, Bruno tells Julia about his strange night. After Julia leaves, Bruno goes to the cellar and finds a locked door. Tony says it contains things that Linda left behind. Bruno asks Tony what Linda was like, and he says she was a "normal kind of girl." Bruno gets a call from Sandra, and she asks to meet later. Angela arrives at the villa and tells Bruno she is looking for Katia, who did not come home. She says Katia had come to get her diary back. Linda would let the two girls swim there, and Bruno tells Angela she can swim whenever she wants. She goes to the pool house to change (Giovanni watches her), and while swimming, she finds the cutter on the bottom. Angela walks into the house (Bruno is at the studio), and a hand with painted fingernails selects a knife from the kitchen. The high-heeled feet walk upstairs. Angela is washing her hair in the bathroom sink. As she reaches for more shampoo, her hand is stabbed. The killer puts a plastic bag over her head and repeatedly slams her head onto the counter, while laughing maniacally. The knife is pulled from Angela's hand, she is placed by the tub and her throat is slit. The killer begins cleaning the floor and counter with tissues.

Bruno leaves a note from Sandra (who did not meet him at the studio) and goes back to the villa. In the kitchen, Bruno sees that the knife is not with the others, and in the bathroom, he finds an empty box of tissues, a cut in the counter and a bloody piece of tissue on the floor. In the cellar, he finds more bloody tissue under Linda's door. Bruno records himself and talks of possibly uncovering a "string of murders," believing Angela and Katia are dead. Sandra arrives, and Bruno tells her what has happened. Sandra mentions the killer not being able to move the bodies, and Bruno tells of the locked door (Sandra knows a Linda but it "couldn't be *her*"). They go to the cellar, where the door is unlocked. When they find a trunk of tennis balls, Sandra says it must be the Linda she knew. She says Linda as a child was the basis for the character in her film. They hear someone in the studio above. In the hallway, Bruno is nearly stabbed by Julia. They all settle down, and Sandra leaves.

Julia tells Bruno that her play was suspended due to obscenity charges. The following day, Sandra telephones Linda and says she is sorry for the way things turned out. She says that she used Linda's story but it was mostly fabricated ("I didn't say anything"). Linda merely whimpers and hangs up. Bruno finds Julia listening to his tape, and the two argue about the murders. Later, Bruno asks Julia to go with him somewhere, but she does not think there is any murderer. Bruno goes to a payphone, calls the director of the theater where Julia worked and asks about the charges of obscenity. The director says it is a children's play, sponsored by the education department, and that Julia left on opening night without an explanation.

Someone walks into the editing room, takes a film canister and cuts up the film reel. Bruno asks Carlo to see the last reel, and they find it in pieces. Giovanni finds the bodies of Angela and Katia, and he is hit on the head with a wrench. Bruno and Carlo splice together as much film as possible and watch the scene, and a woman suddenly appears in the film. Carlo says it is probably the killer. Sandra looks for Linda at the villa, and in the garage she finds a barely living and bloody Giovanni. Linda wraps film reel around Sandra and chokes her. Julia walks into the garage, finds the bundle of reel, a dead Sandra and the garage door shut. Julia runs into the house, and, after being startled by falling tennis balls, hides in a closet. She tries to keep the door shut as Linda pushes the knife in. When Bruno calls her name, Julia jumps out and runs. Linda follows and stabs Julia in the back, then runs towards Bruno screaming. He whacks her on the head with a brick and runs to see Julia dead. Bruno walks back to Linda, and a wigless Tony steps out and swings the knife. Bruno turns Tony's hand and stabs him. He falls ("I'm not a female child"), and Tony/Linda dies. Bruno watches the final reel, and the little boy, sent down the dark stairway, is adorned in a wig.

A Blade in the Dark is a great slasher from director Bava (the son of the great Italian director Mario Bava), with a somewhat predictable but still enjoyable ending. Fellow film director Michele Soavi is great as Tony/Linda, and the murder sequence in the bathroom is wonderfully directed, creating a truly shocking and intense killing.

Blade of the Ripper
(aka *Lo strango vizio della Signora Wardh*; *Next Victim*; *Next!*)
(1970)

Written by Eduardo M. Brochero, Ernesto Gastaldi and Vittorio Caronia; Directed by Sergio Martino; MLR Films, Inc./Laurie International/Devon Films/Copercines/Cooperativa Cinematográfica; 86 min.

Cast: George Hilton (George); Edwige Fenech (Julie Wardh); Cristina Airoldi (Carol); Ivan Rassimov (Jean); Alberto de Mendoza (Neil Wardh); Bruno Corazzari (Killer); Manuel Gil; Carlo Alighiero; Marella Corbi; Miguel Del Castillo; Luis De Tejada; Brizio Montinaro, C.S.C.; Pouchie; Mira Vidotto

Crew: Luciano Martino, Antonio Crescenzi (Producers); Nora Olandi (Composer); Emilio Foriscot (Director of Photography); Fima Noveck (Editor)

A person is driving down the street, and a prostitute gets in the car. They drive and sit in the car by an airport, and as a plane goes by overhead, the woman is slashed with a razor. Julie arrives at the airport with her diplomat husband, and she goes home alone in a taxi. A police officer stops them and tells them that a woman has been murdered (the driver asks if it was the "sex fiend"). Julie recalls running out of a black car in the rain, and being chased, thrown to the ground and attacked. When she gets out of the taxi cab, the same black car is sitting across the street. She goes inside, prepares a bath and answers the door to a delivery boy. The note is from Jean, who says she will "always be his." At a party, Julie's friend Carol introduces her to her cousin George, whom she just recently met after her uncle died (Carol did not know either). Julie sees Jean across the room and angrily leaves; Jean follows. Julie says whatever they had is over. When her husband Neil arrives, he punches Jean, who laughs and walks away. Julie and Neil embrace, and Julie calls Jean a "pervert" and a "maniac."

Julie awakes from a nightmare involving Jean. A blonde woman goes home to shower and is killed with a razor. Julie, talking with Carol, says she only married Neil to get away from Jean, believing Neil would be a "wall" of protection. George is at Julie's house, waiting to speak with her husband. Later, at a restaurant, George sits with Carol and Julie, despite Julie's objection. Carol is called away, and George takes Julie home on his motorcycle, a speedy ride that Julie says helped make the afternoon "stimulating." George calls Julie and tells her he loves her, and Julie says he should not telephone any more because she likes him too much. They are kissing outside later when a car speeds by and scares Julie. The couple goes inside George's place. The car returns, the headlights are turned off and a person gets out to watch.

Julie gets more flowers and another note: "Your vice is like a room locked from the inside and only I have the key." The note is anonymous, but it is written in the same handwriting as the note from Jean. Julie gets a phone call from a person who claims to know about her and George, and demands money to keep it from Neil. Julie tells Carol, who says she is not completely sure it was Jean. Carol says she will go to the appointment ("It's bound to be Jean"). Carol is waiting on a bench for a while, then has a caretaker point her in the right direction for the meeting place. A person with a razor chases Carol down and kills her. The caretaker finds her, and the cops are called. At the station, Julie says she believes Jean is the killer, and tells a cop that he has a black car similar to the one reported near the crime scenes. Jean says that he and Julie were once on "intimate terms." Julie says it was Jean that called her, with a disguised voice, but the cop says Jean has an alibi. Jean suggests Julie is the killer, and Julie furiously leaves with Neil.

George talks to Julie, saying he wants to

tell Neil that he wishes to take Julie away. Julie says they should not be seen together until after the killer is caught. Julie is in a parking garage when a car speeds past her. She runs to the elevator and sees the razor killer standing there. The killer swings, and Julie runs and hides in her car. She quickly drives to the elevator and jumps inside, narrowly avoiding the killer. She bangs on her door until Neil lets her inside, and she tells her husband what has happened. Neil gets his gun and the couple heads over to Jean's place. They find a camera on the floor and a dead Jean in the bathtub. Outside in Neil's car are more flowers and a note. Neil throws them away and they leave.

Neil has the photograph developed, and it is a picture of the person from the garage. George says he is taking Julie to Spain. A woman walks into her place, where the razor killer is waiting to attack her. She struggles and manages to stab him, and the killer dies. George and Julie do some scuba diving, then learn that the razor killer is dead. Julie gets flowers from a boy, with a note signed Jean: "Seeing that the living don't bring flowers to the dead, the dead bring them to the living." Julie is scared, and she runs to look for George. Someone shoots a dartgun at her and narrowly misses. Julie gets in her car, drives to her place and she sees blood behind a curtain. When George appears, Julie passes out and is carried to the bed. George looks behind the curtain and sees a leaky radiator. He calls the doctor and says he fears for Julie's sanity. Julie awakes, walks around and sees feet behind the curtain. She pulls it aside and sees only shoes, but she is grabbed by Jean with a cloth over her mouth, and passes out again.

George, driving back with the doctor, says he has discovered that blood has an odd effect on Julie: It "excites and repels her at the same time." Jean drags Julie into the kitchen, puts her fingerprints on tape and tapes the window shut. He turns on the gas and closes the door (using an ice cube to allow the latch to lock once he leaves). George and the doctor break down the door and open the window, and as George calls the hospital, the doctor performs CPR on Julie.

Neil is told his wife is dead from an apparent suicide. Neil blames George, and he storms out. George goes to see Jean, who says he wants his money. George mentions that the "sex maniac" did not kill Carol. He goes to get Jean's money and shoots him instead, wiping the gun and leaving it in Jean's hand. Neil is picked up at the train station by George, and he tells him they will not pay until the death certificate is signed. George says the best time to kill someone is when a crazy person is on the loose. They did each other a favor; George got rid of Julie, and Neil got rid of Carol (with his cousin gone, George is the only heir). As they are driving away, Neil thinks he sees Julie at the side of the road. Suddenly an assortment of law enforcers are behind her. A chase ensues, and George and Neil go off the road and into the river below. A police officer says the men were "unmasked" because there was a difference in Carol's murder. Julie thanks the doctor who saved her life, and they leave together.

Sergio Martino's *Blade of the Ripper* is a fun slasher, with a deliciously intricate ending and a very good performance from Fenech. Actress Airoldi later appeared in Martino's *Torso* (1972), also playing a character named Carroll and also being killed in a wooded area.

Blood and Black Lace (aka *Sei donne per l'assassino; Fashion House of Death*) (1964)

Written by Marcel Fondato, Joe Barilla and Mario Bava; Directed by Mario Bava; Emmepi Cinematografica/Les Films Georges de Beauregard/Monarchia; 87 min.

Cast: Cameron Mitchell (Max Marian); Eva Bartok (Contessa Cristina); Thomas Reiner (Inspector Sylvester); Arian Gorin (Nicole); Dante Di Paolo (Frank Sacalo); Mary Arden (Peggy); Frank Russel (Marquis Richard Morell);

Claude Dantes (Tao-Li); Luciano Pigozzi (Cesare); Lea Kruger (Greta); Massimo Righi (Marco); Francesca Ungaro (Isabella); Guiliano Raffaelli (Zanchin); Harriet Medin (Clarice); Enzo Cerusico (Gas Station Attendant); Mara Carmosino; Heidi Stroh; Nadia Anty

Crew: Carl Rustic (Composer); Herman Tarzana (Director of Photography); Mark Suran (Editor)

It is a windy night outside a fashion house. One of the models, Nicole, comes out front, and Frank waves her over. He tells her that Isabella has taken his "last" and that he needs something. Later, Isabella is dropped off and begins walking to the fashion house. She is being followed by someone wearing a cloth over the face. The stranger eventually grabs her and kills her.

In the fashion house, Marco asks Cristina if she wants him to fix the sign outside. Later, he takes some pills. Cristina tells Mr. Marian that Isabella has not returned. Cristina then opens a door and discovers a dead Isabella. The next day, Inspector Silvester interrogates the people at the fashion house. Marian introduces Silvester to Cristina; the inspector remembers her from when her husband died in a car accident. Richard, the fiancée of model Greta, comes inside, complaining because the cops grabbed him. Peggy, who lived with Isabella, is in tears. Caesar, the dress designer, suggests the police speak with antique dealer Frank Sacalo. Silvester goes to see Frank and asks him if he and Isabella were lovers. He then shows Frank some cocaine found in the woman's house. Frank says he knew nothing about it.

At a fashion show, none of the models want to wear Isabella's dress. Nicole says she will wear it, and when she goes looking for the broach that goes with it, she discovers a diary. She begins to read it aloud, but Caesar takes it from her to read. Cristina takes it from them both and says it should be given to the police. Nicole offers to take it, puts it in her purse and heads for the runway as everyone eyes the purse. Nicole calls Frank and says she has Isabella's diary. Frank initially says he will be over to look through it, but then calls back and asks Nicole to come over. Nicole asks to borrow Peggy's car. Peggy gets the keys from her purse (next to Nicole's), and Nicole leaves. Nicole arrives at Frank's antique shop. She hears a crash, and the lights go out. Attacked by the faceless killer, she tries to get the locked door open. The killer grabs a clawed hand (from a knight's armor on display) and shoves it in Nicole's face. The killer looks through the purse, finds no diary, goes outside, jumps into Nicole's car and drives away. A man at a nearby gas station watches the car and writes something down.

Peggy arrives home, and Marco is waiting for her. Marco says he will wait with Peggy so that she will not be alone, and he also lets her know that he has fallen in love with her. When Marco goes through Peggy's purse for cigarettes, she quickly snatches it away from him ("Don't touch it!"). Silvester calls and says he found Peggy's abandoned car. She says she lent it to Nicole, and the inspector says he will be right over. After Marco decides to leave, Peggy gets the diary from her purse, flips through it and rips out pages referring to her stealing money from Isabella. She throws the pages and then the diary in the fire. The faceless killer arrives at her door, grabs Peggy and, via a tiny notepad, demands to know where the diary is. Peggy says she burned it, and the killer pokes through the fire. The killer gets an unconscious Peggy outside before the police arrive.

Frank goes to see Richard and Greta, says he found Nicole dead and tells Richard he needs an alibi because the police will think he committed the murder. Frank says they can help each other since Richard essentially had a motive for murder (owing Isabella money). Peggy has been taken to a room with a furnace. She insists the diary was burned, pulls the mask off of the faceless killer and seems to know who it is. The killer shoves her face on the furnace. The cops interrogate the gas station man, who tells them the killer entered the car and quickly turned off the burglar alarm, as if he knew where it was.

At the police station, the men (Marian,

Marco, Caesar, Frank and Richard) are all in a line. Peggy's maid says she has seen Marian in Peggy's car, and she saw Marco with her the night she disappeared. When Caesar tries to blame Marco, Marco gets upset and has an epileptic attack. The other men are asked to stay. The cops believe Peggy may have been murdered, so the alibi for Frank and Richard is fruitless. At the fashion salon, the models are left alone. Greta tries to get Tao-Li (another roommate of Peggy and Nicole) to stay with her, but Tao-Li says she is not frightened since the men are locked up and she is certain one of them is the murderer. Later, Tao-Li gets in her car and drives away. Greta also leaves, and now Cristina is alone.

Greta goes home and discovers Peggy's corpse in her car trunk. She carries the body inside to hide from the butler. She goes to the bathroom to wash off the blood. When she hears a noise, she goes back into the bedroom and sees the body standing. The faceless killer grabs a cushion and suffocates Greta. The police find the bodies; now all the men have alibis. When leaving the station, Marian is handed a notebook similar to the one the killer used earlier.

Later, Marian is in his office. After he speaks with Tao-Li, he goes behind the bookshelf and enters the room with a furnace. Cristina appears and says she burned Peggy's clothes, moved the body and killed Greta. As they talk, it is learned that the death of Cristina's husband was not an accident and that Isabella, upon discovering the murder, blackmailed Cristina and Marian. Marian says that they have to give the police a killer, and that Cristina must kill one more time.

Cristina visits Tao-Li and drowns her, then slits her wrists. Outside, something is being cut. The doorbell rings and there is a loud banging at the door. Cristina, startled, runs to the balcony, tries to climb out and falls. Marian, who was the one creating the ruckus, goes back to the fashion house and opens a box of jewelry. He hears a noise, looks around and then returns to the office to see that a gun previously on the desk is missing. A wounded Cristina appears, saying she knows he did it, because he had told her to go on the ledge if there was any danger. She accuses Marian of wanting nothing but her wealth, but Marian assures her that she is wrong. He says he loves her and they kiss—Cristina shoots him. She tries to telephone the police, but she drops the phone and falls to the floor next to her dead lover.

Blood and Black Lace, one of the earliest *gialli*, is a glorious film from Bava, with radiant and colorful cinematography and a taut and effective mystery.

Blood Hook (1986)

Written by Larry Edgerton and John Galligan; Directed by James Mallon; Spider Lake Films/Golden Chargers Productions/Troma; 92 min.

Cast: Mark Jacobs (Peter van Clease); Lisa Todd (Ann); Patrick Danz (Rodney); Sara Hauser (Kiersten); Christopher Whiting (Finner); Don Winters (Leroy Leudke); Paul Drake (Wayne Duerst); Bill Lowrie (Evelyn Duerst); Sandy Meuwissen (Bev D.); Dale Dunham (Denny Dobyns); Paul Heckman (The Sheriff); Don Cosgrove (Roger Swain); Bonnie Lee (Sheila Swain); Greg Nienas (Irving Swain); Julie Vortanz (Ruth-Ann Swain); Donald Franke (Grandfather); Ryan Franke (Young Peter); Dana Remker (Dickie); John Galligan, Ron Kasier (Emcees)

Crew: Lloyd Kaufman, Michael Herz (Executive Producers); David Herbert (Producer); Thomas A. Naunas (Composer); Marsha Kahm (Director of Photography, Editor)

As a man is fishing, his grandson runs to the dock and asks him about a tape recorder playing music. He shows how it works, turns and smiles, and then seems scared. The boy watches as his grandfather grips his face and seems to jump into the water.

Seventeen years later, Peter, Ann, Kiersten, Rodney and Finner are headed for the Muskie Madness Fishing Contest. Roger and his family visit Leroy Leudke's place for some minnows, and Leroy gives the son, Irving, a stud finder. Before they leave, Leroy reminds the family to treat the water with respect. The friends meet Denny, the "Muskie Maniac," Bev D., the contest hostess, and Wayne, who messes with Rodney's radio and tells him to turn off the "headache machine." They go to Peter's Place, where Evelyn is out on the lawn cleaning his gun. Wayne comes out and tells Peter that he worked for his grandfather but will not work for Peter. Ann finds some records inside and plays "Fishing For Your Love" (the song playing when Peter's grandfather was killed). At a restaurant, Roger and his wife Sheila argue; he says he is there to fish and that she can go to her sister's place. Sheila goes to the dock, answering the call of the loons, and a hook hits her neck. She spins, and a rod pulls her into the water.

Denny is in his place, with a large fish in a tub that he has grown and intends to put in the contest. Wayne walks in when Denny leaves ("Cheatin' bastard!") and dumps the fish into the water. Peter and Ann are sitting on a bed; Ann thinks that he imagined seeing Sheila on the dock because he will not do anything about it (much like his music, he is afraid to "make noise"). Rodney and Finner are fishing, and Finner catches a huge fish (with a red clip that Denny had put on). Bev invites them for breakfast. Later, Bev is exercising while her young son is playing by the water. The hook flies into the water and misses him, but Bev hears him scream, and she runs to him and sees that his leg is cut. Rodney goes to Leroy's place for fishing gear, and Leroy tells him that Wayne and van Clease (Peter's grandfather) used to kill muskies with a "lucky bullet," a copper slug that they would dig out of the dead fish and use again. Wayne once accidentally shot van Clease in the spine with the slug, and van Clease refused to let anyone operate and get the slug out of his spine.

Rodney goes out in his motorboat and runs circles around a fishing Denny. Later, Rodney swims and gets back in the boat and turns on some music. The hook is thrown onto a seat in the boat. Rodney lies on his stomach, the line is reeled in, and he is pulled into the water. Peter, Ann and Kiersten are drinking together. Peter tells Kiersten about different tones, and the "devil's tri-tone" that was thought to drive people crazy. The group hears the sheriff on the radio about a body, and then see Rodney's boat, with blood and bullets inside. Peter says Evelyn killed Rodney (they are M-16 bullets), and he and the sheriff go out to the place and ask for Evelyn's gun. The sheriff shows Peter that the M-16 is not real, and he leaves.

Peter apologizes to the sheriff and says he wants to find Rodney's killer. The sheriff says no one knows that the boy is dead. Kiersten runs away crying and goes to float on an inflatable raft and listen to music, as Wayne prepares to fish, sharpening a hook like the one the killer uses. The hook is thrown towards Kiersten, and she falls into the water and screams at the oncoming boat. Wayne is on the shore with a plastic bag. Wayne is in the contest lead with a 46½ pound fish. Finner and Bev enjoy some time alone in her house, and she tells him to come back later at midnight. Peter tries to call about Kiersten but the phone is not hooked up. Evelyn comes in and talks about vibrations. Wayne tells him to shut up, saying to Peter that the job he had meant a lot to him and that van Clease, despite the accident, gave the job to Wayne. At Leroy's place, Irving takes something from the open cash register, then finds a helmet with a hole in the top (which Leroy got in the Korean War). As Leroy bends over, Irving puts the stud finder near his head and it moves. The boy takes something from the tub.

Roger is out on his boat and Finner is outside with his rod (and a hook similar to the killer's). Finner sees Evelyn and Bev laughing in her house and becomes irate. Roger tries to signal for help (his boat's engine will not start), and he is hooked in the stomach and reeled in. Peter tells Ann that people are being "nailed in the water" like his grandfather, and Finner is one of the few people who knows about it. They go to check Bev's place. Bev turns on some music, goes to the water and gets a hook in her back. She manages to get the hook out, and an oar is swung. Denny tries to cheat in the contest, with a fish that is 60 pounds only because it has a metal bar inside. Peter and Ann find part of Bev's bathing suit and a tassel from Finner's rod, and Evelyn is angry. Leroy is in his place as a drunk Finner sings and plays music, and the man grabs his head in agony. He runs outside, casts and hits Finner in the head. Finner gets the hook off and, as he fiddles with the wound, his ear comes off. Finner tries to hide at the side of the boat, but Leroy sees him, swings his gaff and takes Finner inside to saw and cut.

Kiersten returns on Finner's boat saying someone tried to kill her, and Peter finds Finner's ear ("Finner, you poor bastard…"). Leroy goes to the dock and gathers the dead people submerged in the water. Peter finally realizes that the noise of cicadas and a note in the songs combine to form the devil's tritone, which "sets off the killer." The children arrive, and Irving says Leroy has a plate in his head. Peter and Evelyn go to Leroy's place, Evelyn finds Bev's wedding ring and Peter finds buckets of blood and guts ("There's your friends, man"). Ann is on the dock listening to "Fishing For Your Love," and Leroy casts and hooks her hand. She gets the hook out and runs. Leroy rows her way and casts again, and Ann screams. Peter and Evelyn run when they see Leroy, and Peter returns to an empty dock, turns on the radio and hears the song. Wayne tells the two that Leory is not a killer, but Irving shows Wayne the lucky bullet, which he found at Leroy's place. Peter offers himself as bait, but he is too frightened to turn the music on, and he sits there all night.

The next day, Leroy is the winner of the contest with a 50-pounder. Wayne pulls his gun on him but the sheriff takes him away. Peter tells Wayne to teach him to cast as good as his grandfather. That night, Peter rows to the dock and turns on the music, and Leroy comes out, casts and hits Peter in the chest. Peter casts and hooks Leroy's neck. Leroy pulls the hook out and reels Peter in. Peter awakes inside and turns on the music from a nearby radio as Leroy sharpens his knife. Peter gets Ann, and the radio falls into the tub of water. Leroy goes for them with the knife, and runs away when he hears sirens. Peter, Ann and Kiersten go home, and the sheriff tells Wayne he needs his help finding Leroy. Leroy is in the woods, screaming in agony.

Blood Hook is a very enjoyable film, with a nice amount of humor and an excellent weapon of choice from the killer. Director Mallon, the co-founder of *Mystery Science Theater 3000*, helped direct and write numerous episodes; he also provided the voice for Gypsy (the bot that looked like a purple vacuum cleaner) for a number of episodes.

Blood Rage (aka *Nightmare at Shadow Woods*) (1983)

Written by Richard Lamden; Directed by John M. Grissmer; Film Limited Partnership/Complex Films, Ltd.; 82 min.

Cast: Louise Lasser (Maddy); Mark Soper (Terry/Todd); Julie Gordon (Karen); Jayn Bentzen (Julie); Marianne Kanter (Doctor Berman); James Farrell (Artie); Chad Montgomery (Gregg); Lisa Randall (Andrea); William Fuller (Brad); Doug Weiser (Jackie/Radio Announcer); Gerry Lou (Beth); Ed French (Bill); Dana Dresher (Little Girl); Brad Williams (Teen Boy at Drive-In); Rebecca Thorp (Teen Girl at Drive-In); Bill Cakmis (Maddy's Date); Keith Hall (Young Terry); Ross Hall (Young Todd); Lauren Myers, Amanda Ball (Baby); Ted Raimi (Condom Salesman); Matthew Carlisle, Kevin Williams (Hospital Attendants); Ed Brophy (Terry's Double); Gregg Vontz, Sarah Baker, Fonda Fisher, Joel Girvan, David Girvan, Debra Growe (Football Players); Billy W. Freeman (Institution Guard)

Crew: Jared M. Drescher, William C. Brakefield, Stanley Westreich (Executive Producers); Marianne Kanter (Producer); Bonnie Leslie, Robert N. Morgan (Associate Producers); Richard Einhorn (Composer); Richard E. Brooks (Director of Photography); Michael R. Miller (Editor)

In 1974, at a drive-in showing *The House That Cried Murder*, Maddy is with her date, and her twin boys are asleep in the back. Maddy is worried about the boys, but she and her date keep kissing, and the boys slip out the back door. Todd picks up a hatchet, and Terry takes the hatchet to a car with two nude lovers and chops the man in the face. The woman runs away. Maddy says she thinks she heard screaming. Terry puts the hatchet in Todd's hand, wipes blood on his face and tells his mother that Todd hurt people, as Todd just stands there, apparently unaware that his brother is pinning a murder on him.

Ten years later, Doctor Berman has learned that Todd is beginning to remember what happened on that night, and suspicion is being cast on his twin brother. Todd tells his mother that he did not kill anyone, and he wants the leave the hospital. At the Thanksgiving dinner table Maddy and Brad announce their engagement, and Terry does not seem pleased. Maddy answers the phone, then calls Terry into the kitchen and says that Todd escaped from the "school." Terry agrees to keep quiet, but then returns to the table and tells Brad, new neighbors Beth and Andrea and his girlfriend Karen that his "psychotic brother" is on the loose. Later as Terry answers the door, Jackie nearly shoots him with a tranquilizer gun, but he is stopped by Doctor Berman. Brad suggests places where Todd could be hiding at the ten-acre estate, and Doctor Berman checks the woods, Jackie goes to the patios and Brad sits in his office.

After Brad calls and checks on Maddy, Terry arrives, taps on the doorway with a machete and slices off Brad's beer-holding hand. Jackie stops to smoke some pot; Terry takes a hit from Jackie's joint. Jackie says that Todd claims to have not killed anyone, and Terry ("Yes, he did") stabs Jackie in the stomach. He runs to the woods and approaches Doctor Berman; soon the woman is, literally, in pieces. Todd arrives at Shadow Woods Apartments, and Terry goes to the bathroom, licks the blood on his shirt ("It's not cranberry sauce") and showers. Maddy tries to get hold of Brad at the office, and Terry goes to see the babysitting Andrea. Karen arrives at Terry's place and sees Todd. Believing Todd is her boyfriend, Karen suggests making love. Todd says he is not Terry, but Karen seems nice (and he has not kissed a girl before). Karen quickly leaves, finds Artie and Gregg and tells them that Terry's insane brother is around. Artie looks for him with a baseball bat but finds no one.

Julie and her date, Bill, return home, and Terry and Andrea leave. Karen and the guys see the two, and Karen tells Terry she saw Todd. Terry runs to his mother and says that Todd is there. Maddy tells Terry to find Brad and to put on a sweater. Todd finds the dismembered doctor and cries, and he puts some of her back together and takes her gun. A little girl is out looking for her cat, and Todd tells her that a bad person is out and to go home and not let anyone inside. Julie goes to change into something more comfortable, and Bill answers the door to Terry. Julie walks out and goes to the door, where Bill's head hangs. She runs for her coat, where Terry is waiting for her. Todd gets inside the house and carries his collapsed mother to her bed. "Terry" says that Todd has not been found yet. Maddy kisses her son.

Artie and Karen play video games, then head into the another room, where Andrea and Gregg have become quiet. Artie and Karen are scared by the other two, and they leave. Maddy learns that Brad's telephone number is in "working order." Andrea and Gregg head to the pool, where they spend some confidential time on the diving board. Terry shows up, slices Gregg's neck, swipes Andrea on the face and swings again. Artie and Karen are outside talking, and Karen says that Terry sometimes acts like she is not around. Terry scares the both of them, and says that Andrea and Gregg should not be out with his "crazy brother" around. Artie leaves to tell them, and Terry and Karen go to the house.

Todd, in Artie's backseat, says that Terry is crazy and is killing everyone, and he pulls the gun. The doorbell rings, Terry answers and Todd points the gun at his brother and runs away. Artie and Terry chase him, but they stop when finding some weapons, including the bloody machete ("That isn't cranberry sauce, Artie"). Terry says he sees Todd, Artie looks and Terry stabs a grilling fork in his neck. Karen finds Terry with the machete and suggests calling the cops, but Terry swings and Karen runs. She gets to the house and hides in the shed, but jumps out when she bumps into Jackie's corpse. Terry is outside with a dead Artie, and Karen runs to the little girl's place. But the girl, following Todd's advice, does not let the frantic Karen inside. Karen goes to Julie's place and finds the woman dead and Terry there. Karen hits him, grabs the crying baby and runs.

Maddy finds Terry's bloody shirt in the trash and runs to Brad's office. Touching the man at his desk, she is shocked when his head falls apart. Karen runs to the pool and, as Terry jumps up and down on the diving board, she runs to the bathroom and hides the baby in the cabinet. She finds a dead Angela and Gregg, and hides in a stall. Terry walks inside and then leaves, but when Karen steps out of the stall, Terry swings and hits her shoulder. She runs around and stands behind the gun-toting and still reluctant-to-shoot Todd. Karen takes the gun and gets a click, and Terry puts the machete in Todd's hand and smears blood on his face. Todd throws the weapon away, and the twins struggle and fall into the pool. Terry crawls out and picks up the machete, and Karen helps Todd out of the water. Maddy arrives and shoots Terry several times. She then embraces Todd, saying that it is just the two of them again and that Todd is gone. The twin says that he is Todd and he walks away upset, and Maddy screams "I'm Todd!" many times before shooting herself in the head. Karen runs out with the baby and Todd stands at the wall.

Blood Rage is a fun slasher, with some very good scenes of gore and a number of funny moments. The ending drags a bit; the movie feels as if it is building up to something—but the conclusion is neither surprising nor spectacular. However, the film is still entertaining.

Bloodmoon (1989)

Written by Robert Brennan; Directed by Alec Mills; Michael Fisher Productions/Village Roadshow Productions; 101 min.

Cast: Leon Lissek (Myles Sheffield); Christine Amor (Virginia Sheffield); Ian Williams (Kevin Lynch); Helen Thomson (Mary Huston); Craige Cronnin (Matt Desmond); Hazel Howson (Sister Mary-Ellen); Suzie MacKenzie (Michelle); Anya Molina (Jennifer); Brian Moll (Mr. Gordian); Stephen Bergin (Mark); Christophe Broadway (Scott); Samantha Rittson (Gretchen); Tess Pike (Kylie); Jo Munro (Jackie); Michelle Doake (Linda); Chris Uhlmann (Chip); Justin Ractliffe (Zits); Damien Lutz (Tom); Warwick Brown (Billy); Gregory Pamment (Rich); Sueyan Cox (Sandy Desmond); Narelle Arcidiacono (Mrs. Bacon); Michael Adams (Mr. Owens); Sue Lawson (Mrs. Owens); Jonathan Hardy (Mayor); Elizabeth Williams, David Clendinning, Jane Dormaier, Helen Strube (Teachers); Les Evans (Kevin's Father); Ray Turner, Shawn Kristofer (Policemen); Kate Riley (Daughter Desmond); Sean Anderson (Baby Desmond); Kesha Loy, Lisa Hamilton (Two Girls); Matthew Smith (Murphy); Karen Miers (Susan); Linda-Jo Free (Choir Mistress); Stuartholme Choir (Choir)

Crew: Graham Burke, Gregory Coote (Executive Producers); Stanley O'Toole (Producer); David Munro (Associate Producer); Brian May (Composer); John Stokes (Director of Photography); David Halliday (Editor)

A choir sings in a church, and Virginia Sheffield, headmistress of a girls' Catholic school, talks of Sister Mary-Ellen as a good influence on the girls. Mary consoles a tearful Jackie, who is running away with her boyfriend Rich for fear that her parents will transfer her to another school. She walks into the woods and finds Rich, with his throat open and his eyes cut out. As she runs, barbed wire is wrapped around her neck and she is killed. Sister Mary-Ellen prays about anger that "blinds" her, and Jackie and Rich are kicked into a hole in the ground.

Myles Sheffield, the biology teacher, is working with the girls. Scott and Chip, both from Winchester School for Young Men, get some Winchester pals and start a fight with "townies" Mark, Billy, and Tom. Police officer Desmond breaks up the fight. Mark goes to see his friend Kevin, says that Billy has a plan to crash the Winchester dance and that they need Kevin's truck. Mary is called from Mass to Virginia's office, where she tells Jackie's parents about their daughter wanting to run away with Rich (Mary was the girl's roommate). At the dance, Kevin awaits a signal, and he talks and dances with Mary. Billy nods to Mark from the doorway, and Mark says uncomplimentary things to Scott and his friends. He is chased out of the building. He calls for Kevin and they stand in front of the truck. Billy and others appear from the back to douse the Winchester guys with water.

The barbed-wire killer stands near a kissing Zits and Kylie, but the couple leaves when hearing the noise of the approaching Chip and Gretchen. Mary calls her mother in Los Angeles and asks how the film is going. Her mother complains about it being late, and a woeful Mary says goodbye. Kevin appears at Mary's window, and when she comes down to talk, he invites her for a boat ride. She says she has to go to Mass in the morning, and Kevin asks if he can go with her. The killer attacks Chip and Gretchen and kills them both.

The next day, Michelle and Jenny, planning to steal Mr. Sheffield's biology test, walk into his room and find him there. Michelle asks him about the test, and the two girls leave. Scott has sex with Virginia; while they are lying in bed, Myles comes home. Virginia complains about Myles being home, and she tells him to mind his own business when he asks who she was with. After Scott leaves, Virginia is angry, saying that Myles ruined her day. Kevin and Mary swim in a lake and kiss. Myles cuts Mary's yearbook picture with a knife.

Kevin and Mary enjoy some time on a boat. At the beach, Desmond is told of a Winchester boy who is missing, and he goes to see headmaster Mr. Gordian. Gordian says that they know Chip is missing because, even though it has only been one night, his medicine for "severe diabetes" has been left behind. The headmaster says that both he and Rich were last seen going to Lover's Lane in the woods.

Michelle and Jenny return to Myles' classroom and look around inside for a copy of the test. Jenny is nervous and wants to leave, but Michelle continues to look. Inside a cabinet, she finds a jar of eyeballs and fingers. They see Myles at the door and try to get out the other door, but it is locked. Michelle tries to run, but Myles grabs her and beats her face on a table. Jenny grabs a knife from the desk and swings it at Myles, but he knocks the knife from her hands. Jenny gets away and runs down the stairs, finding the front door locked. Myles stabs her a few times and cries. Now he eyes Kevin and Mary, outside kissing in the truck. Later, Myles showers, and he sees an image of the couple kissing. Desmond arrives at the school about the missing girls, and Myles lets him inside. The teacher feigns calling his wife (and being demanding with her), but Desmond sees Myles keeping the connection closed with his hand. Myles offers Desmond coffee, but the cop leaves.

Myles watches Mary with binoculars as he cuts some phone lines. He calls her and says that Kevin could not get through and had asked Myles to tell Mary to meet in the woods at nine o'clock. Desmond wants to get hold of the California State Police, since he had seen a photograph of the Sheffields at their last school, near cars with California license plates. From a phone booth, Linda, a friend of Mary, calls Kevin and says the phones are dead and that Mary wants to meet. Myles is standing beside Linda as she hangs up, and stabs her in the stomach. Desmond learns that, in California, three couples were found dead, and the authorities were looking for a teaching couple matching the Sheffields' descriptions. Myles, at home with a bloody shirt, apologizes to Virginia. Virginia asks if he has done it again, and says she is not helping him this time. Myles goes for his barbed wire in his room, and Sister Mary-Ellen has it ("You evil, evil man"). The teacher knocks the weapon away from the nun.

Kevin calls out to Mary in the woods, and they greet and embrace one another. In Myles' biology classroom, a jar of acid is picked up. Desmond goes to see Virginia and asks where her husband is, and he fires a warning shot and points his gun at her when she is uncooperative. Desmond surmises that Myles is at Lover's Lane, and he runs out. Myles jumps out and wraps the wire around Kevin's neck. Mary beats the teacher with a limb and they struggle. Myles chokes Mary until Desmond arrives with his gun. As he looks at the couple, Myles lunges forward and stabs him in the chest. Sister Mary-Ellen calls out to Myles, and she throws acid in his face. He whimpers and runs off. The nun falls to her knees, Mary at her side. Myles, with a bloody, mildly deformed face, walks into the headmaster's house, takes a shotgun and bullets from a cabinet and leaves. He walks home, and Virginia reacts to him as he enters. From outside, two gunshots are heard.

Bloodmoon is a mediocre slasher entry from Australia, with a humdrum killer and a trite weapon of choice. There are too many characters for any of them to fully develop, which creates an abundance of uninteresting people and weak subplots.

Bloodstained Butterfly (aka *Una farfalla con le ali insanguinate*) (1971)

Written by Gianfranco Clerici and Duccio Tessari; Directed by Duccio Tessari; Filmes Cinematografica; 94 min.

Cast: Helmet Berger (Giorgio); Giancarlo Sbragia (Alessandro Marchi); Evelyn Stewart (Maria); Silvio Tranquilli (Inspector Berradi); Wendi D'Olive (Sarah Marchi); Günther Stoll (Giulio Cordaro); Lorella de Luci; Carole André

Cast: Gianfranco Clerici, Duccio Tessari (Producers); Gianni Ferrio (Composer)

Marta Clerici returns home, takes off her wig and heads upstairs. Françoise Pigaut and Sarah Marchi are out walking as Sarah's mother Maria gets a massage and manicure and her father Alessandro buys a gift. Giorgio is playing the piano and his father Eriprando is out hunting. Two children are playing in the park, accompanied by their "nurse." There is a scream, and a girl rolls down an incline. A nearby person in hat and coat runs and is spotted by a kissing couple in a car. The cops give chase. The person is seen jumping a wall and running down the street.

At the airport, Marta meets a woman carrying a package similar to one that Alessandro had purchased. Giorgo walks down the alley drunk, and Sarah sees a news report of her murdered friend Françoise. Inspector Berradi is at the scene, where a bloody switchblade and musical record are discovered. There are fingerprints on the knife, and stains (caused by imitation leather found in cars) are found on Françoise's coat. The cops compose scenarios, one in which the girl was driven to the park (by someone she knew) to meet someone else, which does not take into account the fact that her books and the record were not left in the car. Alessandro does a TV report on sports. Giorgo almost runs into Sarah with his car, and the two smile at one another. Gabriela, who had seen the killer from the car, tells the cops that she knows who the person is. Giulio Cordaro, a lawyer, gets a call and goes to Alessandro's place, where the police are looking through his clothes. Maria serves some drinks and mentions sending her husband's muddy coat to the cleaners.

At Alessandro's trial, the closing argument presents the evidence against him, including the prints, car seats, soiled coat and familiarity with the victim. Giorgo and Sarah talk to each other, having apparently known one another from before. Later, Giorgo has a drink with his rich and estranged father. The next day in court, Giulio gives his closing argument, reminding everyone that the switchblade had been stolen and that many cars have seats with the material in question. Giorgo had testified about seeing another running man, Alessandro claimed that a passing car had splashed muddy water on him (and his coat) and Giulio proved that, without glasses, Gabriela could hardly recognize anyone. Afterwards, Sarah talks to Giorgo about Françoise's secret lover, of whom she would not speak. Giorgo seems unsettled.

In court, a woman says that Alessandro had purchased a sexy negligee, and Alessandro tells the court that he did not give the clothing to his wife. Giulio convinces him to admit that he had given the gown to Marta, who had drunkenly stumbled and cut her hand (explaining the blood on his coat). Berradi goes to Marta's place, and he talks to the milkman about the last time he delivered there (Marta is not home). Blood from Alessandro's shirt is discovered to be the same as Françoise's blood type. On the stand, Marta tells of her husband's story that a co-worker had cut his hand. She is accused by the court of hiding the shirt, and Maria says nothing more. Giulio lies in bed naked with Maria later, saying that they no longer have to meet in secret. Giorgo and Sarah spend some time together, and Giorgo says they should not see each other for a while. Sarah returns home, and Giulio tells Maria that he must depart.

Giorgo plays music and loads a revolver as images of a dead Françoise flash. Giulio stops at a gas station and lights a woman's cigarette, and the next day, the woman, Gloria, is found murdered. Alessandro attacks and punches his gabby cellmate (he had mentioned the man killing a schoolgirl). Sarah is angry that her mother almost seems content with the fact that Alessandro is in jail. Sarah calls Giorgo, but the pianist smokes and ignores the phone. Berradi thinks there two different killers for the two murders. Giorgo eats dinner with his parents. When a birthday cake is served to him, he pours his drink on the burning candles.

Giorgo walks on the streets and looks at a butterfly broach in a display window. Berradi receives a call from the killer, who talks of killing twice and killing a third time. Maria looks for Giulio, hears some commotion and finds the lawyer trying to force himself on Sarah. Giorgo walks through the park, where a woman is followed and grabbed, and a switchblade is flicked open. Marta goes on the stand and explains that Alessandro had been her "visitor" that day (photographing a friend). She further explains that she has the same blood type as what was found on the man's shirt. Alessandro, released, goes home to his family. Giorgo, upset, throws things around in his apartment. Berradi talks to a woman who sold switchblades, who says she knows a man who purchased two of them. The cops see Giorgo walking and chase him, but Giorgo eludes the officers.

The Marchi family is at home when Alessandro gets a telephone call. He mentions blackmail and says he will meet somewhere. After a drive, Alessandro walks into a building where Giorgo is waiting for him with a gun. Giorgo makes him say that he is a killer, and he says that he had to kill twice to get Alessandro free so that he could kill him. Giorgo says that Françoise was his, and he asks Alessandro why he killed her. Alessandro tells of making advances towards Françoise and stabbing her when she struggled and threatened to tell his wife and daughter. Giorgo shoots him. When Giorgo approaches and hesitates to shoot again, Alessandro stabs him in the stomach. A flashback shows Giorgo giving Françoise a necklace with a butterfly on it. Giorgo shoots Alessandro many more times until he is dead.

Bloodstained Butterfly is an excellent *giallo*, with strong performances and an intriguing mystery and investigation. The "introduction" of the characters at the beginning (via intertitles) is great, and there are plenty of twists and turns.

Bloody Birthday
(1981)

Written by Barry Pearson and Ed Hunt; Directed by Ed Hunt; Judica Productions; 85 min.

Cast: Lori Lethin (Joyce); Melinda Cordell (Mrs. Brody); Julie Brown (Beverly); Joe Penny (Mr. Harding); Bert Kramer (Sheriff James Brody); K.C. Martel (Timmy); Elizabeth Hoy (Debbie); Billy Jacoby (Curtis); Andy Freeman (Steven); Susan Strasberg (Miss Davis); José Ferrer (The Doctor); Ben Marley (Duke); Erica Hope (Ann); Ellen Greer (Madge); Michael Dudikoff (Willard); Cyril O'Reilly, Sylvia Wright (Couple in Van); Daniel Currie; William Boyett; Ward Costello; Georgie Paul; Norman Rice; Ruth Silveira; John Avery; Nathan Roberts

Crew: Gerald T. Olson (Producer); Steve McGloten (Associate Producer); Arlon Ober (Composer); Stephen Posey (Director of Photography); Ann E. Mills (Editor)

On June 9, 1970, at Meadowvale General Hospital, a baby girl and two baby boys are born during an eclipse. Ten years later, Duke and Ann are kissing in a cemetery, and Duke asks Ann if she wants to play "Ambulance" (a game involving his hand and her leg). Ann is afraid someone will see them, so they move to kiss inside a hole in the ground. They hear some noise, and Duke is smacked with a shovel. A jumping rope is thrown around Ann's neck. She is choked as Duke is hit more with the shovel.

Joyce is enjoying a sandwich as her brother Timmy comes through the window, saying that he was out feeding the dog and the front door was locked. Joyce arrives at the Thomas Jefferson Elementary School the next day, and Sheriff Brody is talking to Miss Davis' class about murder. He shows a handle from a skipping rope and asks if anyone was in the cemetery last night. He then leaves, saying goodbye to his daughter Debbie. After class, Debbie, Curtis and Stephen ask Miss Davis if everyone can be excused for their birthday party. The request is denied. Later, the three children dine on some cookies, and Debbie charges the boys to watch through a hole in the wall. They see Beverly, Debbie's sister, dance and undress. Later, Debbie is skipping rope and calls her father outside. Sheriff Brody narrowly misses stepping on a skateboard (carefully placed on the steps by one of the boys), and Debbie drops her skipping rope (missing a handle). Stephen beats the sheriff with a baseball bat when he bends over. The boys move the body. Debbie spots Timmy watching, and she decides to quickly call for her mother.

After the sheriff's funeral, some kids are playing a game in the junkyard. Curtis, tricking Timmy into hiding in an old refrigerator, locks the boy inside. Timmy, eventually managing to escape, returns home and tells Joyce where he has been. He then admits that the other night he was over at Debbie's house (she was not there) to see the Beverly peep-show. Joyce says she does not want Timmy to play with Curtis any more. Debbie puts a picture of Miss Davis in her scrapbook, which also contains an article about her father's death. At night, Debbie turns off the house's security system, and she and Curtis switch his replica gun with the sheriff's real gun. Later, Curtis stands behind Miss Davis with the gun, and he shoots the teacher. Debbie, outside, says hello to an approaching Timmy and Joyce. Joyce goes inside the school, where Stephen is hiding in the closet. Curtis runs outside and is decked by Timmy. Joyce finds Miss Davis' body in the closet.

Joyce returns home to find a note from Timmy, telling her he is in the junkyard. She goes looking for him there, and she finds Timmy's tiny flashlight in the refrigerator. Stephen (with a cloth covering his face) hotwires a car and tries to run Joyce over, with Curtis assisting in operating the pedals. The two boys finally tie down the gearshift, and the car flies by Joyce and goes over a small cliff. An officer arrives, and Joyce tells him what has happened. That night, Joyce, discussing astronomy with Timmy. She says that the eclipse that occurred during the births of Debbie, Curtis and Stephen would have blocked Saturn, the planet which controls the way a person treats other people. Curtis is outside with the gun, but he decides to go across the street where a couple is kissing inside a van. The man checks a noise and is shot in the head. Curtis enters the vehicle and shoots the woman.

At their birthday party, Debbie tells Curtis that Joyce might know too much, but assures her that no one will believe Joyce if she is thought to be crazy. Curtis begins putting more icing on cakes; Joyce sees him there. When she goes for another cake, she sees Curtis is hiding a bottle of ant poison behind his back. Joyce runs outside and tells everyone that Curtis has poisioned the cake. Curtis' grandfather is upset that Joyce would the accuse the boy of such a transgression, and both he and Curtis try some icing to show that there is nothing wrong with it. At home, Joyce tells Timmy that Curtis did not seem to know he was doing anything wrong. When she investigates a noise, her boyfriend Paul comes out to scare her. The couple hugs.

Beverly inadvertently discovers Debbie's scrapbook ("Clippings of murder?"). Beverly shows her mother, and Debbie says that Curtis left it. Beverly burns the book. Debbie calls up Curtis and Stephen and tells them to come over. She readies an arrow with her bow, points it at the hole in the wall and raps the arrow against the wall until Beverly looks through and is rewarded with an arrow in the eye. The boys arrive at the house ("Why didn't you wait for us?") and move the body out by the trash. Following Beverly's funeral, Debbie's distraught mother goes to the hospital. When Debbie is playing with Curtis and Stephen at her house, Timmy throws some rocks at the windows (the "special glass" will not break). They chase Timmy down, put a garden hose around his neck and cover his mouth. Joyce sees them, and Debbie feigns pleading with the two to stop hurting Timmy. Curtis mocks Joyce for the party incident, and the warped children leave.

Joyce is added to Debbie's scrapbook. Debbie tells Joyce that her mother is back, and asks if Joyce and Timmy can babysit. That night, as Timmy sleeps and Joyce listens to her earphones, Debbie lets her twisted pals inside. Curtis rewires the security system while Stephen cuts the phone line. Timmy awakes in time to see Curtis point his gun. He and his sister dodge bullets (as well as elude Debbie's sinister skipping rope). The siblings cannot open the doors or break the windows, so they run into Debbie's room, where they are under assault by Debbie's arrows. They let Stephen inside and manage to lock him in a trunk. Outside, Joyce grabs the sheriff's gun, and Curtis lets her know it is only a replica. He pulls the trigger, the gun clicks and Timmy tackles him, tying him with cords. Joyce whacks the security system and Timmy runs for help. Debbie sees her mother arriving in her car, and tells her the boys did some bad things for which she will be blamed. The two drive away. The next day, Curtis and Stephen are taken away by the police (Curtis smiles at Joyce). Debbie is outside a motel, messing with a car jack, and her mother comes out and makes sure Debbie knows her new name ("Beth Simpson"). As they drive away, a man is lying crushed underneath a nearby truck.

Bloody Birthday is an odd film, mostly due to the general perturbation surrounding the idea of children murderers. Regardless, the film manages to provide a few thrills; the junkyard pursuit and the concluding scene in Debbie's house are highlights. Actress Hoy and actor Jacoby also appeared together in the pre-credit sequence of *Hospital Massacre* (1981).

Bloody Moon (aka *Die Säge des Todes*) (1980)

Written by Rayo Casablanca; Directed by Jess Franco; Lisa-Films/Metro Films/ Rapid Films; 84 min.

Cast: Olivia Pascal (Angela); Christopher Brugger (Alvaro); Nadja Gerganoff (Manuela); Alexander Waechter (Miguel); Jasmin Losensky (Inga); Corinna Gillwald (Laura); Ann-Beate Engelke (Eva); Peter Exacoustos (Antonio); Antonio Garcia (Elvira); Beatriz Sancho Nieto (Rita); Maria Rubio (Countess Maria Gonzales); Otto W. Retzer (Bueno)

Crew: Wolf C. Hartwig (Producer); Gerhard Heinz (Composer); Juan Soler (Director of Photography)

A woman is being rolled in a wheelchair at night. Miguel, a man with a heavily scarred face, hangs around a dance outside. As a young couple enjoys some time together, Miguel steals the boy's mask and shirt and puts them on. He leads another dancing girl to believe he is Ralph, and they go to her room, where they lie on the bed for some kissing. The girl takes away the mask, sees Miguel's face and kicks him away. Miguel grabs a pair of scissors and stabs the girl repeatedly in the stomach.

When Manuela drives to a clinic to pick up her brother Miguel, a doctor tells her to not remind Miguel of the incident. On the train, a seemingly irate Miguel eyes Angela as she stands in her compartment. Alvaro arrives at the International Youth-Club Boarding School of Languages. He goes to see Manuela, whose aunt, Countess Maria Gonzales, states her belief that she is being plotting against and that Manuela only wants money. That night, as Maria lies in bed, someone shines a light in her face, then moves a flaming torch towards her. The countess screams and burns.

Angela arrives at the school a little later than her friends, and she mentions the "awful experience" on the train. She is staying in Room 13, where (it is rumored) a girl was once killed with a pair of scissors. Angela unpacks, plays some music and prepares to shower. When she wipes the steamy bathroom mirror, she sees Miguel reflected and recognizes him as the "guy from the train." At the estate, Manuela rolls her aunt around in a wheelchair. Angela goes outside, sees Miguel and walks faster. She is scared by her friend Inga, and then both go to see Laura, Eva and the flirtatious gardener, Antonio. Miguel goes to see his sister, and he proclaims his love to Manuela; the two kiss and touch. Manuela stops him, saying that it could be like it was before if they could get rid of the people who would judge them.

After a night of dancing at the disco, Antonio walks Angela home and asks her to play tennis tomorrow. Angela reads in bed, and the lights are turned off ("Who's there?"). A person is in her room with a knife. Angela looks around, finds nothing and goes back to bed. Before the killer can attack, Eva appears at the window; when she is let inside she asks to borrow a pullover. Angela gives her the clothing. As Eva changes, she is stabbed through the back with a knife. Angela finds Eva's body on the bed, screams and runs outside, finding Antonio. She tells him about Eva, but the corpse is gone when they return to the room. Inga and Alvaro also arrive at the room.

The next day, in the Spanish class that Alvaro teaches, the class is listening to tapes of Spanish dialect. On Angela's tape, the voice suddenly changes and threatens to cut her with a hacksaw. Seeing Miguel at the window, she screams—but he is gone when Alvaro is there, and the tape is back to its Spanish lessons. Angela finds bloody clothes and a bloody shower in Eva's place, and decides to look for her friend. At the dock, Angela sees Antonio arguing with Manuela. Later, a boulder rolls down a hill, nearly crushing Angela. She tells Laura that she cannot find Eva. Angela talks to Antonio, who says he did not even know Eva. Manuela talks to her aunt and notices one of her snakes is missing. After agreeing to look for Eva, Antonio sees a snake near Angela and chops off its head with garden shears. Angela turns to see bloody and open shears, and runs. Antonio tries to stop her, but Alvaro calls out to him and tells him to stop bothering his students.

Laura and her pals go to Room 13, where Inga, reportedly with someone named Ralph, is feigning a sexual act inside. She does not see a dead, hanging Eva in the closet; the girls finally see Inga through the window, and they laugh at her. Angela, out walking, sees Inga drive by in a yellow car (similar to one Manuela drove). A person wearing a mask takes Inga somewhere (she has accompanied the person willingly), and she is tied with rope. The person turns on a saw, and Inga slowly moves towards it. A young boy, having seen the couple arrive, walks inside, turns off the machine and runs. The saw is turned back on, and Inga's head is sawed off. The killer gets in the car, chases the boy and runs him over.

Manuela rolls the countess in her wheelchair. Angela goes to her room and packs. After seeing Antonio at the front door and Miguel at the window, she barricades herself in her room and sits and waits with a knife. As she looks around a room, Angela sees a shadow and stabs someone. After she lets Laura inside, she realizes she has only stabbed a dummy. Laura offers to stay for the night, and goes to the disco-club to get some drinks. When Laura returns, the killer clamps large thongs around her neck and kills her. Angela receives a phone call ("Prepare yourself to die!"), and she then finds the detached head of Inga in her bed, a lifeless Eva behind the curtain and Laura's hanging corpse outside. She is grabbed by the killer. Miguel runs in, and the two struggle. Angela runs away. Later, she sees a figure in the dark, which turns out to be Alvaro. Alvaro gets in his car and drives away. Miguel, having been hit on the head by the killer, stands up and walks out the door. Angela runs to Manuela's place and asks for help ("All my friends are dead"). Manuela takes her to a room and gives her something to drink. Angela says that the murderer's eyes seemed familiar.

Miguel is outside when Alvaro arrives at the place. Manuela and Alvaro discuss the killings that he has done, and Miguel hears them talk of blaming the murders on him. Manuela talks of how Miguel thinks she loves him, and she mentions his "repulsive face." Manuela tells Alvaro that he has already been "paid," and she tells him to kill Angela and get out. Miguel goes to a room and, evidently believing that Angela is his sister, chokes the girl until she shoves a spike through his neck. Angela runs downstairs, sees Alvaro and Mauela struggling and goes to a room and screams when seeing the crispy countess. Alvaro grabs her and holds a knife next to her, but Manuela arrives with a power saw and saws Alvaro's stomach. She puts the saw to Angela's throat and tells her to remember that she has saved her life. Angela nods and runs away. Manuela goes to the room and talks to her dead brother, but Miguel sits up and chokes Manuela. As the cops arrive and Antonio embraces Angela, Miguel collapses, holding onto his sister's hand.

Bloody Moon is a good slasher film. Although a few scenes drag and a couple of the murder sequences are unexceptional, director Franco provides some good stalking suspense, and the movie does include a nice sawing murder. Actor Christopher Brugger is actually Christoph Moosbrugger.

Bloody Murder (2000)

Written by John R. Stevenson; Directed by Ralph Portillo; Hemisphere Entertainment; 88 min.

Cast: Jessica Morris (Julie); Peter Guillemette (Patrick); Patrick Cavenaugh (Tobe); Christelle Ford (Drew); Michael Stone (Dean); Justin Martin (Jason); Tracy Pacheco (Whitney); Lindsey Leigh (Jamie); Dave Smigelski (Brad); William Winter (Doug); Michael Prohaska (Sheriff Williams); Jerry Richards (Tom McConnell); Trevor Moorehouse (Himself); Brian Messing (Deputy); Ricky Courtney, Jason Gelber (Paramedics)

Crew: Marc Greenberg, Rich Goldberg, Marc Beinstock (Executive Producers); Ralph Portillo, Jamie Elliott (Producers); Steven Stern (Composer); Keith Holland (Director of Photography); Carlos Puente (Editor)

Bill and his pregnant wife Patricia are driving in the woods when the car breaks down. Bills gets a tank from the trunk and walks until he finds a truck and headlights. He tells of his car trouble, and sees someone in a hockey mask and coveralls carrying a chainsaw ("Trevor Moorehouse"). Bill runs and falls, and screams as the person lifts the running chainsaw.

Among a group on the way to Camp Placid Pines, Tobe discusses the legend of

Trevor Moorehouse. Tobe, Dean, Whitney, Jason and Julie reach the camp and are greeted by Patrick. Brad is already there; he and Jason have a bad history from running track together. Patrick gives the counselors-to-be their jobs and, later, Julie is introduced to her "co-counselor," Drew. In the woods, Julie meets an old man named Henry, who tells her that Nelson is back for revenge. Patrick says the man once ran the camp. In the cabin, Julie tells Drew about her dead mother, and Drew says that she has also lost a parent. Around the campfire, Jason suggests playing "Bloody Murder," in which people hide from the "it" person, and if anyone finds "it," he/she screams Bloody Murder and everyone runs to "home base." During the game, Brad finds a bloody Dean and is almost attacked by an axe-wielding, hockey-mask-adorned person, who turns out to be an amused Jason. After the group disperses, Dean spots Jason and Whitney together in the woods. As Jason dresses, he is approached by someone.

The next day, Julie asks if anyone has seen Jason, saying that his bed was not slept in. Patrick says he will call the sheriff if Jason is not back by dinner. Dean asks Whitney for a row in the boat. Out on the water, he shakes and rocks the boat until she falls in (earlier he had mocked her inability to swim). Dean helps her back into the boat and rows to shore. Patrick tells Julie that Dean told him that Jason had wanted to leave, and Julie tells of the incident in the lake with Dean and Whitney. A group is watching *Sleepover Camp Massacre 14* in the mess hall when Whitney leaves for some food. In the pantry, a person in a hockey mask approaches, and Whitney is stabbed with a knife.

With Whitney missing, the sheriff is called to camp. Patrick asks about Moorehouse, but the sheriff says he does not know of the man's existence. Sheriff Williams talks to Tobe, and Tobe presents a scenario which allows Dean time to kill Whitney and clean up everything. Dean is taken to the police station. Julie and Drew talk, and Drew tells of her father's death (before she was born) and of her own "transference" (anger at other people for the death of her father). Julie runs into Henry again, and he says to ask Tommy McConnell about Nelson (Tommy is Julie's father). She e-mails him that night. Brad goes to the archery range, and the killer shoots two arrows into his back.

Since Brad is now absent, the sheriff releases Dean. He and Patrick believe the culprit is Jason. Julie tells Patrick about Henry's warning of Nelson, and Patrick says that the man is sick, but he will check for a Nelson. Julie gets a note from Drew to meet her at the lake, and on the way, Julie is chased by the killer. At the road, Julie stops Dean in his truck, and he gets out for a flat tire. He says that everything is an "elaborate prank." As Julie walks away, the killer approaches Dean and slits his throat with a garden fork and stabs him in the back.

Julie finds Henry's "creepy old cottage" and looks inside. She e-mails her father, tells of her missing pals and says she found a picture of her father next to someone named Nelson Hammond. Julie gets on her computer and researches Nelson. She learns that, at camp, he almost drowned and later killed Bill. Julie's connection is interrupted (the lines are down). She heads to the office. Jumped by someone, Julie runs and tricks the person into the freezer. It is Jason, and he says that Dean threatened to tell Julie of the Whitney situation if he did not leave. The police take Jason away.

The next morning, Julie receives an e-mail from her father, who says he remembers Nelson and asks what happened to him. Julie runs an obstacle course as a test, and falls while climbing a rope which had previously been partially sliced. Doug goes to find the tug-of-war rope for Jamie, and a dart is thrown through his back.

Julie's father arrives and Drew shows him around the camp. Julie gets a copy of the campers list, runs to the office and compares the counselors' files to Henry's picture. She learns that Drew is the daughter of Bill and Patricia, and that she was enacting her revenge on the counselors. Julie tells Tobe to call the police, then goes to find Drew and her father. Drew tells Tom to check the view at the end of the dock, and he is approached and whacked on the head with an oar. Julie meets Drew in the woods and they go to the docks, where Julie accuses Drew of killing everyone. The killer comes out with a sickle and Julie runs.

She finds Patrick in the woods and says they have to help Drew, but Patrick tells her that Drew is dead because he killed her — as well as her father and all her friends. He shows her the real Patrick hanging in a tree, and he says that he is Nelson. Tom attacks, but dead, hanging bodies fall on the two. Julie runs, and Nelson/Patrick follows with an axe. Julie runs to Tobe, Jason and Jamie, who are not sure what to do about the hysterical counselor. Tobe finally gets a shotgun from a police vehicle, but it only clicks. As Patrick lifts his axe on Julie, Drew shoots him in the arm. The sheriff drives Patrick to the station, says he knows why Patrick killed Brad, Dean and Whitney (they were children of counselors) and asks why he murdered Doug. Patrick says he did not kill Doug and that Trevor Moorehouse must have done it. Julie says bye to everyone, and tells Jason that Tobe is going to the hospital with her. The two drive away, and an irate Jason is greeted by a hockey-mask-wearing, chainsaw-toting person.

Bloody Murder is a mildly entertaining slasher film. Despite incorporating a number of references to horror films (especially *Friday the 13th*), the movie takes itself seriously.

Body Double
(1984)

Written by Robert J. Avrech and Brian De Palma; Directed by Brian De Palma; Columbia Pictures; 114 min.

Cast: Craig Wasson (Jake); Melanie Griffith (Holly); Gregg Henry (Sam); Deborah Shelton (Gloria); Guy Boyd (Jim McLean); Dennis Franz (Rubin); David Haskell (Drama Teacher); Rebecca Stanley (Kimberly); Al Israel (Corso); Douglas Warhit (Video Salesman); B.J. Jones (Douglas); Russ Marin (Frank); Lane Davies (Billy); Barbara Crampton (Carol); Larry "Flash" Jenkins (Assistant Director); Monte Landis (Sid Goldberg); Linda Shaw (Linda Shaw); Mindi Miller (Tina); Denise Loveday (Actress, Vampire Movie); Gela Jacobson (Corso's Secretary); Ray Hasset, Rick Gunderson, Jerry Brutsche (Police Officers); Michael Kearns (Male Porno Star); Rob Paulsen (Cameraman); Jeremy Lawrence (Theatre Director); Rod Loomis (TV Director); Gary F. Griffith (Auditioning Actor); Michael White (Security Guard, Gloria's House); Emmett Brown (Studio Guard); H. David Fletcher (Security Guard, Bellini's); Marcia Delmar (Production Assistant); Phil Redrow (Naked Man); Slavitza Jovan (Saleslady); Jack Mayhall (Jake's Replacement); Alexandra Day, Pamela Weston, Brinke Stevens, Melissa Christian (Girls in Bathroom); Patty Lotz, Barbara Peckinpaugh (Girls in *Holly Does Hollywood*); David Ursin, Casey Sander, Wes Edwards (Men in *Holly Does Hollywood*); Chuck Waters (Jogger); Paul Calabria (Man With Dog)

Crew: Howard Gottfried, Brian De Palma (Producers); Pino Donaggio (Composer); Stephen H. Burum, A.S.C. (Director of Photography); Jerry Greenburg, Bill Pankow (Editors)

Jake Scully is filming a low-budget film, *Vampire's Kiss*. While filming a scene where he is lying in a coffin, he has a claustrophobic attack and cannot continue. He is sent home, and seems happy to have a little time off, but his mood abruptly changes when he catches his girlfriend having sex with another man. He heads to a bar to saturate himself in alcohol, neglecting the bartender's reminder that he quit drinking. The bartender, Doug, asks if he has a place to stay. Jake is allowed to sleep on a tiny loveseat.

The next day, Jake is looking through the casting notices, searching for an "interview only." He runs into a fellow actor and asks him if he knows of any sublets. Sam shows up, and he and Jake are introduced. His friend reminds Jake to go to class later. Jake goes to a couple of interviews and runs into Sam again. At his acting class, he is telling of a game he played when he was younger, one in which he hid from others

("I'm the sardine") and was not able to move. The acting instructor tears into him; Sam, sitting with others, finally stands and tells him to leave Jake alone. The teacher looks at him ("You're not a member of this class, are you?"). Sam leads Jake away.

Jake and Sam are at a bar, discussing his current situation. Sam finally asks where he is staying and tells Jake he has been housesitting for a friend but will be leaving soon. Jake accepts the offer and they go to an extravagant home where Sam shows him around and they have a toast "to Hollywood." Sam then introduces Jake to his "favorite neighbor" via a telescope: and Jake watches a woman perform a seductive dance all the way into her bed. Sam says the neighbor does the dance every night. Jake thanks Sam again and he is left alone. Later, Jake checks on the neighbor, who is now sleeping. Someone enters her home and takes some money. When the woman tries to stop him, he hits her and leaves her crying.

Some time later, Jake's agent tells him that he has been fired by director Rubin ("artistic differences"). Jake goes to the set and argues with Rubin, but he is taken outside. That night, Jake watches the neighbor again and sees an "Indian" working on a satellite dish nearby. The next day, Jake is driving and he sees the woman leaving her place. He also spies the Indian following her. Jake pursues them to the mall. He tails the woman to the phones, where she calls someone, and then to a store, where she tries on and purchases a pair of panties. Jake sees the Indian again and runs after him. He gets on the elevator with the woman before the Indian, who sees Jake with her and does not get on.

After taking her old pair of panties from the trash, Jake continues to follow the woman. They go to a lavish hotel near the beach. Jake stands on a balcony near her hotel room and hears the woman on the phone. Whoever she was planning on seeing is not coming. She walks down to the beach, and Jake sees the Indian nearby. He runs to the beach and stops her: "Excuse me. Someone's following you." She looks at him, and the Indian runs by and grabs her purse. Jake gives chase, following the Indian into a tunnel, where he has another claustrophobic attack. The Indian stops, dumps the purse, takes something and runs away. Jake picks up the things and sees that the woman's name is Gloria Revell. Gloria arrives and helps an unsettled Jake out of the tunnel. The two kiss for a moment, then Gloria stops him and quickly leaves.

Back at the house, Jake is thinking of what to say to Gloria when he telephones her. While he is watching her house, he sees the upstairs blinds open in her bedroom. The Indian is there with a gigantic drill, emptying the contents of her safe. Jake watches in fear for a while and finally calls Gloria, who answers in her bedroom ("Look out, he's right behind you!"). The Indian wraps the phone cord around her neck. Jake runs outside, finds two joggers and gets them to follow him. Jake gets inside the house, but is jumped by the dog. The Indian knocks Gloria to the floor and drills her, which Jake can see from the floor below. The joggers finally get the dog off of Jake, and he runs upstairs, seeing a dead Gloria and narrowly missing her murderer.

Detective McLean tells Jake the Indian took Gloria's card key. He finds the panties in Jake's pocket, and he thinks Jake had sex with his neighbor. He then asks Jake if he knew Alexander Revell, Gloria's husband. Later, Jake is watching late night television and sees a preview for *Holly Does Hollywood*, in which Holly does a very familiar seductive dance. The next day, he calls Adult Film Group to ask about Holly, and he hears the receptionist and a man arguing about auditions. He shows up to audition and sees the gruffy Mr. Corso, reads cheesy dialogue and takes off his clothes for some pictures. Jake gets the part and films a scene with Holly.

After the shoot, Jake pretends to be a big film producer, and he tells Holly he wants her in his next movie. They go to a bar to discuss the scene, which involves a woman alone, and Holly says she is known for a certain number she does ("I know. I've seen it…

a few times"). They head to his place, where he keeps trying to get her to talk about being hired to dance. She says she does not know who hired her, and, irate about there being no part for her, she starts to leave. Sam calls, Jake tells him to wait and Jake lets Holly listen to his voice. She says that it is the man who hired her, and she leaves. Sam watches them from the house.

Jake telephones McLean and tells him he was set up. He says Sam is really Alexander Revell, and he hired the Indian to kill his wife. He also hired Holly to dance so that Jake would watch and eventually witness the murder. Holly, trying to hitch a ride, is picked up by the Indian. Jake goes out to meet McLean, and sees Holly and the Indian in front of him. He follows them to a reservoir, where the Indian is digging a hole. Jake walks over to the hole after the Indian is suddenly gone. He is pulled inside, where he pulls at the Indian's face and removes a mask to reveal Sam. Jake's claustrophobia kicks in, and he cannot move. Sam says Jake ruined his surprise ending, and that he is giving Jake "another take." Jake is suddenly on a movie set with Rubin screaming "Action!" He is helped out, but he stops them and says he can help himself. He crawls back into the coffin, the "scene" starts again and Jake opens his eyes and grabs the shovel from Sam ("Don't be so melodramatic!"). The dog, awaiting in Sam's truck, jumps out and goes for Jake. He ducks, and the dog hits Sam, knocking both of them into the reservoir. Holly suddenly awakes and is angry. Jake returns to filming the vampire movie, while Holly watches with the rest of the crew.

Body Double is a vastly underrated De Palma achievement, with an excellent movie-within-a-movie theme and beautiful, crisp visuals. The title, and the scene at the end (in which a crew is replacing an actress with a body double), are references to De Palma's earlier thriller *Dressed to Kill* (1980), which was criticized for using a body double in a shower scene for actress Angie Dickinson. Annette Haven, star of pornographic movies, was originally cast as Holly.

Body Puzzle (aka *Misteria*) (1991)

Written by Teodoro Agrimi, Bruce Martin and Lamberto Bava; Directed by Lamberto Bava; Produzioni Atlas Consorziate; 98 min.

Cast: Joanna Pacula (Tracy); Tom Arana (Michael); François Montagut (Abe); Gianni Garko (Police Chief); Erika Blanc (Doctor Corti); Matteo Gazzolo (Gigli); Susanna Javicoli (Mrs. Consorti); Bruno Corazzari (Professor Brusco); Ursula von Baechler (Katia Lelli); Sebastiano Lo Monaco (Mortician); Giovanni Lambardo Radice (Morangi); Paolo Baroni (Milani); Gianni Giuliano (Cemetery Director); Giuseppe Marini (Agent Melli); Guido Quintozzi (Ass't Pathologist); Francesco Romano (Lifeguard); Gianna Paola Scaffidi (Mrs. Landi); Mino Sferra (Agent Mino)

Crew: Mario Bregni, Pietro Bergni (Producers); Carlo Maria Cordio (Composer); Luigi Kuveiller (Director of Photography); Piero Bozza (Editor)

A man is sitting in front of a piano and listening to music with earphones. He beats the piano keys, puts his head down and thinks back to driving his car in the rain. He screams for a man on a motorbike to stop, but the man keeps going and wrecks his bike. The man runs out and cries over his body in the rain. The man goes to a bakery near closing and asks for some chocolates. When the bakery owner gets on a ladder, the man stabs him in the back. He stabs him a few more times, and then puts something in a plastic bag.

Tracy wakes up and walks to the kitchen, and does not see the killer just outside her window. She gets a drink and goes back to bed. The killer, now inside the house, goes to the refrigerator. At the bakery, the cops learn that the dead man's ear has been cut off. Tracy is stopped outside by the cemetery director, who drives her to the graveyard to show that someone has dug up the coffin of her husband Abe and taken the corpse. Back at her place, Tracy finds a wrapped object with her name written on it; inside is a severed ear. Michael, a detective, visits Tracy, and she tells him the handwriting on the package is that of her late husband. Michael tells her that the intruder may have used a key (no forced entry), and he is putting her under police protection. He introduces her to his inspector friend; the inspector and Tracy leave for her parents' house.

The killer follows a woman around in the mall and, in the bathroom, ties her hand to a toilet seat and lops off her free hand. The cops later discover that the woman's chest cavity has been gutted. Michael goes to see Tracy at her parents' home and tells her of the most recent murder. She shows him the doors and windows around the house, and Michael leaves. Tracy's dog stands by the door and whines, and a frightened Tracy checks outside. Michael is driving in his car and, noticing blood on his sleeve, he quickly turns around. The front door shuts, and Tracy finds a severed hand hanging on the door. Michael is back at the house, and the two talk about Tracy's husband Abe. They discuss the animal blood incident (all over the bed) following the day Tracy and Abe were married. Tracy says it may have been Tim, an old friend of Abe's.

Michael goes to see Morangi, who had identified Abe's body. He says Abe was always over in a private room (even after his marriage) with both women and men. Michael finds a picture of the killer standing by a mustached man whose photograph is framed in Tracy's house. Michael shows the picture to Morgani, and tells the detective that it is Abe but he does not know the other man. Tracy, at her own place to pick up a manuscript, finds a leather outfit and helmet lying on her bed. The inspector arrives, and they both see blood in front of the refrigerator. A bloody suitcase is inside. The inspector starts to call someone but is shoved into the pool by the killer. The killer grabs the suitcase and runs out.

Michael goes to see a psychiatrist (her number was in an address book found in Abe's private room); she recalls Abe, but he was not her patient. She treated Timothy Bell, a would-be concert pianist who was very close to Abe. He "went crazy" and became very jealous when Abe married Tracy. A lifeguard (with a scar on his back) solo swims after people have gone, and the killer dives in and stabs him underwater. Michael and Tracy find a package by her door, and Michael picks it up and opens it ("It's not a finger"). Michael learns that, with each killing, something was amputated but additionally internal organs were taken. The lifeguard had only one kidney, having just been through surgery. Michael and Tracy have dinner together, and afterwards they kiss. The inspector tells Michael that Timothy Bell was once in a mental hospital but is now out, and that Morangi telephoned, wanting to talk to Michael. Michael goes to the hospital and learns that Bell had "become" Abe to accept the loss, and the doctors were able to "persuade" Bell of his true identity.

Michael goes to see Morangi, who is hiding out in a horse carriage. He tells the detective that he saw Abe the previous night. Michael is told that all three victims were donor organ recipients, and that in each case, the implated organ was taken. The organs all came from Abe's body, and Michael surmises that Bell is trying to put him back together. The inspector learns that there are three remaining recipients, and one of them is deceased. Tracy follows her wandering dog to a room (the same one the killer was in earlier), and she finds pizza and a beer atop a freezer adorned in a tablecloth. She runs out. The inspector shows Michael a picture of Timothy Bell, and Michael recognizes him from the photo with Abe. One of the recipients, Mrs. Landi (kidney), is at the station. The police arrive at a school to find the other recipient, Katia (cornea), who teaches a class for the blind. She plays the children a tape; the killer sneaks up behind Katia, stabs her and cuts out her eyes.

Michael is at Tracy's place, and Tracy tells him what has happened, saying the beer she found was the imported kind that Abe would drink. Michael shows Tracy the photograph of the two men and says that he thinks it is Bell. Tracy says it is a picture of Abe and her deceased brother. Michael points out the killer and asks if that is Tracy's brother, and she corrects him, saying the man with the mustache is her brother, and the other (the killer) is Abe. Mrs. Landi is in labor and is taken to the hospital. Abe, dressed as a doctor, begins to roll her to the elevator, and Michael arrives and pulls the bed from him ("Don't do it, Abe").

Michael arrives at Tracy's place, and as the inspector stays with Tracy, he goes to the room with the freezer to look around. Inside the freezer, under the frozen foods, is a body. Abe jumps up from hiding and whacks the detective. The inspector goes to check on Michael, and locks Tracy inside, before he is hit and his key is taken. Tracy tries to get outside, and she meets Abe, holding a knife. Abe tells her he did the things he has done for her and Abe. He is evidently upset about what he has done, and he runs outside and speeds away on his bike. Tracy follows in her car and chases Abe, until he runs head first into a car and flies through the windshield. The cops arrive, and a weeping Tracy is led away. Michael walks down the dark street alone.

Body Puzzle is a very effective slasher from Lamberto Bava, with plenty of suspense and a very intriguing mystery. Montagut is very good as the tight-lipped killer. Arana has appeared in a number of A-production Hollywood films such as *L.A. Confidential* (1997) and *Gladiator* (2000), but he may be best remembered by horror fans for his maddening performance in Michele Soavi's *The Church* (1989).

Bride of Chucky (1998)

Written by Don Mancini; Directed by Ronny Yu; Universal Pictures/Midwinter Productions; 89 min.

Cast: Jennifer Tilly (Tiffany); Brad Dourif (Chucky); Katherine Heigl (Jade); Nick Stabile (Jesse); Alexis Arquette (Damien); Gordon Michael Woolvett (David); John Ritter (Chief Warren Kincaid); Lawrence Dane (Lieutenant Preston); Michael Johnson (Norton); James Gallanders (Russ); Janet Kidder (Diane); Vincent Corazza (Bailey); Kathy Najimy (Motel Maid); Park Bench (Stoner); Emily Weedon (Girl at One-Stop); Ben Bass (Lieutenant Ellis); Roger McKeen (Justice of the Peace); Sandi Stahlbrand (Reporter); Ed Gale (Chucky Double); Debbie Lee Carrington (Tiffany Double)

Crew: David Kirschner, Grace Gilroy (Producers); Laura Moskowitz (Co-Producer); Corey Sienega, Don Mancini (Executive Producers); Graeme Revell (Composer); Peter Pau (Director of Photography); David Wu, Randolph K. Bricker (Editors)

A police officer goes into the police evidence room, opens a locker marked "Unsolved" and gets out a plastic bag. Next he makes a phone call, reminding someone to bring his money. While waiting, he finally opens the bag to look inside, and he is grabbed from behind and his throat slit. A blonde Tiffany takes the cop's lighter (with "Bailey" inscribed on it) and picks up a mangled Chucky ("Well, hello, dolly"). She takes him to her trailer where there are many dolls, and she pieces and stitches Chucky back together.

Chief Warren Kincaid answers the door to David, the gentleman caller for Jade. After they leave, the chief telephones someone. Inside David's car is Jesse, the true lover for Jade, and the two kiss. Suddenly they must respond to flashing cop lights behind them. In her trailer, Tiffany places Chucky on the floor surrounded by candles, then reads *Voodoo for Dummies*. She recites a chant and nothing happens ("What a crock!"). Damien, a Marilyn Manson–esque goth lover sweet on Tiffany, arrives at the trailer. Tiffany obviously finds Damien exasperating (he has not even killed anyone), but she seems excited upon realizing that Chucky is no longer lying on the floor. He eventually appears next to Tiffany and she screams. Damien laughs at Chucky ("He's so '80s! He's not even scary!"), but when Tiffany sets Chucky atop Damien and dances for the both of them, Chucky turns around, pulls Damien's lip ring out and suffocates him with a pillow. The two lovers are reunited.

David, Jade and Jesse are getting breathalyzer tests from the cop Norton. The chief shows up and takes his niece away. At the trailer, Tiffany tells Chucky about the ring she found on the mantle the night he was killed. She thought he was going to pop the big question, but Chucky says he stole the ring, and he laughs at the idea of marriage. An irate Tiffany puts Chucky in the playpen and padlocks it, and she lies on her bed and weeps.

The next day, Tiffany asks her neighbor Jesse to help her with a heavy trunk (a dead Damien is inside). Tiffany later gives Chucky his bride, a doll in a wedding dress that says, "With this ring I thee wed." As Tiffany bathes and watches TV, Chucky uses the ring from the doll to saw the wooden bar of the playpen. He attacks Tiffany, she kicks him, and he retaliates by sliding the TV stand towards her, knocking the TV into the bath and electrocuting Tiffany. He transfers Tiffany's soul to the wedding dress doll. Tiffany awakens understandably upet, but Chucky tells her they can transfer their souls to humans if they have the Heart of Damballa, an amulet buried with Chucky's corpse. Tiffany calls Jesse and asks him to deliver two dolls. Tiffany changes her attire, and Jesse arrives to five $100 bills and a note saying to deliver the dolls to Forest Creek Cemetery in Hackensack, New Jersey.

Jesse goes to see Jade, excited about the money and the chance for freedom, and he asks her to marry him, which she accepts ("I give 'em six months; three if she gains weight," says a pessimistic Chucky). Chucky and Tiffany watch as the chief gets near the van. Tiffany suggests improvising (like Martha Stewart), and they use a collection of nails aimed at the chief's face. They clean up the blood and throw his body into a compartment in back before the young couple returns. Before they get far, Norton pulls them over. He searches the van and finds marijuana (that the chief had planted). Chucky borrows Tiffany's lighter, crawls to Norton's car and throws a shirt in the gas tank and lights it. The car explodes; and Jesse and Jade quickly leave.

Both Jesse and Jade think the other one is responsible, and David calls to tell them about the discovery of a lighter (belonging to a dead cop) and the missing chief. The couple go into a church to get married, and while Chucky and Tiffany are in the van talking, the chief jumps out and Chucky stabs him multiple times. While Jesse and Jade are in the honeymoon suite, another couple enters the room. Tiffany watches as the woman steals Jesse's wallet, and later she goes into the couple's room. She tosses a champagne bottle up at the mirrored ceiling, and glass falls down in shards, slicing the two people and their waterbed. "I love you," Chucky tells Tiffany after her display of murderous rampage, and he asks her to marry him (using the ring from a detached finger). Tiffany says yes, and they spend a night of plastic-rubber intimacy.

When the maid finds the bodies the next morning, she screams. Jesse and Jade think it best to grab everything and run. They each think the other has killed the couple. David shows up, telling them it is all a misunderstanding (they both called him the night before). David notices a wretched smell, and he opens the compartment and finds the chief. Before the other two see him, he grabs the chief's gun, points it at Jesse and Jade and tells them to pull over. He gets out of the van, and Chucky and Tiffany bring out their guns. A dumbfounded David backs up into the street and is pulverized by a passing semi-truck ("That works, too!").

As they are driving away, they hear over the radio that, at one of the murders, fingerprints belonging to Charles Lee Ray were discovered and that his body is going to be exhumed. The group steals an RV; Tiffany makes dinner and cooks for Chucky. Jesse gets Chucky to start an argument (by implying that Tiffany should wash the dishes herself), and during the fight, Jade kicks Tiffany into the oven. Jesse pushes Chucky out of the window, and the RV swerves off the road.

Tiffany jumps out of the oven, half-cooked, and bites Jade's ear, and is thrown to the side by Jesse. Jesse and Jade are separated when the RV explodes.

Chucky has Jade as a hostage, and he has her get the amulet for him. Jesse has a burnt Tiffany as hostage, and he trades her for Jade. As he and Jade embrace, Chucky throws the knife into his back. Chucky has both guns and he ties the couple up. He begins his chant again but is stabbed in the back by Tiffany, who says they "belong dead." Jade gets free as Chucky and Tiffany begin a shovel fight. Chucky finally stabs Tiffany, and Jesse whacks him with a shovel. Chucky lands in his own dug grave as Lieutenant Preston shows up. Jade picks up a gun and points it at Chucky. Chucky says, "Go ahead and shoot. I'll be back. I always come back!" Jade shoots, and Chucky is killed. After the couple leaves, Preston eyes Tiffany, and she is suddenly awake and screaming, giving birth to a little baby who jumps onto Preston.

Bride of Chucky breathes fresh life into the series with the introduction of the delightful Tiffany and a terrific new look for Chucky. Director of photography Pau won an Academy Award for his beautiful cinematography in *Crouching Tiger, Hidden Dragon* (2000). Director Yu also helmed the Hong Kong classic *The Bride With White Hair* (1993). At the beginning of the film, in the police evidence room, the Jason Voorhees and Michael Myers masks are shown.

Bruiser (2000)

Written and directed by George A. Romero; Le Studio Canal+/Romero-Grunwald Productions; 99 min.

Cast: Jason Flemyng (Henry Creedlow); Peter Stormare (Miles Styles); Leslie Hope (Rosemary Newley); Nina Garbiras (Janine Creedlow); Andrew Tarbet (James Larson); Tom Atkins (Detective McCleary); Jonathan Higgins (Detective Rakowski); Jeff Monahan (Tom Burtram); Marie V. Cruz (Number Nine); Beatriz Pizano (Katie Saldano); Tamsin Kelsey (Mariah Breed); Kelly King (Gloria Kite); Susanne Sutchy (Colleen); Balazs Koos (Chester); Jean Daigle (Fadush); Christ Gilett (Male Executive); Chantal Quesnelle (Rita); Jennifer Foster (Carol); Boyd Banks (Jostor); Neil Crone (Boss); Ted Ludzik (Gas Station Attendant); Dianna Platts (Reporter); Kiran Friesan (Lady Godiva); Murray Oliver (Cameraman); Peter Mensah (Skinhead); Neville Edwards (Derelict); Yan Feldman (Knife); D'arcy Smith (Uniform); Colin Glazer (Police Officer); Monique Osier (Top Hat); Tina Romero (Cleopatra); C.J. Fidler (Captive Woman); Ron Weber (Captive Man); Kevin Rushton (Drunk Attacker); Andrew Romero (Little Devil); J.B. Destiny (Guitarist); Big Poppa Gator (Bouncer); Ari Cohen, David Lyle (Callers); David Harcourt (Rigger); Ron Van Hart (Football Player); Brian Renfro (Train Station Man); Victoria Fodor (Lady in Red); Melanie (Diogee); Bill Vidbert (Stand-In); The Misfits (Themselves)

Crew: Adam M. Shore (Executive Producer); Peter Grumwald, Ben Barenholtz (Producers); Martin Walters, Ric Shore (Co-Producers); Donald Rubinstein (Composer); Adam Swica (Director of Photography); Miume Jan Eramo (Editor)

Henry Creedlow wakes up in the morning and goes through his usual routine, doing things like shaving and brushing his teeth. He then puts a gun to his head and shoots himself, a fatal act that he merely imagined. He eats breakfast, working his way around his incomplete house (it is in the midst of construction) and dealing with an insubordinate little dog. The dog actually belongs to Henry's wife Janine, who seems indifferent to Henry.

At the train station, Henry is waiting with his friend, Jimmy. Apparently, Jimmy has invested some money for Henry, and Henry's return is much lower than he thought. While trying to board the train, an unsettled Henry imagines himself pulling away a pushy lady and struggling with her until she is left under the tracks, allowing the moving train to crush her head.

Henry works for a magazine called *Bruiser*. While at the office, everyone is deciding on which model should be on the cover of the magazine's latest issue. The reprehensible boss, Miles, mocks Henry's choice in front of Henry and his co-workers. Later, Henry is talking to Miles' wife Rosie, and there appears to be an attraction between the two people. While playing tennis with Jimmy, Henry tells his friend that he cannot even get a platnium credit card because his "assets" are "coming up short." Afterwards, there is a pool party for the workers at Miles and Rosie's home. Henry is sitting for a plaster of his face, so that Rosie can add the mask of Henry's face to her "garden of lost souls." From across the pool, Henry sees Miles and his wife in a very intimate moment, for which Henry confronts Janine in the car at home. Janine hardly seems to care that Henry saw her with Miles, telling her distraught husband, "You are going no place. You're nothing. You're nobody." Henry then fantasizes about Janine pulling the car into the garage and getting an axe in her head.

After drinking all night, Henry awakes and goes through his routine, only to see a faceless mask staring back at him in the mirror. When he tries to remove the "mask," he cuts himself. Henry hides as Katie the maid comes home, and he watches her fill her bag with goods from around the house. He exposes himself and bashes her face with the bag (full of solid, silver objects). He wraps the body in plastic and hides again when Janine comes home, overhearing a conversation in which Janine says she is going to leave Henry. Henry follows his wife to the office, but it is Rosie who catches Janine and Miles having sex on the conference table, and she snaps a picture (she is the photographer for *Bruiser*). When Miles chases his wife out of the building, Henry revels his new face to his wife, and he tosses her out of the window to hang to death on an extension cord.

Henry goes home, eludes the cops (who come to his door) and eventually discovers that his pal Jimmy has more than likely been taking Henry's money. After making it appear that he has possibly killed himself and disposing of the maid's body, Henry calls Rosie and tells her not to go out of her house because the police think she has killed Janine. Later, Henry visits Jimmy at the tennis court and points a gun at him in the locker room. Jimmy tells him it was Janine's idea to extort money from Henry and that he will write Henry a check. Henry politely declines and shoots him in the chest. Henry goes to see Rosie at her home to tell her what he has been up to lately ("I've been working on my image"). He then telephones *The Larry Case Show*, a popular radio program, tells them his name and says that he is "Faceless" and has murdered people.

Henry goes to Miles' costume party; Rosie and Detective McCleary, who is investigating the recent killings, are also there. Henry has several men take Miles away, and Henry tells him he will be the grand finale. With the crowd of partygoers underneath, Miles is raised overhead on wires, which people have been doing throughout the party. Henry aims a strong laser (intended for exploded the heads of confetti-filled dummies) at Miles and kills him, while the crowd cheers. As Henry walks away, he puts down the mask and cape, and his face is back to normal. Someone says hello to Henry ("You can see my face?"), and he is spotted by McCleary. Before the detective can arrest Henry, however, Rosie shows up in costume with the blank white mask on, yelling to the detective, "It's me!" She tells Henry she made a plaster of her own face, and it was blank, just like Henry's. Henry is then lost in the crowd, and McCleary cannot get to him in time.

Working in an office as a messenger boy, a long-haired Henry passes by an office with an angry executive yelling at several people. After the man screams at the overly curious Henry, Henry calmly walks by, and the executive demands for him to come back. Henry says, "Coming, sir," turns around, and his blank, anonymous, faceless mask has returned.

Bruiser, Romero's first film in almost nine years, is a visually adept feature that effectively returns the director to his recurring theme of searching for identity (which he also explores in 1976's *Martin*, 1982's

Knightriders and 1993's *The Dark Half*). *Bruiser* had been completed for some time and was awaiting a studio to pick it up and release it theatrically. After Romero fans were forced to wait well over a year, the film made its debut on video and DVD.

The Burning (1981)

Written by Peter Lawrence and Bob Weinstein; Directed by Tony Maylam; Miramax/Filmways Pictures/Cropsy Ventures; 91 min.

Cast: Brian Matthews (Todd); Leah Ayres (Michelle); Brian Backer (Alfred); Larry Joshua (Glazer); Jason Alexander (Dave); Ned Eisenberg (Eddy); Carrick Glenn (Sally); Carolyn Houlihan (Karen); Fisher Stevens (Woodstock); Lou David (Cropsy); Shelley Bruce (Tiger); Sarah Chodoff (Barbara); Bonnie Deroski (Marnie); Holly Hunter (Sophie); Kevi Kendall (Diane); J.R. McKechnie (Fish); George Parry (Alan); Ame Segull (Rhoda); Jeff De Hart (Supervisor); Bruce Kluger (Rod); Keith Mandell (Young Todd); Jerry McGee (Intern); Mansoor Najee-Ullah (Orderly); Willie Reale (Paul); John Roach (Snoop); K.C. Townsend (Hooker); John Tripp (Camp Counselor); James Van Verth (Jamie)

Crew: Jean Ubaud, Michael Cohl, Andre Djaoui (Executive Producers); Harvey Weinstein (Producer); Danny Ubaud (Associate Producer); Rick Wakeman (Composer); Harvey Harrison, B.S.C. (Director of Photography); Jack Sholder (Editor); Tom Savini (Special Makeup and Effects)

At Camp Blackfoot, several boy campers decide to frighten the caretaker, Cropsy. The group heads over to his cabin with a box, and one boy goes inside, puts the box down, lights something and walks out. They rap on the window until Cropsy wakes up, and the caretaker sees a wormy skull with lit candles inside. He screams and inadvertently knocks over the skull, setting the bed afire and burning a gasoline can, which explodes. Cropsy runs out, engulfed in flames, and falls down a small incline into the water. One week later, at St. Catherine's Hospital, an orderly takes an intern to see a man, badly burnt, who was lucky to be alive ("He's a monster, man..."). As the orderly stands by the curtain, Cropsy's charred hand grabs him, and the orderly screams.

Five years later, Cropsy is released from the hospital, deformed from the scorching episode. Cropsy walks the streets and goes somewhere with a prostitute (being sure to turn off the light before he enters). As she is preparing, Cropsy gets close and stabs the woman with scissors. At Camp Stonewater, campers are playing baseball, and Cropsy is out in the trees with his garden shears. In the cafeteria, Karen tells Michelle that she likes Eddy, but she is a little frightened of him. Sally wakes up in the morning and goes to shower. While showering, she hears a noise ("Who's there?"), and she throws the curtain aside and screams. The girls run to the showers and see Alfred running away. Todd stops him and goes to have a talk with him. Alfred says he just wanted to scare Sally and that people are always picking on him. Todd says he knows how Alfred feels because, five years ago, he was sent home from camp. Later, Glazer warns Alfred to "stay away from his girl."

Later, the campers are swimming, and Glazer pushes Alfred off the dock and into the water. Dave helps Alfred back to the dock (Alfred cannot swim). Dave, Woodstock and Fish help Alfred enact his revenge: Woodstock shoots Glazer with an air pistol and hits him on his backside while he is on a raft trying to woo Sally. In the cabin that night, Cropsy is hanging around outside, and Alfred reacts when seeing a "horrible face" in the window, but the others see nothing. At dinner that night, a man talks to everyone about the three-day canoe trip to Devil's Creek.

The next day, a large group of campers are out canoeing. At night, around the campfire, Todd tells the story of Cropsy the caretaker. He mentions the "prank," and says that Cropsy survived and eats people raw. Eddy jumps out in a mask and scares everyone. Later, Eddy and Karen are kissing. Karen seems doubtful, and Eddy decides to

Cropsy the caretaker (Lou David), irked about his scorching disfigurement and armed with his garden shears, searches the woods for more camping victims in Tony Maylam's *The Burning* (1981).

skinny dip in the nearby lake. When Karen joins him and remains unsure about his true intentions, Eddy grows angry, and Karen leaves. She finds her clothes scattered around the trees, and while looking for them, Karen is killed by Cropsy. The next morning Michelle and Todd ask Eddy where Karen is, and he says he does not know. They learn that the canoes are missing, and Todd finally decides that the group needs to construct a raft.

Eddy, Woodstock, Fish and two of the female campers leave on the raft to get help at the camp. They see one of their canoes and row towards it. Cropsy, waiting inside, chops up the rafters with his shears. Glazer and Sally are out in a sleeping bag, and despite the unsatisfying moments of intimacy, they decide to stay with one another. Glazer goes to get some matches so that he can build a fire, and while he is gone, Crospy attacks Sally. Glazer gets the matches, and Alfred gets out of his sleeping bag and follows him. Glazer returns to find Sally dead, and he is killed by Cropsy. Alfred runs back to Todd and wakes him up ("Glazer's dead!"). Todd goes back with him, finds a bloody and lifeless Glazer, and Cropsy swipes Todd with the shears. Alfred screams and runs away from Cropsy, and a wounded Todd awakes.

The campers see the raft return, and Michelle swims out to it and finds various pieces of the rafters. Todd returns to the group, and he convinces the remaining campers to get on the raft and get back to the camp for help. Todd grabs an axe and goes looking for Alfred. The rafting campers make it back, and Michelle and supervisor Jeff jump on a motorboat. Alfred is grabbed by Cropsy and he is bound and gagged inside a building. Todd, having heard Alfred scream, gets to the building, and inside (after finding a dead Karen), he sees Cropsy with a flamethrower. A flashback shows that Todd was one of the pranksters who caused the burning of the caretaker. Cropsy shuts off the flamethrower, Todd hears Alfred scream, and Cropsy appears again; the flamethrower is once more active. As Cropsy is swinging his flames around, Alfred frees himself and stabs Cropsy in the back with the garden shears. Michelle waves the police helicopter down. Cropsy returns once again and grabs Alfred. Alfred moves, and Todd axes the caretaker in the head. Alfred turns the blazing flamethrower, and Cropsy burns. At the end, the story of Cropsy is being told around a campfire.

The Burning is one of the better slashers, due to some good performances and a superb villain-stalker. Some of *The Burning*'s notoriety can be credited to the fact that most of Tom Savini's work was chopped out of the film (evidently someone used Cropsy's garden shears). The film was an early production for Miramax and the Weinstein brothers, and the film debuts for Alexander, Stevens and Hunter. Editor Sholder went on to direct *Alone in the Dark* (1982) and *The Hidden* (1988).

The Cat o' Nine Tails (aka *Il gatto a nove code*) (1971)

Written and directed by Dario Argento; Seda Spettacoli/Terra Filmkunst/Labrador Films/Mondial Films/Transconta S.A.; 112 min.

Cast: James Franciscus (Carlo Giordani); Karl Malden (Franco Arnó); Catherine Spaak (Anna Terzi); Pier Paolo Capponi (Commissario Spimi); Horst Frank (Dott. Braun); Rada Rassimov (Bianca Merusi); Aldo Reggiani (Dott. Casoni); Carlo Alighiero (Dott. Calabresi); Vittorio Congia (Fotografo Righetto); Tom Felleghy (Dott. Esson); Emilio Marchesini (Dott. Mombell); Carrado Olmi (Morsella); Cinzia De Carolis (Lori); Werner Pochat (Manuel); Tino Carraro (Professor Terzi); Ugo Fangareggi; Fulvio Mingozzi; Pino Patti; Umberto Raho; Jacques Stany; Stefano Oppedisano, C.S.C.; Ada Pomett, C.S.C.; Walter Pinelli; Sascha Helwin; Marie Luise Zetha; Martial Boschero

Crew: Salvatore Argento (Producer); Ennio Morricone (Composer); Erico Menczer (Director of Photography); Franco Fraticelli (Editor)

Franco, a blind man, is walking at night with the young Lori, and they pass by a man in a car; Franco hears him mention blackmail. Franco feigns tying his shoe and asks Lori to describe the man, and Lori does, saying she cannot see the face of a second person. Later, as Lori sleeps, Franco hears a noise. Outside, a night watchman is knocked out. A person uses a screwdriver to get inside a building, goes to Doctor Calabresi's room, unlocks it and gets inside. A doctor preparing to leave finds the unconscious night watchman and sees someone run away.

The next day, cops are at the Terzi Institute. Carlo Giordani bumps into Franco on the sidewalk and helps the blind man. He says that he is a reporter, and Franco asks his name. Inside, Carlo learns that nothing was taken from the institute ("Not even a paper clip"). Professor Terzi tells officers that, since nothing is missing, he would rather not reveal the institute's research. Doctor Casoni suggests that pictures may have been taken, but Doctor Braun says to let the cops handle the matter. Calabresi (the man from the car who Franco heard) looks at his files, calls someone and agrees to meet. He tells his fiancée Bianca that he knows who broke into the institute and what was taken, but he does not wish to tell anyone yet, saying it could mean a "big step forward." At the train station, Calabresi approaches a person, and he is pushed onto the tracks as the train arrives.

Franco and Lori are at home, and Lori says that the man in the newspaper is the same one from the car the night before. She describes the picture to Franco and says Giordani wrote the article. The two go to see the reporter at the newspaper office, and Franco asks if the picture had been cropped. Carlo calls Righetto, the photographer who snapped the picture at the last second, and he goes back to the original and sees a moving hand-arm at the far left. As Righetto prepares to print the photograph, he is strangled with a cord and killed; the killer takes the photograph and the negatives. Carlo, Franco and Lori arrive, and Carlo goes inside and finds the body. Spimi, a cop, talks to Carlo about the "maniac." Later, Carlo looks through a pair of binoculars and describes the doctors to Franco as they leave: Mombell, Esson, Casoni and Braun, as well as Terzi and his daughter, Anna.

Carlo goes to see Terzi at his home, and he expresses his desire to talk about Calabresi's "accident." Afterwards, Carlo speaks with Anna, and he evades her questions of what he and her father spoke about. The two drive away together. Franco and Lori had gone to see Bianca, and she says apologetically that she could not find anything in the house. As they leave, Franco asks Lori what he kept hearing while they talked, and Lori says it was the chain and locket around her neck (Bianca was fidgeting with it). Carlo and Anna talk over drinks, and she tells about the institute's research of "chromosome alteration" and "XYY," the extra Y producing a "criminal tendency" in a person. Carlo goes to see Braun at St. Peter's Club, and he talks to the doctor about someone being after the institute's secret drug. Braun does not seem vexed.

Bianca takes a taxi to Calabresi's parked car; inside, she finds a tiny note with an appointment time at the station (and an unseen name) written down. She tapes the note to the inside of her locket. Bianca calls Franco and says she knows who killed Calabresi and will explain when she sees him. As Bianca walks down a hallway, a cord is wrapped around her neck and she is choked. The killer rummages through her purse. Franco shows Carlo a note he received, in which the killer threatens the "puzzle-solver" and "journalist." Carlo talks of Casoni being fired from his last job and Braun inexplicably having a lot of money. Carlo goes to see Casoni, and the doctor talks about the institute's "wonder drug" and the "XYY pattern." Carlo asks Mombell about XYY, and the doctor says that everyone at the institute was tested.

The killer approaches Carlo's door and injects milk cartons with a syringe. Carlo comes home and brings the two cartons inside. Anna arrives, and the two talk and spend some intimate moments together. Afterwards, Carlo pours Anna a glass of milk, and Franco calls, telling the reporter that someone tampered with his gas and may try to kill Carlo. Carlo notices the milk that had bled from the cartons, and he knocks the glass from Anna's hand and smells and tastes the milk. Carlo finds one of his old buddies (who had been in prison), and they break into Terzi's place and discover that Anna is adopted and (via a diary) Terzi apparently "adored" the woman. Carlo learns from Spimi that Bianca often met with Braun and that the cops cannot find the doctor. Carlo runs a story of Braun being suspected, and an older lover of the doctor's tells Carlo where Braun is hiding. Carlo goes to the villa, is attacked and fights with Manuel (Braun's "friend"); he sees the dead doctor lying on the couch.

Later, Franco recalls Bianca's locket and suggests that the note is still in there. He and Carlo head to the cemetery and open Bianca's crypt, and Carlo gets the coffin open as Franco waits by the door. Carlo opens the locket, finds the note behind a metal plate and hands the paper to Franco, who goes back to the door. As Carlo closes the coffin, Franco shuts the crypt door. After Carlo spends some moments in the dark, Franco opens the door again and walks inside without his sunglasses, and with a blade protruding from his cane (with blood). He tells the reporter that the killer said he had Lori. Franco gave him the note, and he says he stabbed the killer. Lori is hit and put in the back of a car, and Franco and Carlo find the taxi (in which the killer and Lori rode) and discover blood in the back seat. The killer calls Franco, saying that Lori will be held for a while. Carlo and the police go to the Terzi house, and Anna comes down the stairs with a cloth wrapped around her hand. Carlo tells of the father-daughter "relationship" and the suspicious milk incident (Anna had the glass for some time without drinking), but it seems she has only cut her hand on a broken vase. She is irate, and Carlo and the others leave.

The group arrives at the Terzi Institute and search the place for Lori, but find nothing. As Carlo walks on a stairwell, he finds blood on his collar, and he thinks back to the room he came from. He returns to the room and sees blood dripping from the ceiling. He climbs to the roof and chases someone; Casoni hits him in the face and kicks him. The two struggle, and Casoni (with a wound in his stomach) goes back to the room with a bound Lori. He pulls his knife, and Carlo jumps the doctor and is stabbed in the chest. The cops are on the roof; Casoni eludes them, but is stopped by Franco with his cane-blade. Franco asks about Lori, and Casoni says he killed her. The doctor tries to run, and Franco swings the cane and pushes Casoni. Casoni falls down the elevator shaft to his death, and Lori calls for Franco.

The Cat o' Nine Tails is not Argento's best work, due to a less-fluid camera and several rudimentary scenes of murder. Nevertheless, the film manages to create some suspense, such as the crypt scene, and for the most part the mystery is intriguing.

Cheerleader Camp (aka *Bloody Pom Poms*) (1987)

Written by David Lee Fein and R.L. O'Keefe; Directed by John Quinn; Daiei Company Ltd.; 89 min.

Cast: Betsy Russell (Alison Wentworth); Leif Garrett (Brent Hoover); Lucinda Dickey (Cory Foster); Lorie Griffith (Bonnie Reed); Buck Flower (Pop); Travis McKenna (Timmy Moser); Teri Weigel (Pam Bently); Rebecca Ferratti (Theresa Salazar); Vickie Benson (Miss Tipton); Jeff Prettyman (Sheriff Poucher); Krista Pflanzer (Suzy); Craig Piligian (Detective); William Johnson, Sr. (Chef Ronnie); Kathryn Litton (Timmy's Girlfriend); Tom Habeeb (Assistant Detective); John Quinn (Ambulance Attendant); Chris Prettyman, Mike Knox, Frank Reinfield, Dave Delgado (Band Members)

Crew: Jeff Prettyman, John Quinn (Producers); Joan Weidman, Jim Silverman (Associate Producers); Murielle Hodler-Hamilton, Joel Hamilton (Composers); Bryan England (Director of Photography); Jeffrey Reiner (Editor)

Alison goes to an empty locker room as a crowd cheers outside. She changes into her uniform, runs outside and is booed by an audience. She sees her mother and father in the apparently empty stands and calls out to them—but is ignored. The pompoms suddenly crowd around her, and Alison screams and awakes in a van of fellow cheerleaders.

The group arrives at Camp Hurrah, and Timmy sticks his bare bottom out of the window for the other cheerleaders to see. Miss Tipton does roll call for the group and leaves out team mascot Cory. Pop, the handyman, takes some of their things for them, and Alison eyes Brent as he flirts with another girl. Brent tries a lame line on the girl, Suzy, who rejects him and walks away.

Pam talks to Bonnie and Theresa about winning the queen contest; Alison, staying in a room with Cory, takes some pills from a bag. Sheriff Poucher watches the girls lying out in their bikinis, as does Timmy, dressed as an elderly woman and videotaping the girls. Later, Alison is in bed, thinking of Brent talking to Suzy, and she gets out of her cabin, walks to another one and finds Suzy dead. Miss Tipton talks to the cheerleaders about Suzy's "suicide." Alison tells Cory she can relate to Suzy, saying that it is difficult to be "perfect." Alison washes in the bathroom sink, looks in the mirror and sees blood on her face.

Miss Tipton makes the mascots stay in their costumes even as they eat, and Cory (as the alligator) complains. Alison goes to the kitchen for sodas, and the weird cook points her toward the walk-in freezer, where Alison inadvertently discovers the frozen corpse of Suzy. Alison runs out and calls the sheriff. Sheriff Poucher and Miss Tipton talk in her office about the incident, and they eventually start a sexual fantasy with Miss Tipton as a cheerleader and the sheriff as the football player. Timmy films the event with his camera. During a routine, Pam flirts with Brent, and Alison says that Cory is a friend. Miss Tipton is preparing to show a video of cheering to the group, and Timmy slips behind Pop and hooks up his camera. The group cheers as they see Miss Tipton and the sheriff together ("Feel the spirit!").

Brent wants to spend time with Alison, and he is angry when she says she is not feeling well. That night, Alison dreams of Brent and Pam together, being cheered by Miss Tipton, Sheriff Poucher, Pop and the cook; Alison is surrounded by mascots with pompoms. The cheerleaders perform, and Pam knocks Alison over. After an argument, the group takes a break by swimming. Alison leaves when Brent massages Pam's shoulders, and Brent and Pam leave together. Pam stops their kissing when hearing a noise, and an agitated Brent leaves. Pam walks alone and is stabbed in the back of the head with garden shears. Alison dreams of approaching a kissing Brent and Pam and slicing Pam with pompoms. Cory wakes her up and stops her from taking more pills.

At the competition, Theresa is upset that Pam is not there. The mascots dance, and they are voted on by cheers. Cory gets the most, but Miss Tipton gives the trophy to a chicken, and Cory is furious. Alison tells Brent that Pam might be hurt or dead. The group decides to try a routine without Pam, and they do fine until Timmy falls over Pop. He laughs, and Pop is angry ("I hope you die!"). As the queen contest nears, Theresa is enraged that they are thinking of the contest when Pam is missing, and she leaves. Bonnie is crowned the Hurrah Queen, and Cory asks if anyone has seen Theresa. Brent goes to look for her, and Cory follows. Miss Tipton tells Pop to keep an eye on them, and soon Alison leaves as well.

Out in the woods, Theresa finds a dead Pam, and she runs to the road, is chased by a van and crushed against a tree. Brent and Cory both find Alison, and Pop tells the three of them to get back to the camp. Timmy kisses a girl at the party and carries her away, and Brent, Cory and Alison ask Bonnie if she has seen Theresa or Pam. They try to talk to Miss Tipton, but she is inebriated. Alison goes to call the police but Brent tries to stop her, saying that he will be suspected of murder. Alison gets on the phone anyway. Miss Tipton, stumbling around in the trees, is stabbed in the back. Sheriff Poucher, sitting in his truck, gets a call about someone reporting "missing persons," and he reluctantly drives away.

Timmy returns to the party with a bloody hand, and he leads Brent and Bonnie to a pulverized and innards-exposed Theresa. Alison finds Miss Tipton with a cleaver in her back, and Cory sees Alison with the bloody cleaver in her hand; she leads her away. Brent stops the band, gets on the microphone and tells everyone that a girl has been killed; the crowd clears out. Cory cleans the blood off of Alison's shirt, and she hears Brent calling their names. The three assemble, and the group gets in the van and learns that the engine has been tampered with. The group decides to walk. In the woods, Pop finds Pam dead and loads his shotgun. He finds the group and fires his shotgun in the air for them to go back. The group splits up, and Timmy sets up his camera and films himself during a call of nature. The others reach the van, and Cory says someone tried to grab her. Brent goes back for Timmy and finds his video camera; they watch the video, which shows Timmy being sliced in the stomach.

The group hides in the shed and sets up a bear trap. When someone walks in, the trap clamps on the face. They see that the sheriff has been killed. Brent grabs an axe and runs outside. Pop is out with his shotgun pointing at Brent, and Cory shoots him twice in the back and once more when he stands again. The four survivors sit in a circle and drink, and Bonnie heads for the phone. Cory goes after her, and Brent rudely slaps Cory's bottom. Brent is a bit forward with Alison; Cory returns, saying she cannot find Bonnie. Brent leaves, and Cory tells Alison that Brent was attacking her and that he was the one who attacked Cory earlier and is, consequently, the killer. She hands Alison the gun and they go outside. Cory peeks around the corner and sees Brent by the phone booth with a dead Bonnie. She cocks the hammer for Alison and points out the killer. Brent screams, and Alison shoots and kills her boyfriend. The cops are at the scene, and an officer tells Cory that, with her testimony, Alison will be charged with the murders. Alison is taken away on a stretcher, and she says she only killed Brent. Cory is in uniform, doing a cheer, as Alison screams her name.

Cheerleader Camp is a slasher with boring kills and uninteresting characters. It is difficult to tell whether Alison's dreams were intended to be humorous or thought-provoking (and neither is wholly successful), but the ending of the movie is clever. Actress Weigel is perhaps better known as the *Playboy* Playmate who went on to became a star of adult films.

Cherry Falls (2000)

Written by Ken Selden; Directed by Geoffrey Wright; Rogue Pictures/Fresh Produce Company/Industry Entertainment; 92 min.

Cast: Brittany Murphy (Jody Marken); Michael Biehn (Sheriff Brent Marken; Gabriel Mann (Kenny Ascott); Jesse Bradford (Rod Harper); Jay Mohr (Leonard Marliston); Douglas Spain (Mark); Keram Malicki-Sánchez (Timmy); Natalie Ramsey (Sandy); Candy Clark (Marge Marken); Amanda Anka (Deputy Mina); Kristen Miller (Cindy); Michael Weston (Ben); Joannah Portman (Sharon); Joe Inscoe (Tom Sisler); Bre Blair (Stacy Twelfmann); Vicki Davis (Heather, Student with Glasses); Bret McKee (Dylan); Clementine Ford (Annette Duwald); Margaret Moister (Annette's Mother); Michael Goodwin (Annette's Father); Steve Boles, David Lenthall, Steve Anyers (Fathers); Candy Aston-Dennis, Deborah Hobart, Beatrice Bush (Mothers); Rick Forrester (Deputy Bean); Tammy Ballance (Young Loralee); Rand Courtney (Dennis); Colin Fickes (Dino); Caroline Perreyclear (Jan); D.J. Qualls (Wally); Anthony Michael Harding (Coroner); Patt Noday (Stan Michaels, TV Reporter); Jessica Driscoll (Diana, Principal's Secretary); Mark Joy (Special Agent Bronhill); Alex Wharff (Young Brent); Chritopher Evans (Young Tom); Michael Cammack (Young Harry); Jesse Janowsky (Young Jimmy); Christine Offutt Thomas, Barry Privett (Couple at Restaurant); Christian Durgano (Young Leonard); Joseph W. West, Jr. (Agent Majestik); Zachary Knighton (Mr. Rolly); Teresa Jones (FBI Agent)

Crew: Joyce Schweickert, Scott Shiffman, Julie Silverman (Executive Producers); Ken Seldon (Co-Executive Producer); Marshall Persinger, Eli Seldon (Producers); Walter Werzowa (Composer); Anthony B. Richmond (Director of Photography); John F. Link (Editor)

At night in a small town, a couple is in a car. The boy, Rod, is trying to smooth-talk Stacy, and she tells him to stop and gets out of the car. Rod tells her he wants his first time to be with her, and Stacy says, "So do I." They get back inside but are interrupted by a car with shining headlights behind them. Rod gets out, believing it is one of his friends, and he is attacked by a long, stringy-haired person in black. Stacy screams and locks the car door. She hears a weak Rod outside calling her name and unlocks the door. A bloody Rod tries to get inside, only to be stabbed again. The killer then goes after Stacy.

Jody and Kenny are kissing in a car. After a few moments, Kenny says he thinks they should "start seeing other people." Jody's mom, Mrs. Marken, comes to the car window and asks Kenny for a cigarette. A furious Jody leaves and tries to sneak back in the house (she was supposed to be home 15 minutes earlier), but she is caught by her father, the sheriff; he grounds her. Early in the morning, the sheriff gets a call, and he heads to the murder site.

The next day at George Washington High, Jody's friend Timmy asks for details on the murders, which Jody was not even

Jody (Brittany Murphy) and Timmy (Keram Malicki-Sánchez) learn that a killer is stalking the virgins of the high school in Geoffrey Wright's *Cherry Falls* (2000).

aware of. The regular classes are canceled so that the teachers can console the students. In Jody's class, Mr. Marliston tries to get the students to talk, but they all argue. Sheriff Marken and the principal enter the room, and the sheriff asks anyone with information to come forward. In the cafeteria, a girl named Annette punches a guy for lying about her sexual deeds. Annette's parents leave that night, and someone knocks on the door ("It's Loralee Sherman"). Annette opens the door, and the killer attacks. The sheriff is called in, and he learns from the autopsy that "Virgin" was carved into the dead teens and that they were in fact virgins. The sheriff talks to Jody later, and asks her how far she has gone ("You know, basewise"). She is still a virgin.

Jody sees Mr. Marliston after school to discuss her T.S. Eliot paper. They think they see somebody, and they look around and find no one. There is an emergency town meeting in the gym, and the sheriff tells them that the killer seems to be selecting only virgins. A fight erupts among the parents; Timmy, watching with Jody, is excited that he has material for the school newspaper. He borrows Jody's phone and calls his friend. He leaves for better reception, and when Jody goes to find him, she discovers Timmy dead in a locker. The killer goes after her and chases Jody around the school. Jody finds her father, but the killer evades capture. Later, Jody works with a sketch artist, who sketches someone with long hair ("That's her!").

While Jody waits in the station, the sheriff calls Tom, the principal, and faxes him a copy of the sketch. He says it is Loralee Sherman. Jody hears the conversation on the other line. Jody's friend Sandy arrives and tells Jody that everyone has decided to have sex at the old Donkey Hal Hunting Lodge ("All we need is floor space"). Jody decides to go to school, where Kenny seems interested in her once again. The principal warns the students not to go to the rumored sex party. Jody goes home to her mom and asks if she knows who Loralee Sherman is. Her mother says no, and she suggests Jody lie down. Instead, Jody sneaks out. The sheriff tells his deputy that he is going to Virginia for a personal reason.

Jody is at the library looking through microfilm, and finds an article on Loralee's disappearance. Her mom finds her, and Jody demands to be told about the mysterious girl. Mrs. Marken tells her Loralee claimed to have been raped by four drunken seniors. Although she had identified who they were, no one was formerly charged because they came from good families. Two of the men left, one of them was the principal, and the other one was Jody's father. Jody, terribly upset, leaves. At the Virginia home of Loralee, the sheriff looks around and finds an empty house with a baby crib in the basement. He gets a call on his radio, and his deputy tells him that he has a message from Tom to meet him concerning Loralee Sherman.

Jody is with Kenny, and she seems interested in being intimate with him. Kenny, however, thinks she only wants to be with him because she is angry at her parents. Jody finally leaves, and tells him she will not be at the sex party. The sheriff arrives at Tom's office and finds him dead with "Virgin Not" carved on his forehead. Sheriff Marken is hit on the head with a trophy. Meanwhile, many of the students are attending the Pop Your Cherry Ball. Kenny is there with Sharon, but he decides to leave her and look for Jody.

Jody goes to see Mr. Marliston at his home, where he is lugging a trunk through the front door. Jody helps him, and she says Mr. Marliston is the only one she can trust. She says she just found out some bad things about her father. Mr. Marliston kicks the trunk down the steps to the basement. Jody asks again what is in the trunk, and he replies, "Your dad. Maybe mine." Jody runs down, opens it up, and finds a duct-taped sheriff inside. She then sees the wig, and the teacher punches her.

Jody awakes strapped to a metal chair. Mr. Marliston demands the sheriff tell the story that happened 27 years ago. The sheriff says he and his friends had just graduated and were drunk, and they saw Loralee by her broken-down car. She would not get in the car, and so they teased her, and after she said something derogatory, they chased her down. They poured booze down her throat, held her down and eventually threw a drunk Sheriff Marken on top of her. Mr. Marliston says that he is Loralee's son, and that she continually beat him ("It's very difficult to look like the one person in the world your mother loves and hates the most"). He says he wanted to deprive the town of its only innocence: its virginal children. He starts to cut Jody's leg (continuing the "Virgin" he began from the earlier assault), and he is interrupted when Kenny rings the doorbell.

Mr. Marliston opens the door with his makeup on. Kenny wants to know where Jody is (her bicycle is outside), and he pushes past the teacher and into the house where he finds her and the sheriff. Mr. Marliston axes his way inside, gets to the basement and, in the ensuing scuffle, murders the sheriff. Jody and Kenny run all the way to the lodge, and Mr. Marliston follows with his knife. "Class dismissed!" he yells, as he begins knifing everyone in swinging distance. Mr. Marliston goes after Jody, and she pulls a defense move she learned from her father which sends the teacher over the balcony, landing on the broken railing of the porch outside. One of the students, Mark, pulls off the wig, the teacher attacks him, and the deputy shoots many times until Mr. Marliston is a bloody mess. Jody later tells the FBI guys that she does not know why her father was in Virginia or why Mr. Marliston was killing everyone. She and her mother leave, and Jody sees a long, stringy-haired figure across the street, who then disappears.

Cherry Falls in an effective slasher. Selden's script is amusing, Wright's direction is strong and precise, and the film is a nice breath of fresh air from the unsubtle self-reflexivity employed in such slashers as *Scream* and *Urban Legend*. Intended for theatrical release, the movie nevertheless finally had a television debut, first showing on the

USA Network in November 2000. Actor Jesse Bradford shares his name with Jess Bradford, the character played by Olivia Hussey in *Black Christmas* (1974); Bradford starred in the 1996 version of *Romeo and Juliet*, while Hussey played Juliet in the 1968 version.

Child's Play (1988)

Written by Don Mancini, John Lafia and Tom Holland; Directed by Tom Holland; United Artists; 87 min.

Cast: Catherine Hicks (Karen Barclay); Chris Sarandon (Mike Norris); Alex Vincent (Andy Barclay); Brad Dourif (Charles Lee Ray/Voice of Chucky); Dinah Manoff (Maggie Peterson); Tommy Swerdlow (Jack Santos); Jack Colvin (Doctor Ardmore); Neil Giuntoli (Eddie Caputo); Juan Ramirez (Peddler); Alan Wilder (Mrs. Criswell); Richard Baird (News Reporter at Toy Store); Raymond Oliver (Doctor Death); Aaron Osborne (Orderly); Tyler Hard (Mona); Ted Liss (George); Roslyn Alexander (Lucy); Robert Kane (Male TV Newscaster); Leila Hee Olsen (Female TV Newscaster); Ed Gale (Chucky Stunt Double); Lena Sack, Tommy Gerard, Michael Chavez, Jamie Gray, Erin Munz, Jana Twomey, Suaundra Black (Bellevue Patients); Edan Gross (Voice of Friendly Chucky); John Franklin (Voice of Walkabout Chucky); Edan Gross, Michael Patrick Carter (Kids in Animated Commercial)

Crew: David Kirschner (Producer); Barrie M. Osborne (Executive Producer); Laura Moskowtiz (Associate Producer); Joe Renzetti (Composer); Bill Butler, A.S.C. (Director of Photography); Edward Warschilka, Roy E. Peterson (Editors)

Two men are running down a dark alley. One man says over the radio that he has the strangler, and the two begin shooting at each other. After his getaway driver abandons him, the strangler runs into a toy store. He is badly wounded from gunshots, and he yells to the detective, "I'm gonna get you for this! No matter what!" Before he dies, he pulls a Good Guy doll out of its box and loudly recites a chant. Lightning crashes and hits the store, and an explosion sends Detective Norris flying across the store. When he manages to uncover the pile of boxes, he sees that Charles Lee Ray is dead.

It is young Andy Barclay's birthday, and he is undeniably a Good Guy fan (even dressing like a Good Guy doll). After making his mother breakfast in bed, he receives a "Super Duper Tummy Gummy," and then it is time to open his gifts. However, there is no Good Guy doll, and Andy is disappointed. His mother Karen says she was not able to save enough money. At work, her friend Maggie says she has found a peddler who will sell her a Good Guy doll for a reasonable price. Karen runs home on her break and gives Andy his present ("Hi, I'm Chucky, and I'm your friend til the end"). That night, Maggie babysits Andy. Chucky wants to watch a news story about the recently escaped Eddie (Chucky's "partner" who left him behind), but Maggie sends them both to bed, only to be provoked later when Chucky turns the TV back on (she, of course, does not believe Andy's protests of innocence). Later, Chucky tosses a Good Guy hammer at Maggie's forehead, causing her to stumble back and fall out of the window.

Karen returns home to an assortment of police figures. Inside, Detective Norris tells her that her friend is dead, and he points out the tiny footprints in the dumped flour on the counter. When he tries to look at the shoes that Andy is wearing, Karen is upset, and she asks the detectives to leave. Before they go, they hear Andy say that Chucky was the one on the counter (he had flour on the bottom of his shoes). Later, Andy insists that Chucky is alive, and that his real name is Charles Lee Ray. He finally says he will "stop making up stories" when he sees that his mother is unsettled. Karen listens at the door after she leaves and hears Andy say to Chucky that he knew she would not believe him. Chucky sees Karen's feet by the door and he says a standard Good Guy line.

The next day, Andy and Chucky sneak out of school and travel to a crummy neighborhood. They find Eddie's house; while

Andy is preoccupied by nature's call, Chucky runs into the house and turns on the oven. When Eddie hears noise around the house, he jumps into the kitchen and fires his gun, annihilating the house (and himself). Karen heads to the police station, where the cops are grilling Andy about his current activities. He tries to get Chucky to talk but the doll is speechless ("Mommy, he's doing it on purpose"). Doctor Ardmore suggests that Andy stay at County General for a couple of days.

Karen goes home with Chucky. She looks at the box he came in, and a package of batteries falls out. She slowly walks over to Chucky, picks him up and opens the compartment on his back. A battery-less Chucky flips his head around and taunts her with "Hi, I'm Chucky. Wanna play?" Karen screams and drops him. She then tries to get him to speak again by threatening to throw him in the fire. Chucky turns against her and attacks by biting her. Chucky gets outside, into the lift and out on the streets. Karen quickly finds Norris to tell him the news and shows him her wound ("Chucky bit me!"). Karen eventually finds the peddler, and (after Norris arrives to keep the man's grubby hands away from Karen) he tells them where he got the doll. Norris tells Karen that he killed Charles Lee Ray there, and that he had threatened to kill Eddie and the detective. Karen says that the Lakeshore Strangler is now in a Good Guy doll, and she goes to find where Ray lived.

Norris gets Ray's file from the station and gets into his car. Chucky attacks with a cable around the neck and then with a knife; Norris loses control and the car flips over, leaving him trapped. Chucky is running around the car when Norris shots and hits him. Chucky screams and sprints away. Norris meets up with Karen at Ray's place and tells her Chucky often spent time with a voodoo-practicing black man. At the same time, Chucky arrives at the man's place. He asks the surprised man why he bled when he was shot, and the man says, "You're turning human." He tries to telephone the police, but Chucky has his voodoo doll and breaks a leg and an arm. The wounded man finally tells him that he must transfer his soul to the first person he let know he was alive. Then Chucky stabs the doll and leaves the man for dead.

Karen and Norris find the bloody man, who tells them they must save the boy, and that Chucky can be killed by hitting his heart. At County General, Andy sees that Chucky is on his way. He manages to get out his room and hide in an operating room. Ardmore finds him and tries to drug him, but Chucky slices him and shocks him to death. Karen and Norris get to the hospital and find out that Chucky was there looking for Andy. Andy makes it home, barricades the home and hides in the closet. Chucky comes down the chimney and eventually knocks Andy out cold. Karen and the detective arrive at the apartment and interrupt Chucky's ritual. After Chucky whacks Norris with a baseball bat, Karen shoots him before the gun jams. She manages to hold him in the fireplace with the fire screen, and Andy sets Chucky afire. Chucky screams and burns until he stops moving.

The two go to check on Norris in the bedroom. Andy goes to get the first aid kit and sees that Chucky's burnt body is missing. Chucky trips the running Andy then chases the boy and his mother around the house until Karen shoots him multiple times with Norris' other gun, knocking off his head, arm and foot. Norris' partner Santo, arrives and is told that Chucky is alive. He picks up Chucky's head from the hallway, puts it on the TV in the bedroom, says "It's dead! Look!" Chucky's one-armed, one-legged, headless body attacks one more time (while his head screams, "Kill him!"), and Norris finally shoots him in the heart, spraying blood on the wall. Norris is taken away in an ambulance. Andy takes one last look at Chucky, turns off the light and shuts the door.

Child's Play is a terrific slasher, with a great mix of horror and humor. It is difficult to imagine anyone else's voice other than Dourif's. Producer David Kirschner created the Chucky doll; it was designed and executed by Kevin Yagher. Director Holland also scripted *Psycho II* (1983).

Child's Play 2 (1990)

Written by Don Mancini; Directed by John Lafia; Universal Pictures; 84 min.

Cast: Alex Vincent (Andy Barclay); Jenny Agutter (Joanne Simpson); Gerrit Graham (Phil Simpson); Christine Elise (Kyle); Brad Dourif (Voice of Chucky); Grace Zabriskie (Grace Poole); Peter Haskell (Sullivan); Beth Grant (Miss Kettlewell); Greg Germann (Mattson); Raymond Singer (Social Worker); Charles C. Meshack (Van Driver); Stuart Mabray (Homicide Investigator); Matt Roe (Policeman in Car); Herb Braha (Liquor Store Clerk); Don Pugsley, Ed Kreiger, Vince Melocchi (Technicians); Edan Gross (Voice of Tommy Doll); Adam Ryen (Rick Spires); Adam Wylie (Sammy); Bill Stevenson (Adam)

Crew: David Kirschner (Producer); Laura Moskowitz (Co-Producer); Robert Latham Brown (Executive Producer); Graeme Revell (Composer); Stefan Czapsky (Director of Photography); Edward Warschilka (Editor)

Mr. Sullivan arrives at the Good Guy factory as Chucky is being put back together again. His assistant Mattson tells him the story of Andy Barclay and his claims of a "killer doll." Mattson says someone obviously tampered with the voice cassette (the doll was saying it was the Lakeshore Strangler), but they were fixing the doll. Just as a machine is putting the finishing touches on Chucky (inserting his eyes), a worker is electrocuted, and the factory alarm goes off.

Andy is playing cards with a social worker and telling him about his nightmares; he seems to have convinced himself that Chucky was only a dream. Back at the factory, Mr. Sullivan tells Mattson to cover up the situation (concerning the injured worker), and Mattson asks what he wants done with the doll. Social worker Grace Poole is talking to Phil and Joanne Simpson about Andy and the "fairy tale" he created. The couple agrees to take him in and watch him until his mother Karen "gets better" from her psychiatric evaluation.

Phil and Joanne take Andy home, where he meets Kyle, another temporary foster child who will be "on her own next year." Andy is shown to his toys-laden room, where a Good Guy doll falls out of the closet. Joanne apologizes and tells Andy she will get rid of it. Out on a rainy night, Mattson tosses Chucky in the back seat (he would not fit in the trunk) and heads for the liquor store. While Mattson is inside, Chucky opens Mattson's briefcase, finds the telephone number of the place where Andy was staying and calls Grace on the car phone ("I'm trying to reach Andy Barclay. This is his Uncle Charles"). Mattson comes back out, and Chucky puts a gun to his face and has him drive to Andy's new place. He has Mattson park the car and then puts a plastic bag over his head. Inside, as Joanne is singing to Andy upstairs, Chucky meets Tommy, the other Good Guy doll, who "likes to be hugged." "Hug this!" says Chucky, as he bashes Tommy's face in and buries him in the backyard.

The next day, Phil and Joanne are discussing a broken antique statue (Chucky's murder weapon) with Andy and Kyle. They are both grounded until one of them "fesses up." Later, Andy hears the couple saying that he (Andy) may need more attention than they can give him, and he goes to see the Good Guy doll. Andy makes sure the doll has batteries, and he carries him around so that Phil and Joanne will see that Good Guy dolls do not frighten Andy. That night, Andy awakes tied to the bed and with a sock in his mouth. Chucky is standing over him; he wants to play Hide the Soul (and Andy is "It"). Chucky begins his chant but must stop when Kyle crawls through the window. Andy pleads for help, and Phil tries to calm him by throwing Chucky in the cellar. Chucky realizes he is bleeding; he is "turning human again."

Andy and Kyle go to school; once they have left, Phil suggests to Joanne that they send Andy back with the social workers. As Andy's school bus drives away, little Good Guy feet can be seen underneath. In class, Andy's teacher Miss Kettlewell finds a paper from Andy with something quite rude on it (a Chucky masterpiece, of course). Andy finds Chucky in a cabinet of toys, but before he can do anything, Miss Kettlewell reprimands Andy and makes him sit with his head on his desk, throwing Chucky, the potential toy, into the closet. She locks the door and leaves him there; Andy crawls out of the window. The teacher returns to hear someone banging on the closet door. She looks inside for Andy and is stabbed and beaten by Chucky.

Andy gets home, but Phil and Joanne had already been called by Miss Kettlewell and know about the obscenity and his detention. Andy tries to say Chucky did it; Phil opens the cellar door to show him Chucky is still there. That night, Andy arms himself with an electric knife and heads into the cellar. After he fights with Chucky for a while, Phil goes to investigate the noise. Phil slowly walks down the steps when he sees Andy with a knife; Chucky trips him, causing Phil to fall and break his neck. Joanne, horrified, wants Andy out of the house. Grace the social worker returns and takes Andy away. "He's still in the cellar," Andy warns Kyle. After the police leave, Kyle throws Chucky in the garbage and sits on the swing, only to find a Tommy buried underneath. She heads back to the garbage can; Chucky is gone. She hears a noise in Joanne's room and finds her foster mother strangled. Kyle is attacked by Chucky, who finally holds her at knifepoint and forces her to take him to Andy.

Andy is in his room when the fire alarm goes off. He separates from the other children, and sees Kyle holding Chucky at the bottom of the stairs. Grace finds them and is irked at Kyle for setting a false alarm; she takes them all into her office. Chucky kills her when she grabs him, and Grace falls and lands on the Xerox machine, photocopying her dying face. Kyle tries to leave, but Chucky slams the door on her, holding the knife to the stupefied Andy ("Snap out of it! You act like you've never seen a dead body before!"). Chucky and Andy get in the back of a newspaper truck, and Kyle gets into her car and follows them to the Good Guy factory. Chucky knocks Andy out and begins his chant ("No more Mr. Good Guy"). He completes his ritual, but nothing changes because he was too late. Kyle shows up and gets Andy away from Chucky. A gate is slammed unto Chucky's hand, and he tears it off to free himself. He affixes a knife blade to his stump and screams in pain ("I hate kids!"). A factory worker gets in Chucky's way and gets plastic eyes shoved into his eye sockets.

Chucky attacks Kyle and Andy again, and he is restrained and sent the wrong way on the assembly line, causing the machine to malfunction and turn Chucky into a gob of melted plastic. But Chucky is still alive, and he crawls towards Andy on his little cart (he has no legs). Andy releases a load of hot wax onto Chucky and he really is turned into a mass of bubbling plastic. Chucky attacks one more time, and Kyle shoves an air tube into his mouth, which causes Chucky's head to swell and explode. Kyle and Andy walk away from the Good Guy factory.

Child's Play 2 is an admirable sequel, managing, like the original, to create a nice blend of wittiness and suspense. Greg Germann earned fame later on the popular television series *Ally McBeal*, while Grace Zabriskie is perhaps best known as Laura Palmer's mother Sarah from the cult television show, *Twin Peaks*.

Child's Play 3 (1991)

Written by Don Mancini; Directed by Jack Bender; Universal Pictures; 90 min.

Cast: Justin Whalin (Andy Barclay); Perrey Reeves (De Silva); Jeremy Sylvers (Tyler); Travis Fine (Shelton); Dean Jacobson (Whitehurst); Brad Dourif (Voice of Chucky); Peter Haskell (Sullivan); Dakin Matthews (Colonel Cochrane); Andrew Robinson (Sergeant Botnick); Burke Byrnes (Sergeant Clark); Matthew

Walker (Ellis); Donna Eskra (Ivers); Edan Gross (Voice of Good Guy Doll); Terry Willis (Garbage Man); Richard Marion (Patterson); Laura Owens (Lady Executive); Ron Fassler (Petzold); Michael Chieffo (Security Guard); Henry G. Sanders (Major); Lois Foraker (Sergeant Frazier); David Ellzey (Ghoul); Mark Christopher Lawrence (Cop); Richard A. Pack (Nelson); Michael Renna, Ryan Austine, Kent Winfrey, Matt Daniels (Cadets); Aimee Joy Slutske (Carnival Teenager); Alexis Kirschner, Jessica Kirschner, Sophie Owen-Bender, Hannah Owen-Bender (Carnival Kids); Kim Stockdale (Mother): David Sosna (Trash Picker)

Crew: David Kirschner (Executive Producer); Laura Moskowitz (Co-Producer); Robert Latham Brown (Producer); Cory Lerios, John D'Andrea (Composers); John R. Leonetti (Director of Photography); Edward Warschilka (Supervising Editor); Edward A. Warschilka, Jr., Scott Wallace (Editors)

Inside an old factory collecting dust, a crane picks up the melted body of Chucky, causing blood to drip into melted plastic used for Good Guy dolls. Mr. Sullivan is in a conference, discussing the future of the Good Guy company. Everything seems okay, and so Mr. Sullivan says they are "moving ahead." One of the men hands Mr. Sullivan a Good Guy in a box ("It's the first one off the assembly line"). That night, Mr. Sullivan is in his office, not realizing that the Good Guy box is empty. After playing with some toys, Chucky whacks Sullivan with a golf club, throws a dart in his back and one in his hand (as he goes for the phone) and strangles him with the string from a yo-yo. Chucky gets on the computer and looks for Andy.

Andy is on a bus, heading for Kent military school. He first meets eight year-old Tyler, who gives him a knife as a gift. Andy goes to see Colonel Cochrane, who calls him a "trouble maker" and tells him to grow up and forget about killer dolls; then Andy gets his head shaved by Sergeant Botnick. In his room, Andy meets a bound Whitehurst in the closet. Whitehurst tells him Lieutenant Colonel Shelton and his "lackeys" tied him up. He offers Andy words of his support for his first day: "Welcome to hell, Barclay."

The next day, with all the other privates, Andy encounters the uncompromising Shelton as well as the tough-minded female private De Silva. Tyler goes to check his mail, and he is asked to give a package to Andy. On the way, he drops the package and sees the Good Guy logo (he was in awe of the Good Guy commercial). He takes it to the armory and opens it; Chucky is in the box. Chucky jumps out and demands to know where Andy is, and then he realizes that Tyler is in actuality now the first person Chucky revealed his humanness to. He tries to play Hide the Soul with Tyler, but they are interrupted by Cochrane and another officer. Cochrane takes the doll from Tyler. Andy, on the field with fellow privates and their rifles, sees Cochrane carrying Chucky. Chucky is thrown into a trash bin and ends up in a garbage truck. When he screams for help, the truck driver searches the back. Chucky runs the compactor and kills him.

Back in his room, Andy is still putting his things away while Whitehurst polishes Shelton's shoes. Chucky picks up Andy's knife. Whitehurst leaves, and Chucky takes the opportunity to slice Andy's foot ("You just can't keep a Good Guy down"). Chucky says he no longer needs Andy because he has someone new. Andy knows he means Tyler, and he grabs Chucky and beats him against the floor. Shelton walks in, finds one of his scuffed shoes and tells Andy that he is Shelton's new "slave." He gives Andy five demerits and leaves with Chucky.

That night, Andy sneaks into Shelton's room with a knife, but Chucky is gone ("Where's the doll?!" demands Shelton). Shelton makes the privates run around in circles until he finds the doll. Meanwhile, Tyler is playing a game with an irritated Chucky. The game leads them into a room where they are discovered by De Silva and her friend (looking for a file on Andy). The group leaves when they hear someone coming, and Chucky is alone. Cochrane walks in and sees Chucky lying on the floor; Chucky disappears as soon as Cochrane turns away. Chucky jumps out with a knife and screams, and Cochrane has a heart attack and dies.

The next day, everyone has a moment of silence for Cochrane in the cafeteria. Andy finds Tyler to warn him about Chucky, and gives him the knife. Later, Whitehurst is in for his haircut from Botnick. After he leaves, Botnick finds Chucky in a cabinet, puts him in the chair and tries to give Chucky a haircut. Chucky responds by slicing Botnick's throat. Whitehurst sees Chucky ("Boo!") and runs away.

The school prepares for the Annual War Games. Two teams, a red and a blue, tries to capture the other team's flag, utilizing rifles with red and blue paint pellets. Chucky reloads all the red guns with live ammunition ("This oughta slow the punks down"). Andy, Whitehurst, and De Silva are on the blue team, and Tyler is on the red. At night, Andy decides he had better find Tyler. With a reconnaissance map he stole from Shelton's tent, Andy knows where the red team might be. After he leaves, the team moves out (instead of the original plan of leaving at dawn). When Shelton sees that Andy is AWOL, he surmises that he stole the map and that he is "doubling for the reds."

Chucky wants to play Hide the Soul with Tyler, but Tyler has no desire to. Chucky eventually grows weary of Tyler and pulls out his knife, only to be stabbed by Tyler. The blue team finds Andy, and then they capture Tyler, their "P.O.W." Chucky calls on the radio, says he wants Tyler, and tells them he has De Silva. He then calls the red team and tells them that the blue team has been spotted. The blue team finds Chucky and they shoot and hit him with blue paint pellets. The red team arrives and fires upon the blue team with their live ammunition. Shelton is shot and killed before the red team realizes what they have done. When everyone is fighting and arguing about the situation, Chucky tosses a grenade. Whitehurst sees him do it, jumps on it and is killed by the explosion. Chucky follows Tyler to the nearby carnival; Andy and De Silva are right behind them.

Tyler heads for the Security and Lost and Found tent, but Chucky has beaten him there. Andy and De Silva arrive to find a dead security guard. De Silva grabs his gun. Chucky and Tyler go into the haunted rollercoaster, and during a gunfight in a cemetery, De Silva is hit in the leg. She hands Andy the gun. Inside the rollercoaster, a Grim Reaper statue brings down its scythe and part of Chucky's face is chopped off. Chucky finally knocks Tyler out on a hill of skulls, and Andy fires until he hits Chucky. Once atop the hill, Andy is attacked by Chucky, and he slices his hand with a knife. Chucky falls into a giant fan and is chopped into many pieces. De Silva is taken away in an ambulance, and the cops take Andy away.

Child's Play 3 is a little watered-down, with a humdrum military school setting, but Chucky is still as charming as ever, with that wonderful Brad Dourif voice. Horror buffs might best remember actor Robinson from the classic *Hellraiser* (1987).

Color Me Blood Red (aka *Model Massacre*) (1965)

Written and Directed by Herschell Gordon Lewis; Box Office Spectaculars; 79 min.

Cast: Don Joseph (Adam Sorg); Candi Conder (April); Elyn Warner (Gigi); Patricia Lee (Sydney); Jerome Eden (Rolf); Scott H. Hall (Farnsworth); Jim Jaekel (Jack); Iris Marshall (Mrs. Carter); Bill Harris (Gregorovich); Cathy Collins (Mitzi)

Crew: David F. Friedman (Producer); Herschell Gordon Lewis (Director of Photography); Robert Sinise (Editor)

At the Farnsworth Galleries, Farnsworth looks at a painting he evidently admires and reluctantly picks the canvas up and takes it outside. He drops it on the ground, saturates it with gasoline and sets it afire. Blood pours out of the canvas as it burns.

Adam Sorg stands before a blank canvas, paints a bit and then angrily throws it aside. He selects another canvas, places it on the easel, but is upset because he cannot get the right color. Gigi enters the room, and

Adam Sorg (Don Joseph), almost out of red paint, needs another model-beatnik April (Candi Conder) for posing *and* blood in Herschell Gordon Lewis' *Color Me Blood Red* (1965).

Adam accidentally hits her with paint. Gigi tells Adam that he is due at Farnsworth Galleries in one hour and that critics will be there. Adam arrives at his showing, where an art critic is talking to Farnsworth. The critic, Gregorovich, tells Adam that, due to his less-than-impressive use of color, he is an "artistic imposter." Adam argues with the critic and leaves, passing by Mrs. Carter, who admires the artist's work.

Farnsworth goes to Adam's home by the beach to pick up a new painting. He tells Adam that he feels the same way as Gregorovich about Adam's use of color, and Adam agrees, beating a painting and leaving the broken frame on the floor. Farnsworth takes another painting and leaves. Adam and Gigi spend some intimate time in another room; afterwards, Gigi bends over to pick up the destroyed painting and cuts her finger on a nail. Adam sees the smeared blood on the canvas and checks it outside and with other paintings. Gigi comes into the room and apologizes about the blood. Adam picks up a rough sketch of a woman and places it on the easel. He asks Gigi to open the wound, and he cuts the finger with a razor and "paints." Gigi pulls her hand away and says that if he needs more to use his own. Adam cuts his fingers and paints with his blood until he is weak and collapses on the loveseat.

After resting, Adam looks at his painting. Gigi talks of how the artist telephoned Farnsworth and said he had something big, and she wonders where he is going to find blood to finish the painting. Adam stabs Gigi in the face and uses her bloody head as a brush. April is with her mother, Mrs. Carter, and she is going on a picnic with Rolf, Jack and Sydney. Adam buries Gigi in the sand, then goes to the gallery to show his new painting. He shows the painting, and Gregorovich declares it Adam's "finest." Mrs. Carter agrees to Farnsworth's high price of $15,000, but Adam says it is not for sale. The critic challenges Adam to paint another masterpiece, and Adam accepts.

Back at his house, Adam prepares to cut his finger again, but he sees April and her friends at the beach, as well as Norman and Betsy, kissing on a towel. Betsy wants to ride the water bikes; when the two are out in the water, Adam approaches in a boat. He stabs Norman in the chest with a spear, and he falls into the water as Betsy screams. Later, Adam is painting with a bowl of blood. He goes to the other room, where Betsy is tied to the wall with her intestines and innards hanging out of her stomach. Adam squeezes some more blood into his bowl. The artist takes the painting to the gallery and again refuses to sell. After Adam storms out, Gregorovich notes that the painting is still wet, and he says that Adam forgot to varnish it.

After a few weeks (Adam has not painted in a while according to Mrs. Carter), April and her pals go to the beach. Adam watches the group arrive, and when April is near his house, Adam pretends to be painting outside. He tells the curious April that he is looking for a model, and he asks her to pose. He tells April his name, and she says that her mother wants to buy one of his paintings. Adam says that if April poses, she can have the painting for free, and she tells him she might be by later in the evening. Later, at the beach with her friends, April tells Rolf of the man who wanted her to pose for a picture.

Adam lets April into his home. April notes the blood-like paint in his picture, and after she makes a joke of putting blood into the work, Adam explodes and tells her the joke is not funny. April wants to leave, but Adam convinces her to stay, and has April stand on a small stepladder. In order to keep her hands still, Adam ties April's wrists and restrains her.

Jack and Sydney look for some wood, and Sydney finds Gigi's corpse and screams for Jack ("Holy bananas! It's a girl's leg!"). They show Rolf, and he runs to the house with a light on in search of a phone. Adam tells April to turn away for a few seconds and he will be done — and he lifts an axe. Rolf runs inside, where he acts rudely towards Adam: "Listen, pal, you'd be rude, too, if you saw your girl tied up, and a man with an axe in one hand and a bloody mess in the other, and a corpse outside there on the beach." Rolf grabs a nearby gun, but Adam knocks it away. He talks of "immortalizing" Gigi by keeping her alive in his painting. When Jack and Sydney enter the room, Rolf grabs the gun. Adam lifts his axe and Rolf fires, hitting the artist in the face. He stumbles and falls with his face on a blank canvas. Gregorovich arrives as Farnsworth burns Adam's painting, and Farnsworth says he is burning Adam's "funeral pyre."

Color Me Blood Red is an enjoyable and campy classic from director Lewis, often referred to as "The Godfather of Gore." Despite its campiness, the movie creates an interesting character of Adam, so intent on finding the right color that he will kill and mutilate for it. Don Joseph is actually Gordon Oas-Heim, who starred in Lewis' *Moonshine Mountain* (1964), credited as Adam Sorg (his character from *Color Me Blood Red*).

The Comeback (aka *The Day the Screaming Stopped*) (1978)

Written by Murray Smith; Directed by Pete Walker; 100 min.

Cast: Jack Jones (Nick Cooper); Pamela Stephenson (Linda); David Doyle (Webster Jones); Bill Owen (Mr. B); Sheila Keith (Mrs. B); Holly Palance (Gail); Peter Turner (Harry); Richard Johnson (Macauley); Patrick Brock (Mr. Paulsen); June Chadwick (Nurse); Penny Irving (Girl Singer); Jeff Silk (Police Officer)

Crew: Pete Walker (Producer); Stanley

Myers (Composer); Peter Jessop, B.S.C. (Director of Photography); Alan Brett (Editor)

Gail walks into what looks like a deserted building ("Harry?") and rides the lift to the top, where she unlocks a door and walks into a beautiful penthouse. She answers the phone and says that it is Mr. Cooper's place but that she is no longer Mrs. Cooper.

Nick Cooper arrives at the airport, and he is picked up by Linda, Webster Jones' secretary. At the penthouse, a sickle is picked up by a gloved hand. Gail gets her purse, and on the steps, a person dressed as an elderly woman and with a mask attacks her. Her hand is sliced off; a bloody Gail falls.

Nick goes to see Webster, who shows him a picture of an estate and says that Harry has fixed a room with electronic equipment. Webster says Nick's last album sold six million copies, but that was six years ago. Nick goes to the estate and meets Doris and her caretaker husband Albert. Nick goes to his tiny studio and plays a recording, and Doris brings by a glass of brandy, having read in "fan magazines" that Nick likes brandy before bed (she further says that she and Albert have all of Nick's records). That night, Nick awakes to a crying child (Doris had said she had no children), but he looks around the estate and finds nothing. Nick records a song in the studio, and Webster arrives afterwards. He talks of Nick quitting his career for Gail, saying she tried to "destroy" him, and he says now there will be no "interference."

Nick takes Linda to dinner, where they talk about his music and Gail. Harry sits by the couple, and he says he wants to get Nick's things out of the penthouse so that Gail cannot take them. Nick does not want to go, but Linda would like to see the place and she agrees to go with Harry. On the lift, Harry says that Linda is beautiful and talks about her breasts, and at the door, there are many flies buzzing (Gail is still inside decomposing). Linda wants to go, and Harry complies, since he has brought the wrong key. Linda visits Nick in his room, and she says she "sensed something" at the penthouse. Webster walks in on the couple as they are kissing, and he tells Nick that they have an offer based on the completed tracks. Webster eyes Linda, and Linda tells Nick that she has to go and leaves with Webster.

Later, Nick awakes to a woman screaming, and outside his door is a decomposed body in a wheelchair. He slams the door shut, hears noises and screams. Doris comes inside and settles the singer down. The next day, Nick finds Albert reading a book of Chinese mythology. Albert talks to Nick about trees and "tree surgery." Linda arrives and suggests that Nick take the day off. Harry goes to Webster's office to get the penthouse keys. Webster thinks back to Gail telling him to let Nick go to "do his own thing" in America. When Webster tells her that Nick is not ready, Gail says she is used to getting her own way.

Nick and Linda are outside kissing, and he tells her of his nightmare. They move to the car, where they spent some intimate moments together. At the penthouse, Harry finds the rotted body of Gail. He runs to the lift; at the bottom, he is stabbed by the masked person. In the car, Linda mentions Webster and their "casual kinda thing," and Nick suggests that they all go to dinner to get things straightened out. The couple head to Webster's house, but he is inside looking in the mirror with make up on his face and he does not answer the door. He sees the couple kissing and he cries. Nick and Linda head back to the estate and go upstairs. In the kitchen, Doris cries and tells Albert that it is due to "those people" ("scum"). Albert calms her by giving her a rosebud. Nick awakes at night to crying, and Linda is not in the bed with him. He runs around the house until he finds a giant box with a bow in the cellar. He opens the box and finds the maggoty remains of Gail.

Webster, Doris and Albert are at the estate as Nick is taken away on a stretcher. Doris says she found Nick huddled in a corner and sucking his thumb, and she tells the doctor that the singer seemed to be imagining things at night ("Too much coffee; I warned him!"). Webster tells the doctor that they had looked for the "decomposing head" that Nick mentioned but had found nothing. The doctor says it is a "touch of hysterical exhaustion." Nick awakes after a five-day sleep and tells the doctor he still believes the things in the house really happened. The doctor says, due to "classic nervous fatigue," he experienced hallucinations, and he only needs to convince himself that the things are in his mind. The doctor suggests that he goes to the penthouse.

Nick asks Webster about Linda, and Webster says Linda left a note and went away. Nick returns to the estate. That night, after turning off the radio, he hears the crying. He turns the radio back on and goes to sleep. The next day, he drives to the penthouse, which is clean and "corpse-less." He calls Webster and says there is something strange about the new carpet, scrubbed walls and "antiseptic" smell. Nick says he is going back to the house, and Webster says he will be right there. Nick goes to the kitchen and tells Doris that he thinks Harry has been killed, but when he turns to look at her, Doris is gone. The killer appears with an axe, and Nick runs out the door and is stopped by a blade-wielding Doris at the end of the hallway. She tells Nick that she and Albert had a daughter they called Rosebud and that Nick was her idol. The day that Nick announced his marriage to Gail, Rosebud killed herself. Albert swings the axe, Nick ducks and Doris is hit. Albert takes off his mask and cries over Doris.

Webster is at the house when Nick hears tapping upstairs. He goes up the steps and hears Linda's voice; he breaks through a wall and finds Linda in Rosebud's room, with Rosebud's dead body inside. The cops arrive, and Linda is taken away in an ambulance. Webster seems happy that Nick is not crazy, and he suggests getting back to work on the album. Nick looks up in a window and sees Gail waving at him. He almost tells Webster and then decides against it. Nick stares at the window, seemingly perturbed.

Although slow in some spots, *The Comeback* is an effective outing for Walker, with some startling attacks from the killer and an uncanny atmosphere around the estate. Actress Keith, who also appeared in Walker's *Frightmare* (1974) as the murderous and cannibalistic mother, is splendid as the quirky Doris/Mrs. B.

Crawlspace (1986)

Written and Directed by David Schmoeller; Empire Pictures/Altar Productions, Inc.; 80 min.

Cast: Klaus Kinski (Karl Gunther); Talia Balsam (Lori Bancroft); Barbara Whinnery (Harriet Watkins); Carol Francis (Jessica Marlow); Tané (Sophie Fisher); Sally Brown (Martha White); Jack Hiller (Alfred Lassiter); David Abbott (Hank Storm); Kenneth Robert Shippy (Josef Steiner)

Cast: Charles Band (Executive Producer); Ron Underwood, Roberto Bessi (Producers); Pino Donaggio (Composer); Sergio Salvati, A.I.C. (Director of Photography); Bert Glatstein (Editor)

A woman is in an apartment building, looking for "Mr. Gunther." She walks into a room and the door locks behind her. Inside she finds rats in cages, as well as a woman in a cage. Karl Gunther appears and says of the caged woman, "She can't talk. I cut her tongue off." He presses a button and a blade is shoved through the woman's back. Karl smears blood from his finger onto an inscribed bullet and loads a revolver. He points the gun to his head and the gun clicks. "So be it."

Sophie is in her room as a man watches from the window and Karl watches from behind a vent. The man crawls through the window, but it is only Hank; the two kiss and enjoy some time together on the bed. A man goes to Karl's door and inquires about the vacant apartment advertised in the newspaper. Karl tells him it has been rented, but when Lori asks about the place shortly afterwards, Karl hospitably shows her the room.

As Lori looks around the kitchen, Karl holds his hand over the flame on the stove and asks if she will take the apartment. She says yes, and they shake hands. Later, Karl writes in his diary and says he believes he is addicted to killing (it makes him feel alive). Martha, the tongueless woman in the cage, gives him a note saying, "Please kill me." Karl says he cannot kill her because he would have no one to talk to.

Harriet arrives at her apartment, and Karl (with a bandaged hand) helps her with her groceries. Harriet talks to him about "vices," but he seems reluctant to discuss it. The women of the apartment building have a get-together, and Karl watches from the vent. He runs some controls, a tiny door opens and a rat comes out into the room. The women scream and jump on furniture, but Lori just sits and laughs. In her apartment, Lori hears clicking sounds and goes to Karl's door. She tells him of the sounds, and he says it is probably just rats. In his diary, Karl writes of once being a doctor, practicing euthanasia ("mercy killing") and being ashamed when learning (from his father's diary) that the Nazis used the same word when killing the Jews. Sophie plays the piano and sings, and Karl watches from the window. He ducks away when he sees Hank. When Hank notices Karl nearby, Karl brings out his switchblade. Later, Karl has put two eyeballs in a jar. He goes to his room, points the gun — and it clicks ("So be it"). He tries the gun again and gets another click.

Josef Steiner arrives at Karl's door and says he has been looking for Karl for three years. Karl reluctantly lets him inside, and Steiner calls him a murderer. He says that, in the five years Karl was chief resident at a hospital in Buenos Aires, 67 people under his care (all with "routine illnesses") died, one of the people being Steiner's brother. He shows Karl a photograph of his father, who designed instruments of torture for concentration camps and was executed for "crimes against humanity." Karl tells Steiner to leave, and the man brings out a picture of a young Karl, saluting in Nazi uniform. Karl weeps.

Karl writes in his diary about accidentally killing a healthy patient and feeling no remorse. He began to understand the feelings his father wrote about; it was "god-like" to be able to give life and take it away.

In his crawlspace by the vent, Karl sees Alfred arrive at the apartment with soap opera actress Jessica. Karl makes clicking sounds by hitting his knife on a steel ball, even when the couple move to the bed. He hears a scream from his room and quickly crawls out to see that a cat had inadvertently set off one of his traps, leaving only a detached tail ("Sorry, kitty!"). Alfred is irritated about the clicking noises and leaves. He hears something outside and goes to Karl's room. Later, a finger (with Alfred's ring) is resting in a jar. As Lori is preparing to bathe, she hears clicks; a rat jumps at her from the vent. She goes to Karl's door and knocks, but there is response. In his room, Karl pushes the button on the arm of a chair and spear shoots out from the seat.

Steiner goes to Lori's apartment and tries getting information from her. Karl is in his crawlspace and he loads a dartgun and prepares to use it, but he changes his mind (surmising that it is not painful enough). Lori asks the nosy Steiner to leave. He heads up to Karl's door and walks inside, where he sees swinging steel balls. He sits in a chair and reads some of Karl's diary on the table. He sees Karl nearby, turns and accidentally sets off the chair-trap. Karl pulls the trigger three times and is rewarded with three clicks. Karl runs a film projector, showing a movie of Hitler and Nazis. "I am my own god, my own jury and my own executioner." He puts on his Nazi hat and salutes ("Hail, Gunther!").

Lori finds rats in her refrigerator. Karl calls and mentions her tub, and she finds a dead Steiner floating in water with a swastika carved on his forehead. Karl is at the window, hitting the knife on the steel ball. Lori runs, but steel bars at the end of the hallway prevent her escape. She sees Sophie dead in her apartment, then finds the body of Harriet. She runs upstairs to Karl's room. From her cage, Martha points to a hanging key. Lori tries to unlock the cage, but the two women hear Karl coming; Martha points Lori to the crawlspace entrance. When Karl nears Lori, she crawls inside, and Karl releases a cage of rats into the crawlspace. Lori crawls around and goes back to the entrance, only to be frightened by the hanging body of Jessica. Karl gets inside and crawls after Lori, but she makes it back to the room again. A blade shoots down, and Lori and Martha hear a reaction from Karl. They see the blade sticking from his chest, and they run outside. Karl's eyes move, and he removes the "blade" from his chest. As Lori gets on the phone, Karl is in the doorway with a knife. As he approaches, she grabs the gun. It clicks several times, and finally there is a gunshot ("So be it").

Crawlspace is an effective film, providing a strong and intriguing character study of a man with murderous impulses (bolstered by a good performance from Kinski) and mixing in a bit of black humor. Schmoeller also directed the eerie cult gem *Tourist Trap* (1979).

Curtains (1983)

Written by Robert Guza, Jr.; Directed by Richard Ciupka; Simon Limited; 88 min.

Cast: John Vernon (Jonathan Stryker); Samantha Egger (Samantha Sherwood); Linda Thorson (Brooke Parsons); Anne Ditchburn (Laurian Summers); Lynne Griffin (Patti O'Connor); Sandra Warren (Tara Demillo); Lesleh Donaldson (Christie Burns); Deborah Burgess (Amanda Reuther); Michael Wincott (Matthew); Maury Chaykin (Monty); Joann McIntyre (Secretary); Calvin Butler (Doctor Pendleton); Kate Lynch (Receptionist); Booth Savage (Amanda's Boyfriend); William Marshall, James Kidnie (Attendants); Diane Godwin (Actress); Janelle Hutchison (Stroker); Virginia Laight (Screamer); Kay Griffin (Thief); Bunty Webb (Tickler); Daisy White (Roommate); Vivian Reis (TV Laugher); Sheila Currie, Frances Gunn, Katya Ladan, Suzanne Russell, Jenna Louise, Anna Migliarese, Elaine Crosley, Mary Durkin, Angela Carrol, Julie Massie, Pat Carroll Brown, Teresa Tova, Janice Nicholson (Inmates); Alison Lawrence (Nurse); Jeremy Jenson, Donald Adams (Ward Attendants); Jo-Anne Hannah (Killer); Richie Pierce (Gas Station Attendant)

Crew: Richard Simpson (Executive Producer); Peter R. Simpson (Producer); Paul Zaza (Composer); Robert Paynter, B.S.C. (Director of Photography); Fred Guthe (Additional Photography); Michael MacLaverty, C.F.E. (Editor)

Samantha Sherwood is on stage practicing a role while director Jonathan Stryker watches by the spotlight. Stryker later drives Samantha to an institution to have her committed. After Doctor Pendleton mentions Samantha's placid composure, she attacks Stryker with a letter opener; attendants run inside and place her in a straitjacket. Stryker asks for a moment alone with Samantha, and the two seem very happy. It seems Samantha is a Method actress ("What a performance!"), and she decides the best way to play the insane title character of *Audra* is to stay in an asylum.

Samantha resides in the institution for some time, surrounded by the eerie and unstable residents. Stryker occasionally visits Samantha, until the one day she sees, in the latest issue of *Variety*, that the casting for *Audra* has begun. Samantha escapes from the asylum and throws photographs of the potential stars into the fire. She tells her friend, "What I have to do won't take long." One of the hopefuls, Amanda, has a sexual role-playing game with her boyfriend and talks about the casting sessions. Later, Amanda is driving in the rain, when she sees her freaky doll in the road. She gets out to look at it, it seems to grab her, and someone gets in the car and drives towards her. Fortunately, it is only a dream, and Amanda stands up to look for her boyfriend. A person wearing an eerie and ugly mask grabs her by the hair, stabs her and takes her doll sitting by the bed.

The different actresses hoping to play *Audra* arrive at Stryker's snow-covered dwelling: Patti, the comedienne–aspiring actress, always telling jokes; Brooke, the vet-

Aspiring actresses are more than willing to kill for a sought-after role in Richard Ciupka's *Curtains* (1983).

eran actress; Tara, the tall, attractive actress; Laurian, the timid and hesitant dancer; and Christie, the ice-skating queen. Stryker arrives with the actresses sitting around the table ("One of you is missing"), and the odd Matthew sits down with the women. Samantha arrives and sits at the table with the others. Later, Tara is out in the "casting Jacuzzi" (as Patti calls it) with Matthew. Stryker and Samantha are arguing about Stryker's decision to have someone else play Audra. Christie listens at the door, and Stryker tells her that he and Samantha were rehearsing a play he wrote. He leads Christie to his room. After someone outside picks up a sickle, Stryker leaves Christie alone in bed to weep.

The next day, Christie goes out to the frozen lake to skate. The music from her boom box abruptly stops. Christie skates over to the boom box and she finds the freaky doll buried under the snow. The masked killer is there on the ice, skating towards Christie with sickle in hand. The killer swings and Christie is hit, but the skater knocks the killer down with the doll and runs. When Christie stops to rest at a tree, the killer grabs her and kills her.

Stryker is in a room with Patti, Tara, Laurian and Brooke when Samantha enters the room, saying that she wants to act. Stryker has her sit in front of the others and puts the killer's mask over her face. He tells Samantha to seduce him without using words ("Make me love you"). Samantha does not do anything; Stryker tears off the mask and points her face to the mirror ("This is a mask, too").

Stryker talks to Patti, who tells him a couple of jokes; he says he does not think a casting session is necessary. Patti screams at him, claiming that she is as good as the other actresses. Stryker almost smiles and says that he is "enjoying a little bit of Audra." Later, Stryker asks Samantha where the mask is. Brooke, reading the script in her room, hears a noise and goes into the bathroom, where she discovers Christie's head in the toilet. She runs into a room where Stryker is working with Tara and Laurian. The director follows her to her room, where he finds nothing wrong in the bathroom. He calms Brooke, and they kiss.

Samantha sees Stryker in bed, with a sleeping Brooke next to him. When Stryker and Brooke are talking about Audra, someone walks into the room and fires a gun, and they both fly out of the window. Tara sees the bodies and screams. She runs around looking for the others, but she does not see a dead Matthew floating in the Jacuzzi. She encounters the masked killer and hides in a vent, but is discovered and killed. Later, Samantha walks into the kitchen, where Patti is opening a bottle of champagne. Samantha tells her about the institution, and she says to Patti that she killed Stryker. She tells Patti to forget about the role and just go back wherever she came from, and assures Patti that she will not hurt any of her friends. "It's only me," Patti says, and she tells Samantha that she killed the others. She stabs Samantha, Samantha screams and Patti ends up doing her comedy bit in an asylum.

Curtains is a very good slasher film, with an eerie doll and a very frightening mask. The ice-skating murder sequence is truly great and horrifying. Ciupka directed the film under the pseudonym "Jonathan Stryker," the name of the director within the film. Egger is perhaps better known as the loving mother from David Cronenberg's cult film *The Brood* (1979).

Cutting Class
(1989)

Written by Steve Slavkin; Directed by Rospo Pallenberg; Gower Street Pictures/April Films; 91 min.

Cast: Donovan Leitch (Brian Woods); Jill Schoelen (Paula Carson); Brad Pitt (Dwight Ingalls); Roddy McDowall (Mr. Dante); Martin Mull (Williams Carson III); Brenda Lynn Klemme (Colleen); Mark Barnet (Gary); Robert Glaudini (Shultz); Eric Boles (Mr. Glynn); Dirk Blocker (Coach Marris); Nancy Fish (Mrs. Knocht); Robert Machray (Mr. Conklin); David Clarke (Crusty Old Man); Norman Alden (Office Fondulaz); Tom Ligon (Mr. Ingalls); Bill Striglos (Mr. Quint); Ronnie Sperling (Mr. Tork); Jeff Rochlin (Nicholas); Alexander Folk (Mr. Nicholson); Neil Stanoff (Little Boy); Julie Hayden (Mother); Logan Clarke (Police Officer); Joel Michaley (Kid in Crowd); Dog Thomas (Bartender); Lara Rugraff-Lyon (Student in Class); Eric J. Van Wagoner (Student); Holly Hayes Jones (Head Cheerleader); Steven Kobrin (Newspaper Boy); John Glenn High School Eagle Band (Band); Joy Griglione (Drum Major); Kevin Beck (Basketball Player)

Crew: Peter S. Davis, William N. Panzer (Executive Producers); Rudy Cohen, Donald R. Beck (Producers); Jill Frasier (Composer); Avi Karpick (Director of Photography); Natan Zahavi, Bill Butler (Editors)

Paula Carson walks out of her house in the morning to retrieve the newspaper. She encounters her father, who is in his hunting gear. He will be gone for a week, leaving Paula alone, so he lays out the rules: (1) do her homework, (2) no boys in the house, and, most importantly, (3) no cutting class. He leaves, not noticing the headline in the paper, "Boy Who Killed Father Released From Institution." He heads out to a marshy area to hunt. Someone calls out, "Mr. District Attorney, over here!"—and Carson is perforated with an arrow in the chest.

Paula's boyfriend Dwight shows up late to chemistry class. Paula is there, and Brian is sitting near the back of the classroom. In gym class, Brian is staring at Paula, and the gym coach tells him to "keep it in his pants." Dwight witnessed Brian's gazing time, and he tugs and pulls on the rope as Brian tries to climb it. Later, Paula and her friend Colleen are hanging out, and Brian watches them both. Dwight tells Paula to wait in the car. He then says to Brian, "We were friends once," and he makes it clear that he does not want Brian around either Paula or himself, despite Brian's claims that the hospital made him better.

The next day, Paula is posing for an art class, and Dwight voices his objections. Brian watches in the back of the room, and the irritated art teacher makes him come up front and pose with Paula. Later, Mr. Dante, the principal, asks Paula to the office, where he shows her the new cheerleading outfit and enjoys the view as she bends over to pick it up. The art teacher, bringing sculptures out of a stove, is shoved inside and the heat is turned up. Paula heads to her car, and Dwight is waiting for her. He is upset because she says she has school work to do.

At home, Paula sees Brian watching from the yard across the street. Dwight arrives with Colleen and Gary; he wants the key to the school files to look at Brian's files (Paula has the key because she is "responsible"). She goes with the group, since Dwight has taken her books, and Brian follows. At the school, they learn that the hospital declared Brian a "violent schizophrenic" and gave him daily shock treatments. Crouched behind the water cooler in the principal's office is Brian.

The next day, Brian is mocked by others in class. On a field trip with the science teacher, the students narrowly miss a wounded but still-living Mr. Carson. At a basketball game that night, Mr. Nicholson, a university scout, is there with Dwight's father to watch Dwight play. Dwight plays poorly and even starts a scuffle on the court; the scout tediously departs, making the father angry ("Your scholarship just walked out the door"). Gary and Colleen, under the bleachers for some fun, are murdered as the crowd cheers the game.

In shop class, Dwight and Brian reminiscence about when they were once friends and worked on cars. In math class, the teacher reproaches Dwight for not paying attention; when Brian stands and tells him to take it easy on Dwight, the teacher sends both boys to see Mrs. Knocht, the vice principal. Dwight does not seem to care that Brian stuck up for him. Waiting outside the office, Paula is nice to Brian and offers some friendly advice. In the office, Mrs. Knocht tells Brian that none of his teachers want him; when he mouths off, she suspends him. Later, while working at the Xerox machine, the vice principal is attacked and her face is beaten against the machine, which Xeroxes the murder in progress. Paula discovers the body. Dwight inspects the corpse and points out Brian as the murderer. He gives chase, but loses Brian when they get outside.

Police cars and a helicopter are searching for Brian. Paula's dad is still out in the woods, and a search dog steals his biscuit but does not get help. Paula finds a tape recorder of her father practicing the final argument against Brian. The next day she gives Dwight a police report of the accident involving Brian's father. He told the police someone had taught him how to cut brake lines, but he refuses to say who because "you don't betray a friend." Brian hears the entire conversation.

In gym class, Dwight gets in trouble for not wearing his gym clothes, and the coach demands that he come in tomorrow (thereby missing Mrs. Knocht's funeral). Dwight is angry and points an arrow at the coach (his back to him) until Paula stops him; he turns and scores a bullseye. When Brian arrives at Paula's house, she thinks he is going to kill her. He picks up a pair of scissors and hands them to her, and tells her to kill him if she thinks he murdered anyone. She relaxes, and Brian stays at her house for the night. The next morning, Dwight telephones Paula; he is still obviously upset. Brian shows Paula a Xerox copy of the earlier murder; Dwight's ring is on the killer's hand.

Dwight arrives at the gym, mouths off to the coach and goes to get dressed. Paula and Brian sneak into the school and are separated when Shultz, the janitor, attacks Brian, believing him to be the murderer. The coach is enjoying the trampoline until someone places a flagpole underneath, and he is impaled. Paula finds a dead Colleen and Gary in the science room, and locks the door when she sees Dwight. She finds the math teacher, and they both take cover in a classroom. A song is played over the intercom in the room they are in, even when they run to other rooms, and they finally stop at a room with a math problem on the chalkboard. The teacher believes he has figured it out, goes to a door and is axed by Brian ("He didn't account for the different time zones").

Brian talks to Paula about deciding that murder was his "profession," and Dwight breaks down the door; he and Paula run. They reach the shop classroom, where there is a struggle, and Brian manages to get Dwight's head in a vice. Paula talks him away from Dwight, gets Brian to close his eyes, and she whacks him in the head with a hammer, letting him fall back onto a running saw. Later, the cops say the Xerox copy with Dwight's ring was from when Dwight was inspecting the corpse. As they are driving later, Dwight realizes the brake line has been cut, and they nearly run over Paula's father. After hearing about Brian, he says to Paula, "You're not cutting class, I hope!"

Cutting Class is a fairly enjoyable slasher, with interesting kills and some humorous moments. It is perhaps best remembered as an early film for actor Pitt, who became a star later in such films as Neil Jordan's *Interview With the Vampire* (1994) and David Fincher's *Seven* (1995). It is fun to watch actress Schoelen, who has an impressive résumé of horror films.

Dead of Night
(aka *Lighthouse*)
(1999)

Written and Directed by Simon Hunter; Winchester Films/The Arts Council of England/British Screen/Tungsten Pictures; 95 min.

Cast: James Purefoy (Richard Spader); Rachel Shelley (Doctor Kristy McCloud); Chris Adamson (Leo Rook); Paul Brooke (Captain Campbell); Don Warrington (Prison Officer Ian Goslet); Chris Dunne (Chief Prison Officer O'Neil); Bob Goody (Weevil); Pat Kelman (Spoons); Peter McCase (Prison Officer Hopkins); Jason Round (Spitfield); Howard Attfield (Sykes); Stuart Callaghan (Ship's Mate); Yolanda Davis (Young Prison Officer); Norman Mitchell; Neil Johnon, Kenny Ingrams, John Kearns, Bob Woodkuft (Guards); Jake West (Voice on Radio)

Crew: Gary Smith, Chris Craib (Executive Producers); Mark Leake, Tim Dennison (Producers); Sara Bingaman (Associate Producer); Peta Inglesent (Co-Producer); Debbie Wiseman (Composer); Tony Imi, B.S.C. (Director of Photography); Paul Green (Editor)

The *Hyperion* is at sea, transporting prisoners to the Marshalsea Island Prison. Inside, Leo Rook is chained within a cage. Later, a guard sees that Leo is not in his cage, and a chain is wrapped around the man's neck. A female guard (who evidently helped Leo out) is there; Leo lightly touches her face, then snaps her neck. Leo rows away in a boat and reaches the shore at the Gehenna Lighthouse. On the *Hyperion*, Doctor McCloud goes to a room of prisoners to check on the sickly Spoons; she gives the man medicine. She asks Goslet about the man who spoke to her, and he says the prisoner is Spader, a man charged with killing his wife (he claims he had an epileptic seizure and that a stranger shot his wife).

One of the men in the lighthouse sees Leo on the shore, and they run out to him. Leo slices one of the men with a machete, and the other runs away and hides. A bearded man still in the lighthouse opens the door, and Leo is standing there. Leo shuts down the power at the lighthouse.

The *Hyperion* hits an obstruction in the sea, and water rushes into the ship. The prisoners scream for the guards to let them loose. Weevil is too frightened to move, and the guard O'Neil handcuffs him to Spoons and leaves. Spader holds the door open for Weevil and Spoons; when they get through, the water slams the door closed and the ship goes under (with Spader still inside). A flare is shot from the shore; the cuffed prisoners are there with the others. McCloud saves the other flare. The group walks to the lighthouse, and Captain Campbell heads for the communications area. Spader collapses, and is aided by McCloud. Prison officer Hopkins goes down to the generator room as O'Neil goes outside with Weevil and Spoons. In the medical room, Spader sits up in bed and tells McCloud that no one else got out. After Hopkins cranks up the generator, Leo slices his neck and pulls off his head.

Outside, Weevil finds what looks like blood in the water. Goslet opens a door, a headless body falls on him and he screams. Spader and McCloud are there, and they call for Hopkins in the generator room below. Campbell has the radio operational, but it shorts out. In the generator room, Spader says he thinks McCloud is hiding something. Campbell walks up the spiraling stairs to the bathroom and sits inside the stall. He hears a noise and sees Leo's feet walking around the room. Campbell stands on the toilet and knocks off a can, which lands quietly on his scarf. Leo walks down the stairs and Campbell takes his scarf; the can now rolls to the very edge of the stairs. The wind pushes the window open, and the can falls. Campbell sits back in fear, and Leo pulls the stall door open and swings with his machete.

McCloud admits to the prisoners that Leo Rook was also being transported on the boat (she is a criminal psychiatrist studying Leo). O'Neil and the three prisoners find the radio on fire. In the bathroom, O'Neil flushes the toilet, and an excess of blood pours onto the floor ("Let's get the bastard!"). O'Neil suggests fighting Leo, but the others decide it best to leave. They find a burning boat. A distressed Goslet runs and Spader gives chase. O'Neil follows them both, loses them and drops his flashlight in the water. McCloud calls him on the radio and says that Spader and Goslet are back. O'Neil finds the boat with *Hyperion* on the side, and when he sees Leo approaching, he hides in the bottom of the boat. Leo places a new head next to the three decapitated ones sitting on the boat, and blood drips on O'Neil's face. After Leo finally leaves, O'Neil crawls out; McCloud loudly comes over the radio. O'Neil turns, and Leo is standing behind him.

Weevil finds a "Morse transmitter," but in order to send a signal, they would have to be outside; Weevil is too terrified to try it. Spader comes up with an idea. All the doors are sealed except the main entrance. He removes panels from the floor above, and the group plans to wait for Leo to arrive, trap him inside and throw flaming bottles at him. As they wait, McCloud nods off to sleep, and she dreams of a little girl watching Leo kill her mother. McCloud thinks she sees Leo in front of her, and she is startled awake. The doctor is consoled by Spader, who looks out the window and sees Leo approaching. As Leo walks inside, the generator stops and the power goes out. Goslet throws down his fiery bottle, and the others throw theirs; Leo screams and burns. Spoons grabs a hatchet, and he and Weevil run outside. McCloud and Spader put the fire out and kick over the body to see the lighthouse man, who had hidden from Leo earlier. Spader tries to call the two men, but they do not have a radio.

The prisoners see Leo and they run. As they go over a tiny cliff, Spoons is knocked unconscious. Weevil tries to cut the chain with the hatchet and finally, apologizing to Spoons, cuts off the prisoner's hand. Goslet and McCloud fill the generator and start it. Weevil gets to the lighthouse and bangs on the door, but the two cannot hear him. Spader, outside by Leo's "head boat," hears Weevil call his name, and he runs to the lighthouse. McCloud finally shuts off the generator, believing she heard something, and glass breaks. She and Goslet go up and Weevil is at the door; his head falls off. Leo stabs Goslet in the stomach. He goes for McCloud but is hit on the head with a fire extinguisher by Spader.

The two run up the spiral staircase to the top and close the door and lock it. They throw out a rope to climb down, and a flashing light gives Spader a seizure. McCloud knocks out the light, and the two climb out to the edge. The doctor begins her descent. Leo lifts his axe to cut the rope, but Spader hits him with a pipe. The rope is hit, and it uncoils quickly and stops, letting the doctor hang. Spader goes up higher, above the light, and a still-living Goslet gets on the radio. Spader yells at him to get the generator running again. As Leo reaches Spader, he swings, and the two men fall. Leo crashes into the light. Goslet starts the generator and Leo is electrocuted. Goslet falls over and dies.

Spader starts down the rope, but Leo is at a window, trying to cut the rope. Spader knocks him down and he holds onto McCloud as the rope starts burning. Spader, barely holding the doctor by her hair, manages to get her through the window. Face to face with Leo, McCloud flashes back to the images of the little girl. Leo tries to push her out of the window, and Spader hits him in the face, grabs the flare from McCloud's pocket and shoves it in Leo's mouth. McCloud sets the flare off and it blows through the back of Leo's head as Spader and McCloud swing back on the rope. There is an explosion and Leo falls out of the window the doctor and the prisoner swing back and into the building. As the sun comes up, a helicopter arrives.

Simon Hunter's *Lighthouse* may have a flimsy script, but it is hardly noticeable with his aptitude for masterful scenes of visual suspense. Hunter's film is exciting and terrifying, complete with an excellent villain (effectively hidden in shadows) and visually stunning scenes, often *sans* dialogue (Campbell's horrific moments in the bathroom are highly memorable).

Deep Red (aka *Profondo rosso*; *Dripping Deep Red*; *The Hatchet Murders*; *The Sabre Tooth Tiger*) (1975)

Written by Bernardino Zapponi and Dario Argento; Directed by Dario Argento; Rizzoli Films S.A./Seda Spettacoli; 126 min.

Cast: David Hemmings (Marcus Daly); Daria Nicolodi (Gianna Brezzi); Gabriele Lavia (Carlo); Macha Meril (Helga Ulmann); Eros Pagni (Calcabrini); Giuliana Calandra (Amanda Righetti); Glanco Mauri (Professor Giordani); Clara Calamai (Carlo's Mother); Piero Mazzinghi (Mario Bardi); Aldo Bonamano (Carlo's Father); Liana Del Balzo (Amanda's Maid); Geraldine Hooper (Carlo's Lover); Iacopo Mariani (Young Carlo); Furio Meniconi (Rodi); Fulvio Mingozzi (Agent Mingozzi); Salvatore Puntillo (Police Agent); Piero Vida (Fat Agent); Nicoletta Elmi (Olga); Vittorio Fanfoni; Dante Fioretti; Lorenzo Piani

Crew: Salvatore Argento (Producer); Claudio Argento (Executive Director); Giorgio Gaslini, Goblin (Composers); Luigi Kuveiller (Director of Photography); Franco Fraticelli (Editor)

While a child's song is playing, a scream is heard, and a bloody knife is thrown onto the floor. A youngster's feet stand by the knife. Marcus Daly, a jazz pianist, is conducting music. At the same time, Helga Ulmann, a clairvoyant, is at a lecture with Professor Giordani and Mario Bardi, and Helga is showing off her psychic ability. During the presentation, Helga reacts violently to a premonition of a "twisted mind" ("You have killed, and you will kill again!"), mentioning a singing child. Someone in the audience stands up and leaves. Later, Helga tells Giordani that she now knows who the killer is, and she will write it down and tell him tomorrow.

That night, Helga is writing about her premonition when she hears a children's song being played. She nears the door, but just as she responds to bad psychic vibes, the door opens and the killer attacks her with a cleaver. Down in the square, Marcus is talking with his frequently inebriated friend Carlo. Shortly after Carlo leaves, Marcus sees a bloody Helga crash through her apartment window. He runs up to her place, helps her out of the window and sees a person in a black coat running away in the square. The police arrive and question Marcus. Gianna, a reporter-photographer, shows up for the story. After his interrogation, Marcus speaks with Carlo again, and Marcus tells him he thinks he remembers a painting when initially entering Helga's apartment but later was not able to locate it.

At Helga's funeral, Gianna suggests that she and Marcus work together on the murder case. Marcus thanks her for printing his photograph in the newspaper and declaring him the witness, so that the killer can find him more easily. After discussing Helga's premonition with Giordani and Mario, and seeing Carlo to talk about the mysterious missing painting, Marcus goes to his apartment to compose some music. He soon hears the child's song, followed by the sound of his door creaking open. As the phone rings, Marcus jumps up and pulls the room's door shut. The killer whispers threats to him and eventually leaves.

The next day, Marcus goes through albums of children's music and finds the song he had heard. Mario tells him a folktale involving a haunted house in which a singing child is heard, followed by the shrieking of someone being murdered. Marcus goes and looks up the folktale in a book, and finds a picture of the house. The book offers no name or address of the person who lived there at the time, so the pianist decides to speak with Amanda Righetti, the book's author. Before he can, however, she is forcibly submerged in hot water. As she lies on the floor dying, she writes the killer's name on the steamy mirrored wall.

Marcus finds Amanda's body and runs away. He proceeds to interview gardeners who might know the plants surrounding the house, until one gardener tells him about the rare plants. After telling Giordani about Amanda (and her "pointing" at the wall), Marcus locates the house and speaks with the present owner (who does not know who owned the house before 1963). Marcus checks out the house and finds a child's drawing on the wall behind plaster. Meanwhile, Giordani realizes Amanda has "writ-

Marcus (David Hemmings) snoops around the dark, mysterious house in search of a killer's identity in Dario Argento's *Deep Red* (1975).

ten" something on the wall, but before he can tell Marcus anything, he is murdered. Marcus continues to tell Gianna that they should leave but after she has gone to pack, Marcus notices something about the photograph of the house. He returns to the estate and sees that a window in the picture is now missing. He beats in the wall and discovers a room containing a badly decomposed corpse. Marcus is then knocked unconscious.

The pianist awakes outside, with Gianna by his side and the house in flames. While at the owner's place, Marcus sees a picture similar to the one on the wall. He asks the owner's daughter where she had seen it before, and she tells him about the files in her school. Marcus and Gianna go there, but when Gianna goes to telephone the police, she is stabbed. Marcus now knows who drew the pictures. After discovering the wounded Gianna, Marcus encounters a gun-toting Carlo. Carlo says he has no choice but to kill Marcus, but soon the police arrive and Carlo must flee. He momentarily escapes, but he is sideswiped by a truck, his foot is caught on the back and he is dragged down several streets until finally being thrown off. A car approaches while Carlo is lying in the street, and his head is crushed under a wheel.

Later, Marcus realizes that Carlo could not have been the murderer because Carlo was with the pianist when Helga was being killed. He returns to Helga's apartment and sees that what he had thought was a painting that was later removed was actually a mirror. He had seen the reflection of Martha, Carlo's mother. Soon Martha has arrived with a cleaver; she tells of how she killed Carlo's father. She swings her cleaver at Marcus. He runs but is wounded when she attacks him again. Martha's necklace gets caught in the gate near the lift, Marcus operates the lift, and the necklace is pulled, creating a guillotine and slicing off the murderer's head.

Deep Red, one of Argento's most popular slasher movies, is a fascinating film and the first collaboration for Argento and Nicolodi (they collaborated off-screen as well) and for Argento and the music group Goblin. Not pleased with Giorgio Gaslini's score, Argento asked Goblin to compose the film's music. The band's score went on to spend 15 weeks at number one on Italian album charts. *Deep Red* was released in Japan as *Suspiria 2*, although Argento completed the film before *Suspiria* (1977), and as *The Hatchet Murders* in America, although a hatchet is never used to murder a character in the film. When the killer enters Marcus' apartment, he defends himself with a statue of a bird, a reference to the earlier Argento film *The Bird with the Crystal Plumage* (1969).

Dementia 13 (1963)

Written and Directed by Francis Ford Coppola; American International; 75 min.

Cast: William Campbell (Richard Haloran); Luana Anders (Louise Haloran); Bart Patton (Billy Haloran); Mary Mitchel (Kane); Patrick Magee (Justin Caleb); Ethne Dunn (Lady Haloran); Peter Read (John Haloran); Karl Schanzer (Simon); Ron Perry (Arthur); Derry O'Donavan (Lillian); Barbara Dowlin (Kathleen)

Crew: Roger Corman (Producer); Marianne Wood (Associate Producer); Ronald Stein (Composer); Charles Hanawalt (Director of Photography); Mort Tubor, Stuart O'Brien (Editors); Jack Hill (Second Unit Writer-Director)

John Haloran decides that he wants to go out on a boat alone, but his wife Louise reluctantly goes with him. Out on the lake, Louise suggests to John that they talk his mother into changing her will so that all of her money will not go to a charity in the name of Kathleen. An apparently concerned Louise tells John he is rowing too vigorously, and John says that if he dies, Louise will no longer be a part of the family. John suddenly clutches his chest and lies down, and Louise, seeing that John has no pills with him, begins rowing quickly ("Row faster, Louise. If I die, there's nothing in it for you!"). John dies, and Louise tosses him into the water. She packs a few of John's things and writes to his mother (signing the notes as "John"), explaining that her son will miss the memorial ceremony. Louise decides she is going to make John's mother change her "ridiculous will."

At Castle Haloran, Louise tells John's brother Billy that the castle seems haunted, and he says it is haunted by Kathleen. Louise asks about his sister, and he tells her that she died by drowning. Billy goes to the airport and picks up Kane, the special lady friend of Billy's other brother Richard, who makes metal statues. At a table, Lady Haloran lets Louise knows she is not invited to the ceremony, and she tells Richard (when they are alone) that she does not care for Kane. Richard tells her not to hurt Kane or he will "never forget it." Later, Kane is riding a horse as Richard watches, and Louise approaches and talks to the man. Richard mentions Louise "squirming" when the will was read, saying that she gave John "enough dirty looks to give him a heart attack." Louise asks him not to make a mockery of John's "bad heart."

Billy is at the pond later, thinking about a time he was playing with Kathleen near the water. Kane greets him, and Billy tells about the ceremony, which involves umbrellas (since it rained the day of Kathleen's funeral), flowers and the collapse of his mother. He spots Simon, a poacher, hiding in the bushes, and tells him to leave. At the ceremony, Lady Haloran collapses, and Louise rushes to her side and helps her get to bed. At her bedside, Louise tells the mother that she has heard a child begging for her mother to listen and that she wants her mother to watch for signs. That night, Louise gets into Kathleen's room and takes some dolls as someone follows and watches her. Louise bumps into Richard ("Are you lost?"), and she goes outside to the pond and ties the dolls together with a wrench on the other side. She strips to her underwear, dives in the pond and leaves the dolls at the bottom. Louise sees what looks like the body of a young girl there, screams and swims back to the surface, where someone is waiting with an axe. Louise is killed and her bloody corpse dragged away.

At the house the next day, Doctor Caleb tells Lady Haloran that, aside from working herself into hysterics for her annual collapse, she is fine. The woman asks Lillian the maid to find Louise for her. Outside for breakfast, the group sees the dolls bobbing on the surface of the pond, and Lady Haloran believes Kathleen is telling her that she wants her tiara. Caleb is angry, thinking that someone has planted the dolls there. As Billy gets the toys out of the water, he flashes back to a time he was standing by the pond and then ran away. Later that night, Simon is out in the trees and shrubbery "hunting" and comes across the body of a young girl. The person with the axe decapitates the poacher.

Caleb asks Arthur, an elderly man who works at the castle, to drain the pond. Lady Haloran goes to a small building where some toys are kept, and she places the tiara onto Kathleen's body, which is sitting in a chair. The murderer arrives and begins chopping away at the building. The woman screams and runs, and the killer takes Kathleen's corpse away. Lady Haloran runs until she collapses, and Kane finds her and calls for Richard. The two brothers arrive and carry their mother inside. Billy tells Kane about a recurring nightmare involving a man climbing into his window, saying he was crazy and acknowledging that Billy's mother was also insane; the dream ends with Billy being tossed into the pond by his mother. As Billy and Kane are leaving, he says he suddenly realizes that Richard was the madman from his dream.

Arthur goes to see Caleb later and leads him to the drained pond, where a shrine made of stone rests for Kathleen. Richard says he does not work with stone, but Caleb says he did once. Richard, recalling the tiara his mother was clutching, suggests that Louise is trying to get her hands on the valuable jewelry. Caleb rejects the idea, but afterwards tells Billy that they should look for Louise. Kane follows Richard to a room full of tools and stone sculptures, where Richard's father once worked; the couple does not see Kathleen's body in the room.

Caleb and Billy head to a bar to ask about Louise and sit for a drink. Caleb says Billy once told him that he watched Kathleen drown, which Billy denies. The doctor then tries to induce Billy ("C'mon, drink up") into telling him what happened to Louise, and a seemingly dazed Billy recites a nursery rhyme involving "little fishies." Later, after the wedding, Richard and Kane go out to the hay to get away from everyone (Caleb had been telling Kane that he had discovered things in the house that made him "uneasy") and to kiss. Caleb, recollecting a part of Billy's nursery rhyme about being "caught on a hook," finds a hanging Louise, with Kathleen in the same room. Richard and Kane hear a scream, and they see a group of people surrounding Kathleen's body near the pond. Kane nears the corpse, and Billy ("Don't touch her!") raises his axe. Caleb comes out from hiding and shoots and kills Billy. Billy thinks back to trying to get a toy from Kathleen and pushing her into the water. "Forgive me, Kathleen," he says. Caleb tells the others that Billy made a wax doll to "relieve his guilt," and the doctor swings an axe into Kathleen's face.

Dementia 13, with quirky and eerie moments and good performances, effectively avoids becoming camp, and it is easy to believe that the director went to produce such classics as *The Godfather* (1972), *Apocalypse Now* (1980) and *The Conversation* (1974). Anders is terrific as the malevolent Louise. Jack Hill, credited as the second unit writer and director, also directed the cult film *Spider Baby* (1964), starring Lon Chaney, Jr., as well as *Coffy* (1973) and *Switchblade Sisters* (1975). Actor Magee starred as the crippled and tormented writer in Stanley Kubrick's *A Clockwork Orange* (1971).

Don't Open Till Christmas (1984)

Written by Derek Ford; Directed by Edmund Purdom; Spectacular International Films; 86 min.

Cast: Edmund Purdom (Inspector Harris); Alan Lake (Giles); Belinda Mayne (Kate); Mark Jones (Detective Sergeant Powell); Gerry Sundquist (Cliff Boyd); Kelly Baker ("Experience" Girl); Caroline Munro (Herself); Kevin Lloyd (Gerry); Wendy Danvers (Housekeeper); Nicholas Donnelly (Doctor Bridle); Pat Astley (Sharon); Lawrence Harrington (Kate's Father); Ken Halliwell (Restaurant Commissionaire); Ray Marioni (Matire d'hotel); Wildfred Corlett ("Experience" Santa Claus); Ricky Kennedy (Theatre Santa Claus); Sid Wragg (Dungeon Santa Claus); Max Roman (Store Santa Claus); George Pierce (Market Santa Claus); Ashley Dransfield (Drunken Santa Claus); Derek Ford, Adrian Black (Circus Santa Clauses); John Aston (Santa Claus in Car); Marla Eldridge (Girl in Car); Des Dolan (Detective Constable); Derek Hunt (Police Constable); Paula Meadows (Dungeon Secretary)

Crew: Al McGoohan (Writer-Director, Additional Scenes); Dick Randall, Steve Minasian (Producers); Des Dolan (Composer); Alan Pudney (Director of Photography); Ray Selfe (Editor).

A woman greets a man dressed as Santa Claus, and they head to a nearby car to kiss. Someone approaches the car, and the Santa steps out and is stabbed in the stomach. The woman gets out of the car and is killed. At a party, Kate and Cliff introduce Kate's father, dressed as Santa, to the crowd, and a spear is thrown, hitting Santa in the back and coming out of his mouth. Inspector Harris and Detective Sergeant Powell go to see Kate and Cliff, and Harris tells Kate that her father was a "victim of another Santa murder." A Santa is standing in the street by a grill, and something is wrapped around his neck. His face is shoved in the grill, and Santa is left there to cook and burn.

A package ("Don't open till Christmas") is delivered to Harris' place, and he tells the housekeeper to leave it on his desk. Kate tells Cliff that Harris asked about him, inquiring whether they were going to get married. A man named Giles calls Powell, saying he is from *The Daily News*. He asks if Powell would like to solve the Santa murders and says he will be in touch and hangs up. A drunken Santa is stumbling in an alley, and a gun is put in his mouth and fired. Giles tries to talk to Kate on the street, and she says he would not bother her if he had ever lost a parent like she had. He tells her he has, and Kate leaves.

Cliff is out playing the flute and Kate is holding a hat for money. Gerry the photographer sees the two, and he and Cliff go for a drink. At the bar, Gerry asks Cliff to the studio and tells him there might be something for him, especially if he brings Kate. Cliff tells Kate that Gerry has invited them for tea. The couple walk into the studio, where Sharon is posing. Cliff tries to persuade Kate to do some shots ("It's a quick 50"), but when Gerry brings out a Santa outfit, Kate storms out. Gerry convinces the irate Cliff to stay. Later, Cliff is outside with Sharon (mostly nude under her Santa costume), and he tries to go back in when he sees cops, but the door is locked. He tells Sharon to run, and she follows and loses him. She sees the killer, who holds a razor over her and leaves. The cops find the frightened Sharon and lead her away. Harris and Powell talk to Sharon, and she says she can only remember the killer's eyes, which seemed to smile. At a peep show, a Santa Claus sits to watch a woman. After the woman dances a bit, the man is attacked and stabbed in the neck.

Cliff and Kate argue. Harris arrives and tells the couple that Sharon was attacked. Giles sees Powell in his office and suggests keeping an eye on Harris. Powell trails Harris at the mall but loses him outside. A Santa Claus hangs around in a museum, where the killer stabs him twice in the stomach. Harris goes to see Powell and talks about the "decoys" being sent out. Two police officers as Santa Clauses are at a carnival, and the killer kicks a Santa in the crotch with a boot-knife and punches him with a studded glove. He shoves a broken bottle into the eye of the other Santa-cop. Powell talks to the woman from the peep show, and she says she can only remember the "smiling eyes." Kate calls Harris' private number, and his housekeeper tells her that it is the day the inspector visits Parkland's.

The woman returns to her job at the peep show, and the killer arrives and punches through the glass. She is chased into the streets, where she is grabbed, dragged into a room and thrown unto a bed. She says she did not tell the cops anything and has not seen the killer's face, but when she turns to look, the killer says it is now too late. The woman is restrained with a chain and left alone. Powell releases Cliff "once and for all," because he thinks he knows the "right man." An inebriated Santa is chased into a building where "Miss Munro" and her band are about to perform on stage. The Santa hides backstage but is found and gets a blade in the face. At Kate's place, she tells Powell that Harris was at Parkland's, a "lunatic asylum." She says she cannot find a record of his name and that Harris irrationally implies that Cliff is the killer, despite the fact that Cliff was beside Kate when her father was murdered. Powell takes Kate's comments lightly. Kate goes to see Doctor Bridle at Parkland's Mental Hospital.

A jolly ol' St. Nicholas goes to the bathroom, and the killer uses a razor to slice off a particular body part. Kate goes to see Harris, who has been suspended. She says Cliff has been acting differently. It is Christmas Eve, and the two decide to dine together; Kate asks what Harris' first name is. Cliff arrives and is taken out of the restaurant (he is not dressed appropriately), and he and Kate see one another. Back at Kate's apartment, Giles is there, and he pushes her against the wall before she can get to the phone. Kate says she has figured out that Giles is Harris' brother, and that Harris changed his name from Harrison when Giles was put in the institution. Giles said he threatened his brother by saying he would go to the newspapers if he did not visit him. Kate says Giles killed her father, and Giles says that her father, like the others, reminded him of Christmastime. Powell calls Kate and she goes for the phone, but Giles pulls her back with tinsel and stabs her in the stomach.

Powell and an officer find Kate dead, and Powell is told that Harris has been in his apartment all night. Outside, Powell spots Giles running and chases him to a parking garage. Giles hooks cables to a car and Powell is electrocuted. Giles returns to the chained woman with some food. She talks of Christmas and, with her hands now free, she hits him on the head with a piece of wood. Giles declares her the "supreme sacrifice" for the evil of Christmas, and the woman runs out of the door. She is chased upstairs, and Giles swings the chain around. The woman grabs the chain over the railing and pulls Giles over, letting him fall. At the bottom of the stairs, he attacks again, and Harris stirs in his sleep. A flashback shows a young Giles at Christmastime walking in on his father (as Santa) with a woman. Giles' mother also sees the couple, the father angrily hits his wife and she falls down the stairs. Harris awakes, takes the gift from his desk (from his "loving Brother") and opens it to see a tiny box with music and a dancing Santa. He sits it on his desk and rests in a chair, and the box explodes.

Don't Open Till Christmas, the British answer to *Silent Night, Deadly Night* (1984), is an average slasher. It is helped out with a hefty Santa body count, but the suspense is nearly non-existent and the ending is predictable.

The Dorm That Dripped Blood (aka *Death Dorm; Pranks*) (1981)

Written by Stephen Carpenter, Jeffrey Obrow and Stacey Giachino; Directed by Jeffrey Obrow and Stephen Carpenter; Jeff Obrow Productions; 84 min.

Cast: Laurie Lapinski (Joanne); Stephen Sachs (Craig); David Snow (Brian); Pamela Holland (Patti); Dennis Ely (Bobby Lee Tremble); Woody Roll (John Hemmit); Daphne Zuniga (Debbie); Jack Jones (Bill Edgar); Robert Frederick (Tim); Chris Morrill (Jack); Chandre (Alice); Billy Criswell (Rick); Richard Cowgill (Debbie's Father); Kay Beth (Debbie's Mother); Jimmy Betz (Officer Lewis); Thomas Christian (Officer Dean); Robert Richardson, Chris Schroeder (Policemen)

Crew: Jeffrey Obrow (Producer); Stacey Giachino (Associate Producer); Stephen Carpenter (Director of Photography); Chris Young (Composer); Jeffrey Obrow, Stephen Carpenter (Editors)

A young college male is running from an unseen pursuer. As he is hiding, hands grab his throat and he is killed. Dayton Hall is a dormitory that is about to be torn down and turned into an apartment complex. Five students have volunteered to help with cleanup, supervised by Joanne. At a party, Joanne's boyfriend Tim tries to convince her to move into an apartment with him, but Joanne wants time to think about it. After she says goodbye to Tim (who is leaving with some friends to go skiing), Joanne prepares the schedule for the next two weeks. She learns that one of the five students, Debbie, has to leave that night with her parents, leaving Joanne with Patti, Brian and Craig.

Debbie helps for as long as she can and then goes to wait for her parents. Before she leaves, she heads to the roof to get the inventory list from the storage room. Debbie's mother and father arrive and wait for her in the truck. The father walks up the stairs to see what is taking her so long, but on the stairwell he encounters someone who beats him with a nail-studded baseball bat. While the mother continues to wait, the back door of the truck slowly opens. Debbie comes down the stairs and sees her dead father. She runs to the truck, only to find her mother's body inside. Debbie is hit on the head and she falls to the ground unconscious. The killer drags her to the truck's back tire, puts the vehicle in reverse and mashes Debbie's head. The bodies are put in the truck and driven away.

The next morning, Patti goes to the supply room. She sees a bum scavenging in the trash bin. When she tells the others about him ("that weird-looking guy with the fuzzy hair"), Brian says his name is John Hemmit; he often hangs around Dayton Hall. Bill Edgar talks to Joanne and complains about someone stealing his drill. Afterwards, Joanne meets Bobby Lee Tremble, who has arrived about the desks being sold from Dayton Hall. Bobby Lee mentions occasionally driving by the dormitory. That night, after playing pool, Patti goes for a beer and is startled when she sees Hemmit at the window. Brian runs outside to get Hemmit, but returns without even seeing him. The group splits up to search for the bum. At home, Bobby Lee gives Joanne a ring and asks if she would like to "get together." His lady friend Alice nags him about the phone call, and Bobby Lee decides to go out for a drive.

The next day, Bill goes to the bathroom to clean up. While he is washing his hands, his drill is returned to him, right to the back of his head. Brian and Craig are outside when Hemmit walks by. Craig confronts and threatens him while Brian tells him to "Lay off!" An elaborate dinner is planned for the evening, but while Craig is getting candles, some food is stolen. Assuming Hemmit is in the house, Craig searches for the bum, while Joanne goes to get the others. When she finally finds Brian, they all meet back at the table to see that someone has beaten the food and dishes with a baseball bat. The group gives a description of Hemmit to a police officer, who tells them it sounds like someone the cops had picked up earlier.

While on the telephone with her mother, Joanne hears noises on the roof. She calls Patti, who comes over to Joanne's room. Joanne then realizes the phones are now dead. Brian is playing pool when the power goes out. When running up the stairs, he is attacked by a man with a machete. Craig joins the two girls, and he and Patti go to check the fusebox. Once there, Craig is knocked unconscious, and Patti is murdered. Craig gets back to Joanne and tells her what has happened. The two of them see Hemmit walking around outside, carrying a bloody machete. Arming themselves, Joanne and Craig go out into the hall to confront a killer.

Soon they run into Hemmit, who knocks out Craig. Joanne runs and eventually finds Brian's body. Joanne grabs the machete from Brian's corpse and wounds Hemmit, not believing him when he tells her, "You've got to trust me." Joanne meets with Craig again. While Joanne gets Hemmit's attention, Craig begins to struggle with him until Joanne hits Hemmit in the head with a baseball bat. Craig seems very pleased and he says to Joanne, "It's been me the whole time." Joanne runs away.

Bobby Lee arrives and hears the screams and cries of Joanne. While hiding, Joanne is knocked out by Craig, and soon the murderer and Bobby Lee are fighting. When Bobby Lee gets the best of Craig and is standing over him with a knife, the cops show up and tell the man to freeze. Craig, acting like a scared victim for the police officers, whispers to Bobby Lee that he is a "dead man." When Bobby Lee lunges for Craig, he is shot and killed by the officers. They help Craig up, and he tells them his friends need help on the seventh floor. When the officers run out, Craig picks up the unconscious Joanne, carries her to the incinerator and drops her inside, leaving the policeman to wonder what the horrible stench is.

The Dorm That Dripped Blood is a decent slasher entry, hampered by drab acting and uninspired scenes of murder and pursuit. It was the film debut for actress Daphne Zuniga, who later achieved fame on the television series *Melrose Place*. The *Dorm That Dripped Blood* score is humdrum, but composer Young went on to write many others, including ones for Clive Barker's *Hellraiser* (1987), George A. Romero's *The Dark Half* (1993) and Sam Raimi's *The Gift* (2000).

Dr. Phibes Rises Again (1972)

Written by Robert Blees and Robert Fuest; Directed by Robert Fuest; American International Pictures; 89 min.

Cast: Vincent Price (Doctor Phibes); Robert Quarry (Biederbeck); Hugh Griffith (Ambrose); Peter Jeffrey (Trout); Fiona Lewis (Diana); Valli Kemp (Vulnavia); John Cater (Waverley); Gerald Sim (Hackett); Lewis Fiander (Baker); John Thaw (Shavers); Peter Cushing (Captain); Beryl Reid (Miss Ambrose);

Terry-Thomas (Lombardo); Milton Reid (Manservant); Keith Buckley (Stewart)

Crew: Samuel Z. Arkoff, James H. Nicholson (Executive Producers); Louis M. Heyward (Producer); John Gale (Composer); Alex Thomson (Director of Photography); Tristam Cones (Editor)

Three years after Doctor Phibes put himself in a comatose state to "sleep" with his wife, the moon shines upon the crypt, and life blood flows back into Phibes. He crawls out of his crypt, dusts off his organ and begins playing music. Vulnavia appears out of nowhere, and Phibes tells her to bring him one of his maps—a map that leads to a pharaoh's tomb, underneath which, every 2,000 years, flows the River of Life. Unfortunately, the map has been taken, and Phibes immediately suspects a man named Biederbeck.

Phibes visits Biederbeck and hears the man speaking with Ambrose about the map and the Temple of Ibisis in Egypt. When the two men leave with Biederbeck's girlfriend Diana, Phibes and Vulnavia murder the butler and steal the map from a safe. Inspector Trout arrives at the scene and learns that Biederbeck is concerned more about the missing map than his deceased butler. The group of people looking for the temple travel on a ship to Egypt. Biederbeck has a small bottle containing the "elixir of life" and, according to his notes, if he fails in Egypt, he is "doomed." While on the boat, Ambrose goes to look for a model of the mountains for Biederbeck, but he instead finds a glass case displaying Victoria's body and Phibes' clockwork band. The case lights up and the band begins to play, as Phibes wraps his hands around Ambrose's throat.

Doctor Phibes and Vulnavia reach the temple, and through a doorway behind a statue's feet, they already have the place decorated to resemble Phibes' old domicile. After Ambrose's body, enclosed in a giant glass bottle, washes ashore, Trout and his boss, Waverley, interrogate Lombardo to ask about the passenger list. Lombardo tells them that none of the passengers were odd, except for a man who wanted an organ and who had clockwork musicians. The officers suspect Phibes. Ambrose's cousin arrives and notices a map sitting on Waverley's desk. She tells the two men that Ambrose and Biederbeck were not headed towards the place marked on the map, but somewhere else.

Biederbeck and Diana arrive in Egypt, where Hackett and other men already have a site set up. One of the men, Shavers, is at the mountain alone. While walking through the tunnels, he is attacked by a bird that is guarding Victoria Phibes. Afterwards, Phibes asks the bird, "Did you have a good dinner?" Later, Diana finds a corpse in the ground under her tent. Doctor Phibes moves Victoria into a compartment inside a coffin. That night, Vulnavia entices a man named Stewart to follow her. He is restrained, and a key for his release is placed inside a statue. When he breaks open the statue, he lets loose many scorpions which proceed to dine on his flesh.

Trout and Waverley are now in Egypt, searching for the others. Biederbeck tells Hackett they have discovered a gold sarcophagus (the very one with Victoria inside). The two police officers arrive at the campsite, where they have recently discovered a dead Stewart. The cops suggest that Phibes committed the murder. The people want to leave, but Biederbeck says that he must stay. At night, the winds are heavy (only because Doctor Phibes is operating a gigantic fan), and Vulnavia straps a sleeping Baker into something. The assistant takes over the fan, and Phibes heads to Baker's tent to squeeze the man in a giant vice. Doctor Phibes and Vulnavia take the sarcophagus and Victoria from Baker's tent.

Biederbeck still insists on staying, and Diana leaves with Hackett. However, Phibes tricks Hackett into believing help has arrived, and when he leaves his vehicle to check, Diana is taken. Hackett comes back, is killed, and his vehicle rolls down a dune until it returns to the campsite with Hackett's corpse behind the wheel. Biederbeck heads to the mountains to get Diana back from Phibes. Trout and Waverley follow him.

Phibes has Diana strapped to a table. Biederbeck has a key that he had taken from a snake statue (which was part of the sarcophagus). The key unlocks the gate to the River of Life, and in order to save Diana, Biederbeck must use the key to release the water (which prevents a wall of snakes killing Diana) and open the gate. Biederbeck needs the River of Life, however, to acquire more of his elixir, which he has been using for almost a hundred years to maintain his youth. Biederbeck finally gives in and releases Diana from the trap. The gates open for Phibes and he passes by them. As Diana and the two police officers enter the room of the gate, Biederbeck is crying for Phibes to let him through. His time runs out and Biederbeck suddenly becomes an old man, as Phibes sails away with Victoria.

In this worthy *Dr. Phibes* sequel, Price gives another superb performance as Phibes. A still-uncredited Caroline Munro reprises her role of Victoria Phibes. Virginia North was not able to reprise her role of Vulnavia from the first film because she was pregnant. Co-writer Robert Blees also co-wrote the quirky horror film *Frogs* (1972).

Dressed to Kill (1980)

Written and Directed by Brian De Palma; Cinema 77 Films/Filmways Pictures/Warwick Associates; 105 min.

Cast: Michael Caine (Doctor Robert Elliott); Angie Dickinson (Kate Miller); Nancy Allen (Liz Blake); Keith Gordon (Peter Miller); Dennis Franz (Detective Marino); David Margulies (Doctor Levy); Susanna Clemm (Betty Luce); Ken Baker (Warren Lockman); Brandon Maggart (Cleveland Sam); Amalie Collier (Cleaning Woman); Mary Davenport (Woman in Restaurant); Anneka De Lorenzo (Nurse); Norman Evans (Ted); Robbie L. McDermott (Man in Shower); Bill Randolph (Chase Cabbie); Sean O'Rinn (Museum Cabbie); Fred Weber (Mike Miller); Samm-Art Williams (Subway Cop); Robert Lee Rush, Anthony Body Scriven, Robert McDuffie, Frederick Sanders (Hoods)

Crew: George Little (Producer); Pino Donaggio (Composer); Ralf Bode (Director of Photography); Jerry Greenberg (Editor)

Inside a pleasant house, a man is shaving in the bathroom as a woman showers. While watching the man through the door, the woman is attacked by someone in the shower. The shaving man hardly seems to notice. The woman yells, and the whole episode turns out to be a fantasy.

Kate Miller goes to see her son Peter, who has been working on a science project all night. She then pays a visit to her psychiatrist, Doctor Robert Elliott, and talks about her mother driving her crazy and being upset over her husband's "wham-bam special" that morning. She asks the doctor if he considers her attractive enough for a closer relationship. He responds affirmatively, but asks if she thinks it would be worth jeopardizing her marriage. Kate is not sure.

At the art museum, Kate is sitting on a bench when a stranger in sunglasses sits next to her. The man seems to interest Kate, and when he stands up, she follows him. Soon he is waiting around a corner smiling at her, and he begins to follow her. The man goes back to the bench and retrieves Kate's glove (which she unknowingly dropped earlier), and he later touches her shoulder with the glove on his hand. Kate mistakes the touch as an advance and walks away, only to realize what she has lost and what the man was trying to return. She walks outside, throws her other glove to the ground and sees the stranger in a taxi, motioning with her glove. The other glove is picked up by someone else. Kate tries to apologize, but the man kisses her before she can say anything. She gets in the taxi and the two get very close.

Later that evening, at the stranger's house, Kate gets out of bed, finds a phone and calls her house. She hangs up when her husband answers. She leaves her afternoon lover a note. Inside his desk drawer, Kate finds a notice from the Department of Health stating, "You have contracted a venereal disease!" Upset, she runs out and to the elevator, while a blonde woman is watching from the stairway. On the elevator, Kate realizes that she left her wedding ring in the apartment. She goes back up, and waiting for her is the blonde, who begins slashing her with a razor. At the same time, Liz is leaving with a man; the man runs away when the elevator opens. Liz sees a dying Kate, and she narrowly misses an encounter with the blonde, who decides to simply drop the razor. Liz picks the weapon up. A maid sees her and screams.

At his office, Elliott has a message from Bobbi, saying she has "borrowed his razor." Detective Marino calls and tells him that his patient was murdered. At the police station, Marino interrogates Elliott, and the detective suggests that Kate may have been overly flirtatious with one of Elliott's patients. While Marino says goodbye to Peter and his father, Elliott takes a peek at a folder on Marino's desk, which is labeled "Elizabeth Blake." Elliott says he cannot let Marino see his appointment book. Later, Elliott calls an escort service and makes an appointment with Liz. Marino talks to Liz next and tells her she is a suspect. Knowing what her profession is, Mario gives Liz 48 hours to find the client she was with that evening.

Peter stands in front of Elliott's office and times patients walking from the door to the gate. After working with some blueprints, he returns, chains his moped in front of the office and sets up a hidden camera. Liz goes out for a job, and a blonde is following her. A cab driver races her to the subway, and the nice cabbie knocks the blonde out as Liz runs. At the subway, however, is the murderous blonde Bobbi. Liz apparently eludes Bobbi and inadvertently mouths off to some hoods, who chase her onto the train. She gets away and stands next to a cop, but when he exits the train, the hoods return and chase Liz. In between compartments, Liz is attacked by Bobbi, and the hoods run away. Peter appears and sprays Bobbi with something; the killer shrieks and runs away.

Peter and Liz now want to find Bobbi (Peter saw her come out of Elliott's office), and Liz tells Marino to get Elliott's appointment book. Marino says he is not able to without a search warrant, but a "paranoid murder suspect" might be able to get it. Elliott goes to see Doctor Levy and says his previous patient Bobbi is out on the streets and very dangerous. Peter and Liz watch the time-lapse film and see Bobbi walk out ("She must be his last appointment").

Liz goes to see Elliott for an appointment. She describes a made-up sexual fantasy, trying to seduce him. She says she is going to "powder her nose," and when she returns, she hopes he might be ready. Outside the office, Liz finds Elliott's appointment book and flips through it. Peter is outside watching and he gets closer to the window. Peter is grabbed by someone, and a blonde in the office looks outside. When Liz returns to the room, she sees Peter and a blonde outside banging on the window; Bobbi is behind her with a razor. The blonde pulls a gun and fires, and the killer is hit in the neck. Elliott lies on the floor wounded.

At the station, Doctor Levy explains about Elliott and his female side Bobbi, and Marino tells Liz he had Betty Luce, the blonde police officer, following her. In an institution, a nurse goes to check on Elliott. He attacks her, chokes her and steals her clothes. At Peter's house, Liz is showering and she hears something. She turns the shower off and sees a pair of legs and feet just outside the door. She slowly steps out of the shower, keeping an eye on the feet. But soon it is revealed that the feet are really only shoes, and before she can reach the razor in the cabinet, her throat is cut wide open. Liz sits up in bed from her nightmare and screams, as Peter runs to her side.

Despite its somewhat predictable unveiling of the killer, *Dressed to Kill* is a good film from director De Palma, with a shocking elevator attack and a suspenseful chase sequence on the train. The blonde killer Bobbi is played by Susanna Clemm, who also portrayed Betty Luce, the police officer following Liz and who was frequently used in the film as a decoy.

The Driller Killer
(1979)

Written by Nicholas St. John; Directed by Abel Ferrara; Navaron Films; 95 min.

Cast: Jimmy Laine (Reno); Carolyn Marz (Carol); Baybi Day (Pamela); Harry Schultz (Dalton Briggs); Alan Wynroth (Landlord); Maria Helhoski (Nun); James O'Hara (Man in Church); Richard Howorth (Carol's Husband); Louis Mascolo (Knife Victim); Tommy Santora (Attacker); Rita Gooding, Chuck Saaf (TV Spot); Gary Cohen (Voice Over); Janet Dailey, Joyce Finney (Girls at Audition); Butch Morris (Sidewalk Beggar); Paul Fitze, John Fitze, Karl Metner, Chris Amato, Rich Bokun, Michael Canosa, Greg Schirrira, Thomas Baeza (Kids on Street); Frank Hazard, Jack MacIntyre (Waiting For Bus); John Coulakis (Hallway); Lanny Taylor (Rooftop); Peter Yellen (Bus Stop); Steve Cox (Empire State); Stephen Singer, Tom Constantine (Street Corner); Anthony Picciano (Sidewalk and Street); Bob De Frank (Fire Escape); Rhodney Montreal (Tony Coca-Cola/Guitar); Dicky Bittner (Ritchy/Bass); Steve Brown (Steve/Drums); Laurie Y. Taylor (Tony's Girlfriend); Trixie Sly (Manager); Andrea Childs, Hallie Coletta, Victoria Keiler, Claire Mailer, Paula Nichols (Friends)

Crew: Rochelle Weisberg (Executive Producer); D.A. Metrov (Associate Producer); Joseph Delia (Composer); Ken Kelsch (Director of Photography); Orlando Gallini (Editor)

Reno walks to the front of a church where a bearded man is kneeling. He unclasps a hand and grabs Reno's hand; Reno runs, grabs Carol and leaves. They ride in a taxi, and Reno calls the man a "degenerate" and "bum." (Evidently he had a piece of paper with Reno's name and number.)

The next morning, Reno hears Pamela trying to drill a hole in the door, and he does it for her. He complains about long distance phone calls that Carol and Pamela have made, and he throws the phone out the window. Later, Reno dreams of the bearded man and a drill, and he sees himself running with a drill. Reno goes to see Dalton and says he is currently working on a masterpiece (a giant painting of a buffalo). He says he needs another week and asks Dalton to lend him $500, but Dalton refuses. Carol writes a check (she later says it is her alimony check) to Al, the super, who says that they are still a month behind.

Tony Coca-Cola and The Roosters move in an apartment nearby, and Reno can hear them practicing their music. At night, Reno, Carol and Pamela see a television commercial for Porto-Pack, which allows a person to walk around with appliances. At two o'clock in the morning, while trying to work on his painting, Reno hears the music. He sees an image of himself saturated in blood, goes outside, meets a sleeping bum and stands him up. It seems he is going to accost the man, but the two watch as a group chases someone down the street. Carol gets a letter from her old flame, Stephen, who sends a photograph of the couple and a $100 bill. Reno complains to Al about the band's music, and Al gives him a gift of a skinned rabbit. Reno takes the carcass home and repeatedly stabs it. Reno eyes the Porto-Pack at a hardware store, then walks inside. Later, he hears voices calling his name and sees an image of Carol with her eyes cut out, as well as his bloody self again. He goes to a sleeping homeless man and drills him in the chest.

Reno, Carol and Pamela have tickets to see The Roosters at a club. Reno avoids the crowd and loud music, leaving the club as Carol and Pamela dance. Reno goes on a drilling killing spree, drilling and killing a man on the ground, someone in the subway station, a drinking man on the street, a weird guy hanging around the bus station and two more men on the street, chasing one down and drilling him in the back. He ends his spree by approaching a man sleeping in the trash and drilling his forehead. Reno then returns home. Tony visits the place and asks Reno if he will paint a portrait of him. Tony agrees to Reno's demand of $500, and he says he will need it right away.

The next morning, Carol reads the paper, which tells of a man killed with an electric drill. Reno sees an image of his initial drill killing and his own bloody image, and he snatches the newspaper from Carol and accuses her of trying to drive him crazy. Later, while the three roommates eat pizza, Reno tells Pamela to ask Carol if she would like some pizza with peppers on it (even though Carol is sitting right beside him), and Carol angrily throws a slice of pizza in Reno's face. Carol goes to a payphone and telephones Stephen, and she returns to the apartment to find a silly picture proclaiming "I'm Sorry." Reno paints Tony as he poses and, at various times, plays guitar and makes out with Pamela. A man in the alley, restless and indignant due to all the noise Tony made, is attacked by Reno, who drills his hands to the wall and kills him.

Reno shows his completed buffalo painting to Dalton, and Dalton declares the work of art "unacceptable." Carol screams at Dalton; she is angry with Reno for just sitting in the chair with a blank expression on his face. The next morning, Reno awakes to an empty bed, and he chases Carol in the street, but she keeps walking. Later, a slightly demented Reno (he "talks" to Carol on the phone but is really only listening to a dial tone) invites Dalton over to show him something, and Dalton says he will be there soon with some wine. Dalton arrives at the apartment, and Reno appears to drill him. Pamela returns from being with the band, and she sees a bloody drill bit in the door and a dead Dalton hanging. She backs away and is grabbed by Reno. Carol is with Stephen and, while she showers, Stephen prepares some tea; Reno drills him in the back. Carol, done showering, walks into the bedroom where a lump is lying under the bed covers. She tells "Stephen" to "come here."

The Driller Killer is an enjoyable early outing from director Ferrara (who plays Reno under the pseudonym Jimmy Laine). The scenes of drilling and slashing are perhaps the least interesting moments of the film, and the movie fares best with Reno's demanding (and sometimes humorous) living situation. Ferrara's urban, documentary-like style and his violent Catholic overtones, highly prevalent in later films such as *Ms. 45* (1981), *Bad Lieutenant* (1992), and *The Addiction* (1995), are quite prominent even in *The Driller Killer*.

Drive-In Massacre (1976)

Written by John Goff and Buck Flowers; Directed by Stu Segall; S.A.M. Productions, Inc.; 74 min.

Cast: Jake Barnes; Adam Lawrence; Douglas Gudbye (Germy); Verkina Flowers; Newton Naushuas (Austin); Catherine Barkley (Kathy); Norman Sherlock (Orville); Frank Hollowell (Jim); Valdesta (Arlene); Michael Alden; Marty Gatsby; Patricia James; Tiffany Jones; Myron Griffith

Crew: Rochelle Gail Weisberg (Executive Producer); Stu Segall (Producer); Lon John Productions (Composers); Kenneth Lloyd Gibb (Director of Photography); T. Howard Chapman (Editor)

A couple arrives at a drive-in movie theater, park and talk about having a baby. The woman suggests procreating at the drive-in, but the man wants to see the beginning of the movie. As he reaches out for the speaker, he is beheaded with a machete. As the woman screams, the blade is shoved through her throat.

The next day, police officers Larry and Mike go to the drive-in to see the manager, Austin Johnson. Austin talks of the carnival that was once there before the "trash heap" was opened. He says that Germy, the drive-in cleaner and the man who discovered the bodies, was once a carnival geek. The cops mention Germy once being a sword swallower, and he says that the theater owner (who is away in Hawaii) lets him use his private sword collection. Germy talks of a troublemaker who is at the drive-in every night looking for kissing couples. He describes the man and his car to the police, and the officers ask Germy to get a license plate number if the man returns.

That night, David and Lori are at the drive-in, and Lori tells him that she is pregnant. David seems happy, and the two kiss, but Lori is uncomfortable due to the recent murders. A man spies on the two. A sword is fatally pushed through David and Lori. Germy is brought into the station, and he says the sword discovered with the corpses was not from the owner's collection. He mentions that Austin also worked at the carnival but was not very good with "blades" and chased around girls. He gives the officers the license plate number of the troublemaker.

Larry and Mike go to see Orville. The cops press the man about being at the drive-in for the last two nights (Mike is playing the "bad cop"), and he says he only looked at the people. Orville tells them he did not murder anyone and will not return to the drive-in. He lets the officers look in his car; when a bloody cloth is found, he runs. When Larry and Mike catch Orville, he says that the blood is from a dog he ran over.

The cops are told the blood really is from a canine, and Orville is released. He goes back to the drive-in. Larry and Mike are staking the place (Mike is dressed as a female), waiting for Orville's move. A man tries to kiss a woman, but she is too into the film, and the man angrily leaves her alone. Germy goes up to the officers' car and talks to them, and he is pulled away by Austin, who tells him to get back to work. Mike has to answer a call of nature, and Larry helps him when he gets out of the car. The man returns to the car, his lady's head falls off and he screams for help. The cop discovers Orville dead. Austin is brought in, and the cops talk to him about once being a knife thrower. He is furious when they tell him to shut down the drive-in, and he mocks them for being so close to the killer. Austin is told to go since the officers have nothing to charge him with; he tells Germy to go back, get his things and leave. Germy goes to a carnival and hears voices talking to or about him.

Larry and Mike get a call that the man is "cornered" in a warehouse after killing two people with a machete. In the warehouse, a man has a girl hostage; she bites his hand and runs away. He chases her and talks of cutting the "poison" (meanness) out of her. Larry and Mike run inside and, following gunfire and a pursuit, Mike shoots and kills the man. The girl comes out and says that the man was her sick father, who killed her mother and aunt and broke out of the hospital that morning. The officers suddenly realize that Austin can leave the projection booth between "reel changes" (he had previously said he was in the booth all night), and they go to pick him up. Arlene tries to stop Germy from going to see Austin, but Germy says that Austin owes him money and that he has a gift for the manager (Germy has the owner's sword collection with him). The cops arrive and see, on the screen, the shadow of Austin being stabbed. They run inside and find the man dead; in another room, Germy is also dead.

The scenes at the movie theatre in *Drive-In Massacre* are enjoyable (although no killing comes close to topping the first one), but the scenes of the officers' interrogations and even the warehouse gunfight are sterile and occasionally excessive. A disclaimer at the end of the film says that the killer's murderous rampage spread throughout other theaters in the country: "The killer could strike again. Anywhere... Anytime... Who will be next...?"

Edge of the Axe (aka *Al filo del hacha*) (1988)

Written by Joaquín Amichatis, Javier Elorrieta and José Frade; Directed by Joseph Braunstein; Calepas International, Inc.; 91 min.

Cast: Fred Holliday (Frank McIntosh); Barton Faulks; Christina Marie Lane; Page Moseley; Patty Shepard; Alicia Moro; Jack Taylor; Conrado San Martín; Joy Blackburn; May Heatherly; Elmer Modlin

Crew: Lara Polop (Executive Producer); José Frade (Producer); Javier Elorrieta (Composer); Tote Trenas (Director of Photography); Barry B. Beirer (Editor)

A woman drives her car through a car wash. Someone is outside in the car wash with her, and a person in a white mask appears and axes through her windshield.

Gerald rides his motorbike home, and an elderly man named Brock tells him "one of those electronic contraptions" arrived. Gerald excitedly takes his new computer to his room. Katherine is working in her kitchen at night, and someone out by the pigpen grabs a pig. Katherine hears squealing, goes to check but then runs back inside and locks her door. In her bedroom, she finds a pig's head lying on her bed.

Katherine's husband Trevor demands that police officer Frank McIntosh find the man who put the pig head in his house, but Frank does not seem interested. Richard picks up Gerald, and he tells him that they are exterminating bugs that day. They head to a bar to help Mike locate the source of a very strong smell in the cellar, and they discover a rotting corpse. The cops arrive and the body is taken away. They believe the woman committed suicide, and Frank suggests that no one talk about the incident (Paddock is a quiet town). Richard and Gerald go to pick up Richard's wife Laura (who Richard thinks is too old) at Nebbs Fishing. Richard flirts with Susan while Laura is out on a boat, and Gerald goes inside and meets Lillian.

Gerald shows Lillian his new computer, then offers to install his old computer in her house so that they can communicate with one another. The two then share a kiss. Rita is in a bar, and she gets a telephone call from someone wanting to meet her somewhere. Rita complies and heads past the railroad tracks. She runs when someone begins following her. She stops and turns, and she sees someone she knows ("Oh, it's you"). The person puts on the white mask and proceeds to axe Rita. The next day, Frank is told that Rita was "hamburger meat," and that it was most likely not the result of the train pulverizing her. Frank decides to momentarily write it up as an accident.

Frank goes to see a man working on church pews. He tells him that his name was in Rita's little book; the man says that he had slept with Rita and she was blackmailing him. Frank tells him they found blood on the ticket booth, so they now believe the death was not an accident but the result of Rita being hacked to death. Katherine is working in the kitchen during a windy storm. When the lights go out, she sees the killer, screams and runs to a room and shuts the door. The door is axed; Katherine gets out to the pigpen to hide, but the killer is out there. She is axed in her back and then in the head.

Lillian is on her computer, trying to access Gerald's computer, and she finds "Gerald Martin's File," which lists the names of the murdered women and the locations of the killings. At a restaurant, Lillian talks about her close relationship with her father, then asks Gerald about his list; he shrugs it off as just a list of facts. Later, at the church, the choir is singing as Lillian walks in late and joins the group. Richard and Susan are out on a boat. When the motor won't turn over, Susan checks the boat's propeller and finds a severed head. Richard tells Gerald that the woman was Maureen Adams and she worked in a psychiatric clinic, and he reveals his suspicion that Laura is having an affair with Nebbs. Anna Bixby is in the church, discussing the recent murders. She goes home, calls for her dog and finds it dead upstairs. The killer, hiding in the closet, chops off her fingers, chases her and then chops her up.

Lillian tells Gerald about an incident that occurred years before. She had been pushing her cousin Charlie on the swing, and when he told her to stop, she persisted; he fell and fractured his skull. Lillian says he was released from a mental hospital two years ago, and she had a dream of Charlie coming at her with an axe. Lillian and Gerald are on a swing later, and she tells him that he is mysterious. She pushes him on the swing, and gets upset when thinking back to Charlie. They get on Gerald's bike, Lillian asks how he got his scar and Gerald says it was caused by a motorcycle accident. Later, he finds Lillian in his room, working on his computer. Gerald turns on the screen and sees names of doctors, and Lillian says that all the women killed worked in a psychiatric ward. She says she saw the name Phillip Martin and asks if it is Gerald's father. He says it is his stepfather, who married his mother after his father's death.

Laura goes to see her banker and learns that she is bankrupt. She goes to a bar with Christopher, the church organ player, and she drives him home. After a near-wreck, the slightly inebriated Laura gets out to relax and returns to the car to see the killer there rather than Christopher. She is chased by the killer. The next day, Richard tells Gerald that Laura is missing, and that she took all of the money. The murders are discovered, and the priest is brought out to identify Christopher. Police officer Sam shows Frank a pin, which is worn at Nebbs' place, discovered at the murder site (Lillian had given Gerald one earlier). Frank suggests stopping at Nebbs' house.

Lillian is trying to get hold of Gerald on the computer, but she receives no response. She hears a noise, arms herself with a familiar axe and checks around the house. She goes back to her bedroom to hide, then throws down the axe and steps outside her room to confront the person ("Charlie, is that you?"). Gerald appears and says he is not Charlie, and that Charlie does not exist. He tells Lillian that she is Charlie. He researched her medical history and discovered that she had been admitted to a psycho ward when she was eight (having fallen from a swing), and she suffered from psychoamnesia and was an "acute psychopath." Gerald says he loves Lillian, but she grabs an axe and says he is Charlie. Gerald tells her again that she is Charlie, and they struggle. Lillian screams and runs outside; the police are out there. Gerald is following her, now holding the axe, and Sam fires once with a shotgun, knocking Gerald down. Frank holds Lillian and tells her that the nightmare is over ("There'll be no more murders in this town"). Lillian smiles a malevolent smile.

Edge of the Axe has multiple plot devices, and it is difficult to tell whether the many subplots are red herrings or the result of poor writing. In either case, the movie is moderately intriguing, and the performances are adequate.

Evil Ed (1995)

Written by Anders Jacobsson, Göran Lundström and Christer Ohlsson; Directed by Anders Jacobsson; Evil Ed Productions; 88 min.

Cast: Johan Rudebeck (Eddie); Per Löfberg (Nick); Olof Rhodin (Sam Campbell); Camela Leierth (Mel); Gert Fylking (SWAT Team Lieutenant); Cecilia Ljung (Barbara); Mikael Kallaanvaara (Tom McClane); Hans Wilhelmsson (Welder); Anders Ek (Janitor); Memory Garp (Office Girl); Christer Fant, Odile Nunes (Man/Woman in Swedish Film); Ulf Landergren (Art Film Dept. Boss); Jenny Forslund (Art Film Dept. Editor); Therese Malmer, Estelle Milburne, Sanna Hansson, Niklas Hättström, Thomas Lewart (Splatter Dept. Bimbos/Hunks); Vasa (The John/Doctor Wrench); Monia Gotngärd (Prostitute); Fredrik Johansson (Dude in Theatre); Gun Forss (Senior Neighbour); Carina Tell (Stripping Neighbour); Fredik Hauge, Johan Harnesk (Screamer); Therese Malmer (Sexy Patient); Göran Lundström (Bandage Face); Estelle Milburne (Secretary); Kelly Tainton (White Demon); Natahlie Kauklua (Emmy); Danne Malmer (Zip); Kim Sulocki (Crackhead); Anders Jacobsson (Car Driver); José Jimenez, Andreas Beskow (Police Officers); Fredik Hauge, Göran Lunström, Heming Kulø (Medics); Lena Neogard, Hans Wilhelmsson, Pia Berg, Magnus Wadling (Patients); Roger Olsson (Doctor West); Carina Ristholm, Åsa Svegen, Karin Hallheden, Carina Sundgren, Hanna Elfvin, Jenny Wigge (Nurses); Marie Bergenholtz (Doctor Dinkelspiel/Demonic Doc); Pia Berg, Hans Wilhelmsson, José Jimenez, Carina Ristholm, Sten Grettve, Åsa Svegen (Lunatics); Sven-Erik Olsson (Psychiatric Ward Guard); Robert Dröse (Paranoid Lunatic); Joakim Lindman, Kurt Nilsson, Joel Rhodin, Hannes Rhodin (SWAT Team); Kaj Steveman (Mop Boy)

Crew: Göran Lundström (Producer, Creature & Makeup Effects Supervisor); Kaj Steveman, Göran Lundström (Assistant Directors); Henriksson & Lindh (Composers); Anders Jacobsson (Director of Photography, Editor)

Tom McClane is in the cutting room, screaming and throwing film reels everywhere. His boss Sam Campbell is outside, demanding the door to be opened, and finally he has a man blowtorch the door. Sam walks in and McClane puts a grenade in his mouth. The grenade explodes, and Sam is covered in blood ("You're fired!").

Eddie, a film editor, is lent to the Splatter & Gore Dept., where Sam tells him he will have to cut and censor the *Loose Limbs* series for distribution in other countries. Sam goes to a house to do his work; his wife Barbara telephones to remind him of daughter Emmy's upcoming birthday party. Eddie edits a scene, watches his heavily edited work, and goes to bed. Nick and his pal are watching *Loose Limbs 5: The Anatomy of Fear* and cheering as a Doctor Wrench chops a patient with a cleaver. Nick's girlfriend Mel sits beside them. Sam walks into the screening room and tells Nick to deliver new films to the editor. After more editing, Eddie goes to cut some bread and sees a severed arm under the slicing knife. Eddie goes to see Sam and tells him he does not think he can continue the work with all the blood and violence. Sam says that if Eddie is not able to give him results, he will be fired.

At night, Eddie is playing a line from one of the films over and over. When he finishes, an eerie person appears in the house and says the line ("My God, what's happening to me?"). Nick goes to the house the next day to deliver *Loose Limbs 7*, and Eddie seems upset that Nick would say it is a great movie. Later, Eddie sees flashes of events, and he enters a room where a bandaged and demonic McClane tells the editor that he has the potential to "correct" the world and free it of evil. When he touches Eddie's face, the editor awakes in bed. Eddie goes downstairs, where he sees the refrigerator shaking. Inside is an odd creature that laughs and throws a tomato at Eddie. Eddie gets a knife to stab it, but the creature is gone.

Eddie is nailing boards to the door when Sam stops by and asks to see his work. They go to the room (Eddie sees the creature again in the refrigerator), and Sam complains that the unoffensive "beaver rape scene" has been taken out. As Sam continues to speak, his voice changes, and he turns to Eddie with bizarre eyes. Eddie runs downstairs and through rocky corridors, where Sam (as a white demon) chases him. McClane appears again ("Evil has shown itself to you!") and tells Eddie he will be the editor's guide. The demon is there; Eddie turns its head, snapping Sam's neck. He laughs and gets a saw.

The next morning, Eddie throws Sam out with the trash. Nick is at the house with more film canisters, and Eddie invites him inside for coffee. Eddie dips his tongue in the coffee and thanks Nick for *Loose Limbs 7*, saying he loves the "concept of pain." Eddie says there is something wrong with Nick's brain and he can help. Nick stands to leave, and Eddie whacks him with a champagne bottle and punches him in the face many times. Eddie cuts up some of the film, and a bloody Nick stands and walks outside as Zip and Crackhead arrive to rob the dark house. Zip goes inside, where he encounters Eddie and fires his shotgun twice, grazing Eddie's cheek. Eddie attacks and beats Zip, and when Barbara calls (Eddie is late for the birthday party), he picks up the phone and beats Zip some more. Crackhead goes inside and sees Zip's head on the floor. Eddie attacks him; following a struggle, Crackhead's head is thrown out of the window.

Barbara and Emmy arrive at the house to see Eddie. Eddie's elderly neighbor finds Crackhead's head in the rain barrel and calls the police. Barbara cannot find Eddie until she and Emmy see the crazed editor at the door with a pair of scissors. The mother and daughter go to hide as Eddie walks around and talks of cutting and killing them. He opens the closet where Barbara is hiding, and she lifts Zip's handgun and shoots Eddie in the shoulder. A screaming Eddie is taken away into an ambulance.

Eddie continues screaming as he is rolled into the psychiatric ward, where he is injected with a syringe. Once he is pacified, his wounds are cleaned and bandaged. He imagines a female doctor's face changing horribly, and he screams and grabs her by the throat, punching a nurse and throwing the doctor and an attendant. He puts on a doctor's coat and walks into a room full of lunatics, where he electrocutes a paranoid patient. Eddie uses a card to open the gate; a guard asks where he is going. Eddie looks at him and turns to keep walking, and the guard sets off the alarm.

Mel goes to see Nick in the hospital. Eddie sees the two kissing and walks in, angry that Mel is ruining his "work" (a purification of Nick). Eddie punches Nick and takes Mel away. Nick pulls out his IV and runs. As the SWAT team arrives, Nick follows Eddie to a taped-off area of the hospital. Eddie takes Mel to a room and gasses her; Nick jumps the editor as he prepares the syringe. Eddie throws Nick over a stair railing, and Nick falls through glass and lands on an operating table. The SWAT team starts shooting at Eddie, who manages to kill four members and shoot and kill the captain in a hallway showdown. Eddie returns to the room and stabs Mel with the metal tube holding the IV bag. Her eyes open and her face changes, and she sits up, telling Eddie (with the voice of the demonic McClane) that he has failed and must pay for his failures. Eddie picks up a scalpel and lifts it (Mel is not actually dead). Nick uses the captain's shotgun to blow off Eddie's hand and arm, hits him in the stomach, and shoots the editor's head clean off. Nick stands over his girlfriend on the table.

Evil Ed is a charming slasher film with many grotesque scenes, an abundance of humor and a number of references to other horror films, including Sam Raimi's 1987 *Evil Dead II* (note the name of Sam Campbell: director Sam Raimi/actor Bruce Campbell). The rated version of *Evil Ed* seems to suffer the same heavy censoring as the *Loose Limbs* series; look for the much gorier unrated print, where Eddie's demise can actually be seen.

Eyeball
(aka *Gatti rossi in un labirinto di vetro*; *Wide-Eyed in the Dark*; *The Devil's Eye*; *The Eye*; *The Secret Killer*)
(1974)

Written by Felix Tusell and Umberto Lenzi; Directed by Umberto Lenzi; Estela Films S.A./National Cinematografica/Pioneer; 88 min.

Cast: John Richardson (Mark); Martine Brochard (Paulette); Ines Pellegrini (Naiba); Andrés Mejuto (Inspector Tudela); Mirta Miller (Lisa); John Bartha (Hamilton); Marta May (Alma); George Rigaud (Reverend Bronson); Daniele Vargas; Silvia Solar; Raf Baldassarre; José Maria Blanco; Olga Pehar; Olga Montes; Veronica Miriel; Richard Kolin; Rina Mascetti; Vittorio Fantoni, C.S.C.; Tom Felleghy; Fulvio Mingozzi; Francesco Marducci; Lorenzo Piani, C.S.C.

Crew: José Maria Cunilles, A.T.C. (Executive Producer); Bruno Nicolai (Composer); Antonio Millan (Director of Photography); Amedeo Moriani (Editor)

A woman at an airport asks about her flight to New York, and then she changes her destination to Barcelona. On the plane, she seems dazed and takes a pill. In Barcelona, a group is on a tour bus with the guide, Martinez. As the people check into their hotel, Martinez scares young Peggy with a mouse and laughs. As the tour stops at one of the sites, Hamilton looks for his granddaughter Jenny, and Lisa takes a few pictures of Naiba. A girl (not a part of the tour) says goodbye to her boyfriend, picks up a chrysanthemum (which Naiba had just "modeled" with), and asks someone about it. She is stabbed in the eye. Bronson, Rommy and Paulette discover the eyeless woman. Mark suddenly appears, and he goes away with Paulette for drinks; they discuss Alma and her "ill health." Mark says Alma went to get treatment in New York, and that when she is better, they will get a divorce.

Soon-to-retire Inspector Tudela and young Inspector Lara go to an autopsy, where they are told of Pepeita, the young girl who was killed. The tourists dine, and Mark and Paulette join them. Rommy's wife Gale tells Reverend Bronson that she knows Mark's wife Alma. Martinez gives Jenny a box, and a toy spider jumps out and scares her; the guide finds this amusing. It is pouring rain, and Martinez passes out red rain slickers as they stop at another site. Naiba and Peggy get on a carnival-esque ride (in separate carts) inside the building, and Peggy is stopped by the raincoat-adorned killer, who swings a knife. A dead and one-eyed Peggy comes out of the ride. Tudela talks to the people and suggests that one of them is the murderer; Hamilton refers to a similar killing in Burlington, Vermont. The toy spider was found in Peggy's hand, and Jenny says that Martinez likes to scare people. The cops take the guide away.

The tourists all sit inside their hotel rooms. Mark calls St. George Clinic in New York and is told that Alma is not a patient, and he cannot reach her in Burlington. Mark goes to where Pepeita was killed, and her boyfriend accuses him of killing her. Mark punches him and runs. Bronson gives Mark a message at the hotel; the note says that his wife is waiting at the Hotel Presidente. He goes to the hotel and manages to get inside the room, but Alma is not there. Mark finds a photograph of Alma and himself, and a bloody knife on the floor causes Mark to think of Alma clutching a bloody knife, lying near a pool. Later, Mark sits with Paulette, refusing to tell her why he is upset. As the tourists are convened at a location, a servant girl carries a basket and feeds the hogs; the killer stabs her eye. The people look for one another, and Gale sees Paulette cleaning her shoes at the fountain. The cops arrive, and Rommy has scratches on his hand. Gale tells of Paulette's shoe-cleaning (it was muddy near the hogs), and Paulette explains that she changed her shoes and wanted them clean before she put them in her purse.

Mark returns to the hotel. Alma has checked out, leaving behind the photograph of the couple. He goes to the airport and learns that Alma canceled her flight. He sees Lisa (who is seeing Peggy's parents off), gives her the photograph and says that if she sees the woman, to get a picture of her. Paulette goes to see Mark in his room, and Mark mentions the Burlington murder, for which a man was convicted. Mark says on that day he came home early and found an unconscious Alma lying by the pool, with a bloody knife in one hand and a "human eye" next to the other. Mark tells Paulette that Alma is in Barcelona. Lisa and Naiba go to the discotheque. Lisa has no desire to dance, so Naiba gets on the dance floor with someone else. Lisa returns to the room, and the killer sneaks in and tears Alma out of the photograph. Lisa is stabbed in the stomach and sliced across the throat; the killer looks through her negatives. Naiba returns, and the killer knocks her down and runs. Naiba screams at the sight of Lisa. Rommy and Hamilton run to the room, where Mark is already helping the woman. They run downstairs and find a discarded raincoat (with blood) in the garden.

The inspectors arrive at the scene, and Mark does not tell them of seeing the torn photograph. Martinez says that all the tourists have identical red raincoats. Gale says she got rid of hers, Paulette lost hers and Mark was not present when the slickers were passed out. Jenny notes a familiar odor to the raincoat in question (a perfume that Paulette wears), but the guide says that the perfume had been accidentally spilled earlier. Tudela has the people turn in their passports. The group rides on the tour bus again, and Jenny finds a roll of film on the bus floor. Bronson offers to give it to Naiba. Tudela tells Lara that Lisa's murder was different (her eye was not taken) and that she may have found incriminating evidence. Mark and Paulette talk of Alma, and Mark says that "one little detail" is bothering him about the incident in Burlington (but he is not sure what the detail is).

The reverend goes to see Naiba in the hospital with a suitcase and flowers, but he is gone after the nurse has checked with the officer (on guard at Naiba's door). As the cop is absent, the killer attacks. Naiba hides in another room and passes out. Tudela talks to Bronson, and he shows the inspector that the suitcase is empty (he had just purchased it). Some members of the group attend the flamenco, and Mark returns to the hotel in a taxi. Jenny, bored, heads for bed. The killer attacks her near the pool and stabs her shoulder; Jenny jumps into the water and screams. The killer is chased, and a cop gets Mark, who says he was just about to catch the murderer. Lara notes that the discovered knife has Mark's initials on it.

The cops talk to Mark at the station about a possible affair with the woman killed in Burlington. The passports are returned, and the reverend suggests that Naiba go through Lisa's things (in particular the film roll) to find clues. The cops give Jenny's description of the attack, and a knifing right hand is mentioned. Mark recalls that Alma is left-handed (he had found her by the pool with the knife in her right hand). Tudela shows him the victims' eyes (lined up in a tiny case), and Mark thinks of "glass" and notes something being identical. Naiba receives the developed pictures, reacts to one of the photographs and runs out to find Bronson.

The reverend is at a castle, talking to a girl about his deceased daughter Martha (the girl has the same color eyes). Naiba makes it to the castle and discovers Bronson with a slit throat. She spots a red-gloved Paulette over the dead girl, preparing to switch eyes with her, and she screams and is chased. Paulette stops her and talks about a friend ripping out her eyeball when "playing doctor." Mark arrives, Paulette goes for him with the knife and is shot by Tudela. Naiba shows the picture, in which Paulette is in the background with a knife. Mark finally gets hold of Alma, and he says goodbye to the inspectors. It is the day of Tudela's retirement, and he is ready to fish for trout.

Umberto Lenzi's *Eyeball* is a fun slasher, with adequate direction and good performances. Despite the somewhat large cast, a number of characters are made to look suspect, and the plethora of red herrings is quite enjoyable.

Eyes of Laura Mars (1978)

Written by David Zelag Goodman and John Carpenter; Directed by Irvin Kershner; Columbia Pictures; 103 min.

Cast: Faye Dunaway (Laura Mars); Tommy Lee Jones (John Neville); Brad Dourif (Tommy Ludlow); Rene Auberjonois (Donald Phelps); Raul Julia (Michael Reisler); Frank Adonis (Sal Volpe); Lisa Taylor (Michele); Darlanne Fluegel (Lulu); Rose Gregorio (Elaine Cassell); Bill Baggs (Himself); Steve Marachuk (Robert); Meg Mundy (Doris Spencer); Marilyn Meyers (Sheila Weissman); Gary Bayer, Mitchell Edmonds (Reporters); Michael Tucker (Bert); Jeff Niki, Toshi Matsuo (Photo Assistants); John E. Allen (Billy T.); Anna Anderson, Deborah Beck, Jim Devine, Hanny Friedman, Winnie Hollman, Patty Oja, Donna Palmer, Sterling St. Jacques, Rita Tellone, Kari Page (Models); Dallas Edward Hayes (Douglas); John Randolph Jones, Al Joseph, Gerald Kline, Sal Richards, Tom Degidon (Policemen); Paula Lawrence (Aunt Caroline); Joey R. Mills (Makeup Person); John Sahag (Hairdresser); Hector Troy (Cab Driver)

Crew: Jack H. Harris (Executive Producer); Jon Peters (Producer); Laura Ziskin (Associate Producer); Artie Kane (Composer); Victor J. Kemper, A.S.C. (Director of Photography); Michael Kahn, A.C.E. (Editor)

A person wearing gloves flips through a book of photographs and cuts out a picture of a woman. The woman from the photograph is followed into a kitchen, where an icepick is lifted and swung. Laura Mars wakes up, dials a number and hangs up after a few rings. She walks into another room and looks at her book *The Eyes of Laura Mars*, gets on the phone again and receives no response.

Laura arrives at her photo exhibit, where she is greeted by her agent, Donald. Reporters follow her, referring to her work as being "offensive to women" and "desensitizing" people to violence (her photographs often portray murder or violent images). Laura asks if anyone has seen Doris, the editor of her soon-to-be-published book. She meets John Neville who, unaware who she is, has uncomplimentary things to say about the pictures. Donald tells Laura that Doris was murdered, and Laura is upset.

Laura goes to a photo shoot in which models pose next to a couple of cars that appear to have just been involved in a collision. Laura suddenly sees the point of view of someone, who is watching her friend Elaine walk up some steps. She stops the shoot, saying she is "dizzy," but then continues. She later leaves a taxi when it is stuck in traffic, and at a crosswalk, the alternate perspective returns. Laura sees Elaine walking down the steps; Elaine is grabbed, stabbed with an icepick, thrown down the stairs and kicked down a few more. Laura runs to the apartment; cops are already there. Laura tells Sergeant Volpe she saw it happen from a few blocks away.

Many of the models and Laura's associates are at the police station. Tommy, Laura's driver, is asked about a switchblade he carries. Policeman John talks to Laura, showing her photos of unsolved murders (never before shown) and comparing them to photographs in her book. They are identical. Laura tells John that two years earlier, she began to see violence and murder, and it went into her photography.

John takes Laura to Elaine's place and asks her if she recognizes the man's clothing inside the closet. Laura says it belongs to Michael, her ex-husband. Back at her place, Laura is grabbed by Michael (he still has a key), and he tells her he did not kill Elaine. The couple argues over their bad marriage, and Laura gives Michael a drink and $50. Donald yells at Tommy in the car before picking up Laura. While driving, Tommy, against the wishes of Donald, explains to Laura that he had been in prison before for armed robbery and assault with a deadly weapon. He and Donald yell some more, and Laura tells them to be quiet and leave her alone. They reach a garage where Donald is dropped off. Tommy drops off Laura, they apologize to one another and Laura heads up to her studio. She begins to see the killer approaching the door and runs screaming for Donald as she watches herself running. Donald shows up, and the killer is gone ("I saw him looking at me!").

Donald convinces Laura to do the photo shoot, but her mind flashes through the recent events, and she walks away dazed, followed by John. Laura and John are left alone, and she demonstrates the killer's perspective by employing a video camera ("What you're seeing through that lens is what the killer sees"). John advises Laura to stay inside as much as possible, then leaves. Later, John talks to models Lulu and Michelle and asks them about any letters they have received concerning Laura's work. Laura is in the darkroom, and she sees through the killer as Lulu answers her door and is murdered. The killer walks to the room where Michelle is; Laura manages to find a phone and dial the number to warn Michelle, but no one answers. After a funeral for the models, Robert loudly blames Laura for the murders. John takes her away, and he consoles an upset Laura until they kiss and spend the night together. In the morning, he gives Laura a gun and shows her how to use it.

At Donald's birthday party, Laura arrives with Tommy. She tells Tommy to come back for her in an hour, and Donald slams the door on Tommy's face. Laura gets a phone call from Michael, who is drunk and talking of commiting suicide. To avoid leading the police to Michael (they are watching her for protection), Laura has Donald leave in her clothes so that the cops will follow him. They see that it is actually Donald, and they leave. The killer is nearby, now trailing Laura's agent. Laura, driving in her car, sees the killer attack and kill Donald, and she runs her car through a wall of glass. Later, John is with Laura in her apartment, and Volpe arrives to tell John that they have found some evidence and might have the killer. John hugs Laura and leaves with his cop buddy.

At Tommy's place, the police find Laura's pictures on the wall. Tommy calls and asks to talk to John. John sends the others away, and Tommy walks in and is told one of his playing cards was found underneath the body of Donald. Tommy's alibi story has some confusing lapses, and he thinks the cops want to put him in Bellevue. Volpe walks in and tries to grab Tommy, but he pulls his knife, stabs a cop, and runs out on the streets. Volpe catches up to Tommy first, and he shoots and kills him. John is angry with Volpe.

John calls Laura and tells her that it is all over and to pack her bags. They say they love one another. John gets to the elevator in Laura's apartment building, and Michael is there. Laura suddenly sees someone (with hands over face) being killed in the elevator. Someone bangs at the door ("Go away!"); the banging stops, and John breaks through the window. He and Laura embrace. John tells Laura that Tommy is dead, and that his mother was a hooker and would leave him in the room while she was working. Laura says that is not Tommy, and John continues, saying a man came home, saw the condition of the boy and slashed the mother's throat. Laura realizes John is talking about himself, and the cop begins talking in the third person and then says, "I'm the one you want." Laura is chased to her bedroom, where John stabs the mirror at his own reflection. Laura has her gun, and John says, "If you love him, kill him." He points Laura's hand grasping the gun towards his stomach, says he loves her and is shot. Laura gets the telephone and calls for help.

Eyes of Laura Mars has a very interesting premise, but the love story is contrived and the ending is rather weak and disappointing. Regardless, Dunaway is very good as Laura, and it is always fun to watch Dourif as an ambiguously insane character.

Faceless
(1989)

Written by Pierre Ripert, Fred Castle, Jean Mazarin and Michel Lebrun; Directed by Jess Franco; Ibero Films Internacional S.A./René Chateau Productions; 94 min.

Cast: Helmet Berger (Doctor Frank Flamand); Brigitte Lahaie (Nathalie); Telly Salvas (Terry Hallen); Chris Mitchum (Sam Morgan); Stephanie Audran (Mrs. Sherman); Caroline Munro (Barbara Hallen); Christiane Jean (Ingrid); Anton Diffring (Doctor Karl Moser); Tilda Thamar (Mrs. Francois); Howard Vernon (Doctor Orloff); Florence Guerin (Florence); Lina Romay (Mrs. Orloff); Gerard Zalcberg (Gordon); Henri Poirier (Police Officer); Laure Sabardin (The Receptionist); Amelie Chevalier (Melissa); Marcel Philippot (Maxance); Tony Awak (Doudou); Mony Dalmès (Baroness); Doris Thomas (Singer); Antonina Laurent (Karen); Isabelle O. (Gina); Nick C. (Woman Parking); Jean Tolzac (Desk Clerk); Jacques Coudrec (Man in Morgue); Pascale Vital (Barmaid); Daniel G. (Brian Wallace); Thierry F. (Secretary)

Crew: René Chateau (Producer); Romano Musumarra (Composer); Maurice Fellous (Director of Photography); Christine Pansu (Editor)

Doctor Frank Flamand drives in a limousine with Nathalie and his sister Ingrid. In a parking garage, a woman drives to the group and says that the doctor operated on her a year ago (her face is badly scarred). As a "surprise," she throws acid towards Frank. He ducks, the acid hits Ingrid's face and her skin peels.

Ingrid awakes in bed, and Frank and Nathalie are at her side. Ingrid considers herself a "monster," and she is upset when looking into a mirror. At a photo shoot, Nathalie leads Barbara away to try some cocaine. Gordon grabs her from the back seat, and Nathalie injects the model with something and takes her gold watch. At the clinic, Mrs. Sherman, one the patients, believes "something weird" is happening. Frank and Nathalie look at the female captives, and they agree that Barbara is perfect. One of the "patients" attacks Nathalie and chokes her, and Gordon slices her arms off ("Kill her!").

Frank goes to see his patients in the clinic. Mrs. Sherman is angry that she has been in the wheelchair for two months, and she says she knows what is going on. She asks the doctor to meet later, and he asks her if it is blackmail ("Absolutely"). Private investigator Sam Morgan goes to see Terry Hallen, Barbara's father, who hires the PI to go to Paris and find his daughter (even if he has to "dirty his hands"). Sam checks into the Hotel Concorde La Fayette (where Barbara stayed) and gives the clerk money for Barbara's mail. Sam goes to see a headless body in autopsy, feels the corpse for a "discreetly placed mole" and surmises that it is not Barbara. Mrs. Sherman talks to Frank again and says that if she does not come to her room that night, she will call the cops. The doctor asks what she knows, and she says, "Everything."

Frank tells Nathalie that they need Professeur E. Orloff to perform the surgery, and they go to see him. He talks of a successful "total face graft" during the war, and he says the man who performed the operation was sentenced to death for experimenting on humans. He changed his name and is living in Spain as Doctor Karl Moser. Gordon goes to Barbara's room, kisses her, and hits her when she struggles. Frank and Nathalie find Barbara with a marked face, and Nathalie punishes Gordon by making him succumb to the desires of Ingrid. Mrs. Sherman calls Frank, and she threatens again to tell the police that he is a "mastermind" of crimes. Nathalie (as a nurse) goes to Mrs. Sherman's room, stabs a syringe into her eyeball and injects something. She takes the dead woman's pearl necklace and tries it on.

Believing that they cannot use Barbara for the operation (due to Gordon's work), Frank and Nathalie choose to invite an old patient, Melissa, to their place. Sam goes to see the photographer who was working with Barbara, and the man is upset that Barbara left while wearing a very expensive gold watch. Melissa is with Frank and Nathalie, and they talk of once working on her face. They become intimate, and Frank leaves the women with Nathalie, telling Melissa that he has a "surprise" for her. Doctor Moser arrives, and at the dinner table, the group discusses "total face transplants." Moser says that Orloff was reluctant to work with "living flesh." Melissa is on the operating table, and as Frank watches, Moser slowly slices the skin around the patient's face with a scalpel. The flesh is too soft, and the operation is "ruined." Moser apologizes to Ingrid, and Gordon chainsaws the body's head off.

Moser says that the donor's fear and panic help keep the muscles tight, which makes it easier during the operation. Frank and Nathalie go to the club to find a new donor, and they pick up Florence the actress and take her back to their place. Sam goes to see the French cops to look at Barbara's file, and they learn that Melissa's headless body was found (a tattoo made it easy to identify her). She, like Barbara, was last seen with a blonde. Nathalie, giving Barbara her injection, says she will help her if she gives her the code to her credit card, and Barbara writes the code down. Nathalie goes out driving with Gordon, and she picks up a man to take back to Ingrid. The man undresses and nears Ingrid, and he takes off her mask. Ingrid is perturbed and calls for Nathalie. Nathalie shoves a pair of scissors into the man's neck.

Sam talks to Melissa's boyfriend Rasheed, but he does not know where Melissa is. Terry calls Sam and says that Barbara's credit card has recently been used in St. Cloud. Sam goes to his files and sees the name of a clinic in St. Cloud. He drives to the clinic and asks about one of Frank's patients disappearing. Barbara seduces Gordon into unstrapping her, and she runs for the door and locks him in. She gets near Frank and Sam, but Nathalie pulls her away and takes her back to the room. Nathalie asks if Sam needs help, and he sees her watch. He leaves, and Frank is angry that Nathalie used the credit card. Sam checks with a picture of the watch. Gordon comes out of the door (leading to the secret place), and the nosy receptionist walks in and sees the prisoner-patients. She runs to a room and finds a rotted maggoty corpse in a locker, then she hides from approaching footsteps. Gordon walks in, sees part of her shirt sticking from the locker and locks her inside. The receptionist bangs on the door, so Gordon drills through the door and into the woman's head.

Florence awakes on a table. Moser is sure she cannot feel anything, and Frank draws a line around her face. Nathalie injects her throat (to keep her from screaming), and Moser begins slicing the skin. He pulls the face off and shows it to Florence ("Look at how beautiful she's going to be"), and Frank puts the skin on his sister's face. Sam, snooping around the clinic, is jumped by Gordon, and the two struggle. Sam finally pushes him against one of the hooks in the locker room. He grabs the keys and runs to find Barbara's prison room. Nathalie finds Gordon dead, and she manages to lock Sam and Barbara inside the room. After the operation, the room of prisoners is bricked up, which Sam sees happening ("This is going to be our tomb"). Fifteen days later, the scars have healed; Ingrid's operation is a success. Frank, Nathalie, Ingrid and Moser have a toast. Terry checks his messages, hears Sam mention the clinic and tells his secretary to book a flight to Paris.

Faceless is an effective and occasionally grotesque slasher (showing Florence her own skinned face is exceptionally gruesome). The performances are good, especially from Lahaie, who makes a wonderfully malevolent pseudo-nurse as Nathalie. Franco, the director of a thousand pseudonyms, is perhaps best known for his *Orloff* movies, and actor Vernon, who appears in *Faceless* as Orloff, portrayed the doctor in Franco's films. Co-writer Castle is actually producer René Chateau. Actor Mitchum is the son of the lazy-eyed actor, Robert Mitchum.

Final Exam (1981)

Written and Directed by Jimmy Huston; MPM/Peninsula Management; 90 min.

Cast: Cecile Bagdadi (Courtney); Joel S. Rice (Radish); Ralph Brown (Wildman); Deanna Robbins (Lisa); Sherry Willis-Burch (Janet); John Fallon (Mark); Terry W. Farren (Pledge); Timothy L. Haynor (Killer); Sam Kilman (Sheriff); Don Hepner (Doctor Reynolds); Mary Ellen Withers (Elizabeth); Jerry Rushing (Coach); Shannon Norfleet (Student in Car); Carol Capka (Student in Car); R.C. Nanney (Mitch); Gene Poole, Fritz Jon Goforth (Cafeteria Workers)

Crew: John L. Chambliss, Lon J. Kerr, Michael Mahern (Executive Producers); John L. Chambliss, Myron Meisel (Producers); Todd Durham, Carol Bahoric (Associate Producers); Gary Scott (Composer); Darrell Cathcart (Director of Photography); John A. O'Connor (Editor)

At March College, some time at night, a male and female student are kissing in a car. The girl seems reluctant, but the boy convinces her to move into the back seat by telling her that he loves her and that he cannot afford another hotel room. The girl stops when she hears something, but the boy thinks it is only his football buddies. Suddenly a man jumps onto the car, cuts open the convertible top and manages to pull the jock out of the vehicle. He stabs him on the car hood as the female screams.

It is final examination week at Lanier College. Courtney and Mark are walking on campus when the bookworm Radish approaches and asks if they heard of the mass murderer. Lisa meets with one of her teachers, with whom she is having an affair. At one of the exams, Radish and an unconcerned Wildman (a goofy football jock) finish their tests early and leave the room. Outside, a van arrives on campus, and men with ski masks and guns jump out and begin shooting at various students. Mark quickly finishes his exam inside as the professor looks to see what is happening. The gunmen pick up the bodies, put them in the van and drive away, as Radish runs into an office and telephones the sheriff. Lisa and Courtney are laughing, however, because they saw a Gamma fraternity sticker on the back of the van's window.

Another van follows Lisa and Courtney to the cafeteria. They sit with the young couple in love, Janet and Gary (rushing for Gamma). Mark tells Gary to see him outside, where he orders the pledge to steal a test out of a professor's office. As Courtney leaves the cafeteria, the van from earlier is sitting outside and someone steps out. The sheriff arrives on campus ("We was told there was a shootin', a multiple shootin' at that"). Radish gives him the van's license plate number, and the sheriff sees that the van belongs to Wildman. The coach talks him out of arresting the football player. The mysterious person from the van is still following Courtney. Later, after Courtney has left her dorm room for a while, she cannot find a book she left on her desk. Janet comes to see Courtney and Lisa, and she tells them that Gary gave her his frat pin, but they have to keep the information to themselves, or the Gamma guys will tie Gary to a tree and cover him with ice until she can rescue him.

Wildman and Mark visit Radish's room, and stick it to him for calling the cops. Mark takes something from his room. Gary manages to weasel his way into a building, steal the test and leave, only to be grabbed by his frat brothers as soon as he makes it outside. The guys see that his frat pin is missing, so they strip him to his underwear, douse him with water, ice and thick cream and tie him to a tree. Back at the fraternity, Mark answers the phone: "Gamma House. Test or pills?" Someone wants speed, so Mark sends Wildman to the weight room with Radish's keys. Another student, Elizabeth, tells Janet that Gary has been "treed," and Janet goes to look for her boyfriend. At the tree, Gary hears a noise and is cut free. He looks for his rescuer, and then the van driver jumps out of the tree and stabs Gary. Janet arrives at the tree and finds a few of Gary's things. She sees someone off in the distance ("Gary, is that you?") and she heads towards the person. After finding Gary's pants, Janet is grabbed by the killer.

In the weight room, Wildman trashes the office, finds the pills but is found and killed. Back at the Gamma House, Mark tells the potential pill buyers to wait for him. Radish goes to see Courtney in her room, talks about psychopaths, asks her to lock her door and then tells her that her face is even prettier than Lisa's. Mark goes to the weight room and finds a dead Wildman in the locker. He runs outside and his car headlights are turned on. The killer eventually catches up to him and stabs him in the chest. Radish arrives at the gym, and he finds Mark's body in a locker. He calls the sheriff, who thinks it is another prank.

Radish runs to Courtney's room and bangs on the door, but the killer punches through and grabs him. Courtney sees a dead Radish hanging in the broken door. The door shuts, and she runs down the hallway screaming for help (most people have already left). Lisa, awaiting the arrival of her professor lover, is murdered by the killer, who eventually finds Courtney. The student is chased to the cafeteria and soon she is at a building with a spiral staircase. The coach shows up to go hunting with Mitch the janitor, and Courtney screams, "There's a killer up here!" The coach grabs his bow and arrow, runs inside and shoots at the killer, who catches the arrow and runs down the steps to kill the coach. The killer attacks Courtney again, and she hits him with a piece of wood. He falls down the tower. At the bottom, he grabs Courtney. She picks up the knife and stabs him numerous times. She walks outside and sits on the steps.

Final Exam is an unexceptional slasher. The murders are dull, and the killer, although interesting in his ambiguity, is anything but frightening.

The Final Terror (aka *Campsite Massacre; Bump in the Night; Forest Primeval*) (1983)

Written by Jon George, Neill Hicks and Ronald Shusett; Directed by Andrew Davis; Samuel Z. Arkoff/81 min.

Cast: John Friedrich (Zorich); Adrian Zmed (Cerone); Daryl Hannah (Windy); Mark Metcalf (Mike); Ernest Harden, Jr. (Hines); Rachel Ward (Margaret); Akosua Busia (Vanessa); Lewis Smith (Boone); Cindy Harrell (Melanie); Joe Pantoliano (Eggar); Irene Sanders (Sammie); Richard Jacobs (Mr. Morgan); Donna Pinder (Mrs. Morgan); Jim Youngs (Jim); Lori Lee Butler (Lori); Tony Maccario (Eggar's Mother)

Crew: Joe Roth (Producer); J. Stein Kaplan (Co-Producer); Susan Justin (Composer); Andreas Da Videscu (Director of Photography); Paul Rubell, Erica Flaum (Editors)

A young couple, Jim and Lori, are out in the forest cruising on a motorcycle. They crash, and Jim's leg is seriously injured. Lori helps him to the side of the road and runs to get help, but when she returns, Jim is gone. She finds him hanging upside down with his throat cut. Lori hurries away, only to set off a booby trap of swinging tree limbs affixed with tin can lids that slice the girl.

Mike is organizing an excursion in the woods for clearing limbs from creeks. Eggar has been asked to drive the crew in a bus to Mill Creek, but Eggar is not happy. He believes the outing is merely an excuse for Mike to be with his lady friend Melanie, and for the boys to be with the girls. The guys—Cerone, Zorich, Boone and Hines—are not fond of Eggar, who not only disturbed their sleep the night before, but is simply bizarre. After picking up Melanie, Margaret, Vanessa and Windy, the group is on the way. Eggar relentlessly advises them to choose an area to camp other than Mill Creek, as it is a dangerous place and "somebody's gonna get hurt." On the way, they pass a mental institution, and Zorich says, "Hey Eggar, isn't that your old home?"

After a day of working in the forest and taunting the eccentric Eggar, the people sit around the campfire. Boone tells a story about a young girl who was raped by her malevolent lumberjack uncle. Afterwards, she went insane and was placed in an institution, where it was soon discovered that she was pregnant. She gave birth to a baby boy, but the doctors took the child from her. Nineteen years later, the woman's son showed up and took his mother away. Not knowing what to do with her, the son put the woman out in the woods. The story leads to a cheap fright on the part of Zorich, and everyone enjoys a laugh. Eggar, on the other hand, is angry, and he says he is going to leave (which is fine so long as he drops off the boats at the specified location).

That night, Zorich, Hines and Cerone go deep into the woods looking for marijuana. Zorich tells Cerone to be the lookout for a couple of hours and to howl every 45 seconds until he sees someone. In the morning, Cerone is gone, and Zorich and Hines admit to having left him out in the woods. The two men, along with Mike, go looking for the missing person. Zorich and Hines head back to camp to comb the area near the creek, and Melanie searches for Mike. They meet near a pond where Mike has decided to go for a swim, and the couple spends a few intimate moments together when suddenly Mike is murdered. A frightened Melanie is taken along with the killer.

Zorich and Hines discover a cabin in the woods. Inside, they find a can of peaches (which had been on the bus earlier) and Eggar's hat. They seem content with the discovery of a jar of magic mushrooms, but when they find women's clothing and an animal's severed head in the cabinet, Zorich says, "He's sicker than I thought he was." Back at the camp, everyone is scared, and they decide to take turns keeping watch, with Zorich going first. While they are sleeping, a figure with long, dirty hair approaches and strokes Margaret's head. Margaret awakes and screams. After they try to calm down Margaret, the group sees someone running in the creek. It is Cerone, who says he was not lost, but only continuing the search for marijuana (and he has found some). Vanessa is angry about the infantile attitude the boys seem to have. She heads to the outhouse and comes across a dead Mike.

The next day, everyone camouflages themselves and heads towards the cabin in search of Eggar. Inside, they find nothing, although the hairy figure is restraining Melanie underneath the floorboards. They grab the raft from behind the cabin and start rafting down the creek. Some time later, Melanie's body is dropped unto the raft. The group finally reaches a place where they can see Eggar's bus. At night, they check inside, gather some food and clothing and get some sleep. The figure arrives and crashes through the windows, getting inside through the windshield. Everyone gets outside, and Windy is somehow left behind. She is attacked and wounded, but the others manage to find her and nurse her injury.

The following day, the group finds an area for attack, and they prepare to defend themselves against Eggar. Zorich, tripping on the mushrooms, talks gibberish about the Vietnam War. Later, Cerone is calling out Eggar's name, and Eggar wraps a rope around his neck. The others jump out and begin beating Eggar, but Zorich simply stands and watches. The hairy figure comes out from hiding and cuts Zorich's foot, causing him to fall to his death. As the figure shrieks, the group see a filthy woman standing in front of them, as Eggar cries, "Mom!" She runs towards them, hits a wire and is pummeled by a large tree trunk and pierced with the sharp limbs that are attached. The group of campers gaze in silence as the insane woman and the trunk swing back and forth.

The Final Terror, which was completed in 1981, is an effective slasher with minimal gore and worthy frights. Director Davis began his career as a cinematography; Da Videscu (the cinematographer for *The Final Terror*) is reportedly a pseudonym. Davis later directed "A" productions such as *The Fugitive* (1993) and co-wrote and directed Steven Seagal's film debut *Above the Law* (1988), which was co-scripted by *Final Terror* co-writer Ronald Shusett.

Four Flies on Grey Velvet (aka *4 mosche di velluto grigio*) (1971)

Written by Dario Argento, Luigi Cozzi and Mario Foglietti; Directed by Dario Argento; Marianne Productions S.A./Seda Spettacoli/Universal Productions France S.A.; 95 min.

Cast: Michael Brandon (Roberto Tobias); Mimsy Farmer (Nina Tobias); Jean-Pierre Marielle (Arrosio); Bud Spencer (Godfrey); Aldo Bufilandi; Calisto Calisti (Carlo Marosi); Maria Fabbri (Amelia); Oreste Lionello (Professor); Fabrizio Moroni (Mirko); Corrado Olmi (Porter); Stefano Satta Flores (Andrea); Costanza Spada (Maria); Francine Racette (Dalia)

Crew: Salvatore Argento (Producer); Ennio Morricone (Composer); Franco de Giacomo (Director of Photography); Françoise Bonnot (Editor)

At various times, while playing drums alone or with his group, Roberto sees a man in sunglasses and a suit and tie. After a session, Roberto sees the man again and follows him to an apparently abandoned opera house, where he confronts him and asks why he has been trailing him for the last week. The man denies such actions, and he pulls a knife on Roberto when the drummer gets too close. Roberto grabs the knife-holding hand, and the man is stabbed, and he falls to a lower level. Lights are turned on from a balcony above, and a masked person snaps some photographs of Roberto holding onto the bloody knife.

That night, Roberto lies in bed awake as his wife Nina lies beside him. The drummer reads in the papers of a dead person, and he receives a letter containing the identification of Carlo Marosi, the man Roberto stabbed. At a get-together, a man talks of executions and beheadings, and Roberto looks through some albums and sees a photograph of the incident. Amelia, the maid, sees him. Roberto dreams of an execution in a coliseum and awakes before the person is decapitated. He hears a noise and looks around, and a cord is wrapped around his neck. The masked person says that Roberto could be killed now, and Roberto awakes on the floor. Nina asks her husband what is wrong, and Roberto finally admits to the accidental stabbing and subsequent harassment, and he says they cannot go to the police.

Roberto goes to see Godfrey (his nickname is God), and Godfrey suggests having the bum-like Professor keep an eye on him. Later, Roberto jumps a person in the rain and beats him with a stick, but it is only the mailman with a special delivery. Amelia calls someone and says that she knows what the person is doing. She demands money or says she will go to the police. Amelia waits on a park bench. As night falls and the crowd dissipates, she stands to leave and hears a person say her name. When she is locked inside the park, she runs to a wall and calls for help. A couple on the other side hears her, but the man is unable to jump the stone wall. Before he can leave for the gate entrance, Amelia screams and is killed.

Nina's cousin Dalia joins the group for another get-together (Roberto does not seem to want her there). Mirko, Roberto's band mate, mentions the drummer not being at rehearsal that day. Nina gets a phone call and learns of the dead Amelia. Roberto has the coliseum dream again, and he awakes to noises in his place and his cat hissing. The next morning, there is a note from the killer, and Nina is frightened. Carlo, alive and well, is in a restaurant, and he calls someone and asks to meet, referring to someone actually getting killed. Professor tells Roberto that he saw someone last night in the garden, with a cat wrapped in a blanket. He tried to stop the person but was hit on the head. Carlo tells the person that what they had agreed on is not enough, and he mentions the "toy" (a knife with a trick blade). The killer picks up a blunt object and bashes Carlo on the head, then gets a wire and twists it around the man's neck.

Roberto goes to see Arrosio, the flamboyantly gay private investigator. After the drummer tells the PI his story, Arrosio admits to having never solved a case (but is optimistic that his bad record can be broken). Arrosio asks Roberto questions in the car, and Roberto mentions Nina getting a big inheritance. Roberto returns home to Nina, who is leaving with officers (it is about Amelia); she says she does not want to stay at the house any more. Roberto decides to stay and Dalia suggests he take a bath, where the two get very close. Roberto gives Arrosio some photographs, and he finds his cat dead and in plastic. That night, he has his nightmare again, and Dalia is lying with the drummer.

Arrosio looks through the pictures, and he calls Roberto and tells of a strange resemblance which might only be a red herring. The PI visits the Villa Rapidi, a mental hospital, and a doctor tells him of a patient with paranoia and homicidal mania. When the father had died, the patient was deemed cured, and the doctors suspected the man was not the patient's father. Arrosio talks to various people and then visits an estate, where he follows someone from the place to a subway train. He gets off at the person's stop and heads to a bathroom, where he is attacked in a stall; a syringe of blue liquid is injected into his chest. The killer leaves and the PI clutches his chest ("I was right…").

Roberto learns of the dead Arrosio, and he, Godfrey and Professor meet at a place where coffins are being sold. Roberto tells of his nightmare and says it seems like a premonition. Godfrey suggests that someone is trying to drive Roberto crazy and that maybe the drummer should get out of the house. Dalia calls the studio for Roberto, but he is busy recording music. As Dalia packs a suitcase, she hears a noise and is frightened. She slips off her shoes and sneaks up to the attic, where she gets a knife and hides behind a door. The killer comes inside; when she thinks the killer is gone, Dalia steps out. A knife hits her forehead, Dalia slides down the stairs and the knife is brought down as the woman screams.

After finding the body, the cops tells Roberto about tests they will do on Dalia. By removing the eye and shooting a laser through it, they are able to see the last image Dalia had seen (the image is retained on the retina for several hours after death). They see what looks to be a small group of flies. That night, Roberto loads a gun and waits in his dark house. He nods off, and his dream goes all the way until the beheading. Godfrey calls to ask if the drummer is okay, and the phone line goes out. Nina arrives, Roberto puts down the gun, tells his wife to get away and pushes her out the door. Nina's necklace (a fly enclosed in glass) swings, giving the appearance of more than one fly, and Roberto pulls her back into the room and shuts the door. He hits her, saying that she killed the people and terrorized him, and Nina grabs the gun. She shoots Roberto in the shoulder and talks of her father beating her and her mother dying in an asylum. She shoots Roberto in the leg and says he looks like her father. Nina shoots some more, Godfrey runs inside and Roberto knocks the gun from Nina's hand. Nina runs to the car and speeds away, slamming into the back of a truck. She is decapitated and the car explodes into a mass of flames.

Four Flies on Grey Velvet is an underrated slasher from director Argento. There are some effective scenes of suspense, as well as a number of humorous moments, particularly the bumbling mailman and the charming Arrosio. Bud Spencer (born Carlo Pedersoli) might be remembered by some viewers as the burly Bambino from the wonderful spaghetti Western parodies *They Call Me Trinity* (1971) and *Trinity is Still My Name* (1972).

Frenzy (1972)

Written by Anthony Schaffer (from the novel *Goodbye Piccadilly, Farewell Leicester Square* by Arthur La Bern); Directed by Alfred Hitchcock; Universal Pictures; 115 min.

Cast: Jon Finch (Richard Blaney); Barry Foster (Robert Rusk); Barbara Leigh-Hunt (Brenda Blaney); Anna Massey (Babs Milligan); Alec McCowen (Chief Inspector Oxford); Vivien Merchant (Mrs. Oxford); Billie Whitelaw (Hetty Porter); Clive Swift (Johnny Porter); Bernard Cribbins (Felix Forsythe); Michael Bates (Sergeant Spearman); Jean Marsh (Monica Barling); Clive Swift (Johnny Porter); Madge Ryan (Mrs. Davison); Elsie Randolph (Gladys); Gerald Sim, Noel Johnson (Men at Bar); John Boxer (Sir George); George Tovey (Mr. Salt); Jimmy Gardner (Hotel Porter)

Crew: William Hill (Associate Producer); Ron Goodwin (Composer); Gil Taylor, B.S.C. (Director of Photography); John Jympson (Editor)

In a crowd of people gathered to hear a man speak, someone turns and tells everyone to look at a dead body floating in the water below. The woman has a necktie around her neck ("That's not my club tie, is it?"). Richard Blaney puts on his tie, goes down to the pub where he works and gets himself a drink. Pub owner Forsythe sees Richard and fires him, claiming the man has been stealing booze. Babs disputes Forsythe's claim, but the pub owner demands Richard pay back his salary advance and leave. Richard goes to see his friend Bob Rusk at the fruit market and tells him what happened. He declines Bob's offer of money, but he accepts a box of grapes and a tip on a horse race. Later, Richard is in a bar, and two men are discussing the recent necktie murders. Richard, almost out of money, sees Bob again, and Bob mentions Coming Up, the horse he advised, winning twenty to one. Richard, who did not have enough money to bet, thanks Bob, saying he "made a fortune." Bob departs, and a frustrated Richard throws his grapes to the sidewalk.

Richard goes to see his ex-wife Brenda at The Blaney Bureau: Friendship & Marriage, and asks Miss Barling, the secretary, to inform Brenda that "one of her less successful exercises in matrimony" is there. Richard starts an argument with Brenda, and Brenda sends Miss Barling home. Richard calms down and explains his situation, and the two go to dinner, where he argues some more and breaks a glass in his hand. Later, Richard is at a hostel, and he stops a man

Richard (Jon Finch) talks to Bob (Barry Foster) while the necktie murderer is on the loose in Alfred Hitchcock's *Frenzy* (1972).

lying in a bed next to him from stealing a fold of money. Bob goes to see Brenda in her office (she calls him Mr. Robinson), and Brenda tells him that she cannot find a match for him because he has "certain perculiarities." He says he "likes" Brenda and that she is "his type of woman," and he stops the apprehensive woman from making a phone call. Bob restrains Brenda and tells her that he has locked the door (Miss Barling is at lunch). Finally, Brenda does not struggle with Bob as he repeats "lovely" many times. A seething Bob moves his tie pin to the side and begins taking off his tie. Brenda screams (now aware that he is the killer), and Bob strangles her. Richard is at the office afterwards, knocking on the door and getting no response. Miss Barling sees Richard walk away, and she discovers Brenda dead.

When the police talk to Miss Barling, she says an irate Richard was there yesterday and he may have hit Brenda (it was Richard hitting his hands on the desk); the secretary gives the police a detailed description of the man. Richard and Babs go to a hotel (he tells her he collected an old debt). The hotel porter reads the newspaper the next morning and realizes that the person described as a murder suspect is staying at the hotel. He telephones the police, but when they get to the room, Richard and Babs are gone. In a park, Richard proclaims his innocence to Babs. He says earlier he was ashamed to admit that Brenda had given him money (which he did not realize until he was at the hostel), and he tells Babs that he only has two ties. Johnny, an old squadron friend of Richard (Richard was a squadron leader), sees the couple and invites them to hide in his apartment. Johnny's wife Hetty is upset that a murder suspect is staying there. Johnny tells Richard and Babs not to worry, and he offers them jobs at his English pub in France. Richard asks Babs to meet him later.

At Scotland Yard, Chief Inspector Oxford mentions the petition discussing reasons for divorce (Richard told Hetty earlier that "extreme cruelty" was cited to speed up the divorce process), and he learns that Richard's money from the hotel was traced back to Brenda. Forsythe calls the police and tells them his barmaid Babs is with Richard and he is afraid she is in danger. Babs returns to the pub, and Forsythe tells her the police are on their way to talk to her. Babs angrily quits; Bob asks her if she has a place to stay. He says he is leaving that night, and she can stay at his place. As they enter his place, Bob tells Babs that she is his "type of woman." Later, Bob wheels a full potato sack to a truck and throws it inside. At his apartment, he realizes that his tie pin is missing, and he recalls that Babs grabbed it during the murder. He runs to the truck and gets inside, and Bob has to continually hide in the moving vehicle before he finally gets the body out and pries the pin from the clenched fingers. Bob gets out when the truck driver stops at a café; police officers spot the body hanging out of the truck further down the road.

The next day Hetty, hearing of Babs' murder, makes Richard leave, despite the fact that, because he was at the apartment, he now has an alibi. Richard goes to see Bob, they discuss the killings ("That man must be a sexual maniac," Bob theorizes) and Bob tells Richard that they will go to his place taking surrogate routes. At the apartment, Richard thanks Bob, and Bob leaves. The police quickly run into the room and arrest Richard. At the station, they find Babs' things in Richard's bag ("It's Rusk!"). Richard is found guilty in court, and he screams that Bob is the killer as he is being taken away.

Deciding to check on Bob, the inspector talks to Miss Barling about Bob (Mr. William Robinson), who wanted women with "certain perculiarities." Richard is walking with two officers and he feigns a fall down some steps. Oxford is at home with his gourmet-cooking wife when Sergeant Spearman enters. The sergeant says a woman at the café remembered Bob and said he was dusty and he borrowed a clothes brush that smelled like potatoes. Richard is in the hospital, and he manages to escape with the help of some other inmates. He walks into Bob's place and beats the lump in the bed with a lug wrench. Throwing the sheets aside, Richard sees a dead woman with a necktie around her neck. Oxford runs into the room, and before Richard can say that he is innocent, they both hear thumping. They keep quiet, and Bob walks into the room dragging a trunk. "Mr. Rusk," the inspector says, "you're not wearing your tie."

Frenzy is a film from an unrelenting Hitchcock, and it is quite proficient, with humorous moments and macabre scenes intermingled. The scene with the rape-murder of Brenda in particular is potent, but also horrendous. Hitchcock, in his trademark cameo, appears in the crowd at the beginning of the film, wearing a derby.

Friday the 13th (1980)

Written by Victor Miller; Directed by Sean S. Cunningham; Paramount Pictures/Georgetown Productions, Inc./SSC Films; 95 min.

Cast: Betsy Palmer (Mrs. Voorhees); Adrienne King (Alice); Jeannine Taylor (Marcie); Robbi Morgan (Annie); Kevin Bacon (Jack); Harry Crosby (Bill); Laurie Bartram (Brenda); Mark Nelson (Ned); Peter Brouwer (Steve Christy); Rex Everhart (The Truck Driver); Ronn Carroll (Sergeant Tierney); Ron Millkie (Officer Dorf); Walt Gorney (Crazy Ralph); Willie Adams (Barry); Debra S. Hayes (Claudette); Dorothy Kobs (Trudy); Sally Anne Golden (Sandy); Mary Rocco (Operator); Ken L. Parker (Doctor); Ari Lehman (Jason)

Crew: Alvin Geiler (Executive Producer); Sean S. Cunningham (Producer); Stephen Miner (Associate Producer); Harry Manfredini (Composer); Barry Adams (Director of Photography); Bill Freda (Editor); Tom Savini (Special Makeup Effects)

At Camp Crystal Lake, 1958, campers are singing around a fireplace. The girl playing the guitar smiles at a boy, she hands off the guitar, and the couple goes somewhere together. While they are lying down and kissing, someone enters the room. The boy smiles at the person ("We weren't doing anything") and is stabbed. The killer turns to the girl, and she screams.

It is Friday the 13th, and Annie is walking into town. She goes into a diner to ask how far it is to Camp Crystal Lake. The people in the diner stare at her like she is crazy (one woman refers to the camp as Camp Blood), but the waitress says that a truck driver might be able to take her halfway; the man agrees. Outside, the two meet Crazy Ralph, who warns them about the camp ("It's got a death curse!"). On the way, the truck driver tells Annie to quit, telling her about the murders in 1958 and the drowning the year before. Annie does not take his suggestion earnestly but thanks him for the lift.

Marcie, Jack and Ned drive into camp, where they meet Steve Christy, the owner of the camp. He calls over Alice and asks her about the other workers, Brenda and Bill. Steve talks to Alice later, and she says she might have to leave, but Steve asks her to stay a little longer. Steve gets in his Jeep and drives into town. At the archery range, Brenda becomes irate when Ned shoots an arrow at the target next to her. Annie hitches a ride with someone and says she is going to Camp Crystal Lake. She is worried when the person drives past the turnoff; when the person refuses to stop the Jeep, Annie jumps from the moving vehicle. She is chased into the woods, where she is caught and her throat slit.

The group of counselors put the rafts together, and Ned feigns drowning so he can get some mouth-to-mouth from Brenda. Alice finds a snake in her cabin; Bill and the others come in and flush out the reptile until Bill chops off its head with a machete. Officer Dorf arrives at the camp to tell the group he is looking for Crazy Ralph. Before he leaves, he cautions them that the people "ain't gonna stand for no weirdness out here." When Alice finds Ralph in the food cellar, he tells the group to leave ("You're doomed if you stay") and rides off on his bicycle. The power is reportedly bad out at the camp, so Jack fires up the generator, and the lights come on. Later, Ned spies Jack and Marcie kissing, and he walks off alone, sees a figure in a dark building and goes inside. A storm is approaching, so Jack and Marcie run to their cabin, light a candle and proceed to make out.

Alice, Brenda and Bill are in a cabin together, and Brenda proposes playing strip Monopoly ("Instead of paying rent, you pay clothes"). Jack and Marcie are intimate in the cabin, and Ned is on the top bunk with his throat sliced. When Marcie goes to the bathroom, Jack is grabbed by someone underneath the bed, and an arrow is shoved in the bed and out his neck. Someone walks into the bathroom with Marcie who gets an axe in the face. Brenda leaves Alice and Bill, believing she left the windows open in her cabin (it is now pouring rain). Steve is at a diner, and he finally decides to head back to the camp. On the way, his Jeep dies; Sergeant Tierney comes by and gives him a lift. Brenda hears a child's voice ("Help me!") while she is reading in her cabin. The voice leads her to the archery range, where the lights are turned on, and Brenda screams.

When Bill returns to the cabin, Alice says she thought she heard a scream and that she saw the lights on at the archery range. The two look for Brenda and find a bloody axe in her bed. They cannot find any of the other couselors, and they run to the office. The phone and the nearby pay phone are dead. Ned's truck will not start. Alice wants to hike out, but Bill assures her that Steve will be back soon and they can use his Jeep if they need help ("We'll be laughing about this tomorrow"). Tierney is called in about a car collision, and he drops off Steve to walk the rest of the way. At the camp's entrance, Steve is killed. The lights around the camp go off, and Bill goes to check the generator. Alice goes into the kitchen and begins preparing coffee. She gets a lamp and goes outside for Bill. In the generator room, she finds

Bill's raincoat and lamp, and sees Bill hanging on the door, with arrows sticking in him.

Alice runs back to the cabin and secures the closed door with tied rope and furniture around it. Brenda's dead body is thrown through the window. She sees headlights approaching, quickly moves the things away from the door and runs out of the cabin. A woman comes out of a Jeep and says she is Mrs. Voorhees, a friend of the Christys. A terrified Alice lets her know what has happened, and the woman goes to check the room and finds Brenda ("What monster could have done this?"). Mrs. Voorhees tells Alice that Steve should not have opened the place again, and she mentions her son Jason, who drowned years ago when the counselors were supposed to be watching him (it is his birthday). Alice asks where Steve is, and Mrs. Voorhees says she could not let him open the camp. She brings out a knife and Alice runs away, finding a dead Annie and Steve. Mrs. Voorhees, in a child's voice, says, "Kill her, Mommy," and she lets Jason know she will not let Alice get away.

Alice goes for a gun but cannot find any bullets. Mrs. Voorhees gets the generator running, and all the lights come back on. The woman comes into the room, and Alice gets away from her again and hides in another room. When Jason's mother beats the door with a machete and unlocks it, Alice whacks her with a frying pan. She goes to sit on the dock, and Mrs. Voorhees attacks again. Alice finally gets hold of the machete and lops off the woman's head. Alice floats out on the lake in a boat, and the next morning, the police arrive. She waves at them, and Jason comes out of the water and pulls her under. Alice awakes in a hospital, and she is told everyone is dead and that the cops found her in the water. She asks about a boy, and the cop says they found no boy. "Then he's still there," Alice says.

Friday the 13th is often credited (with 1978's *Halloween*) with sparking the run of slashers in the early 80s. Cunningham's slasher is a classic, with a great stormy locale, multiple murders and sudden appearances of corpses. Look for a very funny parody of Crazy Ralph ("You're doomed!") in Trey Parker's *Cannibal! The Musical* (1995).

Friday the 13th, Part 2 (1981)

Written by Ron Kurz; Directed by Steve Miner; Paramount Pictures/Georgetown Productions, Inc./Greengrass Productions; 87 min.

Cast: Amy Steel (Ginny); John Furey (Paul); Adrienne King (Alice); Kirsten Baker (Terry); Stu Charno (Ted); Warrington Gillette (Jason); Walt Gorney (Crazy Ralph); Marta Kober (Sandra); Tom McBride (Mark); Bill Randolph (Jeff); Lauren-Marie Taylor (Vickie); Russell Todd (Scott); Betsy Palmer (Mrs. Voorhees); Cliff Cudney (Max); Jack Marks (The Cop); Jerry Wallace (The Prowler); David Brand, China Chen, Carolyn Lauden, Jaime Perry, Tom Shea, Jill Voight (Extra Counselors)

Crew: Tom Gruenberg, Lisa Barsamian (Executive Producers); Steve Miner (Producer); Frank Mancuso, Jr. (Associate Producer); Dennis Murphy (Co-Producer); Harry Manfredini (Composer); Peter Stein (Director of Photography); Susan E. Cunningham (Editor)

Alice, having survived Mrs. Voorhees' reign of terror, is lying on a bed, having a nightmare. She dreams of Mrs. Voorhees and Jason, and she finally sits up in bed. She answers the phone and talks to her mom, and then she goes to take a shower. The phone rings again but no one responds. Alice seems unsettled, so she locks her door. She hears a noise, sees an open window in the kitchen and gets an icepick. She then finds a decapitated head in the refrigerator. She gets the icepick shoved in her head, and the killer moves the screaming kettle from the hot burner.

Jeff and Sandra stop at a gas station, get on a pay phone and call Ted for directions. Crazy Ralph stops by ("You're all doomed"), and the couple realizes their truck is being towed. They chase the tow truck down but the driver ignores them. Around a corner, Ted is laughing at his humorous joke. Jeff, Sandra and Ted are driving in the truck, and they stop for a tree limb in the road. Sandra looks around and finds an old sign for Camp Crystal Lake. Ted calls it Camp Blood but avoids any discussion of the camp. The trio reaches the Counselor Training Center, and Paul talks to the group about the center. Ginny arrives late in her noisy red car, and Paul talks to her for a little bit and then tells her to move her car. Ginny's car refuses to start as Paul lays out the rules for the potential counselors. Paul returns to Ginny, looks at the engine and the car starts. Ginny moves the vehicle.

Around a campfire, Paul talks about Jason, claiming the body was never found. He says the survivor of Camp Blood saw Jason and she disappeared two months later. Jason saw his mother beheaded and he seeks his revenge, having now been "dormant" for five years and ready to kill. Ted jumps out in a mask and scares everyone. Paul says now the Jason legend should be out of everyone's system. Scott asks to dance with Terry but she turns him down, so he dances with her dog, Muffin. Ginny beats Paul at chess and leaves for bed. Sandra tells Jeff she wants to check out Camp Blood, but Paul said it is off limits. Ginny is scared by Paul in her cabin, and the two kiss. Crazy Ralph is hanging around outside. A wire is looped around his neck and he is killed.

The next day, the group is out jogging. Ginny chainsaws some wood for the fire, and Terry, looking for Muffin, is called to lunch. Later the group is swimming, and Sandra and Jeff go looking for Camp Blood. In the woods, they find a mangled animal (which might be a dog), and a cop finds them and tells them to get back to the center. Back in his car, the cop sees someone running in the woods. He chases the person to an old shack deep in the forest. Inside he finds a room and reacts ("Oh my God"), and a hammer is swung into his head. Paul lets the people have a night in town (except Sandra and Jeff, who he says "volunteered" to stay), but several decide to stay at the camp. The others leave for some drinking.

Terry goes down to the lake for skinny dipping, and Jeff arm wrestles with the wheelchair-bound Mark until Sandra suggests wrestling with her. Terry's clothes are taken away, and she sees Scott, who makes her chase him for her clothing. He gets his foot caught in a rope and is pulled upside down. Terry goes to get something to cut him down; while she is gone, Scott's throat is cut with a machete. Terry heads back to Scott with a Swiss Army knife and finds him dead. At the bar, Ginny ponders the possible existence of Jason, saying he would be grown by now and would have seen his mother killed. Paul tells Ginny that Jason is nothing but a legend.

Sandra leads Jeff upstairs, as Mark and Vickie talk downstairs. Mark and Vickie kiss, and Vickie wants to get a cabin with him and she leaves to get a few things. Vickie heads to her cabin and changes clothes. Mark, waiting for her, calls Vickie on the porch; a machete is cut into his face and he rolls down some steps. The killer walks inside, takes a spear and walks upstairs, where he shoves the spear through both Jeff and Sandra, occupying the bed. Ginny and Paul decide to head back to camp and let Ted get drunk by himself. Vickie returns to the cabin looking for Mark, and she heads upstairs for Jeff and Sandra. She sees a shape under the sheets the killer (with a sheet over his face) sits up and cuts her leg. She backs up and sees a dead Jeff behind her. The killer approaches with a knife and stabs.

Ginny and Paul are back and find the lights on but the cabin vacant ("Think something's wrong?"). They go upstairs and find blood-soaked sheets before the lights go out. The couple heads back downstairs, and Ginny sees the killer behind Paul and yells a warning. The killer and Paul struggle. Ginny runs into a room, shuts the door and goes for the window, only to be blocked by the killer. She runs to the kitchen, finds a dead Ralph and gets out the window. She runs to her car, which does not start. The killer cuts the convertible top with a pitchfork and reaches his hand in, and Ginny kicks open the passenger door and knocks him down. She runs for

Jason (Warrington Gillette) checks all the cabins, looking for the campers responsible for his mother's death in Steve Miner's *Friday the 13th, Part 2* (1981).

Vickie's car, finds it locked and hides from the killer. She crawls under a bed in a cabin, but the killer waits for her to come out. Ginny runs to a cabinet, gets the chainsaw fired up and swings. The killer falls, the chainsaw stops and Ginny bashes the killer with a chair.

Ginny runs to the old shack, calling for help. The killer follows, and she hides in a room with dead people and a woman's head on a table. The killer chops through the door with a pickaxe, and Ginny puts on the sweater resting near the head. Once the killer is inside, Ginny says, "It's all done, Jason." Jason sees his mother ("Mommy is pleased"), and the confused killer kneels down as his mother suggests. Ginny lifts a machete, Jason sees the head behind her and he blocks her attack and cuts her leg. Paul enters and he and Jason struggle until Ginny swings the machete and hits Jason's neck. Ginny lifts the mask of the fallen killer, and she and Paul react. They go back to the cabin and hug; the door has suddenly been shut. Ginny has the pitchfork, and Paul checks the door to find Muffin there. Jason jumps through the window behind Ginny. Ginny is then being taken away on a stretcher and put in an ambulance. She is driven away, and Mrs. Voorhees' head continues to rest on the table.

Miner's film is a worthy sequel, creating some good frights and introducing the world to a pre–hockey-mask-wearing Jason. Ginny is a marvelous character, outmaneuvering Jason many times with her strength and intelligence, and she is wonderfully portrayed by actress Steel. Watch *Friday the 13th, Part 2* along with Mario Bava's *Bay of Blood* (1971); there are a number of similarities.

Friday the 13th, Part 3 (1982)

Written by Martin Kitrosser and Carol Watson; Directed by Steve Miner; Paramount Pictures/Georgetown Productions, Inc./Jason Productions; 95 min.

Cast: Dana Kimmell (Chris); Paul Kratka (Rick); Tracie Savage (Debbie); Jeffrey Rogers (Andy); Catherine Parks (Vera); Larry Zerner (Shelly); David Katims (Chuck); Rachel Howard (Chill); Richard Brooker (Jason); Nick Savage (Ali); Gloria Charles (Fox); Kevin O'Brien (Loco); Charlie Messenger, Terry Ballard, Terence McCorry (State Troopers); Annie Gaybis (Cashier); Cheri Maugans (Edna); Steve Susskind (Harold); Gianni Standaart (Newswoman); Perla Walter (Mrs. Sanchez); David Wiley (Abel); Steve Miner (Newscaster); Betsy Palmer (Mrs. Voorhees); Amy Steel (Ginny); John Fuery (Paul); Steve Daskawisz (Jason Voorhees)

Crew: Lisa Barsamian (Executive Producer); Frank Mancuso, Jr. (Producer); Peter Schindler (Associate Producer); Tony Bishop (Co-Producer); Harry Manfredini (Composer); Gerald Feil (Director of Photography); George Hively (Editor)

As Paul leads Ginny away, Jason takes the machete from his neck and crawls away. Harold is out by a clothesline, and his wife Edna yells at him. On television is a discussion of the recent massacre of eight people, with Ginny as the only survivor and the murderer still at large. Edna complains about Harold eating in the store and the rabbit being inside, then Edna returns to her sewing by the TV. Harold goes to the bathroom and is whacked in the chest with a cleaver at the door. Edna looks around and is grabbed, and a knitting needle is shoved in the back of her head.

A group arrives in a van to pick up Vera. Chris mentions something happening at the lake a long time ago. A guy with a mask approaches Chris, Debbie and Andy, and "stabs" Andy, but it is only Shelly the jokester (Vera's "date"). Debbie makes an observation ("Hey, the van's on fire!"), and the group sees pseudo-hippies Chuck and Chill smoking inside. On the road, cops with sirens are behind them, and Andy tells the smoking couple to eat the dope, which Chuck does. But the cops speed past to a place with paramedics carrying out a body bag. Later, the van stops for a man sleeping in the street, and they quickly leave when he shows them an eyeball. At Higgins Haven, Chris finds the house's door open; Rick is inside. They move some hay into the barn using a pulley, and the couple runs into the house, where they hear a scream. Chris finds Shelly in the closet with a hatchet in his head. The others run in, Andy touches Shelly's stomach and the jokester laughs. Everyone is angry, and Shelly leaves with Vera (in Rick's car) to go to the store.

At the store, Vera and Shelly have a run-in with a rude gang of bikers, Fox, Loco and

Ali. In the car, Shelly inadvertently knocks over their bikes, and Ali punches the windshield and the side door before Shelly drives off. Shelly turns around and runs towards Ali, forcing the biker to jump away from his bike. The two return to the others and explain what happened to Rick's car ("We had a slight misunderstanding with a motorcycle gang"). Rick is a bit steamed, and he and Chris leave in his car. Later, the gang is there to steal gas from the van. Fox has fun swinging on the pulley, and Loco (with a tank of gas to pour in the barn) sees her; then she is suddenly gone. He goes inside, finds Fox dead and is killed with a pitchfork. Ali goes in the barn and Loco's corpse falls next to him. He sees Jason and attacks him with a machete, but Jason knocks him down and beats him.

Shelly and Andy are having a juggling contest, and Debbie asks Andy upstairs. Shelly tells Vera that he likes her a lot, and she stops him from speaking, and says they will talk later, leaving Shelly incensed. Chris is out with Rick, and she decides to finally tell him what happened to her that scared her so much. She tells of a night when she was angry with her parents and decided to punish them by staying all night in the forest. While sleeping under an oak tree, she was awakened by a noise and saw a hideous man ("almost inhuman") who attacked her with a knife. She was grabbed and dragged, and she blacked out and woke up the next morning in her bed. She did not know what happened after that, and her parents refused to talk about the incident. The car's headlights go out, and Rick realizes that the battery is dead. The decide to walk back to the others.

Chuck goes to the outhouse. When it starts to shake, he goes outside and thinks he sees Shelly walk into the barn. He and Chill look inside but they find no one. Vera is sitting by the dock, and her foot is grabbed by Shelly. Vera is mad, but Shelly just wants her attention, and he becomes irate when he surmises that she does not like him. He leaves and investigates a noise in the barn. Vera is looking at Shelly's wallet (he gave it to her in the store for money), and she drops it in the lake and wades in the water to retrieve it. She sees a person in a hockey mask (with a spear gun), and tells "Shelly" she is getting his wallet; Jason aims the spear gun and shoots a spear into Vera's eye. Debbie and Andy are inside enjoying the hammock. Debbie goes to shower, and Andy impresses her by walking on his hands. He "walks" down the hallway, sees Jason and is sliced. Debbie gets out of the shower, lies on the hammock, and flips through a magazine. Blood drips on the pages, she sees a dead Andy and a knife is shoved through the back of her neck.

Chuck is making popcorn when the lights go out. Chuck goes to check the fusebox in the cellar. Shelly shows up at the door with his throat slit and dies, and Chill hardly notices ("Stop foolin' around, man!"). Jason throws Chuck in the cellar and electrocutes him. When Chill realizes Shelly is not faking it, she runs up to tell Debbie and Andy. Jason stabs Chill with a firepoker and carries her away. Chris and Rick return to find popcorn burning. Rick goes outside to look for others before Chris can follow him. She calls for Rick, but he is being restrained around the corner by Jason, who squeezes his head and pops out an eyeball. Chris goes upstairs and finds the tub overflowing with water and bloody clothes soaking inside. She runs outside calling Rick again, finds a dead Loco and runs back inside the house. Rick's body is thrown through the window.

Chris goes upstairs and hides in the closet, finding Debbie and screaming. Jason axes the door, and Chris pulls the knife from Debbie's corpse and stabs Jason's hand. She swings the knife at him, stabs his knee and runs downstairs. She gets in the van and drives, but it stops on a bridge (out of gas). She hits the "Reserve" switch and the van starts, but the bridge begins to collapse. Jason attacks again, and Chris runs to the barn and hides. She whacks Jason with a shovel, wraps the pulley's rope around his neck and lets him hang. At the door, the suspended Jason pulls himself from the rope, knocking up his mask ("It's you!"). Ali returns for an attack, getting his hand chopped off. Jason turns around, and Chris swings an axe into his head. The next morning, Chris awakes in a boat on the lake, and she thinks she sees Jason running from the barn; she is pulled underwater by a wormy Mrs. Voorhees. The cops arrive to take Chris away, saying that she is the only survivor. Jason lies in the barn with the axe in his head.

While not as good as its predecessors, *Friday the 13th, Part 3* is still an enjoyable film and certainly notable, since Jason first uses his hockey mask. The movie was originally filmed in 3-D, which is evident when seeing many things shoved towards the camera. Debbie looks through an issue of the horror movie magazine *Fangoria* and passes an article on Tom Savini, who created the special effects in the first *Friday the 13th*.

Friday the 13th: The Final Chapter (1984)

Written by Barney Cohen; Directed by Joseph Zito; Paramount Pictures/Georgetown Productions, Inc.; 91 min.

Cast: Kimberly Beck (Trish); Peter Barton (Doug); Corey Feldman (Tommy); E. Erich Anderson (Rob); Crispin Glover (Jimmy); Alan Hayes (Paul); Barbara Howard (Sara); Lawrence Monoson (Ted); Joan Freeman (Mrs. Jarvis); Judie Aronson (Samantha); Camilla More (Tina); Carey More (Terri); Tom Everett (Flashlight Man); Lisa Freeman (Nurse Morgan); Thad Geer (Running Man); Wayne Grace (Office Jamison); Bonnie Hellman (Hitchhiker); Frankie Hill (Lainie); William Irby (Helicopter Pilot); Paul Lukather (Doctor); Bruce Mahler (Axel); Arnie Moore, Robert Perault (Medics); Antony Ponzini (Vincent); Gene Ross (Cop); Abigail Shelton (Woman); John Walsh (TV Newscaster); Robyn Woods (Girl in Shower)

Crew: Lisa Barsamian, Robert M. Brasamian (Executive Producers); Frank Mancuso, Jr. (Producer); Tony Bishop (Co-Producer); Harry Manfredini (Composer); João Fernandes (Director of Photography); Joel Goodman (Editor); Daniel Loewenthal (Co-Editor); Tom Savini (Special Make-up Effects)

Following the events of the last film, Jason is lying in a barn with an axe in his head. Many flashing lights arrive, and paramedics are told that everyone is dead, including Jason ("This time, they got him"). Jason's body is taken to a hospital, where Axel flirts with a nurse and invites her to the "cold room." In the room, the two kiss next to Jason's covered body and are startled when Jason's hand falls and hits the nurse's leg. Later, Axel's head is grabbed and neck sawed by Jason. Jason finds the nurse and stabs her in the stomach.

Trish is jogging with her mother, and they return home to Tommy. Trish asks about the house next door and is told that it is being rented by six kids. Paul is driving with his girlfriend Samantha, Doug, Sara, Jimmy and Ted. They pass by a hitchhiker, who sits for a banana and is killed by Jason. As the kids arrives at the house, the family dog, Gordon, and Tommy check out the people unpacking. Trish and Tommy go out and introduce themselves to the group. The next day, the six friends are walking a trail and they meet twins Tina and Terri. They all decide to go to the lake; Sara says she is going back for the car and will meet them there later. Trish and Tommy go out to the lake, and Tommy follows Gordon and enjoys the skinny-dipping people until Trish turns him around.

As Trish and Tommy are driving back, the engine cuts out. Tommy pops the hood and looks for a screwdriver. The backpacking Rob shows up and uses a knife to get the engine started. Trish offers Rob a ride, and he tells her that he is hunting bear. He asks if anyone is at the lake or vacationing, and Trish tells him about the kids next door. Tommy invites Rob inside and shows him all the masks and animated creatures he has made. At the house, Jimmy's music is replaced by something slow, and Paul and Sammy dance. Ted kisses Tina but she stops him, goes for a drink and hits on Paul when

Sammy is gone. Trish says good bye to Rob and offers him a place to stay if he ever needs one. Tina wins a drinking contest between the twin sisters, and she dances with Paul. Sammy is angry, and goes outside for a swim. Ted is upset that Paul took the twin he was interested in.

Sammy undresses outside, swims to an inflatable boat on the lake and lies inside. She hears a noise in the water, thinks it is Paul and is grabbed by Jason and stabbed through the boat. Paul decides he cannot be with Tina, and he goes outside to be with Sammy. Tina asks Jimmy to dance and then suggests going upstairs, which only makes Ted more indignant. Paul swims to the boat, finds Sammy dead and screams. He swims to the dock, and Jason points a spear gun at Paul's crotch. Paul screams again, and Rob, resting nearby in a tent, hears him. He looks around, armed with a machete, and sees someone back at his tent, where he finds his gun broken. Ted finds an old film, and he, Sara, Doug, and an obviously bored Terri watch it. Terri goes upstairs, knocks on a door and asks Tina to leave. Tina tells her to go alone, and Terri goes out in the rain, calling her sister a slut. Jason is out there to stab the twin.

Trish and Tommy's mother arrives home, and the lights will not come on. She looks around in the house, and then outside, and screams when she sees something. Trish and Tommy come home in the car and look for their mother. Trish tells her brother to stay and fix the lights, and she goes looking in the woods for Rob, who scares her with a machete. Tina and Jimmy complete their time together, and Tina goes for a drink. Jimmy walks downstairs, proud of himself, and he looks in the kitchen for the corkscrew. Jason finds it for him and shoves it into Jimmy's hand, then swings a cleaver into his face. Tina returns to the room with no Jimmy, and she looks outside the window to see both her and her sister's bike still by the tree. As she is standing by the window, Jason breaks through, pulls her out and tosses her atop the car. Rob is talking about his sister Sandra, who was murdered by Jason, and he says Jason (whose body disappeared from a morgue where two people are missing) is still alive. Ted stands and the filmstrip is cut, stopping the movie. He turns around, and Jason stabs him through the screen.

Sara and Doug finish up their time together in the shower, and Sara leaves to blow dry her hair. While she is gone, Jason smashes through the door and squishes Doug's face. Sara finds Doug dead, she runs downstairs calling for her friends, and an axe flies through the door, hitting her in the chest. Rob and Trish get back to the house; Trish tries to call for help but finds a dead phone line. She and Rob go next door, and when the power goes out, Rob goes into the basement. Trish heads upstairs (armed with Rob's machete), finds a dead Doug in the bathroom and runs to tell Rob. Rob is grabbed by Jason and is stabbed several times ("He's killing me!"). Trish runs, and then changes her mind and goes back to Rob, finding him dead. Jason attacks her, and Trish slices his wrist. She runs to the door, sees a dead Tina, and then a dead Jimmy at the other door. She breaks a window in the kitchen and crawls out.

Tommy opens the door for Trish, and as they try to lock the windows and nail the doors, Jason smashes through a window and grabs Tommy. Trish hammers his head, and she and Tommy run to a room upstairs and move shelves in front of the door. Jason axes through, and Trish throws a television set on him. He attacks again outside the room, and he chases Trish back to the other house. Tommy stays behind. Trish runs upstairs, jumps through the window, goes over the balcony and lands on the soft ground underneath. Using a drawing of Jason (from a newspaper article that Rob had) as a guide, Tommy shaves his head. Trish is back at her own house, and before Jason can strike again, Tommy comes downstairs ("Remember me, Jason?"). Trish swings the machete while Jason is distracted, and his hockey mask comes off. Trish drops the weapon, repulsed by Jason's appearance, and Tommy swings the machete into Jason's face. The siblings embrace, and when it looks like Jason is still moving, Tommy chops away at Jason's body. In the hospital, Trish is concerned about the way Tommy acted. She asks to see him, and Tommy hugs his sister, with a somber look on his face.

The Final Chapter is a very good series entry, mostly due to some strong special effects from Tom Savini. The film also introduces audiences to Tommy, the three-movie hero tormented by hockey masks and killers.

Friday the 13th: A New Beginning (aka *Friday the 13th, Part V: A New Beginning*) (1985)

Written by Martin Kitrosser, David Cohen and Danny Steinman; Directed by Danny Steinman; Paramount Pictures/Georgetown Productions, Inc.; 92 min.

Cast: Melanie Kinnaman (Pam); John Shepherd (Tommy); Shavar Ross (Reggie); Richard Young (Matt); Marco St. John (Sheriff Tucker); Juliette Cummins (Robin); Carol Locatell (Ethel); Vernon Washington (George); John Robert Dixon (Eddie); Jerry Pavlon (Jake); Caskey Swaim (Duke); Mark Venturini (Victor); Anthony Barrile (Vinnie); Dominick Barscia (Joey); Tiffany Helm (Violet); Debisue Voorhees (Tina); Ron Sloan (Junior); Dick Wieand (Roy); Richard Lineback (Deputy Dodd); Corey Feldman (Tommy at 12); Suzanne Bateman (Nurse Yates, The Receptionist); Todd Bryant (Neil); Curtis Conway (Les); Bob De Simone (Billy, Male Nurse); Jeré Fields (Anita); Ric Macini (Mayor); Maguel A. Nunez, Jr. (Demon); Corey Parker (Pete); Rebecca Wood-Sharkey (Lana); Sonny Shields (Raymond); Ed Shinstine, Chuck Wells (Deputies)

Crew: Frank Mancuso, Jr. (Executive Producer); Timothy Silver (Producer); Harry Manfredini (Composer); Stephen L. Posey (Director of Photography); Bruce Green (Editor)

Tommy, walking in the rain, comes upon Jason's grave. He watches as two men arrive with flashlights and dig up the ground. The coffin is pried open, and a wormy Jason stabs one of the men in the stomach with a machete and the other in the neck with a screwdriver. He walks over to a stunned Tommy and lifts the machete. An older Tommy awakes in the backseat of a van. He is coming from the Unger Institute of Mental Health and is being dropped off at the Pinehurst Youth Development Center. Assistant director Pam manages to get the quiet Tommy to follow her to Matt's office, where he is told about the center. Tommy goes to his room, where he meets Reggie and shows him the masks that he creates. Reggie says he is only visiting the center because his grandfather works there, and he runs outside when he hears sirens.

Sheriff Tucker is at the center to tell Matt that he found two kids in the woods enjoying themselves. Ethel and her son Junior show up on Junior's motorbike, and she is upset about the children being on her property. She threatens to shoot anyone else she sees near her farm. Later, Victor is outside chopping wood. The irritating Joey walks over to Robin and Violet hanging clothes, and they tell him to leave when he gets chocolate everywhere. He watches Victor, and the man tells Joey to leave him alone; he chops the chocolate bar that Joey lies down for him. When Joey tells Victor he is "out of line," an irate Victor chops Joey in the back. The cops and paramedics arrive, Victor is arrested and Joey's body is taken away. That night, Vinnie is working on Pete's car. When Pete goes into the woods for a bit, Vinnie gets a flare shoved into his mouth. Pete returns to see Vinnie lying under the hood, he tries the car and it starts. He is grabbed from the backseat, and his throat is slit with a machete.

The next morning, the people are called to breakfast. Matt asks if Tommy could tell Eddie to come downstairs, and Eddie suddenly jumps out in a mask and scares Tommy. A few people laugh. When Eddie playfully hits Tommy on the chest, Tommy flips Eddie and punches him on the ground until Matt pushes him off. A strange man arrives at Ethel's door looking for some work, and the cops are on the scene with the dead Vinnie and Pete. Billy (who works at the mental hospital Tommy came from) drives to a diner and calls out Lana, who goes inside to get ready. Billy snorts some cocaine while waiting, and he gets an axe in the head. Lana goes out to the car with no Billy. She sees some cocaine on the car floor, leans over to get some and sees Jason's feet. The axe is swung into Lana's stomach. The next day, Tommy thinks he sees Jason standing outside. The mayor is yelling at the police to catch the murderer, and Sheriff Tucker suggests that Jason is back and killing everyone.

Tina and Eddie go out into the woods and spend a little bit of time together. The man working for Ethel is out there watching, and he is stabbed in the stomach. Eddie leaves to wash up, and while he is gone, Tina is attacked with garden shears. Eddie comes back to find Tina dead with her eyes gouged out. He steps back, and a leather strap is thrown around a tree and over Eddie's eyes, and twisted and turned until it snaps. Pam and Reggie are going into town to see Reggie's brother Demon. Matt tells Pam to take Tommy with her, and Tommy agrees to go. At the trailer park, Tommy stays back at the truck, and Reggie and Pam visit Demon and his girlfriend Anita. Tommy is scared outside by Junior on his motorbike, and when Junior realizes Tommy is from "the looney bin," he says his mother is going to chop him up. They fight, until Pam stops Tommy, and he runs away. Reggie and Pam leave, and Demon goes to use the bathroom, only to be scared by Anita shaking the building. They sing a song back and forth, and Anita is suddenly quiet. The building starts to shake again, and Demon opens the door, sees a dead Anita and is attacked and killed when a metal bar is shoved through the walls.

Pam is told that Matt went out looking for Tina and Eddie. She tells Jake, Violet, Robin and Reggie to stay inside while she goes and finds the others. Junior returns home, upset about losing a fight, and he drives around screaming until his head is lopped off. Ethel is fixing dinner inside, and a cleaver is punched through the window and into her face. The truck putters to a stop, and Pam has to get out and walk. While watching a film, the stuttering Jake tries to tell Robin that he would like to make love with her, and she laughs. He angrily heads upstairs and goes to Violet's room, but she is too busy dancing to music. In the hallway, Jake is killed with a cleaver. Robin turns off the TV, and she covers Reggie and lets him sleep on the couch. She goes to her room, lies on the top bunk and sees a dead Jake. She is killed with a machete through the bed. A bloody hand opens the door to Violet's room, and she is eventually grabbed by the neck and stabbed in the stomach.

Reggie awakes, goes up to Tommy's room and sees the three dead people. Pam comes back, and after she sees the corpses, she and Reggie run downstairs, where a killer in a hockey mask bursts through the door. Pam and Reggie run outside and are separated. Pam finds Matt dead with a railroad spike in his forehead, and when she hides in a building, the body of Reggie's grandfather is thrown through the window. She runs outside. Before the killer can get her, Reggie drives a bulldozer out and knocks the killer down. He attacks again, and Pam and Reggie run to the barn and hide.

In the barn, Reggie is hiding in the hayloft. Pam jumps out, and she and the killer have a chainsaw-machete duel until Pam's chainsaw stops working. Tommy is at the door, and Pam and Reggie tell him to run. Tommy is frozen ("Jason?"), and the killer swipes his chest with the machete. Tommy stabs him in the leg with a pocket knife and stumbles up to the loft with the other two. The killer follows, finds Reggie hiding and is beaten on the back by Pam with a bar. Pam moves during an attack, and the killer goes over the edge. When they look over, he is only hanging, and he grabs Reggie. Tommy picks up the machete and cuts his hand, and the killer falls and is impaled on spikes of the farming equipment below. The mask has fallen off, and the killer is actually Roy, a paramedic. At the hospital, the sheriff tells

Pam that Roy was Joey's father ("I guess he used the Jason thing to cover up with"). Tommy has a dream in which he kills Pam, and he awakes to see an image of Jason, who fades away. He gets out of bed and gets a hockey mask from a nearby desk. Pam goes to see Tommy, hears a window crash, and runs inside. Tommy is standing behind the door in the mask, and he lifts a knife.

Although one of the weaker entries, *A New Beginning* still proves entertaining, offering a questionable Tommy and some comedy with Ethel and her inane son Junior.

Friday the 13th, Part VI: Jason Lives (1986)

Written and directed by Tom McLoughlin; Paramount Pictures; 87 min.

Cast: Thom Matthews (Tommy); Jennifer Cooke (Megan); David Kagen (Sheriff Garris); Kerry Noonan (Paula); Renee Jones (Sissy); Tom Fridley (Cort); C.J. Graham (Jason); Darcy Demoss (Nikki); Vincent Guastaferro (Deputy Rick Cologne); Tony Goldwyn (Darren); Nancy McLoughlin (Lizbeth); Ron Palillo (Allen Hawes); Alan Blumenfeld (Larry); Matthew Faison (Stan); Ann Ryerson (Katie); Whitney Rydbeck (Roy); Courtney Vickery (Nancy); Bob Larkin (Martin); Michael Swan (Officer Pappas); Michael Nomad (Thornton); Wallace Merck (Burt); Roger Rose (Steven); Cynthia Kania (Annette); Tommy Nowell (Tyen); Justin Nowell (Billy); Sheri Levinsky (Bus Monitor); Temi Epstein (Little Girl); Taras O'Har (Little Boy)

Crew: Don Behrns (Producer); Harry Manfredini (Composer); Jon Kranhouse (Director of Photography); Bruce Green (Editor)

Tommy is driving with his friend Hawes, coming from the institution. Tommy wants to "make sure" Jason is going to Hell. They dig up Jason's grave, and Tommy grabs a metal rod from the surrounding gate and stabs Jason's rotting, wormy corpse many times. He throws the hockey mask inside and goes for a gasoline tank. Lightning strikes and hits the rod and electricity goes through Jason's body. His eyes open, he pulls out the rod, and he grabs Tommy. Tommy throws gasoline on Jason and lights a match but the rain puts the flame out. Hawes hits Jason with a shovel, and Jason rips out his heart and lets the body fall into the open ground. Tommy speeds away in his truck, and Jason puts on his hockey mask.

Tommy runs into the police station and tells Sheriff Garris that Jason is alive. The sheriff recognizes his name as the boy involved with earlier Jason attacks. The sheriff's deputy, Rick, comes in, and when a frustrated Tommy goes for a gun, the two police officers throw him in a cell. The sheriff says the name of the town has been changed to Forest Green so people can forget about Jason. Darren and Lizbeth are driving, and Lizbeth stops when she see Jason in the road ("I've seen enough horror movies to know any weirdo wearing a mask is never friendly"). Jason does not move, so Darren gets out of the car to confront him with a gun; he is impaled with the metal rod. Lizbeth screams, gets out of the car and tries to offer Jason money. He declines the offer by stabbing her.

The next day, Garris' daughter Megan is at the station with Sissy, Paula and Cort. Tommy (from his cell) says that Jason is out in the woods, and the sheriff tells Megan to stay away from the dangerous Tommy (Megan thinks he is cute). Martin, the cemetery caretaker, shovels the dirt back into the open grave (thinking Hawes' foot hanging out belongs to Jason). The group of friends discuss the existence of Jason, and the children arrive for the camp ("Think I'd rather deal with ol' Jason," says Sissy). Larry and Stan, two businessmen, are out playing paintball, and they are both hit by Katie. She has already hit Burt, who is alone and angry swinging his machete. Jason grabs his swinging arm and pulls and throws Burt. The man's face runs into a tree limb, and Jason has both the machete and Burt's arm. Katie says the game is over, but Larry and Stan remind her that Roy is still out there. Jason suddenly appears and beheads all three of the people with one swipe of his machete. Roy is standing behind them, he fires and hits Jason with a paintball and Roy quickly runs away.

The sheriff and deputy are escorting Tommy out of town, but Tommy makes a sharp turn and goes to the cemetery. He runs to Jason's grave and finds it covered again; as the cops take him away, Tommy tells Martin that it is friend in the coffin and to dig the hole again ("Does he think I'm a farthead?"). The sheriff takes Tommy to the edge of town and tells him to stay away. At night, Martin is outside drunk, and Jason catches his tossed empty bottle, shatters it and shoves it into Martin. Lovers Steven and Annette hear Martin's scream, and Steven runs over to see Jason by the body. Steven runs back, and he and Annette jump on his bike, only to be killed with a machete stab. Sissy and Paula are waiting in a cabin, and Paula is worried about her sister Lizbeth. They hear a scream, and little Nancy tells them she saw a monster. Cort is out in a RV with Nikki. Jason unplugs the hook-up, and the RV's power goes out. Cort goes outside, and when he finds the cord torn, he decides that the couple should leave. Cort drives the RV, cranks up the music and enjoys driving so much that he does not realize Nikki is grabbed and killed by Jason. Jason approaches Cort, shoves a knife in his ear and the RV flips and wrecks. Jason crawls out.

Sheriff Garris learns about the counselors, killed "using Jason's M.O." The sheriff thinks it is Tommy trying to prove that the Jason legend is true. Tommy flips through a book on the occult and calls the sheriff's office. Megan answers and tells him her father is looking for him. She asks where he is and says she will come to pick him up. At the scene, Rick finds bloody glasses (belonging to Roy) and body pieces. Sissy hears some noise, and she pours soda out of the window in case someone is hiding. Jason jumps up, pulls Sissy through the open window and twists her head off. A slumbering Paula ignores the ruckus, thinking it is Sissy and Cort. Megan is driving with Tommy, and she successfully avoids a roadblock. A cop calls it in, and the sheriff recognizes the description of his daughter's car. He creates his own roadblock, stopping Megan and her car with a shotgun.

Nancy goes to see Paula, having found a bloody machete outside. Paula tells her it is Sissy and Cort playing a joke. Paula takes Nancy to bed and walks back to the cabin. She finds the phone dead (Jason had already chopped the line), and she sees that the machete is gone. The door is open, but no one is there. The wind pulls the door shut, Jason walks in and Paula screams. While Tommy is in the cell, he and Megan feign an argument, he grabs her, and they kiss. When Rick gets close, Megan gets his gun, puts the cop in the cell and runs out to her car with Tommy. Tommy says the only way to stop Jason is to return him to his original resting place. Jason stands over Nancy, the girl prays, and he is gone when she opens her eyes (he had heard a car door). The sheriff finds a bloody cabin, and Jason murders a police officer by the dock. Another cop finds a crying Nancy ("There's a scary man!"), and he shoots Jason a couple of times before his head is squished. The sheriff finds Nancy and tells her and the other children to hide under their beds. He sees Jason, shoots him many times and finally runs away.

Tommy and Megan are at the camp. When Jason turns at hearing Megan call for her father, the sheriff comes out from hiding, tries to stop Jason and is bent backwards. Tommy wraps a chain around a heavy rock and padlocks it, and he goes out on the lake in a boat. He calls Jason out, and Jason walks until he is underwater. Tommy pours out some gasoline and sets the lake afire; Jason jumps out and grabs him. Jason lets go and attacks again; Tommy gets the chain wrapped around his neck. The rock hits bottom, and Jason pulls Tommy along and chokes him. Tommy floats to the top, and Megan jumps in to pull him out. Jason grabs her foot. Megan starts the boat's motor, slices Jason a bit and pulls Tommy out of the water. She revives him, and the couple hugs ("It's finally over!"). The next day, Jason is chained underwater, and an eye opens.

Jason Lives is a great addition to the series, with a nice tongue-in-cheek approach (evident from the beginning with a James Bond parody for the title credit). The abundance of humor and the rapid pace make for an exciting film. Actor Palillo might be remembered as Horshack from the hit television series *Welcome Back, Kotter*. Actor Mathews has starred in *The Return of the Living Dead* (1985) and *Return of the Living Dead, Part II* (1988).

Friday the 13th, Part VII: The New Blood (1988)

Written by Daryl Haney and Manuel Fidello; Directed by John Carl Buechler; Paramount Pictures; 88 min.

Cast: Lar Park Lincoln (Tina); Kevin Blair (Nick); Susan Blu (Mrs. Shepard); Kane Hodder (Jason); Terry Kiser (Doctor Crews); Susan Jennifer Sullivan (Melissa); Elizabeth Kaitan (Robin); Jon Renfield (David); Jeff Bennett (Eddie); Heidi Kozak (Sandra); Diana Barrows (Maddy); Larry Cox (Russell); Craig Thomas (Ben); Diane Almeida (Kate); Jennifer Banko (Young Tina); John Otrin (Mr. Shepard); William Butler (Michael); Staci Greason (Jane); Michael Schroeder (Dan); Debora Kessler (Judy); Delano Palughi (Rescue Worker)

Crew: Iain Paterson (Producer); Barbara Sachs (Associate Producer); Harry Manfredini, Fred Mollin (Composers); Paul Ellott (Director of Photography); Barry Zetlin, Maureen O'Connell, Martin Jay Sardoff (Editors)

A man is arguing with his wife, and their daughter, Tina, is listening outside. She hears her father hitting her mother, and she runs out to the dock, followed by her father. Tina gets on a boat and floats out on the lake, and she tells her father that she hates him and wishes he was dead. The lake begins to bubble, and the dock shakes and collapses. The father falls into the water, and Tina screams. Tina (some years later) awakes in a car with her mother. Tina has just been in the hospital, and she and her mother are headed to Crystal Lake to see Doctor Crews. The two return to their old place, and Nick, from next door, helps Tina when her suitcase opens. Later, Tina sits for a session with Doctor Crews, who points a video camera at her. The doctor puts a matchbook on a desk in front of Tina and tells her to move it by thinking about it. Crews says he is trying to help Tina overcome her guilty feelings concerning her father's death, but Tina believes he is more interested in her telekinetic ability.

Tina heads out to the dock and thinks about her father. She feels something and concentrates, and underneath the water Jason awakes. The chain snaps, he swims to the top and Tina passes out. Tina's mother and the doctor find her, and she tells them what happened. Crews thinks it is a hallucination. Michael and Jane are at the side of the road with a broken-down vehicle, and Michael wants to camp out there. Jane would rather head back, and she admits that there is a surprise birthday party waiting for Michael. Nick goes to see Tina to give her some clothes that fell from her open suitcase and to invite her to the party. Michael answers a call of nature and returns to find Jane stabbed with a metal spike. He runs, and Jason pulls the spike from Jane's neck and throws it into Michael's back. Nick takes Tina to the party and introduces her to everyone. David, the stoner, pops a cold one and downs it, and as he coughs, Tina sees an image of Jason stabbing Michael, and she drops her drink. Tina runs back to the house, and there is a metal spike stuck on the porch.

Tina says she saw the man again, this time killing someone. Crews says it was another delusion, and he checks the porch and finds nothing. Dan and Judy are outside by a campfire and tent. Dan goes out to gather some firewood, and Jason punches him through his back, snaps his neck and steals his machete. He goes to the tent, where Judy is waiting for Dan in her sleeping bag, and cuts open the tent. Jason drags Judy out in the sleeping bag, picks her up and slams her against a tree. The next day, Nick talks to Tina and she tells him how her father died and says she was in a mental hospital. The two kiss as Melissa watches them. At the house, Melissa and Eddie mock Tina by Eddie wearing his jacket the wrong way, like a straitjacket. Tina is angry, and Melissa's pearl necklace comes apart. Tina runs out.

Tina is arguing with Crews (he does not want her to leave), and she uses her telekinesis to throw a TV at him. Nick is there, and Tina asks to see a picture of his cousin Michael ("I think he's dead, Nick."). Russ and Sandra decide to go skinny dipping, but Russ gets an axe in the face before he can take his clothes off. Sandra comes up from underwater, screams when she sees Russ and is grabbed and pulled under by Jason. In an attempt to make Nick envious, Melissa flirts with Eddie. Tina's mom finds the metal spike in Crews' office, and outside the doctor finds Michael dead with a bloody spike nearby. In the office, Tina's mother confronts Crews about the spike, and accuses him of not wanting to help Tina (and only wanting her to "perform"). Tina hears Crews say that she is dangerous and needs to be committed, and she drives away.

While driving, Tina "sees" Jason stabbing her mother, and she runs the car off the road. Maddy goes outside looking for David, and she runs into Russ, who falls lifeless out of a tree. She screams and runs to hide in a building, but Jason finds her and kills her. Tina meets Nick, and they look for her mother, as Tina's mother and Crews find the wrecked car. Ben and Kate are enjoying the privacy of the van outside, and Jason arrives to squeeze Ben's head and shove a noisemaker in Kate's eye. Jason cuts all the electricity in the house, but David and Robin do not seem to mind. Tina and Nick find his dead cousin. David goes downstairs to the refrigerator and is stabbed in the stomach. Tina runs to the office to get a gun from the desk, and she finds articles on Jason Voorhees ("It was him in the lake").

Eddie, having been sexually rejected by Melissa, is in the living room, and Jason gives him a machete to the neck. Robin goes looking for David, and she manages to find at least his head before Jason grabs her and throws her out the window (from the second floor). Nick goes looking for the others with the gun while Tina waits. Tina's mother and Doctor Crews see Jason in the woods, and the mother is stabbed in the back (as Tina had seen) while the doctor runs away. Nick finds a dead Eddie, and he runs back to a Tina-less house. Melissa is there, and Nick tells her that Michael and Eddie are dead. Tina finds Crews in the forest, and he tells her that her mother is back at the house. Tina sees blood on the doctor (it belongs to her mother), and she runs away. Jason chases the doctor down and saws into his stomach.

Tina finds her mother and several of Nick's friends dead. Jason is near, and Tina uses telekinesis to restrain him with limbs as a power line comes down and runs electricity through a nearby puddle. Despite the electrocution, Jason stands and pursues Tina to the house, where Tina "throws" things at him and causes the porch to collapse on him. Tina runs back to Nick, and Melissa does not believe Tina's story until she opens the door and gets an axe in the face. After Tina knocks Jason through the steps, she tightens his mask, and it snaps off, revealing Jason's ugly face. An electrical cord picks Jason up and drops him through an open part of the floor. Jason pulls Tina down there with him, and she tosses nails at him, douses him with gasoline and pops open the furnace door to set him afire. Tina and Nick run outside, and the house explodes. Jason attacks again on the dock, and the lake bubbles, and Tina's father ("Daddy?") comes up, wraps a chain around Jason and pulls him under. Tina and Nick are taken away in an ambulance.

Missing most of the humor from *Jason Lives* (and not being quite as exciting), *The New Blood* manages to provide some thrills with a hefty body count and some intriguing kills (the slamming-against-the-tree-in-a-sleeping-bag killing is great). Tina's father is named John Shepard; actor John Shepherd played Tommy in *Friday the 13th, Part V: A New Beginning*.

Friday the 13th, Part VIII: Jason Takes Manhattan (1989)

Written and directed by Rob Hedden; Paramount Pictures/Horror, Inc.; 100 min.

Cast: Jensen Daggett (Rennie); Scott Reeves (Sean Robertson); Barbara Bingham (Colleen Van Deusen); Kane Hodder (Jason); Peter Mark Richman (Charles McCulloch); Martin Cummins (Wayne); Gordon Currie (Miles Wolfe); Alex Diakun (Deck Hand); V.C. Dupree (Julius); Saffron Henderson (J.J.); Kelly Hu (Eva Watanabe); Sharlene Martin (Tamara Mason); Warren Munson (Admiral Robertson); Todd Shaffer (Jim); Tiffany Paulsen (Suzi); Timothy Burr Mirkovich (Young Jason); Fred Henderson (Chief Engineer); Roger Barnes (Irish Cop); Amber Pawlick (Young Rennie); Vinny Capone (Street Urchin); Peggy Hedden (New York Waitress); David Longworth (Sanitarion Engineer); Sam Sarkar, Michael Benyaer (Gang Bangers); Ace (Toby)

Crew: Randolph Cheveldave (Producer); Barbara Sachs (Associate Producer); Fred Mollin (Composer); Bryan England (Director of Photography); Steve Mirkovich (Editor)

Jimmy and Suzi are out in a boat on Crystal Lake. Jimmy tells Suzi that they are near the camp were many murders took place, and he talks about Jason and his sanguinary ways. The anchor pulls on an underwater cable, a chained Jason is electrocuted and the power goes out at the nearby camp. Jimmy goes to investigate a noise, and he returns to scare Suzi by wearing a hockey mask. Jimmy and Suzi go back to the bed, and Jason shows up (wearing Jimmy's mask) to kill Jimmy. Suzi runs away, but Jason finds where she is hiding, and he kills her.

Rennie and her teacher Colleen drive up to the dock. Charles McCulloch, Rennie's uncle and legal guardian, tells Colleen that she should not have brought Rennie. As people board *Lazarus*, Admiral Robertson gives his son Sean a sextant, and he offers him control of the boat. The captain is disappointed when his son forgets to send a signal and broadcast before starting the voyage, and Sean leaves the bridge. Jason hangs onto the boat, and the deck hand says to anyone who is listening, "This voyage is doomed." Sean and Rennie talk, and he gives her a necklace with the Statue of Liberty on it. Rennie's uncle asks why she has come along. He talks of the upcoming storm and about Rennie overcoming her fear. J.J. is playing guitar in the boiler room, and Jason shows up to chase her and whack her with the guitar.

Rennie is in her room with her dog, Toby. She hears a child say, "Mommy?" and in the window she sees an image of a drowning child. Toby whines and runs out the door. Tamara convinces Eva to try a little bit of cocaine, and Rennie walks by and asks if they have seen her dog. Charles walks in later and asks if the two girls are using drugs. Tamara thinks that Rennie was a temporary narc, and she decides to get her back. A boy enjoys the sauna for a short while, and Jason comes in and smashes a rock into his chest. Tamara walks by Rennie on the deck and feigns bumping into her, knocking her into the water. Rennie has a vision of the boy pulling her underwater, and Sean jumps into the ocean and helps her back on the boat. An irate Charles tells Colleen and Sean to stay away from his niece. Rennie goes to wash her hands and imagines the water turning to blood and the boy coming from the mirror to grab her ("Help me!").

Charles goes to Tamara's room to collect her biology project, and she throws aside her robe to reveal the organs drawn on her body. She throws Mr. Culloch on the bed, and Wayne, having filmed them, walks in and lets Charles know what he shot. Charles leaves, and Wayne says he has the hots for Tamara, but she makes him leave. After Tamara showers, she watches Jason enter the room. As she waits behind the bathroom door, Jason punches through, breaks the mirror and stabs Tamara with a mirror shard. Sean and Rennie head to the bridge and find Sean's captain father dead. Sean calls everyone to the bridge, and he tries to find someone on the radio, but Jason destroys the antennae. The deck hand lets the people know they are "all gonna die" because Jason is on board. Julius suggests they go looking for Jason. Charles stops Rennie from dropping the anchor (due to the storm).

Eva sees Tamara dead in the bathroom, and she runs from Jason until he catches up and chokes her. The males of the ship grab some weapons and split up. Wayne goes looking for J.J. in the boiler room, and after losing his glasses, he accidentally kills the engineer with a shotgun. He sees Jason's feet, and he runs and trips over J.J.'s bloody guitar. Jason throws Wayne, who is electrocuted. Sean finally gets the ship back on course, and Jason, due to a fire started from Wayne's corpse, sets the fire alarm. Jason grabs Miles' axe and throws it, and as Miles tries to climb away, he is tossed off and impaled by the antennae. Jason grabs Julius and throws him overboard. Rennie (locked in her room by Charles) has another image of the boy, and Jason punches through and grabs her. She stabs him in the eye with a pen, and Sean gets her out of the room. The two find the engine room flooded, and Sean tells Colleen that there is no restaurant (the teacher had locked some people inside). After finding the deck hand with an axe in his back, Sean, Rennie, Colleen and Charles jump in a small boat. Toby makes it, and Julius jumps from under the water and gets in.

The group rows the boat for a long time until they finally see the Statue of Liberty. They dock and walk into New York, and Jason crawls out of the water. Two punks mug the group and take Rennie along with them. Rennie is injected with some cocaine, and while one punk is gone, Jason stabs the other in the chest. The dead punk's friend returns, and Jason slams his head against the wall. Rennie manages to run away. Julius runs to a pay phone to call the police, and Jason attacks him. A chase leads to the roof of a building, and Julius tries his best boxing punches on Jason to no avail. He is finally worn out, tells Jason, "Take your best shot"—and Jason knocks his head clean off. Sean finds a drugged and dizzy Rennie, and Charles and a cop find Colleen. They convene, get in the officer's car and see Julius' head on the dashboard. Jason attacks and kills the cop, and Rennie gets behind the wheel, but wrecks the car when she sees the boy again. The group gets out, but not Colleen, who explodes into flames with the car.

Rennie flashes back and learns that her uncle tried to teach her to swim by throwing her into the water and saying that Jason pulls under those who cannot swim. She angrily runs away, and Sean follows her. Charles finally sees Jason, and he runs into a building but is tossed out the window and dunked into a bucket of filthy water. Jason chases Rennie and Sean to the subway station and onto the train. Sean pulls the emergency brake, he and Rennie leave and he knocks Jason to the track and electrocutes him. They walk into the street, but Jason comes back, and the couple runs into an alley and crawls into a manhole. They meet a sanitation worker in the sewer, and he says toxic waste will be flooding the corridors soon. Jason grabs the worker and beats him with a wrench, then chases Rennie until she finds a bucket of toxic waste and dumps it on him. Jason's mask comes off and his face partially melts, and Rennie runs back to Sean. They climb up a ladder, and Jason grabs Rennie's hand. The toxic waste engulfs Jason, who melts; and the two see a little boy lying there. They are out in the streets again, and Sean gives Rennie back her necklace (it was lost during the scuffle with the punks). Toby returns, and they embrace their furry pal.

The different approach for *Friday the 13th, Part VIII*, with a rock-music score and the boat and city settings, does not really work, and it seems to lose some of the earlier films' energy. It is possibly the weakest *Friday the 13th* film. Jason hardly "takes" Manhattan; he spents most of the film on the boat and mostly hangs out in the alleys and sewers of New York. The boat, *Lazarus*, is named after a character from the Bible, who, like Jason, rose from the dead. Although Jason has to steal a hockey mask (his mask in *The New Blood* was destroyed), the axe wound from *Part 3*, interestingly enough, returns.

Frightmare (aka *Frightmare II*; *Once Upon a Frightmare*) (1974)

Written by David McGillivray; Directed by Pete Walker; Peter Walker (Heritage) Ltd.; 86 min.

Cast: Rupert Davies (Edmund Yates); Sheila Keith (Dorothy Yates); Deborah Fairfax (Jackie); Paul Greenwood (Graham); Kim Butcher (Debbie); Fiona Gurzon (Merle); Jon Yule (Robin); Tricia Mortimer (Lillian); Pamela Farbrother (Delia); Edward Kalinski (Alec); Victor Winding (Detective Inspector); Anthony Hennessey (Detective Sergeant); Noel Johnson (The Judge); Michael Sharvell-Martin (Barman); Tom Wright (Nightclub Manager); Andrew Sachs (Barry Nichols); Nicholas John (Pete); Jack Dagmar (Old Man); Leo Genn (Doctor Lytell); Gerald Flood (Matthew Laurence)

Cast: Tony Tenser (Executive Producer); Pete Walker (Producer); Stanley Myers (Composer); Peter Jessop (Director of Photography); Robert C. Dearberg (Editor)

In London, 1957, Barry Nichols walks through an empty carnival and knocks on a trailer door. He tells the person who answers that he has no one else to turn to, and he is let inside. Later, the man is dead, with one side of his head missing, exposing the brain. A judge sentences Edmund and Dorothy Yates to a mental insitution until they are deemed sane and can re-enter society.

Debbie, Alec and their biking friends enter a discotheque, where the barman refuses to serve the 15-year-old Debbie. She goes back to Alec and says the man called her a "tart," and Alec returns to fight, but he and his friends are thrown out. Later, the group waits for the barman to come out, and they jump and beat him. Alec sees an old man and they all run, leaving Debbie alone for a while. Alec is ready to leave, and Debbie tells him to go without her. Jackie is home reading late at night, and Debbie returns to the flat. The two sisters argue, and Debbie mentions her dead parents; she says that Jackie is not waiting for her, but waiting so that she can leave. The cops talk to the old man, and the barman is nowhere to be found.

Jackie visits her father Edmund. She has brought something wrapped in paper, and Edmund says he thinks Dorothy is trying to make him think she is better. Dorothy comes out and says hello, and she says she has not had a migraine in a long time, and Jackie suggests that she does not need the parcels any more. Dorothy thanks her for the parcel (leaking a red liquid), and she leaves. Jackie tells Edmund that she does not think her mother has guessed what they are doing. Later, Jackie is alone in a train compartment, and her pale mother appears, offering a parcel, with blood dripping from the package and from her mouth. Jackie answers the buzzing door to police officers, who talk to Debbie about the barman and her biking pals. After they leave, Jackie tells her sister that, if she does not have a job by the end of the week, she can get out and fend for herself.

While working at her make up job with her friend Merle, Jackie gets a call from her father, and the two leave to talk. Lillian visits Dorothy's place (there was an advertisement in the newspaper), and they sit for a reading of tarot cards. Edmund asks Jackie to visit that night and talk to Dorothy, and he shows her a pig's head he found. Jackie and her psychiatrist friend Graham are on a date, and she tells him that she has to leave early and she drives away. Graham returns to Merle and Robin, saying that Jackie gave him an excuse for a premature departure, and Merle blames her "delinquent" sister Debbie. Jackie arrives at the house, and Edmund shows her tarot cards he found. Jackie confronts her mother ("Have you started again?"); Dorothy is upset, believing Jackie is trying to trick her back into the asylum. She mentions her baby being taken away and her child not knowing that she exists. Edmund settles his wife down, and Dorothy asks Jackie to continue bringing parcels.

Graham is at Jackie's flat speaking with Debbie about the orphanage and her parents. Jackie returns home and tells Debbie to go to bed, and Debbie angrily walks out the door. Graham tells Jackie to stop treating Debbie like a child. Dorothy goes to the barn, finds the body of Lillian and drills the corpse. Graham says that Debbie seems cold because she has no "roots," due to Jackie not speaking of her parents. He wants to help, but Jackie says she does not need his help. Alec meets Debbie at her storage area, where she shows him the body of the barman in a car trunk. Alec tells her he did not murder the man, and she says that, regardless, he and his friends had better hide the corpse in the quarry.

Graham goes to see Doctor Lytell about getting in touch with someone from the hospital where Jackie's (still-living) parents were committed. Delia goes to see Dorothy for a reading, and Dorothy acts in a peculiar way, not telling the woman about her future and throwing her money back at her. Delia observes that Dorothy is "quite mad," and she tries to get out, but the doors have been locked. Dorothy takes a burning stick from the fireplace and shoves it into Delia's stomach, then asks a person behind the curtain for help after licking some blood. Edmund has returned, and he walks through the door to see Dorothy over the dead body. She tells her husband she had to do it, and he asks her if it was the first. She says no, and Edmund asks Dorothy what she has been doing with the bodies.

Graham is at the hospital with Matthew Laurence, who tells the psychiatrist that Dorothy was a cannibal. He talks of her childhood and how, with the help of her husband, she killed six people, in the form of a "pathological cannibalim." He mentions the daughters (Jackie is from Edmund's previous marriage), and he says that he believes Edmund feigned his insanity to be with his wife and that, now released, Dorothy is "completely cured." Edmund throws the body in the barn, and he realizes that Dorothy started killing as soon as she was out of the hospital. Jackie tells Graham that she found blood on Debbie's jacket, and Debbie told her that Alec had killed the barman. Jackie, Graham and a couple of cops go to the storage area, and the cops think the dead barman is the result of more than a bicycle chain.

Alec and Debbie are at the farm, and Debbie knocks on the door. Edmund asks who she is, and she says, "Hello, Dad." He learns that Debbie has always known her parents were alive, and Debbie says that Jackie told her. Alec goes to the barn and finds the bodies; Dorothy stabs him repeatedly with a pitchfork as Debbie watches. Jackie tells Graham that she had been taking Dorothy meat from the butcher to make the woman believe that Jackie was doing the killing for her. Debbie suggests that Jackie must be killed next because she is trying to break up the family. Graham arrives at the place, and Dorothy hides Debbie as Edmund answers the door. Graham asks for a reading, and he tells Dorothy that his name is Robin. She senses that he is worried about two girls, and she asks why he is lying to her (he called her Mrs. Yates when Dorothy had been using an alias). Debbie comes out and says it is Jackie's doctor friend, wanting to put Dorothy back in the institution.

Debbie calls Jackie and tells her she is at the farm with her mother and father, and Jackie is on her way. At the house, she asks her father where Graham is, and she sees marks on Edmund's face and thinks that Dorothy has hit him. He says that Dorothy has had a "serious relapse," and that Debbie is looking after her now since they have so much in common. Jackie looks around and she finds Graham in the attic, lying on a table and being drilled in the face by Dorothy and Debbie. Edmund walks in and locks the door, and he reluctantly ignores his daughter's pleading as Debbie approaches her sister with a cleaver.

Pete Walker's *Frightmare* is an effective, eerie film, with strong performances and touches of black humor. After a film was released in 1982 as *Frightmare*, subsequent releases of Walker's film were titled *Frightmare II*, evidently to avoid confusion.

The Funhouse
(aka *Carnival of Terror*)
(1981)

Written by Larry Block; Directed by Tobe Hooper; Universal Pictures/Mace Neufeld Productions; 96 min.

Cast: Elizabeth Berridge (Amy); Kevin Conway (Freak Show Barker/Strip Show Barker/Funhouse Barker); Cooper Huckabee (Buzz); Miles Chapin (Richie); Largo Woodruff (Liz); Sylvia Miles (Madame Zena); William Finley (Marco the Magnificent); Wayne Doba (The Monster); Shawn Carson (Joey); Jeanne Austin (Mrs. Harper); Jack McDermott (Mr. Harper); David Carson (Geek); Sonia Zomina (Bag Lady); Ralph Marino (Truck Driver); Herb Robins (Carnival Manager); Mona Agar (Strip Show Dancer); Susie Malnik (Carmelia); Sid Raymond (Strip Show MC); Larry Ross (Heckler, Girlie Show); Frank Grimes (Strip Show Voyeur); Frank Schuller (Poker Player #1); Peter Conrad (Midget With Tall Lady); Mildred Hughes (Tall Lady); Glen Lawrence (Spectator); Shawn McAllister, Sandy Mielke (Garbage Collectors); Mike Montalvo (Spectator)

Crew: Mace Neufeld, Mark L. Lester (Executive Producers); Brad Neufeld (Associate Producer); Derek Power, Steven Bernhardt (Producers); John Beal (Composer); Andrew Laszlo, A.S.C. (Director of Photography); Jack Hofstra (Editor)

An unseen person enters a bedroom and looks around. Amy prepares to shower as the person takes a hanging knife from the wall and puts on a mask. The bathroom door is open, the shower curtain is thrown aside, and Amy screams. The knife hits her, and it is only rubber. A little boy takes off the mask ("Joey!"), laughs and runs away. Amy finds Joey in the closet and says that she is not taking him to the carnival on Saturday and that she is going to get him back when he least expects it.

Amy's father tells her he does not want her to go to the carnival because it is the same one in which two girls were found dead. She says she is only going to the movies. Her date, Buzz, arrives, and as they are sitting in his car, a man on the radio mentions the murders from last year. Amy suggests that they go to the movies instead of the carnival. The couple goes to pick up Liz and Richie, and a stubborn Joey sneaks out of the house. At the carnival, Amy initially seems distant, but she lightens up after the group rides a few rides and tries out the bumper cars. A woman in the bathroom tells Liz and Amy that God is "watching them" and that "He hears everything." A truck driver pulls over and asks Joey if he needs a lift. He points a shotgun at him, Joey runs and the man maniacally laughs.

The four friends go to the freak animals tent, where they see a two-headed cow and a deformed fetus in a jar. Joey arrives at the carnival, and Amy decides that the group should go see the magician, who performs an act that involves staking someone through the heart. They see Madame Zena, the fortune teller, next. As Amy gets her palm read, the group continually snickers. Zena is understandably enraged, and she kicks them out of her tent. Later, Buzz and Amy partake in some kissing time in a semi-private place, and Joey heads for the funhouse, being strapped in by a man wearing a mask of Frankenstein's monster.

The barker at the strip show tent carefully eyes Amy, much like the barker at the freak animals tent and the one at the funhouse. After spying through a hole at the strip show tent, Richie decides that the group should spend the night in the funhouse. Liz telephones her mother and says she is staying with Amy, and Amy does the same with her parents. Joey sees each couple get strapped in by the masked man, but he does not see them come out. He hangs around the funhouse for a while as the crowd of people dissipates. He is eventually frightened by the old woman from the bathroom, and he runs away and jumps the fence.

Inside the funhouse, the couples are making out. A light suddenly appears from the floor underneath, and they watch as the masked man gets money for Zena. After he gives her $100, she moves around a bit in her skimpy clothing, but she refuses to let him touch her. He wants his money back, but she tells him it is too late. The man chokes Zena and kills her. The group decides it is probably a good idea to leave. As they head for a door, Richie goes into the room with a dead Zena to "make sure she's dead." The door is locked, and they all look for a way out. Unable to find anything, they return to their room from earlier.

The light comes on again, and the masked man is with the funhouse barker. "You killed one of the family!" the barker yells at the whimpering man. He says they will dump the body and blame it on the locals. The masked man hands the barker the hundred dollar bill, but when he goes to the box of cash, it is empty. As he is demanding to know where the rest of it is, Richie drops his lighter from above, and the barker hears it land. He asks whoever is up in the room to come out, but no one answers. He whispers to the man to take his gloves off because they "have work to do." Richie is the one who took the money, and he says he was going to split it. Joey is hanging around the funhouse, and the masked man, now no longer wearing his mask, grabs the boy. Joey runs, and he is stopped by an old man.

The barker is loading his gun, and he apologizes to the man, mentioning his brother "on display," and saying, "I don't want that for you." He says he will only have to do one last bad thing. After a prop skeleton jumps out and scares the group, Richie is strung up with rope from above and pulled away. Joey's parents arrive to take him from the old man, who is letting the boy rest on a bed. Back in the funhouse, a cart rolls down the track with a dead Richie, and Liz falls through a trap door. Through a giant running fan, Amy sees her parents nearby with Joey, and she screams at them but they cannot hear her. Liz awakens in a dark corridor, and the man appears. He gets near and Liz stabs him, and he attacks.

Buzz and Amy run into the barker with his gun ("I'm just protecting my family"). Buzz tries to get the gun, and the barker is eventually impaled by a prop. The man is there, and Amy runs away until she hears a gunshot. She turns around, and sees a dead Buzz rolling down the track. The man, now clearly visible without his mask to expose his deformed face, catches up to Amy in a room of running gears, and she beats him with a crowbar until he is caught on a hook. He grabs Amy, but she pulls away from, and the man is caught in one of the gears and crushed. Amy gets outside into the daylight, takes one last look at the funhouse, and walks away crying.

Director Hooper, who gave the world the classic *The Texas Chainsaw Massacre*, offers a fun slasher, with hysterical parodies of *Halloween* (1978) and *Psycho* (1960) in the beginning scene. Actor Finley is perhaps best known as the tormented Winslow in Brian De Palma's cult musical *Phantom of the Paradise* (1975). Actress Miles was nominated for an Oscar for a six-minute cameo in *Midnight Cowboy* (1969).

Graduation Day (1981)

Written by Anne Martisse, David Baughn and Herb Freed; Directed by Herb Freed; 97 min.

Cast: Christopher George (Coach Michaels); Patch Mackenzie (Anne Ramstead); E.J. Peaker (Blondie); E. Danny Murphy (Kevin); Michael Pataki (Gugilone); Richard Balin (Roberts); Carmine Argenziano (Halliday); Virgil Frye (MacGregor); Beverly Dixon (Elaine Ramstead); Hal Bokar (Ronald Corliss); Linnea Quigley (Dolores); Denise Cheshire (Sally); Billy Hufsey (Tony); Tom Hintnaus (Pete); Carl Rey (Ralph); Karen Abbott (Joanne); Vanna White (Doris); Ruth Ann Llorens (Laura); Patrick Wright (Truck Driver); Aaron Butler (Photographer); Viola Kates Stimpson (Mrs. Badger); Erica Hope (Diana); Grant Loud (Singer)

Crew: Hal Schwartz (Associate Producer); David Baughn, Herb Freed (Producers); Arthur Kempel (Composer); Daniel Yarussi (Director of Photography); Martin Jay Sadoff (Editor)

During a track meet, Laura, a female runner is pushed by the crowd and by her coach ("Move it, move it, move it!"). Apparently, the pressure is too much for Laura, who collapses right after crossing the finish line.

Anne Ramstead, returning from the Navy, is getting a ride into town. She asks to be dropped off when she sees a girl running by. The girl, Paula, runs into a wooded area with her earphones on. Someone is following her, and a pair of black-gloved hands starts a stopwatch. The person catches up to Paula and slits her throat. At the Midvale School, the track team is waiting for Paula so that they can have their photograph taken. Coach George Michaels decides to have the picture taken without the student. Anne arrives home to see her mother and her crabby stepfather, Ronald. Anne and her mother discuss the death of their sister/daughter, Laura, and Anne goes upstairs to unpack her things, including her black gloves.

Later, track member Sally is walking through the wooded area and she has an encounter with Anne, who is looking for the auditorium. Anne acts strangely towards Sally ("Boy, is she weird!" Sally later tells her friends). The students have a graduation rehearsal, with Anne as a "special guest." Later, Anne goes to see Laura's boyfriend, Kevin. He shows her a photo album of Laura, and Anne gives Kevin one of Laura's medals. Sally is in the locker room when the lights are shut off. She runs into Doris and Joanne and frightens them. Sally searches the area but finds no one. Later, the gymnast does her routine on the bars for a photographer, but she is not able to concentrate and continually fails, despite Coach's words of encouragement: "Don't disappoint me." Sally heads back to the locker room, where the killer is in fencing garb and stabs her in the throat with a sword. Later, Principal Gugilone is in his office, and he removes a switchblade from his coat pocket to slice his apple. He places the blade into his desk drawer, where a stopwatch resides.

While Dolores is on the bench with her boyfriend Tony, smoking marijuana and kissing, MacGregor, the "narc," shows up and says he had better not catch them with drugs again. Anne goes to the metal shop to see Coach Michaels. The coach is angry about being blamed for Laura's blood clot, and he says to Anne, "I didn't kill your sister! I loved her!" Anne leaves, still indignant towards Michaels. In the wooded area, another member of the track team, Ralph, is running in his football gear, tossing a football back and forth. Doris and Joanne are there, and they playfully toss the football into some trees. The killer is already waiting, with a football affixed with a blade. Ralph goes behind the trees and says, "Hi. Gimme my ball." The killer abides, giving Ralph his football right in the stomach.

That night, there is a skating party for the students. They are skating to the tune of "Gangster Rock," played by men donning black and white make up. Tony and Dolores head into the woods to make out, and when Tony answers a call of nature, his head is chopped off with garden shears. Dolores is attacked, and a chase begins, as "Gangster Rock" continues to play. Dolores is murdered with a sword.

The next day, parents continue to call about their missing children. The principal, believing the kids are out "raising hell," takes it lightly. Inspector Halliday arrives to investigate. Pete is out pole vaulting, and when completing the vault, he lands on the mat, with spikes hidden underneath. Halliday goes to speak with the coach, who has now been fired. Inside his desk are black gloves and a stopwatch. In the locker room, Joanne and Doris find Sally's body stuffed in a locker. Coach Michaels is nearby, and he checks the corpse. Kevin runs into the room and, believing the coach is the murderer, he begins a struggle. Coach gets away, and Kevin gives chase. Out in the wooded area, after discovering the body of Ralph, Coach pleads his innocence, but Kevin says, "You killed Laura! You all killed her!" Kevin then admits to the murders and pulls out a knife. When Michaels gets the knife away from Kevin, Halliday shows up and sees him standing over the student. He shoots and kills the coach.

Anne goes over to Kevin's place later. When no one answers the door, she heads upstairs to find him, and she discover the corpse of her sister sitting in a rocking chair. Kevin shows up, and when Anne refuses to give Laura a kiss, Kevin says, "You're as bad as the others!" He attacks her, but Anne runs away. Kevin pursues her to the track and field, and while fighting under the bleachers, Kevin is finally killed when backing into the spikes lodged into Pete's corpse. Anne goes home that night and imagines Kenny walking into her room, but it is only her drunk stepfather. The next day, she says good bye to her mother and leaves.

Graduation Day is a campy slasher, with fairly sterile performances and scenes that are perhaps more humorous than intended, such as the "Gangster Rock" chase scene, which never seems to end. Actor Pataki directed the gory eye-catching *Mansion of the Doomed* and an erotic version of *Cinderella* (both 1977).

Halloween
(1978)

Written by Debra Hill and John Carpenter; Directed by John Carpenter; Falcon Films; 91 min.

Cast: Jamie Lee Curtis (Laurie Strode); Donald Pleasence (Doctor Sam Loomis); Nancy Loomis (Annie); P.J. Soles (Lynda); Charles Cyphers (Brackett); Kyle Richards (Lindsey); Brian Andrews (Tommy); John Michael Graham (Bob); Nancy Stephens (Marion); Arthur Malet (Graveyard Keeper); Mickey Yablans (Richie); Brent Le Page (Lonnie); Adam Hollander (Keith); Robert Phalen (Doctor Wynn); Tony Moran (Michael, Age 23); Will Sandin (Michael, Age 6); Sandy Johnson (Judith Myers); David Kyle; Peter Griffith (Laurie's Father); Nick Castle (The Shape)

Crew: Moustapha Akkad (Producer); John Carpenter (Compser); Dean Cundey (Director of Photography); Tommy Wallace, Charles Bornstein (Editors)

In Haddonfield, Illinois, Halloween night of 1963, someone is snooping around a house. Inside, a boy and girl are kissing and cuddling, and they head upstairs. The person walks through the back door, gets a knife from the kitchen and, after the boy leaves, walks up the stairs. He puts on a mask, stabs the girl to death and walks outside. A six-year-old Michael Myers stands dazed, clutching onto a bloody knife.

Fifteen years later, in Smith's Grove, Doctor Sam Loomis is driving with a nurse, Marion. When they reach the institution to see Michael, patients are wandering around the estate. Loomis goes to see what is wrong, and Marion is attacked in the car. She jumps out, and the attacker springs behind the wheel and speeds away ("The evil has gone!").

It is Halloween in Haddonfield. Laurie Strode is dropping the key off at the Myers place (her father is a realtor), and she meets with young Tommy (whom she is to babysit that night). Tommy tells her that the Myers place is haunted. Michael watches the two of them leave. In class, Laurie sees the stolen car that Michael is using sitting outside. Later, Tommy is tormented by classmate bullies, who tell him "The Boogey Man" is coming. Loomis calls someone and says that Michael is headed for Haddonfield, and that they "must be ready for him." As Laurie is walking home with her friends, Annie and Lynda, they see Michael's car drive by, and the brakes are slammed when Annie yells at the driver. The car moves on, but later, when walking with Annie, Laurie sees Michael standing a few yards ahead on the sidewalk. When in her bedroom, Laurie sees Michael once again, standing in the backyard.

At the cemetery, Loomis and the keeper see that Judith Myers' headstone is missing. Laurie and Annie are driving around, and they stop to talk with Sheriff Brackett, Annie's father. He tells them (with a loud alarm ringing) that a store was robbed, and some rope, a couple of knives and a Halloween mask were taken. Loomis arrives afterwards to talk to Brackett about Michael. Laurie and Annie discuss the upcoming dance, unaware of the fact that Michael is following them. Loomis and Brackett enter the Myers home and find a dead dog. Loomis says he wants to wait for Michael at the house.

While Laurie is reading to Tommy, he asks her about The Boogey Man. Annie calls and tells Laurie about a very excited Ben, who has just been told about an interested Laurie. Tommy sees a shape near Annie's house, but when Laurie looks, there is no one there. After Michael ensures that the barking dog will no longer bark, Annie spills some butter on her clothes and heads outside to the laundry room. She is accidentally locked inside, and then gets her foot stuck when trying to crawl out of the window. Lindsey, the girl Annie is babysitting, finally helps Annie out when her boyfriend, Paul, telephones.

Annie wants to see Paul, so she drops off Lindsey with Laurie and Tommy, and heads back home. Waiting for her in the car is Michael. While hiding and trying to frighten Lindsey, Tommy sees Michael carrying the now-dead Annie, and he scares Lindsey by claiming that The Boogey Man is outside. Lynda and her boyfriend Bob arrive at Annie's house, and after learning that Annie is gone and Lindsey is with Laurie and Tommy, they heard upstairs to engage in a sexual tussle. Afterwards, Bob goes to get a beer, and Michael kills him. Lynda calls Laurie (without knowing Bob is dead), but before she can say anything, Michael strangles her. Laurie only hears grunts, and, believing it is Annie, she asks if she is okay. Loomis, still waiting at the Myers home, turns and sees the stolen car. Laurie checks on the kids, and goes over to Annie's place. There she discovers her dead friends and is attacked by Michael.

Laurie runs into the streets screaming, but she is ignored by her neighbors. She manages to wake up Tommy and Lindsey and get inside, only to learn that the phone lines are dead. Michael gets inside and attacks again, but Laurie stabs him with a sewing needle. Laurie momentarily believes she is safe, but Michael reappears on the stairs, and Laurie takes refuge inside a closet.

Michael breaks inside, Laurie stabs him with a coat hanger and then picks up Michael's dropped knife and stabs him again. She tells Tommy and Lindsey to go get help. They run outside screaming, and Loomis sees them. Inside the house, Laurie does not see Michael rise behind her. Loomis runs in as Michael is attacking Laurie. After his mask is pulled off, Michael backs away and Loomis fires his gun. He walks into the room and shoots Michael five more times until he falls over the balcony. "That was The Boogey Man," Laurie says, to which Loomis replies, "As a matter of fact, it was." When the doctor looks over the balcony, Michael is not there.

Carpenter's frightening and influential slasher film, along with *Friday the 13th* (1980), is often credited as initiating the run of slasher films in the early '80s. The character Sam Loomis is named after a character from Alfred Hitchcock's *Psycho* (1960). Look for *The Thing from Another World* (1951) shown on the television; Carpenter directed the remake *The Thing* in 1982. The arm and hand of young Michael Myers at the beginning of the film belong to producer–co-writer Debra Hill. The mask worn by Michael is reportedly a William Shatner mask, spray-painted white and with the eyes and hair altered. Co-editor Tommy Lee Wallace went on to direct the Michael Myers–less series entry *Halloween III: Season of the Witch* (1983).

Halloween II (1981)

Written by Debra Hill and John Carpenter; Directed by Rick Rosenthal; Universal Pictures/De Laurentiis; 93 min.

Cast: Jamie Lee Curtis (Laurie Strode); Donald Pleasence (Doctor Sam Loomis); Charles Cyphers (Leigh Brackett); Lance Guest (Jimmy); Pamela Susan Shoop (Karen); Hunter von Leer (Gary Hunt); Tawny Moyer (Jill); Ana Alicia (Janet); Nancy Stephens (Marion); Gloria Gifford (Mrs. Alves); Leo Rossi (Budd); Ford Rainey (Doctor Mixter); Jeffrey Kramer (Graham); Dick Warlock (The Shape); Cliff

Emmich (Mr. Garrett); John Zenda (Marshall); Catherine Bergstrom (Producer); Alan Haufrect (Announcer); Lucille Benson (Mrs. Elrod); Howard Culver (Man in Pajamas); Dana Carvey (Assistant); Bill Warlock (Craig); Jonathan Prince (Randy); Leigh French (Gary's Mother); Ty Mitchell (Young Gary); Nancy Loomis (Annie); Pamela McMyler (Laurie's Mother); Dennis Holahan (Laurie's Father); Nichole Drucker (Young Laurie); Ken Smolka, Roger Hampton, Dick Warlock (Patrolmen); Adam Gunn (Young Michael); Robin Coleman (Medic); Jack Verbois (Bennett Tramer); Tony Moran (Michael Myers, Age 23); Kyle Richards (Lindsey); Brian Andrews (Tommy); Anne Bruner (Alice)

Crew: Debra Hill, John Carpenter (Producers); John Carpenter, Alan Howarth (Composers); Dean Cundey (Director of Photography); Skip Schoolnik, Mark Goldblatt (Editors)

The film begins the same night as the previous film ended. Michael Myers has walked away after being shot six times and falling from the second floor. Doctor Loomis jumps into the car with Sheriff Brackett ("He's not human!"), and Michael heads to a house and steals a knife from an elderly couple. He goes next door, where a girl is on the phone discussing the news on the radio. She hears some noise, checks it out and is killed.

Back at the initial crime scene, Laurie is put into an ambulance and taken to a hospital. Jimmy, one of the paramedics, apparently knows Laurie. "Don't put me to sleep," Laurie pleads from the gurney. Loomis and Brackett are circling the block with a spotlight. Loomis sees someone with a mask similar to Michael's. He follows the man, but the evasive person walks into the street, where he is hit by a cop car. The car smashes into another vehicle, creating an explosion and incinerating the person. Now Loomis cannot be sure whether it was Michael. A cop arrives and tells Brackett about three bodies discovered. At the scene, Brackett finds his daughter Annie dead, and he curses Loomis. Loomis says he wants to make sure the body is Michael.

Meanwhile, the still-living Michael enters the hospital. Jimmy tells Laurie that it was Michael Myers who was after her. The head nurse, Mrs. Alves, realizes that the phones are out. Mr. Garrett, the security guard, hands Nurse Janet a radio and says he is going to check outside. He later tells her on the radio that someone has broken into the store room and that Janet needs to call the sheriff, but the nurse only hears static on her end. Soon Garrett is killed by Michael. At the coroner's office, Loomis still cannot be sure the body is Michael, but he convinces the police to continue with the presumption that Michael is still alive. At the Myers home, where a riot has ensued, two boys tell a police officer that they are worried about their friend, who left a party drunk and wearing a mask.

Laurie has a dream-flashback in which a woman tells her, "I'm not your mother." In the meantime, Budd, another paramedic, wants to head into the therapy room with Karen. While the couple is enjoying the hot tub, Michael turns up the heat. Budd goes to check on it and is murdered. Michael then goes into the room and drowns the nurse in the scorching water. Loomis and the cops investigate the school, which was broken into by someone. Nurse Marion arrives and tells Loomis that he has been ordered back to Smith's Grove by the governor, and that a marshal is waiting to escort him. At the hospital, Jimmy discovers a catatonic Laurie. Janet goes to look for Doctor Mixter, but she finds him in his study with a syringe in his eye. The nurse is killed by Michael. Jimmy goes to look for Mrs. Alves, and nurse Jill is buzzed by someone and leaves Laurie's room. Michael enters the room with a scalpel, but only pillows are on the bed. Laurie is on the lam, and she hides in another room.

Jimmy finds Jill, and tells her, if she cannot find anyone else, to get the sheriff. Jimmy later finds Mrs. Alves with a tube in her arm, and her blood all over the floor. He turns and slips in her blood, knocking himself unconscious. Jill's car will not start, and she sees flat tires on all the cars in the parking lot. The nurse heads back inside, and as soon as she sees Laurie, Michael comes out from the shadows and murders her. Laurie manages to elude Michael and hides inside a car. Marion tells Loomis of a recently unsealed file proving that Laurie is Michael's sister. Loomis now believes Michael is destined to kill Laurie since he has already killed a sister, and the doctor points his gun at the marshal and tells him to turn around. A dazed Jimmy gets into a car—Laurie's hiding place—but passes out.

Loomis, Marion and the marshal reach the hospital and go inside before Laurie is able to scream for help. She runs from Michael, who is now outside, and Laurie is let inside by the marshal. Michael bursts through the glass door and is shot by Loomis. Marion runs to call the cops, and the marshal gets too close to Michael. Loomis and Laurie run into another room, and Loomis hands Laurie a weapon. Eventually she fires two shots into Michael's eyes and blinds him. He responds by swinging the scalpel wildly. Laurie and Loomis turn on the gas in the room, and Laurie runs out, leaving Loomis to flick his lighter and the room to explode. Michael walks out engulfed in flames but falls down after only a few feet. Laurie is taken away in another ambulance.

Although borrowing some John Carpenter techniques, Rosenthal generates suspenseful moments and keeps the film moving at a dynamic pace, making *Halloween II* a worthy successor to the original. Actor-comedian Dana Carvey made his film debut in a minor role. Jamie Lee Curtis had to wear a wig so that her hairstyle would resemble the 1978 version. Co-editor Skip Schoolnik went on to direct the slasher *Hide and Go Shriek* (1988).

Halloween 4: The Return of Michael Myers (1988)

Written by Alan B. McElroy; Directed by Dwight H. Little; Trancas International Films, Inc.; 88 min.

Cast: Donald Pleasence (Doctor Loomis); Ellie Cornell (Rachel Carruthers); Danielle Harris (Jamie Lloyd); Michael Pataki (Doctor Hoffman); Beau Starr (Sheriff Meeker); Kathleen Kinmont (Kelly); Sasha Jenson (Brady); Gene Ross (Earl); Carmen Filpi (Jack Sayer); Raymond O'Connor (Security Guard); Jeff Olson (Richard Carruthers); Karen Alston (Darlene Carruthers); Nancy Borgenicht (Woman Attendant); David Jensen (Man Attendant); Rand Kennedy, Don Glover, Robert Conder, Richard Jewkes (Troopers); Jordan Bradley (Boy); Stephanie Dees (Girl); Leslie L. Rohland (Lindsey); M.J. McDonnell (Female Staffer); Harlow Marks (Power Worker); Richard Stay (Wade); Danny Ray (Tommy); Michael Flynn (Deputy Pierce); Beverly Booth Rowland (Elderly Woman); George Sullivan (Logan); Ron Harrison (Hick Kid); Tami Sanders (Anchorwoman); Walt Logan Field (Unger); Michael Ruud (Big Al); Eric Hart (Orrin); Donré Sampson (State Policeman)

Crew: Moustapha Akkad (Executive Producer); Paul Freeman (Producer); M. Sanousi (Associate Producer); Alan Howarth (Composer); Peter Lyons Collister (Director of Photography); Curtiss Clayton (Editor)

On October 30, 1988, an ambulance drives to the Ridgemont Federal Sanitarium to transfer patient Michael Myers to Smith's Grove. The medical administrator, Doctor Hoffman, tells the male attendant he hope's that, now that Michael is gone, Doctor Loomis will transfer, retire or die. They roll Michael to the ambulance, and the man and a female attendant sit in the back. The man mentions Michael's niece in Haddonfield, and Michael (with his face wrapped in bandages) grabs the man's face and presses his thumb in his forehead.

Jamie Lloyd is up at night watching the rain until her foster sister Rachel takes her back to bed. Jamie looks at a photograph of her deceased mother Laurie and cries, and she has a nightmare in which Michael is after her. The next morning, the babysitter cancels for that night, and Darlene asks her daughter to watch Jamie. Rachel, despite having to cancel or postpone a date, agrees to do so. Loomis goes to see Hoffman, angry that he was not told about Michael's transfer. They respond to a call of the accident, and Loomis looks inside the wrecked, bloody ambulance ("He's gone") and then leaves to find Michael. Loomis drives the car to a gas station, fills up and goes inside to find a dead mechanic. He runs to the adjacent diner and sees a dead person and the phone crushed. Michael is there, and Loomis tells him to leave the people of Haddonfield in peace. He fires his gun but Michael is gone. Outside, Michael crashes a tow truck through the garage and hits the gas tanks. Loomis' car explodes.

Jamie is mocked at school for her Boogey Man uncle and her dead mother, and she runs out to meet Rachel. Jamie now wants to go trick-or-treating like the other children, and she and Rachel go to the discount mart to get a costume. Rachel greets Brady there, they kiss and she says she has to watch Jamie. Michael (who parked his tow truck outside) picks up his mask in the costume aisle. Jamie has selected a clown costume, and she looks in the mirror and imagines a boy in the costume with a bloody knife. She backs away and is scared by Michael and screams. When Rachel runs to her, Jamie says, "It was the Nightmare Man." Loomis hitches a ride with a reverend who looks like a wino and says he is looking for armageddon. Jamie's foster parents leave, and Rachel calls Brady and is told he is not back from work yet. The two leave for trick-or-treating. Michael is in the house, looking through photographs.

Loomis goes to the station and meets Sheriff Meeker. He says Michael is after his niece, and that the doctor has seen dead bodies on the way. Deputy Pierce gets on the phone to check it out but the lines are down. The sheriff and Loomis go to find Jamie. Jamie and Rachel trick-or-treat at the sheriff's house, and Kelly answers. Rachel sees Brady by the staircase. Brady follows her to the sidewalk, trying to give an excuse, and Jamie leaves with other trick-or-treaters as the couple argues. Rachel walks away from Brady angrily and is frightened when realizing that Jamie is gone. Earl, the bar owner, hears a story on the news about people getting off the streets and businesses shutting down. He calls the police station ("Just rings"), and then he and some of the drinkers leave to see what is going on. Meeker and Loomis find a dead dog at the Carruthers' house ("He's been here"), and the sheriff tells Officer Logan to stay in case the girls return. Michael visits the power grid and throws a power worker against a box to electrocute him and knock some of the power out.

Jamie and Rachel are looking for one another. After Rachel runs from an approaching figure, she finds her foster sister. The sheriff and Loomis pull up, and they get the two girls in the car. They see Michael standing nearby, and then two more appear, but they all turn out to be three punks in masks. At the station, they find a mess of dead cops, and Meeker asks Loomis what they are dealing with: "Evil." Earl and the others arrive, and the doctor tells them that it is Michael on the loose, and they leave to "fry his ass." Logan leaves the Carruthers' to meet at the sheriff's house (with Michael in the back seat), and the parents return home looking for Jamie and Rachel. Earl and his pals inadvertently shoot and kill Ted, a man they know. Brady and Kelly are interrupted during some special time when Meeker pulls in the driveway. Rachel eyes Brady, and the sheriff tells the people to lock everything and gives Brady a shotgun and tells him to secure the attic.

Logan sits by the front door; the sheriff tells him it is the only way in or out and gives him the key. Meeker gets on a radio and calls for help, and he finally gets through and is told to wait for more information. Loomis asks if Jamie is okay, then leaves for the Carruthers' residence to find Michael. The sheriff hears about the lynch mob killing Ted, he tells Rachel to wait by the radio and he leaves to stop Earl and his buddies. Kelly brings Logan some coffee and talks to him but he does not reply. She lights a candle and sees Logan dead. Michael stands by the chair and impales Kelly with the shotgun. Rachel hears that more troopers are on the way, and she goes to tell Logan and finds the officer and

Kelly dead. She runs upstairs and Jamie is not in the room. Brady fires at the metal deadbolt and says that they are trapped. Rachel sees Jamie upstairs, and she and Brady head up, as Michael approaches. Brady tries to reload in time, but he and Michael struggle until Brady's neck is crushed.

Rachel breaks the window in the attic and she and Jamie climb out onto the roof. Rachel ties a cable around Jamie and lowers her. Michael attacks, and Rachel slides and falls to the ground. Jamie cries over her fallen sister and runs when she sees Michael. Jamie finds Loomis and they run to the school and get inside. The doctor is thrown through a door. Michael comes after his niece, and Rachel hits him with a fire extinguisher. Earl and his cronies are outside; agreeing to let the troopers handle Michael, they drive the girls away. Michael climbs onto the truck bed, stabs and throws off two men, and pushes a third man out. He grabs the driving Earl's neck and rips it. Rachel pushes the dead man out and takes control of the wheel. She slams on the brakes and Michael rolls off, and then she rams him with the truck.

Rachel goes to meet the cops, and Jamie walks over to Michael and touches his hand. She is told to get down, and she complies, as the sheriff and other cops fire multiple times, and Michael falls into a hole. Jamie and Rachel return home to their parents, and Darlene goes to take a bath. Jamie puts on her mask and stabs her foster mother with a pair of scissors. Loomis sees Jamie at the top of the stairs with the bloody scissors, and Meeker stops the doctor from shooting her, as the others stare in awe.

Halloween 4 is a decent sequel, but, despite good performances, it seems more like a stand-alone episode, since it does not really further the story of Michael Myers. The movie was the film debut of Danielle Harris, who steals the film with a wonderful performance as Jamie.

Halloween 5: The Revenge of Michael Myers (1989)

Written by Michael Jacobs, Shem Bitterman and Dominique Othenin-Girard; Directed by Dominique Othenin-Girard; Trancas International Films, Inc./Magnum Pictures, Inc.; 96 min.

Cast: Donald Pleasence (Doctor Loomis); Danielle Harris (Jamie); Ellie Cornell (Rachel); Beau Starr (Meeker); Wendy Kaplan (Tina); Donald L. Shanks (Michael Myers); Jeffrey Landman (Billy); Tamara Glynn (Samantha); Jonathan Chapin (Mike); Matthew Walker (Spitz); Betty Carvalho (Nurse Patsey); Troy Evans (Charlie); Frank Como (Deputy Nick); David Ursin (Deputy Tom); Karen Alston (Stepmother); Max Robinson (Doctor Hart); Stanton Davis (Young Policeman); Jack North (Gardener); Russ McGinn (The Announcer); Jon Richard Platten (Cop at Pageant); Jay Bernard (Tall Policeman); Angela Montoya (Little Girl); Patrick White (Mole Man); Steve Anderson (Cop in Field); Fenton Quinn (Eddy); Frank Kanig, Donre Sampson (Troopers); John Gilbert (Fat Sniper); Tom Jacobsen (Jail Cop)

Crew: Moustapha Akkad (Executive Producer); Ramsey Thomas (Producer); Alan Howarth (Composer); Robert Draper (Director of Photography); Charles Teoni (Editor)

Following the events of the previous film, Michael falls down a hole and crawls through a shaft as the officers drop an explosive down. Michael makes it to a creek and floats until he reaches a rundown place that belongs to an old man. Michael grabs the man, and then falls to the ground.

One year later, on Halloween Eve, Jamie is in the Haddonfield Children's Clinic, having a nightmare about stabbing her foster mother, and Nurse Patsey runs in to console her. The nurse goes to get the doctor, and the mute Jamie, in a trance, scribbles "He's coming for me" on a tiny chalkboard. As Michael kills the old man, Jamie convulses. She is rolled onto a stretcher, and a doctor goes for her throat with a scalpel (to open her trachea). Loomis stops him, saying she will "stabilize." ("She has something to tell us.") The next day, Rachel is with Jamie in her room, and Tina comes by with Max the dog and a princess costume for Jamie. Loomis is also there. A rock is thrown through the window with a note: "The evil child *must* die!"

Rachel goes home, and Max barks at moving bushes (with Michael in them). In class, Jamie is frightened, and she draws a picture on the wall and mouths "Max" to Billy. Loomis is there, and he telephones Rachel to make sure Max is okay. Rachel goes downstairs, the door is open and Max is gone. Loomis tells her to get outside and go for help. The cops check the house and find nothing, and Max comes running down the sidewalk. Rachel calls Jamie, and Loomis tells Jamie that Rachel is fine. He tries to get the girl to write what she knows, but she is too upset. Rachel hears Max barking again, and she sees that he is outside barking at the house. She looks around, finds a broken frame with a picture of Jamie and is stabbed by Michael with a pair of scissors as Jamie has another seizure.

Tina arrives at the house and opens the door with the key atop the frame. She looks around for Rachel, and her friend Sammy shows up. Tina and Sammy are walking to the clinic to see Jamie, but they go instead with Tina's boyfriend Mike. Jamie thinks she sees Michael outside, and she runs out of her room and to the boiler room, where she is scared by the gardener. Nurse Patsey leads her away. Loomis goes to see Jamie and says he needs her help to find Michael. He says the coffin of a nine-year-old girl was dug up at the cemetery, and the nurse tells him to leave Jamie alone. A bus arrives in town, and a man in black exits. Loomis looks for Michael at his house. Tina, Sammy and Mike go to see Spitz at the store where he works, and Mike drives the car around back so he and Spitz can load the cases of beer. While waiting alone, Mike sees Michael scratch his freshly waxed car with a garden fork. When he confronts Michael, he gets a garden fork in the forehead.

At a Halloween costume party, Jamie is backstage with Billy, and he gives her flowers and a bracelet for good luck. Michael shows up in Mike's car to pick up Tina (Michael is wearing the mask that Tina gave her boyfriend). During the pageant, Jamie falls back and screams. Tina tells Michael/Mike to stop for some cigarettes, and a convulsing Jamie manages to describe (with Billy's help) the gas station where Tina is. Michael switches masks as he waits in the car, and many policeman arrive to pick Tina up. Tina goes to tell Mike, but the car is gone. She is taken to see Jamie, and they hug. Jamie pleads with Tina not to leave, but she does, despite Loomis' warning that he and Jamie believe she is in danger. The doctor tells two cops to follow her, and they give her a ride to the tower farm.

The man in black is outside, and Nurse Patsey tells Loomis that Jamie is gone. Jamie meets Billy, who says he knows where Tina went. The cops are waiting outside in their car, and Spitz, Sammy and Tina play a joke on them (with Spitz dressed as Michael). The three go to a barn to play with some kittens, and Tina leaves the two alone. Spitz and Sammy kiss a bit and seem to be enjoying themselves until Michael shoves a pitchfork through the back of Spitz. Sammy pulls out the pitchfork and attacks Michael, but he grabs the weapon and swings a scythe her way. The two cops see Michael outside with the pitchfork and call him over to the car. The people are leaving the party, but Tina stays for her two friends. Tina goes to the barn and finds a dead Sammy and Spitz, and she runs for help and sees the two dead cops. Jamie and Billy arrive, and Michael (in Mike's car) begins chasing the group until he slams into a tree. He gets out with a knife and heads for Jamie. Tina stops him and is killed, and the cops are there. Jamie cries as she sees Tina being carried away, and Loomis asks her if she is willing to help.

Loomis goes to the trees and yells to Michael that he and Jamie will be waiting at the house. Jamie sits in a room with a number of policeman surrounding the place. Jamie reacts to something ("Billy?"). The cop in the room, Charlie, gets Loomis. Loomis tells the cops that Michael is at the clinic, and cop cars drive away. The sheriff says to take Jamie to the station. Loomis goes to the room, locks the door and tells Charlie that he is not taking Jamie anywhere. Charlie's partner Eddy calls in about an approaching car, and they hear Eddy being beaten over the radio. Loomis pulls a gun on Charlie, says that Michael is outside and tells him to stay with Jamie. Loomis leaves, and Charlie barricades the door.

Loomis meets Michael downstairs and says he knows he wants Jamie so that he can "stop the rage." He goes for the knife, and Michael swipes and throws him. Charlie drops a rope ladder out the window, and Michael bursts through the door, hits Charlie and tosses him outside with the ladder around his neck. Jamie climbs into a laundry chute and hangs. Michael opens the door and tries to grab her, and Jamie falls down the chute. In the cellar, Michael tries to get the door open, and he stabs through the metal as Jamie slowly climbs up to the door and crawls out. Jamie reaches a room of candles and finds a dead Max and Rachel. When Michael is in the room, she lies inside the open coffin. Michael lifts the knife, and Jamie says, "Uncle… Boogey Man… Let me see." Michael takes off his mask ("You're just like me"), and as a tear falls from his eye, Jamie reaches for him. He jumps back, puts the mask on, and Jamie runs.

Loomis grabs Jamie ("You want her, here she is") and leads Michael into a room, where he drops a chain net on him and shoots him with a tranquilizer gun. Michael keeps moving, and Loomis pulls a board from the window and beats him until he collapses atop Michael. At the station, Michael is in a cell, and an officer goes to take Jamie back to the clinic. The man in black has entered the station, and there is an explosion and gunfire. The cop goes inside, and Jamie follows, walking by dead cops. Michael's cell down is open, and he is gone ("No!").

Halloween 5 is another weak sequel, with a number of dull stalking scenes and few scares. However, the mysterious man in black is an intriguing addition, and Pleasence and Harris provide another set of excellent and enjoyable performances.

Halloween: The Curse of Michael Myers (1996)

Written by Daniel Farrands; Directed by Joe Chapelle; Dimension Films/Miramax Films/Nightfall Productions; 88 min.

Cast: Donald Pleasence (Doctor Loomis); Paul Stephen Rudd (Tommy Doyle); Marianne Hagan (Kara Strode); Mitchell Ryan (Doctor Wynn); Kim Darby (Debra Strode); Bradford English (John Strode); Keith Bogart (Tim Strode); Mariah O'Brien (Beth); Leo Geter (Barry Simms); J.C. Brandy (Jamie Lloyd); Devin Gardner (Danny Strode); Susan Swift (Mary); George P. Wilbur (The Shape); Janice Knickrehm (Mrs. Blankenship); Alan Echeverria (Doctor Bonham); Hildur Ruriks (Dawn); Sheri Hicks (Paramedic); Tom Proctor (Motorist); Bryan Morris (Attendant); Lee Ju Chew (Nurse); Raquelle Anderson (Ballerina); Kristine Summers (College Coed); Elyse Donalson (Lunatic); A. Michael Lerner (Additional Shape)

Crew: Moustapha Akkad (Executive Producer); Malek Akkad (Associate Producer); Paul Freeman (Producer); Alan Howarth (Composer); Billy Dickson (Director of Photography); Randolph K. Bricker (Editor)

A screaming woman is rolled down a hallway. She is pregnant, and she gives birth. A person in black takes the baby away, ignoring the pleading woman. A man's voice says that six years ago, on Halloween night, Michael Myers and Jamie Lloyd disappeared. The man believes the two have been hidden away by someone who tries to control and protect Michael. A nurse runs into the room with the woman, hands her the baby and leads her away. The new mother, Jamie, runs down the hallway, with Michael, having just killed the nurse, in pursuit. Jamie gets into a truck and drives away. Inside a dark room, a voice says, "Danny, kill for him," and a man in black is standing with a knife. The young Danny calls for his mother, Kara, and she consoles him and says goodnight. On the radio, Barry Simms is discussing Michael. Haddonfield has banned Halloween since 1989. Kara is in her bedroom, and she sees a man watching her from another house. That man is on the phone with Barry, telling him he will be ready for Michael.

Doctor Sam Loomis is at home, typing and listening to the radio. His friend, Doctor Wynn, is at the door, and he asks Loomis to come back to Smith's Grove. The radio show receives a call from Jamie, from a pay phone at a bus station, and she tells him that Michael is coming. She then says, "Doctor Loomis, are you out there?" and Loomis hears her. Jamie's call is cut off. When she is in the bathroom with her baby, the lights go out. She gets outside and back in the truck, but now Michael is right behind her in a van. She is run off the road, and she takes refuge in a barn. Michael finds her and attacks. Jamie says, "You can't have the baby, Michael," and he kills her. Back at the truck, the baby is not there.

The next morning, Kara deals with her unmannerly father, John, and then leaves with her brother Tim and his girlfriend Beth. At Smith's Grove, Loomis insists that it was Jamie on the radio the night before. Doctor Wynn's secretary tells the two that Jamie's body was discovered. The weird man from earlier plays back a recording of Jamie's phone call and hears an announcement in the background. He goes to the bus station and finds a trail of blood that leads to the restroom. Then he hears a baby crying, and inside a cabinet is the infant. He takes the baby and leaves.

In the barn, Loomis sees a rune burned unto the haystack. ("It's his mark. He's come home.") The weird guy meets Loomis at the hospital and tells him that he is Tommy Doyle, who Laurie had babysat for during Michael's 1978 killing spree. He says that the baby belongs to Jamie, and that relatives of the Strodes are living in the Myers house. Loomis heads to the house and meets Kara's mother, Debra. He tells her that he is there to help her family. He tells her about Michael, and in Loomis' subtle way, describes how some "pure evil" had "contaminated his soul."

Danny is walking around and sees the man in black standing by the van, and he is frightened by Tommy. Debra calls John and tells her about Michael and the house's shady history, but John does not seem to care. Afterwards, she receives a phone call from the "Voice Man" (as Danny calls him), who tells her, "We want the child." Michael appears and gets blood all over Debra's white sheets. Kara comes home, and her mother is not there. She finds Tommy and Danny sitting in a room together. Tommy convinces Kara to go to his room, and he tells her about Michael and Michael's rune (which Danny had drawn earlier). It is Thorn, a demon that brought sickness and death. One child from each tribe would be inflicted with the curse of Thorn to offer a blood sacrifice; sacrificing one family would spare the lives of the whole tribe. Jamie's baby is Michael's final sacrifice.

Doctors tell Loomis and Wynn that Jamie had recently given birth before her death. Danny talks to Mrs. Blankenship, who runs the boarding house where Tommy stays, and she tells the boy that she babysat for Michael. She says that a voice told Michael to kill his family. Meanwhile, John comes home drunk and is killed by Michael. Tim and Beth are at a fair, on a stage and talking to Barry Simms (doing his radio show from Haddonfield). Beth tells him that Tim lives in Michael's house, and Barry says that he wants to do the show live from there. Barry gets on the phone, heads for his van and is whacked by Michael. Tim and Beth are back at home, and they go up to Tim's room for some quality time. Back at the fair, Tommy watches as a dead Barry falls from a tree. Loomis is there, wanting to know where the baby is.

From Tommy's room, Kara sees a light on at the house. Tim comes out of the shower and asks for a towel, but Michael kills him instead. Kara calls Beth to tell them to get out, but she is too late, as she watches

Michael kill Beth. Danny hears the Voice Man, and he heads over to the Myers home. Kara sees him, grabs a fire poker and follows her son. She and Danny are attacked by Michael, but they get away and get back to Tommy's place. Tommy and Loomis are there, but the baby is gone. The Voice Man says, "Danny, come to me." Danny obeys, and the rest follow him.

The man in black is in the other room, and he reveals himself to be Doctor Wynn. Other men in black come out and restrain Tommy and Loomis. After being drugged and left behind, Tommy and the doctor go to the sanitarium to save Kara, Danny and the baby. Loomis goes to see Wynn in his office and holds a gun on him ("You are a madman," he tells the man in black). Loomis is knocked out by a henchman. Tommy manages to get Kara out of a room before a slowly approaching Michael can reach them. He and Kara see Wynn and other doctors in an operating room with the infant and Danny. An angry Michael gets a blade and starts hacking everyone in the operating room. Tommy and Kara get the children and run. Michael follows them, and the two are able to keep him away from the children by drugging him with multiple syringes and continually beating him with metal pipes. He is finally left on the floor, drugged and beaten.

Loomis and the others get away and outside. Tommy wants Loomis to go with them, but the doctor says he has "a little business to attend to." Tommy, Kara, Danny and the baby drive away as Loomis goes back inside the hospital. On the floor there is only a mask. An unseen Loomis screams for an unknown reason.

Halloween: The Curse of Michael Myers is a decent sequel, although it certainly does not add anything to the series, aside from a weak story to explain Michael's origin. An alternate cut of the sixth installment surfaced (most commonly referred to as the "Producer's Cut"); it includes many different scenes and alternate takes. Additionally, in the "Producer's Cut," Jamie lives through Michael's attack and ends up in the hospital, where she spends half the movie before being shot and killed by the man in black. The film's ending is also different, with a transferral of the "mark," and essentially explaining why Loomis was screaming. The sixth *Halloween* was the great Donald Pleasence's last film.

Halloween: H20 (1998)

Written by Robert Zappia and Matt Greenberg; Directed by Steve Miner; Dimension Films/Nightfall Productions; 86 min.

Cast: Jamie Lee Curtis (Laurie Strode/Keri Tate); Adam Arkin (Will Brennan); Michelle Williams (Molly); Adam Hann-Byrd (Charlie); Jodi Lyn O'Keefe (Sarah); Janet Leigh (Norma); Josh Hartnett (John); L.L. Cool J (Ronny); Joseph Gordon-Levitt (Jimmy); Branden Williams (Tony); Nancy Stephens (Marion); Beau Billingslea (Fitz); Matt Winston (Matt); Larisa Miller (Claudia); Emmalee Thompson (Casey); David Blanchard (Waiter); John Cassini, Jody Wood (Cops); Lisa Gay Hamilton (Shirl); Chris Durand (Michael); Tom Kane (Voice Over)

Crew: Moustapha Akkad (Executive Producer); Bob Weinstein, Harvey Weinstein, Kevin Williamson (Co-Executive Producers); Paul Freeman (Producer); Malek Akkad (Associate Producer); John Ottman (Composer); Marco Beltrami (Additional Music); Daryn Okada (Director of Photography); Patrick Lussier (Editor)

In Langdon, Illinois, two days before Halloween, Nurse Marion returns home to find her porch light broken and her door ajar. She goes next door and tells Jimmy and Tony that someone has been in her house. They call the police, and Jimmy goes to check the place out while Marion and Tony wait outside. He finds the office trashed, takes a couple of bottles of beer out of the refrigerator and leaves, telling Marion it is okay. Marion goes inside (the lights do not work); in the office, she sees that Laurie Strode's folder is empty. The front door creaks open, and she sees the back door is open. Marion runs to her neighbor's house again and finds Jimmy dead with an ice skate in his face. Tony is dead at the door, and Michael walks inside, taking a knife from the kitchen. Marion is attacked as the cops arrive at her place and her throat is slit. The cops check next door, and Michael drives away. At the scene, two cops talk of Marion's obsession with Michael (newspaper articles are everywhere). One cop says that Michael's body was never found, and an article says that Laurie died in an automobile accident.

Laurie awakens from a nightmare in which her name is written on the chalkboard (she is living under the name Teri Kate). Her son John runs inside and gets her pills from the cabinet. It is Halloween in Summer Glen, California, and Laurie and John discuss the upcoming camping trip at Yosemite. Laurie tells John that he is not going on the trip. John tells the news to his friends Charlie and Sarah, and they learn that John's girlfriend Molly is likewise not going to Yosemite. Charlie suggests the four friends have a Halloween party. Casey and her mother stop at a rest area (Michael's stolen car is nearby). Because the women's bathroom door is locked, they go to the men's bathroom. While sitting in the stall, Casey's mother sees Michael enter and take her purse. She runs out when Casey screams ("Spiders!"). Michael discards the purse and drives away in the woman's vehicle.

Charlie and Sarah get out of the Yosemite trip, and Will Brennan visits Laurie in her office, where they kiss. Ronny, the security guard, reads some of his novel to his girlfriend over the phone. John and Charlie beg him to let them out of the gate, and he finally agrees. Laurie and Will sit and talk in a café, and Laurie refers to a "back story" that she has not told him. He leaves for a moment, and she chugs some chardonnay. Charlie steals some alcohol, and Laurie sees them both out of school. She tells Charlie to wait in the car, and she yells at her son for doing something stupid on Halloween. John tells her that Michael is dead and that she told him she "watched him burn." Laurie drives the boy back, and Michael follows them.

Molly meets John in the basement, and he tells her he has never celebrated Halloween due to a "psychotic serial killer in the family." After class, Laurie gives John a permission slip for Yosemite, and later she watches the buses leave. Her secretary Norma tells her "Happy Halloween!"

Ronny is still reading to his girlfriend when he sees Michael's vehicle by the gate. He opens the gate and looks in the car, and Michael walks behind him and through the gate. Laurie leaves her office and goes outside, where she thinks she sees Michael approaching. She closes and opens her eyes a few times, and Michael still gets closer, until Will scares her. The group crawls through a building window, and Laurie has some vodka and mouthwash before Will shows up. At the party of candles and music, Charlie leaves to get a corkscrew. Laurie tells Will her real name and that her brother Michael killed her sister and tried to kill her. She says she faked her death and went into hiding. Laurie suddenly realizes that John is 17 (the age of both her and her sister when Michael was murderous), and she gets on the phone to find it dead. She sees John's camping gear still in his closet, and she gets her gun from under the pillow. Ronny tells Laurie and Will that there was a strange car at the gate.

Sarah finds Charlie in the kitchen, and he gets in the dumbwaiter to find a corkscrew upstairs. He finally gets one and turns to see Michael. Sarah goes to the dumbwaiter and finds Charlie with a slit throat. Sarah gets in the dumbwaiter as Michael appears with a knife, and he slices her leg before she gets the door shut. She tries to crawl out upstairs, Michael cuts the rope, and the dumbwaiter falls and breaks Sarah's leg. Michael stabs Sarah as she tries to crawl away. John and Molly go to check on a noise (the dumbwaiter crash), and they find Sarah hanging on the light. They get out of a window, and Michael grabs Molly outside. In a struggle, John is stabbed in the leg, and Molly hits Michael with a rock. They get inside a gate, Molly drops her keys and Michael picks them up. They bang on a door until Laurie and Will finally let them in, and Laurie stares at Michael through the glass window on the door. She reaches for her gun, but Michael is gone. Will asks who the person was, and Laurie says, "My brother."

John and Molly hide, and Will sees a figure approaching, grabs the gun and shoots, hitting Ronny. Michael appears, stabs Will in the back and goes after Laurie. Laurie hits him with a fire extinguisher and then gets the two kids out from hiding; they all run to her truck. They drive to the gate, where Laurie gets out, opens the gate and tells them to go get help. Molly drives, and Laurie shuts the gate and destroys the gate's control panel. When Michael shows up, she axes his chest, and he cuts her arm. Laurie runs and hides in a room full of tables and eventually stabs Michael with a flagpole. She runs to the kitchen and throws knives at her brother. Laurie runs and hides, and she jumps out at Michael with two knives and stabs him until he falls over the balcony and lands on a table with one knife still in his chest. Laurie goes downstairs to stab him some more, but Ronny stops her ("He's dead").

The cops are at the scene, and Michael is rolled in a body bag. Laurie grabs a gun and, also holding her axe, steals the coroner's van with Michael inside. She drives and checks the rearview mirror until she sees Michael moving. He climbs out of his body bag, and goes for Laurie. She slams on the brakes, causing her brother to fly through the windshield. She waits until he stands, and she rams him, goes over a cliff and flies out. Laurie picks up the axe and walks to where Michael is pinned between a fallen tree and the van. She says his name, and he looks up and holds out his hand. Laurie reaches out, and their hands nearly touch, and Laurie swings the axe and decapitates her brother.

Halloween: H20 is one of the weakest entries in the *Halloween* series, due to a desire to replicate the recent overabundance of yuppie and perfunctorily self-reflexive slashers. (Kevin Williamson, writer of the *Scream* movies and *I Know What You Did Last Summer* [1997], was one of the producers; look for *Scream 2* [1997] on the television.) There are a number of amusing references to Hitchcock's 1960 classic *Psycho* (listen for Bernard Herrmann's score lightly played as actress Leigh walks to her familiar car).

Happy Birthday to Me (1981)

Written by John Saxton, Peter Jobin and Timothy Bond; Directed by J. Lee Thompson; Columbia Pictures/Famous Players/The Canadian Film Development Corporation; 110 min.

Cast: Melissa Sue Anderson (Virginia); Glenn Ford (Doctor Faraday); Lawrence Dane (Hal Wainwright); Sharon Acker (Estelle); France Hyland (Mrs. Patterson); Tracy Bregman (Ann); Jack Blum (Alfred); Matt Craven (Steve); Lenore Zann (Maggie); David Eisner (Rudi); Michel-René Labelle (Etienne); Richard Rebiere (Greg Hellman); Lesleh Donaldson (Bernadette O'Hara); Lisa Langlois (Amelia)

Crew: John Dunning, Andre Link (Producers); Bo Harwood, Lance Rubin (Composers); Miklos Lente, C.S.C. (Director of Photography); Debra Karen (Editor)

On the Crawford Academy campus, Bernadette is leaving to meet her friends. After an encounter with the authoritarian Mrs. Patterson, she gets into her car, but is attacked by someone with gloved hands. She momentarily feigns death and manages to elude the attacker, until she sees someone she apparently knows. ("Thank God. Oh, please help me.") The person slices her with a razor.

At the village's inn a group of students are drinking. Virginia arrives and joins everyone, and soon the Norman Bates–esque taxidermist Alfred is there too. After Rudi angers the local folk (with a prank involving Alfred's pet mouse, George, and someone's cup of beer), the students run outside. Seeing that the bridge is going up, Steve says, "Let's play the game." They all plan to jump the opening bridge. When Virginia, in a car with Greg and Amelia, goes over the bridge,

Hal (Lawrence Dane) is invited to sit with the (dead) guests and enjoy some cake as the birthday girl, Virginia (Melissa Sue Anderson), sings her birthday song in J. Lee Thompson's *Happy Birthday to Me* (1981).

she screams "Mother!" Visibly upset, she demands the car be stopped, and she gets out and runs away. Virginia goes to the cemetery and visits her mother's grave. Another student, Etienne, offers to walk her home, and she declines. At home, Virginia goes to her room to shower and change. When she returns from the bathroom, she sees that the recently shut window is now open. She screams in fright, as Etienne (who Viriginia does not see) jumps down and flees into the night.

The next day in chemistry class, the teacher is shocking a pair of frog legs with static electricity, and Viriginia flashes back to an operating room, where she is lying on a table with her head wrapped up. She later tells her doctor, David Faraday, of the eerie recollection. David tells her that, after being injured in an accident, Virginia had been an experiment (a "very successful guinea pig"). She was able to remember something she had prevously forgotten due to a "regeneration" of her brain cells. David says that she will remember more later.

At a dirt bike race, Virginia and her friends are cheering Etienne, who wins. Being the hopeless romantic that he is, he shows Virginia that he won because he had a pair of her underwear next to his heart. Virginia is obviously angry, as is Albert, watching from afar. That night, as Etienne is cleaning his bike, someone approaches and throws his scarf into the running wheel, which pulls his face closer. Then the person revs up the bike, letting the wheel do the rest. Everyone is together later, awaiting Etienne and Alfred. Viriginia and Ann go to see what "evil deeds little Alfred's been up to." They climb through his window and discover Bernadette's head on a tray. Alfred is suddenly there and he shows the girls that the head is a fake, calling it his "latest masterpiece." The next day, Virginia and Ann are reprimanded by Mrs. Patterson because she does not believe their claims that they do not know the whereabouts of the missing Bernadette and Etienne.

After the group of students view *High Noon*, the uninvited Rudi arrives and starts a fight with Steve, who accompanied Maggie (with whom Rudi had been with). Rudi threatens Greg after Greg pulls him away from Steve. That night, Greg is lifting weights. Someone he evidently knows comes in, and at Greg's request adds more weights. When it is too much, the person refuses to spot Greg, and drops a weight onto his crotch, allowing the heavy barbell to fall and crush his throat.

Viriginia and Rudi go to the bell tower together. Rudi mentions that Viriginia is new, but she tells him she was at the academy four years ago for a few weeks. Rudi talks about cutting the bell's rope and brings out his knife, disturbing Virginia. Later, Virginia is with David, flashing back to when her head was cut open in the operation, and the doctors declared her dead. She tells David about Rudi and the knife, and that she panicked and cannot remember anything. David hears about the discovery of a bloody knife and the possibility of foul play, and he finds Virginia to tell him exactly what happened. Before long, however, Rudi turns up, and a skull found in the garden bed is only a joke. The students are assembled later, and Virginia is unsettled and goes to the cemetery again. She is followed by Alfred, but when he gets close, she turns around and stabs him.

Virginia's father is leaving, but he promises to be back by Sunday, which is Virginia's birthday. At a school party, Virginia invites Steve over to her place. While dining on shish kabob, Virginia is feeding Steve, and she shoves the metal bar into his mouth and kills him. The next morning, Ann arrives and tells Virginia, "I wanna hear all the gory details about you and Steve last night." Virginia says she does not remember anything. As Virginia is showering, she flashes back to a rainy night with her irate mother. As they are on the bridge, it opens, and the car falls into the river below. Virginia manages to get out of the car, but her mother is trapped and she drowns. Virginia awakes to a bathroom flooded with water, and she sees that Ann is dead in the overflowing tub.

David comes to Virginia's house, but Ann's body is no longer there. He stays the night and eludes the cops looking for a missing Ann. He tells Virginia that she has to remember what happened to her. She recalls that her mother wanted Virginia to have a birthday party, but none of the other students showed up because there was a party at Ann's house. Her mother is angry, and she drives over to the house and demands to be let inside. "I can't be bought off again!" she yells from the gate.

Virginia, distressed, runs out of the room, only to return with the fire poker, which she uses to beat David to death. Virginia's father comes home, sees all the blood in the room and runs outside looking for his daughter. After finding David's corpse, the father heads for the cottage, and discovers, all around a table, the bodies of the dead students, along with Virginia's mother. Virginia walks into the room with a birthday cake, singing, "Happy birthday to me." Virginia puts a birthday hat on her father as he sobs, then slices his throat.

Virginia walks over to Ann, lying face down on the table, and lifts up her head. It is actually Virginia at the table. She awakes and struggles with her evil twin (who says "I've done it all for you, sister, dear"). She inadvertently tears off a mask and sees Ann standing there. Ann tells Virginia that she would drug her before each murder and kill the people disguised as Virginia. Virginia's mother was Ann's father's mistress (which means the two really are sisters), and the mother would not let Ann's father ever forget it. Virginia suddenly turns against Ann and eventually stabs her. A police officer walks in as Virginia is standing there with a bloody knife. "Dear God, what have you done?"

Despite the over-the-top ending, *Happy Birthday to Me* is a superb slasher, with a good cast, some great killing sequences and a first-rate performance from Anderson. Anderson gained much popularity from the hit television series *Little House on the Prairie*.

Hatchet for the Honeymoon (aka *Il rosso segno della follia*; *Un'accetta per la luna di miele*; *Blood Brides*; *The Red Mark of Madness*; *The Red Sign of Madness*) (1969)

Written by Santiago Moncada; Directed by Mario Bava; Pan Latina Films/Mercury Films; 88 min.

Cast: Stephen Forsyth (John Harrington); Dagmar Lassander (Helen Wood); Laura Betti (Mildred Harrington); Jesús Puente (Inspector Russell); Femi Benussi (Alice Norton); Antonia Mas (Louise); Alan Collin (Vences); Gérard Tichy (Robert Kane); Verónica Llimer (Betsy); Silvia Lienas (Vicky); Monserrat Riva (Bride on Train); José Ignacio Abadal

Crew: Manuel Caño (Producer); Enzo Ferla (Assistant Producer); Sante Romitelli (Composer); Mario Bava (Director of Photography); Soledad López (Editor)

John Harrington is walking down the corridor on a moving train. He closes his eyes, sees a set of stairs and then sees a little boy reflected in the train's windows. He opens the door to a compartment, where a bride's gown is on a bed and a couple is kissing. A cleaver is brought out, and the woman screams. John sees a series of distorted images, and someone calls his name. He uses the wedding gown to clean his cleaver, puts a "Do Not Disturb" sign on the door and leaves.

John is in the bathroom shaving, and he introduces himself with a voice over, saying that he is "completely mad." He has killed five women and buried three in the hothouse. "I must go on wielding the cleaver. It's most annoying." He "must kill" to find out "the whole truth." John is eating breakfast with Mildred, and he asks her if she thought about what they had discussed. She tells him she will not give him a divorce, and that they will be together until death. Mildred says that all of John's wealth is accredited to her money, despite John inheriting his mother's home and fashion house, both of which his wife claims were in a "mountain of debt." Mildred wants John to accompany her to a seance that night.

Model Helen Wood is waiting in John's office, and she says that her friend Rosie told her about the place. John tells her Rosie left not long ago. John's business, Harrington & Co., specializes in wedding dresses or anything a bride might use on her wedding day. John offers Helen a one-month trial, which the model accepts. Once Helen leaves, John enters through a secret door into a room full of mannequins in wedding gowns. At the seance later, a seemingly possessed Mildred yells out things like "John, behave yourself!" and "Don't be naughty!" John demands the session be stopped. Inspector Russell goes to see John in the hothouse. He asks about the incinerator, which John tells him is for burning leaves. Russell asks about Rosie, and then he says he might be back later ("Just routine").

Another model, Alice, tells John that she will have to quit because she is getting married. John asks her to stay that night after the other women leave. He shows Alice his room of mannequins, and he tells her that the dresses are all the designs created since his mother founded the company. He tells Alice to select a dress as a wedding gift, and while she tries the dress on, John gets his cleaver. Adorned in her dress, Alice dances with John, as he imagines the steps again ("Someone is tiptoeing inside my brain"). His name is called, and John brings out the cleaver. He wants to know why the woman in his mind keeps calling his name, and each time he kills he sees her face more clearly. He murders Alice and puts her in the incinerator.

The next morning at breakfast, Mildred tells John that she is going to see her sickly cousin, so he can pretend he is divorced for a week. John sees Helen at the airport, and the two go to dinner together, where Helen implies she is Rosie's sister and asks what John did with her. He says he killed her, raped her and buried her in the hothouse, and Helen laughs. Later, John and Helen kiss. John goes home and sits to watch some television. He sees a light coming from a room upstairs, and there is Mildred reading in bed. She laughs ("I'm not a ghost, my dear"), and says she will not leave John and will always be at his side. John sits beside her and reminds Mildred that they were once happy, and Mildred agrees. John leaves and returns with his cleaver on a tray as Mildred is composing herself. "I hated these last years with you, and now, finally, it'll be all over." John, with a wedding veil and wearing lipstick, swings his cleaver, and a wounded Mildred starts down the stairs. John follows and kills her. There is loud banging and ringing at his door. He throws off the veil, wipes his mouth and goes to answer the door.

Russell and Alice's fiancé Robert are at the door, demanding to know where Alice is. They say they heard a woman screaming. John takes them to his television set, where a woman is screaming. Russell talks of Alice's disappearance, while blood drips from Mildred's arm and hand and hits the carpet below (Mildred's body is also reflected in the steel table next to John and the inspector). Russell and Robert leave, and the inspector notes that John is sweating on a cold night. As John buries Mildred, the younger version of himself realizes he saw his mother dead, and now he wants to know who killed her. The next day, the maid pours a cup of coffee for Mildred's vacant seat. John asks her why she poured the drink, and she says that his wife asked for it. Throughout the day, people continue to speak to Mildred when John is around, but when John looks, he cannot see his wife. Russell sees John later and says he asked about the movie on TV the night before; there was no screaming before the scene they saw. He says he will trap the murderer with patience.

Later, John goes to his bedroom and calls Mildred's name. She appears and says that she will never leave John and that everyone but John will see her. John digs up Mildred's body, burns her in the incinerator and puts her ashes in a bag. He goes to a bar with the bag, and the waiter asks what "madame" would like. John grabs a passing woman and she resists his advances, saying he has company. He says his wife can watch, the woman smacks him and John is thrown out of the bar. He drops the bag in the river, then returns home to see the drenched bag waiting for him; he throws the ashes around outside. Helen sees John later, and he tells her to leave. John says he has one more step to go and he will know everything. He goes to Betsy's house (earlier she had spoken to John of her wedding), but the cops burst inside. Russell arrives at John's house and asks where he has been, and Helen appears and says that he has been with her all night.

John is dancing with Helen (wearing a wedding dress) in the secret mannequin room. John sees the steps and, as a little boy, he looks through a keyhole and sees his mother with a man. John tells Helen he has to know who did it, and he swings his cleaver at her; then he sees himself as a boy killing his mother with a cleaver. ("I killed my mother. I didn't want her to marry again.") Helen goes to the door and lets the police inside. John is taken away and passes by Helen, and he says she was a "pawn" who was "introduced" by Russell. John is put in a truck and the bag is placed beside him. Mildred is there, and she tells him now only he will see her. John tries to escape, and he sees himself as a little boy.

Mario Bava's *Hatchet for the Honeymoon* (a hatchet is never used) is not the director's best work, but it still entertains with that quirky Bava atmosphere and crisp, colorful visuals. Actor Collin is actually Luciano Pigozzi, who has also appeared in the Bava films *Blood and Black Lace* (1964) and *Baron Blood* (1972). The film on television (which John claims is what the two men heard as screaming) is Bava's own *Black Sabbath* (1963).

Henry: Portrait of a Serial Killer (1986)

Written by Richard Fire and John McNaughton; Directed by John McNaughton; Fourth World Media; 82 min.

Cast: Michael Rooker (Henry); Tracy Arnold (Becky); Tom Towles (Otis); Mary Demas (Dead Woman, Dead Prostitute); Anne Bartoletti (Waitress); Elizabeth Kaden, Ted Kaden (Dead Couple); Denise Sullivan (Floating Woman); Anita Ores, Megan Ores, Cheri Jones (Mall Shoppers); Monica Anna O'Malley (Mall Victim); Bruce Quist (Husband); Erzsebet Sziky (Hitchhiker); David Katz (Henry's Boss); John Scalidi, Benjamin Pressman (Kids With Football); Flo Spink (Woman in Cadillac); Kurt Neebig (High School Jock); Mary Demas, Kristin Finger (Hookers); Lily Monkus (Woman in Beauty Shop); Ray Atherton (Fence); Eric Young (Parole Officer); Rick Paul (Shooting Victim); Peter Van Wagner, Tom McKearn, Frank Coranado (Bums); Lisa Temple, Brian Graham, Sean Ores (Murdered Family); Pamela Fox (Hair Stylist); Waleed B. Ali (Store Clerk); Donna Dunlap (Dog Walker); Augie the Dog (Delores)

Crew: Waleed B. Ali, Malik B. Ali (Executive Producers); John McNaughton, Lisa Dedmond, Steven A. Jones (Producers); Robert McNaughton, Ken Hale, Steven A. Jones (Composers); Charlie Lieberman (Director of Photography); Elena Maganini (Editor)

A bloody dead woman is lying in the grass. Henry finishes his meal and pays the waitress ("Real nice smile you got there"). Two people are dead in a convenience store, and the sounds of their murders can be heard. A woman is dead in a motel room, another is dead in a bathroom, and a woman is lying dead in a creek. Henry sits in a shopping mall parking lot and watches women get into their cars. He follows one woman to her house, but leaves when he sees a man greet her in the driveway. Henry drives on and picks up a guitar-carrying hitchhiker. Otis meets Becky at the airport, and he tells her she looks terrible. In the car, Otis says he knew Leroy was no good before they married. Becky is not sure how long she will be there.

Otis and Becky are at the table when Henry comes back and gives Otis a guitar as a gift. Otis introduces Henry to his sister, and Otis tells Becky that Henry is on his way west. Later, Henry is spraying a kitchen, and his boss tells him that is all the work for a while and to hold onto the spray. Henry drives to the house of the woman he had followed earlier; he still has the tank with him. She lets him inside. Afterwards, the woman is lying dead on the couch with a cord wrapped around her neck. A young boy visits the gas station where Otis works and asks him if he has any of what he had last week. He gives Otis money, and they agree to meet later.

Becky is in the kitchen, and she asks Otis how he met Henry. He tells her they met in prison, and that Henry was inside for killing his mother and one of her friends with a baseball bat. After dinner, Otis leaves, and Becky asks Henry about his father, telling of how her own father raped her. She asks Henry if he killed his mother, and he tells Becky he stabbed her. She would make Henry watch her when she was with men and would beat him when he refused. When Henry then mentions shooting his mother, Becky reminds him that he had told her stabbing; Henry corrects himself.

On another night at the table, Becky tells of her new job at a beauty parlor, and Otis mentions Becky dancing naked and asks when she will dance for them. Otis tells Becky to get him a beer. When she comes back, he pulls her by the arm as if to give her a kiss. Henry grabs Otis' hair ("Don't do that, Otis; she's your sister!"), and he makes Otis apologize and promise not to do it again. Otis seems upset, so Becky suggests the two men go get a beer. Henry and Otis pick up a couple of women; in the back seat, Henry murders one of them. The other woman, in front with Otis, screams, and Otis grabs her, while Henry reaches up and snaps her neck. He pulls the bodies out and leaves them on the street. Otis is unsettled, but Henry pacifies him by getting him something to eat. In a motel room, Henry talks about killing, and Otis seems to agree with Henry's philosophy that it is either "you or them."

At home, Otis is getting bad TV reception and kicks in the screen. He decides that he has to have a television, and he and Henry go see a portly man surrounded by television sets. They discuss different TVs and a $500 video camera before Otis settles on a $50 black-and-white TV. The man is angry that they wasted his time and he is rude towards Henry, who stabs him in the hand and then in the stomach as Otis holds him. Then the two bash the $50 TV over his head and plug it in. Later Otis, Henry and Becky are playing with the video camera.

Otis goes to see his parole officer and later meets the young boy in the parking lot for the dope transaction. Otis touches the boy's leg and receives a punch in the face. Otis, furious, tells Henry he feels like killing someone. Henry and Otis feign car trouble, and Henry lets Otis shot and kill a man who stops to offer help. When out filming with the video camera, Henry advises Otis to kill in different ways so that the police will not find a pattern; he also says it is important to keep moving. The two men head over to a house where Henry films Otis tormenting a woman (her husband is lying on the floor, bound and with a cloth over his head). The son returns home; Henry drops the camera, runs to the boy and snaps his neck. Otis breaks the woman's neck, and Henry stabs the man. Otis fondles and kisses the dead woman, and Henry orders him to stop. Later, the two are watching the video, which Otis rewinds ("I wanna see it again").

Otis and Henry are filming in a car; as Otis leans out, the camera is hit and broken. Otis throws it out the window and the two men argue. Otis says he wants a beer, and Henry makes him get out of the car. Back at the apartment, Becky tells Henry that she quit her job so she and her daughter could go live with her mother, and she asks Henry to go with her. Henry suggests getting a steak dinner so he can try out his new credit card. The couple returns to find Otis passed out on

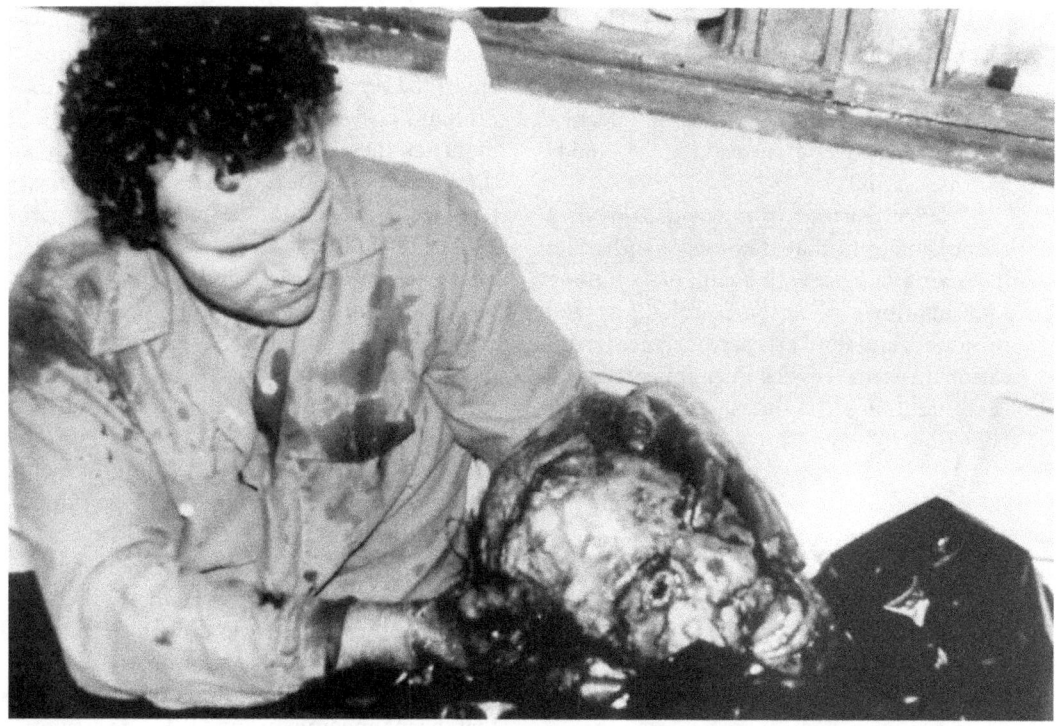

Henry (Michael Rooker) puts a bloody head in a trash bag for proper disposal in John McNaughton's *Henry: Portrait of a Serial Killer* (1986).

the couch. Becky leads Henry to her room, takes off her shirt and begins unbuttoning Henry's shirt. Henry seems reluctant. Otis is suddenly in the doorway ("I ain't interruptin' nothin', am I?"). Henry leaves for some cigarettes. Outside in the alley, he meets a woman with a dog. He follows the two for a while, then walks the other way and heads back to the apartment.

Henry finds Otis on top of a partially unclothed Becky, choking her with her shirt. Henry kicks him off and beats him until Otis breaks a bottle over his head. Before he can attack with the shattered glass, Becky stabs him in the eye with the sharp end of a comb. Henry crawls to the screaming Otis and stabs him in the stomach. Becky yells to get the cops, but Henry tells her to shut up and let him think. Henry chops up Otis in the tub, then he and Becky drive to the bridge, where Henry drops the garbage-bagged pieces into the water. While driving, Henry says they are going to his sister's ranch, and they will send for Becky's daughter. Becky tells Henry she loves him ("I guess I love you too"). They go to a motel, and the next day Henry leaves by himself. He stops the car at the side of the road, opens a trunk and pulls out Becky's suitcase. He drives away, leaving the bloody suitcase behind.

Henry: Portrait of a Serial Killer is a remarkable film that flawlessly synthesizes horrifying violence with quaint black humor. McNaughton's direction is relentless and profound, and Rooker's performance is sensational. Actor Towles also appeared in a McNaughton sci-fi outing, *The Borrower* (1991).

Hide and Go Shriek (1987)

Written by Michael Kelly; Directed by Skip Schoolnik; New Star Entertainment; 90 min.

Cast: George Thomas (David Hanson); Donna Baltron (Judy Ramteize); Brittain Frye (Randy Flint); Annette Sinclair (Kim Downs); Scott Fults (Shawn Phillips); Ria Pavia (Malissa Morgan); Sean Kanan (John Robbins); Bunky Jones (Bonnie Williams); Jeff Levine (Fred); Scott Kubay (Zack); Michael Kelly (Wino); Ronald Colby (Phil Robins); Donald Mark Spencer (Vince); James Serrano, Larry Lyons (Cops in Car); Robin Turk (Hooker); Joe White (Man at Newstand)

Crew: Robby Wald (Executive Producer); Dimitri Villard (Producer); John Ross (Composer); Eugene Shlugleit (Director of Photography); Mark Manos, Adam Wolfe (Editors)

An unknown man is using a dirty mirror to apply mascara, lipstick and blush. He straightens his tie, brushes his head and heads for the red-light district. After picking up a female hooker, he takes her into an alley, stabs her with a switchblade and walks away.

Several couples are getting together: Kim and Randy, Malissa and Shawn, the recently engaged Bonnie and John and the virginal and nervous Judy and her boyfriend David. The group piles into a van and heads for Fine Furniture, a department store owned by John's father Phil. When they arrive, John and Shawn encounter the "creepy" Fred, who loads and unloads trucks. Then everyone enters the store and pretends to look around. Phil and co-worker Vince close up for the night; as they are leaving, Vince tells Phil that he does not believe an ex-convict (the tattooed Fred) should be working at Fine Furniture. Phil assures Vince that Fred has already served his time and that Fred must be a good worker since no one has broken into the store since he has been working there. The doubtful Vince credits the shatterproof windows for keeping the potential thieves out.

Back inside the dark store, the group of people come out, and Bonnie and John jump out and scare everyone. When bringing out the beer, Shawn comments that he can smell something cooking (Fred is in the back, preparing dinner and watching telelvision). John gives everybody a tour of all three floors of the huge department store, pointing out that the mannequins around the store are not to be moved. After David jumps out and scares Bonnie, Kim is apparently inspired and suggests that the gang play Hide and Go Seek. They all agree and run to hide, declaring Kim "it." She counts loudly and begins looking for everyone.

Bonnie and John grab themselves a bed and prepare for a time of intimacy. They pop the cork of a champagne bottle; the cork lands next to a pair of mannequin feet which prove to be moving human feet. Kim finds the couple in bed, says they are "it" and tells everyone to come out. Meanwhile, the group is unknowingly locked inside by someone. Shawn and Malissa are in bed kissing. She tells him to wait for a surprise (a negligee borrowed from Kim) and he strips to his underwear. Malissa is attacked in the bathroom and her head dunked into a sink full of water and beaten on the counter. When Shawn is looking for her later, he sees the killer in negligee and laughing a girlish laugh. Once close enough, he sees the hairy arms and chest and surmises that it is not Malissa. However, the killer grabs him and tosses him onto spikes.

The people are getting bored so they decide to reconvene for their midnight dinner. They all go looking for the absent Malissa and Shawn. Judy eventually sees someone running around in Shawn's clothes but later only finds a mannequin lying in bed, which upsets John. The group decides the missing couple is being devious, and they all head for bed. While Bonnie and John are in bed, the person in Shawn's clothes reemerges and shows them both his middle finger and his bare bottom. An irate John gives chase and learns that the person is actually a stranger. The two begin a fistfight; the killer gets the better of John, leaving him on the ground. The killer returns to shove a mannequin arm into John's stomach. Later, a frightened Bonnie hides under the bed and sees a mysterious foot covered in tattoos.

Kim sees someone in Randy's clothes (which were stolen from the bedside when Randy was sleeping). She screams and heads for the elevator, but the killer follows. Randy jumps up, throws some pants on and runs into Bonnie. The two find Judy and David in bed, and they all go looking for the others (not realizing that Kim is bound and restrained atop the elevator they are using). After discovering many mannequins in beds and rearranged, the group sees the killer dancing and dressed as Kim. Randy asks what they just saw, and Judy responds, "Kim's clothes, but that's not Kim." Everyone decides to call the police.

After discovering that the phones are dead and the back door padlocked, the group heads for the front of the store and try to break the shatterproof windows. Their attempts to get the attention of a wino, and later a couple of cops, prove unsuccessful. They finally decide that the only thing they can do is make a stand. Outside, a news stand owner sees the group walking around in the store and telephones the police. After the people find the corpses of Malissa, Shawn and John, they encounter Fred. They tackle him, beat him and restrain him with rope. They head for the elevator, and the killer is on top, struggling with Kim. She frees herself somewhat, ducks her head into the elevator screaming for Randy and is beheaded by the elevator and the floor.

As everyone waits in a room, the killer arrives with a razor and attacks. Fred jumps the killer and the two fight. They know each other, and Fred tells the killer (calling him Zack), "I told you it was over!" Fred is stabbed in the throat with his own knife. Judy picks up Zack's razor and swings up at him. He laughs and backs away, only to slip on Kim's blood and fall down the elevator shaft. After the police and John's father arrive, a wounded Fred explains that Zack was his "friend" in prison. He apologizes, and then dies. Outside, a stretcher is brought with Zack's body, and his tattooed foot hangs out. As the group is led into an ambulance and driven away, the stretcher is shown to be containing someone else's body. Following everyone is a second ambulance, driven by a seemingly content Zack.

Hide and Go Shriek is a moderately enjoyable slasher. Despite the cast's mediocre acting, the film is helped with some amusing moments (especially the killer's constant changes of attire) and the nice confined setting. Actor Kanan is perhaps best known for his soap opera performances, having appeared as a regular in *General Hospital*, *Sunset Beach* and *The Bold and the Beautiful*.

The Hitcher (1986)

Written by Eric Red; Directed by Robert Harmon; Silver Screen Partners/HBO Pictures/Tri-Star Pictures; 98 min.

Cast: Rutger Hauer (John Ryder); C. Thomas Howell (Jim Halsey); Jennifer Jason Leigh (Nash); Jeffrey DeMunn (Captain Esteridge); John Jackson (Sergeant Starr); Billy Greenbush (Trooper Donner); Jack Thibeau (Trooper Prestone); Armin Shimerman (Interrogation Sergeant); Eugene David (Trooper Dodge); John Van Ness (Trooper Hapscomb); Henry Darrow (Trooper Hancock); Tony Epper (Trooper Conners); Tom Spratley (Proprietor); Colin Campbell (Construction Man)

Crew: Edward S. Feldman, Charles R. Meeker (Executive Producers); David Bombyk, Kip Ohman (Producers); Paul Lewis (Co-Producer); Mark Isham (Composer); John Seale, A.C.S. (Director of Photography); Frank J. Urioste, A.C.E. (Editor)

Jim Halsey is driving at night, fighting to stay awake. He nods off and is awakened by the lights and horn of a semi-truck, and sees a hitchhiker at the side of the road. He opens the door for the man ("My mother told me never to do this."), and the hitcher says his name is John Ryder. Jim asks where he is going, and the hitcher only stares at him. As they pass a car at the side of the road, the man grabs Jim's leg. An unsettled Jim stops the car and tells him to get out. The man opens the door but stays in his seat, and Jim asks him about the car they passed. The man says he ran out of gas, so Jim heads for a station. The man finally says that he does not need gas, and he tells Jim about cutting off the legs, arms and head of the last man who picked him up, which is what he will do to Jim. They reach some road construction, and the hitcher shows his switchblade and holds it near Jim's crotch; the "sweethearts" are let by. The hitcher talks about puncturing eyeballs and slitting throats, and he tells Jim to say, "I want to die." Jim sees the "Door Ajar" light and pushes the man out of the car.

Later in the day, a station wagon passes and Jim sees the hitcher inside. He drives to the side and screams for the people to pull over. A bus comes by the other way and Jim's car is clipped, but he drives on. Further down the road, he sees the wagon, stops, looks inside and is sick. Jim gets to an old gas station and goes inside; the hitcher shows up and throws Jim's keys to him. The man goes outside and hitches a ride in a truck, and Jim gets in his car and drives away. The hitcher shows up later to ram the back of Jim's car (in his new truck). At another gas station, he drives through the garage door, knocks over some tanks and lights a match. Jim jumps in his car and speeds away in flames as the station explodes.

Nash gets off a bus and heads to a diner. Jim bangs on the door and says he has to call the police. She lets him inside and Jim makes his call, telling the cops that he will wait. He cleans up in the restroom as Nash prepares a burger and fries. Nash goes to the freezer and lets the preoccupied Jim eat his food. Jim nearly chomps on a severed finger and runs outside, where two police officers arrest him and find a bloody switchblade in his pocket. At the station, Jim tells them the car is a drive-away, and he is on his way to San Diego (his wallet and identification are missing). They call the company but the office is closed, and there is no response at Jim's brother's number. Jim is put in a cell where he lies down and sleeps. He awakes and finds the cell door is not locked. He looks around the station and finds three police officers dead. Sirens and cops arrive, and Jim grabs a gun and runs out the back.

He reaches a pay phone. A cop car pulls up, and Jim quickly points his gun and has the officers get back in the car. He asks the driver to get someone in charge, and Captain Esteridge gets on the radio. Jim tells the captain that he has not killed anyone. Jim decides to trust the man and tells the cops to take him in. The hitcher passes in his truck and shoots and kills the two cops. Jim stops the car and jumps out. He enters a café, orders a coffee and sits at a booth. The hitcher sits across from him, and Jim pulls his gun under the table. The hitcher looks and tells Jim that he has no bullets. The hitcher feigns having a gun and slaps the table, and Jim pulls the trigger repeatedly. The hitcher leaves a cloth on the table and walks away. A bus arrives outside, and Jim takes the cloth (with bullets) and sneaks onto the bus, hides in the bathroom and loads the gun.

The bus moves, and Jim comes out and sits in the back. Nash heads down the aisle, and Jim pushes her into the bathroom and tells her he is not a killer. They get out and sit in the back together as cops pull the bus over. Jim willingly walks to the front and out of the door and throws down his gun. One cop is enraged (his friends have been killed) and tries to get Jim to wipe spit from his wrist. The cop cocks his hammer. Nash fires into the air with Jim's gun and has the cops drop their weapons. Jim empties their pistols and the two get in the cops' car and drive away. They speed away from two cop cars, and the police ignore Nash when she gets on the radio and says they want to turn themselves in. Jim causes the two cars to wreck (by shooting their shotguns at each other), and soon a helicopter and more cars are after them. The hitcher arrives in his truck and shoots at the helicopter. The helicopter crashes in the road, taking out the cars. Jim stops the car and he and Nash get out and walk.

They reach a motel and sit in a room. Jim goes to shower, and Nash calls someone to say that she is okay. The hitcher walks inside and lies down beside her, and he puts his hand over her mouth when she sees him. The television comes on. Jim pulls the towel rod from the wall and sees that Nash is gone. He goes outside and is stopped by a police officer and Captain Esteridge, who lead him to where Nash is tied to a parked trailer and a running semi, with the hitcher behind the wheel. Jim gets inside and sits beside the man. The hitcher puts a loaded gun in front of Jim and has him point it at his forehead. ("You know what to do. Now do it.") Jim refuses to do anything, believing that Nash will die, and the hitcher calls Jim a "useless waste" and lets the truck roll. Jim screams.

At the station, the cops say they do not know anything about the hitcher (even after running his prints) and that he will not answer questions, except to say that he is from Disneyland. Jim asks to see him, and he spits in the hitcher's face and is taken away. The hitcher is taken away on a prison bus, and Captain Esteridge drives away with Jim in his truck. While driving, Jim pulls the captain's gun from his holster, has him stop the truck and get out, and turns the vehicle around. Jim drives to the bus and hears the shotgun sounds from inside; the hitcher blows open the bus' doors and jumps onto the truck's windshield. Jim slams on the brakes and the hitcher flies out. The man stands and fires repeatedly at the truck as Jim frantically tries to start the vehicle. The engine comes alive and Jim sits up ("Come on!" challenges the hitcher). Jim drives and smacks into the man. Jim gets out, picks up the shotgun and sees that the hitcher is still. He turns to leave, and the hitcher stands and throws his cuffs and chain. The hitcher smiles, and Jim turns around and shoots him a few times.

The Hitcher is a tremendous film, with a strong atmosphere, an appropriately eerie score and loads of suspense and action. The dialogue is solid but the film is just as effective in the stretches of silence. Although the usually dynamic Leigh is under-utilized in her role, Hauer supplies a powerhouse performance as the murderous and excitement-seeking title character.

Home Sweet Home
(aka *Slasher in the House*)
(1981)

Written by Thomas Bush; Directed by Nettie Peña; 82 min.

Cast: Jake Steinfeld (Killer); Vinessa Shaw (Angel); Peter De Paula (Mistake); Don Edmunds (Bradley); Charles Hoyes (Wayne); David Mielke (Scott); Leia Naron (Gail); Lisa Rodriguez (Maria); Collette Trygg (Jennifer); Sallee Young (Linda); J. Kelly, R. Fouts (Cops); Victor Paddock (First Victim); Rochelle Costanten (Old Woman); Anne Cribbs (Witness)

Crew: Rick Whitfield, Alex Rebar (Executive Producers); Don Edmunds (Producer); Jack Petty (Associate Producer); Rich Tufo (Composer); Don Stern (Director of Photography); Nettie Peña (Editor)

A man sitting in a car listening to the radio looks up at someone approaching ("Hey, you want a beer?"). He is pulled out of his car and choked by a muscular madman. On the radio, the deejay says Jay Jones escaped from a mental institution after being locked away eight years for killing his parents. The killer shoots his tongue with a syringe (on the radio it is said that he might be on PCP) and he drives away, with "Home Sweet Home" on the back of his hand. On the way, he runs over an old woman at a crosswalk while laughing maniacally.

Scott and Jennifer are headed towards their Thanksgiving dinner. Mistake is out playing guitar (with an amplifier strapped to his back and Kiss-esque make up on his face), and Bradley tells him to stop and then goes for a beer. The killer stops somewhere and uses a water hose to clean his blood-drenched windshield. Mistake bothers a kissing Scott and Jennifer, and Scott chases him until Mistake runs into a room where Bradley and Linda are making out; he is chased by Linda. In the house, Wayne is watching his girlfriend Maria (who speaks only Spanish) play some guitar and sing. Gail and Linda go to get some wine, and Scott lends them his car. The killer watches the women pull away, then drives his car to the house.

The killer hits the switches at a fuse box, and the power goes out. Bradley says it happens once in a while and goes outside to fire up the generator. He then leaves to get more gas. Bradley drives until he sees the killer's stolen car sitting in the road. He stops, looks around and opens the gas lid to transfer the fuel to his gas can. Bradley's Jeep will not start, so he decides to steal the car's battery. The killer, watching from the trees, jumps out and lands on the car hood, crushing Bradley underneath. Mistake is playing guitar for the little girl Angel and showing her some magic tricks while the killer cuts the phone lines outside. Meanwhile, Gail and Linda are lost.

A hungry Wayne, upset that Bradley has not returned, gets on the phone to see if Bradley is at the gas station, only to find the phone line dead. Scott says that Gail and Linda may have run out of gas. Wayne gets in his car to look for the others, but he is killed by the maniac, who was waiting in the back seat. Scott, Jennifer and Maria set the table for Thanksgiving, and Mistake appears to hit on Maria. Scott takes Jennifer to show her his apartment, and the two lovers kiss. Gail and Linda are pulled over by a couple of police officers, but Linda manages to flirt her way out of a ticket; the cops let them off with a warning. Scott's car will not start, and so the women grab their things and begin walking.

Mistake and Maria are playing music together as the killer is watching Angel in the kitchen. Scott and Jennifer come out of his room and the group goes to check on Angel. They find some of the food destroyed, but Angel is unharmed and dining on some turkey underneath the table. Gail and Linda find Wayne's car and see the killer in the dark, thinking it is Wayne. They scream when they realize their mistake. The killer grabs Gail and throws her, and her head smashes into a rock. Linda throws the wine bottle at the killer and runs. He follows her, and he eventually finds her and kills her with the broken bottle.

The people at the house have started their dinner. Mistake spills something on

Maria and goes to his room to find her a shirt. Maria finds a dead Linda in the shower, and the killer grabs her. Mistake finds them, and the killer tells him not to make a sound. Mistake follows them to the trees, pleading to be taken instead, but the killer decides to stab Maria. Mistake runs away. The maniac catches up to him and, with the aid of the guitar, he electrocutes Mistake. Scott goes to get firewood and finds Maria dead. He runs back and, believing Mistake has gone crazy, he tells Jennifer to get inside with Angel and lock the doors. The killer gets inside before the door-locking commences.

After Jennifer takes Angel to the bathroom, they go to sit by the fire. Scott gets a knife from the kitchen, and the lights go out. Scott looks around some more, and he says that they are all "perfectly safe." Angel has to go to the bathroom again, and Scott takes her. The killer jumps out and tries to strangle Scott. He tosses Jennifer to the side when she beats on his back with a poker, and the woman stabs the killer with the knife. She and Scott run out, and Jennifer tries to go back for Angel. Scott goes back instead, and the killer pulls him through the door and slices his throat. Jennifer runs to Scott's apartment and hides. She passes out (presumably from exhaustion) while the killer looks for her and continues to laugh. The next morning, the cops find Gail dead. Jennifer comes out from hiding and is attacked by the killer (with the knife still in his back). The police arrive and shoot him a few times until he collapses. Angel is in the cop car (they had found her wandering around) and Jennifer embraces the little girl. The bloody and fallen killer opens his eyes.

Home Sweet Home is quite an amateurish film, with few scares and dull moments, but it has the saving grace of humorous characters like Mistake and Maria.

Hospital Massacre (aka *Be My Valentine, or Else...*; *Ward 13*; *X-Ray*) (1981)

Written by Marc Behm; Directed by Boaz Davidson; Cannon Group, Inc.; 89 min.

Cast: Barbi Benton (Susan Jeremy); Chip Lucia (Harry); Jon Van Ness (Jack); John Warner Williams (Doctor Saxon); Den Surles (Doctor Beam); Gloria Morrison (Nurse Dora); Karyn Smith (Nurse Kitty); Michael Frost (Ned); Jimmy Stathis (Tom); Lanny Duncan (Hal); Miriam Beller (Mrs. Edelman); Ely Wold (Mrs. Fedrow); Jonathan Moore (Mrs. Perry); Gay Austin (Doctor Jacobs); Bill Errigo (The Janitor); Beverly Hart (Suzy); Ann Charlotte Lindgren (Nancy); Judy Baldwin (Desk Nurse); Tammy Simpson (Eva); Elizabeth Hoy (Young Susan); Michael Romano (Young Dave); Billy Jacoby (Young Harry); Don Grenough (The Doctor)

Crew: Geoffrey Rose (Executive Producer); Menahem Golan, Yoram Globus (Producers); John S. Thompson (Associate Producer); Arlon Ober (Composer); Nicholas von Sternberg (Director of Photography); Jon Koslowsky (Editor)

It is 1961, and young Susan and David are playing with a train, with paper hearts all around the room. A boy watching from outside leaves a red envelope at the door and knocks. Susan answers, and she shows David the Valentine's card from Harold; the two laugh and crumple it up. Susan goes to the kitchen to cut some cake, and when she walks back into the room, David is dead and hanging on the coatrack. Susan turns and sees a smiling Harold standing by the open window. She screams, and the young killer runs away.

Nineteen years later, on Valentine's Day, Susan Jeremy has to go to the hospital for test results and she tells her ex-husband Tom to watch their daughter Eva. Susan's fiancé Jack takes her to the hospital, and he asks if it is the same hospital where a patient once "ran amok." Susan goes inside and heads for Doctor Jacobs' office. In the elevator, Susan meets hospital patient Hal, who at first appears bloody and dead but is only napping after enjoying a burger with excessive ketchup. Susan inadvertently goes to the cloudy ninth floor, where three men in gas masks are fumigating and tell her to leave. The elevator stops, and Susan bangs on the door for help. Doctor Jacobs is called to the ninth floor (she uses the stairs) and is murdered by someone wearing OR scrubs and a doctor's mask.

The elevator is started again, and Susan gets off on the eighth floor. The killer goes to Jacobs' office, takes Susan's file and writes her name on another folder. Susan knocks on the door, looks inside the empty office and waits on the bench outside. The janitor goes to the room on the ninth floor and finds Jacobs' body hanging upside down in a locker. The killer is at the door, and the janitor follows him to another room ("Hey man, where are you?"); the janitor's face is dunked into a sink full of acid (the killer is wearing the appropriate rubber gloves). Susan calls Tom, but her stubborn ex-husband refuses to answer and will not let Eva pick up the phone. A doctor suggests that Susan check the doctor's lounge for Jacobs. Susan meets Harry there, and they go to Jacobs' office, where Harry looks at Susan's file. After checking the X-ray, Harry says he needs to find an MD to sign the report (he is only an intern).

Harry and Susan go to Doctor Saxon's office, where Harry (by whispering something) gets the doctor to look at the report. Harry leaves; after Saxon excuses himself, Susan calls Tom again, and Eva answers. She tells Susan that Tom has left her alone, and Susan tells her daughter that she is going to be a little late. Nurses Dora and Kitty take Susan to another room, where Saxon tells Susan that the results are inconclusive and that more tests are necessary. Saxon checks Susan, takes some blood and sends her to a room occupied by three strange elderly women. Susan telephones Tom again, but the receiver is off the hook (Tom is at the house with Eva).

Suzy is in a room typing Susan's report, and Nancy comes in and asks her for a bite to eat. Suzy stays to finish the report, and the killer murders the woman, takes the report out of the typewriter and puts another one in its place. Harry comes in, sees no one and takes the report sitting in the typewriter. He gives the report to Saxon and Doctor Beam, and they determine among themselves that it is "practically a death warrant." Nancy finds a dead Suzy, and she runs until she finds the killer, who breaks her neck. Saxon tells Susan that she has to stay for a while due to "discrepancies" in her tests, and he admits to her that it is serious. Susan leaves the room to get away from the eerie women and sees Harry in the hall; the two go to Jacobs' office and look at her files. He reads a file, and then tells Susan that someone is playing a "con job" on her and to wait in her room. He goes to Saxon's office, answers the ringing phone and says he will be "right up."

Jack awakes, still waiting in his car. He walks into the hospital and is sent to the eighth floor for Susan. He gets to her room and Susan tells him that they will not let her go. The two head for the elevator but they are stopped by Saxon and the two nurses. Susan is taken back to her room, and Jack is told to wait on the bench by Saxon's office. While waiting there, Jack is called to the ninth floor. He enters a room to see someone sitting in a wheelchair behind a dressing curtain. A voice tells him to "come closer"; a dead body is sitting in the wheelchair. The killer appears and attacks Jack with a surgical drill.

Susan is alone in her room (the three women were on the ninth floor when Jack was walking around), and the killer enters with a big red box, leaving it on the stand next to the bed. Susan sits up, opens the box and finds Jack's head inside. She screams and runs to hide in the doctor's lounge. Saxon and Kitty enter the room, take Susan back to her room, and find only a cake inside the box. Susan tells Saxon about her file in Jacobs' office (which Harry has).

Susan goes to the elevator and hides behind a dressing curtain in the hallway when she hears someone approaching. She sees the killer standing by the elevator with a hatchet. She is almost discovered when she drops her lighter, but the killer leaves on the elevator. Susan runs down the stairs to the archives (for another copy of her file). Saxon is there, and the killer arrives to put the hatchet in the doctor's head. Susan screams and runs down the hall, but she is strapped to a bed by Dora, Kitty, and another doctor. Doctor Beam comes in to see her and Susan bites his finger. Dora is walking down the hall when she is attacked by the killer with a giant syringe. Beam gets a large blade through his neck as he is looking at Susan's X-ray.

The killer unstraps Susan and puts her on an operating table. She tears off the mask and sees Harry. ("It's not Harry, it's Harold.") Susan asks him what he wants, and he replies, "What I've always wanted: your heart." Before he can attack, Susan stabs him with a blade and flees. They run to a room where Susan dumps a jar of flammable liquid on Harry; now the chase leads to the roof. Susan beats Harry with a pipe a few times, and when he attacks again, she flicks her lighter and sets Harry afire. Harry jumps over the edge of the building and drops to his fiery death. The next day, Susan leaves the hospital and is greeted by Tom and Eva.

Hospital Massacre has a nice setting, but the story is too watered-down and suspense is almost completely absent. Some humorous moments do help (the "bloody" introduction of Hal is particularly amusing). Actress Benton is possibly best known as a *Playboy* Playmate. Reportedly, the original title *Be My Valentine, or Else...* was changed when *My Bloody Valentine* made it to theaters first.

House of Death (aka *Death Screams Night Screams*) (1983)

Written by Paul C. Elliott; Directed by David Nelson; ABA Productions; 88 min.

Cast: Susan Kiger (Lily); Martin Tucker (Neil Marshall); William T. Hicks (Sheriff Avery); Jennifer Chase (Ramona); Jody Kay (Sandy); John Kohler (Diddle); Andria Savio (Kathy); Kurt Rector (Bob); Josh Gamble (Tom); Hans Manship (Casey); Helen Tryon (Edna Sharps); Mary Fran Lyman (Agnes Bottomly); Monica Boston (Sheila); Mike Brown (Walker); Sharon Alley (Sara); Larry Sprinkle (Ted); Penny Miller (Angie); Bill Ison (Arch Johnson); David Lenthall (Jackson); Debbie Ison (Girl at Kissing Booth); Gene Poole (Hippie at Kissing Booth); Jimmy Bouskos (Boy in Store); R.C. Nanney (R.C.); Barbara McClarty (Sara's Mother); Bob Melton (Carnival Barker); Gail Minton (Beaula the Waitress)

Crew: Charles Ison, Ernest Bouskos (Executive Producers/Producers); John Hay (Executive Assistant to Producer); Parrish Todd (Associate Producer); Dee Barton (Composer); Darrell Cathcart (Director of Photography); Jerry Whittington (Editor)

Ted and Angie are out kissing on a motorcycle, waiting for the train, which apparently augments their dual orgasm. Unfortunately, someone shows up, kills the couple and kicks the bodies into the river. The next day, Sheriff Avery is at the store looking for Ted, who has not shown up for work. Bob and Kathy are at the ballfield, assisting baseball coach Neil Marshall. They see the slow and weird Casey watching them, and he runs away when he realizes he has been spotted. Neil takes his assistants out for a pitcher of beer, and Bob walks Kathy home. Bob asks her to the river, but Kathy says she has to work at the carnival tomorrow and she asks him along to help. Ted and Angie continue floating down the river. Lily leaves work and heads home, continually looking around for anyone following. She gets home to her grandmother.

The next day at the carnival, Tom and Ramona hang around with Sheila, Walker, Sandy and the irritating Diddle. At the booth, Bob tells Kathy that he thinks he is in love, and the two kiss. Lily is rolling her grandmother in her wheelchair; they speak with Agnes. Sheriff Avery asks the six friends if they have seen Ted or Angie. The group later tells Bob and Kathy about their bonfire party that night. Lily talks with Neil, and he tells her his mother used to live in the town when he was younger. Bob and Kathy tell Neil about the party, and Neil asks Lily to accompany him. She politely declines, but accepts his invitation to a potential movie in the future. Sara, upset that Neil seemed more interested in Lily than her, covers his car in shaving cream, which Casey evidently witnesses. Later Sara, sitting by a fountain, is shot with an arrow. She runs to an abandoned merry-go-round and the ride starts moving. A plastic bag is thrown over her head and Sara is suffocated.

At home, Casey's mother Agnes tells her son that it is wrong to steal things like ballfield equipment (which Casey has been accused of). Bob is dropping Kathy off, and they both tell Lily that she should go to the party. At her house, Lily's grandmother expresses her skepticism of Neil, and she calls his mother a "common whore." Neil is in the shower, and Ramona walks in on him and kisses him. Neil carries her to the shower and turns it on. He tells her to go home, and he lets her know that he does not like "cheap thrills" because he had a "lifetime" of that with his mother. Ramona storms out. The sheriff sees her outside, and he mocks her for her flirty ways. Ramona says something about Avery's son and he becomes irate, but Ramona tells him that Casey was driving. Agnes cannot find her son, and she calls to tell the sheriff. Out in his garage, Neil sees a soccer ball fall from the upper level. He climbs the steps, and a machete is swung.

Out at the bonfire, Ramona, upset, tells Tom to leave her alone for a while, but she later hugs him and apologizes. Diddle had been dancing with Sandy, but he passes out, right when Sandy wants to go for a swim. At Neil's house, Sheriff Avery sees something on the windshield of Neil's car, and something falls from above. No one wants to swim with Sandy, so she goes off alone; out in the water, she bumps into the floating corpses of Ted and Angie. She screams, gets to shore and is chopped with the machete. Diddle wants to find Sandy, so he, Tom and Walker look around. They meet Bob, Kathy and Lily and sit around the bonfire, deciding that it is time to go to the cemetery. Lily is reluctant, but Bob suggests leaving a note by the fire in case Neil arrives afterwards.

At the Sunset Cemetery, the group sits in a circle, each holding a lit candle, and Lily is chosen to tell a ghost story. She tells of a frightened girl staying alone during a storm, and her dog constantly reassuring her by licking her hand in the dark. The girl hears a dripping sound, and she checks her shower and finds her dog hanging, bloody and dead, and "Maniacs lick hands, too" written on the mirror in blood. They run to an old house for shelter when it begins to rain. Diddle goes back out to occupy the outhouse. Tom suggests scaring Diddle, and after giving him some time, the group heads out to the outhouse and find Diddle hanging, bloody and dead. ("Somebody slit him from ear to ear.") They carry his body inside; Walker heads for the truck, followed by Sheila. When Sheila reaches the truck, Walker is there, but his head falls off and Sheila is grabbed. Tom finds the both of them dead and headless, and runs from the killer but falls into an open grave. When he tries to climb out, the killer chops off his hands.

Kathy hears someone approaching. Bob opens the door in time to see a raised machete and quickly slams the door shut. The killer breaks the window, and Ramona heads for the stairs and falls through the unstable steps. Bob tries to pull her up, but Ramona's body hanging in the cellar is sliced. The remaining three run upstairs, followed by the killer. They barricade the door, and Bob is hit when leaning against it. Neil bursts into the room and yells to Lily that she is just like the others. Flashbacks show Neil's mother having sex with a strange man as a young Neil watches her. Lily picks up a glass shard from the broken window and slices Neil's throat. Neil attacks again, Lily moves out of the way and Neil flies out of the window. The sheriff arrives, sees the dead Neil and shoots the corpse several times. Avery walks Lily to his car and lets her inside.

House of Death is a somewhat enjoyable slasher film, with a nice assortment of characters and a decent killing spree (although it starts a little late). The title house does not appear until near the ending, and only one person actually dies inside the house. Casey's predilection towards baseball equipment is possibly a reference to the popular poem "Casey at the Bat." In the outhouse, Diddle is humming "Singin' in the Rain." Actress Kiger was the *Playboy* January 1977 Playmate of the Month.

I Know What You Did Last Summer (1997)

Written by Kevin Williamson (from the novel by Lois Duncan); Directed by Jim Gillespie; Columbia Pictures/Mandalay Entertainment; 100 min.

Cast: Jennifer Love Hewitt (Julie James); Sarah Michelle Gellar (Helen Shivers); Ryan Phillippe (Barry Cox); Freddie Prinze, Jr. (Ray Bronson); Muse Watson (Benjamin Willis/Fisherman); Bridgette Wilson (Elsa Shivers); Anne Heche (Melissa Egan); Johnny Galecki (Max); Stuart Greer (Officer); J. Don Ferguson (MC); Deborah Hobart (Mrs. James); Mary McMillan (Mrs. Cox); Rasool Phan (Deb); Dan Albright (Sheriff); Lynda Clark (Pageant Official); Shea Broom, Jennifer Bland (Contestants); John Bennes (Old Man); William Neely (Hank); Jonathan Quint (David Egan); Richard Dale Miller, Mary Neva Huff, David Lee Hartman (Band Members)

Crew: William S. Beasley (Executive Producer); Neal H. Mortiz, Erik Feig, Stokely Chaffin (Producers); John Debney (Composer); Denis Crossan, B.S.C. (Director of Photography); Steve Mirkovich, A.C.E. (Editor)

At night, a young man is sitting alone on a small cliff. Fireworks suddenly explode in the sky. There is a queen contest in Southport, and Julie, Ray and Barry are watching Helen in the pageant. Helen wins and is awarded a crown as the Croaker Queen. At a party afterwards, Max hits on Julie, and he and Barry have a scuffle that Ray breaks up. The four friends decide to head to Dawson's Beach, where they tell alternate versions of the man-with-a-hook-for-a-hand urban legend around the campfire. When they are alone, Julie expresses her sadness to her sweetheart Ray that the two of them will be separated after high school.

The group gets Barry's car keys away from him, and Ray drives them back. Down the road, Barry's inebriated behavior is so distracting that Ray inadvertently hits something, and the car squeals to a stop. Seeing blood on Barry's face ("It's not mine") and the severe damage to the car, they initially think they hit a deer, until Julie finds a bloody boot and then a body near the road ("Is he dead?"). Ray checks for a pulse and surmises that the man is dead. Believing the police will surmise that a drunk Barry was driving and wishing to avoid the potential consequences, they decide to dump the body. After dodging an encounter with Max, who drives by, they carry the man to the dock. Julie is very uncomfortable with what they are doing, and no one wants to kick him in the water. Helen bends over to finish the act, and the man jumps up and grabs her crown. They knock him into the water, and Barry dives in to retrieve the crown. He takes it from the man, whose eyes pop open. Back on the dock, Barry demands that everyone make a pact to never tell anyone about the incident.

One year later, Julie comes home from college. She seems distant and world-weary, and her mother complains about her poor grades. Then she reads a mysterious letter that says, "I know what you did last summer." Julie goes to see Helen's sister Elsa at her shop to ask for Helen's phone number in New York, but the ambitious model is a few feet away in Fragrances. She shows Helen the note, and the frightened females go to see Barry. They discuss the incident; Julie says that the man's name was David Egan, and that his body had been discovered three weeks after that night. Barry thinks the note-writing culprit is Max, and they head to the dock, where Barry shoves Max around and threatens him. The three run into estranged fisherman Ray, and Julie tells him about the note. Later, Max is alone working, a hooded figure appears, and Max gets a hook in the neck.

After working out at the gym Barry hears a noise in the locker room and finds a Polaroid of his car in his locker, with "I know" written on the back. He looks around the room, and returns to find his locker standing open and his jacket missing. He runs outside and sees his car being driven away. Barry chases the driver, who turns around and chases Barry, smacking into him and leaving him wounded. The man in the slicker stands above Barry with a hook.

The next day the group visits Barry in the hospital. Helen suggests that the fisherman is somehow related to David Egan. She and Julie get on the computer, and they find an article on the accidental death of Susie Willis, who was engaged to Egan (Julie had seen the name tattooed on his arm). They go to see Egan's sister Missy. The two girls feign car trouble, Missy lets them inside and they get her to talk about her brother. Helen pretends to remember Egan and his friend, and Missy recalls someone saying the name, "Billy Blue."

Helen goes home, unaware that the fisherman has walked into her house. She heads upstairs and goes to bed. The next morning she awakes with some of her hair cut and the word "Soon" written on her mirror. She calls Julie, who rushes over. On the way, she hears rattling in her car, pulls to the side of the road and finds the lifeless body of Max covered in crabs in her trunk. She runs to Helen's house, and the girls and Barry discover an empty trunk. They encounter Ray, and Barry punches him, believing he is the one tormenting them. The group finds no trace of Billy Blue in Elsa's 1992 yearbook, so Julie decides to take it to Missy so she can point him out. Helen and Barry go to the parade (Helen has to be there as the "outgoing queen"). Ray, deeming the Billy Blue search preposterous, goes back to his boat.

At Missy's house, Julie says David's death was not an accident. Missy says it was a suicide, showing Julie a note ("I will never forget last summer") written in the same thick black ink as Julie's letter. Julie says it was a death threat, and she tells Missy what happened last summer, mentioning David's tattoo. When Missy says her brother had no tattoo, Julie finally realizes that they did not hit David Egan. At the talent portion of the contest, Barry calms Helen, who had seen the man in the slicker during the parade. While sitting on stage, Helen sees the fisherman appear behind Barry on the balcony. Barry is attacked and killed. A police officer investigates after Helen screams hysterically, and he finds nothing and takes Helen home. On the way, the officer stops to help a motorist and is hooked by the killer fisherman. Helen gets out of the car and runs to Elsa's store. Inside she calls the police and tells Elsa to lock to back door, but Elsa is too late and is murdered. Helen is chased around the store until she manages to get back outside. The killer catches up and slashes her in an alley. Meanwhile, Julie returns to the original article on Susie Willis, and she learns that Susie was survived by her father Benjamin Willis.

Julie finds Ray on his boat. She tells him what she has learned, and he tries to persuade her onto the boat — but Julie sees the boat's name: Billy Blue ("You!"). She runs away, and Ray follows. A fisherman knocks Ray down and tells Julie to get on his boat. She does, and in another room, she finds many pictures and articles relating to her and her friends. The fisherman appears: "Kids like you should be out having fun, drinking, partying, running people over, getting away with murder — things like that." Julie realizes it is Benjamin Willis ("You!"). He chases her around the boat, now out at sea. Ray gets on board, and there is a lengthy chase and fighting, until Willis' hand is caught on a rope, his hand is chopped off and he flies off the boat. Later, the police find a hand gripping a hook but no body.

A happy Julie is back at college, and she gets her mail given to her in the locker room. She sees a note written in black ink, but it is only a party invitation. Inside the shower room, however, "I still know" is written on steamy glass, and the evil fisherman breaks through.

I Know What You Did Last Summer is a hohum slasher, which was released soon after the 1996 *Scream*, attempting to capitalize on screenwriter Williamson's recent popularity. The name of Dawson's Beach in the film is a reference to the Williamson-created television series *Dawson's Creek*.

I Still Know What You Did Last Summer (1998)

Written by Trey Callaway; Directed by Danny Cannon; Columbia Pictures/Mandalay Entertainment; 100 min.

Cast: Jennifer Love Hewitt (Julie James); Freddie Prinze, Jr. (Ray Bronson); Brandy (Karla Wilson); Matthew Settle (Will Benson); Mekhi Phifer (Tyrell Martin); Bill Cobbs (Estes); Muse Watson (Benjamin Willis/Fisherman); Jennifer Esposito (Nancy Murphy); Jeffrey Combs (Mr. Joseph Brooks); John Hawkes (Dave); Ellerine Hurding (Olga, the Maid); Benjamin Brown (Derrick); Red West (Paulsen); Michael P. Byrne (Thurston); Michael Bryan French (Dr. Smith); Dee Anne Helsel (Nurse); John Harrington (Todd); Mark Boone Junior (Pawn Shop Owner); Dan Priest (Professor Krueger); Sylvia Short (Old Woman)

Crew: Neal H. Mortiz, Erik Feig, Stokely Chaffin, William S. Beasley (Producers); John Frizzell (Composer); Vernon Layton, B.S.C. (Director of Photography); Peck Prior (Editor)

Inside a church, Julie walks down the aisle and into a confessional booth. "It's been a year since my last confession," she says. She confesses to killing a man, and she says she is having bad dreams. She says the man's name, "Ben Willis." The priest says he knows. When Julie looks up, he turns and says, "I know what you did last summer." A hook crashes through, and Julie wakes up screaming in a classroom. She quickly leaves, and Will chases her down. She tells him she is still having dreams of the fisherman. She says it has been a year since the incident. Julie meets Ray, and the couple talks. Julie says she cannot go back to Southport, and an upset Ray leaves.

Julie wakes up that night to a sound in the dark. She gets a knife, looks around and is scared by her friend Karla. Karla convinces her to go to a club with her. They meet Will there (Karla slyly invited him), but before he and Julie can have a drink, Julie thinks she sees the fisherman in the club. She heads his way, but he disappears, and she decides to go home. The next morning, Karla answers the phone, and *Mark in the Morning* from the radio show says she will win a contest if she tells him the capital of Brazil. She finally says Rio and wins four tickets to the Tower Bay Islands in the Bahamas. Julie calls Ray to invite him along; he becomes agitated because she is going away with her friends but would not go with him. He then says he is too busy, but Julie asks him to try to make it. Ray's fishing pal Dave sticks it to him, and Ray shows Dave a ring. Dave convinces Ray to surprise Julie in the Bahamas.

On the road, Ray and Dave pull over to help someone lying on the road. Ray uncovers a mannequin, and quickly turns around just in time to see Dave killed by the fisherman. The killer gets in the truck and chases Ray until he jumps down a small incline. Julie and Karla are waiting for an absent Ray. Karla's boyfriend Ty shows up with Will, Julie relaxes a bit and the group head out to the Tower Bay Islands. They arrive at a beautiful resort and encounter Titus, a quirky white male with dreadlocks and an exaggerated Jamaican accent. Inside the hotel, they sign in and speak with hotel owner Brooks, who tells them that the storm season has started and that the hotel is in its off-season.

At the hospital, a man says to a police officer that an injured Ray mentioned the name Ben Willis. Then there is an alert for a flatline, and Ray is gone, leaving the window open. Ty and Will go to a bar and meet Nancy the bartender. When Julie and Karla arrive, Nancy points them all to the karaoke machine. The others push Julie to try it out, and she sings, "I Will Survive." When she finally lightens up, she turns back to the screen, and the words suddenly say, "I still know ... what you did last summer." No one else sees it, but Julie is upset and she goes back to her room, where there is a note sitting on a table. She opens it and sees "Surprise!" Will appears with glasses, flowers and champagne, and Julie is startled. Will apologizes and leaves the room.

Darick, the dockhand, is pulling in a boat, and he is frightened by Titus, who invites him to a party. Titus leaves, and the fisherman arrives to kill Darick. Ray is on a pay phone calling the hotel, but no one at the front desk is answering. The maid finds bloody sheets and is killed by the fisherman. Karla and Ty's private time in the Jacuzzi is interrupted by Titus, who swims away, and then again by Will, who sits with them. In her room, Julie hears creaking in the closet and discovers Darick's dead body. She runs out to the others ("It's happening again!"), but when they check with Brooks, the closet is empty. Julie demands to be taken off the island, but Brooks says the last ferry has gone and the phones are down. The porter is in his room later, using a candle flame to burn a toothbrush (which Julie had lost earlier). Titus checks on his plants and prepares to smoke some marijuana, but the fisherman kills him before he has a chance to blaze.

Ray goes to a pawn shop and sells the ring for money and a gun. The storm has already begun at the Bahamas, and the four people are all sleeping in the bed. Ty, angry, blames Julie for ruining the getaway. He and Will go to find Titus, who might have something for them to do. Karla and Julie go to the gym to work out some stress, and Karla decides Julie needs a tan and leads her to a tanning bed. Karla goes back to working out, and she hears the dryer making noise and discovers the dead maid inside. Ty and Will find Titus' bloody corpse. The fisherman secures the tanning bed shut, and Julie screams when she realizes she is trapped. The group get her out and head to Brooks' office, finding a bloody mess. The boats are all missing; Ty decides that the porter is responsible, so they go to his room. They find their personal items and believe the porter is practicing voodoo.

Julie and Karla wait in the lobby while Ty and Will look for flashlights. Julie sees a globe and finds Brazil. The porter appears and tells her that Brasilia is the capital of Brazil (they had told him about winning the contest earlier). Ty and Will return. The porter says the radio is dead, and that he had taken their things to protect them. Julie says the radio contest was a set-up. Ray finds the boat guy, pulls his gun and says that, despite the storm, he has to get to the islands that night. The porter talks about Ben Willis, saying that he murdered his wife and disappeared with his children. In the cemetery, they find an open grave with Julie's name on the headstone. The porter leaves, and Will goes after him.

Ty, Julie and Karla find some knives in the kitchen and discover Nancy hiding in the freezer. The group is arguing in the kitchen when the fisherman appears and murders Ty. The females run and climb into the attic. Karla's foot gets caught, and she and Ben Willis fall through into the room underneath. Karla eventually crashes through a greenhouse, and Julie and Nancy get her outside before the fisherman can reach her. They get to the storm shelter and find all the dead bodies. Will leads them outside and back into the hotel. He is bloody, and Karla and Nancy go to get a first aid kit. Julie says she cannot find a wound, and Will tells her, "That's because it's not my blood"—and imitates the radio guy's voice. He grabs her and pulls her away. Nancy and Karla find the porter, who has been impaled with a spear through the back, and he falls on Nancy. The fisherman shows up, shoves the spear through into Nancy, and swings at Karla, who falls back through a mirror.

Will takes Julie to the grave, and the fisherman arrives ("Hi, Dad!"). Ray is suddenly there with his gun, but he only gets a click when he pulls the trigger. He and Will struggle, until Will stands him up for his father to kill. Ray moves, and Ben Willis accidentally kills his son. He goes for Ray and is shot repeatedly by Julie. When the sun comes out, Julie helps a limping Ray, and the Coast Guard arrives. Miraculously, Karla is still alive. Julie later comes home to Ray. She hears a noise, looks around and returns to her room, where she sees the fisherman waiting under her bed. He hooks her feet and pulls her under.

I Still Know What You Did Last Summer is fairly watered-down, with minimal scares and uninteresting characters, aside from Titus (played by the charming, and uncredited, Jack Black). The title is essentially a mistake, since what the killer "still knows" did not happen last summer, but the summer before last.

The Initiation (1984)

Written by Charles Pratt, Jr.; Directed by Larry Stewart; Georgian Bay Productions, Ltd.; 97 min.

Cast: Vera Miles (Frances Fairchild); Clu Gulager (Dwight Fairchild); Daphne Zuniga (Kelly/Terry); James Read (Peter); Marilyn Kagan (Marcia); Robert Dowdell (Jason Randall); Patti Heider (Nurse Higgins); Frances Peterson (Megan); Deborah Morehart (Alison); Paula Knowles (Beth); Trey Stroud (Ralph); Peter Malof (Andy); Christopher Bradley (Chad); Joy Jones (Heidi); Mary Davis Duncan (Gwen); Rusty Meyers (Night Watchman); Christi Michelle Allen (Kelly, 9 years old); Cheryl Foster, Diane Page, Traci Odom, Melissa Toomin, Jennifer Suttles (Sorority Girls); Dan Dickerson (Detective); Ronald M. Hubner (Motorcycle Cop); Jerry L. Clark (Orderly); Kathy Lee Kennedy (Nurse); Lance Funston, Andrea Vaccarello (Students)

Crew: Bruce Lansbury, Jock Gaynor (Executive Producers); Scott Winant (Producer); Gabriel Black, Lance Ong (Composers); George Tirl (Director of Photography); Ronald LaVine (Editor)

On a stormy night, a young girl crawls out of bed and walks to the room at the end of the hallway. She sees a couple making love, and after seeing herself stab the man, another man enters the room and there is a struggle. Booze is poured on the man, he is engulfed in flames when nearing the fireplace, and the mother carries her daughter out of the room. Kelly jumps up in bed, awakened from her dream.

Kelly is at a sorority, and she and three other pledges (from an initial 15 pledges) are led into a room. Megan tells them about hell week and "prank night." The prank involves breaking into the Fairchild building (owned by Kelly's father) and stealing the night watchman's uniform. Kelly tells her pledge friend Marsha that she had the dream again, the third time that week.

At the Fireside Sanitarium, a nurse is yelling at patients and she is angered by a scarred man working in the garden. Later, the nurse is leaving, and she runs to her car when numerous inmates surround her. Inside her car, a person wearing plastic gloves stabs the nurse with a garden rake (which the gardener was using earlier). The next day, Kelly's father Dwight gets a call from the sanitarium, and he tells his wife Frances that seven inmates escaped. Frances starts to say something, but Dwight stops her and tells her not to worry. Kelly arrives, and they crack open a bottle and give her a gift for her birthday. Kelly sees Peter and tells him she wants to do a paper on dreams because she has a recurring nightmare. She fell out of a treehouse when she was nine years old, and she does not remember anything before the accident. Peter, who is doing his thesis on dream analysis, shows Kelly his place used for monitoring a dreaming person.

At home, Frances talks to Dwight about the "horrible lie," and Dwight gets his gun out to investigate a noise outside. Kelly is at Peter's place, "hooked up" and dreaming. After recounting the dream, Heidi, Peter's assistant, says that Kelly had REM and the standard muscle contractions, but her brain was "snoozing." Peter thinks the machine malfunctioned, but Heidi says that psychic phenomenon would explain it. Heidi leaves for class, and Kelly seems dazed standing in front of a mirror (the mirror seems important in her dream). Kelly tells her mother about having her nightmare again, and Frances tells her not to see Peter any more. Dwight, who will be leaving for a couple of days, is on the phone, and Kelly hears him talking to another lover. Outside, while preparing to leave, Dwight is stabbed with the rake and beheaded with a machete. Frances goes outside to give him his forgotten eyeglasses, but the car is already leaving. ("Sometimes I think that man would forget his head if it wasn't attached.")

At a frat party, Andy persists in bothering Kelly, but he is there with Megan. Kelly is with Peter, and they eventually leave the party and engage in some smooching. The next day, Kelly is being videotaped while in a hypnotic state, and Peter tries to help her remember when she was nine years old. She yells about a man ("Make him stop!") and a fire. Frances walks in, and when Peter tries to awaken Kelly by saying her full name, her mother says to call her Kelly Randall. After Kelly awakes, Frances tells her to leave and threatens Peter with the loss of his job. Peter tells Heidi that Kelly's dream is a memory, and that Kelly tried to stab her father and, to explain the mirror, she perceives herself as two different people. Her parents did not take her to a psychiatrist because they did not want it known that their daughter was homicidal.

At the Fairchild Building, the night watchman hears a noise and looks outside. Inside, the music playing stops. After looking around, he is stabbed. At the sorority house, Beth is reluctant to do the prank, saying that it is juvenile and that Megan is crazy, and she decides to quit. Frat boys Andy, Ralph and Chad are waiting by the building, and Kelly is standing by the door (she has the keys). Marcia and Alison are dropped off, and the three pledges go inside, leaving Megan the keys. Inside, Kelly tells Alison to distract the night watchman while she goes for the spare uniform in the lounge. Alison steals some skates from a store and skates past a display of knives (which is now missing a few items). Andy and Megan spend some time alone, and Ralph and Chad roll a bowling ball by the three pledges, scaring them until the frat guys laugh their recognizable laughs. The girls realize they are locked inside, so they go to find the others and get the keys.

A playful Megan is running away from Andy while lights are shutting off around the building. Andy chases Megan to the elevator, but when the doors open, he gets a hatchet in his head. Megan goes into a store of lamps, and someone shoots an arrow into her chest. The girls find Ralph and Chad, who scare them with masks. Heidi shows Peter an article telling of burnt Jason Randall and his wife Frances; it also says that Dwight was "rumored to be in the house." Peter surmises that Randall is actually Kelly's father and that she tried to stab Dwight, the man sleeping with her mother. Peter learns that an inmate groundskeeper, Randall, escaped from the sanitarium, and a nurse was found murdered. Peter tries to reach Kelly at the sorority and then at her home, then runs out, headed for the Fairchild estate.

The people in the Fairchild building are sitting around the table, enjoying themselves. Alison finds a dead night watchman and then sees that Chad has been murdered. She tells Kelly, and Alison goes to the security desk while Kelly heads for the bathroom, finds a dead Chad and sees "Kelly" written in blood on the mirror. Alison is murdered at the desk, and Kelly hears her screams. Peter visits Frances, who tells him her husband has been murdered. Peter calls the sorority house again, and Beth finally answers and tells him about the prank. Peter tells Frances to call the police, and he runs out. Ralph, in bed with Marcia, is hit with a speargun. Marcia runs.

Kelly and Marcia take refuge in the lift, but they are discovered, and Marcia is pulled away before Kelly can help her. In the boiler room, Kelly sees Randall walking around and follows her to the roof ("Kelly?"), where she whacks him with a pipe and sends him over the edge. Peter arrives, gets inside and embraces Kelly, but she stabs him. Kelly runs down and sees herself standing over Peter ("It's like looking in a mirror, isn't it, Kelly?"). Terry, Kelly's evil twin sister, says she "got out," and after the murders are blamed on their father, she will "become Kelly." Before Terry can kill her sister, she is shot and killed by Frances. Kelly is standing by an injured Peter on a stretcher, and she watches the police take her mother away.

The Initiation is a good slasher film with favorable performances and a moderately scatterbrained conclusion. The film "introduces" actress Zuniga (as the opening credits say), but audiences actually saw her before in *The Dorm That Dripped Blood* (1981).

Intruder (aka *Night Crew: The Final Checkout*) (1988)

Written and Directed by Scott Spiegel; Phantom Productions; 83 min.

Cast: Elizabeth Cox (Jennifer); Renée Estevez (Linda); Danny Hicks (Bill); David Byrnes (Craig); Sam Raimi (Randy); Eugene Glazer (Danny); Billy Marti (Dave); Burr Steers (Bub); Craig Stark (Tim); Ted Raimi (Produce Joe); Alvy Moore (Officer Dalton); Tom Lester (Officer Matthews); Emil Sitka (Mr. Abernathy); Bruce Campbell (Officer Howard); Lawrence Bender (Officer Adams); Scott Spiegel (Bread Man); Douglas Hessler (Townie at Door); Greg Nicotero (Townie in Car); Mike Jonascu, James Hanson, Jim Reickel, Paula Major, Laura Schwartz, Mark Saticoy, Steve Patino (Customers); Mara Massey, Christopher Salzgeber (Love Birds)

Crew: Lawrence Bender (Producer); Douglas Hessler (Co-Producer); Fernando Arguelles (Director of Photography); King Wilder (Editor)

The Walnut Lake Market is closing in five minutes, and the last few customers are exiting. Jennifer and Linda are working the registers, and the bearded and shady Craig approaches Jennifer's register ("Long time no see!"). Craig is angry that Jennifer seems to have no desire for a relationship with him. Craig grabs Jennifer and pushes Linda away. Jennifer refers to Craig as "crazy," and he hits her. Dave and Bill jump Craig. As others arrive, Craig gets away. Danny tells the people to look for Craig, and the group splits up and looks around the store. Jennifer is on the phone, on hold with the police, and Craig reappears and grabs her. Danny and Dave pull Craig away, Danny tells him not to come around any more, and the group pushes the man out the door.

Danny tells the night crew that they are marking everything in the store half price because he and Bill are selling the place to the city. Their jobs will be gone by the end of the month. After Danny leaves, Bill tells the upset group that he wanted to keep the place but Danny owns just a little more of the market than him. Craig gets on a pay phone and calls Jennifer, telling her he can see her ("This guy is a total creep," Linda says). Jennifer tells Linda that she went out with Craig about a year ago, and she tried to break up with him in a bar. Craig was upset, a bouncer intervened and was killed, and Craig was sent to prison. The phone rings again, but it is only Teddy, Linda's boyfriend. Dave talks with Jennifer in the back, and he asks her out. Bill recommends a place for Jennifer to work after the market job is gone.

At break, Bill talks about when he was a volunteer firefighter; at the scene of an accident, a man named Parker found the missing head of a victim and carried it in one hand while eating a sandwich in the other. Two police officers finally arrive to check on the place. Linda goes out to her car with a bag of groceries and sees a person with a knife who grabs her neck and swings the blade. In the office, Danny tells an upset Bill to sign the contract, which he reluctantly does. Down by the trash, Bill hears a noise and looks around with a hammer in his hand. He goes outside and sees Craig standing by the bathroom window. The two struggle, and Craig grabs the hammer and hits Bill on the head.

In the office, Danny is grabbed and choked; he goes for the intercom but only gets feedback. Teddy calls and asks if Linda is still at the store, and Jennifer tells him she left a while ago. While sitting in his office, Danny has his face shoved into the spike for keeping notes. Jennifer is scared by Dave, and she tells him she is worried about Craig and the fact that Linda is evidently missing. Tim watches as the couple kisses; he is secretly being watched by someone else. Joe, back in produce, is cutting up the carrots and listening to music with headphones on. A knife is swung into his head and he falls over dead.

In the aisles, Bub borrows Dave's cutter. Randy the butcher goes looking for Danny and Bill at the office. Tim is working in the back with the beverages, and the door opens. He goes to look and is stabbed in the stomach. Bub sees a dead Tim in the freezer. He talks to Tim (not realizing he is dead) and is pulled through the shelves into the freezer. Bub is carried to the trash compactor and his head is held underneath and crushed. In the meat locker, Randy finds a packaged severed hand. He is picked up and thrown unto a meat hook.

Dave tells Bub to throw back his cutter. The cutter is thrown, and, still open, it cuts Dave's hand. Dave complains and goes to get a bandage. He finds shoes with bloody stumps in the bathroom (he thinks they are pigs feet) and sees blood flowing from underneath the meat locker door. Dave climbs a ladder to a tiny attic, where he is scared by a still-living Danny (with a wounded eye). He freaks and runs to a window, where he sees Craig standing in an aisle behind Jennifer at the register. He bangs on the window, but she cannot hear him. Dave runs out of the room and is kicked down by someone. His head is sliced with a cleaver and he is dragged to the saw, which is kicked on as Dave screams.

Jennifer calls for Dave and goes looking for the others. She finds a hanging, dead Randy, screams and hides in the meat locker. She arms herself with a hook; when some meat moves, she screams, runs and slams the door on a person's hand, cutting it with the hook. She runs to the office calling for Danny and Bill and sees blood under the door. Jennifer falls down a chute, finds other dead people and runs to the front, where a customer had tried to enter through the locked doors. Craig is behind her, and she swings and hits him with the hook. He falls, and Jennifer runs crying to Bill when she sees him approach. He calms her, and Craig's eyes open. Bill goes to call the police. After seeing the blood on her hands, Jennifer notices Bill's wounded hand. Bill chases her and grabs her hair and tells her he killed for the store ("I guess I just got a little carried away"). Jennifer hits Bill with a bottle and runs. Bill gets the cleaver, finds Jennifer and chases her until she bonks him on the head again.

Jennifer runs to the front, where a man delivering bread is killed. She sees a wounded Danny calling for help. She then realizes that it is Bill, imitating Danny's voice with Danny's head. He swings the head in one hand while munching on a sandwich in the other. Jennifer runs into Craig, who says he was knocked out by Bill and saw Bill kill Linda. He says they can get out of the bathroom window (which is how Craig got inside). Craig is hit by Bill, and Jennifer runs to the bathroom, crawls out of the window and finds a dead Linda inside her Jeep. Bill grabs Jennifer, drags her under the vehicle, and she stabs him with a knife. Jennifer runs to the pay phone and calls the cops. Bill punches through and pushes the booth over. Craig arrives, grabs the cleaver and chops Bill. Two officers show up and arrest Jennifer and Craig. A dying Bill says that the couple killed everyone inside, and one cop checks the store and finds a "bloodbath." Bill's eyes open, and Jennifer screams as her Miranda Rights are read to her.

Intruder is a very enjoyable slasher, with good performances, inventine killings and over-the-top visualization from director

Spiegel. Spiegel, an old pal of director Sam Raimi and actor Bruce Campbell (who both appear in *Intruder*), co-wrote *Evil Dead II: Dead by Dawn* (1987) with Raimi. (Notice actor Hicks, who appeared in *Evil Dead II*, and a repeat of the "Suck on this!" line.) Ted Raimi, who plays Joe, is Sam Raimi's brother. Producer-actor Bender also produced Quentin Tarantino's *Pulp Fiction* (1994) and other Tarantino-related projects. Actress Estevez is the daughter of actor Martin Sheen and the sister of actors Charlie Sheen and Emilio Estevez.

Just Before Dawn (1980)

Written by Mark Arywitz and Gregg Irving; Directed by Jeff Lierberman; Oakland Productions Limited; 90 min.

Cast: George Kennedy (Roy); Mike Kellin (Ty); Chris Lemmon (Jonathan); Gregg Henry (Warren); Deborah Benson (Constance); Ralph Seymour (Daniel); Kati Powell (Merry Cat); John Hunsaker (Mountain Twins); Charles Bartlett (Vachel); Jamie Rose (Megan); Hap Oslund (Pa Logan); Barbara Spencer (Ma Logan)

Crew: Doro Vlado Hreljanovic, V. Paul Hreljanovic (Executive Producers); David Sheldon, Doro Hreljanovic (Producers); Joseph Middleton (Associate Producer); Brad Fiedel (Composer); Joel King, Dean King (Directors of Photography); Robert Q. Lovett (Editor)

Ty and his nephew Vachel are inside an old abandoned church. Ty mockingly prays, and he sees a man standing on the roof through the hole in the ceiling. He goes outside to look, and now sees nothing. Vachel's truck rolls and hits a tree, and Ty calls to his nephew. As Vachel walks to the door, a giant man stabs him in the crotch with a machete and laughs. Ty sees the man put on Vachel's orange hat and jacket, and he quickly runs into the woods.

Warren, Connie, Jonathan, Danny and Megan are traveling in an RV. On the road, Warren hits a deer and gets out to look. He sees no deer, and he walks back inside and tells Connie that it ran away. Forest ranger Roy is performing "surgery" on a plant, and Agatha, his horse, is upset. He goes outside and sees the RV come by. He stops it and tells the group that there is no campsite up ahead and that he cannot let them continue. Warren has a deed ("At least tell me where you're goin', so that when you don't come back, I'll know how to fill out the report!"). As the RV drives away, Roy says that he warned them. Later, they stop because Danny says he saw someone. Ty jumps out and says he is trying to get away from "demons." Warren and Jonathan agree that they cannot take Ty with them, so they get in the RV, Jonathan throws him a couple of sandwiches and the group leaves. Ty sees the killer jump on the back of the RV as it moves down the road, and he laughs.

The group sets up a camp. Warren and Jonathan head back to the RV for more of their things. Night falls, and Connie, Danny and Megan sit around the campfire. They hear noises; Connie points a flashlight and sees a hand on a tree, and Warren and Jonathan jump out from behind and scare the trio. The next morning, Connie is upset that she was so frightened ("helpless") the night before. The group hears a female singing voice, and they see a girl by the water, but she leaves when Connie calls to her. The group slowly walks on a rope bridge and goes to a small lake and waterfall, where Jonathan and Megan swim and Danny takes pictures. A hand from underwater touches Megan, and she laughs until she sees Jonathan stepping onto dry land. She screams and gets out of the water.

At home, Roy finds Ty leaning over and floating in the trough, and he tells the forest ranger that a "demon" killed his nephew and is going to get the group in the RV. The friends dance around the campire until a man fires a shot in the air. The man, accompanied by a woman and the singing girl, tells them to leave the land (despite the fact that Warren owns it). Connie suggests leaving, and Roy rides around on Agatha. The next day, Megan thinks a raccoon stole some of her make up, and Jonathan goes to look in the trees. He sees the girl, Merry Cat, and she kisses him and runs. He follows her to the rope bridge, where she hides behind a rock. Jonathan demonstrates how to walk across the bridge, but when he looks back, the girl is gone. The killer is at the other end, and he cuts Jonathan's hand and cuts the bridge ropes. Jonathan falls and hangs on the rope and blows a whistle. Jonathan manages to pull himself to the top, where a booted foot kicks him in the face and knocks him back into the water.

Danny goes to the old church and walks inside. Megan meets him there and mentions a "bad smell" (a dead Vachel is in the back pew). They go to the graveyard in the rear, and Danny takes some pictures of Megan. Connie and Warren play and kiss in the creek as the body of Jonathan floats their way. Warren pulls his friend to land and tries to give him mouth-to-mouth. Connie recalls hearing the whistle, and she thinks that Jonathan has been killed. Megan playfully poses for Danny. They hear a noise and believe it is Jonathan. The two feign kissing as someone approaches (Danny can hardly see, having left his sunglasses in the church). Danny is stabbed in the stomach, and Megan screams and runs into the building. She sees Vachel, ducks down and looks out the window as the killer plays with Danny's camera. The twin killer (still in Vachel's hat and jacket) appears behind Megan, puts on Danny's sunglasses and approaches a screaming Megan, as his brother snaps some pictures.

Connie and Warren call for Danny and Megan; Connie believes they are dead. The couple goes to the house of the "old people," and the man comes out with his shotgun. Connie says a friend has been killed and asks why they wanted them to leave and Warren asks what is out there. They receive no answer, and they leave, as Merry Cat watches from inside. Warren gets a lantern and goes for the body of Jonathan (he has the keys to the RV). Jonathan's corpse has been moved and is now wearing Danny's sunglasses; Warren grabs the keys. Roy reaches the house and asks the man if he has seen five campers. Merry Cat runs out and says she saw them, but she is pulled back inside, and the man eludes further questions from Roy. Inside, the girl is told not to go against her family (the killers are her brothers). She leaves, chases Roy down and offers to take him to the camp.

Connie hears the whistle, looks around and then sits back by the fire. One of the killers sits next to her and whistles, and Connie screams and runs. She climbs a tree as the killer chops away with his machete. Roy and Merry Cat find Warren as Merry Cat runs off. The tree and Connie fall, Connie runs and the killer lifts the blade. He is shot three times by Roy. Roy helps Connie up and tells her and Warren to get their things and leave. At the site, they pack their things, and a tent falls down. The twin killer comes out and stabs Warren. Connie jumps on his back. The killer knocks her off and grabs her, but Connie gets free. The killer then gives her a deadly bear hug; as the killer laughs, Connie punches her hand down his throat and forces it inside until the killer stops moving. There is more movement in the bushes, but it is only Merry Cat, who runs out, looks at Connie and runs away. The day brings light; a wounded Warren cries, and Connie embraces him.

Just Before Dawn is a very good slasher film. The "Mountain Twins" make for a couple of interesting killers, and the forest locale is attractive and beautifully photographed, particularly the waterfall and lake. Chris Lemmon is the son of actor Jack Lemmon.

Killer Workout (aka *Aerobicide*) (1986)

Written and directed by David A. Prior; The Winters Group/Maverick Films Ltd.; 85 min.

Cast: Marcia Karr (Rhonda); David James Campbell (Lieutenant Morgan); Fritz Matthews (Jimmy); Ted Prior (Chuck); Teresa Vander Woude (Jaimy); Richard Bravo (Tom);

Diane Copeland (Debbie); Laurel Mock (Diane); Lynn Meighan (Cathy); Teresa Truesdale (Rachael); Denise Martell (Marsha); Michael Beck (Curtis); John Robb (Weight Lifter #1); Joel Hoffman (Weight Lifter #2); Larry Reynolds (Officer Peterson); Deborah Norris (Office Girl); Sharon Young (Locker Room Girl); Kellyann Sabatasso, Elizabeth Keeme, Veronica Davis, Sheila Howard, Kris Hagerty, Andrea Drever, Monica Karlson, Kathi Miller, Lorain Joyner, Lori E. Forsberg, Kima Lingquist, Eddie Swilling, Richard Turner, Krysia Javid (Aerobic Dancers); Charles Vernniro, Pat Statham (Paramedics); Irene Korman, Carol Maxwell (Locker Room Girls); Wes Montgomery, Joseph Chandler, James Steele, Ronald Dais (Weight Lifters)

Crew: David Winters, Marc Winters (Executive Producers); Peter Yuval (Producer); Thomas Baldwin (Associate Producer); David A. Prior (Co-Producer/Editor); Sheila Howard (Choreography); Todd Hayen (Composer); Peter Bonilla (Director of Photography)

Aerobics dancer Valerie arrives home and checks her answering machine to learn that she has gotten a modeling job for the cover of a magazine. She heads to the Second Sun for some tanning, but her tanning ban short circuits and flames burn her.

At Rhonda's Work-Out, Rhonda is teaching Jaimy's class. Jimmy asks Rhonda out and she turns him down; Rhonda then angrily tells Jaimy to stop arriving late. In the women's locker room, Rachael stays in the showers after everyone leaves, and the lights are turned off. Someone stabs the woman to death with a large safety pin. Jaimy almost walks into the locker room, but decides instead to go into the men's locker room, where she checks out the jockstraps. Rhonda walks in and laughs at Jaimy. Jaimy goes to the women's locker room to clean up. After being frightened by an artificial arm falling from one locker, she is startled by Rachael's body falling from another.

Police officers investigate the scene. Lieutenant Morgan finds a bloody knitting needle inside the locker-coffin, goes to see Rhonda and Jaimy and asks about Diane Matthews, whose locker was the storage area for the corpse. The next day, a couple of weightlifters are talking about Rachael, but they quickly shut up when Rhonda scolds them. Rhonda tells Jaimy to teach her class and to stop "showing off." Rhonda finds Chuck Dawson in her office, looking through her files. He says that Rhonda's "senior partner," Mr. Erickson, has hired Chuck. Outside, Jimmy tells Chuck to stay away from Rhonda, and the two men fight. Debbie, evidently impressed by Chuck's combat skills, offers the man a ride, and they head to Debbie's house, where Chuck asks for Jimmy's address. While Debbie is inside, Chucky calls Mr. Erickson and tells him he is "working on it." Debbie gives Chuck the address, and the two kiss.

Jimmy is watching some aerobics later as Diane eyes him. She asks him out, and Jimmy declines. Diane walks home and is followed by someone in a car (who checks on a gun in the glove compartment). Diane gets home, and Morgan is outside by his car. He knocks on her door, but she backs away, too frightened to answer. The killer is inside; Diane is stabbed with the pin. Morgan bursts inside as the killer jumps out the window. The lieutenant returns to his car and is told that the knitting needle belonged to Diane but is not the murder weapon, a fact which Morgan recently surmised. Rhonda is surprised by Jimmy at the gym ("Just relax, I'm not some kind of a crazy killer"). Debbie, Marsha and Curtis deface the gym's front windows with spray paint (painting "Aerobicide" and "Death Spa"), then run away. Curtis is stabbed in the neck. Marsha is looking for him when the killer grabs her and slits her throat. Debbie finds Curtis and runs back to her car. The killer jumps on top of the convertible roof and stabs through until finally hitting and killing Debbie.

A weightlifter is working on a weight machine that has been loosened, and he is hit and falls to the floor. The killer is waiting to whack him in the face with a weight. The man's weightlifting friend finds him dead and is subsequently stabbed in the head with the pin. Tommy finds the men dead. When Jaimy sees him by the bodies and screams, Chuck runs in and beats Tommy. The bodies are taken away, and Morgan mentions the coincidence that Chuck began work as soon as the killings started (and that he took Tommy out "like a pro"). Tommy, handcuffed and waiting alone in a locker room, is murdered. His body is taken away ("See you tomorrow, Lieutenant," one of the paramedics says), and Morgan tells Chuck things have "picked up" since he has been there.

Morgan sees Rhonda in her office, and after pointing out that she seems "handy" with a letter opener, he tells her he has several suspects but needs a motive. Chuck snoops around Jimmy's place and discovers an assortment of guns as well as many pictures of Rhonda. Later, Chuck goes to Rhonda's place where Jimmy starts another fight. Chuck is finally kicked into the pool, and Jimmy leaves. Chuck comes around in Rhonda's house, and Morgan is there. The lieutenant says he knows Chuck is a PI, and Chuck tells him he was hired by Mr. Erickson and tells about Jimmy's place and his locker (Rhonda asks what kind of pictures he had). Morgan tells Chuck to get out of town.

Cathy cleans out her locker and says she is leaving. She goes to say good bye to Jaimy, and finds her dead. Later, Officer Peterson finds both women murdered. Morgan gets a call from someone who has checked on Rhonda. Chuck is leaving from the back of the gym when Jimmy runs him down, gets out of his car and stabs him. Morgan goes to see Rhonda (who has just put a wig on her scarred head) and says he knows she is Valerie, who was burned five years ago. Morgan arrests her, thinking she killed the people because they were beautiful. In the car, he is told that Chuck was killed, and that witnesses saw Jimmy.

Morgan chases Jimmy down, and he says he knows he did not kill anyone, suggesting that Rhonda did it all. Jimmy hits the officer, leaving to see Rhonda. He turns the lights on in the locker room and reacts to Rhonda's nude burnt body; she gets a gun out of her locker and shoots him. Jimmy says he loves Rhonda and he did not want her to be caught, and Rhonda thanks him by killing him. Later, Morgan takes Rhonda to a secluded area. He tells about his law-enforcing father and the mysterious disappearance of a guilty man who the courts let go. Morgan gets out his gun and says he will be "crossing that line" because he knows that Rhonda murdered at least 12 people. Rhonda quickly grabs a shovel and pounds the lieutenant in the head. At the gym, she is read an advertisement for Rhonda's Work-Out and is assured the gym will be "packed with gorgeous bodies." Rhonda says she is counting on it. When she is alone, she brings out her keychain, which is a large safety pin.

Killer Workout has few scares and multiple scenes of aerobic dancing. A somewhat tongue-in-cheek approach keeps the film from becoming completely flat.

The Last Horror Film (aka *The Fanatic*) (1984)

Written by Judd Hamilton, Tom Klassen and David Winters; Directed by David Winters; Twin Continental Films/Shere Productions Ltd.; 87 min.

Cast: Caroline Munro (Jana Bates); Joe Spinell (Vinny); Judd Hamilton (Alan Cunningham); Devin Goldenberg (Marty Bernstein); David Winters (Stanly Kline); Stanley Susanne Benton (Susan Archer); Mary Spinell (Vinny's Mother); Glenn Jacobson (Bret Bates); J'len Winters (Girl in Jacuzzi/Beach Girl Teaser); Sharon Hughes (Stripper); Sean Casey (Jonathan); Don Talley (Cowboy); John Kelly (Man in Theatre); Simone Overman, Malgosia Casey, Patty Salier (Women in Theatre); Chip Hamilton, George Valismis, Peter Darcy (New York Men); Mai Britt Finseth, Valerie (Bikini Girls); Robert Paget, Katia Malmio, Dennis Beasnard, Richard Masner, Jenny Lipman, Holly DeJong (Screening Room Jury); Tony McCann (Blowtorch Man); Jane Wellman (Burn Effect Girl); Valerie Devereaux (Girl Fan); Joanne Hicks, William Whittington (Miss Bates' Secretaries); John Claude (Delivery Boy); Noreen Kantala, Corina Burkli (Girls in Lobby); Lavanna Hakim, Marika Laususer, Mai Britt Finseth (Beach Girls); George Altschul, Ronald Dessautels (Bouncers); Marie Jose Welsch (Topless Girl on Pier); Marty Ollstein (Door Man); June Chadwick, Robin Leach, John Austin (Reporters); Jane Rawlins (Old Lady, Alley Scene); Mark Hutchinson (Young Boy); David Jones (Rock Star); Melissa Carr, Judy Duckett (Girls by Pool); John Hamilton, Luke Walter (Bodyguards); Tammy Hamilton (Jana Bates' Lookalike); Marty Heckleman, Tom DeNove (Policemen); Henri Marchal (Announcer)

Crew: David Winters, Judd Hamilton (Producers); Sean Casey (Associate Producer); Jesse Frederick, Jeff Koz (Composers); Tom DeNove (Director of Photography); Chris Barnes, G.B.F.E., Edward Salier (Editors)

At night, a woman gets into a hot tub. Someone cuts a cable which is slid into the water, switches on a fuse box are hit, and the woman is electrocuted. "The End" appears on the screen; Vinny is sitting in an audience watching the film.

Vinny is in his taxi cab reading about Jana Bates ("queen of horror films"), and imagines working with Jana on *The Life of Vinny Durand* and Jana presenting him with an Oscar. He goes home to his mother and packs his bags for the Cannes Film Festival. Vinny says he is going to be a "great director" (which his mother considers one of his many "crazy ideas").

In Cannes, the wall of Vinny's hotel room is filled with pictures of Jana. A screening room jury nominates Jana for Best Actress for her performance in her most recent film, *Scream*. Vinny later tries to get into a Studio Circus party but security keeps him out. The next day, Vinny calls Bret Bates, the producer of Jana's films and her ex-lover; Bret will not let him talk to her. Jana gets flowers and a note that says, "You've made your last horror film. Goodbye." Bret receives a bottle of champagne and an identical note. Jana goes to see Bret; when there is no response, she walks inside and finds the man dead in the bathroom. Secretly being filmed, Jana runs away.

Later, Jana's current lover Alan tells her that Bret is probably playing a joke (the hotel people found no body). Vinny is watching girls at the beach, and they mock him. Vinny goes around filming Jana doing different promotional things. After agent Marty Bernstein shrugs off Vinny, the ambitious filmmaker calls his mother and tells her he is making a movie with Jana. Marty, director Stanly Kline and actress Susan Archer tell police they have all received notes like Bret, but the police think Bret's disappearance is a publicity stunt. Marty gets a letter from Bret to meet him in a screening room, where the agent is axed to death as a camera is rolling. Vinny calls his mother again and tells her that everyone wants to buy his film. At a press conference, Jana is asked if anyone has become obsessed with the actress. At a club, Vinny runs up to a stripper during her performance ("I love you, Jana!"), and he is pulled away by bouncers.

Vinny goes to see Stanly Kline's *Caller in the Night*, which begins with a woman knocking a man down and cutting up his body. Vinny, sick, sprints from the theater and runs into Stanly outside. Vinny tells him he should not be alive to make such films. Susan is scared and wants to leave, but Stanly first takes her to a building and playfully runs around and hides from her. While hiding from Susan, Stanly is stabbed and killed; Susan finds his dead body on the roof. She is shot while being filmed and falls off the tower. Vinny, on the phone with his mother, says he is going to be famous. He imagines himself sitting in the director's chair, but people are laughing at him.

Vinny gets a bottle of champagne and enters through Jana's bathroom window after the actress gets out of the bath. He wants to talk about his movie, but Jana tells him to leave. He breaks the bottle and points the broken end towards her. Vinny turns when the doorbell rings, and Jana runs screaming to the lobby (still only in her towel). The people in the lobby think it is another stunt and applaud; Vinny stops for them and smiles. Jana runs to a crowd of reporters ("What a fabulous entrance!") and then to Alan. He takes her back to her hotel, calms her and says they will go to his friend's castle tomorrow. Vinny, at the window, overhears, and follows the couple to the castle. Alan tells his friend Jonathan that they will be staying for a night. Vinny gets inside the castle, says to himself "This is perfect!" (a little too loudly) and runs when bodyguards chase him. Jonathan tries to stop Vinny, and the bodyguards, having fired at the running Vinny, unknowingly hit Jonathan.

The next day, Alan and Jana go to the awards ceremony. Vinny writes a letter to his mother, explaining that his film will be great and that Jana will be his bride. He looks in the mirror and says, "Don't worry, Miss Bates, you need protection. Someone's trying to hurt you." Michelle, Jana's decoy, goes with Alan to sit in the audience as Jana waits backstage with Joanne, not realizing they are being filmed. Joanne goes to get Jana a glass of water, Vinny puts a cloth over Jana's mouth, carries her to his car and drives away. Alan is asked backstage (Jana has just won the Best Actress award), where they find Vinny's letter.

Vinny, driving with the unconscious Jana, says that someone was trying to kill her. He mentions "that stupid Vinny" as a crazy fan, and he tells her about the upcoming scene in the castle for his film, *The Loves of Dracula*. Vinny films a scene in which he (as Dracula) stakes Jana through the heart. The actress awakes (the staking was only an effect), and Vinny thanks her for being in his movie. Bret shows up with a camera and a gun, and he says that Vinny is the perfect fall guy. Vinny throws his cape over Bret and runs, but Bret grabs Jana. Outside, Vinny turns on headlights and blinds Bret. After Jana gets away, Vinny swings at Bret with a chainsaw and decapitates him. The police and Alan arrive as Vinny stands over the body and screams. The film ends, and Vinny and his mother are sitting in a screening room. His mother says she is proud of him. As Vinny tries to talk about his next picture idea, the woman asks her son for a joint.

The Last Horror Film re-teams Spinell with Munro (following the much more violent *Maniac*). While not outstanding, the film provides enough humor to make it fun, and the many movie posters at the different Cannes sites are a treat for film buffs. *For Your Eyes Only* (1981) is the Bond film poster shown during the film; actress Munro had appeared with Roger Moore in the 1977 007 movie *The Spy Who Loved Me*. The character of Stanly is credited as "Stanlee" on the *Caller in the Night* movie poster and as "Stanley" in the movie's opening credit; Vinny is credited as "Vinnie" for his completed film.

Leatherface: Texas Chainsaw Massacre III (1990)

Written by David J. Schow; Directed by Jeff Burr; New Line Cinema; 81 min.

Cast: Kate Hodge (Michelle); Viggo Mortensen (Tex); William Butler (Ryan); Ken Foree (Benny); Joe Unger (Tinker); Tom Everett (Alfredo); Toni Hudson (Sara); Miriam Byrd-Nethery (Mama); R.A. Mihailoff (Leatherface); Jennifer Banko (Little Girl); Ron Brooks (TV Newsman); David Cloud (Scott); Beth DePatie (Gina); Duane Whitaker (Kim); Michael Shamus Wiles (Checkpoint Officer)

Crew: Robert Engelman (Producer); Michael DeLuca (Associate Producer); Jim Manzie (Composer); James L. Carter (Director of Photography); Brent Schoenfeld (Editor)

Only one member of the chainsaw family, W.E. Sawyer, was brought to trial, and he was put to death in the gas chamber in 1981. The jurors presumed that Leatherface was an "alternate personality." A woman screams and is pounded with a sledgehammer. Leatherface cuts and sews a new skin mask as a girl watches from a window.

Michelle is driving with Ryan; that night, they are held up by a checkpoint. A "body pit" has been discovered, and the police are investigating the scene. An officer asks where the two are going, and Michelle says she is dropping the car off for her father. The cop tells her to keep moving and not to stop for anyone.

The next day Michelle hits an armadillo. She gets a large rock to put the animal out of its misery, but she cannot do it, and Ryan kills it for her. Tex is dropped off at the Last Chance gas station, where Michelle and Ryan stop for gas. After Ryan goes to the bathroom, Alfredo the attendant takes Michelle's picture and tries to get her to pay it. Michelle gets out of the car as Alfredo fills up the tank, and Tex asks Alfredo if he is bothering Michelle. When Ryan returns, Tex asks if they can give him a ride, but Ryan says they are on a tight schedule. Michelle leaves for the bathroom, and Tex suggests a road for Ryan to take. Alfredo is pulled away from the wall as he watches Michelle in the rest room, and Tex pushes the attendant outside. Alfredo gets a shotgun and Tex tells the couple to leave. The two drive off, and Alfredo shoots at the car and then at Tex. Ryan tells Michelle to take Tex's route.

Night falls, and a truck is driven away from the Last Chance gas station as Alfredo laughs. The truck is suddenly behind Michelle and Ryan, a dead body is thrown on the windshield and the car stops. They blew a tire, so they quickly jack up the car and put the spare on. When Leatherface appears with his chainsaw the two jump into the car, and Michelle backs into Leatherface. He grabs the trunk, which is pulled off as the car speeds away. Down the road, Ryan wants Michelle to stop so that he can tighten the lug nuts, and an apparently wounded Tex runs out in front of them, causing both Michelle and Benny (in his Jeep) to run off the road. Ryan crawls out and is scared by Benny, and the men get Michelle out of the car. Ryan tries to tell Benny what is going on, and he gives the couple "painkillers," which makes them both sleepy. Michelle says that Tex may be on the road, and Benny goes to check.

Benny tells Tinker of the accident. Tinker gets in his truck (the same one that frightened Michelle and Ryan), and Benny, having been told of the maniac with a chainsaw, sees a chainsaw in the back of the truck. He tells Tinker to wait and goes to his overturned Jeep and gets his gun and bullets. An impatient Tinker runs toward the Jeep, and Benny jumps over the edge and rolls down an incline. Leatherface attacks Benny, and the chainsaw is kicked away. Benny is cut with a small surgical saw, and Leatherface lifts the chainsaw. The girl from earlier gets his attention, and he chases after her.

A sleepy Michelle and Ryan get up and walk. Benny sees a bloody hole in the girl's hand, and she tells him she is the only one left from an attack the previous week. Benny hears the couple calling him, and he stands. The girl decides to stay, and she tosses him her lighter. Leatherface finds the girl and chainsaws her, and he chases after Michelle and Ryan. Ryan is caught in a bear trap; he tells Michelle to run, and Leatherface chainsaws him. Michelle runs to a house and finds a seemingly frightened little girl. She tries to console her, and the girl stabs her with a shard of bone. Michelle is grabbed by Tex. Her hands are nailed to the arms of a chair, and Mama arrives in her wheelchair. Tinker drags in Ryan, and his legs are hooked; still alive, he is hung upside down. Tape is put around Michelle's mouth.

Benny watches Alfredo throw body parts into a pond. Leatherface plays around with Ryan's Walkman, and Tex brings in Leatherface's gift of a brand new chainsaw, with the inscription "The Saw is Family" on the blade. Tinker is angry that Benny is still alive, and he throws Leatherface's Walkman into the fire. Leatherface grabs Tinker and makes him retrieve the Walkman with his hand. Alfredo fights a trap "sprung," and Benny is there with his gun against the gas station attendant. Benny knocks Alfredo into the pond ("One down!"). Benny sees Leatherface play with an electronic toy in the shed.

A sledgehammer contraption is used to bash in Ryan's head. Leatherface starts the saw and prepares to chop Michelle. Benny is at the window and he fires repeatedly, hitting the chainsaw, killing Mama and shooting Tinker in the hand and blowing his ear off. Michelle gets free by pulling her hands out of the spikes. When Tex grabs her, she stabs him. The little girl turns on the lights, and Leatherface drives his truck and Benny and Michelle run. Benny turns to fire but is out of bullets, and ducks under the truck. Leatherface chases after Michelle with the chainsaw. An injured Tinker tells Tex to "go get the meat," and Tex swings an axe at Benny as he crawls out from under the truck. Benny grabs the axe and hits the gasoline tank sitting on the truck. Tex attacks Benny with a chain, and during a struggle, Tex is doused with the leaking gasoline. Benny flips the lighter and throws it, Tex is set afire and the truck explodes.

Michelle's ankle is caught in a rope, but she is stopped by the pond, and she pulls the rope off. As she gets out of the water, Leatherface attacks, but he is jumped by Benny. The chainsaw runs free in the pond as the two men fight, and Leatherface pushes Benny on the saw. Michelle grabs a rock and beats Leatherface in the head. Michelle is walking the next morning when a truck from the Last Chance gas station pulls up beside her, with Benny behind the wheel. He is hit with a sledgehammer by Alfredo, who bashes on the truck to get to Michelle. He finally grabs her on the passenger's side, and she grabs a shotgun, and fires. Michelle leads Benny to the passenger side, and she drives away. Leatherface watches them leave and angrily runs his chainsaw.

Leatherface: Texas Chainsaw Massacre III diminishes any chance for frights by having an assortment of murderous family members but only a handful of potential victims. It also suffers from heavy editing of the gore. However, it is fun to watch the chameleon-like Mortensen as well as the charming Foree, who also starred in George A. Romero's classic *Dawn of the Dead* (1978). Caroline Williams, who starred in the second *Texas Chainsaw Massacre*, appears in a cameo near the beginning of the film (when Michelle and Ryan are stopped by the police).

Maniac
(1980)

Written by C.A. Rosenberg and Joe Spinell; Directed by William Lustig; Magnum Motion Pictures; 88 min.

Cast: Joe Spinell (Frank Zito); Caroline Munro (Anna D'Antoni); Gail Lawrence (Rita); Kelly Piper (Nurse); Rita Montone (Hooker); Tom Savini (Disco Boy); Hyla Marrow (Disco Girl); James Brewster (Beach Boy); Linda Lee Walter (Beach Girl); Tracie Evans (Street Hooker); Sharon Mitchell (Second Nurse); Carol Henry (Deadbeat); Nelia Bacmeister (Carmen Zito); Louis Jawitz (Art Director); Denise Spagnuolo (Denise); Billy Spagnuolo (Billy); Frank Pesce (TV Reporter); Candace Clements (First Park Mother); Dian Spagnuolo (Second Park Mother); Kim Hudson (Lobby Hooker); Terry Gagnon (Woman in Alley); Joan Baldwin, Jeni Paz (Models); Janelle Winston (Waitress); Randy Jurgensen, Jimmy Aurichio (Cops)

Crew: Joe Spinell, Judd Hamilton (Executive Producers); Andrew Garroni, William Lustig (Producers); John Packard (Associate Producer); Jay Chattaway (Composer); Robert Lindsay (Director of Photography); Lorenzo Marinelli (Editor); Tom Savini (Special Makeup and Effects)

A couple is lying on the beach. The woman asks the man to fetch some wood for their fire. While he is gone, someone approaches the woman and slits her throat with a razor. The guy returns, and a wire is wrapped around his neck and pulled.

Frank Zito sits up in his bed screaming. His room is full of mannequins (one is lying on the bed beside him), and there is a framed picture of a woman on the wall, surrounded by candles. He takes off his shirt and examines the scars on his chest. He dresses, puts on his gloves and leaves.

Frank is walking downtown when a prostitute stops him and asks if he would like a date. The two go inside the nearby hotel. In the room, Frank asks the woman if she has ever modeled ("Show me, like in the magazines"). After she dances a little bit, the woman and Frank kiss, and she relaxes him after he stops. When they resume kissing,

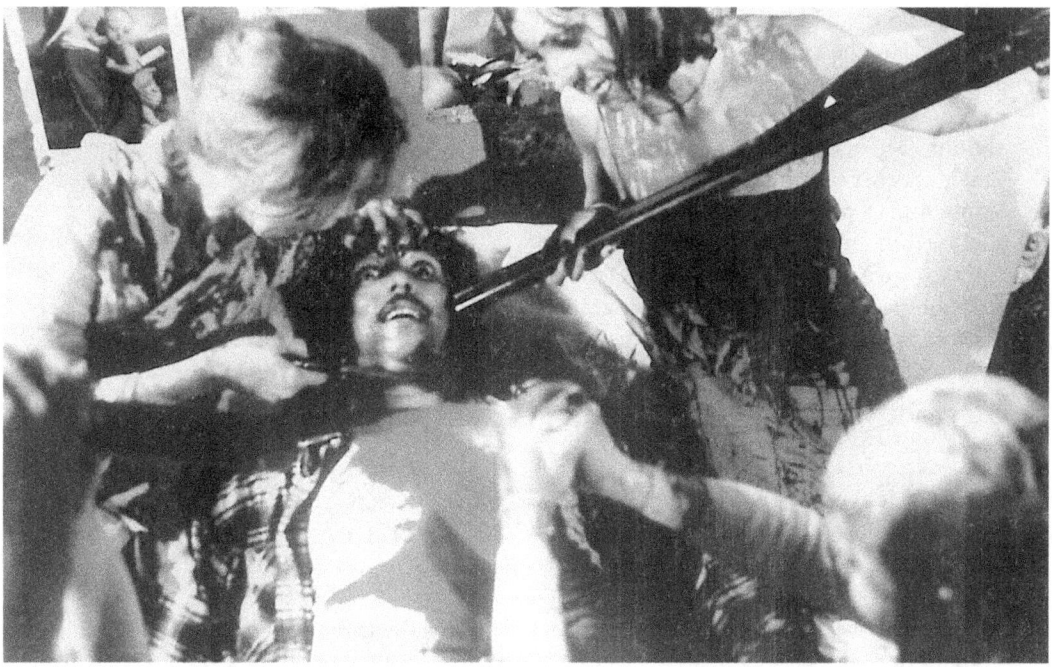

Frank (Joe Spinell) is stabbed, chopped and mutilated by his mannequin victims in William Lustig's *Maniac* (1980).

Frank suddenly becomes angry and begins choking her until she dies (with images of choking the woman in the picture). He gets sick ("Why'd you make me do that?") and then scalps the woman. Frank goes home with a new mannequin and puts it on his bed. He dresses it in the hooker's clothing and nails the bloody wig to its head. A newspaper headline screams of a mutilated couple of the beach. Frank packs his shotgun, puts his gloves on and leaves, telling the mannequins he will "be right back."

Frank watches a couple getting into a car. The man and woman park, and the man persuades the woman to join him in the back seat. Frank gets out of his car, and the woman stops their session when she sees Frank at the window. She is upset and wants to go home, and the couple returns to the front seat. When the headlights come on, Frank is standing in front of them. He jumps on the hood, fires his shotgun and blows the man's head off. The woman ducks down inside the car as Frank approaches, points the gun at her and fires. Later, Frank is in the room, talking to himself and/or the mannequins. He mentions another person "stopping" the "fancy girls," and he says the person must stop ("They'll take you away from me...").

In the park during the day, Frank stops a little girl on a bicycle and tells her to be careful. He sees a woman snap a photograph of him from afar, so he follows her, sneaks a peek at her bag and sees her name (Anna D'Antoni) and address. Two nurses are leaving the hospital, and one mentions the killer on the loose. One woman is picked up, and the other continues to wait. Frank starts to follow the nurse, but she realizes someone is behind her and runs to the subway station. She gets through the gate, but the train leaves without her. Seeing Frank approaching, she runs and hides in a bathroom stall. Frank walks inside, looks around and leaves, and the nurse calms down. Happy that she is okay, she walks to the sink to wash her face. Frank, standing behind her, stabs her with a knife and then washes the bloody blade.

Anna is in the darkroom developing photographs when the doorbell rings. Frank is at the door, and he tells her he is the man she photographed in the park. Anna lets him in, and they talk about photographs. Anna says she sells the pictures, but Frank says she should keep them to preserve the beauty. Frank asks her to dinner. That night, Frank shows Anna a picture of his mother, who he says died in an automobile accident. Frank wants to see Anna again, and she invites him to a show on Thursday. At a photography session, Frank gives Anna a teddy bear and is introduced to the model Rita. Anna and Rita go back to shooting, and Frank eyes the two women together. He steals a necklace and leaves.

Rita, at home, answers her buzzing door to Frank, who returns her necklace (claiming he found it at the studio) and slyly pushes in the door's lock. After her bath, Rita is getting some hot tea when she is grabbed by Frank. Frank ties and gags Rita to her bed, and says that her hair is different but he knew he would find her. He says he is going to keep her so she will not get away, then he stabs her, saying "Mommy." Frank takes Rita's hair.

In his room, Frank sits in the front of the woman's picture and talks about hiding in the closet when his mother said. Frank calls Anna, asks her to a show and picks her up. Anna thanks him for sending flowers and attending Rita's funeral. They go to the cemetery to visit the grave of Carmen Zito, and Frank begins to cry. He says that Rita knew, and he grabs Anna by the neck. Anna hits him and runs, and Frank gives chase. Anna wounds Frank with a shovel to the arm, and runs away as Frank screams, "Mother!" He hears his mother's voice and the voice of a young Frank ("Mommy has to punish you"), and he pleads not to be locked in the closet. He kneels at the grave, and the rotting corpse of his mother grabs him. Frank sits alone and cries.

Frank goes home and lies on the bed with a wounded arm. As he looks around the room, the mannequins turn into the murdered women they represent, and they all approach Frank with weapons. They stab him in the stomach, chop off an arm and pull off his head. The next day, a couple of police officers run into Frank's place and find him lifeless on the bed (with only a knife in his bloody stomach), with the mannequins standing around the room. The cops leave, and Frank opens his eyes.

Maniac is a somber cinematic venture, adeptly produced, and featuring a killer who is both pitiful and atrocious. Spinell's performance is uncomfortably uncanny and at times almost too realistic. The man who has his head blown off is played by Tom Savini, who also created the film's special effects.

Maniac Cop (1988)

Written by Larry Cohen; Directed by William Lustig; Shapiro Glickenhaus Entertainment; 85 min.

Cast: Tom Atkins (Frank McCrae); Bruce Campbell (Jack Forrest); Laurene Landono (Theresa Mallory); Richard Roundtree (Commissioner Pike); William Smith (Captain Ripley); Robert Z'Dar (Matt Cordell); Sheree North (Sally Noland); Nina Aversen (Regina Sheperd); Nick Barbaro (Councilman); Lou Bonacki (Detective Lovejoy); Barry Brenner (Coroner); Victoria Catlin (Ellen Forrest); Jim Dixon (Clancy); Corey Eubanks (Bremmer); Jill Gatsby (Cassie Phillips); Rocky Giordani (Fowler); John Goff (Jack's Lawyer); William J. Gorman (Desk Sergeant); Jon Greener (Tactical Sergeant); Teddy M. Haggarty, Patrick Wright (Prison Guards); Danny Hicks (Squad Leader); Erik Holland (Doctor Gruber); Dennis Junt (Assistant Squad Leader); Marcia Karr (Nancy); Judy Kerr (Motel Maid); Jake LaMotta (Detective); Judy Levitt (Woman in Car); Jason Lustig (Squad Commander); William Lustig (Motel Manager); Vic Manni (Jail Guard); Tito Nunez (Chico); Daniel Ortiz (Ramos); Louis Pastore ("John"); Frank Pesce (Watchman); Bernie Pock (Sam); Ed Polgardy, Tom Taylor (Men in Bar); Sam Raimi (Parade Reporter); Carla Y. Reynolds (Police Officer); Jef Richard (Witness); Adele Sparks (Nurse); Ingrid van Dorn (Waitress); Luke Walter (Musician); Nicholas Yee (Patrolman); Lee Arnone, Nay K. Dorsey, George "Buck" Flower, Bill Waldron, Alma Washington (People on TV)

Crew: James Glickenhaus (Executive Producer); Larry Cohen (Producer); Jef Richard (Co-Producer); Jay Chattaway (Composer); Vincent J. Rabe (Director of Photography); David Kern (Editor)

Cassie leaves the bar at night and is attacked by two punks who try to take her purse. She runs and hides, then calls out to a police officer she sees standing nearby. She gasps when she sees his face; he grabs her neck, picks her up and kills her as the punks watch. The next day, the punks are picked up, and they say that an officer was responsible. Detectives Frank McCrae and Lovejoy see the woman's body at the medical examiner's office, and Frank believes the punks' claim of a murderous policeman. A man and woman are waiting at a red light, and a cop raps on the window with a billy club. He takes the man to the front of the car for a sobriety test, and the woman watches as he pulls a blade from the billy club, swipes twice and throws the man on the windshield. She screams, gets in the driver's seat and speeds away.

Frank goes to see Commissioner Pike and suggests giving policemen mental tests. Pike tells him to keep it quiet and talks about Frank trying to shoot himself after his partner was killed in the line of duty. A man is thrown against his car and handcuffed, and he runs away when the officer pulls a blade. The cop catches up and shoves the man's face in wet cement; and he is jackhammered out the following day. Frank meets with his news reporter friend Regina and gives her information on the recent killings. After the news story of a maniac cop runs, a woman has car trouble; when a policeman knocks on her window, she shoots and kills him.

Jack Forrest is putting on his police uniform as he and his wife Ellen argue about his job. She says she is sometimes afraid that he might hurt her in his sleep. He leaves, and Ellen receives a phone call from a person who has called before, suggesting that Jack is the killer. Ellen gets her gun, follows Jack to a hotel and catches him in bed with another woman. She points the gun without letting Jack explain, storms out and is grabbed and pulled into a van.

A maid at the hotel finds Ellen dead in a room. Captain Ripley tells Jack that his wife is dead, and he arrests the officer after he admits to being at the hotel. In the interrogation room, Ripley and Frank show Jack the collection of "Maniac Cop" articles (belonging to Ellen), and read a page of Ellen's diary saying that she thinks he is the killer. Jack tells his lawyer that he has a witness but would like to keep her out of it. Frank believes Jack is protecting someone and goes to see Jack in his cell, where he finally admits he was with Theresa Mallory. Theresa is posing as a prostitute, and she is attacked by the killer cop. Frank arrives, and they both fire at the maniac. They settle down with drinks, and Theresa says the only person she told about her and Jack was Sally, a cripple who works in the Clerical Room. Frank goes to talk to Sally and tells her about Theresa being attacked.

Later, Frank follows Sally in his car to a pier, where he watches her talk to the stout cop. She tells the killer that if he relaxes, the police will think Jack did it and let their guard down, and he can go after the commissioner and the mayor. She calls him "Matt," and tells him to save his murderous rampage for the people who did wrong to him. Frank goes to see Clancy and reads about Matt Cordell, who had been thrown in Sing Sing for "violating people's rights." He says Cordell had a girlfriend who jumped out of a window to kill herself but was only crippled. Cordell thinks back to being sentenced and then led into the prison. As he showers, three men attack him, and he beats them until he is stabbed in the back. He falls, and the men slice his face with a shiv.

Frank and Theresa go to see Jack in prison, and they tell him Cordell may not have died in prison and may be committing the murders. Theresa and Jack are left alone to kiss, and Frank goes to the Clerical Room, where he is beaten by Sally with a cane ("He knows I'm no good to him!"). She leaves and sees a dead cop ("He's here!"), and Cordell grabs her as Frank leads her away. Cordell slams Sally up against the wall, and Frank pulls his gun but is thrown by the cop. Theresa sees dead cops outside, and Jack grabs a gun and tells Theresa to wait in Frank's car. Frank is tossed out of a window on a high floor and lands on a taxi next to Theresa. Lovejoy points a gun at Jack, thinking he is murdering everyone, and he goes for the phone and reacts to touching Sally's dead fingers. Jack punches him, gets the gun and runs away.

Jack and Theresa visit Doctor Gruber at Sing Sing's infirmary (Jack says he is Frank, who had an appointment). After preliminary questions, Gruber finally admits that, on the day Cordell was attacked in the showers, the doctor discovered that he was still alive, and he revived the officer. He said he thought the man was legally dead and did not see any harm in making people believe he had actually died. The St. Patrick's Day parade is that day and, while Jack waits on the sidewalk, Theresa goes to warn Pike that Cordell might be after him. Theresa tries to tell the commissioner who the murderer is, but he and Ripley think Theresa aided in Jack's escape and killings. A cop stays to arrest Theresa, and Pike and Ripley leave and are stabbed and killed by Cordell. The cop handcuffs Theresa to him, and as they are walking down the hallway, the office is stabbed in the stomach. Theresa gets into a room, gets the key and uncuffs herself as Cordell breaks through the door. She climbs unto the ledge as Jack watches. A group of policemen see Jack, arrest him and throw him in the paddy wagon.

Cordell pulls the driver out and drives away with Jack. Theresa gets in a cop car with another officer and they follow them to Pier 14. Cordell stops the vehicle and Jack jumps out as he starts to axe the door open. Cordell picks up Jack and throws him on Theresa as she approaches with a shotgun. Cordell picks up the weapon and blows away the other cop as he runs in. Jack knocks the gun away from the maniac cop, and he is punched and thrown before Cordell hears sirens and drives the paddy wagon away. Jack jumps on, and they run into a suspended tube that crashes through the windshield and pierces Cordell's chest. The truck, Cordell and Jack fly off the dock and into the water. The paddy wagon is pulled to the dock, and the cop is not inside. Down in the water, Cordell's hand comes out.

Maniac Cop is an exciting and action-packed slasher, with a great villain and likable characters. Lustig's direction is taut and keen, and Cohen's script is kinetic. Look for Lustig in the motel office and director–Campbell pal Sam Raimi as the reporter at the parade.

Maniac Cop 2 (1990)

Written by Larry Cohen; Directed by William Lustig; The Movie House Company Ltd./Fadd Enterprises, Inc.; 87 min.

Cast: Robert Davi (Det. Sean McKinney); Claudia Christian (Susan Riley); Michael Lerner (Edward Doyle); Bruce Campbell (Jack Forrest); Laurene Landon (Theresa Mallory); Robert Z'Dar (Matt Cordell); Clarence Williams III (Blum); Leo Rossi (Turkell); Lou Bonacki (Det. Lovejoy); Paula Trickey (Cheryl); Charles Napier (Law Brady); Santos Morales (Store Clerk); Robert Earl Jones (Harry); Andrew Hill Newman (Citizen); Angel Salazar (Traffic Officer); Vincent Russo (Cab Driver); Hank Garrett (Tom O'Hanion); Bo Dietl (Detective); Charlie Alfano (Color Guard); Kurek Ashley, Joe Cirillo (Police Officers); Nick Barbaro (Captain of the Guards); John Barnes (Prison Guard); Barry Brenner (Medical Examiner); Marc Chamlin (Pedestrian); Charlie Croughwell, David Graves (Trustees); Shelly Desai (Convict); James Dixon (Range Officer); Jude Farese (Sergeant); Henry Fehren (Priest); Lisa Kramer (Ambulance Attendant); Lennon (Club Host); Frank Pesce (Strip Club M.C.); Sam Raimi (Newscaster); Debra Sarrategui (Bartender); Linda Stockwell (Woman Cop); Danny Trejo (Prisoner); Audrey Marlyn, Patrick S. Harrigan, Glen Lloyd Hahn, Maria D'Alessio (Interviewees); Cynthia Banks, Heather Dalberg, Nancy Dregan, Robin Hansen, Manuella Mora, Krystal Sather, Mildred Smedley, Ysobel Villanera (Strip Club Girls)

Crew: David Hodgins, Frank D'Alessio (Executive Producers); Larry Cohen (Producer); Anthony De Felice (Associate Producer); John S. Engel (Co-Producer); Jay Chattaway (Composer); James Lemmo (Director of Photography); David Kern (Editor)

A man stumbles into a convenience store and shows the store clerk his shotgun. The clerk says he does not know the combination to the safe, and he hits the silent alarm. With the register nearly empty, the potential thief and the clerk scratch off lottery tickets. After getting a $5,000 winner, the man sees Officer Matt Cordell in the back of the store and fires his shotgun. Cordell takes the gun from him, beats him in the head and shoots the clerk, who was happy about his winning ticket. The officer hands the gun back to the crook and the man runs outside, where police are waiting. He says that one of the cops is responsible for the murder, and he is gunned down for not dropping his weapon.

Commissioner Doyle tells Jack and Theresa that they are cleared, and Theresa says if they have not found a body, Cordell must still be alive. The commissioner says that Cordell died in jail, and he has the two officers see police psychiatrist Susan Riley. Susan suggests that the "Maniac Cop" was someone other than Cordell. Theresa is angry at Jack's willingness to accept that theory in order to keep his job.

When Detective Sean McKinney shoots and kills a suspect, he is sent to see Susan; they discuss his indifference towards killing a man and also McKinney's old partner, who committed suicide. Jack talks to Harry, a blind newsstand vendor, and Cordell stabs Jack through the throat with the blade of his billystick. At the coroner's office, McKinney shows Theresa her lover's dead body, then rails her about their mild argument earlier. Doyle had McKinney put "pressure" on Teresa so she would not go to the press with the story. McKinney sticks it to Susan for being a doctor.

A man tries to talk a cop out of towing his car away, and Cordell helps a bit by beating the officer and driving the tow truck away with the cop hooked on the back. Susan talks to Harry, who says he brushed against Jack's killer and was reminded of the cold, dead flesh of lifeless bodies surrounding him in a war. The man who avoided having his car towed is arrested, and he tries to tell the officers that a cop killed the cop. McKinney and Doyle are discussing the killings; the commissioner avoids the detective's suggestion that Cordell is the murderer. Theresa packs her bags and tells Susan she is going on a show to alert people of the killings. Susan gets in the cab with her; when the cabbie stops for an apparently flat tire, Theresa sees Cordell behind them, gets behind the wheel and speeds away. Theresa crashes the cab, gets out and is thrown through a window by Cordell. The maniac cop handcuffs Susan to a steering wheel and rolls the car away. After Theresa attacks with a chainsaw, he snaps her neck. Susan manages to get inside the car and turn off the road, flipping the vehicle.

Susan goes on the television show *Criminals at Large* with Doyle and discusses the still-living Maniac Cop. After the show, Doyle suspends Susan. In a strip club, Turkell watches Cheryl on stage. Later, Cheryl is in a seedy hotel, talking to her mother on the phone and lying about her job and place of residence. Someone starts shaking the door, and Cheryl tries to call for help, but the person evidently leaves. Turkell crashes through her window, knocks the woman to the floor and puts his hand around her neck. Cordell breaks through the door and starts choking Cheryl, throws two cops across the room and helps Turkell escape.

Turkell excitedly talks to Cordell and compliments his "gimmick." They go to Turkell's apartment, where the man shows the officer pictures of his girls (now dead strippers). He goes to get pencil and paper for Cordell to write his name, and the cop manages to whisper it. Later, Turkell asks what happened to Cordell, and he thinks back to his sentencing and his attack in the shower. The cops have put the word out that Cheryl died so that the serial killer will relax.

Susan sees Cheryl's neck bruises and asks what the cop's hands felt like ("Like ice!"). McKinney, Susan, Detective Lovejoy and Cheryl go to a strip club, the woman points out Turkell, and the man is arrested. McKinney goes to Turkell's apartment and finds the photographs of the dead strippers, including one of Cheryl.

Susan is at Turkell's cell, wanting to talk of Cordell. Turkell says if she wants to know, she should stick around. Cordell kills a number of officers in the shooting range (from behind the targets), grabs a gun and walks into the station shooting; Susan is taken hostage. Turkell and his cellmate, Blum, get some guns. Turkell tells Susan they are going to Sing Sing to break out the prisoners on Death Row. They get on a prison bus, and Turkell plows through some cop cars. McKinney rides with Doyle, and he tells the commissioner that only he can stop Cordell, by reopening the case and signing a confession, admitting to setting the officer up for finding out about "payoffs."

Turkell and the bus are let inside (Turkell is wearing an officer's uniform). A cop calls the warden and says that Blum has been "delivered," and the warden says he got word that Blum was broken out of jail and tells the man to seal off the ward. Over an intercom, Doyle tells Cordell that his conviction has been reversed due to perjury at the trial. As Turkell calls after him, Cordell walks past the Death Row inmates into general population. One of the prisoners who attacked him in the shower throws a burning bottle at him, and a fiery Cordell grabs, kicks and throws his enemies against the wall. As Cordell burns a fourth man, a forlorn Turkell stabs him with the cop's billystick knife. Cordell grabs Turkell, the man burns and the both of them break through the wall and fall all the way down into the prison bus, which explodes. Cordell is awarded a proper funeral and burial, and McKinney drops the officer's badge on the casket. After McKinney walks away with Susan, Cordell's hand pushes through his coffin and grabs the badge.

While not as engaging as the first film, *Maniac Cop 2* provides a number of thrilling sequences (Cordell's police station carnage in particular) and exceptional performances, especially from Davi and Christian in the two leading roles. The final credit reads: "Dedicated to the Memory of Joe 'Maniac' Spinell."

Maniac Cop 3: Badge of Silence (1992)

Written by Larry Cohen; Directed by William Lustig and Joel Soisson; Neo Motion Pictures/First Look Pictures; 85 min.

Cast: Robert Davi (Det. Sean McKinney); Robert Z'Dar (Matt Cordell); Caitlin Dulany (Doctor Susan Fowler); Gretchen Becker (Kate Sullivan); Paul Gleason (Hank Cooney); Jackie Earle Haley (Frank Jessup); Julius Harris (Houngan); Grand Bush (Willie); Doug Savant (Doctor Peter Myerson); Bobby Di Cicco (Bishop); Frank Pesce (Tribble); Lou Diaz (Leon); Brenda Varda (Lindsey); Vanessa Marquez (Terry); Denney Pierce (Pedestrian Heckler); Ted Raimi (Reporter); Vinnie Curto (Kenyon); Jophery Brown (Degrazia); Jeffrey Anderson-Gunter (Janitor); Jeffrey Hylton (Teen Witness); Barbara Pilavin (Nora Sullivan); Victor Manni (Shotgun Cop); Tony Capozzola (Nelson); Barry Livingston (Asst. Coroner); Jason Lustig (EMT Driver); Bill Irving (Elderly Patient); Harri James (Radiation Therapist); Katherine Marie Elledge (Nurse); Amanda Finnigan (Doctor Dennison); Claudia Templeton (Doctor Chad); Hillary Black (Doctor Everett); Henry Fehren (Priest)

Crew: W.K. Border (Executive Producer); Joel Soisson, Michael Leahy (Producers); Larry Cohen (Co-Producer); Joel Goldsmith (Composer); Jacques Haitkin (Director of Photography); David Kern, Michael Eliot, A.C.E. (Editors)

Houngan, a voodoo-esque priest, recites a chant while surrounded by candles. As he stabs a decapitated head, Matt Cordell, lying inside his coffin, opens his eyes and punches through his casket.

Detective Sean McKinney talks to Officer Kate Sullivan on a shooting range. She complains about being in trouble for using excessive force (she has been dubbed "Maniac Kate"). Since that day is Kate's birthday, McKinney gives her a watch.

McKinney goes to a crime scene, where a headless corpse is found with a chicken stuffed inside. The detective talks of *Palamayumbe*, a ritual which uses heads; the chicken is left to let the soul "take flight." Kate and her partner are at a scene where the crazed Frank is inside a store, shooting anyone who enters. Reporters Bishop and Tribble are listening to the police scanner for stories, and they are excited to hear that the notoriously aggressive Kate is at the scene. After Kate's partner is killed, she runs inside with an automatic and shoots at Frank until he runs into the pharmacy (with shatterproof glass) for refuge. McKinney describes to Houngan (standing by a barrel of fire) a symbol resting next to the corpse, and Houngan says it is the symbol of "anti-justice." Kate runs to the roof, loads hollow bullets into her revolver and jumps through the roof and into the pharmacy. Frank holds the girl from the pharmacy in front of him, and Kate shoots him. The girl says, "You shot Frankie," and Kate realizes that she had buzzed Frank into the pharmacy. They both fire, and the girl is hit in the head as the two reporters are filming.

Cordell goes to see Houngan, and the man tells the cop that he allowed Houngan to bring him back and that his spirit is not at rest. Cordell hears the news of Kate on the radio (the video of the incident has been edited a bit and the pharmacist's assistant is thought to be innocent), and he is angry. McKinney asks Doctor Myerson about Kate, and he is told that the officer is brain dead. Outside the hospital, a man says uncomplimentary things about Kate, and Cordell throws him and shoots him in the air. McKinney talks to his friend Willie and learns that Frank is suing the police; due to Kate's employment of illegal weapons, Frank has been given a six months suspended sentence in exchange for dropping the suit. McKinney goes to the hospital and asks Doctor Susan Fowler if he can talk to Frank. The detective tries to help Frank remember more about the shooting by cutting off some of his oxygen.

A comatose Kate dreams of walking down the aisle to meet an ugly Cordell at the altar, and she opens her eyes and grabs a nearby McKinney when she sees Cordell behind him. The detective tells Susan about her movement and her heart monitor speeding up, but the doctor sees no change in Kate. Regardless, she tells Myerson what has happened and asks for another brain scan, but Myerson thinks it would just be a waste of money. Later, Myerson is enjoying some time with a woman in the lounge, and Cordell knocks on the door. When the doctor comes out, Cordell shocks him with pads. He chases Myerson to the roof, where he places the pads on the doctor's face. Afterwards, Susan sees Cordell and follows him to the basement, but he disappears. Later, after the cops have discovered the body of Myerson, Susan tells McKinney about seeing a cop leave Kate's room. McKinney goes to the basement and finds the old church with Houngan, who talks to the detective about resurrection. He says that McKinney and Cordell walk the "same path."

Hank Cooney goes to see Doctor Powell and tells him that cutting off Kate's life support would save the city some trouble. Cooney has a letter of consent, signed by Kate's mother. Powell says he can take care of it that afternoon. Later, Powell hears glass break in the X-ray room, where Cordell grabs him and straps him underneath the X-ray machine for a fatal treatment. Cordell takes the letter of consent from Kate's bed and crumples it. Bishop and Tribble go to a scene of a drive-by shooting (which sounds intriguing since it was reportedly a child shot). At the scene, Bishop callously interviews the brother of the victim. He then looks for Tribble, finding him dead inside an ambulance with two attendants. Bishop is stabbed through the back by Cordell. The next day, McKinney watches the unedited version of the shooting and sees that the girl had buzzed in Frank.

Cordell places a gun by Frank's pillow,

uncuffs him and leaves the keys. As Cooney and Gina Lindsey, Frank's lawyer, discuss clearing Frank's record (so he can get the benefits of film or literary rights), Frank and his hospitalized criminal roommates escape. The three men shoot and kill Cooney, Lindsey and the guard, and Cordell picks up Kate and carries her away. McKinney rolls down on a hospital bed and kills two of the would-be escapees. He follows Frank to the women's bathroom, where he kicks a stall door, is grazed by a bullet from Frank (hiding behind a woman on the toilet) and kills the trigger-happy criminal.

Susan bandages McKinney's arm and they kiss. The detective is told that Kate has been taken away. McKinney and Susan run to the church, where Houngan is standing over Kate's body and Cordell is standing behind him with a shotgun. McKinney tells Cordell that Kate is at peace now and to "let her go," but Cordell tells Houngan to "finish it." Houngan says he cannot "recover" because Kate will not allow him, and Cordell shoots Houngan. He picks up a flaming Kate and they burn together, as McKinney and Susan run outside and avoid an explosion. They get in an ambulance as the building burns, but down the road, a scorching Cordell follows. The driver jumps out, and McKinney gets behind the wheel as Cordell tries to reach his hand inside and literally pushes cars out of the way. McKinney tosses an oxygen tank in Cordell's backseat, but the maniac cop latches his arm onto the passenger's side door. The detective drives by a road sign, slicing off Cordell's arm, and the ambulance flips. Cordell stops the car, turns and slams it into drive, but the car explodes. McKinney lights a cigarette with Cordell's flaming arm, and he walks away with Susan. The crispy bodies of Cordell and Kate lie side by side on tables, and Cordell lovingly touches Kate's body.

The third film of the *Maniac Cop* series is hampered by a weak subplot involving the chants and voodoo-like scenes, but makes up for this with enjoyable gunfights and an over-the-top but very fun car chase at the end. That *is* an uncredited Robert Forster as Doctor Powell. Actor Haley is perhaps better known as one of *The Bad News Bears*.

Mikey (1991)

Written by Jonathan Glassner; Directed by Dennis Dimster-Denk; Tapestry Films, Inc.; 92 min.

Cast: Brian Bonsall (Mikey); Josie Bissett (Jessie); Ashley Laurence (Gilder); Mimi Craven (Rachel); John Diehl (Neil); Whitby Hertford (Ben); Lyman Ward (Mr. Jenkins); David Rogge (David); Mark Venturini (Detective Reynolds); Laura Robinson (Grace); Peppi Sanders (Mary Ellen); Frank Sprague (Levinson); Frank Bridge (Mr. Fineberg); Beverly Piper (Mrs. Packard); Jean Fowler (Hancock); Emily Ragsdale (Captain); Elayne Stein (Mrs. Fineberg); Eli Marder (Katherine); Shawna Leavell (Stewardess); Bob Gottlieg (Fireman); Stephen Hart (Harold); Keeley Marie Gallagher (Beth); Tori Page (Sarah); Matt Hammer, Jonathan Furedy (Kids); Elijah Crain (Stevie); Sanford Gibbons (Cornell); Diana Baines (Mary Raynee); Gary M. Johnson (Dan Raynee); Joseph Bernard (Doctor Schaefer); Kathleen Bonsall (Eva)

Crew: J.P. Guerin (Executive Producer); Peter Abrams, Robert L. Levy, Nathan Zahavi (Producers); Stan Foster, Edward L. McDonnell (Associate Producers); Sam Bernard (Co-Producer); Tim Truman (Composer); Tom Jewett (Director of Photography); Nathan Zahavi, Omer Tal (Editors)

When Mikey's mother finds her son burning papers in the garage, she yells at him and takes his sister Beth away with her. Mikey says he hates her and that she is not his real mother. He takes Beth's doll away, runs to the pool and drops the doll from the diving board. Beth reaches for her doll, and Mikey jumps on the board, causing Beth to fall in and drown. Mikey walks in on his mother, saying that the woman does not love him any more. He picks up a blow-dryer, turns it on and throws it to his mother, who is electrocuted. Mikey puts ball bearings on the floor; when his father comes home and runs out to the pool, he slips and crashes through the glass door. Mikey beats his head with a baseball bat as a video camera records. Detective Reynolds arrives at the scene and Mikey describes a man leaving the house. Katherine takes Mikey away.

Mikey lies to a doctor about a man being at the house ("I hate him!"). The sister of Mikey's mother refuses to take care of him, and so Rachel and Neil Trenton adopt him. The couple brings Mikey home, where Mikey asks to take care of the baby fish in the aquarium. He meets his neighbor and peer Ben and his teacher and Rachel's friend, Shawn Gilder. Neil takes Mikey to an archery range, and Mikey is a natural with the bow and arrow. In class, Mikey learns of "marble time." A student adds a marble to a collection and, when full, the door opens for a prize. Rachel and Neil looks at a Mikey drawing of a "swimming girl" and believe it is symbolic of something good. Mikey and Ben are together, and Mikey eyes a photograph of Ben's sister, Jessie, who is away at school.

After class, Mikey adds marbles to the collection. Shawn sees him and tells Mikey to let his parents know what he has done. Later, Shawn learns that Mikey did not tell Rachel of the marble incident, but she says nothing. The class draws pictures, and Mikey draws a turkey "fixing" a pilgrim (chopping his head off). Shawn shows the picture to Mr. Jenkins, believing Mikey has "unattached syndrome" (psychotic behavior), but Jenkins thinks her assessment is premature. Shawn goes to Eva to find information on Mikey and learns that Mikey's records are sealed. Jenkins talks with Mikey, who says that his real parents were "bad." He admires a skeleton in the room.

When Jessie comes home, the two boys pretend that Mikey is unconscious. Jessie gives him mouth-to-mouth (Mikey had a ball under his arm so that Jessie could not find a pulse). That night, Mikey crawls into Jessie's room through the window and watches her sleep. In class, Mikey wins a spelling contest and refers to a triumph in Oklahoma City. Shawn calls a teacher and asks about Mikey, and she talks about the "tragedy" of Mikey's murdered family. Mikey goes to see Ben (knowing he is gone), and he and Jessie go for a boat ride. That night, after watching the video of his previous father crashing through the door, Mikey is tucked in bed, and he asks Neil how someone knows if he loves a girl. Mikey films through Jessie's window, and he is upset when seeing her with David, throwing a rock through the window. David runs outside as Mikey sits in the bushes and snaps the neck of Rosie the cat. Jessie is now tired and tells David to leave. He gets in his truck, hears something and sees that he has "run over" Rosie. He tells Jessie.

Behind a propped-up book in class, Mikey incessantly stabs his arm with a thumbtack. Shawn asks to see the book he is reading, and she sees his arm. Shawn and Jenkins tells Rachel and Neil that Mikey should see a doctor, and the couple is agitated. At home, Mikey throws a fit because a man bought the baby fish, and he tells Rachel that she does not love him any more. Later, as Rachel is in the tub, Mikey walks in and picks up a curling iron, talks of throwing it in the water, and then unplugs it. Mikey watches David apologize to Jessie, and he is perturbed by the apparent success of the apology. That night, as David and Jessie play in the pool, Mikey dials Jessie's number and puts the phone by the TV. As Jessie answers the phone, Mikey approaches the Jacuzzi and kicks the radio into the water. Jessie returns to a dead and floating David.

Shawn talks on the phone with Reynolds and asks to see the police reports. He says he will Fax them to the school in the morning. Jenkins gets a call and is told that Mikey and Ben will not be at school due to the accident at Ben's house. Mikey talks to a melancholy Jessie and tells her that, now that David is dead, she can love just him. Later, Jessie goes to see Rachel and says that she believes Mikey loves her and that he is dangerous and may have killed David. Mikey listens from the stairs. After Jessie leaves, he takes the phone off the hook. Shawn reads the Fax from Reynolds and learns of an electrocution. She tries to call Rachel but the phone is busy. She is leaving the school grounds, and Jenkins goes with her.

Rachel hears screaming and sees Mikey watching *Mikey's Funniest Home Videos*. She tells him to go to his room, and Mikey whacks her hand with a hammer and swings and hits the aquarium. Downstairs, Rachel wraps her hand, Mikey beats her arm and she pushes him down and runs to her room, locking the door. Mikey breaks the glass door and gets in the room. He attacks with a glass shard, and the two go over the railing. Shawn and Jenkins find them on the stairs (the shard is in Rachel's neck). He takes Shawn's gun as she waits outside. Jenkins puts the gun on the counter as he goes for the phone, and Mikey picks it up and returns it. Mikey appears with a bow and arrow and, since Jenkins has no bullets, shoots an arrow into the man's stomach. Shawn goes inside and sees Jenkins dead. Mikey slingshots a marble (evidently made of steel) at her face.

When Neil calls, Mikey says Rachel is not well. He brushes his hair and turns the oven's gas on. He goes to Jessie's house and asks if he can come in, and she says no. Mikey appears in her bedroom and asks if Jessie does not like him. She pushes him out of the door, but goes downstairs when hearing the TV. Mikey has his bow and arrow; Jessie runs to her room as he shoots.

Neil is home, and Mikey is waiting for him. Jessie tries to warn him, but Neil thinks she is only waving. Inside, Neil sees the dead people and Jenkins' skeleton at the table. As he screams, Mikey tosses a flaming bottle, and the house explodes. Jessie is told that the remains of a ten-year-old were discovered. A man tells a couple prepared to adopt that a boy (called "Josh") was found suffering from amnesia, and Mikey walks into the room.

Mikey mostly thrives on the eeriness of a child killer, and the film stretches plausibility by making the nine-year-old virtually unstoppable. Bonsall is okay, but his character is more irritating than frightening. The appealing Ashley Laurence (who also appeared in Clive Barker's 1987 classic *Hellraiser*) is wasted in a dreary role.

Mommy (1995)

Written and Directed by Max Allan Collins; M.A.C. Film Productions; 89 min.

Cast: Patty McCormack (Mommy); Rachel Lemieux (Jessica Ann); Jason Miller (Lieutenant March); Brinke Stevens (Beth); Michael Cornelison (Mark Jeffries); Majel Barrett (Mrs. Withers); Mickey Spillane (Attorney Neal Ekhardt); Sarah Jane Miller (Janitor); Marian Wald (Principal); Mark Spellman (Detective); Janelle Vanerstrom (Substitute Teacher); Judith Meyers (Hallway Teacher); Nathan Collins (Gleeful Kid); Tom Castillo, Tom Summitt (Ambulance Attendants); George Michael (Mr. Sterling); Dewayne Hopkins (Daddy); Crusin' (Band at Charity Ball); Debi Hahn (Mrs. March); Gary Coderoni (Plainclothes Cop); Jason Shepley (D.A.'s Office Rep); Greg Meyers (Little Boy); Gary Meyers (Little Boy's Father); Lucie Nelson (Little Girl); Barb Trainor (Little Girl's Mother); Dick Lafrenz (Little Girl's Father); Elly Lloyd (Bus Driver); Max, Alex (Junkyard Dogs); Don Phelps (Deputy Sheriff); Jeffrey Benson (Highway Patrol Officer); Brian Hammer, Howard Hughes, Tom Tovar (Detectives); Jerry Ewers, Kevin McCarthy (Fire Dept. Rescue Unit); A.P. Anderson, Al Dobert, Phil Sargent, Rob Yant (Police Officers); Tami Allison, Michelle Levenhagen, Paula Lofgren, John Maw, Patti Meyer, Melanie Poock, Kerry Powell, Stephanie Quade, Jim Renkes, Allison Sohr, Kathy Sternberg (Treachers); Patricio Cadena, Renee Dunakey, Shannon Lael, Elizabeth Maurus, Lindsay Trumbull, Robyn Vedvik (Jessica Ann's Classmates)

Crew: Max Allan Collins (Executive Producer); James K. Hoffman (Producer); Phillip W. Dingeldein (Co-Producer/Director of Photography/Editor); J. Douglas Miller (Associate Producer); Richard Lowry (Composer)

Young children rush out of the building after school and are taken away by bus or by parent. Jessica Ann awaits her mother, Mrs. Sterling, and they walk into the school. "Mommy" goes to see Mrs. Withers alone, upset that her daughter will not be awarded the Outstanding Student of the Year plaque for the fourth consecutive year. The award is going to a Hispanic boy, crudely referred to by Mrs. Sterling as a "foreign student," and Mommy thinks Jessica Ann is being "punished" because she is white. An irate Mrs. Withers ends the "conference" and continues decorating for the Spring Fling. While on a ladder to hang a banner, Mrs. Withers is knocked down by the angry mother. Mrs. Sterling goes to the swing set and tells Jessica Ann that she discovered a dead Mrs. Withers, who had apparently fallen and broken her neck. The police and ambulance arrive, and Mrs. Sterling, the "witness," is questioned by Lieutenant March.

The mother and daughter return home to Aunt Beth cooking their dinner. Later, Beth comforts a tearful Jessica Ann in her bedroom; Jessica Ann talks of her father, who drowned when she was young (her stepfather, Mr. Sterling, also died). The girl says she believes Mommy doesn't miss Daddy, and Beth tells her niece that, when they were younger, Jessica Ann's mother was "pampered" and used to getting her way. Mark, Mommy's new beau, arrives, and the group sits at the dinner table for dessert. Beth has trouble opening a jar, and Mark tries to no avail. Mommy opens it with ease, and Mark tells her, "Remind me not to cross you." At the school, the janitor bothers Jessica Ann in the hall, telling her that she saw her mother go into Mrs. Withers' room and stay awhile. In the office, Lieutenant March tells Jessica Ann that the medical examiner believes that hands broke the teacher's neck. He mentions the plaque (others knew of Mommy's complaints), and he tells the girl to let him know if she finds it, suggesting that her mother took it. Jessica Ann storms out.

At home, Jessica Ann tells her mother of the janitor's "teasing," and Mrs. Sterling suddenly decides to get some fresh ground coffee. She heads to the school and speaks with the janior, who says she saw the woman go in and heard talking. The janitor alludes to a possible bribe. Jessica Ann looks through her mother's room and finds the plaque in a bureau. At the school, the lights are shut off, and the janitor goes to check the boiler room for the fuse. After she turns the lights back on, water is splashed on her and a bucket is thrown, and the janitor is electrocuted. Mommy returns home with Chinese food and a movie.

The next day in class, Jessica Ann hears the news of the janitor's tragic death. Already questioning the deaths of her father and stepfather, the girl now believes that Mark might be in danger. At a charity ball, Mark and Mrs. Sterling dance, and Mark mentions that Jessica Ann seems to be avoiding him lately. Lieutenant March later talks to him. Mark is angry, believing the lieutenant will "blow his cover," and he says that no one knows Mrs. Sterling has killed anyone. Later that night, Mark is beeped; he goes downstairs to the phone and tells someone not to contact him. Jessica Ann hears him on the stairs, and Mark goes to her room and asks her what is wrong. The girl admits that she wanted him to leave because he would be a "good daddy," and she thinks that her mother has killed people. Mark admits to working for an insurance company, investigating the death of Mr. Sterling, and says that Mommy needs help. Mrs. Sterling walks inside, pulls a gun ("Close your eyes, dear") and shoots Mark twice in the chest, as Jessica Ann screams and cries.

Mrs. Sterling consoles her daughter and tells her that they have to stick together and tell things to fit a puzzle. She goes to the phone, feigns hysteria and says that she shot Mark for molesting her daughter. The cops arrive, and Mrs. Sterling is questioned for a long time. Alone in the kitchen, Beth asks Jessica Ann what really happened, but they are interrupted by Mommy, who rejects Beth's invitation for her niece to stay with her for the night. The next day, the mother and daughter are questioned separately. When they return home, Mrs. Sterling begins to pack and tells Jessica Ann to do the same. They drive for a while and reach a motel. Jessica Ann changes into her pajamas, brushes her teeth and goes to bed.

Jessica Ann awakes from a bad dream and hears her mother (believing that Jessica Ann is still asleep) talk of making "hard decisions." Mrs. Sterling jumps for her daughter, but Jessica Ann runs to the bathroom and crawls out of the window. She is chased to the junkyard, where a junkyard dog scares them both and jumps Mrs. Sterling. Jessica Ann takes cover, picks up a pipe and returns to find the dog dead. Mommy appears and Jessica Ann whacks her with the pipe. Jessica Ann cries as her mother wraps her hands around her neck, but she cannot do anything. Lieutenant March fires his gun in the air, and Beth leads Jessica Ann away (the mother and daughter had been followed). Mrs. Sterling tells March that, for a moment in the moonlight, Jessica Ann had looked like her. As Mommy is arrested a cop car drives Jessica Ann and Beth away.

Mommy is a good slasher. A number of scenes seem to move at a lethargic pace, but the film does not bore, and it is a treat to watch McCormack as the evil, murderous mother; she also played an evil, murderous child in *The Bad Seed* (1956). Lemieux is also very good in her film debut. Viewers might recognize actor Miller as the dedicated and determined priest in *The Exorcist* (1973).

Murder Rock (aka *Murder-Rock: Dancing Death*; *Murderock—uccide a passo di danza*; *Giallo a disco*) (1984)

Written by Gianfranco Clerici, Vincenzo Mannino, Roberto Gianviti and Lucio Fulci; Directed by Lucio Fulci; Scena Films; 92 min.

Cast: Olga Karlatos (Candice Norman); Ray Lovelock (George Webb); Claudio Cassinelli (Dick Gibson); Cosimo Cinieri (Lieutenant Borges); Giuseppe Mannajuolo (Professor Davis); Berna Maria do Carmo; Belinda Busato; Maria Vittoria Tolazzi; Geretta Marie Fields (Margie); Cristian Borromeo (Willy); Robert Gligorov (Bert); Carlo Caldera; Riccardo Parisio Perrotti; Giovanni de Nava

Crew: Gabriele Silvestri (Executive Producer); Augusto Caminito (Producer); Keith Emerson (Composer); Giuseppe Pinori, A.I.C. (Director of Photography); Vincenzo Tomassi (Editor)

At the Arts for Living Center, a group of dancers dance in a studio. After the number, they are told it needs "perfecting." Dick, Steiner and Morris watch a video of the dance, and Candice, the teacher, learns that the men only need to select three dancers. Candice says that if the dancers know only three will be picked, they will "tear each other to shreds." Willy and Susan stay after the others leave. The school is closing up, and Susan is left alone to shower. After the water is turned on, a gloved hand puts a cloth over Susan's face, and she falls to the floor. The person stabs Susan in the chest with a pin.

Lieutenant Borges Davis and other cops arrive, and some of the dancers are there (Margie, the choreographer, had found Susan). Borges learns that Dick, the school administrator, and Candice cannot be found. At home, Candice answers her phone and hears heavy breathing, and Dick buzzes at the door. They talk of potential relationships with Dick and the dancers (Jill, Janice or Susan), and Dick says there is nothing between him and Susan. Bob, the deejay (and Jill's brother), calls Candice and tells her the news. The next day, the group dances, and Willy is upset that they hardly seem to care about Susan's death. Borges talks to Dick about a possible rivalry among the dancers. Janice dances alone for an audience and walks home, where Willy is sitting in her place, wanting to talk. Janice goes for a photograph she has of Willy and Susan, but when she calls out to him, Willy is gone. Janice goes to the front door, hears chirping and returns to find her bird dead with a pin in its stomach. Janice runs, a door is slammed and she is attacked and killed.

Candice dreams of a man in black, chasing her with a pin. At the scene, Borges tells Davis to hide the pin and not tell anyone. The lieutenant talks to the dancers, and they blame one another for the murders. As they are leaving, Davis tells Borges that he tape-recorded the entire conversation. Candice is upset by a billboard advertisement with the man from her dream. She goes to the Fulton Hotel and gives the clerk money for the key to Mr. Robinson's room. She looks around and finds photographs of the man. He returns to his room drunk and tries to grab Candice; the woman runs, leaving behind her purse (and ID).

The killer makes a phone call to the police and threatens to kill again. Candice meets with George (Mr. Robinson), and he gives back her purse. They go to a restaurant where Candice tells George of her dream. Using Davis' tape, the phone voice is matched to the voice of Bert, one of the dancers. The cops pick him up and he admits to the murders, saying he killed Susan because she said he was crazy and Janice because she was Puerto Rican. As Bert is locked up, Borges states his belief that Bert is not the killer, just a born liar. Dick goes to see Candice, but she shrugs him off and returns to bed with George. The next day at the studio George goes to see Candice. Gloria, another dancer, recognizes him (George says later that they once modeled in a fashion show together). Dick sees George and Candice via a security camera, and he points out George to Borges, saying he is the killer and telling of Candice's dream.

Candice tells George of an "idiot on a motorcycle" who ruined her potential Broadway career, and she says she was told that the psychological impacts were worse than the physical ones. She says she does not know who the biker was. A Chinese man reads George's fortune with sticks and says he is a murderer. Phil, who had looked for an acting job for George, tells Candice that George once had an affair with a young girl who later died. While alone in the studio, Candice is attacked and nearly killed by Margie (using the killer's M.O.). Margie tells Dick she hates Candice but could not murder her. Jill goes to babysit the wheelchair-bound Molly, who takes pictures of Jill as she sits downstairs on the couch. Jill gets two heavy-breathing calls, and then a call from someone who wants to talk. Jill answers the door to a person she knows, and the killer attacks. Molly frantically snaps away. The cops see Dick run out of the building. Chased and caught, he says that he found Jill dead.

When questioned, Dick admits to having an affair with Jill (and denies affairs with Susan and Janice). Borges and Davis look at slides of Molly's pictures, and there is only a shot of the killer's leather jacket. Since it is clearly not the suit-and-tie–wearing Dick, Borges says to release the man. He then notices something about the slide, and he flips it around.

The killer attacks and kills Gloria in the locker room. At George's place, Candice finds a pin and a bottle of chloroform (used to knock out the victims) and quickly leaves. George looks in the drawer, sees what Candice has found and rushes to his car. George goes to Candice's place and buzzes at the door, but no one is home.

Candice tells Borges of her discovery, says George is the murderer and names the hotel where George is staying. Candice finds Gloria dead in the school, phones Borges and says she will wait for him. George is there, and he turns on the music. Candice runs to the manager's room, and she sees videos of the dancers who have been killed. Candice, greatly agitated, screams loudly. George walks in with the pin and asks if it is the evidence. Candice says that George killed her hopes and ambitions when he hit her with the motorcycle (she calls him George Webb). She says he will be blamed for the murders when she is found dead, and that will be Candice's revenge ("You have to pay!"). She pulls George's pin-holding hand and is stabbed in the chest. Borges and Davis arrive, and the lieutenant says they had come to arrest Candice. They realized that she was the killer when Borges saw that the slide was the wrong way (it was a woman's jacket) and Candice had known of the "lion's head" on the pin when only Borges and Davis knew the murder weapon. George leaves the studio as the cops investigate the scene.

Lucio Fulci's *Murder Rock* is much less gory than many of his later films, but his visual flair shows, with beautiful dark scenes in the school (the flickering lights are exceptional) and a superb utilization of mirrors. The dancing scenes might not be to everyone's tastes, but they are certainly well choreographed.

The Murder Secret (aka *Non aver paura della zia Marta; Don't Be Afraid of Aunt Marta; The Broken Mirror*) (1989)

Written and Directed by Robert Martin; Alpha D.C. Productions; 89 min.
    Cast: Peter Gabriel; Jessica Moore; Norren Parker; Lucy Arland; Sacha M. Darwin
    Crew: Luigi Nannerini, Antonino Lucidi (Producers); Gianni Esposito (Composer); Silvano Tessicini (Director of Photography); Vincent P. Thomas (Editor); Lucio Fulci (Supervisor)

    Richard is driving in a car with his wife Nora and their two children, Georgia and Maurice. Richard thinks back to doctors telling his mom and a young Richard that there is not much hope for Aunt Martha's recovery. A seemingly catatonic Martha, strapped to a bed, stares at her nephew. Richard tells Nora that Aunt Martha (whom he had never spoken of before) had been living in South America for the last 30 years and is now coming back. A young Richard is told by his mother the secret of Aunt Martha, and she says he will understand someday and that he must write a letter to the doctor. She kisses him good bye. After walking out the door, Richard hears a scream. He returns and looks out the window. His mother is lying dead on the ground outside.

Richard thinks back to the letter he had received from Martha, expressing a desire to meet the family. On the way, he nearly plows into a truck. He pulls over to the side and finally drives on when everyone relaxes. They reach the estate and are greeted by Thomas the caretaker, who tells them that Martha will arrive tomorrow. As he shows them around, Richard asks about a locked door; Thomas says it leads to a basement with unsafe stairs. Richard answers the ringing phone but there is no response. Later, the phone rings again, and no one responds. As the family sleeps, a person with a shotgun and walks into the house. It is only Charles, Richard's son from a previous marriage. He says he is just staying for one night.

The next morning, the family is up for breakfast, and Charles grabs some food and leaves to check the woods for "game" and then to meet some friends in a nearby town. In the woods, Charles meets Thomas, says he was just about to tell the family that Martha is unable to make it until tomorrow. Thomas goes to the house and tells them the Aunt Martha news. She hears her name called. Later, Richard awakes to a banging noise and he goes outside and shuts a gate, not seeing a dead, bloody Charles hanging in the tree. In the morning, Richard goes to the children's room, where Maurice's bed is empty. He finds his son downstairs, lying on the floor in front of the television. Georgia awakes and sees "June 16th, 1958" written on the mirrored closet.

At breakfast, Georgia tells what she has found and Richard reacts to the news. Richard and Nora drive down the road; he gets out to find Thomas' cottage as Nora drives on for some shopping in the village. Georgia showers and throws aside the curtain to see Maurice holding a lizard. Georgia tells her brother to go away. As she continues his watery recreation, she hears a voice that says now she is really going to die. Thinking it is still Maurice, Georgia moves the curtain and screams at a knife. She is stabbed in the face and stomach many times. Maurice comes back inside, and the bathroom is empty. As Maurice walks, a chainsaw comes from around a corner and beheads him. Nora returns home, calls for her children and looks around, not seeing blood on the wall.

Richard reaches a house and asks two workers about a caretaker for the house nearby; and the two men do not know Thomas. Richard calls St. George Clinic and agrees to call back in five minutes. In the attic, Nora finds a letter from St. George Mental Health Clinic which mentions a patient, Martha Thompson, with "serious mental problems and autism symptoms." While reading, Nora is grabbed, her head is pushed over the open trunk and she is decapitated when the trunk lid is slammed shut. Richard calls the clinic again and learns that Martha was released last March. On the way back to the house, he finds a tiny cemetery. Each headstone has a family member's name (there is one for him), with November 23, 1988, as the date of death.

Richard returns home to find his dead family at the dinner table. Aunt Martha arrives and she says she does not know what happened. She talks of being rich and being locked in the "inferno" so others could enjoy her wealth. Martha suddenly disappears, and Richard hears her calling his name. He walks to the previously locked door and goes down the stairs. He sees a bed-ridden, rotted corpse with maggots on the face. Thomas moves some maggots, kisses the corpse and says good morning to Martha. Thomas says what he did to the "bad" and "cruel people" who wanted Martha's money, and then the "caretaker" sees Richard and says he is going to kill him. The two men engage in a scuffle, and Thomas finally gets on top and punches Richard. He gets an axe and lifts it high, and Richard screams and throws up his hands. The truck from earlier comes to a stop, and the family car is crashed. Nora appears dead in the front, as do the children in the back, and a dazed and bloody Richard is still alive in the front, thinking back to Aunt Martha lying on the clinic bed.

The Murder Secret is a slasher that is more interesting than frightening, but the ending is pretty fun (although very similar to the 1962 cult classic *Carnival of Souls*).

Director Robert Martin is Mario Bianchi, and editor Vincent P. Thomas is Vincenzo Tomassi, who edited a number of Lucio Fulci films.

The Mutilator (aka *Fall Break*) (1983)

Written and Directed by Buddy Cooper; OK Productions; 82 min.

Cast: Matt Mitler (Ed); Ruth Martinez (Pam); Bill Hitchcock (Ralph); Connie Rogers (Sue); Frances Raines (Linda); Morey Lampley (Mike); Jack Chatham (Big Ed); Ben Moore (Ben); Trace Cooper (Young Ed); Pamela Weddle Cooper (Ed's Mother); Jimmy Guthrie (Bartender); George Sutton (Gentleman at Bar); Steve Davis, Tom Outlaw, Pat Jodan (Students at Bar); Hallock Cooper, Michell Rach, Miriam Mason, Jennifer Price (Cheerleaders); A.B. Cooper, Sr. (Professor at Dorm); Jan Case, David Bell, Phil Collins, Chris Sarosy, Dee Clodfelter, David Sledge (Students at Dorm); Fred Tillery (Storekeeper); Jenny Grice (Storekeeper's Wife); Kay Case (Woman at Store); Wendy Case (Girl at Store); John Bode (Deputy Wall); Bruce Taylor (Deputy Driver); Darryl Case (Doctor); Andrea McLean (Nurse with Doctor); Dail Lowery (Nurse with Tray); Greta Groves (Nurse at Door)

Crew: John Douglas (Co-Director); Buddy Cooper (Producer); Neil B. Whitford (Associate Producer); Michael Minard (Composer); Peter Schnall (Director of Photography); Stephen Mack (Editor)

A woman is working on a birthday cake in the kitchen. In another room, her son puts a sign on the gun cabinet ("Happy Birthday Daddy. All cleaned by me!") and takes out a rifle to polish. He playfully aims the gun and pulls the trigger, and a shot fires through the door and hits his mother. The woman's husband returns and sees his dead wife. He hits his son, the boy runs out and the man drags his wife to the other room. He sits, has a drink and puts his son's sign on his wife's corpse. The boy watches from the kitchen.

Ed is drinking with his friends, and they are complaining about their monotonous fall break. Ed gets a phone call from his father, and Pam tells the others about the accident with Ed's mother that "drove his father crazy." Ed's father tells him he wants him to close the condo for the winter, and after telling his friends and making the job sound simple, they suggest going there for their break. Ed, Pam, Ralph, Sue, Mike and Linda jump into Ed's car and drive.

At the condor the group finds the door open and many empty bottles inside. Pam wants to report it to the authorities, but Ed tells her that the cops are usually not around and the beach patrol enforces the law. They go to the father's trophy room and find animal heads, a gaff and a photograph of a dead, bloody guy (Ed's dad ran over him with a ski boat). Ed shows them a pyramid stinger in the wall and tells of a throwing contest between his father and friends. Pam points out an empty space on the wall, and Ed says his father's battle axe was there. Pam thinks it has been stolen, so Ed tells her he will call his dad in the morning to ask about the condo and the axe. Ed's father, having awoken from a slumber in the garage, grips the axe.

Big Ed dreams of choking, shooting and slicing the throat of his young son. Linda and Mike look at the things in the garage but are called back inside before they can open the door where Big Ed is hiding. After dinner, Pam's "duty roster" shows that she and Ed are cleaning up. Mike and Linda go for a walk while the others play a board game. Pam is worried about the couple being gone for a while, so they all go to look for them on the beach. Mike and Linda find a pool, strip and dive in the water. While they are splashing around, Linda is pulled underwater and drowned; her body is taken away without Mike seeing anything. Mike gets out and sees that his clothes are missing. He follows a trail of his own clothes, puts them on as he goes along and finally sees Linda's bra near the garage ("I think I'm getting your message"). He checks the door with Linda's hanging panties; another door opens to reveal Big Ed, who has a boat's motor to slice open Mike's chest.

Ben of the beach patrol finds the others, and is told they are at Big Ed's place and that someone may have been at the house. Ben looks around the house and is beheaded by Big Ed's battle axe. The group head back to the place and decide to play Blind Man's Bluff. Sue offers to be first, so the other three go outside and drink a beer as Sue turns off the lights and hides. They finish their beer and go inside, and Big Ed goes around to the back of the house. Pam finds Sue hiding behind the cooler and hides next to her under the kitchen table. Ralph finds them both and hides, and Big Ed walks around the house. Ed finally ends the game by walking in the kitchen and offering everyone a beer. His father walks outside.

Everyone goes to bed. Ralph and Sue are kissing on the bed, and she tells him they forgot to lock up. Ralph leaves to find Linda and Mike, and he goes to the open garage door thinking they are inside. He finds Linda's panties and throws a pyramid stinger at the door and hits it. Big Ed jumps out and stabs Ralph in the throat with a pitchfork. Pam hears a noise and tries to wake Ed. Sue goes looking for Ralph, and Big Ed gets inside and takes the gaff off the wall. Pam gets Ed awake, and they go looking for the others and find Sue, who says she does not know where Ralph is. They split up to look. Sue is grabbed by Big Ed, taken to the garage and chopped with his axe.

Pam and Ed make it to the garage and find their dead friends. They see the shadow of an approaching Big Ed, and Ed throws Pam in a room. He struggles with his father, and Big Ed knocks his son down and ties his hands and feet. He lifts the axe, but Pam comes out to throw things at him. The man shoves part of an axe in Ed's leg, and Pam tosses a pyramid stinger at him, hitting his forehead. She picks up a knife and stabs Big Ed in the chest. Pam and a freed Ed run to the convertible, but the vehicle won't start. Suddenly Big Ed is atop the car and axing through the top. He grabs Ed, Pam burns him with a cigarette lighter and the car is backed out. Big Ed tries to get on the car's back, and Pam throws it in reverse, crushing him into two pieces. A cop is there, and the top half of the killer jumps up to cut him with an axe. Later, Ed goes to see Pam in the hospital, and they observe a moment of silence.

The Mutilator has an interesting premise, with a father out for revenge against his own son (and consequently killing his son's friends), but the implications of such a relationship between the killer and potential victim are never touched upon. A bland and weak killer, as well as underdeveloped characters, make the film a hohum slasher.

My Bloody Valentine (1981)

Written by John Beaird; Directed by George Mihalka; Paramount Pictures/The Canadian Film Development Corporation/Famous Players; 90 min.

Cast: Paul Kelman (T.J.); Lori Hallier (Sarah); Neil Affleck (Axel); Keith Knight (Hollis); Alf Humphreys (Howard); Cynthia Dale (Patty); Helene Udy (Sylvia); Rob Stein (John); Tom Kovacs (Mike); Terry Waterland (Harriet); Carl Marotte (Dave); Jim Murchison (Tommy); Gina Dick (Gretchen); Peter Cowper (The Miner, Harry Warden); Don Francks (Chief Newby); Patricia Hamilton (Mabel); Larry Reynolds (Mayor Hanniger); Jack Van Evera (Happy); Jeff Banks (Young Axel); Pat Hemingway (Woman); Graham Whitehead (Mac); Fred Watters, Jeff Fulton (Supervisors); Pat Walsh (Harvey Smith); Marguerite McNeil (Mrs. Raleigh); Sandy Leim (Ben); John MacDonald (Rescuer)

Crew: Andre Link, John Dunning, Stephen Miller (Producers); Lawrence Nesis (Associate Producer); Paul Zaza (Composer); Rodney Gibbons (Director of Photography); Jean Lafleur (Editor)

Two people are walking in a mine shaft garbed in mining gear and gas masks. A blonde woman takes her gear off, and the man leaves his on and sets his pickaxe to the side. He looks at the woman, and then pushes her against the pickaxe in the wall.

It is Thursday, February 12, in the town of Valentines Bluff, and miners are leaving work and showering. The men head to a building where people are decorating for the first Valentine's dance in 20 years. T.J. watches Axel with his ex-girlfriend Sarah. The mayor comes by, and someone gives him a heart-shaped box that was left for him. In the truck with Chief Newby, the mayor reads the note ("From the heart comes a warning filled with bloody good cheer; remember what happened as the 14th draws near") and inside is a bloody heart ("It can't be happening again!").

The group of friends congregate in a bar, and the bartender talks about a curse. Twenty years ago, two supervisors left five miners below to go to the Valentine's dance, neglecting to check the methane gas levels. The five men were buried alive; six weeks later, a survivor, Harry Warden, was finally discovered. He was put in the hospital, and one year later he returned to town. He cut out the hearts of the two supervisors, put them in heart-shaped boxes and left a warning to never have a Valentine's dance again.

Sarah talks to T.J. and tells him it is his fault they are not together. A doctor tells the mayor and Newby that the heart is one from a woman, and they surmise that Harry is back in town. Mabel is in the laundromat, and someone leaves a heart-shaped box for her. She finds and opens it ("Roses are red, violets are blue; one is dead and so are you"), and a pickaxe is swung. Hanging out in the junkyard, Axel tells T.J. to stay away from Sarah, and T.J. says they both know who she wants.

On the day before Valentine's Day, Newby is told that the hospitals cannot find any record of Harry Warden. Newby heads to the Madame Mabel's Laundromat to discuss canceling the dance, and he finds Mabel dead inside a dryer. In the mines, T.J. and Axel almost fight but are stopped by coworkers. At the laundromat, Newby says to tell everyone that Mabel died of a heart attack, and a note is found inside the body. ("It happened once, it happened twice; cancel the dance or it'll happen thrice.") T.J.

leaves the mine, picks up Sarah and they go somewhere to talk. T.J. says he loves Sarah and apologizes, and the two kiss. At the bar, the bartender claims that Mabel was murdered. T.J. suggests having a party in the mine. The bartender warns them against having a party. Later, he is irked about his unheeded warnings, and sets up a dummy with mining gear and a pickaxe to jump out when a door is opened. He keeps opening the door and laughing, until the killer appears and pickaxes him.

Valentine's Day has arrived, and the people gather for a party. Sarah shows up with Axel, and T.J. is there, too. Dave checks out the hot dogs in the kitchen, and his face is shoved into the pot of boiling water. Newby leaves the station for the mine, and a bloody heart-shaped box is outside ("You didn't stop the party"). Sarah is becoming angry with Axel, and T.J. tells him to back off and that Sarah wants to be with him again. Sarah is now irate with both guys, and the two men fight until Hollis pulls them apart. Axel pops open a beer and storms out. T.J. tries to apologize to Sarah, but she tells him to leave her alone. Axel cries outside.

John and Sylvia are together and kissing, and John leaves to get her a beer. Gretchen adds water to the hot dog pot and finds the cooked heart inside (but does not know what it is). John opens the refrigerator for beer and does not see a dead Dave inside. As Sylvia waits for John, the killer turns on the building's showers. Sylvia finds the dead body of the bartender, and she is grabbed by the killer and taken to the showers. John returns and finds Sylvia impaled on a water pipe. Mrs. Raleigh from the hospital had called Chief Newby and said it was urgent. Patty suggests going to the mine, and she, Hollis, Mike, Harriet, Howard and Sarah go inside, ignoring T.J., who tries to stop them. Hollis gives a tour of the mine, and Mike and Harriet go off on their own, saying they will meet the others later. Gretchen runs into the main room having found Dave dead. John is next, frightened from the discovery of a dead Sylvia. Axel thinks it is Harry Warden, and he tells everyone to leave. T.J. learns that the phones are dead, and he and Axel split up and go into the mine to find their friends.

Hollis is walking with Sarah and Patty, and they are all three scared by Howard. Patty is worried about Mike and Harriet (who are somewhere else kissing), and the group hears smashing as the killer breaks the lights along the corridors. Tommy, John and Gretchen find Newby and tell him that Harry is killing people and that some friends are in the mine. Newby speeds away and requests that men be rounded up at the mine. T.J. finds the group of four and says that Harry has killed Sylvia and Dave. Hollis and T.J. split up and tell Howard to stay with the girls. Hollis finds Mike and Harriet dead, and the killer shoots a nailgun at him. Hollis gets back to the girls and collapses, with nails in his head. The group sees the killer; Howard flees, leaving the girls behind, but Axel shows up and leads Patty and Sarah away. They run into T.J. and tell him what has happened.

The group finds a smashed control panel at the lift. Axel leads them up a ladder. Near the top, Howard's body drops down on a rope and his head comes off. They go back down and head for the railcars. As Axel provides back-up from around a corner, the other three hear a grunt, followed by a splash, and they run to see Axel's light in the water. T.J. is separated from the girls, and Patty gets a pickaxe in the stomach. Sarah runs and finds a bloody T.J., who says he has been hit. T.J. and Sarah get a railcar moving as the killer approaches. Newby and many cops start running down the track.

T.J. fights the killer shovel to pickaxe, and they fall off the railcar. T.J. loses the shovel, and Sarah hits the killer with a rock. The pickaxe gets stuck, the killer brings out a knife and Sarah lifts the mask to reveal a tearful Axel. He flashes back to a young Axel watching his father (the supervisor) being killed by Harry. T.J. hits Axel with a rock, and he and Sarah run as the ceiling falls. They find the cops, and Newby says he learned that Harry had died. The men move some debris and find a moving hand, and T.J. and Sarah run back to the room. Through a small hole in the rubble, everyone watches a one-armed Axel run further into the mine while laughing maniacally.

My Bloody Valentine is an average Canadian slasher. There are few frights in the film, but the Valentine's theme is nicely incorporated.

Nail Gun Massacre (1985)

Written by Terry Lofton; Directed by Terry Lofton and Bill Leslie; Futuristic Films; 84 min.

Cast: Rocky Patterson (Doc); Ron Queen (Sheriff); Beu Leland (Bubba); Michelle Meyer (Linda); Sebrina Lawless (Mother); Monica Lawless (Baby); Jerry Nelson (Victim #1); Mike Coady (Mark); Staci Gordon (Mark's Girlfriend); Randy Hayes (Brad); Tom Meyers (Hitchhiker); John Prince (John); Charles Ladeate (Tom); Joann Hazelbarth (Maxine); Frances Heard (Storekeeper); Terry Lofton (Truck Driver); John Rudder (Hal); Shelly York (Ann); Mike Bendall (Ben); Connie Speer (Trish); Roger Payne, Kit Mitchell (Lovers on Car); Taleesa Van-Tassel, Amy Deitrich (Waitresses); Aaron Carrol, Aaron Chadwick (Carpenters); Rob Slyker (Barbecued Victim); Pamela Rene (His Daughter); Kim Mathis, Diana Bober (Girl Victims); Thomas Freylac (Killer's Voice); Michael Cullis, Martin Smith (Rapists); Mark Woodcock (Boy Walking Down Street); John Holden (Old Man in Town)

Cast: Linda Bass, T.L. Lofton (Executive Producers); Terry Lofton (Producer); Whitey Thomas (Composer); Bill Leslie (Director of Photography); Lynn Lenau Calmes (Editor)

Six men pin down a woman and rape her. A woman is hanging clothes on the line, and inside the nearby house, a man walks out of the bathroom, calling her name because he does not have a clean shirt. A person wearing camouflage and a motorcycle helmet covered in electric tape loads a nail gun, walks past the woman and enters the house. The man sees the person ("Who the hell are you?"), and the person nails the man several times. The woman goes to the house with her baby, sees the nailed man and runs into the woods.

Mark gets out of bed and goes to cut wood with Brad. They leave the truck at the side of the road and go into the woods with a chainsaw. The killer pulls up behind the truck in an old hearse. Brad goes to "take a leak," and the killer appears and nails him in the stomach and crotch. Mark revs up the chainsaw, and the killer comes up behind him and shoots the nail gun. Mark falls and inadvertently cuts off his hand. Maxine tells Tom and John in a store that someone is letting them stay in a house for free, and the elderly storekeeper says that dead bodies were found near the area. When Doc arrives at the scene, the sheriff shows him the corpses of Mark and Brad. The doctor mentions that three bodies have now been discovered on Old Lady Bailey's property. The sheriff asks if her husband was a carpenter before he died, and he leaves to call the "meat wagon."

The killer stops for a hitchhiker, nails him in the stomach and gets out of the car to nail him to the road. The sheriff and Doc go to a store where a dead nailed woman was found behind the store, and they are called out to where a truck driver found the hitchhiker. Maxine, John and Tom are eating, and Maxine mentions Old Bailey letting them have the house because someone had been killed. John looks outside after hearing a noise and finds nothing. The next day, John and Tom load the truck with lumber, and Linda (the woman who had been raped) yells at them for forgetting their receipt. Hal and Ben, with Ann and Trish, arrive at the lumber yard and ask Bubba if he is hiring. He tells of the place where they are fixing a house, and after they leave, Linda asks Bubba if the two men were construction workers.

The group goes to the house, and since no one is out at the door, they sit on a blanket for a meal. Hal and Ann go for a walk and end up having sex by a tree, where they are nailed by the killer. Trish is worried about the two, and Ben goes to look for them. He sees the killer, who tells him to put his hands around the tree, where he is nailed and left alone. John finds a very upset Trish, who had heard shots; he tells her that hunters are out there, and leads her away. The sheriff arrives to see John and Tom, who have found the three bodies. Afterwards, John and Tom unload the truck, and Maxine suggests the noise the other night was the killer. Tom asks John where the nail gun is. Two carpenters are playing with nail guns, and they go back into the partially constructed house. The killer shoots one, and when the other says he did not do anything, the killer says to think back six months ago. The man says, "It wasn't me who raped you," and the killer nails him.

A man and a woman get something to eat, and then enjoy some time in the car. The killer shows up and nails them both. A man looking through a newspaper tells his daughter that he is going to check on the steaks. Outside, the killer, having cleverly hidden in the pool, splashes out and nails the man, who falls and lands on the grill. The daughter finds her father cooking with the steaks and she screams. Doc calls a Dallas hospital, tells a fellow doctor the situation and asks for a profile of the killer. The sheriff and Doc talk to the daughter, and she says her father had been reading about his friends being killed. The sheriff tells the doctor that six of the dead people worked at the construction site where Linda had said she was raped after delivering supplies. At a diner, Doc says that he talked to Linda after the incident and she gave no indication that she would murder anyone. He goes to check the Dallas reports.

Two women walking out in the woods are nailed. Doc calls Linda and asks for Bubba. He drives over there and demands Linda tell him the truth. He asks where Bubba is, and Linda says he is out in his hearse. Doc and Linda follow the hearse until the killer gets out and runs and eventually falls to his death. Linda takes off the helmet and sees her brother Bubba. Doc says that at least the killings are over. ("Is it? Is it over?") Linda takes the helmet, and she and Doc walk away hand in hand.

Nail Gun Massacre is a low-budget slasher with amateurish performances, feeble direction and an unfrightening and monotonous killer (the "voice disguiser" the killer uses is particularly annoying).

New Year's Evil (1981)

Written by Leonard Neubauer and Emmett Alston; Directed by Emmett Alston; Golan-Globus Productions; 84 min.

Cast: Roz Kelly (Diane Sullivan); Kip Niven (Richard Sullivan); Chris Wallace (Lieutenant Clayton); Grant Cramer (Derek Sullivan); Louisa Mortiz (Sally); Jed Mills (Ernie); Taaffe O'Connell (Jane); Jon Greene (Sergeant Greene); Teri Copley (Teenage Girl); Anita Crane (Lisa); Jennie Anderson (Nurse Robbie); Alicia Dhanifu (Yvonne); Wendysue Rosloff (Make-up Girl); John London (Floor Manager); John Alderman (Doctor Reed); Michael Frost (Larry); Jerry Chambers (Clerk); Barry Gibberman (Hotel Guest); Mike Mihalich (Policeman, Hotel); Jerry Zanitsch, Mark L. Rosen (Drunks); Bob Jarvis, Richard E. Kalk (Policemen); Richard Brown (Swamper); Mark Defrain (Teenage Boy); Julie Kay Towery (Space Girl); Lyle Baker (Space Boy); Tim Cutt (Ambulance Attendant); Jay Happstein (Ambulance Driver); Don Grenough (Punker); Ryan Collier, Mark Korngute (Bar Hustlers); Edward Jackson, Celena Allen, Bill Blair, Christine Davis, Ricky Israel, Clarisse Kotkin, Cynthia MacArthur, Roxanne Orbis, Justin Rubin, Michelle Waxman (Punkers in Car); Randy Gould, Jodie Mann, Karen Mills, Adrienne Upton (Phone Girls); Jim Amormino, Doug Le Mille, Larry Lindsey, Lyle Pearcy (Clayton's Men)

Crew: Billy Fine (Executive Producer); Menahem Golan, Yorum Globus (Producers); Christopher Pearce (Associate Producer); W. Michael Lewis, Laurin Rinder (Composers); Edward Thomas (Director of Photography); Dick Brummer (Editor)

Diane Sullivan is getting her make up put on. Her friend Yvonne tells her over the phone that her husband Richard is in Palm Springs at a club and will probably not be back to see Diane's show. Yvonne is in the bathroom, and after turning the shower faucet to stop the dripping, she hears the door open ("Who's there?"). She sees no one, shuts the door and walks back to the bathroom. Yvonne goes to turn on the shower faucet again, and she is grabbed by a person in black and stabbed with a switchblade.

Derek, Diane's son, enters his mother's hotel room and tells her about a part he got in a new series. Diane is too busy getting ready and she does not seem to be paying attention to Derek, who is evidently perturbed. Diane, wearing a gaudy dress, a studded collar and too much make up, leaves to host *Hollywood Hotline* (her stage name is Blaze, the "first lady of rock"). She is hosting a rock countdown called New Year's Evil, in which everyone will be watching different time zones to celebrate midnight several different times. People can call in to vote for the best song. One of the callers is a man, using something to disguise his voice, who asks to be called "Evil." He tells Diane that he is going to kill someone she knows at midnight (for the first time zone).

A man in black sneaks into the back of a mental institution through the cafeteria. When a nurse finds him, he is appropriately dressed and he tells her that he is new. She offers to show him around, he asks her for a little drink, and they dance to Diane's show on the radio. The cops tell Diane to try keeping Evil on the phone longer if he calls again.

Diane calls Derek in the room and asks if he has heard from Yvonne. Derek says there is something important Diane should know, but she says she has to go, and Derek takes a few pills. The man and the nurse are kissing as it nears midnight in Manhattan. He casually presses the record button on his radio and then viciously stabs the woman several times as the radio crowd cheers. Evil telephones Blaze again ("I just made my first kill right on schedule"). He plays the recording for her, says he will call back in an hour and tells Diane where the body can be found (Crawford Sanitarium).

As Derek cuts a red stocking and puts it on his head, Evil glues on a mustache and goes into a club to pick up a woman. Lieutenant Clayton tells Diane that the "creep" is for real, and he says it seems that the killer means to kill at midnight at each time zone. A woman in the club, Sally, agrees to meet Evil out front, and brings her roommate Lisa along. They are driving in his Mercedes and Evil becomes agitated as it nears the hour of kill. Evil hands Lisa some money and tells her to buy a bottle of champagne. Evil hits RECORD (the car radio is on), shows Sally something in a plastic bag and wraps the bag around her head and suffocates her. When Lisa comes back out, the car is gone. She finds Sally's shoe, sees some cloth hanging from the trash bin, and opens the bin only to see Evil inside; he pulls her in. Evil calls Diane, plays her the recorded murder and tells her where the bodies are.

Evil, now dressed as a priest, is driving, and he accidentally hits a biker from a gang. He speeds off, and the bikers follow him into a drive-in. While hiding, Evil sees the bikers looking around. He gets out of his car and sees one of the bikers ("I'm a man of God, not a man of violence"). He pulls his blade, stabs the biker and runs. Evil finds a car with two couples kissing, he yanks the man out and drives away with the girl in back. The girl jumps out when Evil stops for two drunken men, and he chases her down with his switchblade and radio. The drunks point cops Evil's way, and the officers prevent Evil from getting the girl and cause him to miss his scheduled kill.

Clayton has the floor (where the show is being held) sealed off and the guards are ordered not to let people inside. Evil heads over to the parking garage, where two officers guard the entrance. One cop leaves, and Evil, from another the corner, calls the other officer over ("I think I found a drunk!"). He bashes the cop on the head, puts on his uniform and gets inside. An officer gets a call that another cop was found knocked out, so he follows Diane to her room, where he checks the room and yells "Freeze!" to Derek. Derek, angry, tells Diane he had a surprise for her, but now he does not care. He storms out.

While the officer is waiting outside, Evil comes out of the bathroom wearing a funny mask. Diane screams, Evil takes off the mask and Diane relaxes, calling him Richard. Richard goes to identify himself to the officer outside and tell him he was in the bathroom. Richard tells Diane that the surprise was Derek's idea and that he decided to come back when he heard Evil calling on the phone. As Richard is leaving, the cop asks him how he was able to get in, and Richard tells him that Ernie okayed it. Clayton tells others that they found Richard's car at a drive-in where someone was knifed, and that Richard was once a patient at Crawford. Ernie says he did not give the okay for Richard to come in. The police officer and Diane get on the elevator, but Richard, at the control box, stops the elevator and maneuvers it to his floor. He opens the door, kicks the cop and drags him away. Richard goes to Diane as she awakes, and he plays the tape of murders for her. Richard tells his wife he is "fed up" with the way she acts around other men and how she treats her son. "This has been a very bad year for me," he says, and he takes Diane away.

As police officers are looking for Diane, Richard handcuffs his wife to the bottom of an elevator, then goes back to the control box to move the elevator up and down. The cops arrive, a gunfight ensues and the open circuit board is hit, causing the elevator to stop when the punks inside hit the emergency stop. Richard, chased to the roof, drops his gun and knife, puts on the mask and throws himself off of the building. In the street, Derek cries at the sight of his dead father and he takes off the mask. Diane is taken away on a stretcher and put in an ambulance. In the vehicle, Derek is behind the wheel and wearing the mask, and the other paramedic is next to him and dead. They drive away as it hits midnight.

New Year's Evil is a fairly uneventful slasher full of mediocre acting, with the exception of Kip Niven, who makes a fun killer. When the car radio is on (and Richard is the priest), the deejay mentions that William Fine has been named secretary general; Billy Fine was the film's executive producer.

The New York Ripper (aka *Lo squartatore di New York*; *The Ripper*; *Psycho Ripper*) (1982)

Written by Gianfranco Clerici, Vincenzo Mannino, Lucio Fulci and Dardano Sacchetti; Directed by Lucio Fulci; Fulvia Films; 93 min.

Cast: Jack Hedley (Lieutenant Frank Williams); Almanta Keller (Fay Majors); Howard Ross (Mickey Scellenda); Andrew Painter (Peter Bunch); Alexandra Delli Colli (Jane Forrester Lodge); Paolo Malco (Doctor Paul Davis); Cinzia De Ponti (Rosie, Ferry Victim); Laurence Welles (Doctor Lodge); Daniela Doria (Kitty); Babette New (Mrs. Weissburger); Zora Kerowa (Eva, Sex Show Performer); Paul Guskin (Desk Sergeant); Anthon Kagan (Santos); Josh Cruze (Morales); Marsha MacBride (Policewoman); Rita Silva (Scellenda's Landlady); Giordano Falzoni (Doctor Barry Jones, Coroner); Lucio Fulci (Chief of Police); Barbara Cupisti (Heather); Martin Sorrentino (Police Detective); Violetta Jean (Hospital Nurse); Cesare Di Vito (Red Volkswagen Owner); Elisa Cervi (Maid); Chiara Ferrari (Susy Bunch)

Crew: Fabrizio De Angelis (Producer); Francesco De Masi (Composer); Guglielmo Mancori (Director of Photography); Vincenzo Tomassi (Editor)

A man out walking his dog throws a plank of wood for the dog to fetch. The canine goes into the bushes and retrieves a rotting severed hand.

Lieutenant Williams talks to a landlady who identifies Anne Lynn (her "working name") and says that last Friday she received a call from a person who sounded like a duck. Rosie is riding her bike, and a driver yells at her after she accidentally runs into his door. Later, on a ferry, Rosie sits in the driver's empty red car and writes on his windshield with lipstick. Someone gets into the car with her, quacks and speaks like a duck and pulls out a switchblade. Rosie tries to get out, but she is pulled back in and stabbed and sliced.

Barry the coroner tells Williams that the

killing was non-sexual and in the same style as the earlier murder. The lieutenant is told he had a phone call from a person who sounded like a duck. Williams goes to see Doctor Davis for some "expert help," and the doctor says they will have to wait until the killer strikes again. Mickey, a man with two fingers missing from his right hand, enters a place to watch people have sex on stage. Jane is in the audience with him. One of the stage performers is backstage when the lights go out. She looks around and calls for someone named Joe, and a hand comes out and, after a quack, she is stabbed with a broken bottle. Williams gets a phone call while lying in bed with a prostitute. The killer calls, mocks the lieutenant and refers to his companion as a whore. The doctor listens to a recording of the killer, and he speaks of the killer's intelligence. Jane goes to a diner and eyes a couple of men. They sit with her and humiliate her, and she runs out to her car.

Fay is on a subway train, and the three-fingered man is with her. As Mickey nears her, Fay runs out of the train when it stops. She moves into the street and suddenly a quacking and a knife are in front of her, and she is stabbed. The killer swings again, and Fay runs, letting the knife hit the wall.

Fay sits in an empty movie theater, and she is attacked from under the seats. She runs again and sees the face of Peter, who repeatedly slices her with a razor blade. Fay screams and awakes in the hospital with only the initial knife wound. Peter goes to see Fay in her room, and she tells him of her nightmare. The police are now looking for Mickey. Fay tells Peter she believes she dreamed he killed her because of the bad things she said about Susy, but Peter assures her it is okay.

Mickey ties up Jane in a hotel (she had given him money) as a tape records. He turns up the radio and calls someone on the phone, but Jane cannot hear him. Later, the man lacking two fingers is sleeping, and Jane (with cuts on her chest) hears the radio report of the cops' search for the three-fingered man (the "ripper"). Jane manages to untie herself, puts on a coat and leaves. Before she can get a door open or get on the elevator, the killer is there, and Jane is stabbed in the stomach and throat. The cops learn Mickey's identity when a hotel clerk picks him out of a mug file, and they ransack Mickey's place.

Peter helps Fay into a house. Doctor Davis visits them to see how Fay is doing. After noticing a chalkboard, he asks if Peter is a mathematician (he is a physician). The doctor asks Fay if she is sure that Mickey attacked her. Later, the doctor notes that Fay is holding out, and he says that the phone calls make the killer seem intelligent, which seems uncharacteristic of the three-fingered man. Fay climbs a ladder and goes into a little girl's room, and a window is broken and unlocked with a three-fingered hand. As Fay looks at a paper from the Memorial Hospital, the lights go out. The man attacks her, but runs when Peter arrives, knocking the physician down the stairs.

The police are awaiting a phone call since the killer said he would telephone and that he had a surprise for Lieutenant Williams. The killer makes his call and tells Williams that he wants to dedicate a killing to him and that Kitty said hello. The cops get a trace and rush to a phone booth, where the killer has a walkie talkie next to the phone's receiver. The killer is with Williams' companion Kitty; tape is pulled off her mouth so that the lieutenant can hear her scream. The killer quacks and slices Kitty with a razor blade. Williams rushes over to the place, but by the time he arrives, Kitty is dead and the killer gone. Afterwards, Mickey's corpse is discovered. Williams is told that he has been dead for about eight days, while Kitty had been killed only four days ago.

In a hospital bed, within a plastic tent, lies a little girl with one arm and no legs. Fay, looking into the room, cries. Outside, she passes the movie theatre and sees the mark the knife left when it hit the wall. Davis talks to a nurse about the little girl, and he is told that one parent is in Brazil and the other pays money but never visits. The doctor tells Williams to put Peter under surveillance. In the kitchen, Fay sees a knife with the tip of the blade broken. Peter answers the phone, and a duck-voiced person says they have not played in a long time. Fay hangs up the phone in another room. Peter looks for Fay and he heads up the stairs, telling Fay not to go in Susy's room. Fay stabs Peter in the chest and he falls down the stairs. At the bottom, Peter jumps up, knocks Fay down and sits over her with the knife, quacking and speaking as the duck. Williams shoots a hole in Peter's face. The nurse asks Susy if she wants to play ducks on the phone with her father. Davis tells Williams and Fay that the duck became an "avenger" for the unfortunate Susy. Little Susy is on the phone, and she cries when her father does not answer: "Daddy, please."

While not the best of Fulci's work, *The New York Ripper* contains some effective scenes of stalking, and the duck-voiced killer is original and fun. Fulci, notorious for his films' exceptionally gory scenes, is a talented filmmaker, frequently underappreciated or unfairly dismissed by critics. Actor Welles is actually Cosimo Cinieri and actor Painter is Andrea Occhipinti, who also starred in Lamberto Bava's *A Blade in the Dark* (1983).

Night School (1981)

Written by Ruth Avergon; Directed by Kenneth Hughes; Paramount Pictures/Lorimar Productions; 88 min.

Cast: Leonard Mann (Judd Austin); Rachel Ward (Eleanor); Drew Snyder (Vincent Millett); Joseph R. Sicari (Taj); Nicolas Cairis (Gus); Karen McDonald (Carol); Annette Miller (Helen Griffin); Bill McCann (Gary); Margo Skinner (Stevie Cabot); Elizabeth Barnitz (Kim Morrison); Holly Hardman (Kathy); Meb Boden (Anne Barron); Leonard Corman (Priest); Belle McDonald (Marjorie Armand); Ed Higgins (Coronor); William McDonald (Medical Examiner); Kevin Fennessy (Harry the Janitor); Ed Chaimers, John Blood (Construction Workers); Lisa Allee (Lisa); Elizabeth Allee (Lisa's Mother); Patricia Pellows (Screaming Woman); J.J. Wright (Plainclothesman); Patricia Rust (Pat); Jane-Leah Bedrick (Receptionist); Wally Hooper, Jr. (Worker); Kevin King (Policeman); Nancy Rothman (Student)

Crew: Marc Gregory Comjean, Bernard Kebadjian (Executive Producers); Leon Williams, Larry Bob, Ruth Avergon (Producers); Brad Fiedel (Composer); Mark Irwin, C.S.C. (Director of Photography); Robert Reitano (Editor)

At the Jack-n-Jill Daycare Center, teacher's aide Anne Barron is saying goodnight to young Lisa. Anne sits alone on the merry-go-round, and a person arrives on a motorcycle, clad in leather and helmet. The person spins the merry-go-round and holds out a knife at Anne as she passes. Finally the blade is lifted, and Anne screams.

Lieutenant Judd Austin is with Stevie on his day off, but Taj calls him, and Judd leaves for his "lousy job." He arrives at the scene and is told that the killing is similar to an earlier one. Judd is shown Ann's head, resting in a bucket of water. The director of the center, Miss Armand, tells the cops that Anne attended evening classes at Wendell College, girls school. Judd tries to find meaning in the decapitated heads in water (since the head from the previous killing was found in a lake). Judd goes to the school and stands in the back of Professor Millett's anthropology class as the teacher is finishing a lecture. After class, Judd says he is there about Anne, and Millett says that his student Kim was Anne's friend. The professor consoles the student. Eleanor, a foreign exchange student, walks in and tells Millett she has finished his notes. Kim tells the lieutenant that Anne had a boyfriend but would not tell her who he was.

Eleanor goes to the Lamplight Restaurant, where the weird Gus stares at her. Carol, a waitress, asks the student if she is in Millett's class and if the teacher "fools around" with his students. Eleanor walks home alone, and she is frightened by a shadowing Gus. She gets inside her place, where she showers and is scared by Millett. The two kiss, and then enjoy themselves, as the professor paints his student's nude body. Kim is in scuba gear feeding the turtles as people watch through glass. She gets out of the water and goes to the locker room, where the helmet-clad killer jumps out and slices her to her death, dropping her head in the tank so the people can see.

Judd goes to see Millett at his home; Eleanor is there (she is the professor's "research assistant"). In the office, Millett says that man is the only animal who kills for pleasure. Judd mentions the murder of another student, and asks about possible affairs with either student; the teacher denies the charges. As he is leaving, the lieutenant says, "People don't go out and kill just for the hell of it. There's always a reason." A tearful Eleanor says she loves Millett and would do anything for him, but there is always another person. Millett follows the upset woman to the restaurant and apologizes, and Eleanor tells him that she is pregnant. They both seem happy, but Eleanor seems a little irked when Millett flirts with Carol a bit.

Millett goes to see Helen Griffin, dean of the school, and hears her talking to Kathy about an affair with the professor. Helen discusses Millett losing his job, and she offers to let Kathy stay at her place. Carol is closing the restaurant after Gary leaves, and the lights are shut off ("Who's there?"). The killer is there, and the knife is brought out. Carol gets out the back door, but the killer catches up, swings the knife and carries her head back into the restaurant. The next morning, Gary comes in with a couple of construction workers, and they see the mess. He drains the sink full of water and finds Carol's head inside. The cops arrive. Judd and Taj get Gus' address from Gary, and go to visit the man (who did not come in for work). Gus tells the cops he was too sick to go to work. Taj finds a bra, but Judd decides to leave, thinking Gus is only a peeping tom.

Judd goes to Millett's place and picks the lock when no one answers the door. In the office, he finds photographs of Millett and Eleanor posing with tribal people. Eleanor comes in and asks if the cop has a search warrant. He tells her no, and he asks about headhunting (implied by the photographs). Eleanor says that heads are cut off in New Guinea because people believed they could possess lifeforce from the heads of enemies; the heads were put in water to cleanse the evil spirits.

Eleanor goes to Millett's class and walks in on a discussion with Millett and Helen about the professor having an affair. Eleanor storms out, and Millett is angry with Helen, suggesting that her interest in the girls is something other than "welfare." Later, Judd follows Millett on his motorbike but loses him, and Taj calls to tell him Gus is outside Helen's place. As Taj follows Gus up some steps, Helen, having lain in bed with Kathy, goes downstairs to answer the phone and is grabbed by the killer. Kathy awakes, finds Helen's head in the toilet and is killed. Judd breaks down the door, sees Helen's body and is jumped by the killer, who runs outside and speeds away. Taj arrests Gus outside.

The killer returns to a place and takes off the helmet. It is Eleanor. She shows Millett the knife, saying "I did it for us, Vincent, and for our baby." She says she had to kill the women that Millett lusted after because she loved him. She talks about an accepted ritual within a society where women are not allowed to defend themselves. When they both hear sirens, Eleanor says the police are coming for her, and if they kill her, they will kill the baby. Judd bangs on the door, and Millett stops a weeping Eleanor from going to the door. A person in leather and a helmet speeds away on a motorcycle, and the cops gives chase in a pursuit that ends with the bike hitting a car and the person landing on Taj's car. The helmet is taken off, and the cops see Millett. Judd does not seem satisfied with the discovery. At the professor's funeral, Judd asks Eleanor if the ceremony is over, and she cries and says yes. Judd leaves his office later, goes to his car and is attacked by a person in a helmet. It turns out to be Taj just wanting to scare him, and the two cops laugh.

Night School is a half-hearted slasher, with minimal thrills and no real surprises.

Nevertheless, the decapitating murders are interesting (especially with the places the killer finds for sources of water), and the ending is humorous.

Nightmare (aka *Blood Splash*; *Nightmare in a Damaged Brain*) (1981)

Written and directed by Romano Scavolini; Goldmine Productions; 88 min.

Cast: Baird Stafford (George Tatum); Sharon Smith (Susan Temper); C.J. Cooke (C.J. Temper); Mik Cribben (Bob Rosen); Danny Ronan (Kathy the Babysitter); John Watkins (Man with Cigar); William Milling (Paul Williamson); Scott Praetorius (Young George); William S. Kirksey (George's Father); Christina Keefe (George's Mother); Tammy Patterson (Tammy Temper); Kim Patterson (Kim Temper); Kathleen Ferguson (Barbara); William Paul (Steve); Tommy Bouvier (Joe); Candy Marchese (Jogger); Geoffrey Marchese (Tony Walker); Michael Sweney (Burt Daniels); George Kruger (Chief Cotter); Ray Baker (Real Estate Agent); Lonnie Griffis (Gatsby's Singer); Tara Alexander (Woman in Booth); Danielle Galiana (Show World Dancer); Carl Clifford, David Massar (Hospital Attendants); Mary Lee Parise, Randy Arieux, Craig Cain, Mark Davis, Ken Thomas, Robert Tenvodren, Susan Webb, Frank Rothery, Scott Trotter (Police Officers)

Crew: John L. Walkins (Producer); Chris Cronyn, Bill Paul (Associate Producers); Jack Eric Williams (Composer); Gianni Fiore (Director of Photography); Robert T. Megginson (Editor); Les Larrain (Special Effects)

A man, tossing and turning, sits up in his bed to see a woman in pieces. The decapitated head's eyes open, and the man screams. He is now in a straitjacket and wheelchair, and two hospital attendants burst into the room and inject him with something.

In Florida, Kathy is babysitting C.J., Tammy and Kim, who tell her they saw someone outside the window. She tells them to go back to sleep, but she goes outside after hearing a noise and shrieks when she sees someone on the roof. Cops investigate the scene and find nothing, as Susan, the children's mother, consoles Kathy. C.J. sits at the top of the stairs smiling.

In New York, George Tatum, the patient, imagines a young boy walking into a room and seeing a woman tying a man to a bed and beating him. There are sounds of something swinging, flying blood, and the woman suddenly without a head. According to the hospital's report, George has schizophrenia, amnesia, dream fixations and seizures — and he is also homicidal. He is having dreams triggered by something in his childhood, and he is being given experimental drugs to pacify his violent episodes. George tells Doctor Williamson of his recurring dream, referring to an axe or hatchet and saying that sometimes he is the child and sometimes he is looking at the child. The hospital considers George a "success," that he has been "rebuilt." George leaves the hospital and goes to an adult-oriented place, but the women only remind him of his dream, and he falls over foaming at the mouth.

George gets on a ferry and goes to Florida. Doctor Williamson asks his receptionist if George has come in yet. George calls Susan's place, and C.J. answers, but George does not say anything. The children leave for school, and Susan goes to see her boyfriend Bob. A woman drives home from a bar, and George is at her house to cut her throat and stab her in the stomach a few times ("I'm sorry"), licking his bloody fingers after the murder. A very agitated man is speaking to Doctor Williamson about George's disapperance, and despite the doctor's claims that George is "simply not dangerous," the man demands that Doctor Williamson get George back to the hospital. The children return home to an empty house (Susan is with Bob), and when C.J. takes out the trash, he sees George standing across the street looking at him. When Susan calls the house to check on the kids, C.J. walks back in with a bloody stomach. Susan and Bob rush back to her house to discover ketchup all over C.J.; the boy thinks this is hilarious. He is sent to his room until the next day. Susan complains to Bob about a man leaving the day after C.J. was born. George calls the house again and hangs up the phone.

Kathy is babysitting again. While C.J. is in his room working, Kathy is answering multiple phone calls to no reply. She walks to C.J.'s room, and he jumps in bed just before she opens the door. In the bathroom later, Kathy sees someone reflected in the mirror. She screams, and turns around to see C.J. in a dummy (his head sticks out of the dummy's chest). The next day, a distraught Kathy tells Susan to find another babysitter. Susan visits a real estate agent, wishing to sell her house. When Bob takes a picture of the house, he sees a figure in a window. The couple runs inside but sees no one (George is hiding somewhere with his knife). At the beach, C.J. sees George again, and he tells his mother a man is following him. She thinks he is lying. That night, George calls Susan, saying, "I want you."

George telephones Doctor Williamson the following day, and he mentions something that is "stronger than pills"; the doctor tells George it is only a dream. C.J. is riding on his bike later, and a jogger, Candy, goes inside a building upon seeing C.J.'s bike outside. Candy does not see George standing behind a door. C.J.'s friend Tony goes into the building, and C.J., standing outside, calls to him. Tony tells him to come in and see the "neat stuff," but C.J. decides to leave. Tony finds a dead Candy, and he tries to scream as George approaches. The cops pick up Susan and C.J. that night, and an officer shows C.J. the deceased Tony and asks him what has happened and if he "hurt" Tony. C.J. answers none of the man's questions. The mother and son are taken away.

Cops find George's abandoned car. C.J. is sent home early from school, and George calls him (from inside the house) and tells the boy to leave while he can. The doctor is in Florida with two other men (they believe George has family in the state), and Doctor Williamson is told that George's "recurring dream" was found in a police report from 25 years earlier, in which a man and a woman were killed with an axe. Susan calls Kathy and pleads with her to babysit one more time so that she can go to a party with Bob.

At the house that night, Kathy's boyfriend Joey arrives. Following a sexual tryst, Kathy goes to shower. George kills Joey while she is gone. Kathy returns, sees George and believes it is C.J. in his dummy (George is wearing a mask). She goes for the phone to call the pesky boy's mother, and George rewards her with a tiny pickaxe near her wrist. When she tries to get away, George stabs her in the back. C.J. sees what has happened and manages to convince his disbelieving sisters to hide in his room. He slams the door to his mother's room and gets out a gun. As George pickaxes through the door, C.J. shoots his hand and then his stomach. George stands up, and C.J. shoots him three more times. C.J. and his sisters run downstairs, and the boy tries to get on the phone but it is busy. He shoots George one more time when he comes down the stairs.

The children run outside and hear George scream again, and C.J. goes back inside ("It's okay. I've still got the gun"). George is gone. C.J. goes upstairs, and George follows him. When his gun only clicks, C.J. runs and gets a shotgun. George calls C.J.'s name, C.J. fires twice and George tumbles down the stairs, his childhood memory now fully manifested. As a boy, George arrives home to see his parents engaged in sadomasochistic sex, and evidently misinterpreting the reason his mother is beating his father, George gets an axe, beheads his mother ("George, you don't understand!"), chops at the headless body and swings the axe into his father's forehead. Susan and Bob arrive, and the woman screams when George's mask is taken off ("That's my husband!"). A young George licks his bloody fingers, and C.J., sitting in a police car, smiles and winks. Then his smile is gone.

Nightmare is a very effective slasher film. Despite a mildly confusing set of events, the film efficiently provides atmospheric scenes to complement the idea of George's dreams. Actor Praetorius, who plays the young George, only appears in the few flashbacks, but his performance is exceptional. Special effects guru Tom Savini claimed to only have supervised the film's special effects (Larrain having actually done the work), but the movie was nevertheless initially sold with Savini credited with the task.

Open House
(1987)

Written by David Mickey Evans; Directed by Jag Mundhra; Intercontinental Releasing Corporation; 98 min.

Cast: Joseph Bottoms (David Kelley); Adrienne Barbeau (Lisa Grant); Rudy Ramos (Rudy Estevez); Mary Stavin (Katie Thatcher); Scott Thompson Baker (Joe Pearcy); Darwyn Swalve (Harry); Robert Miano (Shapiro); Page Moseley (Toby); Johnny Haymer (Paul Bernal); Leonard Lightfoot (T.J.); Barry Hope (Barney Resnick); Stacey Adams (Tracy); Roxanne Baird (Allison); Tiffany Bolling (Judy Roberts); Dena Drota (The Fan); Cathryn Hartt (Melody); Christina Gallegos (Pilar); Lee Moore (Donald Spectra); Stephen Nemeth (Tommy); Joanne Norman (Agent #1); Richard Parnes (Lenny); Sheila Ryan (Ellen); A. Gerald Singer (Captain Blake); Bryan Utman (Policeman); Susan Widem (Policewoman); Eddie Wong (Mr. Yoshida)

Cast: Victor Bhalla, Sultan Allaudin (Executive Producers); Sandy Cobe (Producer); Gabriella Belloni (Co-Producer); Jim Studer (Composer); Robert Hayes (Director of Photography); Dan Selakovich (Editor)

Tracy is in a phone booth, talking to radio psychologist Doctor David Kelley on *Survival Line*. Tracy wants to kill herself because of the horrible things her father has done to her. Evidently believing that the doctor does not care about her, Tracy shoots herself.

Realtor Melody is showing Mr. and Mrs. Yoshida a house, and after finding ants and pet food in the kitchen, she tells them to look at the origami garden in back. She frantically cleans, but despite the mess, Mr. Yoshida says he will take the house. Melody relaxes and goes to the bathroom, where she finds a bloody corpse in the shower and "Sold" written on the mirror in blood. When cops arrive, Shapiro mentions the dead woman as being "number four." An officer refers to the murderer as "The Open House Killer."

Lisa listens to David on the radio, and he avoids a caller's discussion of the "litigation" because he cannot legally talk about it. A woman in the real estate office gives Lisa a copy of the listings, and the old listings are thrown in the trash and taken out by someone. Resnick talks to Tommy about trashing condos. Katie is showing Joe a house, interrupting the killer's dinner of dog food from a can. The killer takes a plunger, affixes many razor blades to the handle and walks toward the couple, who have now decided to kiss. They run to the bathroom, and Joe loses two fingers. The killer bursts inside and slices and dices his way through the couple.

David gets some fan mail, with an "urgent" envelope containing the listings. He receives a call from Harry, who says the people of "that real estate thing" deserved to die, and complains about them being rich. Mary Lou calls and, in a heavy Southern accent, says she doesn't see enough of her boyfriend. After the show, David gets the "Multiple Listings" (the M and L have been circled) and drives to a highlighted listing. "Mary Lou" (it is actually Lisa) greets him, and they spend the night together. The next morning, David tells Lisa of Harry's eccentric phone call, and he tells her to be "extra careful." Resnick is at an open house and being rude to Pilar. Captain Blake tells Shapiro to check out the man who called in to the radio show. Lisa is leaving the estate, and Resnick tells her to stay away from the house and mentions the condos getting "all messed up." Lisa angrily drives away.

Harry calls the show again, Shapiro listens and the captain tells the officer to order a wiretap. Pilar is closing up the estate; when she goes back for her car keys, she is grabbed by the killer. She is restrained and her mouth is duct-taped. The killer pours wine on her, puts two open wires on the woman and puts a plug in the outlet. The switch is hit, and Pilar is electrocuted. Lisa talks with Donald about filing a complaint against Resnick, but with no witnesses, Donald says there must be something more. David and fellow deejay, Rudy are called into Paul's office, where Shapiro tells them about the wiretap. Paul does not want another lawsuit (David calls it a "professional inquiry"), and Shapiro mentions the girl killing herself on the show. Shapiro tells Paul the phones will be tapped. David drives to his place and listens to a tape of Tracy's phone call. In the parking garage, he is frightened by noise, and he finds a section of listings.

Lisa arrives at David's place, and the paranoid radio psychologist almost attacks her. At the station the following day, the phones are tapped, and David begins the show by asking listeners what they think of the real estate murders. In a conference room, Donald mentions Lisa's suggestion of a "buddy system" for the realtors. Resnick says the "system" might ruin percentages and he nearly threatens Lisa with everyone in the room. Lisa says she sold some condominiums that morning, and Resnick says that it is not possible since he trashed them. Donald says he will go before the licensing board about Resnick, and the meeting is over. Two realtors are at a house; the guy is beeped and leaves to check on his pregnant wife, leaving the other real estate agent alone. Later, the woman hangs dead from a cord.

Lisa meets with David and Rudy in a bar and talks of Resnick threatening her after the meeting. Lisa says Resnick was once more successful, and Rudy believes that Resnick has a motive to commit the murders. In order to get a listing, Resnick meets Allison, in leather and chains, at a house, and she puts a leash on him. Afterwards, she goes to the spa behind the house; the killer has Resnick's head. After swimming around, Allison sees Resnick's decapitated head, and the killer puts a leash around her neck, drags her and strings her up. The next day, Rudy tells David that Resnick is dead and shows him the paper, which states that David refused the wiretap to protect callers' privacy (a story Rudy fabricated).

David starts a new show and Lisa is at the studio. The killer is at the studio and he picks up a phone. Harry's call comes through, and they begin the tap. Shapiro calls on his radio and tells someone to inform the people that Harry is calling from the station. David runs around looking for Lisa, but she and Harry are nowhere to be found. David gets another call, and Harry says he has 30 minutes to find Lisa or she will die. Lisa talks and tells David to not forget Mary Lou. David checks the listings and speeds over to a house, where Harry is with Lisa. Harry asks David where all the news people are, because he has something to say. He says he does not like the houses being so expensive, and he blames the realtors. A SWAT team arrives, and Shapiro comes in and shoots Harry a number of times. Shapiro goes to the balcony, where Harry attacks again. The two struggle, and Harry falls off and hits the ground.

Open House is fairly tedious, with a lack of suspense and a tiresome killer. However, it is always fun to watch Barbeau in a movie.

Opera (aka *Terror at the Opera*) (1987)

Written by Franco Ferrini and Dario Argentol Directed by Dario Argento; ADC/Cecchi Gori Group Tiger Cinematografica/RAI Radio Television Italiana; 107 min.

Cast: Cristina Marsillach (Betty); Ian Charleson (Marco); Urbano Barberini (Inspector Alan Santini); Daria Nicolodi (Mira); Coralina Cataldi Tassoni (Guilia); Antonella Vitale (Marion); William McNamara (Stefano); Barbara Cupisti (Signora Albertini); Antonio Juorio (Baddini); Carola Stagnaro (Alma's Mother); Francesca Cassola (Alma); Maurizio Garrone (Maurizio); Cristina Giachino (Maria); Gyorivany Gyorgy (Miro); Bjorn Hammer; Peter Pitsch; Sebastiano Somma

214 • Opera

Cast: Ferdinando Caputo (Executive Producer); Dario Argento (Producer); Brian Eno, Roger Eno, Claudio Simonetti, Bill Wyman, Terry Taylor (Composers); Ronnie Taylor, B.S.C. (Director of Photography); Franco Fraticelli, A.M.C. (Editor)

While practicing at an opera house, Mara, the star of the show *Macbeth*, is angry at a shrieking raven, throws her shoe at it and storms out. She is surrounded by reporters outside and is hit by a car. Betty is at home listening, and she gets a call from someone who says she will be Lady Macbeth and hangs up. Mira arrives at Betty's apartment, and Betty says she is too young to play the role and would rather make her debut in something else. The understudy also says that *Macbeth* brings bad luck. The director, Mark, and others assure her that she will be fine. In a nearby vent in Betty's bedroom is the silhouette of a person.

While Betty is performing at the opera house, someone goes to a balcony and watches her through binoculars. A flashback shows a woman being chased and screaming, and a woman tied up. A stagehand tells the person that no one is allowed on the balcony, and the man is hit, causing the nearby light to fall and crash to the ground. As the show is stopped, the stagehand is pushed into a coat hanger and killed, and the murderer shakes blood off the binoculars. Betty completes the performance, and the audience cheers. Betty is complimented backstage; Alan visits her dressing room and gives her a flower. She learns that he is an inspector, and she asks Stefano why he is there. He tells her that a stagehand has died.

Another flashback shows a knife held over a woman in bed, and the woman sitting up and screaming. The killer takes the knife from the case and scratches it across the TV screen (Betty's performance is being televised). In the wardrobe room, the killer takes Betty's costume and cuts into it, and the nearby ravens get out of the cage and fly around. The killer kills a few of them and leaves when someone approaches; the ravens angrily peck at the killer's exit door. After an

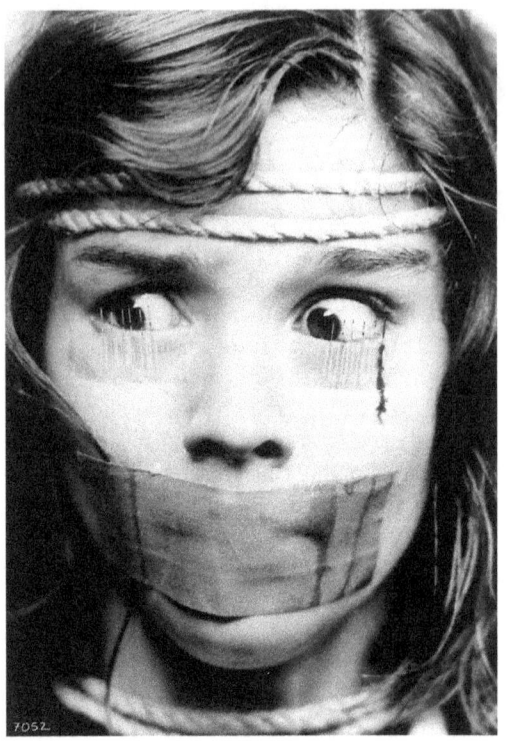

Betty (Cristina Marsillach) is forced to watch a maniac's murderous and bloody handiwork in Dario Argento's *Opera* (1987).

unsuccessful time in bed with Betty, Stefano goes for some tea. The killer grabs Betty, tapes her mouth shut, ties her standing to a pillar and tapes needles under her eyes, forcing her to keep her eyes open and watch. Stefano returns and is stabbed numerous times by the killer, who then cuts Betty free. Betty pulls away the rope and needles and runs away.

Betty runs out in the rain and makes an anonymous phone call to the police. Mark finds her and picks her up. At her apartment, she tells him what has happened. She says it was like a childhood nightmare, concerning a man in a black hood. Mark tells Betty he saw someone watching her from the street, but the man is gone when Betty looks. Through the eyehole, Betty sees a woman talking to a man who Betty cannot see. Betty calls out and asks who the woman is, and she says she is Betty's neighbor and leaves. Betty returns to her room, and a shadow passes by in the vent. She gets a phone call from a person who hangs up, and a child's voice whispers, "Don't cry, Betty."

The next day, Alan is talking to a group from the opera production about Stefano, and he says that feathers were found mixed with blood in the man's apartment. Alan is told that Stefano left the cast party with Betty. The man who cares for the ravens suggests that Mara killed the three ravens, and he says that ravens are vengeful creatures and do not forget.

Julia goes to mend the costume, meets Betty and finds a gold bracelet affixed to the fake jewelry on the dress. She looks for a magnifying glass, and Betty is grabbed by the killer. Julia returns to a restrained Betty (with the needles under her eyes), and the killer beats her back with an iron. She uses the iron on the killer's head and takes the bracelet. She removes the hood and tries to tell Betty who it is, but the killer grabs her neck and stabs her in the stomach with a pair of scissors. The bracelet falls into the dead woman's mouth, and the killer must cut into the body to retrieve it. The ropes are cut and the killer gets rid of the bracelet. Alan sees Betty later and asks about the wounds on her wrists (caused by the rope). She admits to witnessing Stefano's murder and tells the inspector that Julia has been murdered.

In her apartment, Betty puts eyedrops in her eyes, then responds to the buzzing of an officer sent by Alan. She cannot see the man clearly due to the drops, and he says he will look around. Mira comes by and mentions the police officer downstairs, Daniele Soave, the very name of the officer Betty thought was in her apartment. They go to the living room, but only the cop's smoking cigarette is there. Not knowing which officer is actually Soave, the two women hide in the kitchen, and Mira arms herself with a knife. From the kitchen door, Mira sees the cop answer the door and walk outside. There is a knock on the door, and someone outside says the maniac is in the apartment. Mira looks through the eyehole but she cannot clearly see the cop's identification. He shows his police-issued handgun and fires it, killing Mira and hitting the telephone next to Betty. The killer threatens Betty through the door, and she runs and hides in her apartment, where she finds a dead Soave. She grabs his gun and fires at the nearby killer. A little girl calls "Betty" into the vent as Betty's music plays loudly.

Betty and the girl, Alma, crawl to Alma's place, and they duck and hide from the killer as he passes by. Alma's mother, the woman Betty had seen the other night through the eyehole, tells the singer to leave. Betty runs to the opera house and sees Mark, who tells her he has made a change in the show as a way to identify the killer. Betty sleeps there that night and has a dream of a woman screaming as another woman watches and almost smiles; there is a hooded figure nearby ("Is that you, Mommy?"). That night, during the performance, the cage of ravens crashes through the set onto the stage and the door opens. The ravens begin flying out and circling the room, and one raven attacks Alan and shoves its beak into his eye. Alan screams and fires his gun at the stage. Betty runs to her dressing room, where Mark tells her the killer is Alan. The inspector suddenly appears, knocks out Mark, and takes Betty with him.

Alan tells Betty that her mother taught him a game of murder and torture, and he was her slave. He ties Betty to a chair and tells her that all he wanted was her mother's love. Then he blindfolds her, saying he does not want her to look any more. He pours gasoline around the room, puts a gun in Betty's hand and tells her which way to point it. To incite Betty, Alan says he enjoyed strangling her mother. As he lights a match, Betty fires, and the match is dropped. She fires the weapon at the rope and frees herself, and she pulls the key from the fire, but it breaks off in the keyhole. Mark and the others open the door for her, and Betty tells them that Alan is dead.

Later, Mark and Betty are talking about a movie role as Mark stands by his camera. After Betty goes outside, Mark hears on the television that the remains found in the fire were not human, and he finds the maid dead. He yells from the window to Betty that Alan is alive and there, and Betty runs. Alan chases her and is knocked down by Mark, and Mark is killed. Betty tells Alan that she realizes she is like her mother and that she wanted Alan to win. They start to walk together, and after seeing dogs run by, Betty beats Alan on the head with a rock, and many police officers arrive and grab the man. Betty yells to Alan that she is not like her mother and, lying down in the grass, she admires the pretty flowers.

Opera is a superb Argento outing, with a kinetic camera that refuses to stay still (the shot of the raven's perspective in the opera house, in particular, is gorgeous). It is hampered only by a bland heavy metal soundtrack that nearly drowns out the wonderful score. The character name Daniele Soave sounds very similar that of film director Michele Soavi, who, as it happens, portrays the doomed man.

Pandemonium (aka *Thursday the 12th*) (1982)

Written by Michael Whitley and Jaime Klein; Directed by Alfred Sole; MGM/United Artists/ TMC Venture; 78 min.

Cast: Tom Smothers (Cooper); Carol Kane (Candy); Miles Chapin (Andy); Debralee Scott (Sandy); Marc McClure (Randy); Judge Reinhold (Glenn); Teri Landrum (Mandy); Candy Azzara (Bambi); David L. Lander (Pepe); Paul Reubens (Johnson); Gary Allen (Doctor Fuller); Eve Arden (Warden June); Kaye Ballard (Glenn's Mom); Tab Hunter (Blue Grange); Sydney Lassick (Man in Bus Station); Edie McClurg (Blue's Mom); Jim McKrell (Mandy's Dad); Lenny Montana (Coach); Donald O'Connor (Glenn's Dad); Richard Romanus (Jarrett); Izabella Telezynska (Salt); Tammy Alverson, Pam Harlow, Lynn Herring, Jan Speck, Sallee Sunshine Young (60's Cheerleaders); Suzanne Kent (Crying Woman); Phil Hartmann (Reporter); Michael Kless (Photographer); "A Friend" (Candy's Mom); Bradley Lieberman (Chip Jr.); Victoria Carroll (Mandy's Mom); Alix Elias (Joe the Fry Cook); Ebbe Roe Smith (Pete); Randy Bennett (Male Driver); Pat Ast (Bus Driver); David Becker (President); John Paragon, Vern Rowe, Rob Sullivan (Prisoners); Don McLeod (Male Nurse); David McCharen (Chicken Patient); Richard C. Adams (Shock Treatment Patient); Nancy Ryan (Fig Leaf Woman); Jim Boeke (Fletcher); Shirley Prestia (Morgue Attendant); Michael Tucci (Man Leaving Restaurant); Candi Brough (Crystal); Randi Brough (China); Jaime Klein, Daniel Davies, Richard Whitley (Men in Restaurant); Lynne Marie Stewart (Stewardess); Mae Hi, Mildred T. Ogata (Passengers on Plane); Joe Shea (Man in Gas Chamber)

Crew: Barry Krost (Executive Producer); Doug Chapin (Producer); Richard Whitley, Jaime Klein (Associate Producers); Dana Kaproff (Composer); Michael Hugo (Director of Photography); Eric Jenkins (Editor)

At a championship game in 1963, quarterback Blue Grange scores the winning touchdown and the crowd cheers. Bambi goes into the locker room and looks through Blue's locker, talking to the locker about being with Blue. As the people rush in, Bambi leaves and asks the cheerleaders on the field if she can go with them to the mall; she receives a resounding no. Someone takes a javelin from the locker room and throws it at the cheerleaders, passing through all of them. With the prop vegetables that each girl was holding, it is dubbed the shish-kebob killing. After a number of other cheerleaders are killed, Bambi decides to reopen the cheerleader camp anyway.

Bambi, arriving at the school with pompoms and a megaphone, meets Pepe and his mother, Salt. They tell her it is too dangerous to have the camp, and she asks them not to tell the girls the horrible stories of dead cheerleaders. Candy (an inter-title declares her "Victim #1") is at the bus station, and her mother tries to stop her from going to the camp. Candy uses telekinesis (with glowing red eyes), levitates her mother and leaves. Glen, Victim #2, says good-bye to his mother and blind father and rich, toothbrush-happy Mandy, Victim #3, leaves for camp. Victim

#4 is Sandy, who causes everyone at the hot dog stand to run away when asking the way to the cheerleader camp, and Victims #5 and #6 are Andy and Randy, who talk of Randy dating Sandy, the head cheerleader at a rival school.

The group arrives at the school, and Bambi has them sound off: Candy, Mandy, Sandy, Andy, Randy and Glenn, whose surname is Dandy. Cooper, a Canadian mountie, talks to his horse Bob while his assistant Johnson complains about having to do more work than Bob. Cooper learns of the prison escapee Jarrett, who had killed his family with a drill and turned them into bookshelves. He and Bob go to check out the asylum, where they learn that a dangerous patient, Fletcher, has escaped. Later, Fletcher, in an Indiana State Asylum vehicle, picks up a hitchhiking Jarrett.

While the cheerleaders work out in a gym, Pepe guides the dead cheerleader's tour, and Sandy asks Bambi if what Pepe said is true. Bambi assures the group that, while there have been "a few mishaps," there is no danger. After visiting the morgue to see a dead prison guard (killed by Jarrett) and discussing the cheerleader killer, Cooper goes with Bob to the school, where he and Candy gaze longingly into each other's eyes. While practicing a trampoline jump, Glenn is too focused on looking suave in his tuxedo that he forgets to catch Mandy, and she breaks her ankle. Bambi tells the cheerleaders that practice is over for the day, and they all leave.

Candy, Sandy, Andy and Randy go to a restaurant, and Glenn stays behind to do some trampoline jumps in honor of Mandy. A person with gloved hands pushes a detonator on one of Glenn's jumps, and an explosion sends him out of the window and all the way up in the sky to an airplane ("Pull over!"). Mandy is playing with her tooth pillows, and she goes to the bathroom to brush her teeth, thereby taunting the evil pillow, Mr. Decay. As she brushes, a hand punches through the back of the cabinet, grabs Mandy's neck and points a drill to her mouth and teeth. Mandy falls to the floor with a mouth full of toothpaste. Warden June calls Cooper and tells him that Jarrett was spotted near Lover's Lane. Cooper and Johnson find the asylum vehicle abandoned and go inside the nearby building (Bob waits in the car). They find Fletcher strapped to a table and Jarrett standing over him. Doctor Fuller joins Jarrett's side with a gun. Fletcher stands behind them and stabs Jarrett's "hand saw." The doctor fires at the same time and, somehow, they are all three electrocuted.

While Bambi bathes in a tub of milk and enjoys some cookies, the killer arrives, pulls up her feet and holds her under. The four remaining cheerleaders are playing strip poker, and Sandy suggests going to bed. She and Randy leave, and Candy and Andy kiss. Candy surprises Andy by taking the cover off the bed with telekinesis ("It started when I went on the pill"). Sandy and Randy go to the sex eduation class, and Randy is grabbed by the killer. Later, Andy returns to the room and sees Randy with a horse head on; he takes the prop off to see Randy with pompoms in his mouth. Andy screams and falls on the bed, and hands punch through and suffocate him with pompoms.

Candy answers a knock on her door, and Sandy falls down, with a megaphone shoved in her back. Candy runs to the phone and finds it dead. She discovers Mandy and Bambi dead, and the killer chases her. Cooper and Bob are enjoying dinner as Johnson serves them; Johnson suggests the killer could be at the school at that very moment, and Cooper and Bob leave. Candy eventually runs to the locker room and hides in a locker, and Blue Grange pulls the door open, wearing a football uniform with a cheerleader's skirt. He says that inside the "football machine" is a cheerleader "yelling to get out," and that if he cannot be a cheerleader, then no one can. Candy runs to the football field, and she telekinetically throws things at Blue. After he has caught a hurled kitchen sink, Candy "announces" him. Blue runs for a touchdown, Candy sends a football statue after him and Blue is run over. Cooper arrives and picks up Candy, and the two ride away on Bob.

Despite some stale jokes, *Pandemonium* manages to keep things funny. The concluding chase sequence nearly pulls the film apart at the seams, but it is too short to do any real damage. Reubens is very humorous as Johnson, and the shish-kebob murder is quite an unprecedented slaying. "A Friend," who plays Candy's mother, is Eileen Brennan.

Peeping Tom (1960)

Written by Leo Marks; Directed by Michael Powell; Michael Powell Productions/Anglo Amalgamated Productions; 101 min.

Cast: Carl Boehm (Mark); Moira Shearer (Vivian); Anna Massey (Helen); Maxine Audley (Mrs. Stephens); Brenda Bruce (Dora); Miles Malleson (Elderly Gentleman); Esmond Knight (Arthur Baden); Martin Miller (Doctor Rosan); Michael Goodliffe (Don Jarvis); Jack Watson (Chief Inspector Gregg); Shirley Ann Field (Diane Ashley); Pamela Green (Milly); Bartlett Mullins (Mr. Peters); Nigel Davenport (Detective Sergeant Miller); Brian Wallace (Tony); Susan Travers (Lorraine); Maurice Durant (Publicity Chief); Brian Worth (Assistant Director); Veronica Hurst (Miss Simpson); Alan Rolfe (Store Detective); John Dunbar (Police Doctor); Guy Kingsley Poynter (P. Tate, the Cameraman); Keith Baxter (Detective Baxter); Peggy Thorpe-Bates (Mrs. Partridge); John Barrard (Small Man); Roland Curram (Young Man Extra); John Chappell (Clapper Boy); Michael Powell (A.N. Lewis, Mark's Father); Columba Powell (Mark as a Child)

Mark (Carl Boehm) shows Helen (Anna Massey) how he photographs a woman's fear while she is being killed in Michael Powell's *Peeping Tom* (1960).

Crew: Michael Powell (Producer); Brian Easdale (Composer); Otto Heller, B.S.C. (Director of Photography); Noreen Ackland (Editor)

A man approaches a woman on the street with a running video camera hidden in his jacket. She names a price and leads him to a room, where she begins removing her clothing. There is a metallic clang, and something reflects on the woman's face. The man-camera nears her, and the woman screams. The man watches his footage.

The next day, the same man, Mark, films the cops taking the body away, and he tells an officer that he works for *The Observer*. Mark goes to a newspaper shop and waits as a man looks through a booklet of exotic "views" and purchases the entire set. Mark goes upstairs, where he photographs Milly in lingerie. Another model, Lorraine, has a slightly disfigured upper lip. She was told that her face need not be photographed, but Mark is fascinated by her face, and he brings out his camera and films her.

Mark returns to his apartment complex and passes the window of Helen's room, where she is enjoying her birthday party. As Mark heads for the stairs, Helen stops him and invites him to the party. He declines the offer. Later, as Mark watches his film again, Helen arrives at his door with some cake. Mark lets her in, and Helen learns that the building belonged to Mark's deceased father and that Mark is her landlord. Mark says he works at a film studio, and Helen asks to see one of his movies. Mark takes her to his room in back and shows her a movie of when he was a young boy. His father filmed him growing up, shining lights in his face as he tried to sleep and throwing a lizard on his bed. Helen, upset with the movie, shuts off the projector. Mark tells her that his father was interested in the reaction to fear. Tony arrives at the door, and Helen returns to the party.

Mark is at the camera as a crew films a scene from a movie in production. After the filming is completed and the people leave, Vivian, the stand-in, dodges the night watchman and walks to an empty stage. Mark is waiting, and he turns on the lights and sets up the studio camera and Vivian's positioning. Mark constructs the "set" by moving a blue trunk and opening the lid. Mark is ready to film; Vivian stands in place and asks Mark to set the mood (for being "frightened to death"). Mark stands close to her and tells her to imagine someone wanting to kill her. He says to imagine that the camera's tripod leg is a weapon, and he pulls the bottom off to reveal a blade. He turns away, and then turns back with the camera running. As he nears her, Vivian screams.

Helen reads the newspaper to her blind mother, Mrs. Stephens. Her mother distrusts Mark because he walks quietly. Helen goes to see Mark, and he gives her a broach for a late birthday present. Helen tells Mark that she writes short stories for children, and she says her first book, about a magic camera, will be published in the spring. She talks of children wishing to see the pictures the camera takes, and Mark offers to take the photographs. As cast and crew rehearse, Mark sneaks away, takes his camera and films an actress as she opens the trunk and screams. Chief Greg and Sergeant Miller arrive and question the crew, and Mark films the officers, telling a fellow crew member that he is making a documentary. Mark climbs to the top of the set as the officers investigate the scene, and he films them. He leaves after inadvertently making noise when pencils drop from his pocket.

Back at the apartment, Helen asks Mark to meet her mother. Mrs. Stephens shakes and feels Mark's hand, and she asks him if he knew the murdered woman talked about in the newspaper (Mark says that he did not). Mark and Helen prepare to leave for a date, and Helen asks Mark if he needs his camera. She offers to put the camera in her room, and he reluctantly agrees. He seems liberated and happy until they come across a kissing couple; Mark stops and feels for his camera. After the two dine, they head back to the apartment building, and Helen gets Mark's camera. She playfully points the camera at herself, and Mark snatches it from her ("Not you!"). He tells her that he loses everyone he photographs. Helen kisses Mark, and she retreats to her room.

Mark goes upstairs to his room and begins to watch his footage of Vivian. Mrs. Stephens is standing in the dark corner. Mark nears her (she has the sharp end of her cane raised), and she says she hears him with the projector running every night. She asks what he is watching, and Mark leads her to the screen. When the Vivian scene is over, Mark is upset, saying that it is no good and that he has to find another. He gets his camera, lifts the tripod and walks towards Mrs. Stephens as she calls to him. He says he has to finish for Helen because she wants to see something he has photographed. He exposes the blade and then puts his camera away as he walks the woman to his door. Mrs. Stephens tells Mark that his filming is "unhealthy" and that he needs to get help. She says she does not want him to see Helen, and Mark says he would never photograph her. Mark walks the woman to her room. At the bottom of the stairs, she feels his face ("Taking my picture?"). She asks him what is troubling him; Mark heads back to his room.

On the set, a doctor stands in the back, and Mark asks him if he knew his father, Professor Lewis. He asks the doctor if he knows of his father's interest, the idea of people being peeping toms. The doctor tells him it is scopophilia, the "morbid urge to gaze." Mark asks him about a cure, and he is dissatisfied with the doctor's response of a two-year analysis. Chief Greg asks the doctor what Mark had talked to him about. Mark calls Mr. Peters and says he will be there by six. He goes to the newspaper shop and is tailed by police officer Baxter. He walks upstairs where Milly is waiting and films the officer waiting outside. He shuts the blinds and approaches the woman on the bed. Later, Mark leaves the shop and locks the door.

Helen goes to Mark's room and calls for him. She sits by the projector, turns the machine on and reacts to the horrible images she sees. She is scared by Mark, and she asks if what she has seen is only a film. Mark tells her no, but that she will be safe if he cannot see her frightened. Mr. Peters calls Chief Greg and tells him that he has found Milly. Mark plays audio tapes that his father made, mostly of people screaming, and he says that the rooms are wired for sound. Mark tells Helen that the most frightening thing in the world is fear, and he shows a giant mirror in front of his camera (with the blade at Helen's neck). The women he killed watched their own terror and deaths, and, if it exists, they saw the face of death. The two hear the police arriving outside, and Mark sets up the camera and points the tripod-blade. He runs to the camera ("Helen, I'm afraid, and I'm glad I'm afraid") and pushes himself unto the blade as cameras around the room snap pictures. Mark falls to the floor. Helen lies near him and weeps, as cops run inside. The voice of a young Mark tells his father good night.

Peeping Tom, a classic slasher, was critically skewered at the time of its release, and many people believe that the film ruined (or nearly ruined) director Powell's career. Although the film seems slow, it is enhanced by gorgeous cinematography. Thematically the film is a masterpiece, with a man's longing to capture the image of fear as a person is being murdered, along with the cruelty of forcing the victim to witness her own death. Decades after the film was trampled in the '60s, fellow film director and movie buff Martin Scorsese helped it garner the release and respect that it deserved.

Phantom of Death (aka *Off Balance*; *Un delitto poco comune*) (1987)

Written by Gianfranco Clerici, Vincenzo Mannino and Gigliola Battaglini; Directed by Ruggero Deodato; Globe Films/Tandem Cinematografica; 91 min.

Cast: Michael York (Robert Dominici); Donald Pleasence (Inspector Downey); Edwige Fenech (Hélène Martell); Mapi Galán (Susanna); Fabio Sartor (Davide); Renato Cortesi (Mikey); Antonella Ponziani (Gloria); Carola Stagnaro (Doctor Carla Pesenti); Daniele Brado; Caterina Boratto; Raffaella Baracchi (Laura); Giovanni Lombardo Radice (Father Giuliano); Daniela Merlo (Mother)

Crew: Pietro Innocenzi (Producer); Pino Donaggio (Composer); Giorgio Di Battista (Director of Photograph); Daniele Alabiso (Editor)

Robert is playing the piano in front of an elegant audience. As the music plays, a female scientist checks a microscope and goes home, letting someone inside whom she seems to know. A sword is taken from the wall, and the woman is killed.

Robert is at a reception following his concert, and Susanna tells him she believes success will pull them apart. Inspector Downey arrives to see his daughter Gloria and tells her that a murder occurred before the performance. Robert talks to Hélène, who says it is easy to fall in love with Robert and that many women already have. Later, Robert is battling with wooden swords, but he stops the practice and apologizes to his teacher, saying he cannot concentrate.

The police discuss the expertise in the slicing of the doctor's neck. Susanna spends some time of intimacy with Davide, and Davide is angry that she leaves so soon. She calls Robert and says she wants to be near him and will be over soon. Susanna exits the train at the station, and after being frightened by a man's silhouette (the man leaves with someone else), she is killed with a stab to the back of the neck. The inspector talks with Robert (who discovered Susanna dead), and later interrogates the evidently suspicious Davide, who says he does not have an alibi for the time of the doctor's death. At home, the inspector receives a call from the killer ("You'll never get me, so I can kill as often as I want"), who refers to the inspector's daughter playing her flute. Later, Davide is at practice with the wooden swords. A slightly inebriated Robert goes to see Hélène, and stays for the night. The next morning, Hélène sees that Robert has left her a rose and a note saying that she will be in his heart.

Robert goes to stay with his mother for a few days. He gets winded during his jogging sessions, and his mother tells him he seems like a mature man. In a gas station bathroom, he combs his hair and some of it comes out. A nearby man says that he can relate and then snickers; an indignant Robert viciously beats the man. A flashback shows Robert going to see the doctor and receiving the bad news of his "rare condition" before murdering the woman. Robert goes to see more doctors, and he is told his disease has a long incubation period and that it may be affecting his brain cells and altering his psyche. It is suggested he consider a clinic ("So they can watch me die?"). Robert visits a clinic and sees a small boy affected with the disease. Later, Hélène tells Robert that she is pregnant with his child, and he thinks back to the boy. Robert attacks Hélène in the parking garage and tries to stab her with a switchblade, but he runs when other people approach.

Downey learns that Robert is the father of Hélène's baby and, deciding that Robert's women have been "unlucky," he goes to his house. Robert ignores the police's knocking, and a van of officers arrives for surveillance. Hélène, working with a sketch artist, says an older man (with wrinkles and not much hair) attacked her, but the inspector believes the woman "subconsciously dismissed" Robert's face. Downey is told that the attacker's skin found on Hélène belongs to man of about 50 years. Robert sees the inspector on television later, telephones him and mocks him for the killer's age suddenly changing.

Robert goes to see the first woman he had been with; she says she remembers him and laughs at him, not allowing him to kiss her. Robert, upset, stabs the woman in the throat with a lamp pole. He goes to a church and confesses, and asks the priest if he recognizes him (they knew each other once). Robert says "time is running out," and he and the priest embrace.

It is two months before the child's birth.

A very old and decrepit Robert walks through the park and greets an old, abandoned dog. He says that he hates young people for the lives they will live and old people for the lives they have already lived. Robert telephones Downey and says that he is giving him the opportunity to stop Robert. A number of cops gather in the park, where Robert is sitting with an elderly man on a bench. He walks over to where Corzi, a female cop, is sitting alone in her car, puts a razor to her throat and has her call the inspector. As the inspector alerts the other police, Robert slashes the cop's throat and runs. Downey and the officers gather everyone who was in the park. Hélène looks at them and says that no one looks like her attacker.

Robert telephones Downey ("I never leave things half done") and tells him he is in a nearby café. The inspector runs into the streets, screaming "You murdering bastard!" Later, Gloria is packing some bags, and her father says he cannot join her in Rome now because he has things to do. Robert leaves the inspector a message saying he saw Gloria on the train and refers to cigarettes in her purse. He then calls Hélène and tells her that he will be coming home soon. The cops play the recorded phone call from Robert, and the inspector is told that it is clearly the voice of a very old man. Inspector Downey is finally informed about a malady that quickly ages people, and he recalls the names Hutchison and Gilford (the two scientists who discovered the disease) from Robert's diary.

The aged Robert tells Hélène that Robert sent him and that there is something he needs to tell her. As Hélène fixes a drink Robert pulls the phone from the wall and sits to watch himself on television (Hélène was watching a tape of Robert from his piano concert). He gets himself a drink, and Hélène returns and asks him how he knew where the whiskey was. Robert tells Hélène who he is ("You're not Robert; you're an old man"); he says he cannot allow the baby to be born because it has his blood and could turn into something like him. Robert says he does not have time to await the child's birth, so he brings out his switchblade. The inspector makes it to the house, Hélène embraces him and a sickly Robert clutches his chest, stumbles and collapses outside. The other two run to him, and Robert says he did everything he could to get the inspector to stop him. "They say that death is God's cruelest joke, but not for me."

Despite Robert's vehement and murderous rampage and his tormenting telephone calls to the inspector, the character exudes sympathy as a man inflicted with a disease that cripples him and pilfers his life. *Phantom of Death* is a superb outing for Deodato, the director who gave the world the gut-munching classic *Cannibal Holocaust* (1979). York is excellent as the tortured Robert and Pleasence is, as always, a treat to watch. Look for Deodato as the man who unknowingly frightens Susanna at the train station.

Phenomena (aka *Creepers*) (1984)

Written by Franco Ferrini and Dario Argento; Directed by Dario Argento; DACFILM-Rome; 110 min.

Cast: Jennifer Connelly (Jennifer Corvino); Donald Pleasence (John McGregor); Daria Nicolodi (Mrs. Bruckner); Dalila Di Lazzaro (Head Mistress); Patrick Bauchan (Geiger); Fiore Argento (Tourist); Federica Mastroianni (Sophie); Fiorenza Tessari (Deisela Sulzer); Mario Donatone (Morris Shapiro); Michele Soavi (Police Detective); Franco Tervisi, Fausta Avelli, Marta Binso, Sophie Bourchier, Paola Gropper, Ninke Hielkema, Mitzy Orsini, Geraldine Thomas (Schoolgirls); Tanga (Inga); Francesca Ottaviani

Crew: Claudio Simonetti, Simon Boswell, Bill Wyman (Composers); Romano Albani (Director of Photography); Franco Fraticelli (Editor); Michele Soavi (First Assistant Director); Sergio Stivaletti (Make-up Special Effects); Luigi Cozzi (Special Optical Effects)

A tour bus inadvertently leaves behind a tourist. The young lady heads to a mysterious house where a person chained to a wall inside breaks free. When the girl enters the home, she is attacked, pursued and killed. John McGregor is discussing a recovered head with Detective Geiger and his partner. McGregor determines that the victim was beheaded about eight and a half months ago. McGregor mentions Greta, his assistant who has been missing for some time. Jennifer Corvino, daughter of famous actor Paul Corvino, is heading towards the Richard Wagner International School for Girls with Mrs. Bruckner. When a bee starts buzzing around the car, Mrs. Bruckner is frightened and swipes at the insect. Jennifer remains calm and consoles the bee when it settles on her hand. ("Insects never hurt me. I love them.")

Jennifer and her new roommate Sophie discuss her actor-father and the maniac running around. That night, a tossing-and-turning Jennifer sits up in bed and sleepwalks out of the school. While sleepwalking, she sees a girl murdered and heads out into the street in a daze. She is picked up by two guys but eventually struggles with them so much she falls out of the car and into the woods. In the forest, she is greeted by Inga, McGregor's chimpanzee assistant, who leads Jennifer to McGregor's place. Jennifer talks with McGregor about her occasional sleepwalking, and the entomologist sees that the insects fancy the young girl. McGregor tells Jennifer that if she ever feels herself sleepwalking again, she should say to herself, "I am sleepwalking. I must wake up."

After the headmistress and the doctors attempt to give Jennifer an EEG (they fear she might be developing a new personality due to her sleepwalking), Jennifer fears the killer might have seen her, and asks Sophie to watch her that night. Sophie later goes outside to see her boyfriend. Jennifer begins to sleepwalk, but she is able to wake herself up. She sees that Sophie is gone and suddenly hears a loud scream. Outside, a firefly leads Jennifer to a bloody glove, and a maggot inside a glove shows her a dead Sophie. Jennifer visits McGregor and tells him about her insect assistance. He tells her that insects can be "slightly telepathic." Back at the school, one of Jennifer's schoolmates reads aloud a letter she has written to her father, telling him about her connection with insects. As the girls begin mocking her (chanting "We worship you!"), a vast number of flies surrounds the school, with a seemingly entranced Jennifer saying placidly, "I love you. I love you all." She then passes out.

Jennifer awakes in a room, hooked to an IV. When the nurse nods off, she quietly slips out to see McGregor. The professor discovered that the larva (from the glove) was of a sarcophagus fly (the "flesh eater"). He tells Jennifer that the fly can lead her to the victims' bodies. Jennifer travels on the same bus that the murdered tourist did, getting off at a stop when the fly goes crazy in its glass box. She follows the fly to the mysterious house, but before she can find anything, a man shows up and scares her away. Detective Geiger arrives shortly afterwards and inquires about the house's former tenants. Inside the house, underneath the floor, the fly and some larvae dine on a severed hand.

Jennifer goes to see McGregor again, but he has been murdered. She then calls Morris Shapiro, her father's agent, and says she needs money so that she can leave. Mrs. Bruckner arrives and says that she was called to pick Jennifer up and take her to her place. When they arrive, Jennifer asks about the covered mirrors. She is told that Mrs. Bruckner has a son who does not like to see his reflection ("He stays in his room with his crazy thoughts"). Mrs. Bruckner gives Jennifer a pill to help her sleep. When Jennifer sees the larvae of the sarcophagus fly hanging around the bathroom, she believes the pills are poisonous and she throws them up. When Jennifer tries to call someone, Mrs. Bruckner knocks over the head.

Geiger is at the door as steel walls come down to ensure Jennifer's silence. Geiger asks Mrs. Bruckner about the time she was attacked by an inmate in a mental institution. At the same time, Jennifer tries to escape by getting to a phone. The phone falls down a hole in the floor when Geiger screams from somewhere in the house, and Jennifer crawls underneath to get to it. Geiger grabs her and pulls into another room, but he has been beaten, and now he is chained to the wall. Jennifer falls into a pit of dirty water and maggots. After Geiger frees an arm and restrains Mrs. Bruckner, Jennifer manages to climb out and flee.

Soon Jennifer meets Mrs. Bruckner's young son, a mutated boy with maggots crawling on his face. He chases Jennifer to a boat and tries to stab her, but when Jennifer screams, her insect friends come to her rescue and devour much of the boy's face. Jennifer attempts to start the boat, but it shorts and ignites gasoline. She jumps into the water. Mrs. Bruckner's son attacks her once again, but he is soon overcome by the fiery water and Jennifer makes it to the shore. Morris finally arrives, only to be decapitated by Mrs. Bruckner, who then attacks Jennifer. Inga, the chimpanzee assistant, jumps onto the woman and slices her with a razor. She and Jennifer walk away hand in hand.

Phenomena, an eerie and ghastly adventure employing Argento's crisp visual style, was originally released in America as *Creepers*, with an astounding 28 minutes edited out. Director Michele Soavi plays Detective Geiger's partner. Fiore Argento, who plays the doomed tourist, is Dario Argento's daughter.

Pieces (aka *Mil gritos tiene la noche*) (1981)

Written by John Shadow and Dick Randell; Directed by Juan Piquer Simón; Almena Film Productions/Film Ventures International/Montoro Productions Ltd.; 89 min.

Cast: Christopher George (Lieutenant Bracken); Frank Brana (Sergeant Holden); Lynda Day George (Mary Riggs); Paul Smith (Willard); Edmund Purdom (Dean); Ian Sera (Kendall); Jack Taylor (Professor Brown); Isabelle Luque (Sylvia); Gerard Tichy (Doctor Jennings); Hilda Fuchs (Secretary); May Heatherly; Pilar Alcón

Crew: Steve Minasiani, Dick Randell (Producers); Librado Pastor (Composer); John Marine (Director of Photography); Antonio Gimeno (Editor)

In Boston, 1942, a mother walks into a room and catches her son Timmy doing a jigsaw puzzle of a naked female. Very agitated, she says she is going to burn it. She orders her son to get her a plastic bag with which to dispose of the remains. He chooses an axe instead and murders her. Then he saws her into pieces and sits down to finish his puzzle. The police enter the room and see blood covering the floor. ("Something's been butchered up here. Let's hope it was an animal.") Inside a closet, they find the woman's decapitated head. Timmy is hiding in the other closet. He screams "Mommy!" and the men console him.

Forty years later, a person is looking through a box with shoes and clothes, mostly covered in dried blood. Somewhere on a college campus, a girl is studying in the grass. Nearby, an unknown person is working on some shrubbery with a chainsaw. The person approaches the student and saws off her head. Lieutenant Bracken and his partner Sergeant Holden see the dean of the university about the chainsaw murder (the head is still missing). They still have no suspects ("We're just out buying clothes without labels and trying them on for size"). Willard, the groundskeeper, is outside utilizing a yellow chainsaw similar to the one the killer used.

A girl in the library gives a note to a male student, Kendall, expressing a desire to "do it underwater." The killer finds the discarded note and arrives first to chainsaw the female. Later, Willard turns on the pool lights, sees Kendall run from the area and finds a bloody chainsaw and a girl in pieces. The cops arrive and arrest the groundskeeper. Bracken and Holden are stumped ("I wonder what the hell he's doing with all the pieces that are missing"). After Doctor Jennings arrives to provide a profile of the murderer, Bracken brings in Mary Riggs, a tennis-player-turned-undercover-cop. She is going to pose as a tennis instructor, and

Kendall is going to assist her whenever he can.

Sylvia Costa, a *Boston Globe* reporter, tells Bracken about the rumors she has heard, leading her to believe a maniac is running loose. Meanwhile, the killer is after more pieces (while continually working on his jigsaw puzzle), following a girl who has just finished her aerobics routine. She sees the killer next to her and apparently knows him ("Oh, it's you, sir"), and they get onto a lift together. Soon he reveals his chainsaw, which he had been hiding behind his back. Kendall hears a scream, he and two cops enter and discover the armless woman in the lift. Later, Kendall sees Mary walking around outside at night. While the killer is near, Mary has an odd encounter with the kung fu professor, who attacks her and then explains he is not sure what has happened after Mary has kicked him in the groin. Afterwards, Mary leaves with Kendall, but Sylvia is still snooping around. The killer follows and murders her.

The next day, Mary and Kendall are playing tennis. A fellow tennis player heads into the locker room to shower. She apparently knows the murderer as well ("You!"). The chainsaw is started and the killer cuts into her torso. Mary and Kendall see Willard leaving the bathroom and inquire about music being played loudly over the speakers. They eventually find the bloody, dismembered corpse inside the bathroom.

Holden and Kendall soon learn of the Dean's shady past, with the death of his mother and his name change. They also learn the reason he has been taking pieces of dead women (he obviously likes jigsaw puzzles). In the meantime, Mary is visiting the Dean and is in danger of becoming the next victim. It seems the undercover police officer has nice feet, so the Dean drugs her. Bracken, Kendall and Holden burst into the Dean's place and find Mary sitting there, temporarily paralyzed by the drug. The cops leave Kendall alone, and the Dean comes out from behind the curtain and attacks him. Bracken returns and shoots the Dean. Afterwards, Holden inadvertently discovers the Dean's human puzzle when he leans against the bookshelf and turns it around; the body assembled from various human parts falls unto Kendall. When everyone has calmed down again and they are preparing to leave, Kendall goes for his jacket. The corpse, somehow alive, reaches up with an arm, grabs Kendall's crotch and squeezes.

The somewhat amateurish performances from the actors gives *Pieces* a nice campy feel, with many gory scenes. Lynda Day George was Mrs. Christopher George until the actor's death in 1983. Actor Paul Smith has offered a number of popular performances, from Bluto in 1980's *Popeye* to the malicious guard in *Midnight Express* (1978). Co-writer John Shadow is actually popular Italian director Joe D'Amato. Cinematographer John Marine is also known as Juan Mariné.

Popcorn
(1991)

Written by Tod Hackett; Directed by Mark Herrier; Movie Partners/Century Films; 91 min.

Cast: Jill Schoelen (Maggie); Tom Villard (Toby); Dee Wallace Stone (Suzanne); Derek Rydall (Mark); Malcolm Manare (Bud); Elliott Hurst (Leon); Ivette Soler (Joanie); Freddie Marie Simpson (Tina); Kelly Jo Minter (Cheryl); Karen Witter (Joy); Ray Walston (Doctor Mnesyne); Tony Roberts (Mr. Davis); Scott Thompson (Bearded Guy); Will Knickerbocker (Landlord/Warden); Ethan Ornsby (Two Headed Guy); Ben Stotes (Hatchethead); Ken Ryan (Radio Announcer); Mat Falls (Lanyard Gates); Cindy Tavares-Finson (Gloria Gates); Giana Hanly (Sarah Gates); Barry Jennifer (Lieutenant Bradley); Suzanne Hunt (Doctor Latimer); Robert Dickman (Skeeter); Thom Adcox (Corky); Bruce Glover (Vernon); Munair Zaza (Doctor); Bobby Chisays (Judge); Lori Creevay (Marge); Ed Amairudo (Boy Friend); George O, Nico Bernuth, Rohan Henry (Hoods); Maki Fame (Lab Technician); Kimio Satoh (Scientist); Fumito Naozaki, Hikonori Washino (Miners); Adam Ornsby, Von Von Lindenberg, April Harris, Ray Garoza,

Mike Stephens, Wayne Farnes, Guy Christopher (Students in Theatre)

Crew: Howard Hurst, Karl Hendrickson, Howard Baldwin (Executive Producers); Torben Johnke, Gary Goch, Ashok Amritraj (Producers); Kenneth Schwartz (Associate Producer); Sophie Hurst (Co-Producer); Paul J. Zaza (Composer); Ronnie Taylor, B.S.C. (Director of Photography); Stan Cole (Editor)

Maggie dreams of an explosion, a running girl, a flaming dagger and someone screaming the name Sarah. She awakes and describes her dream to a tape recorder ("same dream"). Suzanne, Maggie's mother, answers the phone to a person who calls her "Miss Judas." Maggie goes to her film class at the University of California and sees her boyfriend Mark, who is upset that Maggie is spending more time on her script than with him. In class, Toby suggests the idea of an all-night horrorthon and showing old films with the original promotional gimmicks to raise money the students can use to make their own films.

The group goes to the Dreamland Theater. Doctor Mnesyne provides them with movie memorabilia, then everyone cleans and decorates the place. Bud finds a film canister with a warning on it, and they decide to watch the single reel inside. The movie begins with an eye and a man saying, "I am the Possessor," followed by "I am the Possessed." The film starts to resemble Maggie's dream, and she is so unsettled that she passes out. Mr. Davis says that the film is *Possessor*, done by a man named Lanyard Gates, leader of a "film cult." After his film was ridiculed, he made *Possessor* and its last part was played out live: Gates killed his family in front of an audience and set fire to the theater, killing a number of people.

At home, Maggie asks Suzane if she knows Lanyard Gates and states her belief that she has been dreaming of him. Suzanne answers the phone to the voice, who mentions the Possessor and says he wants Maggie. He tells an agitated Suzanne that he is at Dreamland. Armed with a gun, she goes to the theater, where *Possessor* is playing. Suzanne sees a figure on the balcony, hears noises and shoots at a figure in the shadows. She is grabbed and pulled through a screen. The next morning, Maggie finds breakfast waiting and a note from her mother.

Maggie is at the horrorthon ticket booth when Mark arrives with Joy. A strange man buys a ticket, mentions *Possessor* and calls the girl Sarah. Maggie runs after him. The people gather in the theater with 3-D glasses as *Mosquito!* begins. Maggie goes to see Toby in the projection booth and says she thinks she saw Lanyard Gates. Toby recalls Mr. Davis saying that Gates' body was never identified amidst the other burnt bodies, and Maggie excitedly realizes that Gates might still be alive. Mark goes to see Maggie in the projection booth. Mr. Davis operates the prop mosquito for the movie, but someone takes over the controls and turns the giant insect around. It returns to perforate Mr. Davis in the chest. The killer makes a mold of the teacher's face.

Maggie tells Mark about Gates, but Mark does not take it seriously. Maggie expresses her contempt for Mark because he is with Joy. *Attack of the Amazing Electrified Man* starts as Maggie returns to the ticket booth to relieve an indignant Tina. Mark finds a big man sitting with Joy; the man punches Mark. Bud is up by the control panel, ready to shock the people's seats during the movie. When Maggie listens to herself on the tape, Gates' voice is on there, calling her Sarah. She and Mark go to find Tina, in case she saw Gates. Tina goes backstage, sees "Mr. Davis" and suggests a "quickie." She kisses the teacher and part of his face comes off. The mask is removed to show a burnt face. Tina screams as she is choked.

Maggie and Mark find Tina (the killer is holding her up and "talking"), and she says she just saw Mr. Davis. The couple is locked out like Toby, and Maggie tells Mark that Gates probably uses disguises. "Tina" goes to the room with Bud, straps him to his wheelchair, hooks him up to the control panel and sets the "shocker" on a timer. Maggie walks in the front with Mark and Bud is electrocuted. The lights in the theater go down. Maggie, Mark and Cheryl walk upstairs in the dark, Mark falls and Cheryl goes down to help him. Maggie goes to the room and finds the control panel destroyed and a person in Bud's wheelchair. The killer sits up and talks to "Sarah" of the things in Maggie's dream. Maggie screams and runs. In her dream, Gates is shot, and Suzanne picks up Sarah and carries her away.

Maggie finds Toby and says she remembers everything. Gates was her father, and he killed her mother, Gloria (Suzanne is Maggie's aunt). She thinks Gates is here to finish the film and kill her. The two go to a cellar to fix the lights, and Toby falls into the darkness. The killer is there ("Welcome home"), and Maggie is grabbed. The lights come back on, and the next film, *The Stench*, starts. Toby tells her that he was there that night, and that Suzanne killed Gates and set fire to the theater. His mother died, and he lost most of his flesh. He shows her his real face, and he tells of having to "make" his face everyday. Toby says he is going to recreate *Possessor*.

In the lobby, Joy tells Mark that she saw Maggie leave with Toby. The big man is there, and Cheryl punches and kicks Joy and the man out of the theater. Mark asks where Toby lives, then runs off. Toby brings out Suzanne in a full body cast (with a gun in her hand). Leon goes to the bathroom and sees himself standing at a urinal next to him. He is thrown into a stall and something is dropped in the toilet, creating a mist that kills Leon. "Leon" goes to see Joanie, who talks about being "madly in love" with Toby; an upset Toby runs out of the room. Mark gets to Toby's house and finds the landlord throwing everything out of his apartment. Mark finds articles of the Lanyard Gates incident and a picture of Maggie with scissors stuck in her eye. Toby stops *The Stench*, begins *Possessor* and puts Maggie in a dress and sets up a camera behind the screen. The screen comes up, and Maggie screams for help as the audience cheers. Toby has the audience help him count down to Maggie's death. Mark wraps his belt around the mosquito's line, slides down and ruins Toby's movie. The mosquito prop falls and Toby is impaled. Outside the theater, Maggie hugs Suzanne, and she and Mark embrace.

Popcorn has its moments (the two versions of Leon side by side in the bathroom is a great scene), but most of the film seems a little plain, and the mock films within the film are probably more enjoyable. Alan Ormsby, star of Bob Clark's *Children Shouldn't Play with Dead Things* (1972), scripted the film as Todd Hackett and is uncredited as a co-director; Clark is credited as special effects make up supervisor.

Prom Night (1980)

Written by William Gray and Robert Guza, Jr.; Directed by Paul Lynch; Quadrant Trust Company/Simcom Productions; 91 min.

Cast: Jamie Lee Curtis (Kim); Leslie Nielsen (Mr. Hammon); Casey Stevens (Nick); Eddie Benton (Wendy); Pita Oliver (Vicki); Michael Tough (Alex); David Mucci (Lou); Marybeth Rubens (Kelly); George Touliatos (McBride); Melanie Morse MacQuarrie (Henri-Anne); David Bolt (Weller); Jeff Wincott (Drew); David Gardner (Doctor Fairchild); Joy Thompson (Jude); Sheldon Rybowski (Slick); Antoinette Bower (Mrs. Hammond); Robert Silverman (Sykes); Rob Garrison (Sayer); Beth Amos (Housekeeper); Sonia Zimmer (Melanie); Sylvia Martin (Mrs. Cunningham); Liz Stalker-Mason (Adele); Pam Henry (Car Hop); Ardon Bess (Teacher); Lee Wildgen (Gang Member); Brock Simpson (Young Nick); Leslie Scott (Young Wendy); Tammy Bourne (Robin); Dean Bosacki (Young Alex); Debbie Greenfield (Young Kim); Karen Forbes (Young Jude); Joyce Kite (Young Kelly)

Crew: Peter Simpson (Producer); Richard Simpson (Associate Producer); Robert New (Director of Photography); Carl Zittrer, Paul Zaza (Composers); Brian Rovak (Editor)

Inside an old building, several children are playing a game in which they all hide while one of them looks for the others, call-

Kim (Jamie Lee Curtis) and Nick (Casey Stevens) enjoy time on the dance floor as a killer stalks selected victims in Paul Lynch's *Prom Night* (1980).

ing out "The killer is coming!" Young Kim and her siblings Alex and Robin walk by and see the children playing. Kim and Alex leave, but Robin lingers, hoping to join in the game. The other children gang up on her, chanting "Kill!" until she finally has nowhere to go. Backing up into a window, Robin crashes through and falls to her death. Nick wants to get help, but Wendy convinces them that the best thing to do is go home and never tell anyone what has happened. Nick, Jude and Kelly swear to keep quiet. Later, Robin's father, Mr. Hammond, and the police are at the scene; they have surmised that Robin was the victim of a sexual attack. They think they know who is responsible, and the cops go to question him.

It is six years later, and the now-grown Kim and Alex are visiting their sister's grave with their parents. A creaky-voiced person is telephoning each member of the guilty party, telling Jude, "I'll see you at the prom!" and upsetting the timid Kelly. Police officer McBride is unsettled because Leonard Murch escaped from the hospital. Murch was the known sex offender who police suspected was responsible for Robin's death; when pursued for questioning, Murch wrecked his vehicle and suffered horrible burns. When the police discover the body of the nurse Murch took for hostage, McBride and Doctor Fairchild believe the man may have returned to town for revenge against everyone.

Nick is Kim's beau, and Wendy, Nick's ex-girlfriend, is certainly not happy that the couple are going to the prom together. Wendy tries to assure Kim that the relationship will not last by telling her, "It's not who you go with, honey. It's who takes you home." Later, school misfit Lou is messing with Kim. Alex steps in to defend his sister; he holds his own against two of Lou's pals until Lou sucker-punches him in the back.

As Lou leaves the school grounds, Wendy tries to talk to him. When Nick and Kim are walking around, Nick tries to tell Kim about that fateful day, but is not able to.

Wendy has made devious plans with Lou. She tells him she does not want anyone hurt, and Lou says he will "take care of it." In the locker room, Wendy finds her school photograph torn from the yearbook and hanging in her locker. When alone, Kim and Kelly hear a loud noise and see that the mirror has been smashed. After checking around the locker room, they return and see that a fragment of the mirror is gone. Jude and Kelly both find their yearbook photographs inside their lockers.

That night, Lou picks up Wendy to take her to the prom. While everyone enjoys the music and dancing in the gymnasium, Kelly and her boyfriend Drew are kissing in another part of the school. Kelly decides she cannot go any further, and an irate Drew goes elsewhere because he knows "plenty who will." The killer quickly approaches the tearful Kelly and kills her. Jude and her prom date Slick are outside enjoying the privacy of Slick's van. After spending a bit of time outside the van, they hear some noises and return to the vehicle to smoke some marijuana. The door flies open, Jude falls back and the murderer stabs her in the neck. Slick tries to escape in his van, but after wildly spinning around, the van goes over a cliff and explodes into flames.

While Wendy is in the bathroom, adjusting her make up, the lights are turned off and an axe is swung aimed at her head. She gets away, eluding the killer in the darkened hallways and classrooms of the school, but in due time the murderer finds her, and Wendy is killed. Back inside the prom, McBride is told by another officer that Murch has been caught and that he was many miles away. Kim is looking for her father (the principal of the school) but cannot find him.

Nick and Kim ready themselves for the announcement of prom king and queen. Nick is accosted by Lou's thugs and Lou takes his place backstage with the crown. The killer, believing Lou to be a Nick-in-waiting, uses the axe to chop off his head, which rolls down the catwalk for the entire student body to see. The students scream and empty the gymnasium. Kim finds Nick and frees him, but soon the killer realizes his mistake and attempts to finish the job. Kim manages to get the axe and wounds the murderer's shoulder. When the killer reacts to the injury, Kim finally sees her brother's eyes staring at her. Alex gets outside the school and sways down the sidewalk. The police have surrounded the place. As Alex falls to the ground, Kim pleads, "Don't shoot him!" and runs to her brother's side.

Prom Night is deservedly a slasher classic, creating genuine frights and a killer who almost seems justified in his murderous rampage. The moment in which Kim looks into the familiar eyes of the killer is terrific. Jeff Wincott, who plays Drew, is the brother of actor Michael Wincott. Actress Eddie Benton is actually Anne-Marie Martin; she is the wife of author-director Michael Crichton. Martin and her husband co-scripted the effects-laden *Twister* (1996).

Prom Night IV: Deliver Us from Evil (1991)

Written by Richard Beattie; Directed by Clay Borris; Norstar Entertainment Inc./Over the Edge Limited Partnership; 92 min.

Cast: Nikki de Boer (Meagan); Alden Kane (Mark); Joy Tanner (Laura); Alle Ghadban (Jeff); Ken McGregor (Father Jaeger); James Carver (Father Jonas); Brock Simpson (Father Colin); Krista Buimer (Lisa); Phil Morrison (Brad); Fab Filippo (Jonathan); Colin Simpson (Larry); Thea Andrews (Louise); Bill Jay (Cardinal); Deni Delroy (Jennifer); Caroline Tweedie (Sister Jude); Tyler Daniels (Dave); Ray Sager (Rafe); Brad Simpson (Rick); Suzanne Valliancourt (Suzi)

Crew: Peter Simpson (Executive Producer); Ray Sager (Producer); Paul J. Zaza (Composer); Rick Wincenty (Director of Photography); Stan Cole (Editor)

Father Jonas kneels in front of a church and asks for help to save the "sluts" and "whores." At Hamilton High in 1957, Brad is alone at a dance. Lisa sits by him and they talk, then they leave to smoke and kiss in the halls. The couple heads to Brad's car, where their kissing progresses. They hear a noise and see candles on the hood of the car. Jonas crashes through the window and slits Lisa's throat. Brad jumps out of the car and is stabbed with the blade of Jonas' cross. Jonas throws holy water and streams of fire hit the car, and the vehicle explodes. Father Jaeger and other priests find Father Jonas in a basement, performing self-flagellation. Father Jaeger calls him an "abomination," and Jonas bleeds from his hands and kisses Father Jaeger. He laughs and is taken away by the priests.

At St. George Church, 1991, young Father Colin is talking to Jennifer about being sent to Africa. However, Father Jaeger tells him that he has been taken out of the program because the church has greater needs. He takes Father Colin to the basement and shows him a bearded, long-haired Father Jonas, strapped to a bed. He tells the young priest that the devil has taken him and that they can only keep the demon "contained." At Father Jaeger's grave, Father Colin hears the priest tell him that he is the new guardian of Jonas (his "life work"), which he is to keep secret. If Jonas should awaken, he is to contact the cardinal.

Laura and Jeff are in trouble with a nun for being in the back seat of a car. Jeff asks Laura to the prom, saying that Mark and Meagan were talking of going. Father Jaeger had told Father Colin that Jonas could not be helped and that he is catatonic from the drugs, exorcisms and treatments used to keep Satan from awakening. The young priest shaves Father Jonas and prepares to inject him with a syringe, then decides not to. Later, Father Colin returns to the room and tells Jonas he wants to help him, but Jonas does not respond. As he walks away, Jonas says some nasty things, but is still lying with closed eyes when Father Colin looks again. The priest becomes more worried and finally decides to give Jonas the injection. He loads the syringe and goes inside. Jonas' feet bleed, his eyes open and he grabs Father Colin and throws him. Mark and Meagan kiss as Mark's brother Jonathan watches. Father Colin sits up and runs to call the cardinal, but Jonas wraps a cord around his neck and kills him.

Meagan, Mark, Laura and Jeff, in gowns and tuxedos, leave in a limousine. The dead Father Colin is discovered and the cardinal tells priests to make it look as if he hanged himself. The cardinal sees the young priest's note, in which he says he did not administer Father Jonas' injection. Jonas gets a ride from a man in a truck. When the group passes by the school, Jeff moons all the students outside. They drive on, eventually passing the truck that Jonas hitched a ride in (with the dead man inside). They reach the summer home of Mark's parents, and Mark says it was once a church retreat. Soon they realize that things have been stolen from the house, but they do not want to call the police since they are not supposed to be there.

Mark and Jeff go to the wine cellar (where the padlock and latch had been torn off). The thieves left behind all the expensive wine, so the two boys take a bottle to start the evening off. The group enjoys dinner and then they dance. Meagan drops a bottle and steps on the broken glass with a bare foot. Laura and Jeff kiss and go upstairs as Mark carries Meagan to the couch. She answers the phone, and Jonas says a few mean things to her. Mark suggests that Jeff made the phone call as a joke. Jonathan is outside, videotaping Laura and Jeff in the bedroom when Father Jonas grabs him and kills him.

After showering, Laura returns to the room to see a bundle under the covers. She hears a noise at the door, and the doorknob is turning. Jonas sits up in the bed and grabs her. Jeff is at the door with wine and glasses, trying to get inside the locked room. He goes to see Mark and Meagan and interrupts their kissing to say that he is locked out of the bedroom. They all go to check, but now the door is unlocked and Laura is gone. Mark and Meagan go to the wine cellar, where Mark discovers a passageway behind the splintered wall. Jeff goes to the attic and sees "Laura" in a rocking chair. Jonas turns around (with blonde hair), grabs him, and squishes his head while reciting the Lord's Prayer. Mark and Meagan find a candle that is still warm and what looks like blood, and go looking for the others.

Mark and Meagan check the attic and find a bloody shirt and blood on the floor. They go to check the woodshed, then see something in the woods. Suddenly, the bodies of Laura and Jeff, hanging on crosses, burst into flames. The couple runs into the house, Mark goes for a gun and Meagan tries to get hold of the authorities. Mark returns and screams when he sees Jonas behind Meagan. Jonas chases Mark before he can load the gun, and they run to the attic. Meagan finds a dead Jonathan outside. Father Jonas hears Mark on the roof, and stabs through the ceiling until he hits Mark's foot. Mark slides and grabs hold of the blade, but falls when the blade is pulled back inside. Meagan runs to Mark's side, and Jonas throws the blade down, hitting Mark in the chest. Meagan runs inside and hides in the wine cellar.

Jonas looks for Meagan, who steps on the broken bottle. Jonas follows her bloody footprints to the kitchen cabinet, where Meagan sprays roach spray in his face. She runs outside, gets Mark's gun and answers the phone to an officer asking if she placed an emergency call. Father Jonas speaks. Meagan runs to the woodshed (after shooting at Jonas a few times), and finally shoots and hits Jonas. He falls, but he comes back and "throws" flames around Meagan. She whacks him with a shovel and runs out of the shed, securing the door with the shovel's handle. The shed explodes. Meagan is taken away on a stretcher when the cops and ambulances arrive. When the charred priest opens his eyes, Meagan opens hers as well. The ambulance drives away.

Aside from a few superficial references, *Prom Night IV* is unrelated to the original slasher (or to the other sequels, for that matter). The film has few frights and monotonous characters. By the end, it is no longer even interesting.

Psycho
(1960)

Written by Joseph Stefano (from the novel by Robert Bloch); Directed by Alfred Hitchcock; Shamley Productions; 109 min.

Cast: Anthony Perkins (Norman Bates); Janet Leigh (Marion Crane); Vera Miles (Lila Crane); John Gavin (Sam Loomis); Martin Balsam (Detective Milton Arbogast); John McIntire (Sheriff Al Chambers); Simon Oakland (Doctor Richmond); Frank Albertson (Tom Cassidy); Pat Hitchcock (Caroline); Vaughn Taylor (Greg Lowery); Lurene Tuttle (Mrs. Chambers); John Anderson (California Charlie, Car Salesman); Mort Mills (Highway Patrolman)

Crew: Bernard Herrmann (Composer); John L. Russell (Director of Photography); George Tomasini (Editor)

In Phoenix, Arizona, inside a hotel room in mid-afternoon, two lovers are getting out of bed. Marion Crane is in the midst of an "extended lunch hour," and she tells her lover, Sam Loomis, that she wants to get married. Sam says he has too much debt for marriage because he is paying alimony to his ex-wife. Back at the office, Marion's boss Mr. Lowery walks in with a new client, Mr. Cassidy. Cassidy is buying a $40,000 home for his daughter's wedding and has his "private money" in cash. Lowery, uneasy, asks Marion to put the money in a safety deposit box at the bank. Marion places the $40,000 in an envelope and she says she is going home after the bank trip because she has a headache. Once home, however, Marion is packing a suitcase; the envelope of money is still in her purse.

After driving out of town, Marion sleeps in her car overnight. She is awakened in the morning by a police officer rapping on her window. He asks to see her driver's license and takes a look at her plates, then lets her go. Marion visits a car lot and asks the salesman if she can trade in her car for another. When she sees the same police officer sitting across the street, Marion becomes anxious. The transaction is completed and Marion quickly drives away.

Further down the road, a heavy downpour begins. Marion struggles to see through the rain, and finally spots a vacancy sign for the Bates Motel. She runs to the office and, upon seeing a woman's figure walk pass the window in the house near the motel, she honks her car horn. Norman Bates walks out of the house and comes down to the office. Marion asks for a room. "We have 12 vacancies—12 cabins, 12 vacancies," Norman grins. Marion signs in and Norman gives her the keys to Cabin One.

Norman asks Marion to have a meal with him. She agrees, and he runs up to the house, where he engages in a verbal fray with his mother ("Go tell her she'll not be appeasing her ugly appetite with my food or my son," Marion hears). Norman returns and watches Marion enjoy her dinner. Marion learns that Norman's hobby is taxidermy, and that his mother is sick. Norman explains that his mother is not a maniac, but that she "just goes a little mad sometimes." Marion ends the conversation by saying that she is going to bed, and that she has a long drive ahead of her. She "stepped into a trap" back in Phoenix, and she would like to make things right. After she leaves, Norman looks at the register and sees that Marion signed in as Marie Samuels from Los Angeles, both pieces of information that Norman now knows are untrue.

Back in the parlor, Norman takes a picture down and peers at a disrobing Marion through a hole in the wall. He then puts the picture back up, heads to the house and sits in the kitchen. Marion is figuring out how much money she has spent out of the initial $40,000, and then she shreds the paper and prepares to shower. While Marion is showering, Norman's mother walks into the room and stabs Marion to death. Norman screams from the house, "Mother! Blood! Blood!" and rushes to Cabin One. He wraps Marion's body in the shower curtain and cleans up the messy bathroom. Then he puts the body in the car trunk, drives to the swamp and lets the car sink.

Lila Crane, Marion's sister, goes to visit Sam at the hardware store. Detective Arbogast sees them and says he was hired to find the stolen money. He goes around, looking at different hotels, and finally arrives at the Bates Motel. At first Norman denies ever having seen Marion, but Arbogast gets him to admit that she stayed at the motel. Norman, nervous, asks Arbogast to leave him alone. The detective calls Lila and Sam and tells them that Marion was at the Bates Motel. He says he thinks the mother (who he saw in the window) might know something, and that he is going to go back and talk to her. Back at the motel, Arbogast sees that the office is empty, and he heads to the house. He climbs the steps, only to be attacked by Mother at the top and viciously stabbed.

Lila is concerned when Arbogast does not return in time, and Sam goes to the Bates Motel to look for the detective. Sam says he saw no one except a sickly old lady who would not answer the door. The two go to see Al Chambers, the deputy sheriff, and tell him about everything that has been happening lately. When told that Arbogast was going to question Norman's mother, Al tells Lila and Sam that Mrs. Bates has been dead for the past ten years. Sam insists that Mrs. Bates was in the window, and Al says, "Well, if the woman up there is Mrs. Bates, who's that woman buried out in Greenlawn Cemetery?" Back in the Bates home, Norman carries his reluctant mother downstairs to hide her in the fruit cellar.

Determined to find Marion, Lila and Sam go to the Bates Motel and register as man and wife. After checking into the room, the two sneak into Cabin One and find torn paper with the number 40,000, which Lila believes proves that Norman knew about the money. Lila wants to talk to the mother, so Sam occupies Norman in the office as Lila heads for the house. Norman quickly becomes unsettled, bashes Sam on the head and runs to the house. Lila hides and sees that the door to the fruit cellar is open. She goes inside and sees Norman's mother sitting in a chair. She turns the woman around to see a mummified corpse. Norman runs in dressed as Mother and wielding a knife, but Sam stops him from attacking Lila.

At the station, a psychiatrist explains that Norman killed his mother and her lover, and that he was split between himself and the personality of his mother. If he was attracted to a woman, the dominant mother side took over. Inside a room, Norman sits as his mother's voice speaks. She says that Norman is going to be put away, as *she* should have done years ago. She maintains composure by not swatting a fly on her hand. Finally, Norman/Mother smiles. Authorities pull Marion's car out of the swamp.

Hitchcock's *Psycho* is a deserved classic, with suspense, a moody Herrmann score and a terrific performance from Perkins. Hitchcock used his television crew (from *Alfred Hitchcock Presents*) to film the movie. Look for Hitchcock in his trademark cameo; he's outside the office as Marion walks inside. The "bird motif" is often discussed in terms of *Psycho*: Norman stuffs birds, he tells Marion she eats like a bird (when Norman himself does, eating seeds), Marion's last name is Crane and she is from Phoenix. Of course, Hitchcock's follow-up movie was the 1963 film *The Birds*.

Psycho (1998)

Written by Joseph Stefano (from the novel by Robert Bloch); Directed by Gus Van Sant; Imagine/Universal Pictures; 105 min.

Cast: Vince Vaughan (Norman Bates); Anne Heche (Marion Crane); Julianne Moore (Lila Crane); Viggo Mortensen (Sam Loomis); William H. Macy (Milton Arbogast); Robert Forster (Doctor Fred Simon); Philip Baker Hall (Sheriff Al Chambers); Anne Haney (Mrs. Eliza Chambers); Chad Everett (Tom Cassidy); Rance Howard (Mr. Lowery); Rita Wilson (Caroline); James Remar (Patrolman); James LeGros (Charlie the Car Dealer); Steven Clark Pachosa (Police Guard); O.B. Babbs (Mechanic); Flea (Bob Summerfield); Marjorie Lovett (Woman Customer); Ryan Cutrona (Chief of Police); Ken Jenkins (District Attorney)

Crew: Dany Wolfe (Executive Producer); Brian Grazer, Gus Van Sant (Producers); James Whitaker (Associate Producer); Bernard Herrmann (Composer); Christopher Doyle (Director of Photography); Amy E. Duddleston (Editor)

The 1998 Psycho *employed the same script as the original and replicated the camera movements and placement that Alfred Hitchcock used; therefore, the synopsis is the same as the 1960 film.*

The *Psycho* remake was quite superfluous, and the decision to use the same Hitchcockian direction proved senseless and banal. Additionally, the performances are weak. It seems that the actors are all trying to reproduce the original performances, which only creates a yearning to watch Hitchcock's movie; actor Vaughan even goes so far as to imitate Perkins' movements, such as the scene with Norman and Arbogast in the parlor, with Norman's bird-like turn to look at the register. Director Van Sant appears outside the real estate office (like Hitchcock's cameo), speaking to a man who resembles Hitchcock. Director of photography Doyle, an Australian, is known for his work in Hong Kong, having provided beautiful cinematography for films such as Wong Kar Wai's *Chungking Express* and *Ashes of Time* (both 1994).

Psycho II (1983)

Written by Tom Holland; Directed by Richard Franklin; Universal Pictures/Oak Industries; 113 min.

Cast: Anthony Perkins (Norman Bates); Vera Miles (Lila); Meg Tilly (Mary); Robert Loggia (Doctor Raymond); Dennis Franz

(Toomey); Hugh Gillin (Sheriff Hunt); Claudia Bryar (Mrs. Spool); Robert Alan Browne (Statler); Ben Hartigan (Judge); Lee Garlington (Myrna); Tim Maier (Josh); Jill Carroll (Kim); Chris Hendrie (Deputy Pool); Tom Holland (Deputy Norris); Michael Lomazow (D.A.); Robert Destri (Public Defender); Osgood Perkins (Young Norman); Ben Frommer (Sexton); Gene Whittington (Diver); Robert Traynor (Desk Clerk); George Dickerson (County Sheriff); Thaddeus Smith (Deputy Sheriff); Sheila K. Adams (Deputy Woman); Victoria Brown (Deputy Clerk); Bob Yerkes (Stunt Man)

Crew: Bernard Schwartz (Executive Producer); Hilton A. Green (Producer); Jerry Goldsmith (Composer); Dean Cundey (Director of Photography); Andrew London (Editor)

Twenty-two years after being incarcerated, Norman is judged "restored of sanity," much to the dismay of the very upset Lila Crane Loomis. Outside the courtroom, Lila yells at Raymond, Norman's doctor, telling him that he will be responsible when Norman murders again. Doctor Raymond drives Norman home and tells him to call if he is ever in trouble. The two shake hands, and Doctor Raymond leaves. Underneath the phone, Norman finds a note that reads, "Norman, I'll be home late. Fix your own dinner. Love, M." He has a flashback in which his mother cries, "What did you put in my tea?!" The bedroom door opens slightly, and a hand falls down.

The next day, Norman is at a diner working as the cook's helper. He meets the nice old Mrs. Spool, Ralph the cook and Mary the new waitress. That night, Mary is arguing with her boyfriend Scott on the phone. Norman asks if she is okay, and she tells him her boyfriend has kicked her out. Norman offers to let her stay at the motel. Once there, Norman gives Mary a room, and first meets the new motel manager, Warren Toomey. Toomey does not seem to care what the tenants do (allowing drugs and other such things to infest the rooms), and Norman fires the listless manager. Norman invites Mary to the house for a sandwich. Even though Scott has already moved someone else in, Mary is too frightened to stay at the motel because she knows of Norman's past. Norman says he "needs" her to stay, and so she sleeps in a room in the house (with a chair propped against the door).

The next day at the diner, Toomey arrives and is rude to Mary (he orders "some of what Norman got last night" from the waitress). When Norman gets a note from Mother (on the order wheel) concerning "that little whore," he blames Toomey and angrily confronts him. Ralph tells Norman to take the rest of the day off. Mary comes by Norman's house and asks if he would still like her to stay at the house. Later, Toomey comes to the office to get his things, and he is making a commotion ("Hey, psycho!"). Norman gets a phone call from someone who says it is his mother. Down in the office, Toomey sees Mother's feet; he is sliced across the face and killed.

Doctor Raymond arrives at the motel and asks Norman why he quit his job. Norman tells him that he is going to be running the motel by himself and that Mary is staying with him. In the bathroom, Mary finds a hole in the wall. The doctor visits Sheriff Hunt, tells him that someone is disturbing Norman and asks the sheriff to check out Mary. When Norman is painting the motel, he sees movement from his mother's window. He heads upstairs and sees that his mother's bedroom has been completely made up. There is a note from Mother in which she threatens to kill "that slut." He hears footsteps, goes into the attic and is locked inside. Two teenagers sneak inside the cellar to smoke joints and kiss. They hear a noise and see Mother walking around, but before the male can get out, Mother stabs him in the back. Later, Mary is calling for Norman. He awakes, goes to the door and discovers that it is unlocked. He heads to the room, but it is vacant, with no note or dresses or anything.

Sheriff Hunt and Deputy Pool are at the house investigating the female teenager's claims that her boyfriend was killed in the cellar. The sheriff asks where Norman has been all afternoon, and Mary gives him an alibi. Norman is distressed, and Mary looks for brandy in the office, where she confronts her mother Lila. Mary says Norman could not have killed the boy because she had locked him in the attic. Lila wants Norman re-committed, but Mary thinks Norman has changed and says she believes someone else is in the house. Later, Norman finds a bloody cloth lodged in the toilet. He believes he really killed the boy, but Mary assures him he did not and tells him to get a drink. While Norman is downstairs, Mary hears a noise and she goes into Mother's room. When she looks through the hole into the bathroom, an eye peers back and Mary screams. Mary calls Lila, but she is not at her hotel. That night, Mary consoles a perturbed Norman ("I'm becoming confused again, aren't I?").

Doctor Raymond goes to see Norman the next day while Mary is gone. He tells Norman that Mary is Lila's daughter, and that they are trying to "destabilize" him. Norman believes that his mother is still alive. Mary is at the hotel with Lila, telling her to leave Norman alone or she will be sorry. The doctor has Mrs. Bates' body exhumed, and Norman seems to accept the fact that his mother is dead. However, when Norman gets a call from Mother later, he believes it is his "real mother," even after Mary tells Norman that she and her mother have been trying to drive him crazy.

The police find Toomey's suitcase at the swamp. After questioning Norman, Hunt says he knows who Mary and her mother are, and he suggests they leave. Lila, followed by Doctor Raymond, is at the Bates Motel. She gets into the fruit cellar and gets Mother's clothes out of a hiding place, but is killed with a knife in the mouth. At the swamp, the police find a car. Mary heads back to the house and tells Norman. Doctor Raymond calls from the office, but Norman thinks it is Mother. Mary cannot get Norman to respond to her, so she heads to the cellar and dresses as Mother. When Norman still disregards her, she gets on the phone upstairs. Doctor Raymond comes from behind, and Mary reacts by accidentally stabbing and killing the doctor. Norman sees what has happened and tries to comfort his "mother." Mary tells him to stay away, swinging the knife in defense. In the cellar, coals fall away and she sees her mother's dead body. "You killed them all," she tells Norman. As she raises the knife, the police enter the room and shoot her.

Hunt tells Norman later that Mary had apparently gone mad, dressed as Norman's mother, and killed everyone. Back at home, Norman is sitting down for dinner when Mrs. Spool visits ("It's Miss Spool, actually"). Norman says he was expecting someone, and he asks her if she is his real mother. She says she is, and that her sister Norma had taken Norman away from him. She also tells him she killed the people who were trying to harm him. Norman whacks Miss Spool on the head with a shovel and takes her body into the room, as his mother's voice says, "Remember, Norman, I'm the only one who loves you."

Psycho II was unfairly treated upon its release, not just because it was a sequel to a Hitchcock movie, but also because it came out during the infamous early-80s run of slashers. Franklin's film is, however, very good, with many enjoyable twists and turns, and a number of eerie moments (especially the eye in the hole to surprise Mary). Mary's alias Mary Samuels (to cover up the fact that she was a Loomis) is a reference to the first *Psycho*, in which Marion Crane signed in at the motel under the name of Marie Samuels.

Psycho III (1986)

Written by Charles Edward Pogue; Directed by Anthony Perkins; Universal Pictures; 93 min.

Cast: Anthony Perkins (Norman Bates); Diana Scarwid (Maureen Coyle); Jeff Fahey (Duane Duke); Roberta Maxwell (Tracy Venable); Hugh Gillin (Sheriff Hunt); Lee Garlington (Myrna); Robert Alan Browne (Ralph Statler); Gary Bayer (Father Brian); Patience Cleveland (Sister Margaret); Juliette Cummins

(Red); Steve Guevara (Deputy Leo); Kay Heberle (Ruthie); Donovan Scott (Kyle); Karen Hensel (Sister Catherine); Jack Murdock (Lou); Katt Shea (Patsy); Hugo Stanger (Harvey Leach); Lisa Ives (Bell Tower Nun); Angele Ritter (Bartender); Diane Rodriguez (Nun)

Crew: Hilton A. Green, Donald E. Zipfel (Producers); Stephen Bray, Carter Burwell, D. Stanton Miranda, David Sanborn (Composers); Bruce Surtees (Director of Photography); David E. Blewitt (Editor)

Maureen, a distraught nun questioning her faith, climbs to the top of a bell tower as if to jump, shrieking, "There is no God!" Several other nuns run up the tower steps. When a nun tries to pull Maureen away from the edge, she resists, and the nun falls to her death. After receiving words of wisdom from a nun ("You'll burn in Hell for this!"), Maureen leaves the convent. While hitchhiking, Maureen is given a lift by Duane Duke, an aspiring rock 'n' roll musician headed for Los Angeles. During a heavy downpour, Duane decides the two of them should sleep in the car. But when he makes advances towards Maureen, she runs away in the rain.

Norman Bates is busy with his favorite pastime: taxidermy. A newspaper article alludes to the still-missing Emma Spool, who claimed to be Norman's mother in the previous film. Duane arrives at the motel, interested in the "Help Wanted" sign hanging in the door. Duane says he only wants extra cash to fix his car brakes, so he will not be staying long. "No one ever does," Norman tells him. Norman heads to a restaurant for lunch and encounters Tracy, a nosy reporter doing a story on the insanity plea. Norman sees Maureen and is reminded of Marion Crane (of the first film). When he sees the initials "M.C." inscribed on her suitcase, he is quite perturbed. He is even more unsettled upon learning that Maureen is staying at the Bates Motel, and that Duane has given her the key to Cabin One, the same cabin in which Marion Crane was viciously murdered.

Duane goes to a bar to pick up women. He meets an apparently uninterested Tracy, who suddenly wants to buy Duane a beer when she learns that he is a Bates Motel employee. She offers to pay him for any information on Norman he can provide. Back at the motel, Mother is restless (much to Norman's dismay), and she decides to pay Maureen a visit. However, when throwing the curtain aside, a suicidal Maureen (soaking in her blood with a razor at the tub's side) does not see Mother with her knife; instead she sees an image of the Virgin Mary bearing a crucifix. Maureen awakes in a hospital, and Tracy learns that the woman had been brought in by Norman, who is considered a hero. The reporter remains incredulous.

Duane returns to the motel with a female. The woman has a run-in with Norman at the ice machine. Later, Duane is being rude, and he hands the woman five dollars for a cab and tells her to leave. She is murdered in the phone booth before she can even place a phone call. The next morning, Duane spots the same five-dollar bill in the register (the bill's edge is torn). Duane tells Tracy about the bill, and Tracy sets about interviewing other people about Emma Spool. She visits Spool's old apartment and dials a phone number written on a magazine. It is for the Bates Motel.

Norman goes out on a date with Maureen. When they return from the motel, there are a number of college people having a party. A slightly inebriated Maureen asks Norman to lie with her on the bed, but she is awakened later by a party goer (concerned about her door standing open), and Norman is gone. Maureen knocks on Norman's door, but Norman refuses to answer because Mother is now angry. To vent her frustration, Mother slaughters a college student in the bathroom and once again leaves the mess for Norman to clean up.

The cops investigate the missing girl, but Maureen gives them Norman's alibi by claiming that he was with her all night. Despite an apparent trust of Norman, Maureen leaves with Tracy because the reporter told Maureen about Norman's shady past.

When Norman returns home, Mother is missing. A note tells him to meet her in Cabin Twelve. Sitting in the cabin playing guitar is Duane, holding Mother hostage, with a desire of blackmailing Norman (believing his land is valuable). Norman decides it best to batter Duane with his guitar. He takes Duane and the other bodies to the swamp and disposes of them.

Maureen, believing she was meant to help him (and the silhouette of Mother in the house was actually the Virgin Mary), goes to see Norman. Once there, she embraces him, but is startled by Mother's voice, and she falls unto a statue pointing an arrow and is killed. Tracy, having uncovered information about Emma Spool, heads to the Bates household. After discovering the body of Maureen, Tracy meets Norman/Mother, who is now very angry. The reporter tries to explain to Norman that Emma Spool was not in actuality Norman's mother, but his aunt, and she killed Norman's mother because she thought the boy was her son. Norman viciously stabs the decomposed body of his mother. Afterwards Norman is arrested. While being driven away, he tells himself he will "finally be free" and gently strokes the rotted arm of his mother.

The beginning of the film seems to be an homage to the 1958 film *Vertigo*, directed by Alfred Hitchcock (who also directed the first *Psycho*). *Psycho III* marked the directorial debut of Anthony Perkins, who provides poignant direction and another good performance as Norman Bates. Actress Katt Shea (who appears in a minor role) has directed and co-written (with her then-husband, Andy Rubin) *Stripped to Kill* (1987), *Poison Ivy* (1992) and the vampire film *Dance of the Damned* (1988).

Psycho IV: The Beginning (1990)

Written by Joseph Stefano; Directed by Mick Garris; Smart Money Productions/Universal TV; 96 min.

Cast: Anthony Perkins (Norman Bates); Henry Thomas (Young Norman); Olivia Hussey (Norma Bates); CCH Pounder (Fran Ambrose); Warren Frost (Doctor Leo Richmond); Donna Mitchell (Connie Bates); Thomas Schuster (Chet Rudolph); Sharen Camille (Holly); Bobbi Evors (Gloria); John Landis (Mike); Kurt Paul (Raymond Linette); Louis Crume (George Emeric); Cynthia Garris (Ellen Stevens); Doreen Chalmers (Mrs. Lane); Alice Hirson (Voice of Mother); Ryan Finnigan (Norman, Age 5); Peggy O'Neal (Nurse); Bob Barnes (Salesman); George Zaloom (Janitor)

Crew: Hilton A. Green, Les Mayfield, George Zaloom (Producers); Graeme Revell (Composer); Rodney Charters (Director of Photography); Charles Bornstein (Editor)

On her radio show, deejay Fran Ambrose is discussing matricide with Doctor Leo Richmond. The doctor, having written a book on "boys who kill their mothers," mentions a 30-year-old case in which a boy committed matricide, and then dressed as his mother and went on a murderous rampage. The next caller, requesting to be identified as Ed, claims to be personally connected with the show's theme. Ed (who is, in fact, Norman) tells Fran and Doctor Richmond that he has killed people before and that he is "gonna have to do it again."

Norman proceeds to tell a story of one of his murders. A young lady arrives at the Bates Motel, with a young Norman sitting on the porch. The flirtatious girl asks to see Norman's room, and when Norman attends to one of the motel guests, she sneaks into the Bates home. After disrobing, the girl lies in bed for a nervous Norman, who decides he had better check on Mother. It seems Norman's mother is upset that a "whore" is in the house, and she wants Norman to kill her. When the girl goes looking for Norman in the bedroom, she sees the mummified Norma Bates, and Norman/Mother murders her.

When Doctor Richmond asks where Ed was when he killed his mother, an agitated Norman hangs up the phone and turns off the radio. Connie, Norman's wife, telephones and asks if he may pick up his birthday cake from the store. After hanging up with Connie, Norman turns the radio back on, and Fran says she would like to hear from Ed again. Norman calls the show and talks about his father, who died (as a result of bees) when Norman was six. Fran reminds the listeners that she is speaking with a man who has killed his mother, and Norman chips in, "Plus her boyfriend with her."

Norman says that he was practically running the motel by the time he was 15. He speaks of an eerily close and intimate relationship with his mother, and of his mother's peculiarities: "She'd be sweet one moment and then she'd suddenly turn mean." Norma Bates would occasionally throw maniacal tantrums, and she seemed oblivious to her sexual frankness towards her son. One day, when the two are rolling around in the grass, Norma realizes that her son is sexually aroused, and she punishes him by forcing him into a dress, smearing make up on his face and locking him in the closet.

During a break for Ed, Doctor Richmond expresses to Fran his suspicions that Ed is actually Norman Bates. He says that if Norman makes a threat, it should not be taken lightly. Fran tells her co-workers to check out California and see if Norman has been released from an institution. Norman then continues his story. It seems Norma is upset about the freeway being constructed so far away from the motel. She reprimands Norman for not showing sympathy and blames him for her bad bladder, saying motherly things like, "I should have killed you in my womb. You sure as hell tried to kill me getting out of it." Fran and the others learn that Norman no longer runs the motel. Norman discusses his mother's new beau Chet, who coaxes Norman into boxing, only to punch him too hard. After inadvertently saying his real name, Norman talks about having a woman at the motel (kissing in her car) and killing her.

Eventually Norman says he must kill his wife Connie because she "let herself get pregnant." He wanted to end the "Bates line," but Connie stopped taking birth control pills. As Norman says, he will kill her with his own hands, "just like the first time." He then tells of a night when he added strychnine to a pitcher of tea and served the poison to his mother and Chet. Norman watched the both of them die, even carrying his not-quite-dead mother to the cellar. Norman then tells Fran that the "show's over," and goes to meet Connie at the Bates home.

At the house, Norman attacks Connie with a knife. Connie manages to talk her husband out of killing her, and a frustrated Norman begins dousing the home with gas and setting everything on fire. Norman, frightened by images of his mother and some of his victims, is finally helped out by Connie. As he walks away from his fiery house, he says, "I'm free," with his mother screaming "Get me outta here! Norman!"

Henry Thomas provides an admirable performance as a young Norman and Olivia Hussey is appropriately monstrous as the evil mother. Norman's mock name for the radio show, Ed, is quite possibly a reference to Ed Gein, the serial killer who provided the inspiration for Robert Bloch's original novel *Psycho*. *Psycho IV* was made for cable television. Film fans might recognize director John Landis as Mike at the radio station. Actress Cynthia Garris is the wife of director Mick Garris.

Psycho Cop (1989)

Written and Directed by Wallace Potts; Smoking Gun Pictures; 87 min.

Cast: Bobby Ray Shafer (Psychocop); Jeff Qualle (Doug); Palmer Lee Todd (Laura); Dan Campbell (Eric); Cynthia Guyer (Julie); Linda West (Sarah); Greg Joujou-Roche (Zack); Bruce Melena (Cop #1); Glenn Steelman (Cop #2); Julie Araskog (Dead Woman); Denise Hartman (Cop #3); David L. Zeisler (Cop #4)

Crew: Cassian Elwes, Jessica Rains (Producers); Rick Catlin (Associate Producer); Marc Tocker (Co-Producer); Alex Parker, Key Pisani (Composers); Mark Walton (Director of Photography); Ian McVey (Editor)

In a room of candles and with a pentagram on the wall, a man slips into a shirt with a badge. He washes his hands in a bowl of blood and puts his sunglasses on. Greg and Barbara are out driving on their wedding night, apparently lost. They see a police motorcycle in a field but no officer, and Greg stops and gets out of the car. Cops on the radio are discussing a woman who has disappeared. Greg is heard gagging and dropping to the ground. Barbara gets out and looks for Greg, and finds a flashlight with "Officer Joe Vickers" written on it. She discovers her husband dead; Vickers is laughing with bloody hands ("Looks like you need a policeman"). Barbara tries to call for help and finds a dead woman. She is tripped by the officer and her neck is snapped.

Three couples are in a car. Eric, driving with Julie beside him, sees a cop car up ahead and tells everyone to hide the beer. They look "sweet and innocent" as they pass the car, and Zack says the cop is not following. Further down the road, Doug sees the car behind them, Eric makes a turn and stops, and the group watches as the car stops and then drives away. Eric drives to an attractive estate and the group unloads the car. Eric meets the caretaker (who says he is like a security guard), and he tells them he lives in a nearby trailer. Vickers is out there, and he draws a pentagram in the dirt.

Relaxing by the pool, the group hears chopping (the police officer is out cutting some wood). The caretaker hears him, sees that his axe is gone and goes into the woods. An axe is thrown at him. He runs to the cop car for help, only to receive an axe in the head. Eric is listening to the radio with earphones, and he tells the others that police found signs of devil worshipping in the yard of a woman who has disappeared. Vickers in the pool shed; a 666 is on the back of his hand.

Zack says he went looking for the caretaker to fix the Jacuzzi switch but was unable to find him. Doug, Zack, and Laura go into the woods to search. Laura finds tire tracks, and Doug shows the other two some crucifixes he found. Eric, Julie and Sarah join them, and an unsure Laura persuades someone to call the police. Eric goes back and finds the outside phone, and Vickers appears ("Something wrong, son?"). The group seems uncomfortable, and a reluctant Zack finally says they will leave, but Eric stops them and says he was told the caretaker hurt himself with an axe. Later, Eric's radio warns people (when no one is around) about the missing Officer Vickers, who is in trouble for brutality. Doug goes to check on the caretaker as Sarah finds the cooler of beer empty. She finds Doug at the trailer and walks back with him to the house.

Doug says the trailer was empty, but they all see that now the TV is on in the caretaker's place. Laura says that the beer was stolen, and Zack leaves to get more. He stops for a tree limb in the road and pops open a warm beer from the car floor. Zack suddenly sees a cop car behind, loses the beer and gets out to see a vacant car. He returns to his car to find his keys missing, and he struggles with Vickers, who finally shoves a billy club in Zack's mouth ("You shouldn't drink and drive; it's against the law!"). When Sarah cannot find her purse, Doug and Laura surmise that a prowler took the purse and the booze. Sarah's purse is later found. Sarah and Julie are angry with Laura, and they decide to move to another room. Doug and Laura go to the trailer and find Eric inside, and he says the caretaker is not there. Julie hears her name mentioned by the pool, and she looks around and returns to find the radio and her brush missing. Believing it is Eric, she goes into the woods, where she is chased and run down by Vickers in his car.

The others look for Julie and find the radio, Julie's shoes and signs of a car out in the woods. They return to the house to call the police, but they see Zack's car in the driveway. Eric and Sarah find beer in the car with Julie's brush, and an indignant Eric goes looking for the two of them. Doug shows Laura footprints he found earlier in the pool shed, and Laura thinks someone was there listening to them. The two get Sarah to leave, but Zack's car will not start. Eric sees Vickers in the woods, and the officer chases him with a zapper. Eric runs and calls for Doug, and Vickers catches him and repeatedly zaps him. Doug and Laura find Eric's radio on the ground. Sarah is alone in the house, and, relieved to see Vickers, she lets the officer inside. Doug and Laura find a bloody cat in a tree and run back for Sarah. When Vickers runs after Sarah with a knife, she heads upstairs and looks a door. ("Sarah, now stop this. You're obstructing justice.") Vickers handcuffs her to a door and comes at Sarah with the knife.

Doug and Laura make it to the house and they find blood in the bathroom. Vickers is there, saying that the "maniac" has been caught, but Doug recognizes his footprints, and he and Laura run upstairs. ("Uh oh! Suspects fleeing the scene!") They climb out of the window, but Vickers grabs Doug, who falls from the roof. Doug and Laura get to Vickers' car to call for help, but the cable has been cut. They find the caretaker's body and try to get his keys, but Vickers attacks again. Laura gets in the caretaker's car, speeds away and picks up Doug. They drive, but suddenly Vickers is on the car roof. After he falls off, Laura stops for the limb in the road. Doug gets out clutching his ribs, and the couple runs from the police officer.

Doug and Laura find two more police officers, and they tell them about Vickers. One of the cops goes to check out Vickers' car and the other tells the couple about Vickers and his mental problems. The cop calls from the radio and says it is Vickers' car, and Officer Joe shoots the cop with a silencer. The cop with Doug and Laura says Vickers "turned to Satan." He then tries to reach his partner, and thinks he is out of range. Vickers shows up and pulls the cop's heart from his chest. Laura and Doug run, and Laura finds her friends dead and hanging on the crucifixes. Vickers pushes Laura down and gets out his gun, Doug attacks and Laura picks up the weapon. She shoots the officer a few times, and he falls but grabs her foot when she gets too close. Doug throws a tree limb like a spear and impales Vickers, and Laura leads Doug away. On TV, a man says fingerprints led police to believe Vickers is actually a serial killer who escaped from prison. The perforated Vickers opens his eyes and smiles.

Although the lengthy chase sequence in the woods makes the ending drag a little, *Psycho Cop* provides enough humor to be an enjoyable film. Shafer is great as the murderous psycho cop who is always prepared with a one-liner.

Psycho Cop 2 (aka *Psycho Cop Returns*) (1992)

Written by Dan Povenmire; Directed by Rif Coogan; Film Nouveau Productions/Penn Eden West Pictures; 80 min.

Cast: Bobby Ray Shafer (Office Joe Vickers); Barbara Lee Alexander (Sharon); Roderick Darin (Larry); Miles David Dougal (Brian/Spongehead); Nick Vallelonga (Mike); Dave Bean (Gary); John Paxton (Mr. Stonecipher); Julie Strain (Stephanie); Alexandria Lakewood (Cindy); Priscilla Huckleberry (Lisa); Justin Carroll (Tony); Kimberly Spies (Chloe); Al Schuermann (Gus); David Androle (Vinnie the Bartender); Adam Rifkin (Man With Video Camera); Alisa Wilson (Anchorwoman); Michael Karp (Big Mike); Brittany Ashland, Sara Lee Froton (Go Go Dancers)

Crew: Cassian Elwes, David Niven, Jr. (Executive Producers); David Androle (Producer); Bobby Ray Shafer, Ed Bates (Associate Producers); Marc David Decker (Composer); Enak Mada (Director of Photography); William G. Bernard (Editor)

Larry and Brian are in a donut shop discussing Gary's bachelor party that night as a cop nearby enjoys coffee and a donut. The party is going to be in the office after hours, and Larry asks Brian if they have everything, including the marijuana. The cop, Officer Joe Vickers, approaches the two, tells them to stay out of trouble and leaves. Inside the officer's police car are bloody symbols and body parts. Larry and Brian are walking to the office, and Brian becomes nervous when he sees the cop following them in his car. Larry walks over to talk to the cop and Brian drops the pot in the mailbox as the police car pulls away. The two men reach the building and go inside, and Vickers parks outside. Larry tells Gary about the party, and Mike shows Larry his file drawer full of booze. Tony and Chloe spend some time together in the copy room, and Larry flirts with Sharon from Accounting. As the sun goes down, Officer Vickers is still waiting outside in his car.

The boss, Mr. Stonecipher, leaves for the night. The four men watch him get in the elevator and then walk out of the building, where Brian sees the police car, believing it is the same cop from the donut shop. Larry goes to the security guard, Gus, and gives him money, and the strippers are let inside the building. Sharon is still at her desk working, and Tony and Chloe, kissing in a room, move down a couple of floors when hearing music from the elevator. Vickers bangs on the door and tells Gus he got a call about a disturbance. The two surmise it is a prank and the officer is allowed inside. Vickers says he saw Gus let the girls inside, and Gus tells him about the party upstairs. Vickers denounces Gus for taking a bribe (he saw him accept the money), stabs the security guard in the eye with a pencil and leaves ("Why don't you keep an eye out while I'm gone?").

The party goers hear the elevator opening and closing, and an irate Mike goes down to talk to Gus. The elevator stops in the midst of its descent, and Mike pulls the doors open and crawls onto the floor. Mike tells Vickers (thinking it is Gus) about the elevator, and the officer points him towards an "Out of Order" sign. Mike is told to take the other elevator on the way back up, where he joins the party again just to get Gus/Vickers a bottle of Scotch. The elevator goes berserk on the way down, and when the doors open, Mike steps off, and the elevator moves along. Vickers is there, and Mike gives him the bottle. The officer pushes Mike down the shaft, telling the falling man that he does not drink while on duty.

A fax of a badge is sent to the party room, and Larry tells an anxious Brian that it is probably Gus. They next receive a fax of Mike. Tony and Chloe are enjoying their time alone, and Sharon inadvertently walks in on them and apologizes. Gary and stripper Lisa are on the roof. Vickers arrives and, upset that Gary is "drunk and disorderly," shoots him in the head. He takes a screaming Lisa to the edge and "lets her go" with a warning, and she lands in the trash bin. Brian is frightened, having seen the body fly by the window, and the group receives a fax of Gary with his driver's license on his forehead (covering the bullet hole). Brian goes to the copy room to find Mike, Gary, and Lisa. Xerox copies cover the floor, and Brian runs out.

Brian tells Larry he thinks something is wrong, and the two men and the other two strippers, Stephanie and Cindy, go to the copy room. Brian points out that Mike never moves in any of the copies. Chloe remembers her panties left behind in the copy room, and Tony goes to get them, but at the door, Vickers runs up with a spear (taken from a statue in the hallway) and stabs them both. Brian shows that a copy of a copy has a different grain than fresh copies, and he thinks the red liquid on the copy machine is blood. Brian suggests the corpses are in the closet, but it is empty. Blood drips from the ceiling, and the group sees a pentagram of blood above them, right before the bodies of Mike and Gary fall down. They all run out and hide in a room, and are scared by Sharon. They tell her what has happened, and she discovers that the phone is dead ("Oh, big surprise!" says a pessimistic Brian).

The group runs to warn Tony and Chloe and finds them dead. Officer Vickers arrives, saying he got a report of a disturbance. They tell him of the bodies, and Stephanie asks about Lisa, and Vickers says she probably called in the report and is okay. He says that Satan worshipper Joe Vickers is doing everything, and Brian notices his badge number (666) and shows Larry the Xeroxed badge with the same number. The officer tells the group that no one is above suspicion, and Sharon reminds him that he said it was Vickers. Vickers introduces himself, and Larry and Brian push a desk against him. The women run as Vickers puts a gun in Larry's mouth and fires. Brian is shot in the back. Sharon grabs Gus' gun, and the women see that the doors are secured with handcuffs. As they run back up the steps, Vickers jumps out and grabs Stephanie. He shoots Cindy and promises not to shoot Stephanie if Sharon drops her gun (he already reached his quota for the day). Sharon puts down the gun and kicks it towards the officer, and he puts his gun away and snaps Stephanie's neck. Sharon runs, and Vickers fires at her.

In the hallway, Sharon swings an axe into Vickers' stomach and picks up his gun, but it has no bullets. Vickers is now armed with the axe. Sharon hides in the bathroom, and when the officer arrives, she sprays hairspray with a lighter, burns Vickers, kicks his axe away and pushes him down the shaft. Sharon runs into a wounded Brian, and they head down the steps. At the elevator, Brian is axed in the back. Sharon runs through the parking garage and out in the streets. Vickers catches up and hits and beats her, and men from a bar come out with baseball bats and hockey sticks and beat Vickers, as a man videotapes the incident from his balcony. Later, Sharon watches the TV report with Brian in a hospital; down the hall, two cops are standing outside a door (Room #666). They hear growling inside, and the cops, a doctor and a nurse go inside, and screaming is heard. Vickers walks out in a doctor's uniform.

Psycho Cop 2 is a humorous slasher and a superior sequel. Shafer is amusing as the one-liner–toting murderous police officer, but this time he is well supported by a strong cast, in particular Dougal as the overly nervous Brian. Director Rif Coogan is actually Adam Rifkin, who appears in the film as the videotaping citizen.

Psychos in Love (1986)

Written by Gorman Bechard and Carmine Capobianco; Directed by Gorman Bechard; Generic Films, Inc./Beyond Infinity; 87 min.

Cast: Carmine Capobianco (Joe); Debi Thibeault (Kate); Frank Stewart (Herman); Cecilia Wilde (Nikki); Donna Davidge (Heather); Patti Chambers (Girl in Bed); Carla Bragoli (Girl in Woods); Carrie Gordon (Girl in Toilet); Angela Nicholas (Dianne); Robert Suttile, Lum Chang Pang, Danny Noyes, Herb Klinger, Wally Gribauskas (Bar Patrons); Peach Gribauskas (Bar Waitress); Ed Powers (Man); Frank Christopher (Man at Picnic); Professor Morono (Joey the Creep); Shawn Light (Girl in Sauna); Scott Sears (Frightened Man); LeeAnn Baker (Heavy Metal Girl); Linda Strouth (Cathy, Herman's Dinner); Eric Lutes (Mechanic); Mike Brady (Redneck); Ruth Collins (Bopper's D.J.); Michael Citriniti (Weather Man); Kate McCamy (Woman); Loren Freeman (Video Store Clerk); Jan Radder (Blood Pumper); Matt Brooks (Asst. Blood Pumper); Kathy Milani (Photographer); Shaun Cashman (Soundman); Joe Murphy (Waiter); Barry Clark (Man in Restaurant)

Crew: Gary Bechard (Executive Producer); Gorman Bechard (Producer/Director of Photography/Editor); H. Shep Pamplin, Shaun Cashman (Associate Producers); Carmine Capobianco (Composer)

Joe is a psycho killer. Even when Dianne, a potential mate, enters his life, he kills her because she likes grapes. Then Kate walks into his bar and sits down. Joe asks if she would like grape juice, Kate says she hates grapes and Joe knows that he has found someone special. The two agree to dinner, a movie and a manicure (Kate is a manicurist). That night, after the movie, Kate works on Joe's nails, and he admits to her that he is a psycho killer, killing women at random. As luck would have it, Kate is also a psycho killer, who kills men at random. They spend the night together and talk of what they do with the bodies, and later they move in with one another. Their "very open relationship" allows both of them to continue occasionally seeing other people for the purpose of killing.

Herman, a plumber, finishes working on a woman's sink and then beats the woman in the head with his wrench. He chops her up with an electric saw, prepares her severed hand with some vegetables and dines alone by the candlelight. Kate goes to see a mechanic for a manicure appointment, and he is too forward and eventually chases her through the woods. He gets her on the ground, and Kate picks up a rock and bashes his head many times. Afterwards, she is upset because of the dull killing. Joe picks up Heather from the bar; she talks at such a rapid pace that Joe can barely even say anything. Joe decides that he is "losing interest" in his murderous hobby; he is in love.

Herman fixes a clogged pipe, and as a big man goes for something in his refrigerator, Herman points a gun at his head. At home, Herman watches television and munches on a snack of fingers. Joe takes Susan home, and Kate seems upset by the woman's presence. After Joe kills Susan and lops off her head to put on a platter, Kate admits to being a little jealous. At the bar, she suggests committing a murder together. Joe brings home Nikki, the dancer at the bar, and as she sits beside Kate, Joe stabs her through the back of the couch. Joe goes to get a drink for Kate, and Nikki stands again and starts to choke Kate. Joe slices her throat, then hits her with a frying pan and shoots her with a shotgun until she stays down. The couple confesses to being tired of killing, and they both agree to get married, as well as chop up Nikki, who stood up one more time and had to be blown away again.

Joe and Kate enjoy a private ceremony, and they visit old slaughterhouses in Chicago for their romantic honeymoon. They pick up a hooker from a bar and agree to later meet in a hotel, where Joe stabs her in the shower. Believing that they both "got the itch again," they return to killing, only to find themselves disappointed again. Joe and Kate accept the fact that they are "ex-psycho killers," and they decide to get a VCR. They go to the video store and rent as many horror films as they can get their hands on.

The couple is having problems with their clogged sink, so they decide to call a plumber. Herman shows up and discovers bloody parts of a human lodged in their pipes. The couple decides to come out of "retirement," and Joe gets a knife, but Herman pulls his gun on the couple. He says he wants the bodies of their future victims, and if they tell him no, he will inform the police that they refuse to let him have their corpses and that Joe tells bad jokes. Herman finally decides to kill them both and garnish them with a special grape juice, which only disgusts the grape-haters. Kate distracts Herman and hits the switch. Following a struggle in the dark, the light comes back on to reveal a bloody kitchen and a chopped-up Herman. Joe and Kate decide to go out to eat, but they leave the French restaurant when the waiter mentions something with grapes. The two lovers walk away and argue about what to have for dinner.

Psychos in Love is a low-budget but very funny slasher. The pseudo-documentary style works well, and Capobianco and Thibeault are terrific, with good chemistry between the two.

Rush Week (1989)

Written by Russell V. Manzatt and Michael W. Leighton; Directed by Bob Bralver; Noble Entertainment Group, Inc.; 100 min.

Cast: Pamela Ludwig (Toni Daniels); Dean Hamilton (Jeff Jacobs); Courtney Gebhart (Jonelle Watson); Don Grant (Byron Rogers); Roy Thinnes (Dean Grail); John Donovan (Arnold Krangen); Gregg Allman (Cosmo Kincaid); David Denney (Greg Ochs); Todd Eric Andrews (Harvan); Laura Burkett (Rebecca Winters); Jay Pickett (Parker); Toni Lee (Alma); Kathleen Kinmont (Julie Ann McGuffin); Dominick Brascia (Peeper); Darrell Zwerling (Professor Cadwell); Edward Rayden (Ichabod); Mark Clayman (Gordo); Johnna Johnson (Cigarette Girl); Heidi Holicker (Sarah); Ray Bickel, Dean Wein (Officers); Pamela Owen (Wendy); Chantel Dubay (Veronica); Pres Seckel (Dean Seckel); Addie

(Band Leader); Eddie Battos (Accordian Player); Francis McCaffrey (Clerk); Tim Topper (GAE Member); Michael Corbin (Freshman); Mitch Watson (Phantom Pledge); Michael W. Leighton (Shadow); Rita M. Saiz (Herself)

Crew: Michael W. Leighton (Producer); George Cook (Associate Producer); The Hamiltons (Composers); Jeff Mart (Director of Photography); Jeff Reiner (Editor)

Toni Daniels, a new transfer student from another school, is a reporter at the newspaper and has been assigned to cover rush week. At the Beta Delta Beta house, Jeff announces that rush week begins tomorrow, and he cuts apart the tied pledges with a battle axe. He tells Byron that he is going for a walk. Julie Ann heads to the science building, where a man takes sexy pictures of her with a cadaver. The man pays her and leaves. As Julie Ann prepares to go, the lights are turned off and someone swings a battle axe at her.

The following day, Toni talks to Harv, president of Gamma Alpha Epsilon, about covering the opening night of rush week at the fraternity. Jeff and his BDB buddies ask how the "GAEs" are doing, and Harv mentions the BDB guys getting kicked off campus. Jeff is introduced to Toni, but when he follows after her to talk, she calls him a "walking ego." In class, a BDB frat member jumps out at a professor while lying in a body bag. Toni talks to Dean Grail, and Sarah asks to see him. Toni waits outside while Sarah tells the dean that her roommate Julie Ann is missing. Toni returns to the room, and Grail talks about fraternities and sororities bringing out corruption. Before leaving, Toni notes the photograph on the dean's desk, and he says it is his daughter, who has died. The professor comes in, complaining about the frat pranks.

At her computer, Toni gets a message from Jeff, and she plays the tape of Sarah (she had left her tape recorder running when she was out of the office). Toni goes to see the hippie Mr. Kincaid about a "missing coed" story, and he tells her to check with the dean and keep writing about rush week. Alma tells Toni later that she knows some rush week stories, and they agree to meet. Toni sees the dean, and he says that, a year ago, Julie Ann left with no explanation, and that she will return soon. At the GAE house, BDB members arrive and pretend to be homosexual frat guys, and they pull off a prank dealing with the video that the rushing people watch. Jeff invites Toni to the BDB party. At the house, Alma is doing some special work for the frat, and she is scared by a cadaver in the bed. Byron and the guys laugh, but an irate Jeff follows her to be sure she does not call the police. Outside, the killer approaches Alma and axes her.

Toni gets a message on her computer: "Drop it — or else!" She goes to see Sarah and asks how Julie Ann got enough money to buy the fancy things she has. Toni finds Julie Ann's bank book and a load of cash (with a red axe symbol on the bills). Sarah tells her that her roommate would get her picture taken by someone in Room 302 of the science building. Sarah says Alma introduced Julia Ann to the photographer. Toni slips into Kincaid's office and finds and calls Alma's number, an escort service that tells the reporter Alma had an assignment at BDB and has not returned. Toni goes into the science building and finds drops of blood in Room 302. She leaves; Jeff is waiting outside. Toni asks about Alma, and Jeff says that he saw her last night and that she is probably away with a rich client.

Toni has the blood analyzed and she learns it is AB-negative, which she later finds out is the blood type of Julie Ann. Her friend Jonelle tells Toni that Jeff has changed in that he seems more distant than he once was. Toni gets another message ("Death purifies"), and a person telephones and hangs up. She meets Jeff in a bar, who tells her he has not been sending the threatening messages. The two dance a bit, and Jeff invites Toni to a picnic. The next day, while waiting at the frat for Jeff, Byron tells Toni that Jeff is "neglecting responsibilities" and he asks her to talk to him. Toni asks Byron what happened last year, and he tells her that Jeff's girlfriend Laura (the dean's daughter) was killed, and that Jeff has not been the same since. At the picnic, Toni and Jeff enjoy time by the fire, and Toni tells Jeff that she thinks she is falling in love. She angers him when she asks about Laura.

Rebecca is getting her picture taken with a corpse, and the photographer is Arnold, the cafeteria cook. Rebecca is paid, and she looks around in the adjacent room, where she is axed by the killer. Toni gets an apologetic message from Jeff, who says he loves her, and she leaves to get more developer at the shop. Arnold asks her if she is into photography, and he slides a $100 bill her way, with the symbol on it. Later, Toni finds his address and breaks into his house, where she finds photographs of the girls in his lab. When Arnold returns, Toni drops her purse and hides in the bathroom, accidentally leaving her identification behind. Arnold goes to shower, and Toni throws the curtain over him and runs away.

The reporter goes to see Grail and tells her that the blood could have been from anyone. He also says that Arnold's position has already been terminated, due to his behavior. Toni is almost disappointed that there is no murderer, but then Jonelle tells her that Rebecca did not come home last night and had gone to meet someone in the science building. Toni leaves a message for Jeff to meet her in the science building. She then calls Arnold, and he says he remembers her (holding her ID). Jeff is at the costume party, in a similar hood and cloak that the killer wears. After getting the Toni message, he grabs the frat's battle axe and leaves.

Campus security does not believe Toni's claims of murders, so she calls the dean and leaves a message for him. Toni goes into the science building and takes the stairs, followed by Arnold. When Arnold reaches the door, the killer is waiting, and the photographer is killed. Jonelle goes into Jeff's room to clean up and finds his collection of clippings of coed murders. She sends a computer message to Toni, which she sees when hiding from a person walking around. Jonelle tells Toni what she has discovered.

The killer walks into a room and sees Toni; the reporter runs and hides in another room. She heads to the boiler room, and when she sees someone approach, she whacks him on the back of the head. Toni sees Jeff lying there in the cloak (without the killer's mask). The killer shows up and reveals himself as Dean Grail, claiming to "bring purification" from the "filthy pictures." Jeff jumps up and the two struggle until Toni stabs the dean in the back. When he returns for another attack, Toni throws Jeff his battle axe, and Grail is beheaded. Later, the new dean tells Jeff that the BDB house is a "model" for other frats, and he mentions to the cops that the boys seemed like gentleman. After the police leave, the frat party resumes.

Rush Week is an okay slasher, with very few frights but decent performances and mildly interesting characters that at least keep things fairly entertaining.

Scary Movie (2000)

Written by Shawn Wayans, Marlon Wayans, Buddy Johnson, Phil Beauman, Jason Friedberg and Aaron Seltzer; Directed by Keenan Ivory Wayans; Dimension Films/Brillstein-Grey Entertainment/Gold-Miller Productions/Wayans Bros. Entertainment; 88 min.

Cast: Anna Faris (Cindy); Jon Abrahams (Bobby); Dave Sheridan (The Killer/Doofy); Shawn Wayans (Ray); Marlon Wayans (Shorty); Regina Hall (Brenda); Lochlyn Munro (Greg); Shannon Elizabeth (Buffy); Cheri Oteri (Gail Hailstorm); Kurt Fuller (Sheriff); Carmen Electra (Drew); Rick Ducommun (Cindy's Dad); Andrea Nemeth (Heather); Trevor Roberts (Dookie); Dan Joffre (Cameraman Kenny); Kelly Coffield (Teacher); Craig Brunanski (Road Victim); David L. Lander (Principal Squiggy); Jayne Trcka (Miss Mann); D.M. Babe Dolan (Grandma); Reg Tupper (Beauty Pageant MC); Tanja Reichert (Miss Congeniality); Kendall Saunders (Miss Thing); Mark McConchie (Drew's Dad); Karen Kruper (Drew's

Mom); Frank B. Moore (Not Drew's Boyfriend); Glynis Davies (Buffy's Mom); Keenan Ivory Wayans (Slave); Lee R. Mayes (Captain); Mark Hoeppner (Whipmaster); Ted Cole, Doreen Ramus, Jessica van der Veen, Jim Shepard (People in Theatre); Ted Gill (Store Clerk); Lloyd Bery (Homeless Man); Mathew Pexman (Annoying Guy); Marissa Jaret Winokur (Garage Victim); Dexter Bell (Shorty's Friend); Chris Wilding (Shorty's Roommate); Peter Hanlon (Suicidal Teacher); Chris Robson (KOMQ Reporter); Susan Shears (Female Reporter); Peter Bryant (Black TV Reporter); Nicola Crosbie, Ian Bliss (Reporters); David Neale, Nels Lennarson (Policemen); Giacomo Baessato, Kyle Graham, Leanne Santos (Trick-or-Treaters)

Crew: Bob Weinstein, Harvey Weinstein, Cary Granat, Peter Schwerin, Brad Grey, Peter Safran, Bo Zenga (Executive Producers); Eric L. Gold, Lee R. Mayes (Producers); Robb Wilson King (Associate Producer); Lisa Suzanne Blum (Co-Producer); David Kitay (Composer); Francis Kenny, A.S.C. (Director of Photography); Mark Helfrich, A.C.E. (Editor)

Drew, at home making popcorn, gets a telephone call. She says she is about to watch a scary movie, and the caller asks her if she likes scary movies. The caller then asks Drew her name, wanting to know who he is looking at (a person in a "scream mask" is flipping through a porno magazine outside). He tells her she forgot to lock the back door, and Drew inadvertently beats trick-or-treating kids with a baseball bat. The killer is in the house, and chases Drew outside. She runs through sprinklers as her skirt and top are torn off. Drew tries to stop her father as he approaches in his car. Her father, busy with Drew's mother, ignores her and hits his daughter with the car. The killer is there, and he stabs Drew.

Cindy is in her room as her boyfriend Bobby comes through the window. Cindy's dad is at the door, and he tells her that he is leaving town for a deal with Colombian guys. The couple kisses until Bobby's groping hand hits an electric fence. He says he does not want to rush Cindy, and Bobby leaves. The next day, Gail Hailstorm (author of *I'm Rich, You're Dead*) is at the school, doing a report on the recent murder. Cindy, Bobby and their friends sit at a fountain and talk about Drew (Ray recalls her attractive brother Steve). Cindy says that the murder happened a year after the group killed a guy. Greg insists it was an accident. A flashback shows the six people in a car, and after a drunk Greg causes a disturbance from the car sun roof, they hit something and Bobby slams on the brakes. "Oh, my God, we hit a boot!" Buffy screams, before they discover a dead man. The man is fine, and he stands to leave and is hit on the head with a empty bottle tossed by Greg (arguing with the others over what to do with the body). They toss the man into the lake and make a pact to never mention the incident again.

Gail tries to get some information from Buffy's simple-minded cop brother Doofy. In class, Cindy gets a note: "I know what you did last Halloween." Later, Greg finds a photograph of a smaller-than-average part of his anatomy ("I know"). Greg is angry, and he shows his friends, and they laugh. Cindy says she also got a note, and Greg tells her not to call the police. At the Teen Beauty Pageant, Greg is left alone to watch on a balcony, and Buffy, during her dramatic reading, screams for help when seeing the killer attack Greg. She goes to help her boyfriend but returns to the stage when she hears that she has won. After talking to Bobby on the phone, Cindy gets a call from the killer, who says he is somewhere in the house. Cindy sees him ("I can, um, see your feet"), and the killer chases her upstairs, where Cindy gets on the computer for help. Bobby comes through the window and drops a phone, glove and knife. Doofy is at the door, and Bobby is arrested.

Outside the police station, Gail says something derogatory to Cindy, who punches the reporter. At Buffy's house, Doofy says that the cops will find the guy the group dumped in the water (he overhead a conversation), and Cindy gets a call from the killer ("You've got the wrong guy!"). Cindy suggests people meet at her place that night, and Shorty announces it to everyone. Bobby has been released, and he is angry that Cindy believes he is a killer. Buffy mocks Cindy in the locker room (with a cell phone), and Cindy is offered condolences by the mannish Miss Mann. Buffy is alone in the locker room later; the killer is there, and she ridicules him, assuming the role of a helpless cheerleader. He stabs her, and Buffy mockily runs around. The killer finally chops off her head with a cleaver and throws it in the Lost & Found basket as Buffy continues to complain.

Gail tries to interview Heather in her car and then the killer as he attacks and kills the teenager. Gail and her cameraman Kenny run as the killer goes after them. Ray and Brenda go to the movies; in the bathroom, something is shoved in Ray's head (through his ears). Brenda is being loud and obnoxious in the theater. When the killer sits beside her, a man grabs the knife and stabs Brenda. Other people in the theater stab and beat her, and Brenda walks to the front and dies. At Cindy's party, a girl sees the killer in the garage and gets stuck when trying to crawl out of the doggie door. The killer runs the garage door and it malfunctions, and half the garage falls down. Bobby arrives, and he and an inebriated Cindy go to her room to enjoy some time together. Shorty and his friends make some phone calls with the killer. Later, the killer tries some free verse, and, with an ice hook and a knife, he slices and cuts the stoners, leaving Shorty alone ("That was the illest rhyme I ever seen, son!").

Cindy and Bobby are dressing, and the killer enters the room and stabs Bobby. Cindy runs downstairs and gets a gun; Bobby is down there. He takes the gun and shoots Shorty (with ketchup on his shirt), and Ray enters the room. Bobby tells Cindy that he and Ray are gay (which Ray adamantly denies) and that the two are copycating the killer to get rid of Cindy. They bring out her father, bound and gagged, and Bobby and Ray work on stabbing each other. Ray overdoes it when stabbing Bobby, and the killer stabs and kills Ray. Cindy and the killer fight, and she eventually kicks him out of the window.

The cops arrive, and Cindy goes outside to find the killer gone. At the station, Doofy brings in a file and the sheriff tells Cindy that the killer cannot be who they killed a year ago because his body was found a few weeks after the accident. The sheriff says the murderer has to be someone connected with everyone, who knew of the accident and could get around without being noticed. Cindy drops her mug of coffee. She thinks of Doofy, and on the bottom of the mug is Doofus Porcelain. Outside, Doofy's usual stumbling turns into a walk, he gets rid of his clothes, tears off a mustache and lights a cigarette. Gail picks him up and they drive away. The sheriff and Cindy run out and find Doofy's discarded bag, with the knife and mask inside. Cindy screams in despair, and she is pummeled by a car in the road.

Although a few jokes take too long to set up or just fall flat, *Scary Movie* still provides plenty of humor and is quite possibly the best slasher parody of them all. Actor Sheridan is not only hysterical as Doofy but also delivers terrific physical comedy as the killer. The ending of the film, a parody of *The Usual Suspects* (1995), is hilarious.

Schizo (aka *Amok*; *Blood of the Undead*) (1977)

Written by David McGillivray; Directed by Pete Walker; Niles International; 109 min.

Cast: Lynne Fredrick (Samantha); John Leyton (Alan Falconer); Stephanie Beacham (Beth); John Fraser (Leonard Hawthorne); Jack Watson (William Haskin); Queenie Watts (Mrs. Wallace); Trisha Mortimer (Joy); Robert Mill (Maitre d'); Victor Winding (Sergeant); Pearl Hackney (Lady at Seance); Lindsay Campbell (Falconer); Wendy Gilmore (Samantha's Mother); Paul Alexander (Peter McAllister); Colin Jeavons (Commissioner); Raymond Bowers (Manager); Terry Duggan (Editor); Diana King (Mrs. Falconer); Primi Townsend (Secretary); Victoria Allum (Samantha as a Child)

Crew: Pete Walker (Producer); Stanley Myers (Composer); Peter Jessop, B.S.C. (Director of Photography); Alan Brett (Editor)

In Northeast England, a man buys a newspaper, then angrily crumbles it after seeing an article on the soon-to-be-wed "ice queen," Samantha Grey. He is denied his request for Samantha's address at the newspaper office, so he packs clothes, a knife, a shard from a broken jar and a framed photograph of a woman into a suitcase and heads out the door.

Alan, Samantha's fiancé, says he is postponing the honeymoon for two weeks so he can work in the office at the carpet factory. Psychiatrist Leonard asks if anyone from Samantha's side will be at the wedding, and Beth, Samantha's friend, tells him she lost contact with everyone after her mother died. The man is on a train, and he imagines a woman screaming "Get out!" and being stabbed in the stomach with a knife. He exits the train and goes to the Men's Welfare Hostel. Samantha is told at the skating rink that a person had called and asked for her, and then asked instead for Gene Longworth. Samantha seems troubled, but she says she does not know the name.

The bride and groom leave the church. As they are driving away, Samantha sees the man standing by a tree. At the reception, the man walks in the back, and he is put to work on the dishes (he is thought to be from an agency). The man switches the knife by the cake with his own knife (crusted with what appears to be blood). The tray is pushed to the newlyweds, Samantha screams when she sees the knife and the man runs away. At home, Samantha receives a mysterious call ("That you, Gene?"), and the man asks if she got his present by the wedding cake. Alan leaves for work in the morning, and Samantha takes a shower. She sees a man's shadow, and the person runs away when the radio comes on. She goes downstairs and is frightend by Mrs. Wallace, the housekeeper, who suggests the ice skater saw spirits.

At the grocery store, Samantha hears her name called out, looks around and sees no one. Soon she hears her name being called from everyone, and she quickly rolls her cart to the register, where she is stopped by a store employee (the butcher's meat cleaver is in her cart). An unsettled Samantha leaves the store and meets Leonard, who says he was calling her name in the market. They go to the clinic, where the two discuss Samantha's mother dying and the loss of contact with her family. Outside the office is Leonard's patient Eric, who threatens the doctor. Leonard tells Samantha that Eric's threats are routine. Samantha goes home and hears a noise upstairs, where she finds an open window and the framed photograph of a woman. Alan comes home and he finds no one in the house. Samantha tells him about seeing someone in the shower, and says that the woman in the photograph is her mother.

Samantha speeds away in her car, and a confused Alan goes for a drink with Beth. He tells Beth he thinks something is wrong with Samantha. Samantha tells Leonard the man following her is William Haskin, her mother's lover. She says her mother's name was Maria Longworth, and Samantha's real name is Gene. A flashback shows a young Samantha/Gene hearing William and Maria arguing, going up the stairs and watching the man stab her mother to death with a piece of broken vase ("He was ripping her to pieces"). Leonard reminds Samantha that William was jailed, but Samantha says he was paroled and is now after her. The doctor says he will try to locate William, and before she leaves, Samantha asks Leonard not to tell anyone what she told him. Shortly thereafter, Alan arrives at Leonard's office looking for his wife, and tells the doctor to stay away from her. Leonard flips through a book on schizophrenia, then goes out to his car. While waiting at a stoplight, the doctor is grabbed and his throat slit. That night, Samantha tells Alan she is okay now.

In the morning, Samantha learns that Leonard is dead and that the cops got the killer, Eric. Later, Mrs. Wallace leaves for a "Psychic Brotherhood" meeting, and Samantha hears a noise and finds broken glass, a knife and blood on the upstairs carpet. She runs and calls the police, sees the man standing outside a glass door, screams and passes out. She awakens to cops banging on the door. They search the house but only find a bottle of spilled nail polish. Afterwards, Samantha shows Beth, who believes the man is a fantasy, a photograph of William (standing by a woman whose face cannot be seen).

The skater and Mrs. Wallace leave for a "Psychic Brotherhood" meeting, where the housekeeper's daughter and founding member, Joy, sits in front of a group of people and speaks through a spiritual guide. After a superficial (and seemingly feigned) message from Samantha's grandmother, Joy suddenly chokes, her eyes turn white and Leonard's spirit speaks through her, saying that his killer is in the room. The lights go out and people run from the room. After Joy recovers from a fainting spell, Samantha asks if she remembers anything. Joy heads to the bus stop, where she is bludgeoned with a sledgehammer and pushed in front of the approaching bus.

The next day, Samantha learns about Joy. She tells Beth that the killer may have thought it was Samatha (Joy was wearing her raincoat). Samantha, alone in the house, gets a knife from the kitchen. Seeing a shadow near the stairs, the woman locks herself in a room. Beth talks with Peter, he tells her that William asked permission to visit London, and he gives Beth the address of the place where William is staying. Mrs. Wallace returns to the house (Samantha is still up in the room), goes to the locked cupboard (she cannot find her key and the skater has the spare) and picks the door with a knitting needle. She reacts to something in the closet and is stabbed in the back of her head with the needle.

Samantha screams at the discovery of her housekeeper. Beth gets into William's room at the hostel, and William returns. The woman grabs the knife from the closet and they struggle. William's face is cut and Beth runs away. Beth goes to Samantha's house, and Samantha drives the upset woman back to her house. She returns home, cleans up the blood around the cupboard and shoves Mrs. Wallace's body back inside after it falls out. Samantha goes to the factory looking for Alan, and William is there ("Time for the reckoning, Gene"). William calls himself "Uncle Bill," and Samantha asks him to not call her Gene. He asks her if she remembers what happened 15 years ago. A flashback shows the young girl, after breaking a jar of paint, going upstairs to find her mother and William in an intimate situation. Her mother screams for her to get out, and the young girl stabs the woman. William says that Samantha must tell the truth, and then he says she is like two different people, perhaps not realizing that she has killed again. He asked her if she put Mrs. Wallace in the cupboard with her weapons. The two struggle, and William falls over the railing and is impaled by one of the factory machines.

Alan, Beth and Samantha are at the home, and the newlyweds are finally preparing to leave for their honeymoon. Alan gets the mail and reads a postcard from Mrs. Wallace, who talks of being away. Samantha goes to get more things upstairs, and she stops and eyes Alan and Beth as they talk and give each other a friendly kiss. Alan says he wishes he could find the key to the cupboard. At the airport, Beth waves good bye as Samantha gives Alan a strange look.

Schizo is a good film from director Walker. The story seems (perhaps retrospectively) a bit predictable, but the movie still has a nice eerie quality, and actress Fredrick is very good in the lead role. Although the voice over in the beginning incorrectly refers to schizophrenia as multiple or split personality, it does seem that the lead character is suffering from schizophrenic symptoms, with a perverted sense of reality.

Schizoid
(aka *Murder by Mail*)
(1980)

Written and Directed by David Paulsen; Golan-Globus Productions; 88 min.

Cast: Klaus Kinski (Pieter Fales); Donna Wilkes (Alison Fales); Mariana Hill (Julie); Craig Wasson (Doug); Richard Herd (Donahue); Joe Regalbuto (Jake); Christopher Lloyd (Gilbert); Flo Gerrish (Pat); Kiva Lawrence (Rosemary); Claude Duvernoy (Françoise); Cindy Donlan (Sally); Jon Greene (Archie); David Assael (Barney); Richard Balin (Freddy); Fredric Cook (Willy); Kathy Garrick (Maxine); Gracia Lee (Bruce); Tobar Mayo (Fritz); Jonathan Millner (Fritz's Friend); Frances Nealy (Housekeeper); Kimberly Jensen (Girl on Motorbike); Jay May (Boy on Motorbike)

Crew: Menahem Golan, Yoram Globus (Producers); Christopher Pearce (Associate Producer); Craig Hundley (Composer); Norman Leigh (Director of Photography); Robert Fitzgerald, Dick Brummer (Editors)

Some time in the night, Julie is in her apartment working at her typewriter. Later, she is with some female friends in a hot tub, while someone is watching them. The women discuss Julie's divorce and her advice column, and then they say good bye and go their separate ways. Julie and Sally ride bicycles, as the person follows in a car. When they split up, Sally is followed. The car trails the bicycle rider and knocks her off her bike, causing Sally to take refuge inside an abandoned house. The person in black gets a pair of scissors out of the glove compartment, chases Sally to the garage and stabs her a few times.

A note with cut-out letters is put together and sent to Julie at the office. Julie shows the threatening note to Doug, her ex-husband (who also works at the newspaper), and he suggests going to the police. He thinks it is one of the "nuts" from her therapy group, which he further thinks of as the cause for their separation. As Doctor Pieter Fales is waiting for his group to arrive, he speaks with his daughter, Alison, who hardly acknowledges him. At the group's session, Gilbert, a janitor, admits that he becomes angry when people do not appreciate the work he does. Alison listens to the session on the intercom in her father's office. Julie stays after the end of the session to speak with Fales about the note. He suddenly kisses her, but the receptionist interrupts any potential discussion between the two by telling the doctor about his next appointment.

Julie drives her friend Pat, also in the group, to the club where Pat works, and the killer follows. At home, Julie is frightened by a tall black man trailing her, but he was only going to see his flamboyantly gay white friend. Fales telephones Julie but does not say anything. After a young couple discovers Sally's body, Fales goes to see Pat backstage at the club, where they spend some intimate moments. Julie goes to see the police about the note, and she first encounters Donahue and Jake. The killer follows Pat while she rides the bus. Then he chases her down the street, catches up and murders her with the scissors.

The murderer hangs around Julie's apartment complex. Fales sits in Alison's room while she is gone and finds a couple of words cut from a magazine or newspaper. Determined to help the note-writer, Julie tells the police she wants to publish a phone number for the person to call. Then, after Donahue has laid out several photographs of dead people to prove the magnitude of John and Jane Does, Julie sees a dead Sally. She calls Doctor Fales, and they both identify the body. Donahue says he does not think the letter writer is Sally's killer. Later, Jake tells Julie all the police can really do is set up a special line for the letter writer's telephone call. He then cites the possibility of someone from her group writing the notes.

Alison meddles in her father's office and pulls a gun from a desk drawer. The police find Pat's corpse, and now Donahue thinks the letter writer might be the killer, despite the letters often referring to guns while the murderer uses knives. At dinner in the Fales household, Alison sits at the table in her mother's dress and continually alludes to her mother. She soon becomes indignant with her father and runs from the room screaming and tearing the dress. Julie later goes to the office; Doug, wallpapering in another room, peeks his head out but does not say anything. Julie runs into Gilbert, and they ride the elevator together. Gilbert acts peculiarly, and refers to Julie and Fales being together. Julie quickly leaves at the next elevator stop. Doug changes to his suit and tie and leaves a message at Julie's place: "I just wanted to make sure you were safe."

Doug later goes to see Julie, but his buzzing is neglected by Julie and Fales, who are engaged in a sexual tussle. Doug climbs the steps in back, but a man from another apartment chases him away. Alison is at home "modeling" in the mirror with a hat similar to the one the killer wears. Fales comes home and tries to talk to her, but Alison tosses the hat aside and heads upstairs. The killer goes to see Rosemary, another member of the therapy group, and stabs her while she relaxes in the hot tub. Fales telephones Julie, wanting to know why the group for that day was so skimpy, and Julie tells him she is waiting for the police (the letter with her telephone number is to be published that day). The receptionist tells Fales she cannot get hold of Rosemary or Pat. Fales finds two more cut-out letters and confronts Alison about writing the notes. She is upset that he seems to be blaming her for the murders, locks herself in the garage and starts the car. A terrified Fales tries to axe through the garage door to save his daughter, but Alison puts the car in gear, crashes through the door and speeds away.

When Donahue and Jake are at the office with Julie, Doug comes out from wallpapering. The cops explain how to access the phone line and leave, with Julie locking the door behind them. After a caller complains about the column, Julie gets a call from Alison, who says she wants to talk to her. Fales goes to the station and tells someone that two more of his patients are missing. He heads to the morgue, but claims not to know Pat when he sees her cadaver. Alison is let into the office, where she shows Julie a blue piece of paper (like all the notes were written on) and points a gun at her and Doug. When asked if she murdered anyone, Alison replies, "Oh, I could." Fales calls and learns that Alison is there. He rushes over to the office, where the door is unlocked and he walks inside.

Fales calls out his daughter's name, and a shot rings out. He is shot at two more times. The doctor gets on a phone and dials the office's number. The phone is picked up and Fales tries to speak with Alison, telling her he did not want Julie to replace her mother. Finally Doug says over the phone, "You make me sick!" Alison and Julie, tied up in another room, get a pair of scissors and try to cut themselves loose. The man at the morgue tells the two cops that scissors were used to kill the women, and that he found traces of a water-based paste — like that used to hang wallpaper. Doug is chasing Fales around the room, and when the doctor falls, he approaches and points the gun to his head. He talks about how the group "dissected" him without even knowing who he was ("You took my wife away from me!"). The gun clicks, and the two struggle. Alison and Julie are free. When she sees Doug beating her father, Alison stabs him in the back. The police run inside as the three survivors embrace.

Schizoid is a good slasher film, with a few slow spots every once in a while but enough red herrings to keep it interesting. Veteran actor Kinski is enjoyable in his underplayed performance as the doctor, and Wasson is effective as Doug. (Compare this performance to the good-natured and wimpy Jake in Brian De Palma's 1984 *Body Double*.)

School's Out
(aka *Schrei—denn ich werde dich töten!*)
(2000)

Written by Kai Meyer; Directed by Robert Sigl; RTL; 93 min.

Cast: Katharina Wackernagel (Nina); Niels-Bruno Schmidt (Philip); Marlene Meyer Dunker (Anna); Nils Nellessen (Tom); Rita Lengyel (Eva); Urs Remond (Michaelis); Sandra Leonhard (Jessica); Raphael Vogt (Jan); Enie van de Meiklokjes (Jasmin); Michael Habeck; Dimitri Alexandrov; Ludgwig Boettger; Oliver Brod; Marietta Burger

Crew: Peter Lohner (Producer); Ludwig Eckmann (Composer); Sven Kirsten (Director of Photography); Irene Abel (Editor)

Jessica is driving a taxi in the rain. After searching for a cassette, she nearly hits a man in the road. There is a car at the side of the road, and Jessica stops for the man, but she changes her mind, keeps her door locked and speeds away. Further down the street, the man calls Jessica (the phone number is on the taxi cab's door), and the two talk to each other about Jessica's graduation party and a prank that a group of her friends is going to pull. The man asks the flirtatious Jessica to return, and she agrees. Back at the car, Jessica gets out to see the man, but he is running around her car, and she quickly jumps back inside. As she is trying to drive the car out of mud, she hears a report on the radio of an escaped scissors-employing lunatic. A person is in the back of the taxi. Jessica accelerates.

Nina and her friend Anna are sitting near the entrance of the school. Anna wants to talk, but Nina is too upset over her boyfriend Tom. Nina mentions that Jessica has been acting weird lately, and then she goes to check on the recently arrived taxi but leaves when she sees it shaking and believes it is presently occupied. Nina and Anne enter the party in the school, where Philip gives Tom keys. Nina sees Jessica's boyfriend John, who she thought was out in the taxi with Jessica, and asks him if he knows where Jessica is (playing on a nearby television is a report of the escaped lunatic and his weapon of choice). Nina and Anna go back out to the taxi; the door is open and the interior muddy and disheveled. There is blood dripping from the back of the taxi, but the girls do not see it.

Tom's older sister Eva drives up, and Tom and Philip unload a crate. The two boys ask Nina and Anna if they would like to join them, and the group enters the school, leaving a large pair of scissors (used to cut the cords holding the crate) in the car. Inside, they discuss the escaped maniac, and Philip tells the story of the lunatic killing women in the school. Someone outside picks up the scissors. Philip takes off a vent from the shaft and positions himself in the way a dead teacher was found, then describes the murder in graphic detail. Outside, a redheaded student (who was with John earlier) is looking for her contact lens, and she is led away by the killer and stabbed. Philip's story leads to a cheap thrill at the expense of Nina, Eva and Anna. The group leaves the room, and Tom is gone. Philip looks for him, and the two scare the girls. As they walk down the hall, a pair of scissors is around a corner behind them.

Philip shows the prepared rooms with dummies filling the seats, one in a harlequin costume at the front of the class. They head to another room and bring out spiders that Eva has been breeding. Tom and Nina decide to get back together, and the couple seems happy. Tom says he forgot to lock up when they came inside, and Nina offers to do so. In the hallway, she runs into Anna, and her friend tells Nina that she thinks she has contracted AIDS. Anna has thought such things many times before, but she says this time she believes it is real. She does not want to tell Nina the name of her partner.

The door to the room (with the infamous shaft) is open; the two girls enter and see that maps have been slashed. They hide when a man enters the room. When they duck away behind some maps, Anna is grabbed. Nina finds her on the floor, and Anna says "one of those costumes" grabbed her. Anna sees something and tells Nina to hide, and when Nina tries to follow her, she is stopped by the harlequin. She realizes it is mostly likely not Philip, so she runs into the shaft, where the killer grabs at her and inadvertently cuts a hand on a screw by the vent. Nina gets to another vent and sees Anna, and tries to pass the key to the vent so Anna can get out. The harlequin is there behind Anna, and Anna is stabbed and killed. The killer shoves the scissors through the gate, Nina screams and the killer runs away.

Eva says she is going home, skates down the hallways and is tripped by the killer. She kicks the harlequin down and crawls over the scissors (her leg is hurt). Eva tries to take the mask off, but the killer flips her scissors-holding hand around and stabs her. Nina gets out of the open vent in the room with the dummies. She hides from an approaching figure, and she is found by Mr. Kaylan. Nina believes the teacher has killed Anna, an idea which is evidently verified when he says he was at the school to talk to Anna (Nina thinks he was the one Anna had been with).

Tom finds a broken display case and streaks on the floor (from Eva's skates) and angrily heads into the room, where he finds a dead Eva and Anna. The killer arrives, and Tom is impaled by a stuffed swordfish. Philip finds a locked door and a puddle of blood, and the harlequin stabs him in the shoulder. Mr. Kaylan and Nina see them, and the teacher attacks and is sliced across the chest. Nina goes out the front door, where she sees a crowd of people and embraces her police detective uncle. The taxi's trunk is open, and a man's body is inside.

The next day, Nina says that the maniac (from the trunk) could not have killed the others because he had been right behind her when she ran from the school. Nina talks to Philip, and he agrees that the lunatic was not the killer, but he angers Nina when he suggests the killer was Jessica, who is missing. At the funeral, they see John, whose right hand is bandaged; he claims he injured it opening the taxi's trunk. Philip goes to see Nina and tells her that Jessica was found, raped and lying in the woods. They go to see Nina's uncle, and he says a hair of the maniac was found on Anna. Philip asks about blood, and Nina remembers the harlequin cutting a hand on the screw. She feigns going to the bathroom, and she steals her uncle's gun. Nina later tells Philip about the screw, and Philip mentions a party in the schoolyard to celebrate that Jessica is okay.

In the schoolyard, Philip suggests going inside and looking for the screw. He tells Mr. Kaylan about the bloody screw, and the teacher says to call the police. Nina and Philip decide to go inside the school (Nina still has the master key). They reach the room, and Philip takes off the vent and gets the screw out. He turns and sees that Jessica has a knife to Nina's throat. Philip drops the screw, and Nina manages to shoot Jessica's hand as she is bending over. Jessica stabs Nina in the back and stabs Philip when he lunges for her, but Philip stabs Jessica in the leg with a screwdriver.

When Mr. Kaylan arrives, Nina points the gun at him and runs to the school's attic. The teacher follows her, and he tells Nina that Anna threatened to report him for "sexual abuse and harassment." Jessica had met the lunatic, and seduced and stabbed him, and she decided to copy his murder spree in order to get rid of Anna for her lover, Mr. Kaylan. Nina's uncle appears and he grabs Nina, but he is whacked with a crowbar when he checks on a bloody Jessica. Jessica stabs the teacher, believing he wanted her to bleed to death, and Mr. Kaylan shoots and kills Jessica. He looks for Nina, and she comes out and stabs him. Nina finds a wounded Philip hiding in the shaft and leads him out of the school.

School's Out is an intriguing German slasher (the harlequin costume is quite clever), but it is a little too derivative of Wes Craven's *Scream* (even the original German title, which roughly translates to "Scream — for I will kill you!").

Scream (1996)

Written by Kevin Williamson; Directed by Wes Craven; Dimension Films/Woods Entertainment; 111 min.

Cast: Neve Campbell (Sidney); Courteney Cox (Gale Weathers); David Arquette (Deputy Dewey); Skeet Ulrich (Billy); Rose McGowan (Tatum); Matthew Lillard (Stuart); Jamie Kennedy (Randy); Drew Barrymore (Casey); Roger Jackson (Phone Voice); Kevin Patrick Walls (Steve); David Booth (Casey's Father); Carla Hatley (Casey's Mother); Lawrence Hecht (Mr. Prescott); W. Earl Brown (Kenny); Lois Saunders (Mrs. Tate); Joseph Whipp (Sheriff Burke); Lisa Beach, Tony Kilbert (TV Reporters); C.W. Morgan (Hank Loomis); Frances Lee McCain (Mrs. Riley); Liev Schreiber (Cotton Weary); Troy Bishop, Ryan Kennedy (Expelled Teens); Leonora Scelfo (Cheerleader in Bathroom); Nancy Ann Ridder (Girl in Bathroom); Lisa Canning (Reporter With Mask); Bonnie Wood (Young Girl in Video Store); Aurora Draper, Kenny Kwong (Party Teens); Justin Sullivan (Teen on Couch); Kurtis Bedford (Bored Teen); Angela Miller (Girl on Couch)

Crew: Bob Weinstein, Harvey Weinstein, Marianne Maddalena (Executive Producers); Stuart M. Besser (Co-Executive Producer); Cary Woods, Cathy Konrad (Producers); Dixie J. Capp (Co-Producer); Marco Beltrami (Composer); Mark Irwin, A.S.C., C.S.C. (Director of Photography); Patrick Lussier (Editor)

Casey answers the ringing telephone. An eerie voice asks who it is, and Casey, thinking it a wrong number, hangs up. The phone rings again, and the person talks to Casey about scary movies and asks for her name again ("'Cause I wanna know who I'm looking at"). Casey, spooked, hangs up, but the person eventually threatens Casey, calling her "blondie" and expressing a desire to see her insides. Casey says her boyfriend will be there soon, but Steve is on the patio, duct-taped to a chair. The person has a game for Casey, and her first response of Michael as the killer for *Halloween* is correct, but she incorrectly cites Jason as the *Friday the 13th* killer. Steve is gutted, and Casey's final question is "What door am I at?" A chair flies through the window, and Casey sees a figure in the house and goes outside. She is attacked, chased and stabbed in the chest, and is not able to scream for her parents, who return home. The parents see the mess, and Casey's mother goes for the phone and hears Casey whimpering. Her husband tells her to get help. Outside, hanging from a tree, is their dead daughter.

Sidney is at her computer as her boyfriend Billy crawls through the window. He discusses their relationship, now "edited for TV," and they kiss a bit, and Billy leaves. The next day, reporters are flocking the school, and Tatum tells Sidney about the murders. Later, the two girls, Billy, Stu and Randy are sitting at a fountain, discussing who the murderer could be. Sidney avoids a TV news story, in which Gale Weathers talks of the rape and killing of Sidney's mother Maureen Prescott.

Her father out of town, Sidney is waiting for Tatum to pick her up; her friend calls and says she is running late. A subsequent call is from the killer, and they discuss scary movies and the possibility of the killer being near. Sidney, thinking it is Randy, says she is going to hang up, and the killer says if she does, she will die like her mother. Sidney hangs up and locks the door, and the killer comes out of the closet behind her. Sidney runs upstairs and calls 911 on her computer, and the killer is gone. Billy crawls through the window, and when he drops a phone, Sidney runs. Deputy Dewey, Tatum's brother, is at the door. Billy is arrested. At the station, Dewey tells Sidney that he cannot locate her father. Gale tries to interview Sidney outside, and after saying she will send Sidney a copy of her book, she receives a punch in the face from Sidney. At Tatum's house, the killer calls Sidney and mocks her.

In the morning, Dewey says that Billy was released because his phone bill was clean. At the school, Sidney talks to Gale about Cotton Weary, the man arrested for Maureen Prescott's murder. Gale did a story on Cotton's innocence, and she thinks that Sidney (who "fingered" the man) is now having doubts. Sidney sees Billy in the hallway, and he says she has not been the same since her mother died. He says he got over it when his mother left, and Sidney angrily walks away. In the bathroom, after Sidney listens to two girls talk about her "slut" mother, the

Sidney (Neve Campbell) receives another phone call from the quiz-loving knife-wielding killer, as friend Tatum (Rose McGowan) looks on, in Wes Craven's *Scream* (1996).

killer jumps out of one of the stalls and chases her. Gale flirts with Dewey and tries to get some information, and Principal Himbry announces that classes are suspended until further notice, in view of the murders. The principal hangs around his office and is, in due time, stabbed and killed.

In the video store, Randy talks to Stu about Billy being a murder suspect, and says that if the police watched *Prom Night*, they would know the formula of everyone as a suspect. Billy hears Randy say he is the killer, and he suggests Randy might be the murderer; Randy agrees. Sheriff Burke tells Dewey that the calls were made from Neil Prescott's phone and, since tomorrow is the anniversary of his wife's murder, they are looking for Sidney's father. Gale is outside the party at Stu's house, and Dewey asks her to join him in looking around inside. Kenny, Gale's cameraman, slips her a tiny camera to place in the house. Tatum goes to the garage, where she meets the killer. Tatum tries to escape through the garage's doggie door. She gets stuck, and she is crushed and killed when the killer opens the garage door.

When Billy arrives, he and Sidney go to talk in Stu's parents' room. They talk for a while, and their kissing progresses. Downstairs, Randy tells a group the rules of a horror film: No sex, drugs or drinking, and never say, "I'll be right back." Gale and Kenny are watching the tiny camera's work, and Dewey says he is looking for a car in the bushes and invites Gale along. Randy gets a call that the principal is hanging from the goal post on the football field, and the others leave to see. Gale and Dewey find Neil's car. Sidney and Billy put their clothes back on. Sidney still seems to think Billy might be the killer — until the killer appears and stabs her boyfriend. Sidney runs to a room, crawls out the window onto the roof and falls off when the killer grabs her. She looks up, and the killer is gone.

Sidney runs to Kenny's van, and they both see the killer behind Randy in the living room. Kenny opens the door, remembers the 30-second delay and is sliced across the throat. Sidney crawls out the back of the van and runs. Dewey runs to the house, and Gale goes to the van to call the sheriff and finds no Kenny. She sees blood and gets in the driver's seat, and Randy scares her. She drives and Kenny falls from the roof. To avoid hitting Sidney, Gale runs the van off the road and hits a tree. Dewey walks out of the house with a knife in his back, and the killer chases Sidney to Dewey's truck. Sidney tries to radio for help, and the killer comes in the back door. Sidney runs. At the door, Randy and Stu arrive, blaming each other for the killings as Sidney points Dewey's gun. She shuts the door on them both and helps a wounded Billy down the stairs. Billy takes the gun and lets Randy inside, where Randy says Stu has gone mad. Billy says, "We all go a little mad sometimes," and shoots Randy.

Billy tastes the corn syrup on his shirt, and Stu arrives, using a box to electronically alter his voice: "Surprise, Sidney." Billy says they framed Cotton for Maureen's murder, and he tells Sidney that, if she would like a motive, he blames her mother for his own mother leaving (she was sleeping with Billy's father). Stu brings out a restrained Neil. In order to play the parts of the survivors, Billy and Stu stab one another. Stu goes for the gun, but Gale has it, until Billy takes it from her and kicks her. Sidney and her father are gone, and Sidney calls Billy and says she called the cops. As Billy looks for Sidney, she comes out of the basement, stabbing him with an umbrella. Stu attacks, and Sidney hits him with a flower vase and drops a TV on his head. Randy is up, and Billy punches him down, lifts his knife over Sidney and is shot by Gale. Billy attacks one last time, and Sidney shoots him in the head. Sidney's father comes up from the basement, and the cops and ambulances arrive. Dewey is taken away on a stretcher, and Gale begins her report.

After a wonderfully tense opening, *Scream* loses some of its footing by the end, with a drawn-out concluding sequence that diminishes all remaining suspense. Williamson's script provides some fun film references, but most of them are so superficial they become presumptuous and excessive. Lillard, as the insane Stu, and Kennedy, as the movie-loving Randy, are both great and steal scene after scene. Look for actress Linda Blair and director Craven in cameos (Craven ostentatiously referencing his own 1984 movie *A Nightmare on Elm Street*).

Scream 2
(1997)

Written by Kevin Williamson; Directed by Wes Craven; Dimension Films/Miramax Films/Craven-Maddalena Films/Konrad Pictures; 120 min.

Cast: Neve Campbell (Sidney Prescott); Courteney Cox (Gale Weathers); David Arquette (Dewey); Elise Neal (Hallie); Jerry O'Connell (Derek); Jamie Kennedy (Randy); Laurie Metcalf (Debbie Salt); Liev Schreiber (Cotton Weary); Timothy Olyphant (Mickey); Sarah Michelle Gellar (Cici); Jada Pinkett (Maureen); Duane Martin (Joel); Lewis Arquette (Chief Hartley); Rebecca Gayheart (Lois); Portia de Rossi (Murphy); Omar Epps (Phil); Paulette Patterson (Usher Giving Out Costumes); Marisol Nichols (Dawnie); Rasila Schroeder (Screaming Girl up Aisle); Heather Graham (*Stab* Casey); Roger L. Jackson ("The Voice"); Peter Deming (Popcorn Boy); Molly Gross, Rebecca McFarland (Theater Girls); Kevin Williamson (Cotton's Interviewer); Sandy Heddings-Katulka (Girl in Dorm Hallway); Dave Allen Clark (Reporter Outside Theater); Joe Washington, Angie Dillard, John Patrick, Stephanie Belt, Richard Doughty, Mark Oliver, Jennifer Watson, Shelly Benedict (Reporters); Craig Shoemaker (Artsy Teacher); Joshua Jackson, Walter Franks (Film Class Guys); Nina Petronzio (Film Class Mopey Girl); Cornelia Kiss (Coroner at Cici's House); Lucy Lin (ER Doctor); Philip Pavel (Officer Andrews); Timothy T. Hillman (Captain Down); Nancy O'Dell (Tori's Interviewer); Tori Spelling (Herself); Luke Wilson (*Stab* Billy); David Warner (Drama Teacher Gus Gold); Greg Meiss (Zeus); Adam Shankman (Ghost

Dancer); Jon Kristien Andersson, Carmen M. Chavez, Anne Fletcher, Erik Hyler, Sebastain Lacause, Lance McDonald, Sarah Christine Smith, Laurie Sposit, Ryan Lee Swanson (Dancers); Jack Baun (Tackled Cell Phoner); Corey Parker (Library Guy); Chris Doyle (Officer Richards); Jason Horgan, D.K. Arredondo, John Embry (Fraternity Brothers)

Crew: Bob Weinstein, Harvey Weinstein, Kevin Williamson (Executive Producers); Cary Granat, Richard Potter, Andrew Rona (Co-Executive Producers); Cathy Konrad, Marianne Maddalena (Producers); Daniel Lupi (Co-Producer); Marco Beltrami (Composer); Peter Deming (Director of Photography); Patrick Lussier (Editor)

At a preview for *Stab*, the movie based on Gale Weathers' *The Woodsboro Murders*, Phil and Maureen are standing in line. Maureen does not like scary movies, so she goes out to get some popcorn, and is scared by Phil on her way back to the theater. Maureen relaxes, and she goes back inside while Phil goes to the bathroom. Phil heads to a stall and puts his ear to the adjacent stall to hear some noise. The screaming-mask killer stabs through the wall and kills Phil. The killer returns to the theater and sits by Maureen in Phil's jacket. She clutches onto the killer, sees blood on her hands—and is stabbed. The killer keeps stabbing as Maureen makes her way through the cheering crowd. In front of the screen, Maureen screams and collapses.

At Windsor College, Sidney answers the phone to an eerie voice, and she reads off the idiot caller's name from the caller ID. Her roommate Hal turns on the TV, and Sidney sees Cotton Weary talking on *Current Edition* of being falsely accused of murder. The two girls learn of the recent killing. In film theory class, Randy and his fellow students discuss the validity of film sequels. Sidney talks to Randy, who thinks the murders are unrelated, and Sidney's new boyfriend Derek sees how she is doing. Reporter Debbie tries to interview Gale, and Dewey arrives and talks to Sidney about someone trying to "follow" Billy. Gale tries to interview Sidney, but she has Cotton with her, and an angry Sidney punches Gale. Dewey tells the reporter to leave Sidney alone. Gale talks to Dewey, who is upset about how he was written up in her book.

Sidney (a potential sorority member) goes with Hal to a party. Cici, the "sober sister," is at a sorority house alone. She receives a call and thinks it is a drunk Ted, but it is really the killer, who asks her if she would like to die that night. Cici is frightened when she hears a noise upstairs, and she walks outside, but has to walk back in the house when she cannot get through to campus security. Another sister answers the ringing phone and hands it to Cici, saying it is Ted. Cici realizes it is the killer, and she hangs up and sets the alarm. The killer calls again and then jumps out. Cici is thrown though a glass door, stabbed in the back twice and tossed over a balcony. The people at the nearby party go to see what the commotion is about. When Sidney goes inside for her jacket, the killer appears and chases her. Sidney gets out back, and Derek runs inside. Dewey arrives and finds Derek with a sliced arm.

Later, pal Mickey talks to Sidney, wondering why Derek would have gone back into the house. Dewey mentions to Derek the "convenience" that he was only cut and not killed. Gale, Dewey and the police surmise that the killer is duplicating the Woodsboro murders, and Chief Hartley says he has detectives following Sidney. In the cafeteria, Derek sings loudly to Sidney and gives her his Greek letters on a necklace. Randy and Dewey discuss the murders as a "sequel," and list the possible suspects, saying those who are not suspects—are targets. Sidney does a performance on stage, but she is frightened by visions of the killer around her. Derek talks to her backstage, and Sidney says she needs to be alone.

Gale, Dewey and Randy are talking on the campus, and Randy answers the phone to the killer ("It's him!"). Dewey says to keep the killer on the phone, and he and Gale run around the courtyard, stopping everyone with cell phones. Randy mocks the killer for imitating Billy and Stu (whom he considers incompetent), and he is pulled into Gale's news van and stabbed to a bloody death. Sidney is at the library on a computer, and she gets a message (without being signed on) that says "You're going to die tonight./The police can't save you." She tells the nearby detectives that the killer is in the library, and they look around. Cotton talks to Sidney about doing a show with him, saying he deserves such exposure after having his name dragged through the mud. The detectives spot and arrest him.

Outside the station, reporters try to talk to Cotton. Gale tells Debbie to leave her alone. Gale's cameraman Joel gives her the camera and footage and says good bye. Gale suggests to Dewey that they watch crowd reactions to see if the killer is returning to the scenes of slayings. In the video archives, Dewey and Gale watch some video, apologize to one another and kiss—until another monitor comes on and plays video of the now-dead people. Dewey runs after the killer, and the killer chases Gale. While the reporter is hiding in a room, the killer attacks Dewey and kills him; Gale sees them through the glass. The killer tries to break the shatterproof glass, Gale screams, and then the killer is gone.

The detectives lead Sidney and Hal to their car, and Derek provides his girlfriend with a good bye kiss. Derek's frat brothers grab him and take him to the theater, where he is strapped to an onstage prop and tormented for giving Sidney his Greek letters. At a stoplight, the killer punches through the window and slashes the throat of the driving detective. The other dick gets out of the car, and the killer gets behind the wheel and drives. The detective lands on the hood, and the killer drives until crashing and killing the man. Sidney pulls the partially punctured gate down, and she and Hal both manage to crawl past the killer and out the driver's side window. They run, Sidney goes back to see who the killer is, and Hal is killed. Gale is scared by a bloody Cotton, who says he found Dewey. She runs outside where Debbie is on the phone, and tells her that Cotton is the killer. Sidney hears loud music and runs to the theater. On stage, the music stops, and the spotlight is turned on. Derek comes down on the prop, and Sidney starts to untie him. Derek says the killer is there.

The killer arrives and pulls off his mask to reveal Mickey ("Surprise, Sidney"). After he calls Derek "partner," Sidney seems reluctant to set him free. Mickey shoots Derek in the chest, and he mocks Sidney for not trusting her boyfriend. He says he wants to get caught and is going to blame the movies when he is on trial. Gale walks in, followed by Debbie with a gun ("Mrs. Loomis!"). Debbie is Billy's mother, and she shoots and kills the superfluous Mickey. Mickey's gun fires, and Gale is hit, falling off the stage. Debbie's motive is revenge for Sidney killing her son, and she blames Sidney's mother for ruining her family. Sidney runs and eludes Debbie for a while, but the killer holds the knife against her. Cotton shows up and fires a gun in the air. Debbie holds the knife against Sidney's throat and says if Sidney lives, Cotton will not be the lead story. Sidney finally agrees to do a show with Cotton, so he shoots Debbie. Cotton gives Sidney the gun, and they help a wounded Gale onto the stage. Mickey jumps up, and Sidney and Gale shoot him multiple times. Sidney shoots Debbie in the head ("Just in case"). Cops and reporters are there, and Dewey is still alive. Sidney points reporters towards Cotton, saying he is the hero. He hands reporters a card and says, "It'll make a helluva movie."

Following the success of the first *Scream* film, *Scream 2* was quickly completed and rushed into theaters the following year. The speedy production shows in the film, with a weak opening and an even weaker conclusion. Regardless, Kennedy as Randy is still terrific. The surfeit of film references that saturated the first *Scream* is toned down a bit. In the film, Randy says that sequels are always inferior, and *Scream 2* is further proof of his contention.

Scream 3
(2000)

Written by Ehren Kruger; Directed by Wes Craven; Dimension Films/Craven-Maddalena Films/Konrad Pictures; 117 min.

Cast: Neve Campbell (Sidney Prescott); David Arquette (Dewey Riley); Courteney Cox-Arquette (Gale Weathers); Parker Posey (Jennifer Jolie); Patrick Dempsey (Mark Kincaid); Liev Schreiber (Cotton Weary); Beth Toussaint (Female Caller); Roger L. Jackson ("The Voice"); Kelly Rutherford (Christine); Julie Janney (Moderator); Richmond Arquette (Student); Lynn McRee (Maureen Prescott); Nancy O'Dell, Ken Taylor (Reporters); Scott Foley (Roman Bridger); Roger Corman (Studio Executive); Lance Henriksen (John Milton); Josh Pais (Wallace); Deon Richmond (Tyson Fox); Matt Keeslar (Tom Prinze); Jenny McCarthy (Sarah Darling); Emily Mortimer (Angelina Tyler); Patrick Varburton (Steven Stone); John Embry (Stage Security Guard); Lawrence Hecht (Mr. Prescott); Lisa Beach (Studio Tour Guide); Kevin Smith (Silent Bob); Jason Mewes (Jay); Erik Erath (Stan); D.K. Arredondo (Office Security Guard); Lisa Gordon (Waitress); Heather Matarazzo (Martha Meeks); Jamie Kennedy (Randy Meeks); Carrie Fisher (Bianca); C.W. Morgan (Mr. Loomis)

Crew: Bob Weinstein, Harvey Weinstein, Cary Granat, Andrew Rona (Executive Producers); Stuart M. Besser (Co-Executive Producer); Cathy Konrad, Kevin Williamson, Marianne Maddalena (Producers); Dixie J. Capp, Julie Plec, Dan Arredondo (Co-Producers); Nicholas C. Mastandrea (Associate Producer); Marco Beltrami (Composer); Peter Deming, A.S.C. (Director of Photography); Patrick Lussier (Editor)

Cotton Weary, host of the talk show *100% Cotton*, is in a traffic hold-up, complaining about his cameo in a "slasher flick." He gets a call on another phone from a woman with a wrong number, and she realizes it is Cotton. She talks about a girlfriend, and the voice changes to a man who says he will kill his girlfriend Christine if he does not tell him where Sidney is. Cotton speeds away. Christine, at home, hears Cotton's voice and is chased to a room, where Cotton yells through the door and says he wants to rip out her insides. Cotton comes through the front door, sees knife punctures in the door at the end of the hallway and gets inside, where Christine swings at him with a golf club. He sees the killer behind her and tries to tell Christine, but she swings again and hits him in the head. The killer stabs Christine in the back and struggles with Cotton until the talk show host is stabbed. The killer says that Cotton should have said were Sidney was, and the knife is lifted and swung.

Sidney walks into her house and gets on the phone for a woman's crisis counseling center, where she advises a caller. Detective Mark Kincaid goes to see Gale (whom Mark considers a "Woodsboro expert") and asks who the woman is in a picture found on Cotton's corpse. Gale says it is a young Maureen Prescott. Sidney learns the news of the murdered Cotton. At Sunrise Studios, currently producing *Stab 3: Return to Woodsboro*, security is tightened. At the studio, Gale meets Jennifer, who is playing Gale in the movie. Dewey, the technical adviser, is there, and Gale talks about the photo of Maureen. Producer John Milton has Gale taken off the set.

That night, Sidney has a vision of her ghostly mother at the window and then the screaming-masked killer breaking through. Sarah goes to the studio the next day to meet with Roman Bridger, the director of *Stab 3*. He telephones, and Sarah complains about her character of Candy, who dies second and is only in two scenes. Roman's voice changes, and the killer threatens Sarah. Seeing an approaching shadow at the door, she runs and hides in a room of the killer's costumes. She is greeted by the killer and stabbed in the back. Dewey tells Gale that a person claiming to be from *Stab 3* tried to get information on Sidney for "research," and that files were ransacked (Dewey had already taken Sidney's).

Jennifer beeps Dewey, and Gale follows him there. Jennifer is upset about the second murder. The actors are being killed in the order their characters die, and, according to the script, "Gale" is next. Gale talks to Mark, who tells her that there are three different versions of the script, with three different characters being killed next. Roman denies calling Sarah and asking her to meet him, but he is taken away by the police. Sidney gets a call and answers as Laura (her counseling name), and a woman says she has killed someone. Sidney realizes she is not on the office line, and the killer (claiming to be "Mother") tells her to turn on the news, where she learns of the new murder. The voice becomes a man, and Sidney looks around with a gun.

Stab 3 is canceled, and the jobless actors convene in Jennifer's house. Gale arrives and tells Dewey that Roman was released because his cell phone was cloned. She says she cannot find anything on Sidney's mother from the time the photographs were taken. Dewey realizes that the second photograph found resembles a Jennifer head shot (same background). Stone, Jennifer's bodyguard, looks in Dewey's nearby trailer and is killed. Dewey and Gale find the actors Jennifer, Tom and Angelina, and a wounded Stone stumbles near the front door and collapses. The lights go out, and they go outside and hear the Faxphone ringing. The killer sends "rewrites" and says one person will be granted mercy. They run out, and Tom goes into the dark house, lights a lighter and learns that the mercy will be for whoever smells the gas. The house explodes, and the people roll down an incline. Dewey stands and shoots at the killer by Gale. Jennifer joins the two, and they find another picture of Maureen with "*I killed her*" on the back.

Sidney shows up at the station, telling them that the killer called her. Gale and Dewey go to show Sidney where one of the photos of Maureen was taken, and the group meets Martha, Randy's sister, who shows them a video of her brother talking of trilogies, involving an "unexpected back-story" and the past coming back. Jennifer tells Gale she is now following her around everywhere since the killer is looking for her, and they both go to the archives. They learn that Maureen was Rina Reynolds in films, and she starred in three Milton-produced features. Sidney walks onto the studio, which is a replica of her house, and she is attacked and chased by the killer. She falls out the window.

Gale, Dewey and Jennifer talk to Milton about Maureen/Rina, and he finally admits to his "private room" from the '70s, in which aspiring actresses would meet men for roles. With Rina, something got "out of hand." Dewey gets a call from Sidney, who says she is going to Roman's birthday party, but Sidney is not there. Roman and Jennifer go to look for Milton's private screening room, and Tyson and Angelina walk together. Roman walks into the basement as Jennifer stands at the top of the steps. Dewey punches in caller ID on his phone, and he and Gale discover a phone and costume in the closet. Gale goes to the basement and finds Roman with a knife in his chest and a frightened Jennifer nearby. They run and tell Angelina that Roman is dead, and the actress freaks, runs the other way and is killed. The group struggles with the killer, Tyson is stabbed in the stomach and Jennifer hides in the closet, inadvertently discovering a secret passage. Tyson is chased and thrown over a balcony. Jennifer is chased through corridors and killed, despite her claim that she plays the killer in *Stab 3*.

Gale calls for help, is grabbed and falls into the basement. Dewey runs to the basement, the knife is thrown, and the handle hits him on the head; he falls down the steps. Sidney is waiting in Mark's office, and she answers the phone to her own voice, which changes into the killer, who tells her about Gale and Dewey and asks if she wants to know who killed her mother. Sidney steals keys and a gun. At the house she is called again and told to use a metal detector and throw the gun in the pool. She goes to her tied friends and shoots the killer with another gun. The killer is gone when she looks again, and Mark is there. The killer stabs the detective, and Sidney runs and finds the private room, where a video of her mother is shown.

The killer shows up, and Roman takes off the mask. He is Rina's son, and after tracking her down and having the door slammed in his face, he showed Billy the video of Maureen with Billy's father. ("I'm a director, Sid. I direct.") He brings out Milton and cuts his throat. The siblings struggle, and Mark gets in the room and is knocked out. Roman shoots Sidney, but she is wearing a vest, and she gets an icepick and stabs Roman in the back and chest. Dewey and Gale get inside, Roman stands, and Dewey fires relentlessly until finally hitting Roman in the head. At Sidney's house, Dewey proposes to Gale. Sidney walks inside and decides not to punch in the alarm code. The door opens, and she walks away from it.

Scream 3 is an adequate slasher, not adding anything particularly interesting to the series (the brother subplot is tottery at best), but certainly no worse than the first sequel. Parker Posey is, as usual, charming and irresistible. Keep an eye out for very funny cameos from B-movie filmmaker Roger Corman, actress Carrie Fisher and from Jason Mewes and Kevin Smith (a.k.a. Jay and Silent Bob).

Scream Bloody Murder (*The Captive Female; Claw of Terror; Matthew*) (1973)

Written by Larry Alexander and Marc B. Ray; Directed by Marc B. Ray; First American Films; 85 min.

Cast: Fred Holbert (Matthew); Leigh Mitchell (Vera); Robert Knox (Mack Parsons)

Crew: Alan Roberts (Executive Producer); Marc B. Ray (Producer); Bob Mitchell, Larry Alexander (Associate Producers); Rockwell (Composer); Stephen Burum (Director of Photography); Alex Furke (Editor)

As a man works on a bulldozer, a young boy gets on the machine, drives and runs him over. Unable to stop the bulldozer, he jumps off, and his arm is run over. The boy is taken away to St. Jude's Mental Hospital.

An older Matthew (with a hook for a hand) reads a letter from his mother Daisy, who talks of her guy friend, Mr. Parsons. Matthew arrives home and sits on the front porch swing, and a newlywed Daisy and Mack Parsons are dropped off. An irate Matthew says that he will not let his mother love Mack, and he runs away. Later, Matthew angrily watches Mack and Daisy kiss. Daisy leaves, and Mack goes to check on a cow, as Matthew and an axe follow. Daisy sees that Matthew is not in his room, and an axe is swung into Mack's chest. Daisy finds her son dragging the dead Mack, and Matthew says that she did not need Mack. An upset Daisy is thrown to the side, her head hits a rock and she dies ("Momma!").

Matthew goes to the gas station and tells Mr. Simpson, the attendant, that he is leaving because his mother does not need him any more. He hitches a ride with the eloping Brenda and Lex, and the group stop for a wade in the creek. Matthew sees images of his dead mother and stepfather, and he throws rocks at Lex and pounds him in the head. Brenda is upset, and as she lies face down in the water, Matthew pulls her up and still sees his mother. He runs and hears voices in his head, and he hitches a ride. Matthew goes to see Vera, who is painting on her porch. Matthew asks to stay there. A sailor arrives at Vera's door, and the two go inside. Matthew looks through the window and sees his mother with a man, and he destroys Vera's painting, takes the pallet knife and sits behind the building.

When night falls and the sailor leaves, Matthew follows him to the dock. He stops the sailor, and Matthew swipes his face, stabs his hand, slits his throat and tosses the body off the bridge. Matthew returns to Vera and says the sailor ruined her picture and stole her "painting knife" (which he gives back). Matthew tells a disbelieving Vera that his father is rich and that he can take care of her so that she will not have to be with men. Vera agrees to visit Matthew sometime. The next day, Matthew approaches a large estate and talks his way inside by telling the maid that his car broke down and that other people will not let him inside because he is a "cripple." In the kitchen, Matthew feigns a call to the auto repair shop as the maid chops a chicken with a cleaver. She goes to the door and responds to the call of an elderly woman, and Matthew now has the cleaver. ("I'm sorry, lady. I need the house.") He chops her, heads upstairs and smothers the woman with a pillow. He leads the dog to the kitchen table and kills it.

Matthew takes Vera to his antique car and drives her to his "mansion." He asks her to move in, and he shows her a nice area where she can paint. Vera says she is fine as an amateur painter and part-time prostitute and that she cannot live with Matthew. Matthew holds Vera to keep her from leaving. She pushes him away, heads for the door and falls down the stairs. Later, Vera is tied and gagged on the bed, and Matthew tells her he will be back soon. Matthew goes around town mugging people so that he can buy groceries, art supplies and clothes for Vera. He shows Vera her new things, and says that the sailor would not buy anything. He also mentions cutting the man's throat for Vera. He says Vera will learn to count on Matthew for everything.

Vera is tied to a chair as Matthew feeds her. He threatens to cut out her tongue if she does not continue. Vera is upset that Matthew keeps calling her Daisy, and she cries. Vera is left alone, and she crawls out under the rope and jumps around with her feet and hands tied. She tries getting to the door as a young boy selling candy rings the doorbell. Then she goes for the ringing phone, hangs up and turns the rotary with her tongue. Matthew returns, says "Wrong number," and hangs up the phone. Later, Vera is in front of a blank canvas and refuses to paint (Matthew has her on a leash). The doorbell rings, and she tries to scream for help, but Matthew puts a gag over her mouth and puts her in the closet with the two corpses. Doctor Epstein, the elderly woman's doctor, is at the door. Skeptical of Matthew's claim that he is a nephew, he lets himself in and looks around. He hears Vera banging with her feet and opens the closet. He is bonked on the head with a statue.

Vera says she would like to take a bath, and Matthew reluctantly agrees. She takes her clothes off in the bathroom and mocks the nervous man ("Poor Matthew!"). After she bathes, Vera pulls the hook off of the bathroom door and goes outside. In the bedroom, the towel-adorned Vera talks about the both of them making love and offers to "teach" Matthew. But as they lie down, Matthew sees his ghastly mother and wraps his hand around Vera's neck. Vera hits him with the hook and runs. At the front door, Matthew cuts Vera in the neck with his hook. The corpse-like Daisy beckons Matthew, and Matthew runs, steals a car and gets to a church, where dead people are all around. As they crowd around him, Matthew stabs his stomach with his hook hand, crawls to the altar and dies in the empty church.

Scream Bloody Murder has a great beginning, and it is fun to watch Matthew's killing spree. Unfortunately, the scenes with Vera as his prisoner are tiring and are perhaps more amusing than horrific.

Shriek If You Know What I Did Last Friday the Thirteenth (2000)

Written by Sue Bailey and Joe Nelms; Directed by John Blanchard; Rhino Films; 86 min.

Cast: Julie Benz (Barbara); Harley Cross (Dawson Dreary); Majandra Delfino (Martina); Simon Rex (Slab O'Beef); Danny Strong (Boner); Coolio (Principal Interest/The Administrator Formerly Known as Principal); Aimee Graham (Screw Frombehind); Shirley Jones (Nurse Kevorkian); Rose Marie (Mrs. Tingle); David Herman (Mr. Lowelle); Tiffani-Amber Thiessen (Hagitha Utslay); Tom Arnold (Deputy Doughy); Chris Palermo (The Killer); Kim Greist (Mrs. Peacock); Steven Anthony Lawrence (Chuckie); Martin Diggs (Cameraman); Mink Stole (Madame La Tourneau);

Artie Lange (Coach Hasselhoff); Kirstin Herold (Tiffany); Renée Graham (Amber); Joe Nelms (Inmate); Sue Bailey (Female Prison Guard); Douglas Fisher (Maitre d'); George E. Roberts (Cabin Man); Kai Ephron (Counselor); Laurel Green, Karen Hartman (Teachers); Jonathan Pressin, Ryan Francis (Drivers Ed Students); Alanna Ubach (Ms. Grossberg); John Gocha (Fisherman); Gavin Grazer (Pizza Guy); Jimmie Walker (Pimp); Christian Everhard (Beefy Boy); Palom Parfrey (Grown-Ups' Lead Singer); Lily Marlene (Guitar Player); Danica O'Brien (Bass Player); Anika Stephen (Saxophone Player); Amy Wood (Drummer); Nicholas Lanier (Kid with Phone); Khrystyne Haje (Sexy Doctor)

Crew: Robert Shaw, Harold Bronson, Richard Foos (Executive Producers); Stephen Nemeth, Andrew Ooi (Producers); Tyler Bates (Composer); David Miller (Director of Photography); Richard LaBrie (Editor)

A girl named Screw is on the phone, and a call beeps in. The caller ID says "The Killer" is on the private line, and Screw answers ("Dad?"). The Killer asks her about scary movies, and asks to play a game involving an intricate math problem. Screw hangs up and puts more icing on a giant cake behind her. She answers the phone again and gets a collect call from The Killer, who is now in the house. He says if she does not get the next question, she is dead: "Who is buried in Grant's tomb?" Screw incorrectly answers Hugh Grant, and The Killer jumps out of the cake and chases her until the phone rings. The Killer answers and gives Screw the phone ("It's Stacy"). Screw is chased outside and runs into a bug zapper. The Killer lights a cigarette and accidentally sets fire to the hockey mask, which melts into a scream mask.

Dawson is registering at Bulmia Falls High School, and "New Kid" is taped to his back. Dawson meets Martina, Slab, Barbara and Boner (pronounced *Bonner*; the O is short). Martina tells the others about Screw's murder. Outside, the group sees Hagitha from Empty V News, who has written the book *Dawson Is a Murderer*, inspired by Dawson's family being murdered under mysterious circumstances while Dawson was at camp. Dawson punches the reporter. Doughy, mall security, helps her up and argues with his sister Barbara. The students go to class, and the janitor sweeps up the dead bodies in the hallway.

In class, Martina gets a note (From the Desk of The Killer): "I no what you did last summer." She corrects it, and thinks to the night when she and her friends hit a deer; she sees a **No Dumping** sign and remembers she forgot to give her grandmother her laxative. In swimming class, Mr. Hasselhoff has Boner act like the victim; the group makes fun of Boner and he passes out. He wakes up with a note in his trunks: "I know what you did last semester." He recalls the deer-hitting night and remembers that he had forgotten to deliver a letter for his brother on Death Row. Slab gets a note at his locker: "I know what you did last Chanukah." He thinks of seeing a **No Smoking** sign and recollects inadvertently smoking the ashes of his dead uncle. Barbara's note (from her bra) is "I know what you did last period" and she remembers removing a tag that was not supposed to be removed.

The group of friends are at lunch, and Dawson finally gets a note (in his hamburger) that tells him he "may already be a victim." He thinks back to Labor Day when, dressed as a deer, he was pummeled by the four friends and dumped in the water. Dawson reminds everyone that it is Halloween, and after coming up with possible reasons as to why anyone from the group would want to kill their friends, they agree to stay together and go to Slab's house that night. Barbara is attacked by The Killer in the bathroom and gets away.

Slab is working on a car in a garage. The Killer drives towards him as he screams against a wall, but The Killer is pulled over by a cop. Martina is running track, and The Killer is behind her. He gets the lead and wins a race. Boner drills a hole into the bathroom and peeks through and sees The Killer showering. A knife is shoved through the hole, and Boner runs away.

In Sex Education class, Dawson goes to

put fuel in the film projector. The Killer appears in the room, and jumps him and but Dawson gets away. The Administrator Formerly Known as Principal is enjoying the hot tub when The Killer arrives. The Administrator stands and is hit by something thrown through the window. He falls into the tub and is electrocuted. The group of people congregate at "The Deserted Location," and Doughy is outside in a golf cart. Hagitha shows up with her cameraman.

While Martina gives the rules on how to survive a "parody situation," The Killer heads upstairs, where Boner is in a room with a drunk, sleeping female. Boner has a heart attack and flatlines. Barbara goes to the refrigerator in the garage, throws things at The Killer and tries to crawl out of the doggie door. The Killer tries to close the door, but a man outside trying to use his garage door opener is making the door move up and down. Barbara pulls out her breast implants and gets through. Barbara runs, but is surrounded by bees and stung until her head swells up and she dies. Martina and Dawson go to Slab's room, where he explodes into tiny bloody pieces, having overdosed on steroids. The Killer arrives and chases the couple around the house while Doughy, Hagitha, her cameraman, and the pizza guy play strip poker outside. Martina finally punches The Killer and he lands on the stairs.

Dawson begins pulling numerous masks from The Killer. Doughy, having heard a noise, goes inside with Hagitha. Dawson gets to the last one, and Doughy's evil twin cousin Hardy is there (looking just like Doughy, except with a mustache drawn on his face). Doughy tells his cousin he is a "disgrace" and goes to hug him. Hardy is shot and killed by Hagitha using a gun as a mirror, and she accidentally shoots her cameraman as well and leaves with the pizza guy. Boner is alive and taken away on a stretcher. The Killer is being taken away and sits up, only to be shot by Doughy. Dawson asks Martina to go for a "walk in the dark scary woods," and he ignores the ringing phone.

The Killer is nearby on a pay phone, and he follows the couple.

Like *Cherry Falls*, *Shriek If You Know What I Did Last Friday the Thirteenth* was pushed away from theaters and debuted on the USA network. However, unlike *Cherry Falls*, it is understandable why *Shriek* never made it to theaters. With an overabundance of pedestrian jokes, it is one of the more boring slasher parodies.

Silent Madness (aka *Beautiful Screams; The Nightkillers; The Omega Factor*) (1984)

Written by Robert Zimmerman, William P. Milling and Nelson Demille; Directed by Simon Nuchtern; Mag Enterprises; 92 min.

Cast: Belinda Montgomery (Joan Gilmore); Viveca Lindfors (Mrs. Collins); Solly Marx (Howard Johns); Sydney Lassick (Sheriff Liggett); David Greenan (Mark McGowan); Roderick Cook (Doctor Michael Kruger); Stanja Lowe (Doctor Margaret Anderson); Ed Van Nuys (Doctor Roger Vandice); Dennis Helfend (Virgil); Philip Levy (Jesse); Tori Hartman (Pam); Katherine Kamhi (Jane); Katie Bull (Cheryl); Rick Aiello (Michael); Jeffrey Bingham (John Howard); John Bentley (Romano Hunter); Paul DeAngelo (Paul); Lori-Nan Engler, Shelly Gibson, Conni Brunner, Michaelene Donati (Flashback Girls); Kathleen Ferguson (Ruth Flannery); William Gibberson (TV Reporter); James Glenn (Professor); Henry Hayward (Mr. Hackler); Elizabeth Kaitan (Barbara); Cindy Lloyd (Skateboarder); Paige Price (Lorraine); Sloane Shelton (Anne Swenson); Bill Shuman (Ralph); Stacey Simms (Stacey); Daisy White (Susan); Noreen Collins (Megan); Marjorie Apollo, Lauren McCann (College Girls); Susan Mordfin (Hand); Chiara Peacock, Kim Plumridge, Laurie Wilson (Pledges)

Crew: Gregory Earls (Executive Producer); Mark Slater, Robert Gallagher (Associate Producers); William P. Milling, Simon Nuchtern (Producers); Barry Salmon (Composer); Gerald Feil (Director of Photography); Philip Stockton (Editor)

At the Cresthaven Mental Hospital, Romano, a patient, seems to think he is going home. Doctor Joan Gilmore asks Doctor Vandice if he signed release papers for Romano, and he responds affirmatively, saying that he and Doctor Kruger believe he is ready for release. Joan thinks they have been releasing too many disabled patients, but Doctor Anderson tells her it is necessary for the hospital to have fewer patients. Later, Kruger sees a John Howard and demands to know why the patient was not released, but Vandice assures him that he added the name to the list. Joan gets on Kruger's computer and sees that a Howard Johns was mistakenly released instead. Somewhere near a lake, Johns approaches a van with a couple kissing inside. He bashes his sledgehammer against the van until the man comes out with a hatchet and is rewarded with a pummeled head. When the woman runs, Johns throws the hatchet, hitting her in the back.

Joan goes to Ward L, where the "paranoid" and "dangerous" Johns was held. Virgil, who refers to the patients inside as "the living dead," tells her she needs permission from Kruger to be let inside. Barbara is leaving her sorority, Delta Omega, to go on vacation, but she only skateboards a few yards before being grabbed by Johns, who takes her somewhere and crushes her head in a vice. Joan gets a key to Ward L and looks at all the patients strapped to tables or inside plastic bags. She finds Johns' empty bed. Virgil and Jesse see her and tell the doctor to leave. Joan goes to see Kruger and she tells him about Johns' accidental release. He tells her not to worry, and that he will let Doctor Anderson know about the situation.

At Delta Omega, a few of the girls are remaining before vacation time. Lorraine playfully feigns a striptease for the others, profoundly disturbing the elderly housemother, Mrs. Collins. Lorraine goes down to the cellar and boiler room, where she is attacked and killed by Johns. At a meeting in Doctor Anderson's office, Kruger says Johns has died, and that the mistake concerned a patient deceased, not released. Joan is not convinced, and Doctor Anderson suggests that she take the weekend off.

Joan heads to the police station in Barrington, the place of the sorority murders (the crime for which Johns was locked away). She asks to see the police records concerning Johns. Sheriff Liggett tells her to check the newspaper. Joan goes to the newspaper office, where she meets Mark and discusses Johns and the killings at the sorority. Mark suggests that Joan pretend to be "an ex-sorority girl" (Ann, who works at the paper, has a sorority ring) and stay there for a few days to get some information. Joan goes to Delta Omega, and Mrs. Collins agrees to let her stay. Joan tries to get some details on the "sorority slaughter," and talks with the housemother. Mrs. Collins mentions her dead son Frances, and Joan gets her to tell the story of the murders. The housemother says Johns, the custodian, was watching the girls during pledge week. When they saw him, they sat him in a chair and teased and humiliated him. He retaliated by shooting all four sisters with a nailgun.

The next morning at breakfast, Cheryl offers to show Joan where the murders took place. They go to the boiler room, where they encounter Mr. Hackler, the security guard. The two females visit the luggage room (Cheryl complains about the stink), and Joan stays to investigate some more. She meets Johns there, weasels her way out of his clutches and finds Hackler. When Hackler looks for Johns, he is gone. Joan calls Doctor Anderson and tells her she has found Johns. Anderson offers to send some people, but Joan says she can get Johns herself. Joan and Mark tell the sheriff, but he says he telephoned the hospital and they said Johns was dead. Kruger returns Liggett's call, and even Doctor Anderson says Johns is dead; they Fax the death certificate to the sheriff. Mark now doubts Joan, and Joan walks out of the office. At the hospital, Anderson discusses having claimed that the patient is dead, and she demands that Virgil and Jesse go the Barrington and find Johns. Krugar later tells the two to bring back both Johns and Doctor Gilmore.

Back at the sorority, Joan and Mark see

a car with a flat tire. Sorority girl Jane wants to leave, and she asks Joan to take her to the lake, where her sister and her boyfriend are camping. Mark agrees to do so, and Joan stays with Cheryl and Pam. Mark and Jane discover the dead couple at the lake and they head to his place, where he tries to telephone the sheriff. He tells Jane to keep trying, loads his gun and speeds over to the sorority. Back at Delta Omega, Joan goes to bolt the cellar door. Pam is hanging upside down on a bar, and she does not hear Johns murder Cheryl over the loud video game Cheryl was playing. Pam sees Johns, and he knocks her out, letting her hang. He ties a jump rope around Pam's neck and ties a barbell to the other. Pam screams for Joan and Joan runs to her rescue, but not before Johns throws the weight out of the window and Pam dies.

Virgil and Jesse, having followed Mark to the sorority, knock him out and throw him in the back of the ambulance. They head inside and run after Joan, and there is a struggle when Johns appears. He beats Virgil and Jesse, and Joan runs out of the room, trips over a medical bag and falls down some stairs. Johns binds her underneath a giant drill in the boiler room. Virgil and Jesse find Joan "wrapped up like a Christmas present." Johns attacks, and they hit him with a cattle prod. Jesse "consoles" the restrained Joan, and he tells Virgil to turn on a light. Virgil hits a switch and inadvertently drills a hole in Jesse's head. Joan gets free and runs while Virgil is attacked by Johns, who stabs him with a crowbar.

Johns chases Joan around the boiler room. Once she is outside (after finding some dead bodies), Mark gives her the gun. Johns gets the gun away from her, and Joan runs inside and arms herself with a shard from a broken mirror. Johns follows. Mark is there with a gun, but he misses when he fires. Johns gets him on the floor, and Mrs. Collins walks inside and stops him, calling him Frances. Joan quickly stabs him with the mirror shard, and Mrs. Collins screams. A flashback shows the elderly woman shooting the sorority girls with the nailgun. Joan learns that Howard Frances Johns was Mrs. Collins' illegitimate son, and she had given him a job on campus to keep an eye on him. Joan and Mark get in her car and leave together.

Silent Madness is a sufficient slasher film, despite the ending chase sequence being a little dragged-out. Actors Helfend and Levy, as the erratic Virgil and Jesse, are a treat to watch. *Silent Madness* was originally filmed in 3-D, which is quite evident even without 3-D glasses.

Silent Night, Bloody Night (aka *Death House*) (1973)

Written by Theodore Gershuny, Jeffrey Konvitz and Ira Teller; Directed by Theodore Gershuny; Armor Films, Inc./Cannon Productions; 81 min.

Cast: Patrick O'Neal (John Carter); James Patterson (Jeffrey Butler); Mary Woronov (Diane Adams); Astrid Heeren (Ingrid); John Carradine (Towman); Walter Abel (Mayor Adams); Fran Stevens (Tess); Walter Klavun (Sheriff Mason); Phillip Bruns (Wilfred Butler, 1929); Staats Cotsworth (The Voice of Wilfred Butler); Ondine (Chief Inmate); Jay Garner (Doctor Robinson); Donelda Dunne (Marianne Butler, Age 15); Alex Stevens (Burning man); Lisa Richards (Maggie Daly); Grant Code (Wilfred Butler, Age 80); Debbie Parness (Marianne Butler, Age 8); Candy Darling, Charlotte Fairchild, Michael Pendrey, George Strus, Barbara Sand (Doctors and Guests); Tally Brown, Lewis Love, Harvey Cohen, Hetty MacLise, George Trakas, Susan Rothenberg, Cleo Young, Kristin Steen, Jack Smith, Leroy Lessane, Bob Darchi (Inmates)

Crew: Jeffrey Konvitz, Ami Artzi (Producers); Gershon Kingsley (Composer); Adam Giffard (Director of Photography)

On Christmas Eve, 1950, a man in flames runs from the house that Wilfred Butler built while a person plays organ music inside. Wilfred Butler was buried on New Year's Day, and his house was left to his grandson Jeffrey Butler. The house remained empty for 20 years, until Jeffrey finally decided to sell it.

At a hospital for the criminally insane, an inmate escapes with a wrench, runs into a car, and speeds away. John Carter, a lawyer from the city, arrives at the Butler estate with his girlfriend Ingrid. Diane drives by a man who is at the side of the road by a car (he beats the windshield). John goes to see Mayor Adams (Diane's father) about buying the house and meets newspaper publisher, Charlie Towman, "communications director" Tess Howard and Sheriff Bill Mason. The inmate arrives at the Butler house, kills a barking dog and walks inside. John tells the group that Jeffrey wants $50,000 in cash by the next day. Tess agrees to connect the phone line for John (who is staying at the Butler house), and John says he has never met Jeffrey and that the man simply called and left a key for him.

John and Ingrid return to the estate and, following a light dinner, head to the bedroom. Tess calls to be sure the phone is working, and John goes to the car for cigarettes and comes back with a tiny gift for Ingrid, which he says she cannot open yet. While the two lovers are in bed, the inmate walks in and chops away with an axe. The killer telephones the sheriff, saying John Carter is not at the house. Leading Mason to believe it is Jeffrey, he has the sheriff come out to the estate. Mason hangs up, and the killer tells Tess at the switchboard that it is Marianne and that the killer is waiting in her dad's house. Tess quickly calls Maggie and tells her to come over. The man Diane saw on the road finds John's car with keys in the ignition, and he drives it to Diane's house and knocks on the door. As Diane holds a gun on him, the man says he is Jeffrey Butler and shows her his identification. He says he wants to get into his house, and Diane says that the sheriff's deputy might have a key.

Tess tells Maggie that, if she has not returned in an hour, to call Mason or Towman and no one else. The sheriff arrives at the cemetery, finds a diary sitting by Wilfred Butler's grave and is whacked in the face with a shovel. Jeffrey returns to Diane's house and says that the deputy was not at home. Diane gets Jeffrey a drink and they talk about the house. She says that a woman keeps calling for her father and says she is waiting in the Butler house. Diane and Jeffrey drive together, and they find the sheriff's car and his sunglasses at the cemetery. The two go to see Towman, and he says that Tess has gone to the estate. Jeffrey and Towman drive to the house (leaving Diane at the newspaper office), but Towman drives to Tess' place, and, finding no Tess, he gets in his car and drives, leaving Jeffrey behind.

The killer calls Towman's office and, after Diane says her name, asks the woman to bring her father to the house. The killer says it is Marianne, and she has a diary, referring to Christmas Eve of 1935. Tess finds Mason's car by the house and calls out his name. She walks inside, and a flashlight is shone in her face. The killer tells her to not be scared and offers her a hand, which falls to the floor. Tess screams and the killer swings. Diane reads old newspapers and learns about Wilfred Butler's daughter Marianne being attacked and raped when she was 15. In 1935, Butler gave his house to Doctor Robinson to be made as an asylum, and he committed his daughter. Towman "cut out" the ending to the story.

Jeffrey returns to the office and Diane asks about his mother Marianne, whom Jeffrey was told died at childbirth. Jeffrey reads the papers, and Diane suggests that his mother is alive and waiting at the house. They drive and find Towman's car in flames. Further down the road, Jeffrey accidentally swipes Towman with the car. Jeffrey stops and sees that the man is dead, and he tells Diane that someone had cut off Towman's hands. They reach the house, and see Mason's car. Jeffrey goes inside as Diane waits. The killer calls Mayor Adams, tells of the "reunion" at the house and says that his daughter will be there. Adams picks up a shotgun.

Jeffrey finds a diary and reads of Marianne's child being taken away and sent to California. Doctors and guests lived in the house, and Wilfred was upset about the way the people acted. One day, as the doctors drank and danced, Wildfred went to Marianne's room (he admits to being the father of her child) and led her away. To save the patients from being "abused" further by the doctors, he freed the inmates. The crowd walked into the house and savagely murdered the doctors. As Wilfred went to the car, Marianne had slipped away, and the inmates, believing she was a doctor, killed her.

Diane walks into the house and Jeffrey tells her that Wilfred is still alive, making the town believe he was dead by frying a squatter. Jeffrey says that the sheriff, Tess, Towman and Diane's father were all inmates at the asylum. The mayor arrives, finds a body on the porch and screams. Diane gives Jeffrey her gun. As Mayor Adams walks inside, the two men shoot one another. At the top of the stairs, Wilfred appears, telling Diane ("Marianne") to not run away. A flashback shows a young Marianne running from her father. Diane goes to Jeffrey's side, grabs the gun and shoots Wilfred three times. Diane runs to a room and cries, leaving at daybreak. A year later, the Butler estate is being torn down.

Silent Night, Bloody Night has a lethargic pace, but it provides enough intrigue and mystery to help a viewer retain interest. Actress Woronov might be remembered from the cult film *Eating Raoul* (1982).

Silent Night, Deadly Night (1984)

Written by Michael Hickey; Directed by Charles E. Sellier, Jr.; Slayride, Inc.; 85 min.

Cast: Lilyan Chauvin (Mother Superior); Gilmer McCormick (Sister Margaret); Toni Nero (Pamela); Robert Brian Wilson (Billy at 18); Britt Leach (Mr. Sims); Nancy Borgenicht (Mrs. Randell); H.E.D. Redford (Captain Richards); Danny Wagner (Billy at 8); Linnea Quigley (Denise); Leo Geter (Tommy); Randy Stumpf (Andy); Will Hare (Grandpa); Tara Buckman (Mother/Ellie); Jeff Hansen (Father/Jimmy); Charles Dierkop (Killer Santa); Eric Hart (Mr. Levitt, Storekeeper); Jonathon Best (Billy at 5); A. Madeline Smith (Sister Ellen); Amy Stuyvesant (Cindy); Max Robinson (Officer Barnes); Vince Mass (Doug), Michael Alvarez (Jim); John Bishop (Bob); Richard Terry (Mac); Oscar Rowland (Doctor Conway); Richard D. Clark (Officer Miller); Tip Boxell (Officer Murphy); Angela Montoya (Girl on Santa's Lap); Mollie Cameron (Girl's Mother); Jayne Luke, Joan S. Forster, Betsy Nagel (Mothers in Store); Barbara Stafford, Paul Mulder (Teen Lovers at Orphanage); Spencer Ashby (Santa at Orphanage); J. Paul Broadhead (Santa in Store); Alex Burton (Ricky at 14); Max Broadhead (Ricky at 4); Melissa Best (Infant Ricky); Dan Rogers (Dispatcher); Spencer Alston, Kristi Ballard, Jacob Peterson, Jonathan Wilde, Susie Massa, Sarah Stuyvesant (Children at Orphanage)

Crew: Scott J. Schneid, Dennis Whitehead (Co-Executive Producers); Ira Ricahrd Barmack (Producer); Perry Botkin (Composer); Henning Schellerup (Director of Photography); Michael Spence (Editor)

It is Christmas Eve, 1971, and Jimmy and Ellie are driving in a car with little Billy in the backseat. They go to the Utah Mental Facility to visit Grandpa, who does not speak or really even seem to acknowledge their presence. When Billy is left alone with Grandpa, the elderly man talks to the boy, saying that Santa Claus punishes naughty children and that Billy had best run from Santa that night. Back in the car, Billy tells his parents what Grandpa said, and he says he is now scared of Santa. Meanwhile, a man dressed as Santa Claus robs a convenience store and kills the cashier when he goes for a gun. Jimmy sees Santa at the side of the road and pulls over, much to the dismay of Billy. Santa pulls a gun, Jimmy speeds away and Santa fires. Jimmy is dead. Billy runs out of the car as Santa pulls Ellie out, rips open her shirt and slits her throat. Infant Ricky cries inside the car. Santa calls out for Billy as he hides by the side of the road.

Three years later, Billy and Ricky are at St. Mary's Home for Orphaned Children. Billy is sent to see Mother Superior because of his drawing of knives sticking in Santa Claus and a reindeer. Mother Superior insists that the boy cannot remember the terrible incident, although Sister Margaret says he gets worse every Christmas. Later, Billy looks through a keyhole and sees a naked man and woman enjoying each other's company, and he flashes back to his mother. Mother Superior pushes him to the side, enters the room and whips the two lovers with a belt. She goes to see Billy outside and tells him what the couple did was naughty and that naughty people are always caught and punished. She whips Billy for leaving his room. Billy has a nightmare about his dead parents, and he screams and runs out of the room. Mother Superior stops him and ties him to the bed. Later, she tries to force Billy to sit on Santa's lap, but Billy punches Santa in the face, runs upstairs and cowers in his room.

In the spring of 1984, Sister Margaret convinces Mr. Sims to give 18-year-old Billy a job at Ira's Toys. Billy is a good worker, but after a while, his co-worker Andy says Billy seems to have an atitude and is not doing work. It is nearing Christmas, and Billy reacts badly to a Santa Claus in the store. Billy dreams of some intimate time with co-worker Pamela and being stabbed by Santa. Mrs. Randall tells Mr. Sims that they are short a worker and need someone to be Santa, and Sims opts for Billy ("Try not to scare the little bastards"). Later, a girl sits on Billy-Santa's lap and will not stop squirming until Billy whispers to her that he punishes naughty kids. That night, the workers of the store have a party, and Billy eyes Andy and Pamela as they walk away to the back of the store. Afterwards, a drunk Mr. Sims asks Billy if he remembers what Santa does on Christmas Eve ("Go get 'em, Santa!").

Billy follows Andy and Pamela to the stock room, where Andy rips Pamela's sweater and pushes her down. Billy flashes back to the Santa incident. He runs out ("Naughty!"), wraps lights around Andy's neck and chokes him. Pamela cries and says that Billy is crazy, and he stabs her in the stomach, then beats Mr. Sims with a hammer. Mrs. Randall finds a dead Sims and she runs for the phone. Billy swings an axe and Mrs. Randall runs and hides. She knocks Billy over, grabs the axe, and heads for the front of the store, where Billy perforates her with an arrow. He unlocks the doors and leaves. Later, Sister Margaret enters and sees the murdered group.

Tommy is banging Denise on the pool table, and Denise thinks she hears the cat outside. She goes upstairs, opens the front door and the cat comes inside. Billy suddenly appears with his axe ("Punish!"), and Denise slams the door. Billy axes his way in, struggles with Denise in the living room and impales her on deer horns on the wall. Tommy (who heard nothing due to loud music) goes upstairs and sees the mess. After a fight, Billy throws Tommy out of the window. Little Cindy appears ("Santa Claus!"), and Billy asks her if she has been good for the year. She replies affirmatively, and Billy gives her a straightedge for Christmas.

Two police officers, on the hunt for killer Santa, nearly shoot a father surprising his daughter. Doug and Jim are preparing to sled, but Bob and Mac muscle them away and go sledding. As one goes down, Billy jumps out and chops his head off, letting the head roll right after the sledding headless body. Captain Richards tells Sister Margaret there have been three more murders. She tells him there is a certain logic to the killings if the tragedy in Billy's life was taken into consideration. Richards says they should be able to predict his next move, and Sister Margaret suddenly thinks of the orphanage.

Officer Barnes reaches the orphanage and shoots and kills a Santa approaching the children (and very near Ricky), but he has shot the wrong person. He tells Mother Superior (now in a wheelchair) to stay in the building and not let anyone inside, and the officer goes to check the grounds. After checking the area, Office Barnes gets an axe in the chest. Little Andrew lets Billy-Santa inside, and Mother Superior tells the children to stay away from him. Billy tells the woman she is naughty, and his brother Ricky realizes who Santa is. Billy lifts the axe, and he is shot and killed by Richards. Billy falls, and the axe lands near Ricky, who angrily stares at Mother Superior and says, "Naughty!"

Silent Night, Deadly Night gained some

notoriety when originally released, due to ads featuring a killer St. Nick. The film is not bad, although the more dramatic parts of the film (involving Billy's traumatic childhood) are more interesting than the slasher section in the second half. Actor Wilson, in his film debut, is good as the murderous Billy.

Silent Night, Deadly Night, Part 2 (1987)

Written by Lee Harry and Joseph H. Earle; Directed by Lee Harry; Silent Night Releasing Corporation; 77 min.

Cast: Eric Freeman (Ricky Caldwell); James L. Newman (Doctor Henry Bloom); Elizabeth Cayton (Jennifer); Jean Miller (Mother Superior); Darrel Guilbeau (Ricky at 15); Brian Michael Henley (Ricky at 10); Corinne Gelfan, Michael Combatti (The Rosenbergs); Kenneth Bryan James (Chip); Ron Moriarty (Detective); Frank Novak (Loan Shark); Randy Baughman (Eddie); Joanne White (Paula); Lenny Rose (Loser); Nadya Wynd (Sister Mary); Kenneth McCabe (Rent-a-Cop); J. Aubrey Island (Orderly); Randy Post (Loudmouth in Theater); Kent Kopasse, Michael Marloe, Larry Kelman (Cops); Stephanie Babbit (Little Girl on Bicycle); Traci Odom, Jennie Webb (Nuns on Street); Janice Carlberg, Jher Tuner (Teen Lovers at Orphanage); Jill K. Allen (Mrs. Rosenberg's Friend); Delia Lambardo (Roxanne); Stephen L. Parks (Photographer); O.J. Ackson (Officer Jackson); Larry Kelman (Paramedic); Fred Griggs, Sally Bedding, Spud Plugman, Richard Levine, Dianne C. Weed, Amy Hamovitz (Moviegoers); John Fitzgibbons, Scottie Simpfender, Erin Davini, Lara Davini, Brian Davini (Kids at Play); Erika Lindquist (Saleslady); Harvey Genkins (Salvation Santa); Samurai Retz (Himself)

Cast: Lawrence Appelbaum (Producer); Eric A. Gage, Joseph H. Earle (Associate Producers); Michael Armstrong (Composer); Harvey Genkins (Director of Photography); Lee Harry (Editor)

Ricky is sitting in a room and smoking when an attendant enters and places a tape recorder on the table. Doctor Henry Bloom enters, puts tape in the machine, sets up a microphone and tells the attendant to leave. The doctor says he is the last chance for Ricky, and he begins his series of questions by asking him who killed his parents. Ricky tells him that Santa Claus was the killer, and tells the story of his parents' murders. He then talks of the stay at the orphanage, where Billy was "taught" about naughtiness and punishment, and where the boy was afflicted with nightmares. Henry switches the tape, and Ricky tells him about Billy's job at the toy store and his subsequent murderous rampage, concluding with his death at the orphanage.

Henry switches the tape again, and Ricky tells of how Sister Mary sent him to live with the Rosenbergs. While on the street with his foster mother Martha, Ricky is frightened by two approaching nuns, and when he sees red, he thinks of Santa's murders. Martha sees Ricky react to the gunshots in his mind, and she leads him away. Despite the incident, Sister Mary convinces the couple to keep watching Ricky. Five years later, Ricky's foster father Morty has died. Fifteen-year-old Ricky is out for a walk, and he sees a couple, Eddie and Paula, lying in the grass. Eddie is too forward with Paula, and he attacks and hits her ("Naughty!" Ricky says to himself). Paula hits Eddie in the crotch, and he goes for a beer at the Jeep. Ricky gets in the vehicle, starts it up and hits Eddie and rolls over him back and forth. Paula then thanks Ricky. The doctor writes down "Red Car!" on his notes.

Ricky says he could not go to college, so he got a job. While taking out the trash, he sees a loan shark trying to collect and beating a man in the alley. The loan shark wipes his face with a red handkerchief, and Ricky throws him and shoves an umbrella through his stomach. Henry wipes his own brow, eyes a red embroidered "B" on the handkerchief and quickly puts it away before Ricky sees it. Henry angers Ricky by asking about Jennifer, and he shows him a photograph of her. Ricky says she was the only one he cared about.

Ricky meets Jennifer when she accidentally bumps her car into his motorbike and knocks him over. They ride on Ricky's bike, and kiss and spend some personal time together. At the movie theater later, Ricky is annoyed by an idiot making noise. As he and Jennifer prepare to kiss, the idiot makes kissing sounds. Jennifer tells Ricky that the movie they are about to see concerns a guy who dresses as Santa and kills. Ricky, apparently inspired ("Punish!"), stands and leaves. Chip sits next to Jennifer and talks about their old relationship. She is mad that Chip cheated on her, and Chip mocks the muscular Ricky. In the back, the idiot is still talking constantly, but he finally shuts up when Ricky attacks him. Chip tells Jennifer that he will be home all summer and to call him, and he leaves with his date Roxanne. When Ricky returns, Jennifer wants to leave, but he says he is enjoying the film.

Later, Ricky and Jennifer are outside walking, and Chip is working on his red car. He makes fun of the two, and he holds onto Jennifer until Ricky confronts him. Chip mentions having had sex with Jennifer, and an enraged Ricky grabs him and shoves jumper cables in Chip's mouth and electrocutes him. Jennifer tells Ricky she hates him, so he rips off the car's antennae and chokes her. A cop arrives and points a gun at Ricky, but he turns the weapon and shoots the cop in the head. Ricky shoots a neighbor who is outside complaining about the noise and another neighbor taking out the trash. A little girl bumps into Ricky on her bicycle ("Excuse me, Mister!"), and Ricky says it is okay. He moves on and shoots at a moving red car, which crashes and explodes. Ricky laughs endlessly. When cops tell him to drop his weapon, he points it at his head and gets a click. Ricky tells Henry it was a shame he was stopped before he was finished, and he passes by the doctor, who is lying dead on the desk. Ricky walks out of the room and begins attacking people outside.

Sister Mary tells a lieutenant that Mother Superior had a stroke and retired and lives alone. Ricky kills a Salvation Santa, telephones Mother Superior from a pay phone and says, "Santa's back!" Ricky arrives at her house, axes his way through and calls for Mother Superior. She rolls her wheelchair into a room and slides a dresser in front of the door. As Ricky axes things around the house, she rolls out of the room and to the stairs, where Ricky attacks and causes her to fall down the stairs. She gets to a wheelchair at the bottom and tells "Richard" to come out and face her. She says she is not afraid and that Ricky is being naughty and needs to be punished. Ricky lifts the axe. The cops and Sister Mary arrive, and they find Mother Superior sitting at the table. Her head falls off. Ricky appears with his axe and is shot until he flies through the glass door. Sister Mary awakens from her faint ("It's over"), and turns and sees Mother Superior's head lying next to her. Sister Mary screams. Outside, Ricky opens his eyes.

The first 35 minutes of *Silent Night, Deadly Night, Part 2* is comprised almost entirely of flashbacks from the first film (to the point where, if planning a *Silent Night, Deadly Night* marathon, the first film may, conceivably, be excluded). The second half avoids a character study similar to the first film in favor of a corresponding killing spree, which, while not very much fun, does provide a few original killings (the umbrella murder, for instance). The movie that Ricky and Jennifer watch in the theater is, not surprisingly, *Silent Night, Deadly Night*.

Sisters
(1973)

Written by Louisa Rose and Brian De Palma; Directed by Brian De Palma; American International Pictures; 92 min.

Cast: Margot Kidder (Danielle Breton/Dominique Blanchion); Jennifer Salt (Grace Collier); Charles Durning (Joseph Larch); Bill Finley (Emil); Lisle Wilson (Phillip Woode); Barnard Hughes (Arthur McLennen); Mary Davenport (Mrs. Collier); Dolph Sweet (Detective Kelly)

Crew: Edward R. Pressman (Producer); Lynn Pressman, Robert Rohoie (Associate Producers); Bernard Herrmann (Composer);

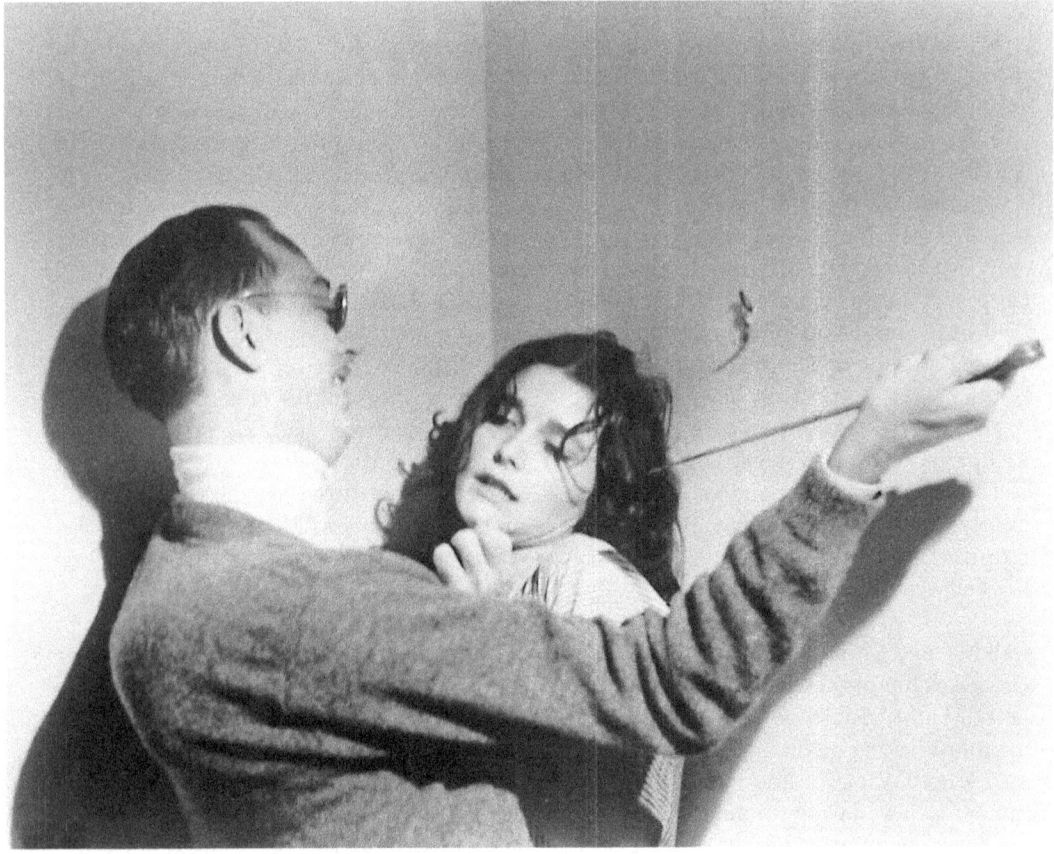

Emil (William Finley) is upset that Danielle/Dominique (Margot Kidder) seems reluctant to accept his proposal of marriage in Brian De Palma's *Sisters* (1973).

Gregory Sandor (Director of Photography); Paul Hirsch (Editor)

A black man is in a locker room when an apparently blind woman enters and begins to take off her clothes. The man, Phillip, is unknowingly a part of a game show called *Peeping Toms*, in which contestants will guess as to whether or not Phillip will continue to peep on the blind woman, Danielle (who is, in fact, not blind). When the game is over, Danielle, the French-Canadian model-actress, is awarded a cutlery set, and Phillip is given dining for two at The African Room. Danielle offers herself as company, and the couple heads for the restaurant, where they encounter Emil, Danielle's meddlesome and discourteous ex-husband. Emil is taken away, but once Phillip and Danielle reach her apartment, Phillip sees Emil standing in the front yard. Phillip pretends to leave, Emil follows and Phillip goes right back to an awaiting Danielle. The two begin to kiss. Phillip does not notice the scar on Danielle's hip.

The next morning, Danielle is moaning in agony. She goes to the bathroom and takes a couple of pills, leaving two more on the sink. A voice calls from another room, and Danielle goes to the bedroom and speaks (in French) to her sister, Dominique, who is evidently angry. Dominique mentions the sisters being "separated," and Danielle pleads with her not to argue on their birthday. Phillip has heard the two talking, and he goes to the bathroom to put some clothes on, unknowingly knocking the last two pills down the sink. Danielle meets Phillip, tells him it is the twin sisters' birthday and asks if he could get her more pills, showing him the empty bottle. While Phillips is gone, she calls someone and says she only has two pills left ("Please hurry!"). She then discovers that the two pills are gone. Phillip visits the bakery and helps the lady write "Happy Birthday to Dominique & Danielle" and heads back, not seeing Emil out in his car. Inside, Danielle is lying face down on the foldaway couch. Phillip prepares the cake with candles, puts a knife on the side (from Danielle's new cutlery set) and sets it next to Danielle ("Surprise!"). It is Dominique lying there, and she grabs the knife and stabs Phillip, who crawls across the floor. Dominique then stabs Phillip several more times and runs away.

From her apartment, Grace Collier, who writes a column for *Panorama*, sees Phillip write something in blood on the window. She quickly telephones the police and runs out to wait for them. Danielle awakes in the bathroom and answers the door to Emil, who gasps when he sees the bloody apartment ("Dominique, what have you done?" Danielle asks). Emil closes the blinds, and he and Danielle put Phillip's body inside the foldaway couch. Danielle composes herself, Emil cleans the apartment and he narrowly avoids an irate Grace (the cops hardly believe her claim) and two police officers in the hallway. Danielle answers the door for the visitors, and the reporter tells Danielle she saw a murder. Danielle insists that she had no company. The cops try to keep Grace from snooping around. She finds clothing in pairs in the closet and asks Danielle if she has a twin, which the woman denies. Later, Grace finds the cake with the two names in the kitchen (and reads the box in the trash). When she goes to show the cops, she slips and ruins the cake. Grace and the frustrated cops leave.

Grace later meets with her mother and, while driving, asks her to stop at the bakery. She asks the women there if they remember someone buying such a cake, and they recall the names Danielle and Dominique. Grace calls *Panorama* to approve the article (with a racist angle since Phillip was black), and they convince her to hire a private investigator. Grace waits in her apartment while Joseph Larch, the PI, sneaks into Danielle's apartment posing as a maintenance man and comes out with a folder. He says he tried to lift the heavy couch, and he presumes that the body is hidden in there. He decides to tail the van (taking the couch away) and wait for someone to pick up the incriminating furniture. Grace goes to talk to someone about the folder, which contains information on the Blanchion twins.

Grace goes to see someone at *Life* magazine about the once conjoined twins. She is shown a video which says that Dominique was the "disturbed one" and that the doctors were forced to perform an operation to separate them. The man tells Grace that a nurse said there were "complications," and Dominique died on the operating table. Grace watches Danielle's apartment. and follows the model-actress and Emil to a building, where she peeks through a window and sees Emil give Danielle a shot of something and then take the bloody murder weapon from his bag. She asks a man trimming the hedges where the phone is. Once inside, she encounters an eerie woman, and then tells a man she is from *Panorama*. He calls the doctor. Emil arrives and says that Grace (who he calls Margaret) is the hospital's newest addition. Grace is taken against her will and, despite her objections, she is injected with something that makes her sleep.

Grace awakens in a hypnotic state with Danielle beside her, and Emil psychologically persuades the reporter that there was no body and no murder. He takes her into a "deeper sleep," and she plays the part of Dominique when the sisters are conjoined. Dominique prevented Emil and Danielle from having a relationship, and when Danielle was pregnant, Dominique tried to kill her baby, who was later lost. Emil tells a dazed Danielle that he is going to marry her. After he says he loves her and kisses her, Dominique "awakes." Emil holds Dominique in a corner and tries to remind her of her previous murder by showing the knife, but Dominique grabs a scalpel and slices Emil a couple of times. The bloody doctor and the sister collapse on the bed where Grace is lying, and Danielle returns and embraces her lover. Grace awakes and screams.

Danielle, arrested for murder, tells the police that her sister is dead. An officer tells Grace that the case is reopened and he would like to know more of what Grace saw that day from her apartment. Grace, however, says there was no body and no murder, a fact of which she is completely convinced. Somewhere, by a grazing cow, is the couch, and hanging from a utility pole is Larch, waiting for someone who will never arrive.

Sisters was De Palma's first thriller (following his *avant-garde* films with a young Robert De Niro), and it is a superb thriller, with an enchanting score by Herrmann and a wonderful performance from Kidder. Actor Finley went on to star in a subsequent De Palma film, the cult *Phantom of the Paradise* (1975).

Sisters of Death (1978)

Written by Peter Arnold and Elwyn Richards; Directed by Joseph A. Mazzuca; First American Films; 86 min.
   Cast: Arthur Franz (Edward Clybourn); Claudia Jennings (Judy); Chéri Howell (Sylvia); Sherry Boucher (Diane); Paul Carr (Mark); Joe Tata (Joe); Sherry Alberoni (Francie); Roxanne Albee (Penny); Elizabeth Bergen (Liz); Paul Fierro (Mexican); Vern Mathison (Police Officer)
   Crew: Gustaf Unger, Gary L. Messenger (Producers); Grady Martin (Director of Photography)

Several girls are wearing dresses and veils, while two pledges are on their knees, awaiting initiation into the "Secret Society of Sisters." The final test is the test of courage: A gun is loaded with a bullet, pointed at pledge Judy's head and fired. There is only a click, and a pendant is put around Judy's neck. Another bullet is placed in the gun, the weapon is aimed at Elizabeth and the trigger is pulled. Elizabeth is shot in the head, and the girls scream.

Seven years later, Judy returns to her apartment and checks her mail. She receives an invitation from "The Sisters," with money inside. Judy calls Sylvia, who also got an invitation and thought that Judy had sent it (since Judy is rich and could afford to send the money). Judy asks Sylvia to come to her place. Penny, a religious fanatic, is letting the "spirits" decide whether she should accept her invitation. Diane hitches a ride, and Francie is pulled over and talks her way out of a speeding ticket, as the women are all on their way to Paso Robles. Waiting for them are Mark and Joey, who are being paid $500 by an unknown person to take the women to a designation. The two men introduce themselves when the "sisters" have all arrived, and they pile into a car.

They eventually reach a big house out in the middle of nowhere. Someone from inside the house is watching them arrive. Mark finds an envelope containing the second half of the payment and a note for the women. The two men drive off ("Enjoy yourselves!"), and the women enter through the gate where a "Welcome Sisters" sign is sitting near a pool. The women have a toast with the champagne that is sitting there. Mark and Joey are still hanging around, and Joey wants to join the party. They head to the fence and see a sign that says the fence is high voltage when the bulb is flashing. Joey declares it safe enough to jump the fence, and Mark makes a clever observation ("Boy, you really are horny, aren't you?"). The women check around the house while Sylvia stays by the pool, where she sees the men arrive and tells them it is a private party. Joey convinces her to let them stay for just one drink, and the others, having found some bathing suits, come out to greet the men. The mysterious person watches them by the pool and turns the electric fence on. Later, the man makes some bullets.

The next morning, the two men are sleeping out by the pool. Judy awakes in her bed, startled from a bad dream. Sitting next to Judy's bed is a photograph of Elizabeth. When the women are sitting around the table anxiously discussing the pictures they received, the man finally makes an appearance. He is Edward Clybourn, Elizabeth's father, and he says he wants the person who murdered his daughter. They try to tell him it was an accident, but Mr. Clybourn says that someone placed a live round on the pillow that fateful night. Penny screams, runs out and heads for the fence but they manage to stop her. Mark throws something at the fence to show that it is electric. Francie tells them a madman is in the house, and Mark runs inside to find the phone dead. Mr. Clybourn, armed with a gun, tells Judy and Mark that one of the women saw the murderer switch bullets at the initiation. They try to get the gun away from the man, but he fires at them and leaves. Mark says they have to turn off the fence.

The group splits up to look for a fuse. Judy finds the estranged Penny, who is outside doing an odd chant. In the cellar, Joey throws a switch. A person approaches Penny from behind and chokes her to death. Everyone runs to the front and sees that the fence is still live. Judy screams at seeing Penny's body. Mark tells them Mr. Clybourn's claim that someone was a "witness," and surmises that someone is working with the man. Mr. Clybourn continues making bullets, including one without gun powder.

That night, the women are all in their rooms while Mark and Joey are waiting downstairs for the "joker" to come out. Mr. Clybourn plays a recording of Elizabeth performing a concert. A frightened Diane (clutching scissors) goes to see Francie, who decides that it is safe enough to take a shower. Sylvia awakes to a spider on her stomach, and she screams and runs to the two men. The spider is brushed to the floor and squished to a gooey death. Diane comes down to see what is wrong. Mr. Clybourn is listening to them in the hallway. Diane runs back to the room and finds Francie dead with scissors in her back.

The next day, the group is sitting outside. Joey suggests making an SOS for planes, but Mark thinks it best to try digging under the fence. Mark goes looking for something to dig with, avoiding a snake in the cellar, and Diane and Joey cut letters from the "Welcome Sisters" sign for an SOS. Sylvia hurts her ankle, and she stays to rest while Judy and Mark go digging with an axe head Mark found. Mr. Clybourn is loading a clip inside the house. Joey locates a secret door to a fuse box. Mark and Judy find a brick wall underneath the fence, Diane tells Mark that Joey needs him and Judy runs to find the now-missing Sylvia. A dog comes out of the house and chases Joey, who runs into the fence and is electrocuted. Diane is shoved into the cellar, where the snake attacks her. Mr. Clybourn knocks Judy out and carries her to his room, while Mark fights off the vicious dog.

Judy is dressed in the initiation attire as Sylvia comes out to stand with Mr. Clybourn. Mark eludes the dog and gets in the room, but he is knocked out by Mr. Clybourn. Sylvia tells Judy she did not see anyone switch bullets, and Mr. Clybourn says the two were waiting for the guilty person to begin killing the possible witnesses. Sylvia, the one who pulled the trigger, says her life has been horrible since the incident, and she and the enraged father decided that Judy, who had asked about every detail of the initiation, was the killer. Judy says that Elizabeth wanted to die because of her overbearing father (music was the world to him, but not to his daughter). A gun is brought out, some bullets live and some blanks, and Mr. Clybourn turns the crank. Mark punches the father, and he and Judy run out, followed by Sylvia, who is hit by Mr. Clybourn's wild shooting. The man runs to the window and fires at them as they run away. Judy turns, shoots at Mr. Clybourn with his handgun and hits him. Mark rolls a barrel of gun powder at the fence, it explodes and the two run out. Mark tells Judy that they made it. "Mark," she says. "I made it." Judy shoots and kills Mark.

Sisters of Death has its moments amid amateurish acting and lifeless direction. Actor Tata might be more familiar to mainstream audiences as the owner of The Peach Pit from the television series *Beverly Hills 90210*.

The Slasher
(aka *Rivelazioni di un maniaco sessuale al capo della squadra mobile*; *Bad Girls*; *Confessions of a Sex Maniac*; *The Slasher ... Is the Sex Maniac!*; *So Naked, So Dead*; *So Sweet, So Dead*) (1972)

Written by Luigi Angelo, Italo Fasan and Roberto Montero; Directed by Roberto Montero; Prodiuzione Cinematografiche Romane; 84 min.

Cast: Farley Granger (Inspector Capuana); Sylva Koscina (Barbara); Cristea Avram (Professor); Susan Scott; Paul Oxen; Jessica Dublin; Femi Benussi; Krista Nell; Phillipe Hersent; Andrea Scotti; Irene Pollmer

Crew: Angelo Faccenna, Mario Pellegrino (Executive Producers); Eugenio Florimonte (Producer); Giorgio Gaslini (Composer); Fausto Rossi (Director of Photography); Rolando Salvatori (Editor)

The police are investigating a murder. A woman has been found with a slit throat as photographs surround her on a bed. Inspector Capuana and the police take the body to the morgue, where the professor says that the killer, who possibly used a razor, is more than likely a sex maniac. The photographs show the woman with a man whose face has been scratched out of the picture. Capuana goes home to talk to his wife Barbara, telling her that the police cannot find the woman's lover and that her husband and his rich friends are above suspicion. He also says that he believes the killer will kill again.

Later, a couple is enjoying some intimacy in a wooded area, and someone in the bushes is snapping some pictures. The woman and man go to her house and enjoy themselves, and the woman mentions her husband. A person with a face covered in black appears; the woman is chased to the beach, where her throat is slit. The killer throws photographs around the corpse. Later, the woman's lover goes to see his lawyer, who advises him not to talk. The professor tells Capuana that the murder is a carbon copy of the first. The inspector goes to see the professor's assistant Gastoni, who tells him that he thinks the woman's lifeless body is "pretty."

Several women are together, and Barbara says that the killer is only killing unfaithful wives. Capuana is told not to "inconvenience" the dead woman's husband, who is involved in politics ("Don't step on too many toes"). The killer is getting some more photographs of a cheating wife. Gastoni shows the inspector his photo developing room, where he has several pictures of corpses. Franka is arguing with her husband Franco (the lawyer); apparently each is both aware of the other's infidelity. Lily is leaving her house, ignoring her crippled husband walking after her. Working at her flower bed, Lily and Franco say hello to one another, and they agree on a time to meet later.

Capuana tells the professor he suspects Gastoni of the killings. The professor says the murderer is not his assistant, and he explains his theories that the killer is an envious homosexual or perhaps an impotent man. Lily spends time with Franco, goes home to her angry husband and says something nice to him: "Your suicide might at least have been fatal." After a party, a young couple are kissing when they hear a noise. The boy goes home and the girl, hearing a struggle, looks next door and sees Lily being murdered. She runs inside her house. Lily's husband is yelling for Lily, he looks around and falls down the stairs and dies.

The next day, the cops discover the slaying, and the girl tells the boy she saw the murderer ("His face was covered with a stocking"). She goes home and her mother, Franka, is leaving (Franco suggested she go to see her mother upon hearing that the killer is targeting unfaithful wives). Franka heads to the train station, and Franco is watching her leave. She gets onto the train, and Franka is killed in her compartment. Capuana talks to Franco later, and the lawyer evades the questions. Capuana is ordered to leave Franco alone. Later, Renata calls her lover and tells him to come over because her husband is gone. The killer is there, and Renata is killed. The lover arrives, sees the murderer crawling out the window and jumps him. The killer cuts him and runs away. The man gets inside the house and finds Renata dead.

The inspector returns home to Barbara after being out all night. She tells him he should quit his job and work in a firm with her father. Later, the cops receive a phone call, race to an address and arrest the man who answers the door ("You never would have found me on your own!"). As it happens, Capuana set up the entire scene, intentionally choosing someone who he thought was a polar opposite of the murderer (he believes the killer will be insulted and come out in the open). Afterwards, the inspector gets a call from someone who calls himself "The Avenger." He says he is going to make Capuana "pay" for what he has done by killing his wife, which, of course, means that the inspector's wife has been unfaithful. He calls to see if his wife is at the barber shop, but she is not there.

Capuana plays back the tape of the phone call and hears a grandfather clock chime that sounds familiar. He goes to Gastoni's place and, in the lab, finds a photograph of his wife with a young man named Roberto. He thinks back to different times when Roberto was around with his wife. Roberto arrives at a place, but leaves when someone calls and says that Barbara's husband is on the way. Barbara shows up, undresses and puts a robe on. The murderer arrives and stabs Barbara as Capuana watches from the window (thinking of how she has cheated on him). The killer throws photographs down, and the inspector walks into house to see the professor standing there with a ripped stocking over his face. Capuana shoots him, sees the photographs and gets on the phone: "Get me the Chief."

The Slasher starts slow but eventually picks up speed and interest, with an intriguing conclusion. Bava fans might recognize Avram as Frank Ventura from *Bay of Blood* (1971). In 1976, *The Slasher* was re-edited as an X-rated film, *Penetration*, altering the plot to involve pornographic films and adding the popular porno actors Harry Reems and Tina Russell.

Slaughter High
(1986)

Written and Directed by George Dugdale, Mark Ezra and Peter Litten; Spectacular Trading International; 91 min.

Cast: Caroline Munro (Carol); Simon Scuddamore (Marty); Carmine Iannaccone (Skip); Donna Yaeger (Stella); Gary Martin (Joe); Billy Hartman (Frank); Michael Saffran (Ted); John Segal (Carl); Kelly Baker (Nancy); Sally Cross (Susan); Josephine Scandi (Shirley); Marc Smith (Coach); Dick Randall (Manny); Jon Clark (Digby)

Crew: Steve Minasian, Dick Randall (Producers); Harry Manfredini (Composer); Alan Pudney (Director of Photography); Jim Connock (Editor)

At Doddsville County High School, Carol leads Marty down the hall, both talking of "doing it." She leads Marty to the girls' locker room as, unbeknownst to Marty, a group of people follow. Marty goes into a shower stall and undresses, and Carol lets the people inside the room. The curtain is thrown aside ("April Fool's!") and the crowd mocks the naked Marty. The coach comes in and tells them all to go to the gym, "suited up." Stella is angry, blaming Marty for the collective punishment. Carl and Ted stop by Marty's locker and, to show there are no hard feelings, give him a joint.

Working alone in the chemistry class, Marty smokes the joint, gets sick and goes to the locker room. In the gym, Skip feigns a brick going through the window (from outside) and leaves to see who is responsible. Skip goes to the chemistry room, adds a white powder to a container and walks away. Marty returns, the liquid in the container pops and a fire starts. He tries to turn off the gas, and a bottle of nitric acid falls and splashes on his face. Marty, with a partially disfigured face, is taken away on a stretcher. As Carol tries to apologize, he grabs her neck. She screams and awakes in bed.

The rich and successful Carol gets a call from Manny, her agent, who tries to convince her to do a movie. Susan visits Carol and tells her that she is recently engaged and will try to make it to the class reunion later. It is the day before April 1, and Skip is driving in his car. He stops for a hitchhiker; it is Nancy, also on her way to the reunion. Skip's car refuses to start, but Joe and Stella arrive, and Joe tows Skip's car to the school. Everyone greets one another at the school, and Frank arrives last on his motorbike. Night falls, and it is still only the small group of friends. Skip and Joe head to the back to get inside the building. As it begins to rain, the rest of the people walk through the front door. They find Skip and Joe inside, and the group looks around the school, eventually coming to a room with a "Welcome Back" sign, school photographs, alcohol and their old lockers. Shirley points out Marty's locker, and they find a rat inside. They also find Marty's yearbook and look through it; Skip talks about Marty's six months of plastic surgery and the fact that he "flipped out."

Someone in a jester's mask (the same one Skip wore during the shower prank) is in the halls. The group smokes marijuana, and Carol shows off her more expensive cocaine. Nancy has to go to the bathroom and Carol goes with her; they are both scared by Skip and Frank. The two guys run into Digby, the old janitor, who says the school will be knocked down soon and that they can take a last look around if they want. After Digby walks on, the jester–mask-wearing person jumps out, shoves Digby's head into a hook and nails his hand to a door. Nancy plays a joke on Skip and pours a drink down his pants. Carl tells Ted to show everyone how to "sink a beer," and Ted demonstrates. He gets sick, his stomach pops open and some of his innards are exposed. Everyone runs away except Shirley, in shock from having some of Ted's blood splash on her face.

The doors will not open, and one of the windows gives Nancy a shock. Carl kicks the fencing, takes Carol's keys and crawls out. When he tries to start Carol's car, the killer shoves a knife through the seat and out Carl's chest. Shirley is in the tub, washing the blood off. When she turns on the faucet for more water, acid fills the tub and she screams. Several of the people run and find Shirley's skeleton in the tub ("Marty's come back!"). Susan arrives, and Skip fruitlessly tries to get her to leave. She walks in the door and sees a life-size picture of Marty at the end of the hallway. Hands punch through. The people convene, and Frank says that Joe saw a tractor earlier. Frank and Skip leave Joe to work on the tractor, with the hopes of plowing through the doors.

Stella flirts with Frank and says she wishes she was with him instead of Joe. The killer visits Joe as he is under the tractor and takes the jack away. Joe holds the tractor up, and the killer starts the machine and cuts Joe's arm, letting the running blades do the rest. The killer then goes to see Stella and Frank during their time of intimacy, hooking up cables to the bed and electrocuting both of them. Nancy goes to check on Joe, finds him dead, and runs back to tell Skip and Carol. They all find Stella and Frank, and Skip screams for Marty to show himself. Nancy is upset, blaming Skip and Carol for everything, and Carol calms her down. Later, a sleeping Skip awakes, goes to the hall, and is grabbed. Carol asks Nancy where Skip is. She says April 1 ends at noon, and they only need to last one more hour. The two women leave the room.

Skip hangs from a rope; he shakes until the rope comes loose and he falls. Carol and Nancy look around and realize that all the corpses are gone. They hear a noise and walk into a room with a video of the shower prank playing. Nancy sees her photograph marked out in a nearby yearbook and she runs, gets outside, and falls into a pit of dirty water. She tries to use a metal pipe to pull herself up, and the killer knocks her back in and leaves. Carol finds Digby dead and hides in the girls locker room until she hears a noise, sees blood in the toilet and flushes, only for the stool to overflow. She eventually picks up a baseball bat and hits Marty with it when he jumps out. Carol hides on stage in the auditorium, and a javelin is shoved through the curtain. From hiding, she hears footsteps and swings a hatchet, hitting Skip in the face. Marty punches through glass, grabbing at her, and she runs.

Marty attacks again, and Carol pushes him through glass, and he lands on the gym floor. Carol sees that it is noon and relaxes, but Marty stands, picks up the javelin and chases Carol to the locker room. He sees Carol hiding in the stall, takes off his mask, laughs and stabs her in the stomach ("I showed ya!"). Marty hears his name being chanted as all of the dead people stalk him around the school. Now he screams and awakes in bed, with bandages over his face. A nurse comes in and tells him to relax. A doctor responds to an alarm and runs into Marty's room, where a nurse stands over him with a syringe. The nurse is actually Marty, who turns around and shoves the syringe into the doctor's eye. Marty then pulls off some of his face.

It is difficult to tell whether *Slaughter High* was intended as a comedy or as a horror-comedy. It has only a few laughs and essentially no frights. Some of the killings are far-fetched (such as the toxic beer and the acid bath) but amusing. The film was originally titled *April Fool's Day*, but the other slasher of the same name made it to theaters first. Actor Scuddamore committed suicide soon after the film's release.

Slaughter Hotel (aka *La bestia uccide a sangue freddo*; *Asylum Erotica*) (1971)

Written by Fernanda Di Leo and Nino Latino; Directed by Fernando Di Leo; Cineproduzioni Daunia 70/Sitoro; 86 min.

Cast: Klaus Kinski (Doctor Franis Clay); Margaret Lee (Cheryl); Rosalba Neri (Anne); Jane Garret (Mara); John Karlsen (Doctor Austin); Gioia Desideri (Ruth); John Ely (The Gardener); Monica Strebel (Helen); Fernando Cerulli; Sandra Rossi; Giulio Baraghini; Ettore Ceri; Anotonio Radaelli; Carla Mancini, C.S.C.; Franco Marlett, C.S.C.; Piero Nistri; Daniela Di Bitonto; Enzo Spitaleri; Marco Mariani; Gilberto Galimberto; Rosanna Braida

Crew: Tiziano Longo, Armando Novelli (Producers); Silvano Spadaccino (Composer); Franco Villa (Director of Photography); Amedo Giomini (Editor)

A person wearing a hood and dark cloak approaches an asylum at night. The person admires some antique weapons, selects an axe and heads upstairs, where an apparently agitated Cheryl is tossing and turning in bed. She presses the buzzer for the attendants, the lights come on and the person runs away.

Ruth is being driven to the clinic. A man tells her to think of her stay as a vacation and that soon she can be back with the children. Ruth, in an apparent suicide attempt, grabs the wheel and tries to run them off the road. At the clinic, as a few attendants and patients play croquet, Helen, a nurse, talks to resident Mara and tells her that she seems to be improving. She says she is there to help Mara, like a friend. Ruth is dropped off; as a man leads her to the building, she tries to whack him with a heavy stick but is stopped. Doctor Francis Clay asks Doctor Austin about the possibility of Cheryl being cured. Outside, Anne tries to follow the gardener, who is walking away from the clinic, but she is called back by Austin, who talks to her of her "impulsive" and "excessive" sexual desires.

Mr. Hume, Cheryl's husband, talks of a

company needing Cheryl back and of her return in one week. Francis says that Cheryl's suicidal urges may relapse, but Hume thinks his wife only needed rest. Anne talks to Peter; he has been told by the doctors that she is getting better. Anne says that no one can calm her "passions" like Peter, but Peter is evidently not as sexually interested in the way that Anne seems to remember. Later, as attendants and patients sit in a room to mingle and play games, Anne sneaks out the front door and runs to the greenhouse. The hooded and cloaked person is outside, and after a nurse walks by (seeing and ignoring the person), she is beheaded with a scythe.

Anne sees the gardener, takes her clothes off, approaches him and seduces him into sex. Helen goes to Mara's room, tells her she can join the others if she wants and says she will check on her later. Doctor Austin is told that Anne is missing, and attendants go to find her. Cheryl asks Francis if, when outside, she will be like she was before, and the doctor tells her she has been cured. Cheryl asks to see Francis afterwards. The gardener tells Anne (after they have had sex) that she must go, or he will suffer the consequences. Anne does not want to leave, so the gardener smacks her. Anne hits him back, calmly puts her clothes back on and leaves. She walks over and kisses the attendants until Austin calls her.

The killer, back inside, gets a knife and unlocks Ruth's door as she sleeps. The knife is placed in her hand, the killer takes off the hood and Ruth awakes. She goes for the killer with the knife, it is knocked aside and her hands are taken and put around the killer's throat. The killer then chokes her and stabs her in the chest. Doctor Austin looks around the hallway with a flashlight and finds Helen, who says she heard a noise. A chauffeur enters the building and drinks all of the drinks leftover from the get-together. After looking around, he is pushed into an iron-maiden–esque device, and his blood pours out. The killer walks around with a sword and angrily hits it on the bed in Cheryl's empty room. Cheryl meets Francis in the hallway, and they leave together.

Mara listens to a radio and takes a bath. Helen enters the room, strips to her undergarments and helps wash Mara for a while. Francis and Cheryl talk of their potential relationship, and he leaves to "do the rounds." The killer walks into Anne's room, shuts her window and takes off the hood. Anne's eyes open, and she asks the killer to lie down with her. The killer chooses instead to axe her to a bloody death. Mara dances a bit for Helen to a song on the radio, and as she looks out of the window, the killer fires a crossbow and hits Mara in the neck. Helen screams, and a crowd gathers outside her door. Doctor Austin and Francis see the dead female, and Austin tells an attendant not to let anyone in the room. The two doctors and Cheryl look around, find blood on the antique weapons and discover the body of the chauffeur. Francis points out that the other sword is missing, and Austin calls the commissioner, stating his belief that the killer is still inside the clinic.

The cops arrive and are angry that Doctor Austin moved some weapons and tried to keep the killings a secret (essentially "helping" the killer). The inspector suggests using Cheryl as bait, and Francis tries to get the woman to rethink the idea after she agrees to it. As Cheryl awaits in a room, the killer approaches with a rope, and removes the hood to reveal Hume. Cops chase Hume out of the room and around the building. The doctors theorize that Cheryl's husband wanted to kill his wife and created the idea of a maniac so that no one would suspect him of Cheryl's murder. Hume knocks out two cops. Upon entering a room of women, he goes on a killing spree. Cops run into the room and shoot Hume dead.

Slaughter Hotel (an inaccurate alternate title since it does not take place at a hotel) is a decent slasher that mostly thrives on the quirky characters residing and working at the clinic. The film, however, drags in a number of moments, particularly in the scenes where the women apparently dream of earlier events, which is both meaningless and tiresome.

Slaughterhouse (aka *Bacon Bits*) (1987)

Written and Directed by Rick Roessler; American Artists/Slaughterhouse Associates; 85 min.

Cast: Sherry Bendorf (Liz Borden); Don Barrett (Lester Bacon); William Houck (Sheriff Borden); Joe Barton (Buddy); Eric Schwartz (Skip); Jane Higginson (Annie); Jeff Grossi (Buzz); Bill Brinsfield (Tom Sanford); Jason Collier (Ronnie); Dave Fogel (Disc Jockey); Hank Gum (Herb); Linda Harris (Barbara); Joel Hoffman (Kevin); Courtney Lercara (Michele); Tom Normand (Ernie); Lee Robinson (Harold Murdock); Jeanette Saylor (Jan); Donna Stevens (Sally Jean); Jeff Wright (Deputy Dave); Herb Pender (Al)

Crew: Jerry Encoe (Executive Producer); Ron Matonak (Producer); Ed Drees (Associate Producer); Joe Garrison (Composer); Richard J. Benda (Director of Photography); Sergio Uribe (Editor)

Deputy Dave and Sally Jean go out parking, and Dave sees Skip's Jeep and Kevin's car, both apparently abandoned. He hears screaming on the dock and pulls his gun, but it is only a group of friends, practicing for Liz's "horror video." After Dave and Sally leave, Liz, Skip, Annie and Buzz get in Skip's jeep and drive away. Michele and Kevin stick around, and she playfully runs and hides from him. Michele conceals herself in an old, rusty bus, as Kevin hits a shovel against a fence (containing squealing hogs). Buddy arrives with a long-handled cleaver and chops Kevin's face. He enters the bus and slices Michele.

Tom goes to see Harold, Lester Bacon's attorney and advisor, and complains about Lester not selling his property. The two of them drive to Lester's place (next to the shutdown meat-packing plant), where they meet the sheriff (Liz's father). Lester answers their knocking, and Tom makes a final offer of $55,000, allowing Lester to stay and work as a consultant. Lester is told that the demolition of the slaughterhouse would create employment opportunities for many people, as well as get the county assessor off his back, but he grumbles about Tom's equipment and bad meat ("Thirty percent fat!"), saying he could do better with hands, knives and fewer men. The sheriff tells Lester that the assessor's office is foreclosing his property and that he has 30 days to vacate.

The group of friends are in a restaurant, talking about the party that night and Liz's video. Buddy takes Lester to a room and shows him the dead Michele and Kevin. Lester is a bit unsettled, thinking they are in a "heap of trouble" ("At least you made good, clean cuts"). He also tells Buddy that Tom, Harold and Sheriff Borden are the ones who deserve such a fate. Liz wants a "creepy" place to film, and Skip suggests the old slaughterhouse. Lester calls Harold and says he has decided to work out the offer with Tom, and he invites the man over. Dave, after being told of the worried parents of Michele and Kevin, checks out the dock and then goes to the slaughterhouse. He walks inside and calls for the two teenagers, and finds a dead, hanging cat (Buddy had eyed the feline earlier). A sliding door is shoved on his gun-toting hand, chopping it off. Buddy shows Lester the dead man ("You've gone hog wild!"). Harold arrives, and Lester takes him to a dark room, where he asks the "jury" (the three dead people) if they believe Harold's claim that he has not deceived Lester. They raise their hands (with Lester's help), and Buddy squishes Harold's face.

The sheriff goes to the Lakeside Hotel (where Dave has been spending his lunch time), and Sally says she has not seen the deputy since that morning. Buddy, in Dave's hat, shades, belt and bloody shirt, gets in the cop's car and drives. Sally waves at the passing "Dave," and she is chased until the cop car stops. She sees Buddy, screams and runs back to her car. He hits her windshield with the nightstick and then drops a rock on it. Sally runs out of the car and tries to hide, but Buddy grabs her and slits her throat.

Tom arrives at the slaughterhouse, and as he and Lester look at an old saw machine, Buddy grabs Tom from behind. Tom tries to say he is sorry, but Lester just laughs as Buddy calmly drops Tom into the machine. The man is sawed and chopped into fleshy, bloody parts.

At The Pig Out, a town dance, the power goes out (due to a storm) and many of the people leave. Buzz says it is the best time for filming in the slaughterhouse. Skip then makes a $20 bet that the girls cannot last one hour at the slaughterhouse. Liz and Annie are dropped off at the place; the boys are sneaking around with their masks (used in Liz's video). Sheriff Borden finds Sally's car with the damaged windshield and Dave's car with the door standing open, and calls in to the county sheriff's department. Liz and Annie realize that the boys are outside trying to scare them, and Liz looks for a way to get behind the two guys and scare them instead. The boys split up, and Buzz gets inside. Skip is at the window, and Annie laughs until Buddy appears and whacks Skip. Annie screams and runs, and Lester grabs her. Liz walks to the front and sees that everyone is gone. Buzz walks into a room, hears a noise and is hit in the face by Buddy.

Liz calls out her friends' names, and she eventually finds a hanging, still-living Anne, as well as the bodies of the other people. The father/son duo are there, and Buddy grabs the girl. The sheriff learns that Tom and Harold have mysteriously disappeared. Buddy holds Liz down on a table and Lester talks of "butcherin'," saying that a meat cutter needs the skilled hands of a surgeon. He slices her fingertip to prove that it is one of the most sensitive parts of the body. When Lester hears to a noise (it is the sheriff walking inside), Liz kicks him and runs away. She runs to her father, and the sheriff shoots at Buddy, hitting his cleaver. The father and daughter run into the rain. As Sheriff Borden pauses at the door, Lester stabs him in the back. Liz picks up her father's gun and shoots Lester, then helps the wounded sheriff to his car. She gets his keys as Lester knocks at the windows. She turns around, and runs over Lester, crushing his head. The sheriff tells Liz to radio for help, but Buddy jumps up from the back seat and swings his knife as Liz screams.

Slaughterhouse is a fun slasher, with adequate performances and a humorous script (Lester managing to compliment his son's butchering while still upset over the murder is particularly amusing).

Sleepaway Camp (1983)

Written and Directed by Robert Hiltzik; American Eagle Films Corp.; 84 min.

Cast: Felissa Rose (Angela); Jonathan Tierston (Ricky); Karen Fields (Judy); Christopher Colley (Paul); Mike Kellin (Mel); Katherine Kamhi (Meg); Paul DeAngelo (Ronnie); Tom Van Dell (Mike); Loris Sallahian (Billy); John Dunn (Kenny); Willy Kuskin (Mozart); Desiree Gould (Aunt Martha); Owen Hughes (Artie); Robert Earl Jones (Ben); Susan Glaze (Susie); Frank Trent Saladino (Gene); Rick Edrich (Jeff); Fred Greene (Eddie); Allen Breton (Frank the Cop); Mike Mahon (Hal); John Churchill (Doctor); Dan Tursi (John); James Paradise (Lenny); Paul Poland (Craig); Alyson Mord (Mary Ann); Carol Robinson (Dolores); Bram Hand (Scott); Brad Frankel (Joey); Dee Dee Friedman (Marie); Julie Delisid (Betsy); Michael Lerman (Greg); Lisa Buckler (Leslie); Colette Lee Corcoran (Young Angela); Frank Sorrentino (Young Peter)

Crew: Robert Hiltzik (Executive Producer); Michele Tatosian, Jerry Silva (Producers); Edward Bilous (Composer); Benjamin Davis (Director of Photography); Ron Kalish, B.A.E., Sharyn L. Ross (Editors)

There is a "For Sale" sign posted in the front of the deserted Camp Arawak. Young Angela and Peter are out on a boat with their father. Marianne and Craig are driving a boat nearby as Dolores water-skis. The kids playfully push their father off the boat, and they all fall in the water. Craig and Marianne switch places so the girl can drive, and Dolores screams at them when she sees the family in the water. The two in front are not paying attention until it is too late. Craig, trying to grab the wheel, hits full throttle, and the boat flies over the father and children.

Eight years later, Ricky and his cousin Angela are sent off to camp by Ricky's eccentric mother, who reminds them not to tell anyone how they got their physicals. The buses arrive for camp, and Artie the cook admires the children in a very suspicious way. Ricky introduces Angela to his friend Paul and shows his cousin around the camp (he was there last summer). Ricky tries to talk to Judy, his flame from last summer, but she hardly acknowledges him. At a meal, counselor Meg tells Ronnie that Angela is not eating, so he takes her to the kitchen and tells Artie to find something the girl will like. The greasy cook takes Angela into the walk-in freezer and goes for his belt, and throws Ricky up against the wall when he sees him, telling him to keep quiet. The cousins run out. Later, Artie is standing on a chair to see into the tall pot of boiling water and corn, and he is pushed. He is steadied on a shelf, asks the "kid" for help and the chair is pulled away. Artie falls and is horribly scarred and blistered by the hot water. Mel, the camp head honcho, tells the cooks to say Artie left for another job.

At a dance, a group of guys are complaining about the shortage of girls. Billy challenges Kenny and Mike to ask Angela to go skinny dipping. They mock her for not speaking, and Ricky sees them and starts a fight. Paul sits and talks to Angela, and she actually says good night to the boy as he leaves. Kenny is rowing in a boat with Leslie at night, and he rocks and overturns the boat. Leslie furiously swims away as Kenny, underneath the overturned boat, is pushed underwater by someone. In the morning, a dead Kenny is found. Despite Ronnie's recollection that Kenny was a good swimmer, a cop surmises that Kenny drowned, a theory of which Mel is quite fond. Angela sits and talks to Paul as the girls play volleyball, much to the dismay of the irritable Judy. Meg tells Angela that she must either participate or do nothing (which includes not talking to boys).

Paul and Angela come from the movie in the rec room hand in hand. Paul is alone with Angela, and he kisses her. She seems uptight, and she goes back to her cabin. The next day at the beach, Paul sits by Angela and leaves when he sees Meg. Meg asks Angela if she is going swimming, and she angrily shakes the silent girl until Ronnie pulls her away. In the cabin, Judy is upset that Angela got Meg in trouble, and she openly mocks Angela for not taking showers with the other girls. When Angela is walking later, Billy and his friends, from a cabin roof, bombard her with water balloons. Ricky is enraged ("I'll kill 'em!"), and Mel reprimands the boys on the roof. Billy's friends go to play baseball and Billy stays behind for a "wicked dump." He is locked in the stall, and someone cuts the screen behind him and shakes a hive full of bees into the room. Billy eventually gets the door open and falls to the floor, with bees covering his face.

Mel is unsettled because he thinks the camp will be shut down, and he says he knows the identity of the killer. Paul and Angela play on the beach, then start to make out. As Paul goes for Angela's shirt, she flashes back to young Angela and Peter watching their father in bed with another man; later the children are in bed, evidently ready to experiment. Angela pushes Paul away and she hastily departs. The next day, while playing a game, Angela and Ricky catch Paul and Judy kissing. Paul chases Angela down and apologizes, and Judy comes by to say that Paul called Angela a "prude." Paul leaves, and Meg joins Judy. The counselor picks Angela up and carries her to the lake as she screams. Ricky tries to run to help, but Mel stops him and accuses him of killing the others for bothering his cousin. Meg drops Angela in the water, and Ricky pulls her out and leads her away as kids throw sand at their feet.

Meg, who has the night off, reminds Mel of a dinner he offered, and they agree to meet. The line for the shower is too long, so

Meg goes next door, where she is stabbed through the shower wall. Paul sees Angela by the rec hall and apologizes again. Angela tells him to meet her at the waterfront after the social. Eddie, camping with the children, takes two of the boys back (they were cold) and leaves the others alone. A person approaches and eyes the nearby hatchet. Mike and Judy are kissing, and Mike hides when Mel stops by to ask where Meg is. Mel leaves, and Mike decides he had better go. Mel finds Meg's corpse and thinks Ricky killed her to get back at him ("I gotta stop him!"). Judy is curling her hair when someone enters the cabin ("Oh, it's you!"). She is punched and then killed with her curling iron.

Eddie returns to find the children bloody in their sleeping bags and screams for help. Ricky is walking outside, enjoying a late dinner, and Mel grabs him and beats him. Ronnie gets a phone call, and he tells Marie to gather the counselors. Mel sees someone at the archery ("It can't be you!"), and he is perforated with an arrow through the neck. As the police arrive, the group splits up to look for missing campers. Paul is waiting for Angela, and she arrives and says, "Let's go swimming." Paul happily begins removing his clothes. Frank, the cop, and Gene find Ricky still alive, and Gene carries him away. Susie and Ronnie hear singing by the beach, and they see Angela there, stroking Paul's head, but she does not respond to them. A flashback shows Ricky's mother speaking with the bandaged child, saying she is happy to have a little girl. She says the child will like the name Angela ("Won't you, Peter?"). Angela jumps up, and Paul's decapitated head rolls. "My God, she's a boy." Angela stands with a bloody body while almost growling or hissing at the counselors.

Sleepaway Camp is a good slasher, with a charming assortment of characters and innovative murder sequences. The jolting and absurd (and also great) ending alone pushes *Sleepaway Camp* to cult status.

Sleepaway Camp II: Unhappy Campers (1988)

Written by Fritz Gordon; Directed by Michael A. Simpson; Double Helix Films; 80 min.

Cast: Pamela Springsteen (Angela); Renée Estevez (Molly); Tony Higgins (Sean); Valerie Hartman (Ally); Brian Patrick Clarke (T.C.); Walter Gotell (Uncle John); Susan Marie Snyder (Mare); Terry Hobbs (Rob); Kendall Bean (Demi); Julie Murphy (Lea); Carol Chambers (Brooke); Amy Fields (Jodi); Benji Wilhoite (Anthony); Walter Franks III (Judd); Justin Nowell (Charlie); Heather Binion (Phoebe); Jason Ehrlich (Emilio); Carol Martin Vines (Diane); Tricia Grant (Girl Sent Home); Jill Jane Clements (Woman in Truck)

Crew: Stan Wakefield (Executive Producer); Jerry Silva, Michael A. Simpson (Producers); Bob Phillips (Associate Producer); James Oliverio (Composer); Bill Mills (Director of Photography); John David Allen (Editor)

At Camp Rolling Hills, T.C., head counselor, is by the campfire telling a scary story involving a girl in the graveyard and her dead boyfriend. Phoebe tells the "true story" of Camp Arawak, with people being killed by a shy girl. Angela interrupts the story and tells Phoebe she should be in her cabin; Phoebe finishes the story, saying the killer was really a boy. After they leave, Sean (whose dad is a cop) says the killer was put in a psycho ward, given a sex change and released two years ago. Angela tells Phoebe that she does not deserve to be at camp, and Phoebe mouths off and walks away. Phoebe gets lost, and Angela finds her, whacks her with a limb and cuts out her tongue for her bad stories and filthy mouth.

Angela wakes up the girls in her cabin for breakfast. She says she sent Phoebe home after finding her with some boys. Angela talks to Uncle John later about kids, and Angela says there are lots of good kids if you "weed out the bad." Uncle John announces in the mess hall that Angela is counselor of the week, and she invites Molly and Ally to the front while the room full of campers sings

Ally (Valerie Hartman) shows what can happen if the sweet and sanguinary camp counselor, Angela, is provoked in Michael A. Simpson's *Sleepaway Camp II: Unhappy Campers* (1988).

"The Happy Camper Song." T.C. invites Angela for a swim (she declines), then asks to discuss what happened between her and Phoebe. At the pool, Ally is upset that Sean is hanging around Molly. The sisters, Jodi and Brooke, are out in the woods, getting stoned. One is passed-out, and the other is kissing a guy. Angela shows up and tells the boy to leave. The passed out sister awakes to Angela dousing her with booze, and she sits up to see her fried, crispy sister. Angela pours gasoline on her, offers some advice ("Say no to drugs") and sets the sister afire.

One of the female campers complains about the camp and says she wants to go home. Angela and Uncle John watch the girl being driven away, and Angela says there are now four gone because she had to send Jodi and Brooke home. John tells her to next time talk to either him or T.C. After lights out, the boys raid the girls' cabin, and Angela returns ("You're all in big trouble"), telling the boys to leave and the girls to clean up. Mare suggests getting the boys back. Later they raid the boys' cabin until Angela walks in. Mare and Angela are in a car, and an upset Mare wants to go home. Angela says she does not have to if she apologizes ("I would rather die first"). Angela looks around the car, and Mare asks if she is looking for a gun. Angela says she is looking for a drill, which she finds and uses on Mare.

The next day, Anthony and Judd tell the girls they are going to scare Angela (the girls will be camping that night). T.C. goes to the front and reads a list of missing things, including a saw, rope, drill and his car battery. Angela is sitting by an abandoned cabin when Molly arrives for advice about Sean. Angela tells her she was once shy and would talk to no one, and she gives her advice from her aunt: "Keep your morals strong and you'll never go wrong." Afterwards, campers are playing a game in which they are blindfolded and feeling what counselors claim are animal parts; Angela's mysterious substance is "dead teenager's brains." Angela finds Charlie and Emilio looking through their Polaroids, and she sees nude pictures of the girls and one of herself dressing. She says she is going to tell Uncle John, and she shows the photos to T.C., who says the boys should not be sent home since they have been going to camp for years. T.C. warns Angela that the boys might try to scare her.

Anthony and Judd are out at night, and Anthony is looking for his glove (he is Freddy). Judd answers the call of nature, and Angela, having found the glove for Anthony, slices his throat. Judd (as Jason) returns, and Angela (as Leatherface) revs up the chainsaw and saws and cuts Judd. Angela goes to the campsite to scare the girls and is told that Ally went to the bathroom. Angela goes there and bangs on the locked door (the chainsaw will not start). Ally is with Rob, Rob hides and Ally leaves with Angela. The following day, T.C. asks if Molly and Sean have seen Anthony or Judd. Ally says some mean things to Molly, and she cries in the cabin and tells Angela about it. Angela suggests she go swimming, but Molly says Ally might be there ("I doubt it"). Ally and Rob have sex, and Ally thanks him and leaves. She finds a note on the mirror to meet Sean, and she goes to the abandoned cabin, where Angela stabs her in the back and throws her into the old outhouse. She forces Ally into the vile toilet (with leeches) and pushes her down with a tree limb.

Rob tells Sean that the disappearance of people is making him think of Camp Arawak and the dead people. Sean says he cannot remember the name of the killer as a female, but Peter was her given name. Demi goes to see Angela and tells her that she called Mare and Phoebe and was told by their families that they were still at camp. As Demi talks and brushes her hair, Angela looks for a weapon, pulls a string off of her guitar and chokes Demi. Lea walks into the cabin, Angela hides and Lea sees a dead Demi hanging out of the window. Angela comes out and stabs Lea. Molly returns, and Angela is inside the nearly vacant cabin, playing guitar and singing ("Looks like you and I are the only two left"). The next day, Uncle John fires Angela for sending so many people home. Molly finds Angela crying and hears what has happened. Molly tells Sean, and she suggests going to see Angela to help if they can.

Molly and Sean go to the abandoned cabin, and Angela tells Molly that T.C. hates her and reminds her of a boy she once knew, who she "fixed" by drowning. Sean opens the door and finds the dead bodies of his friends; Angela beats him with a limb. She grabs Molly when she walks inside. The couple is tied and gagged, and T.C. comes by looking for them. As he walks through the door. Angela throws something on his face which burns and melts ("I knew your battery would come in handy"). When Angela tries to feed the bound Sean, he says he remembers her name, calling her the "Angel of Death." Angela says she did her time and is cured. Sean says his dad helped arrest her, and Angela finally gets an axe and decapitates him. Angela leaves Molly alone, and drags another dead body to the cabin. Molly gets free, hits Angela, takes the knife and runs. Angela chases her ("I just wanna be your friend!"), until Molly falls and hits her head on a rock.

Diane is looking for Molly, and she finds Charlie and Emilio dead outside, and Uncle John and Rob dead in John's office. Angela is there, and she stabs Diane. Molly awakes out in the woods. Angela is hitching a ride with a woman who smokes and has a bad mouth, so she stabs her. Molly, running, stops an approaching truck and sees Angela behind the wheel, wearing the woman's cowboy hat ("Howdy partner!").

Sleepaway Camp II, with tongue firmly in cheek, creates great characters and even greater killings. The performances are very good, especially from Springsteen (Bruce's sister) as the sweet Angela. Many of the principal characters in the movie are named after actors/actresses from the "Brat Pack" of the '80s or actors and actresses appearing in similar films.

Sleepaway Camp III: Teenage Wasteland (1988)

Written by Fritz Gordon; Directed by Michael A. Simpson; Double Helix Films; 80 min.

Cast: Pamela Springsteen (Angela); Tracy Griffith (Marcia); Michael J. Pollard (Herman); Mark Oliver (Tony); Haynes Brooke (Bobby); Sandra Dorsey (Lilly); Daryl Wilcher (Riff); Kim Wall (Cindy); Kyle Holman (Snowboy); Cliff Brand (Barney); Kashina Kessler (Maria); Randi Layne (Tawny); Chung Yen Tsay (Greg); Jarrett Beal (Peter); Sonya Maddox (Anita); Jill Terashita (Arab); Stacie Lambert (Jan); Charles Lawlor (Paramedic); Jerry Griffin (Policeman); Mike Nagel (Ambulance Driver)

Crew: Stan Wakefield (Executive Producer); Jerry Silva, Michael A. Simpson (Producers); Bob Phillips (Associate Producer); James Oliverio (Composer); Bill Mills (Director of Photography); Amy Carey, John David Allen (Editors)

Maria awakes in her bed, gathers her things for camp and heads out the door. On her way down the sidewalk, a garbage truck chases her to an alley and crushes her. A person with similar clothes and hair throws Maria and her things in the back of the garbage truck. A Camp New Horizons van picks up Angela and drives away.

Tawny Richards, a news reporter, is at the camp, talking to the owners, Herman and Lilly. The camp selects kids from higher and lower classes for a "better understanding between the rich and the poor." Tawny then mentions the camp once being Camp Rolling Hills and Camp Arawak, and the murders that ensued at the bloody hands of Angela, the "Angel of Death." Lilly stops her since Tawny promised not to talk of the murders. After the campers leave, Tawny tells Angela she looks older and asks her if she can get Tawny some cocaine. Angela goes to cleaning supply storage area and returns with a white powder ("It'll really clean your pipes"). Tawny drives away, stops and sniffs some coke. Blood comes out of her nose and mouth, and she hangs dead out of the car.

The campers congregate inside a building, and Herman flirts with Jan. Officer Barney Whitmore, the third counselor, arrives. Cindy asks him if he is a cop, and he tells her he is. Riff belches, and he and Tony fight until the officer breaks it up. Barney takes away Riff's knife and asks anyone else with a weapon to give it to him. Everyone puts on their Camp New Horizons shirts. Angela tries to avoid Barney, but he stops her and asks for ID (she is posing as Maria). The campers split into three groups to camp out in the woods.

Barney is with Marcia, Tony, Greg and Anita. He talks of his son Sean, who was murdered at camp last year, and Tony apologizes for his bad attitude. Herman is with Jan, Peter, Snowboy and Angela, and he compliments Angela's axe-chopping skills. Angela fishes with Peter and Snowboy. Peter puts a firecracker in a fish and lights it, and Angela screams and runs off as the two guys laugh. She returns to the campsite and finds Herman and Jan inside a tent. When Herman comes out, Angela beats him repeatedly and finally stabs him with a tree limb. Jan sees Herman and runs away, but Angela hits her and throws the body in the tent. Later, Snowboy spray paints Angela's tent and Peter throws a firecracker at her ("Why did I think this year would be any different?"). Marcia and Tony talk and hold hands out in the woods. Angela crawls to a slumbering Peter and lights a firecracker in his nose. Snowboy awakes and screams at the result, and Angela whacks him with a limb ("Batter up!"). She throws them in a tent, douses the tent with gasoline and sets it all afire, as a still-living Snowboy screams. Angela roasts some marshmallows over the blaze.

Lilly is with Bobby, Arab, Riff and Cindy when Angela arrives, saying that Herman told her to switch with someone from the group. She walks with Arab back to the campsite, where she points her to a tent and kicks her in. When Arab pokes her head out, Angela chops it off with an axe. Back with Angela's new group, Cindy complains about Riff's rap music and uses some racial slurs. Barney's group is asking about Angela, and in response to a question from Tony, Barney says he would kill Angela if he met her. Lilly has her group play a trust game, and they split into groups of two. Angela is blindfolded and Cindy leads her around, using more racial slurs when referring to Riff, and scaring Angela by placing a turtle against her neck. Angela says it is time to switch, and she leads Cindy to the main camp, where she hooks her by the belt at the flagpole, lifts her high up and lets her drop.

Angela returns and says Cindy is at the main camp with a headache. Lilly tells her to go get Cindy, take the trash and get bug spray. She goes to the main camp and thinks back to the happy times when she was a counselor. She comes back, saying that Cindy is resting in a cabin. Lilly has another trust game, and she ties Angela and Bobby together. They go to fish, and Bobby says he likes being tied to Angela and tries to get closer. Angela tells him to meet her later. The two return, and Riff says he does not want to clean the fish. When Angela presses him about it, he pulls a gun ("Bobby, clean the fish"). Marcia and Tony talk some more, kiss and lie down. Angela asks Lilly to play the trust game with her, telling her they can check on Cindy. Angela leads a blindfolded Lilly to the buried trash, pushes her in and throws dirt on her while singing "The Happy Camper Song." When Lilly is buried to her neck, Angela runs over her with a lawnmower. Angela waits for Bobby, ties his arms around a tree (he said he liked being tied) and ties the another end to a Jeep, which she drives away as Bobby screams. Angela returns to Riff and throws him a cassette tape of her rapping. She pulls the tent, beats a spike into his hand and then spikes Riff through the tent.

Angela walks to the remaining group and tells Barney that Herman wants her to switch with Marcia. Barney walks with the two girls, and Angela falls and says her ankle is hurt. Barney wraps the ankle, and Angela complains about Lilly and Herman as counselors. She also admits that Herman did not tell her to switch. Marcia asks if Lilly really does just sit around, and Angela says Lilly is outside right now. ("I'm warning you, it's not a pretty sight.") Marcia sees a headless Lilly outside and runs back to Angela for comfort. Barney checks, then tells Marcia to run to the highway. An angry Barney walks into the room with Angela ("You look just like your son when you get mad"). Barney suggests the different ways Angela could kill him, and he says, "C'mon, Angela, what's it gonna be?" She tells him a gun, and she shoots the officer a few times. Angela chases Marcia in the Jeep and takes her away.

Angela goes to Tony, Greg and Anita, ties all three of them together for another trust game. She cuts down Barney, and lets him hang from the tree. She says the object of the game is to stay alive. Marcia is in one of three cabins, and they have two minutes to find her or they will die. The group hurriedly checks the cabins and finds Marcia in the last one. They set off a booby trap, and axes swing down into the chests of Greg and Anita. Angela tells the two remaining campers they made it, and goes to her Jeep. Marcia gets free and runs to Angela. In the struggle, Angela is stabbed in the stomach many times. Tony and Marcia call the cops, and Angela is taken away in an ambulance. A cop and a paramedic learn that Angela is still alive and suggest killing her since she does not deserve to live. Angela grabs a syringe, sticks the paramedic in the chest and shoves the syringe in the cop's eye. The driver asks what is going on in back, and Angela says, "Just takin' care of business."

Sleepaway Camp III may not be as good as the first sequel, but it comes close, with loads of black humor and another winsome performance from actress Springsteen. Many of the principal characters are named after characters from *West Side Story* (1961) and the children from the hit television series *The Brady Bunch*.

Sleepless
(aka *Non ho sonno*)
(2001)

Written by Dario Argento, Franco Ferrini and Carlo Lucarelli; Directed by Dario Argento; Medusa Produzione/Opera Produzione/Cecchi Gori Group Tiger Cinematografica; 117 min.

Cast: Max von Sydow (Moretti); Stefano Dionisi (Giacomo); Chiara Caselli (Gloira); Gabriele Lavia (Mr. Betti); Rosella Falk (Laura de Fabritiis); Paolo Maria Scalondro (Manni); Roberto Zibetti (Lorenzo); Roberto Accornero (Fausto); Barbara Lerici (Angela); Guido Morbello (Detective); Massimo Sarchielli (Leone); Diego Casale (Beppe); Alessandra Comerio (Mrs. Letti); Elena Marchesini (Mel/Kitten); Aldo Massasso (Cascio); Barbara Mautino (Dora/The Little Rabbit); Conchita Puglisi (Amanda); Brian Ayres (District Attorney); Daniele Angius (Young Giacomo); Robert Camero (Marco); Luca Fagioli (Vincenzo de Fabritiis); Daniela Fazzolari (Maria Luisa); Aldo Delaude (Train Conductor); John Pedeferri (Police Officer); Francesco Benedetto (Porter); Renato Liprandi (Stationmaster); Elisabeth Rocchetti (MacDonald's Girl); Antonio Sarasso, Piero Marchelli (Coroners); Rossella Lucà (Mara); Giuseppe Minutillo (Dwarf); Giancarlo Colia (Adolfo Farina); Francesca Vettori (Giacomo's Mother)

Crew: Claudio Argento (Executive Producer); Goblin: Claudio Simonetti, Agostino Marangolo, Massimo Morante, Fabio Pignatelli (Composers); Ronnie Taylor, B.S.C. (Director of Photography); Anna Napoli, A.M.C. (Editor)

In Turin, 1983, Ulysses Moretti investigates a murder scene and tells a young Giacomo that he will find his mother's killer. Seventeen years later, Angela refuses to let a man do "disgusting things," and he gives her money and tells her to leave. After cleaning up in the bathroom, Angela hears the man mumble in his sleep about killing, and she runs, knocks over a table (with some weapons), gathers her things and leaves. On the train, Angela realizes she inadvertently picked up a "blue file," which is full of articles, photographs of dead people and a copy of *The Death Farm* by John McKenzie. She recalls the "killer dwarf" and calls her friend Amanda, telling her of the file and says to meet her at the station. The killer calls Angela ("Thief!"), and she runs down a corridor, finds the conductor and asks to stay with him until reaching her destination. She returns to get her things, hears a noise and runs, finding the conductor out cold. She tries to hide, but the killer catches her and stabs her. At the station, Amanda looks around the train and finds the blue file. She goes back to the parking lot. In her car, the killer attacks and stabs her in the neck. Beppe, the car lot attendant, finds a gold pen on the ground as the killer takes back his file.

Manni and other cops are at the scene, and the conductor says that Angela had mentioned the killer dwarf. Manni visits Moretti, who was in charge of the case in 1983, and he talks about the "loose ends" of the dwarf suspect being found shot in the head, apparently from a suicide. Moretti says that his memory is not what is used to be. Mel, who dances as a "kitty" in a club, is in her dressing room when the lights go out. She hears a cat howling and is scared by Marco, who says there was a short circuit. He leaves, and Mel heads up the dark staircase. At the top, a figure in a yellow jacket (like Marco wears) turns to her wearing a hood. She scratches the killer's neck, but she is punched and then dragged to a tub of water where she is drowned and her fingernails are cut off. At the scene, cops discover a cutout of a cat, and Marco says he thought he saw a "little person" before Mel was killed. Moretti says that, 17 years ago, cutouts of animals were found with the victims.

Giacomo gets a call from Lorenzo, asking him to come back to Turin, and Lorenzo lets Giacomo stay with him. At the police station, Moretti hears Giacomo talk to Manni and say his mother's name: Maria Gallo. He chases him down, and the two go to the scene of Maria's murder. Giacomo could not see the killer's face as he stabbed his mother with an English horn, but he says he remembers a "whistling" or "hissing." Giacomo eats dinner with Lorenzo's family, and Mr. Betti cannot find his pen. Later, Lorenzo talks about his father wanting an athlete (Lorenzo has asthma) and being sent abroad, and Giacomo talks of fighting with his abusive father. Giacomo goes to see Gloria play the harp for an audience, and he, Gloria, Lorenzo and his girlfriend, and Fausto, Gloria's boyfriend, go to a club. Fausto talks about the dwarf, Vincenzo de Fabritiis (aka John McKenzie), and says he does not think the man is dead. He says that, as children, they would mock him, and he once put a curse on them.

Giacomo and Moretti go to Villa de Fabritiis, and Giacomo thinks he sees Vincenzo in the window. They meet a bum, Leone, who recites a familiar verse to Moretti but says he cannot remember any more. Beppe meets with the killer about the pen and talks about keeping his mouth shut. He gives the pen to the killer, and the killer writes on Beppe's hand and shoves the pen into his temple many times. Giacomo and Moretti find the dead man and read "I'm a bad boy" on his hand. They call the police, and Manni is upset that the two are out there.

Giacomo and Lorenzo meet their friends in a bar. When they sit back down (Mr. Betti had just left the bar), Lorenzo accidentally drinks from Giacomo's glass, notes a "funny taste" and collapses. In the hospital, Giacomo says the poison was meant for him, and Mr. Betti tells him to stay away from his son. Giacomo leaves, and Gloria goes after him. Moretti, up late at night, recalls another verse of the rhyme and believes the killer is murdering to the nursery rhyme. Dora (a friend calls her a "little rabbit") leaves work, gets on a train and walks outside. She goes into the door of a building, and the killer attacks and slams her face against a wall, knocking out a number of her teeth and leaving a cutout of a rabbit.

Moretti tells Giacomo of a manuscript Vincenzo had said was stolen, believing the killer was using it to kill. At the house, they meet Vincenzo's mother Laura, and they ask about his books. Gloria calls Giacomo (on Moretti's phone) and tells him about *Swan Lake*, which she is about to perform. Moretti finds a children's book, *Animal Farm*, with pages missing, and he thinks Vincenzo had hidden the pages of the original text from the killer. He looks in a copy of *Animal Farm* (George Orwell's book) and finds the pages, which contain the nursery rhyme. The last verse, following the one with the rabbit, mentions the killing of a swan. Giacomo quickly drives to the *Swan Lake* performance runs backstage, and finds Gloria alive and well. Mara, who danced to Gloria's harp playing, is grabbed and decapitated.

At the cemetery, Vincenzo's coffin is exhumed, but his corpse is gone. Laura goes to see Moretti at his home, and she says she does not want the "rumors" to start again. She says she knows her son is dead because, not wanting him to go to prison, she shot and killed him. Moretti says a gun was never found, and Laura goes to the estate and retrieves a pistol from a hidden place. She sees a short figure in the dark, backs up and falls over a railing to her death. At home, Moretti leaves a message for Giacomo on Gloria's answering machine. The lights go out, and Moretti hears the sounds of breaking glass and footsteps. He sees a tiny person walking in the dark, fires repeatedly, clutches his chest and falls to the floor. The next morning, Giacomo hears the message, and Moretti talks of the murders being in a small neighborhood in 1983 and all over the city in 2000, a "discrepancy" in his mother's killing and the writing on Beppe's hand. Manni calls and tells Giacomo that Moretti has died from a heart attack.

Giacomo and Gloria get in the woman's car, and they give Leone a lift. He is dropped off, and Giacomo gets out to give him wine he left in the back seat. At the shed at Vincenzo's estate, he sees Leone with a "puppet dwarf," and he runs back to the car. He and Gloria follow Leone to a building, and Gloria goes to her car to call the police, while Giacomo climbs the fence and walks inside. Upstairs, he finds Leone dead from a gunshot wound, and Mr. Betti suddenly appears in the room and shoots Giacomo in the shoulder. Lorenzo and Gloria pound and yell at the door, and Mr. Betti shoots himself. The two run inside, and Lorenzo goes to his father's side ("Forgive me!"). Lorenzo gasps and uses his inhaler.

Lorenzo goes to call the police. As he returns, Giacomo tells Gloria what Moretti had learned. The killings were in a small area because the killer was a child, and now, as an adult, he can go anywhere he wants. Additionally, a child would take the rhyme literally, not realizing "instrument" referred to a weapon. Giacomo takes Lorenzo's inhaler and says the hissing he heard was the inhaler's spray, and he says that Mr. Betti sent Lorenzo abroad to stop him from killing. Lorenzo says he was doing fine on his own and he called Giacomo back because it is a game for the two of them ("I'm a bad boy"). Lorenzo grabs a knife and holds it against Gloria's throat. Giacomo asks why he has not killed in so long, and Lorenzo tells of other places ("They know the nursery rhyme there, too!"). He pushes Gloria to the window, and Manni, outside, shots and blows Lorenzo's face off. Giacomo and Gloria embrace as cops run inside.

Sleepless is a nice return to Argento's *giallo* films. While not his best work, the movie does boast a visually striking camera that refuses to stand still, an intriguing mystery and a few impressive and gory effects. Actor von Sydow is terrific as the aging detective. Actor Lavia also appeared in Argento's *Deep Red*, playing a character who likewise (at least momentarily) takes the murder rap for a family member. The nursery rhyme in *Sleepless* was written by Argento's actress-writer-director daughter, Asia Argento.

The Slumber Party Massacre (1982)

Written by Rita Mae Brown; Directed by Amy Jones; Santa Fe Productions, Inc.; 76 min.

Cast: Michele Michaels (Trish); Robin Stille (Valerie); Michael Villella (Russ Thorn); Debra Deliso (Kim); Andree Honore (Jackie); Gina Mari (Diane); Jennifer Meyers (Courtney); Joe Johnson (Neil); David Millbern (Jeff); Jim Boyce (John Minor); Pamela Roylance (Coach Jana); Brinke Stevens (Linda); Ryan Kennedy (David Contant); Jean Vargas (Telephone Repairwoman); Anna Patton (Mrs. Deveraux); Howard Purgason (Mr. Deveraux); Pam Canzano (Carpenter); Aaron Lipstadt (Pizza Boy); Francis Menendez (Paper Boy)

Crew: Amy Jones (Producer); Mark Allan (Associate Producer); Aaron Lipstadt (Co-Producer); Ralph Jones (Composer); Steve Posey (Director of Photography); Sean Foley (Editor)

A paperboy tosses a newspaper with a headline that screams, "Mass Murderer of 5 Russ Thorn Escapes." Trish awakes, dresses and gathers some dolls. Trish's parents are leaving, and her mother tells her that Mr. Contant is there if she needs help. Her parents leave and Trish throws the bag of dolls in the trash. As she is leaving, someone takes a doll.

Jeff and Neil are talking about girls, and Jeff hits on a telephone repairwoman. The boys keep walking as the woman stands by her van, and she is pulled inside the vehicle and drilled to death. The girls are playing basketball and afterwards are discussing the party at Trish's house that night. Valerie, the new girl, is being ignored until Trish approaches her and compliments her on her basketball skills. Later, Trish suggests inviting Valerie to the party, an idea which Diane rejects. Valerie hears the girls, starts to leave and is stopped by Trish. Valerie says she cannot come over before Trish asks and she leaves ("She heard"). The group is leaving, but Linda returns to the school for a book. She sees Russ Thorn in the hallway and he drills her arm. Linda runs and hides in the dark shower room, but Thorn sees her blood seeping under the door. The killer drills through the door and runs back out to the van.

Diane later meets John and says maybe she can get around the no-boys-allowed rule at the party. Coach Jana returns home and asks the carpenter if she has seen her cat. Trish is on the phone with Diane, and she hears a noise and is scared by Mr. Contant, who offers to sit and wait with her until the girls arrive. At home, the coach hears a noise, and her cat, Muffin, jumps out of the closet. Jackie and Kim are at the house talking about the weed they brought. Mr. Contant does not seem to mind, and he leaves the house. Valerie is home with her sister, Courtney, and Valerie checks outside for a noise to see an overturned trash can. Jeff and Neil watch from a window as the girls change their clothes. Trish suggests ordering a pizza, and Diane goes outside to get more wood for the fireplace. She meets Mr. Contant, who is chopping snails with a cleaver. Diane says good night and leaves. Just as Mr. Contant is preparing to snag another snail, he is drilled and killed by Thorn.

Later, Trish shuts the window and sees someone outside. When she looks again, she sees a melted doll (the one she threw in the garbage) stuck up with a cleaver. She and Diane go to check the garage door and see that it is not locked. Diane calls John (aka "Boo-Boo"), the girls listen on another phone and Diane hears them laughing. When the lights go out, the girls go to the garage to check the fusebox and find some fuses missing. They are scared by Jeff and Neil (Jeff is punched), and they all go inside. Valerie hears a noise again, and outside both trash cans are lying down. John honks his car horn and Diane comes out saying she cannot leave now. He pulls his car into the garage.

Courtney suggets crashing the party nearby while Valerie brushes her hair. Diane and John are out kissing in the car while the others are inside. John suggests going to his place, and Diane goes in and tells Trish that she and John are going for beer ("You don't have to ask my permission, Diane"). Diane returns to the car, and John's head falls off. She screams (while the girls are running a blender) and is killed by Thorn. Courtney thinks she hears honking and screaming. The doorbell rings, and the group thinks it is the pizza guy. Jeff asks through the door, "What's the damage?", and gets the reply, "Six, so far." Kim and Jackie are on the phone with Coach Jana to ask about a baseball game, and the door is open to a dead pizza boy who falls to the floor. Trish tries to use the phone, but Thorn cuts the lines. Coach Jana calls Valerie, suggests checking out the house and then says she will do it herself. The boys arm themselves; Jeff goes out the back door while Neil runs out the front.

Jeff finds Diane dead and is drilled through the back. Neil runs to Valerie's house and knocks on the door, which Valerie either ignores or cannot hear due to the loud television. Thorn approaches and attacks Neil. When Valerie finally goes to the door, she cannot see the two struggling beyond the porch steps. Thorn stabs Neil several times and carries the body to the garage and throws it in the trunk. Thorn counts the bodies and realizes one is missing. Trish, Jackie and Kim are sitting in a circle armed with knives. Jackie goes for the dead pizza boy's delivery and enjoys a slice of pizza. The girls hear Jeff, who has crawled to the door. They are too afraid to open the door, and they hear Thorn drilling Jeff. Coach Jana is driving in her car. Valerie sees her sister walking to Trish's house and runs after Courtney.

Courtney ducks away from Valerie, who knocks on the door and rings the doorbell. She leaves, and Jackie goes to the door to let Valerie in. Thorn is now standing there, and he swipes his drill across Jackie's neck. Valerie sees Courtney in the back, and she says she is going to check the front door again. She walks inside and calls out the girls' names. Kim wants to respond, but Trish suggests Valerie is helping the killer. Valerie goes back outside, and Courtney is gone. Thorn walks in the window behind Trish and Kim, and they knock him down with a baseball bat. He grabs a knife and stabs Kim. Trish runs and hides in a closet. Valerie finds Courtney again, and they go inside Trish's house, where Courtney finds Kim's corpse in the refrigerator. Valerie sees the shadow of Thorn and hides in the basement while Courtney ducks under the couch. Thorn drags the pizza guy away and lies on the living room floor under a cover.

Coach Jana arrives at the house, calls some names and walks inside. Thorn jumps up and goes after the coach with the drill. Courtney trips him, and the coach beats him with a firepoker as Trish runs in and stabs Thorn in the back. He sits up and drills Coach Jana, and he tells Trish, "All of you are very pretty. I love you." Valerie swings with a machete she found in the basement. She chases Thorn outside, chops off his drill bit, lobs off his hand and slices into his stomach. He falls into the pool, and Valerie drops the machete and she and her sister embrace. Thorn crawls out, and jumps atop Valerie, and Trish attacks him again. He moves, jumps for Valerie again and lands on the machete.

The Slumber Party Massacre is a moderately good slasher, with a killer who is not very menacing and a few tedious pre-killing spree exposition moments. The concluding scene, with the girls collaborating to stop the killer, is well done.

Slumber Party Massacre III (1990)

Written by Catherine Cyran; Directed by Sally Mattison; Concorde-New/Horizon Corp.; 80 min.

Cast: Keely Christian (Jackie); Brittain Frye (Ken); M.K. Harris (Morgan); David Greenlee (Duncan); Brandi Burkett (Diane); Hope Marie Carlton (Janine); Maria Claire (Susie); Maria Ford (Maria); Garon Grigsby (Michael); Devon Jenkin (Sarah); David Kriegel (Tom); David Lawrence (Frank); Lulu Wilson (Juliette); Yan Birch (Weirdo); Alexander Falk (Davis); Wayne George (O'Reilly); Marta Kober (Pizza Girl); Ron Smith (Uncle Billy)

Crew: Rodman Flender (Executive Producer); Catherine Cyran (Producer); Jamie Sheriff (Composer); Jürgen Baum (Director of Photography); Tim Amyx (Editor)

A group of friends are playing volleyball at the beach. Jackie is sitting with Diane talking. A strange man sits at the beach near them and stares at the girls, until Duncan tells him to keep his eyes to himself. Duncan mentions being at a party, but they tell him it is a slumber party. Juliette goes to get the volleyball, and talks to Ken. As they are leaving, Jackie goes back for something and drops her address book. Sarah gets into her car, where she is grabbed, and a drill is run through her stomach from behind.

Frank drives Jackie home and they kiss. Jackie's door is open; inside is Morgan, who thought it was an open house (Jackie's parents are moving). Jackie says he can stay and look around. After Jackie listens to a mysterious voice on the answering machine, an apparently nervous Morgan finally leaves. Later, Jackie's friends arrive, saying Sarah did not answer at her home. Morgan calls (he is watching the girls through a telescope from his house) and asks Jackie if he can look at the house again; Jackie responds negatively. Later, when Juliette and Maria playfully perform a striptease, Frank, Tom and Michael scare them with masks. Jackie tells them all to leave.

The weirdo from the beach is hanging around outside. Frank and Tom go to get something for the girls, and Michael goes to apologize. He knocks on the door, and the girls ignore him. Michael has an encounter with a masked person, and he returns to the door and bangs for help. He is impaled with a "House for Sale" sign post. The killer drags his body away and returns the post to the yard. Ken calls Juliette, and she invites him over. Duncan, having paid the pizza girl to switch shirts and let him have the pizza, delivers the pizza to the girls, and they let him inside. The pizza girl (in Duncan's shirt) is walking down the street, and she is chased and drilled by the killer. Jackie is talking with Diane, and they hear a noise and see the weirdo outside. Jackie calls the police, and O'Reilly thinks it is "just a bunch of girls with overactive imaginations." The girls have let Frank and Tom inside, and Ken was right behind them. Frank gives Jackie some flowers and apologizes. The weirdo gets into the basement.

Susie shows Tom a swordfish on display in the basement, and the two kiss. Juliette is with Ken, and when her hand movies to a certain spot, Ken stops her. Janine hears them and tells the others, "They're doing it!" Tom drops pizza on the carpet, and Susie gets some bleach to clean it up. Juliette goes to shower, and Ken leaves. She finds a vibrator in the bathroom, she plugs it in and laughs. Juliette is in the tub, the lights go out and someone turns on the vibrator, throwing it into the water and electrocuting Juliette. Maria goes to the bathroom, dries up some of the water on the floor and opens the closet to discover a dead Juliette. The group gathers together, and Maria suggests that the weirdo killed their friend. Jackie calls the cops, but O'Reilly still does not take her seriously. Ken says he will go find his uncle, who used to be a police officer. He runs out, and Tom goes with him. As the two are running, Ken stops by a lumberyard and suggests getting tools (for better weapons). Tom finds a sledgehammer and gives it to Ken ("It's perfect"), and Ken whacks Tom. The men fight until Ken finally gets a chainsaw and slices into Tom's legs. After Ken leaves, Tom sits up and begins to crawl.

Jackie goes with Frank to check the basement. After seeing the swordfish with its "sword" broken off, they find the missing piece sticking in the dead weirdo in a trunk. Ken calls from a pay phone and tells them that his uncle said it would be safer to stay in the house. Ken goes to a van; inside are pictures of his cop uncle, dead bodies and his drill. Back at the house, Duncan goes to answer a knock, and Ken drills him. Frank jumps on Ken from behind. Moran (still looking through his telescope) calls the police and reports a disturbance. Jackie hits Ken with a lamp, and Frank is knocked down by the drill. Jackie is sitting by Frank, and tells Ken he killed him. The other girls cannot get the back door open (something is lodged between the sliding doors). Maria is separated and Ken approaches her (she sees Tom dead by the window). Janine runs in and knocks him on the head with a glass bowl. She and Maria run to the door. Maria is swiped by Ken's drill, and Janine jumps through the glass door and collapses on the patio. "What a waste," Ken says, as he starts the drill.

Upstairs, Ken walks into a room where both Maria and Susie are hiding. He finds Susie in the closet, pulls her out and throws her on the bed, where he hits her. After Maria comes out and hits Ken on the head with a lamp, she, Jackie and Diane run to the basement. They try crawling through the window, but Ken appears. Jackie shoots him with a spear gun, hitting his leg. They run back upstairs and see Janine and her innards on the patio. Susie puts bleach in a bucket and dumps it on Ken, blinding him. He swings wildly with his drill and hits Maria, who pleads with Ken to not kill her. She says she knows he has been hurt, and she seems to relax him by letting him touch her. He blindly gets on top of her, and Maria reaches for the drill. Ken is upset when her other hand moves around too much. He manages to get the drill and kills Maria.

Ken hears where Susie is in the kitchen (Jackie and Diane are standing by the front door) and heads for her until Diane gets his attention. They knock the drill away from Ken and throw the volleyball net over him, and Diane whacks him. Jackie goes to call the police. Ken awakes and his vision begins to return. He thinks back to his Uncle Billy, and he jumps up and grabs Diane. Susie tries to stab him, but he knocks her to the side and fatally stabs Diane. Jackie seizes the drill and drills Ken to a bloody death. Jackie finds a photograph of Uncle Billy with a young Ken.

Some adequate acting and a bit of humor in *Slumber Party Massacre III* almost make up for a few of the more humdrum scenes involving the characters' relationships. Like the first *Slumber Party Massacre*, the girls manage to work together to get rid of the murderer (with the exception of not helping Maria when they had the chance). The drill-toting killer is not quite as terrifying as perhaps he should be. Actress Carlton was the *Playboy* Playmate of the Month for July 1985.

Sorority House Massacre (1986)

Written and Directed by Carol Frank; Concorde Pictures; 74 min.

Cast: Angela O'Neill (Beth); Wendy Martel (Linda); Pamela Ross (Sara); Nicole Rio (Tracy); John C. Russell (Bobby); Marcus Vaughter (Andy); Vincent Bilancio (John); Joe Nassi (Craig); Mary Anne (Mrs. Lawrence); Gillian Frank (Doctor Lindsey); Joseph Mansier (Technician); Axel Roberts (Larry); Fitzhough Houston (Detective Gilbert); Marsha Carter (Nurse); Maureen Hawkes (Professor); Alan Eugster (Night Orderly); Phyllis Frank (Teacher); Thomas R. Mustin (Steve); Susan Bollman (Cindy); Ray Spinka (Shop Owner); Hammer (Gas Station Woman); Todd Darling (U-Hauler); John Hofferman (U-Helper); Patrick Fahey, Bob Moore (Policemen); Hillary Hollingsworth (Laura); Aimee Brooks (Cathy); Kara Joy (Janet); Ivory Berry (Susan); Shirley Aldridge (Mother); Scott Martin (Father)

Cast: Ron Diamond (Producer); Michael Wetherwax (Composer); Marc Reshovsky (Director of Photography); Jeff Wishengrad (Editor)

Mrs. Lawrence visits the hospitalized Beth to ask what happened. Beth says it started when she entered the house. A flashback shows Beth knocking on the door of a sorority house. A man in a hospital bed imagines a little girl entering an empty sorority house, and he screams. Two attendants run into his room. Linda lets Beth inside and says that after the weekend she will want to join the sorority. Beth dreams of going to the sorority and seeing four little girls in the yard. Inside she sees dolls at the table and blood dripping from the ceiling. Upstairs a jar of marbles breaks. Beth finds blood covering a bed before she finally awakes.

In the morning, Sara asks Beth how she got a scar on her arm; Beth does not remember. Tracy asks Linda and Sara about Beth, and she is told that Beth's aunt, who had raised her like a mother, had died. In her room, Beth sees a man standing in the mirror. He stabs his knife through, and blood drips. The hospital man, having freed himself from the restraints, is banging on the walls. In class, Beth sees a bloody man outside the window, and a knife comes up through her desk. Doctor Lindsey has the man hooked up to a machine to do some "mind reading." Beth returns to the sorority house, where many of the girls are leaving for the weekend. The man says to the doctor "Laura" (he has not spoken before). Beth enters the sorority and sees dead people in the living room and also the man, who approaches with a knife ("Who are you?"). The man screams in his hospital room, and Beth bumps into Mrs. Lawrence. Beth returns to the house, and everything is back to normal. The man is left alone.

Linda, Tracy and Sara return; the four have the sorority house to themselves for the weekend. They go to rich Cindy's room and try on her clothes, and Linda asks a quiet Beth what is wrong. Beth says she is having a recurring nightmare. An attendant goes into the man's room, and the man beats the attendant's head against the wall and walks out. As Beth tells her friends about her dreams, the man jumps the fence and escapes the Peligro Valley State Mental Hospital. The group of girls analyzes Beth's dream (Linda's major is dream imagery), and they talk of the dolls, the man and the phallic knife. U-Haul guys drop off materials for the girls so they can decorate for an upcoming "powwow."

John, Andy, Craig and Steve arrive to scare the girls. Larry the attendant sees that the man is missing from his room. Steve says that he has to go so he can go rafting, and Linda is upset. The lights go out, but the guys claim they did not do it. Larry gives a description of the missing patient to Detective Gilbert. In a circle around the fire, John says the sorority is haunted, and tells of a man who killed his mother and father. Beth, unsettled by the story, goes upstairs for bed. John continues his story, saying that the man went on to murder the rest of his family. Later, John says goodnight to Beth and they give each other a light kiss. Larry leaves a message for Doctor Lindsey on her answering machine. Beth awakes (she is sleeping on a bunk bed in a different room) as the man enters, stabs the bed above her and blood drips down. Beth screams, and the group runs to the room.

Tracy goes to the fusebox, and she is scared by Craig, who suggests they spend the night in the teepee (there for decoration). Beth tells of her dream, saying that this time the man killed someone else. She felt like she knew him and knew that she was next to be killed ("It's like he's already here"). She "sees" the man hide the knife in the fireplace, and the group finds it there. Tracy thinks it is a joke, and drops the knife into the smoldering wood. The doctor gets the message, and she calls Larry and tells him to get the man's file. She says the surviving girl lived with her aunt, and Larry gives Gilbert the address. Andy has to go, and he kisses Sara good-bye and is killed in the front yard. Linda hypnotizes Beth, who says that her brother Bobby is in the house, hurting everyone. Beth, as a little girl, hides as Bobby calls for her ("Laura?"), and he sees her and swings his knife into her hiding place. Linda cannot wake up Beth, and the girl finally comes out of her hypnosis when she is hit on the arm.

Tracy and Craig go to the teepee and make out. The killer, Bobby, cuts open the teepee and, following a struggle, stabs Tracy in the chest. Craig runs inside screaming and tells Linda and Sara that Tracy has been killed. The phone line and Cindy's private line are cut. Beth dreams of four little girls in a picture on the wall, with blood dripping on the girls (only on the arm of one girl); Bobby is after her, calling for Laura. Beth awakes, sees Bobby and moves from the couch, where a slumbering John is stabbed. Beth runs upstairs to the hiding place of the others, and they push a dresser in front of the door. Sara gets a fire ladder and they hang it out the window. Craig goes down first to hold the ladder steady, and he is stabbed in the back as Linda is on her way down. Bobby grabs Linda's foot, but she gets back in the room as Beth and Sara throw the ladder off. Bobby hangs on the window sill, so they slam the window on his hands and spray him with mace until he falls.

The girls run to the front door, see a dead Andy and run back to the room. When Bobby jumps through the window, they run out the sliding door in back of the house. Bobby is outside, and he stares at Sara and sees a little girl ("Janet?"). The girls run, and Sara trips over Tracy's corpse and is killed. Linda and Beth hide in the basement. Beth tells Linda that John's story is true, and that Bobby is after her (Laura is her first name). Doctor Lindsey suddenly realizes that Bobby would not go to the aunt's house, but would return to the house of his original killing spree.

Linda gets the spare key in the basement, and when Bobby arrives, she whacks him with a shovel. They run upstairs, where Bobby sees Linda as a little girl ("Cathy?"). Bobby goes after Beth; Linda swings the shovel, knocking things off the mantel, including Bobby's knife (he is using the original murder weapon he took from the fireplace). Linda bangs Bobby on the head, but as the girls as leaving, he sits up and stabs Linda in the back. A crawling Bobby grabs Beth's foot and stabs her in the legs. She makes her way to the other knife and stabs Bobby in the neck. The police arrive and take her away. In the hospital, Beth sees Bobby push a curtain to the side, and he calls her Beth. She screams and Mrs. Lawrence runs to her side.

Sorority House Massacre is not a great slasher, but writer-director Frank provides some intriguing visuals to show the telekinetic connections with Beth and her murderous brother, and the performances are effective.

Stage Fright (aka *Stage Fright: Aquarius; Deliria; Bloody Bird; Sound Stage Massacre*) (1987)

Written by Lew Cooper; Directed by Michele Soavi; Filmirage/DMV; 95 min.

Cast: David Brandon (Peter); Barbara Cupisti (Alicia); Don Fiore (Police Chief); Robert Gligorov (Danny); Mickey Knox (Old Cop); John Morghen (Brett); Clain Parker (Irving Wallace); Lori Parrel (Corinne); Martin Philips (Mark); James E.R. Sampson (Willy); Ulrike Schwerk (Betty); Mary Sellers (Laurel); Jo Anne Smith (Sybil); Piero Vida (Ferrari); Richard Berkeley (Doctor Porter); Sheila Goldberg (Nurse); Danny Gordon, Claude Jurman, Mark Parkinson, Helen Porter, Dominique Portier, Rackel Roskoff, Frank Senica, Simone Sardon, Albert Schultz, Sandy Schultz (Dancers)

Crew: Aristide Massaccesi, Donatella Donati (Producers); Simon Boswell (Composer); Renato Tafuri (Director of Photography); Kathleen Stratton (Editor)

A woman is walking down the street. As a feather lightly falls, she is grabbed by someone in a pitch black alley. People crowd around the dead woman; a man wearing a giant bird head jumps out and everyone starts dancing. Peter, the director, is watching the dancers on stage, and he angrily stops the performance, telling Alicia (the woman now risen from the "dead") that she is "supposed to be a whore." Peter tells Mr. Ferrari, who is there to "protect his investors," that the show, which opens in one week, has not accomplished its intended eroticism because the actors "stink." Backstage, Alicia is massaging her sore ankle and Betty, who is in wardrobe, convinces Alicia to sneak out and see a doctor. The two persuade Willy to let them out the service entrance. He gives Alicia a key and the two women leave.

Betty and Alicia go to a psychiatric hospital ("Psychiatrists are doctors, too, aren't they?"), and a doctor agrees to look at Alicia's ankle. Alicia asks the doctor about a man she saw behind bars, and he tells her it is Irving Wallace, who Betty knows as an actor who went insane and murdered people. As the two pass Wallace's room, they do not realize that the person in the bed is an attendant with a syringe in his neck. Betty drops Alicia off at the door, and Alicia runs inside to discover that she was "called" while she was away. She goes to see Peter, and he tells her to leave and that Laurel will be taking over her role. Betty returns to her parked car to turn off her lights, and she gets a pickaxe in the mouth when she steps out of the vehicle. Alicia cleans out her room and heads to her car. Outside she hears meowing from Lucifer (Willy's cat). She walks over the Betty's car and finds Betty dead.

The cops leave two police officers to watch (assuming that the escaped Wallace is the murderer). Peter tells his assistant Mark to ask Alicia, Laurel, Corinne, Danny, Sybil and Brett (playing the bird killer) to stay a little longer. He then tells Ferrari that he can open the show in three days, and they go to talk to a journalist. Inside, Peter gives the key to Corinne and tells her to lock the door and hide the key. Peter tells the six actors that have remained that he is changing the script. Brett will no longer play an "anonymous bird," but will be Irving Wallace. They seem reluctant (particularly due to the fact that Peter had told the papers that Betty was an actress to sensationalize the story), but Peter reminds everyone that they accepted their parts because they were desperate and now they all need a hit show.

Lovers Danny and Sybil (now an expectant mother) talk in the bathroom. Mark sends Laurel to wardrobe, where she screams when someone tries to open the locked dressing room door. Laurel thinks it was Brett, who now cannot find his costume. Later, Brett is looking at himself in the mirror; standing behind him, in bird costume, is Irving Wallace. The costumed Wallace walks onto the stage with Corinne, and as Peter tries to direct the scene, Alicia tells him she cannot find the key and that the maniac might be inside. Wallace improvises in the scene and uses a knife to stab Corinne. Alicia screams that the bird is not Brett, Wallace runs away and the people gather around the wounded Corinne. They ask the woman where she hid the key, but she dies before she can answer.

They all bang on the walls, but the two police officers sitting in their car do not hear anything. When the lights are shut off, the group goes to find candles. Mr. Ferrari stays behind to get all of his money, and Wallace murders him. The three men find Ferrari hanging and they run back to the make up room with the women. As Wallace begins playing loud music in the main room, Danny suggests going to Willy's office and getting a skeleton key. Alicia says her ankle hurts too much, so the women and Mark stay behind and Danny and Peter run to find the key. As the group waits in the room, someone tries to open the door. They stand in front of it, and Wallace's arm crashes through and grabs Mark. Sybil screams as Mark is being drilled through the door. Peter and Danny hear her and rush back to find Mark dead, hanging at the door.

They head to the workshop and arm themselves. In the main room, Peter points the spotlight and sees Wallace running above the stage. Peter and the others climb up, but Alicia tugs at Laurel's ankle for her to wait, and Laurel kicks her. Alicia falls to the floor and is knocked unconscious. Everyone else gets inside a room, and Peter axes the bird-costumed man, only to discover that it was a bound Brett. Sybil is pulled through the weak floor, and Peter and Danny grab her arms and manage to only bring up the top half of her body. An enraged Danny jumps in the hole and is attacked and killed by a chainsaw-wielding Wallace. Peter runs to the main door and tries to axe it open. He pushes Laurel to the side, and she is hit with the running chainsaw from an approaching Wallace. The maniac slices off Peter's axe-holding arm, and the chainsaw stops running. Peter goes for the axe with his remaining hand, but Wallace grabs it and beheads the director.

A feather lightly falls, and Alicia awakes. She follows a blood trail to the showers and sees an injured Laurel behind one of the curtains. Alicia hears someone coming and hides in the adjacent shower, and watches Wallace kill Laurel and drag her away. In an office, Alicia finds keys and a gun in the desk, and she runs to the main door and tries different keys. She hides from Wallace, who turns on some music, and goes to sit on the stage, where the corpses are all sitting in various positions. She sees the key sitting in a crack in the floor. Alicia goes underneath the stage and pries the key through with a metal spike. Wallace grabs her as she is walking out, and after the gun only clicks, Alicia stabs him with the metal spike. A chase leads to above the stage, where Alicia uses a fire extinguisher and Wallace falls back and hangs onto an electrical cord. Alicia axes the cord and Wallace falls. As she passes the maniac, he grabs her again, so she dumps a burning barrel onto him and sets him afire. She gets the door open and runs to the cops outside.

Alicia is taken to the hospital, and the next day she goes back to the theater to find her expensive watch (which she lost during the struggle with Wallace). Willy lets her inside and tells her the gun she found had the safety on, which is why it did not fire. Alicia finds her watch, and Wallace appears behind her and raises his axe. Willy shoots him in the head, and the axe falls and breaks Alicia's watch. After a dismayed Alicia leaves, Wallace's eyes move, followed by an odd grunt.

Stage Fright is an astounding feature film debut from Soavi, with a terrific locale and many scenes of pure suspense. Screenwriter Cooper is actually Luigi Montefiori, who also uses the pseudonym "George Eastman," and who might be remembered by some as the villain with the interesting conclusion in Joe D'Amato's *Anthropophagus* (aka *The Grim Reaper*) (1980). Soavi plays the young police officer who thinks he looks a little like James Dean.

The Stepfather (1987)

Written by Donald E. Westlake; Directed by Joseph Ruben; ITC Productions; 89 min.

Cast: Terry O'Quinn (Jerry Blake); Jill Schoelen (Stephanie); Shelley Hack (Susan); Charles Lanyer (Doctor Bondurant); Stephen Shellen (Jim Oglivie); Stephen E. Miller (Al Brennan); Robyn Stevan (Karen); Jeff Schultz (Paul Baker); Lindsay Bourner (Art Teacher);

Anna Hagan (Mrs. Leitner); Gillian Barber (Annie Barnes); Blue Mankuma (Lieutenant Jack Walls); Jackson Davies (Mr. Chesterton); Sandra Head (Receptionist); Gabrielle Rose (Dorothy Finnehard); Richard Sargent (Mr. Anderson); Margot Pinvidic (Mrs. Anderson); Rochelle Greenwood (Cindy Anderson); Don S. Williams (Mr. Stark); Don MacKay (Joe); Dale Wilson (Frank); Gary Hetherington (Herb); Andrew Snider (Mr. Grace); Marie Stillin (Mrs. Fairfax); Paul Batten (Mr. Fairfax); Sheila Paterson (Doctor Barbara Faraday)

Crew: Jay Benson (Producer); Patrick Moraz (Composer); John W. Lindley (Director of Photography); George Bowers (Editor)

Inside a nice house in an attractive neighborhood is a bearded man in glasses, who washes blood off his hands and showers. He shaves his beard, puts in contact lenses, slips into a fresh suit and walks downstairs, where a bloody, dead family is lying in the living room. He walks out the door and rides on the ferry, where he knocks a suitcase of his old clothes into the water.

One year later, Jerry Blake comes home to his wife Susan and stepdaughter Stephanie. Stephanie goes to see her psychiatrist, Doctor Bondurant and talks about her father's death, her trouble in school and her stepfather, of whom she does not seem fond. Jerry, working in realty, shows a family a house. He pushes little Cindy on the swing, talking of his daughter Stephanie and inadvertently calling her Jill. Stephanie tells Jerry and Susan that she has been expelled from school (for causing another outburst) and that she wants to go to boarding school. Jerry refuses to break up the family. Later, Susan talks to her daughter, and Stephanie says she is trying to give Jerry a chance. In the bedroom, Susan mentions that Jerry does not talk about his past.

Jim Oglivie and reporter Al Brennan go to the house where Henry Morrison killed his family a year ago. Jim tells Brennan that Henry quit his job three weeks before the killing, and he suggests that he had set up a new life and is living in a nearby area. He tells the reporter that Henry's wife was Jim's sister. At a get-together in the backyard (with most of the families to whom Jerry sold houses), Herb shows Jerry a newspaper article about a family killer still being sought. When Stephanie is in the basement getting some ice cream, Jerry comes down and has a maniacal outburst. He sees his stepdaughter and says he was letting off some steam. Stephanie reads the article and she tells her friend Karen that she is writing to the *Seattle Examiner* to request a picture of Henry Morrison.

When Stephanie tells Bondurant about boarding school, he thinks it is a good idea for her to get away and tells her he will talk to Jerry. At home, Jerry checks the mail and sees an envelope addressed to Stephanie from the *Seattle Examiner*. Inside is a picture of his bearded self. He hides it from Stephanie. Jerry spends some angry moments in the basement before he is called to dinner. Later, Bondurant calls, but Jerry tells Susan to say that he is not there. Jim goes to see Lieutenant Jack Walls and learns that the police have no leads on the family killer. Jerry talks with Mrs. Leitner, and he gets Stephanie back in school.

Stephanie tells her doctor that Jerry scares her. Bondurant (as "Mr. Martin") makes an appointment with Jerry to see a house. Paul walks Stephanie home, and Stephanie receives her *Seattle Examiner* envelope, with a photograph of another man. Bondurant arrives for his appointment, telling Jerry that he is a bachelor working in "stress management." The doctor asks Jerry many questions, and Jerry notes that he seems more interested in the man than in the house. Bondurant says it is a force of habit and that his wife gets on him for it all the time. Jerry reminds him that he had said he was not married, and the doctor's explanation of being "recently divorced" does not seem to satisfy Jerry, so he beats Bondurant to death with a block of wood. Jerry checks his identification and wraps up the body. He puts the doctor behind the wheel, lights some wrapping in the tank and lets the car roll into an explosion.

The following day, Jerry tells Stephanie

about Bondurant's car accident. Later, Jerry is putting up a birdhouse and Stephanie offers to help. She apologizes about her trouble, and Jerry suggests they bury the hatchet. Jim, having found a magazine with missing pages in the house, goes to a library to find the same issue and sees a story on "great all-American towns." After the family enjoys a Thanksgiving meal, Stephanie is out at a pizza place, and she is given a ride home on Paul's moped. At her front door, they kiss and Jerry storms out. Stephanie is angry, calling Jerry a "crazy creep" and wondering why her mother is with him. Susan slaps Stephanie, who runs away. Susan is upset with Jerry's behavior, and Jerry steps away to think to himself.

Jerry says good-bye to the people at the real estate office. Jim goes to the police station to warn the cops of Henry Morrison possibly being married again. He wants a look at the marriage certificates, and he flirts with Annie for information. Stephanie has an appointment with her new doctor, but she goes to Bondurant's dark office instead, and sees a note with an address, time and "J. Blake." Jerry rides a ferry and, in the bathroom, puts glasses on, removes his hairpiece and affixes a mustache to his face. Jerry (as "Bill Hodgkins") goes to an insurance office for an interview. Jim is visiting houses, and Susan answers the door. She says that Jerry is not in, and Jim learns that the man sells houses. Jerry/Bill greets his new neighbor, a woman with children but no husband.

Susan calls the real estate office for Jerry and is told he is no longer there. Jim goes to another house and shows a picture of Henry, and he is told that it looks like the man who sold the couple the house. At home, Susan tells Jerry what she has learned, and he says it is a mistake and he gets on the phone. Susan says the receptionist probably got his name wrong, and Jerry says that Hodgkins should be easy to remember. He stops himself and asks who he is, and Susan tells him, "Jerry." He thanks his wife, beats her face with the phone and punches her, knocking her into the basement. Stephanie walks in and goes to shower. Before Jerry can get to the door, the doorbell rings. Jim walks in, but Jerry is waiting behind the door. Jim notices blood on Jerry's face and he goes for his gun, but is stabbed in the stomach.

Jerry walks upstairs, and Stephanie, out of the shower, sees him with a bloody knife. He chases her to the bathroom and bangs on the door. When Jerry breaks through, Stephanie stabs him with a shard of mirror. Jerry chases Stephanie to the attic and, as he nears her, he falls through the floor and into the bathroom below. Stephanie gets out of the attic and sees her wounded mother on the stairs. Jerry grabs his stepdaughter and Susan shoots him twice with Jim's gun. He slides down the stairs, then crawls slowly towards the knife. Stephanie grabs it and stabs Jerry in the chest. He falls to the bottom of the stairwell, dead. Stephanie saws the birdhouse down and walks away with her mother.

The Stepfather is an effective slasher, bolstered by a tongue-in-cheek script and good performances by Schoelen and O'Quinn. O'Quinn is especially effective when he has no dialogue and merely eyes the people around him (the table scene, after Jerry has already started looking for another family, is excellent).

Stepfather II (1989)

Written by John Auerbach; Directed by Jeff Burr; ITC Entertainment Group; 88 min.

Cast: Terry O'Quinn (The Stepfather); Meg Foster (Carol Grayland); Caroline Williams (Matty Crimmins); Jonathan Brandis (Todd Grayland); Henry Brown (Doctor Joseph Danvers); Mitchell Laurance (Phil Grayland); Miriam Byrd-Nethery (Sally Jenkins); Leon Martell (Smitty); Renata Scott (Betty Willis); John O'Leary (Sam Watkins); Glen Adams (Salesman); Eric Brown (Hotel Attendant)

Crew: Carol Lampman (Executive Producer); Darin Scott, William Burr (Producers); Jim Manzie (Composer); Jacek Laskus (Director of Photography); Pasquale A. Buba (Editor)

The man whose last alias was Jerry Blake sits up in his bed at night and looks at the scars on his chest. At the Pugent Sound Psychiatric Hospital, Jerry is taken to see Doctor Danvers. The two talk about trust, and Danvers tells Smith, the guard, to remove Jerry's handcuffs. In another session, Jerry tells the doctor that he is the only one he can trust, and Danvers asks Smith to wait outside. Later, Jerry shows Danvers a model house with a male figurine that he has made. He throws them against the wall to express his metaphor of wanting to fix everything. While an appeased Danvers writes notes, Jerry pulls a needle from the man model and stabs the doctor in the back of the neck. He buzzes Smith in and beats him with his nightstick. Jerry puts on Smith's uniform and leaves the hospital.

As a man is trying get his suitcase in the car, Jerry offers to help, but slams the trunk on the man's arms. He drives the car to a hotel, where he watches a television news story on himself and circles an obituary. He then watches a game show called *Dream Houses*, where Palm Meadow is called an "ideal spot." Jerry goes to Palm Meadow, where Carol shows him, as Gene, a house available to lease. Gene says he specializes in family guidance, and Carol tells him she lives nearby with her son. Gene drops the welcome mat by the front door and has an unsuccessful attempt at Video Date-Tronics.

Later, Gene ("Doctor Clifford") is sitting in a session with a group of women, and he speaks to a quiet Carol, who talks of her husband leaving and how it has affected her son. Afterwards, Carol's friend Matty tells her that Gene likes her. Gene comes home later with groceries, and Carol asks him over, where they enjoy some Chinese take-out. Carol's son Todd goes outside and throws a baseball against the garage, and Gene shows him a better way to throw the ball. The two also build a ramp for Todd's skateboarding, with Gene showing Todd how to properly hammer nails. At a later session, Gene sees a car parked in Carol's driveway across the street, and a man getting out. Distracted, he stops the session early. He goes to Carol's house, where he meets her ex-husband Phil, then heads to his garage where he runs the saw and angrily mumbles to himself. Matty is at the door for her mail carrier hat that she forgot, and she walks inside and sees Gene's book (for notes during sessions) with blank pages. Gene is there. Matty gets her hat and says good-bye.

Carol tells Gene that Phil wants a second chance, and Gene tells her to have Phil stop by for a talk. Phil is there later, and Gene tells him that Carol wants no part of him. Phil heads for the door, but Gene stops him and tells him it was a test, to see if he was true. Gene says that Carol is indeed interested, and he gives Phil a drink. He brings out wine ("Think it's time I cracked open this bottle") and cracks open the bottle on Phil's head and stabs him with the broken end. Carol calls and tells Gene to ask Phil to telephone her when he returns to the hotel. Gene relays the message to the dead man, goes to the hotel, takes his things and places everything in the trunk. He goes to the junkyard and smashes and beats the car before leaving it behind.

The next day, Carol tells Gene that she was told Phil checked out of the hotel. Gene says he is not sorry about Phil, and the two kiss as Phil's car is crushed in a compactor. At a party, Gene announces to everyone that Carol has agreed to marry him. Matty, not happy, tells Carol that she does not know enough of Gene. She says he only gets junk mail and local bills; Carol is upset over Matty's apparent paranoia. Later, Carol suggests a time of intimacy with Gene, but he seems reluctant.

Gene and Matty meet at a park bench. Matty has opened a letter from Gene's high school; there is a picture of the basketball team (of which Gene was a member), but all the players are black men. Gene asks Matty to let him tell Carol of his mendacities, and she gives him until five o'clock. Gene goes to Carol and they spent some time in bed, where he tells her that the scars were caused by a patient. Matty calls the house (it is past five), but no one answers. She awakes later on the couch; upon hearing a noise, she gets a letter opener, looks around and is scared by a cat. Matty relaxes until Gene arrives and chokes her. Gene types up a suicide note and leaves Matty hanging in the kitchen. He takes a bottle of wine from her house and goes through the backyard, where his whistling is heard by the blind neighbor, Sam. Gene returns to Carol with the wine.

After Matty's funeral, Gene and a sad Carol are in Matty's house, and Sam arrives. He mentions someone leaving in the middle of the night, and he whistles the tune for the couple. Carol wants to postpone the wedding, and Gene tells her they do not have to have an extravagant wedding and that the marriage is the most important thing. At the church, Todd delivers a few wine bottles (a gift from Matty's parents). After Carol realizes that Gene had the same wine on that particular night, she hears her son whistling a familiar tune out in the hall. She calls him in and asks him where he learned the song, and he tells her that Gene taught him.

Gene walks into the room, and Todd leaves. Carol wants him to explain about the wine and "The Camp Town Ladies" (his whistling tune of choice). An irate Gene says that Carol will never find a better family man. Carol goes for the door, but her finacée grabs her, throws her against the wall and shoves the veil in her face. When Todd comes in, Gene swings a bottle at him and chases him to a storage closet, padlocking him inside. Carol stabs him in the hand with a fork and then with a knife. Gene throws Carol through some doors. Todd takes the hinges off of the door with a screwdriver and runs down the hall with a hammer. As Gene lifts the knife (taken from his chest), Todd hammers his hand. When Gene goes for the knife again, Todd swings the hammer into the man's chest. After Carol and Todd leave, Gene limps to the cake table, where he looks at the broken head of the bride figurine. He lies down, evidently dead.

While not as thrilling or creepy as the first film, *Stepfather II* does provide some humor, and O'Quinn is still very good as the multiple-aliased, murderous "family man."

Stepfather III (1992)

Written by Guy Magar and Marc B. Ray; Directed by Guy Magar; ITC Entertainment Group; 110 min.

Cast: Robert Wightman (Keith Grant); Priscilla Barnes (Christine Davis); Season Hugley (Jennifer); David Tom (Andy Davis); John Ingle (Father Brennan); Dennis Paladino (Mr. Thompson); Stephen Mendel (Mark Wraynal); Jay Acovone (Steve Davis); Christa Miller (Beth Davis); Mario Roccuzzo (Plastic Surgeon); Joan Dareth (Bernice); Jennifer Bassey (Doctor Brady); Adam Ryen (Nicky); Mindy Ann Martin (Tiffany); Joel Carlson (Pete); Sumer Stamper (Maggie); Brenda Strong (Crime Search Reporter); Mort Lewis (Funeral Priest); Adam Wylie (Easter Party Boy)

Crew: Guy Magar, Paul Moen (Producers); Patrick C. Regan (Composer); Alan Caso (Director of Photography); Patrick Gregston (Editor)

A man walks in the rain to a trashed place, and he hands a plastic surgeon a wad of money. The man is strapped to the table; after the surgeon cuts and slices into his face, he passes out. Later, the man looks at a magazine that declares Deer View as one of the "safest neighborhoods." After the surgeon cuts off the bandages, the man compares his face in a mirror to a picture of his old self as Jerry/Gene and then slices the doctor's throat with a surgical saw.

Nine months later, in Deer View, Keith is the Easter bunny for the church's Easter egg hunt. At the Easter dance, Father Brennan and the wheelchair-bound Andy discuss Compu-Tective. Bernice tells Christine, Andy's mom, that she should talk to Keith. Christine asks Keith to dance, and Andy smiles as he watches them. Mark cuts in, asking Christine for another chance. Later, Keith is invited to dine with Christine and Andy, where he discusses once selling real estate, and Andy talks of his love for "computer sleuthing." Keith brings Christine a basket of flowers at the school where she works, and she invites Keith to a picnic. Mark arrives and is angry that Christine broke off the relationship.

Enjoying the day together, Keith asks Christine how Andy ended up in the wheelchair. She tells a story of arguing with her then-husband Steve, and Andy running into the street and being hit by a car. Christine says that doctors claim that, physically, Andy should be able to walk and that his problem may be psychosomatic. Mark follows Keith to his house, where he says he wants to marry Christine and be Andy's stepfather ("Find your own family!"). Keith says he understands and swings a shovel into Mark's leg and then beats his face twice.

Andy tells Father Brennan that there is something about Keith that he does not trust. Christine and Keith are kissing by the fireplace when Andy interrupts them to ask where the printing paper is. Keith says he wants to stay the night but he does not want to take advantage of a single mother. He does not believe it is right until they are married, which evidently is a marriage proposal, and Christine accepts. The two are wed, but Andy remains suspicious. Father Brennan watches Andy when Keith and Christine are gone, and he sees that Andy is running a search on all the Keith Grants in Charleston and Louisville (reportedly Keith's last place of residence and his city of origin). Andy asks the priest to make the phone calls.

Andy tries to watch television, and Keith takes him outside to throw a football around. On the second attempt, Andy falls, and Keith tells him to stand up and walk. He says Andy just does not want to walk, and he finally picks him up ("Stop that damn whining!"). Steve and his wife Beth want Andy to live with them for the summer, but Keith does not want to break up the family. Christine asks Andy about it in his room, and Andy seems happy about the idea. Keith is angry, and he takes his frustration out on a tree stump with a hatchet. At Keith's workplace, Thompson's Nursery, Jennifer and her son Nicky arrive to ask about Keith's cottage. Keith shows them the place, and he learns that it is just Jennifer and Nicky, and he seems content.

Christine says good-bye to Andy, and Keith watches from the window, crushing the model airplane he had given his stepson. Keith goes to throw around a football with Jennifer and Nicky, and Father Brennan stops by. Keith leaves as quickly as possible. Later, Keith learns that Christine will more than likely not be able to give birth, and he is furious. Andy watches *Crime Search USA*, and he sees a report of an escaped family serial killer who seeks single mothers with one child. Keith returns to Christine after being with Jennifer, and an upset Christine says something has changed in the six weeks they have been married. At the nursery, Mr. Thompson tells Keith he knows that Keith has been with Jennifer, and he mocks Keith's family-is-important motto. Keith chops Mr. Thompson in the chest with a garden rake and then hits him again in the throat.

An update on *Crime Search USA* says the police believe the killer may have had plastic surgery and may have surgery scars (Andy had seen a scar behind Keith's ear). Andy takes a picture of the killer's photo on television. Keith goes to confess to Father Brennan, and the priest, knowing who it is, asks personal questions until Keith wonders about the peculiar inquiries. Keith suggests marriage to Jennifer, but he says they would have to move out of Deer View for a "new beginning." Keith goes home with an axe, but he settles down when he sees that Andy is home. Keith says it is nice to have Nicky home and then he corrects himself. Jennifer and Nicky visit Christine's office, and Christine reacts to Nicky's familiar name. Keith goes to see Christine, but leaves when he sees his surrogate family. Christine watches him leave and then learns that the mother and son are living in a nearby cottage.

At night, Keith peeks in and sees Andy scanning a picture of his old and new self. Andy talks to Father Brennan, who says he checked out the names and all of the Keiths still live there. He says he will help in Andy's quest to check Keith's fingerprints to prove that the boy is wrong. The priest joins them for dinner that night. When Keith helps Christine with the dishes, Andy grabs Keith's fork and drops it in Father Brennan's plastic bag. The priest leaves, and Keith says he forgot to turn the heaters on at the nursery. He drives down the road, rams the priest's car and drives past him. Father Brennan stops when Keith's truck is in the way, and Keith breaks through the window and beats the priest's head on the steering wheel. He takes the fork and bag, lights a cloth in the gas tank and pushes the car over the cliff to an inevitable explosion.

Jennifer visits Keith at the nursery and pressures him about moving in. He follows her with a hammer but stops when he sees two women. Keith tells Andy the sad news about Father Brennan's car accident and he suggests a fresh start. The next day, before the priest's funeral, Keith is happy ("It's Father's Day!"). At the funeral, Keith walks away when he sees Jennifer. Christine approaches Jennifer and asks to talk. Keith learns of the meeting, and he says he is going to the nursery to work. Andy expresses his distrust of Keith to his mother. Christine gets a phone call from Jennifer, who postpones the talk because her boyfriend wants to see her. Jennifer arrives at the nursery, and Keith says he must protect his family. He hits Jennifer, turns the woodchipper on and lifts her up, but stops when he sees car headlights.

Christine tells Andy to wait in the car, and she goes inside. She sees Keith and demands to know where Jennifer is. When she spots a beaten Jennifer nearby she tries to run, but Keith grabs her hair. Andy is chilly and he goes for a sweater and finds the bloody bag with the fork. He gets his wheelchair and crawls out of the car. Inside, he sees Keith with the two unconscious women. Andy stands and rolls his wheelchair toward Keith. Keith runs after him; when looking up high on a ladder, Andy pushes him, and Keith falls into the running woodchipper. Andy gets too close, and Keith grabs him.

Christine pulls Andy away, and Keith slides in and is chopped to bloody pieces until Jennifer axes the cable. Christine and Andy hug and the three people walk away.

Stepfather III is the weakest of the *Stepfather* series, mostly due to the absence of Terry O'Quinn and the film rehashing plot elements (mixing up the family names) and killings (the "car accident"). The character of Andy is such a pigheaded brat that it is almost easier to sympathize with the murderous stepfather.

Stripped to Kill (1987)

Written by Andy Ruben and Katt Shea Ruben; Directed by Katt Shea Ruben; Concorde Pictures; 86 min.

Cast: Kay Lenz (Cody); Greg Evigan (Heinaman); Norman Fell (Ray); Pia Kamakahi (Eric/Roxanne); Tracey Crowder (Fanny); Debby Nasser (Dazzle); Lucia Lexington (Brandy); Carlye Byron (Cinammon); Athena Worthey (Zeena); Michelle Foreman (Angel); Diana Bellamy (Shirl); Peter Scranton (Mr. Pocket); Brad David Berwick (Derek); Tom Ruben (Mobile Entrepeneur); J. Bartell (Margolin); Jon Lee Freels (Punk); Debra Lamb (Amateur Dancer)

Crew: Roger Corman (Executive Producer); Mark Byers, Andy Ruben, Matt Leipzig (Producers); John O'Kennedy (Composer); John Leblanc (Director of Photography); Zach Staenberg (Editor)

Angel is dancing on stage for Roxanne, announcer Derek and Ray, the owner of the club, The Rock Bottom. Eric is working on a sculpture, and he heads home to see his sister Roxanne being intimate with Angel. After Angel leaves, Eric is angry about Roxanne being with Angel, then relaxes and hugs his sister. Backstage at the club, Derek asks Brandy out and she declines, and Angel telephones Roxanne ("Well, did he hurt you?"). Roxanne sounds sick and asks her to meet her somewhere. Pocket, a frequent and eerie visitor of the club, bothers Angel, and she calls for Ray. Later, someone pushes an

Angel in waiting off of a bridge and pours gasoline on her as she lies wounded. Cody, a cop going undercover, chases a perp, stumbles over Angel and is doused with gasoline. Her partner Heinaman stops her from firing her gun and pulls Cody away as the stripper is set afire.

Roxanne tells Ray she cannot perform due to family problems, but Ray says she has to if she wants money. Zeena gets mad when she sees Roxanne dancing in Zeena's dress. The cops learn that Angel was a stripper, and Heinaman informs Cody of an amateur contest in which the winner is frequently hired. The contest uses applause meters, and so several officers volunteer to visit the club and cheer for Cody. Cody goes on stage at the contest (as "Sonny") and, thanks to her police buddies, wins first prize. Cinammon (as the "professional entertainment") dances next; evidently strung out on some drugs, she falls off stage and onto Pocket's lap. Cody is hanging around backstage with the other strippers when Roxanne shows up, saying she has nowhere else to go. Ray fires Cinammon because of her drug habit, and she leaves. Zeena mentions Pocket frightening Angel the night before. Ray stops Cody from leaving, and tells her, "You are the worst dancer I ever saw in my life. You're hired."

Cody tells Heinaman that she got the job, and she points out Pocket to him. Cody sits by Pocket and talks to him, and he gives her a paper flower and walks away. Heinaman follows Pocket outside, sees someone try to sell Pocket a butterfly knife, and watches the man expertly handle the weapon. Cinammon is walking home alone, a chain is wrapped around her neck and she is strangled. The killer straps her to the bottom of a semi-truck, and it pulls away. Cody gets home and hears a noise inside her house. She finds Heinaman occupying the bathroom, apparently waiting for her to return. He tells about Pocket, and says that the man took something from the seller on the street, but the cop did not see what it was. Cody says she does not think Pocket has killed anyone. The next day in Heinaman's office, the officer tells Cody about Dazzle and Fanny involved in an assault, and he says that siblings Roxanne and Eric are runaways, having both witnessed their father kill their mother. Cody suggests that the killer could be one of the dancers.

Brandy tries to get hold of Cinammon. Roxanne, while on stage, loudly accuses Pocket of murdering Angel. Outside, Dazzle, Zeena and Fanny accost Pocket, demanding to know where Cinammon is; Cody stops them. The dancers say they assaulted Pocket for Roxanne, who was Angel's lover. Later, Cody suggests to Heinaman that Roxanne may have learned that Angel and Cinammon were together, and she killed them both (Cinammon is still only missing). She says they should check out Roxanne and her brother. Heinaman comes at Cody with a knife (with a trick blade), and he says her reflexes are getting better, and he gives her the knife. At the club, Cody wants to talk to Roxanne, and an unofficial date is set.

Roxanne returns to her home to see Heinaman trying to get inside. The cop gets into a padlocked door to find something wrapped in plastic, which turns out to be a sculpture. A shotgun is pointed at Heinaman; it is Paul Margolin, an ex-cop who lives above the siblings. He says he was with Eric watching Bruce Lee films. The next day, the cops get a call from their superior and Cody is told to stop dancing (Heinaman neglected to tell Cody that she was not actually supposed to dance topless). Heinaman says that Angel was raped, so the killer cannot be Roxanne. Now the cops are looking for Pocket. Cody goes to see Ray and tries to quit, but she feels obligated to go on stage one last time. An irate Heinaman meets Cody backstage, and he tells her Cinammon was found murdered. He further suggests that Cody is more interested in stripping than solving the case. They calm one another by kissing, but their time together is seemingly unsatisfactory, and they angrily depart.

Heinaman finds the street seller and asks him what he sells Pocket; the man tells him he always wants cassette tapes of classical music. Cody finds a connection with Margolin and the brother and sister, and she learns that Margolin used to blackmail young girls into having sex. Heinaman finds Pocket and sees that one of his hands is missing. He telephones a doctor (from a card in Pocket's wallet), and the cop learns something which would prevent Pocket from being the person who raped Angel.

Cody goes to Roxanne's place for their "date," Eric answers the door, and leaves her to sit in the living room. Cody finds Margolin dead in the other room, and Roxanne appears behind her. ("He wanted more, or less, than I could actually give him.") In a struggle, Roxanne is stabbed in the chest, and Heinaman runs inside and gets on the telephone, only to be shot by Roxanne. Roxanne pulls the knife out of her artificial breast, and a wig is yanked off to reveal Eric. He had killed Roxanne to keep her from leaving him. Cody is drenched in gasoline, and she gets out the door with a pyromaniac Eric after her. The chase leads to the club, where Eric shoots Derek and Fanny. Cody manages to pour some gasoline on Eric. Outside, she throws the trick knife at Eric, he fires the gun and is engulfed in flames. The fire is heading towards Cody, and Heinaman (having worn a bulletproof vest) pulls her away. The two embrace.

Although jam-packed with scenes of stripping, *Stripped to Kill* does contain a solid story, and the acting is respectable. Additionally, the choreography and the dancing are strong.

Stripped to Kill II (aka *Live Girls*) (1989)

Written and Directed by Katt Shea Ruben; Concorde Pictures; 82 min.

Cast: Maria Ford (Shady); Eb Lottimer (Decker); Karen Mayo Chandler (Cassandra); Marjean Holden (Something Else); Birke Tan (Dazzle); Debra Lamb (Mantra); Jeanine Bisignano (Sonny); Lisa Glaser (Victoria); Tommy Ruben (Ike); J. Bartell (Assistant Coroner); Virginia Peters (Shirl); Paisley (Mo); Al Guarino (Man in Club); Gregg Cooper (Cop); Charlie Wallace (Charlie); Sandy Ruben (Ike's Mom)

Crew: Roger Corman (Executive Producer); Andy Ruben (Producer); Rodman Flender (Associate Producer); Gary Stockdale (Composer); Phedon Papamichael (Director of Photography); Stephen Mark (Editor)

While dancers are on a stage, Shady is being pursued by a person in a black mask. The person, with a razor in the mouth, kisses Shady, and then the masked person becomes Shady with another dancer. Shady awakes from a dream with bloody lips. Her roommate Cassandra calms her down and makes her some tea. Shady tells her she dreamt that she hurt Victoria. Shady and Cassandra go to the club, Paragon, where they work. Shady asks Ike where Victoria is, and he calls Victoria over from a private dance. Later, Shady tells Victoria she asked Ike to interrupt her private dance (and make her lose money) because she wanted to see that Victoria was okay. Victoria seems happy that Shady would think of her, and asks to meet her later. After dreaming of slicing Victoria's throat with a razor, Shady goes to Paragon and finds Victoria dead.

Police officers are investigating the murder and talking to the dancers. Shady walks in and sees Victoria again, and Sergeant Decker catches her when she passes out. Cassandra takes her friend home, and Decker has what seems to be blood on his hand (from Shady). Later, Cassandra reassures Shady that she has not killed anyone. Decker learns that the blood on his hand was Victoria's (with traces of black spandex), and a broken part of a razor blade was found in Victoria's body. Ike tries to give a dismal Shady a flower, but she says she does not want anything from him. Afterwards, Shady apologizes to Ike, and he seems to accept. Decker visits the club for a private Shady dance, but she leaves when he asks too many questions.

Decker goes to see Shady outside the club. He shows her a razor, she tells him of her dreams and admits to finding a murdered Victoria. The two kiss. Ike sees them and angrily walks away. Decker stops the kissing session. Shady, believing the sergeant considers her cheap, goes home. In his office, Decker is told that traces of saliva were found on the razor blade, and that Shady was once in an institution. Shady is smoking in the alley outside of the club, and Decker calls her by her real name and asks about the man she "cut up." She tells him, and then asks why Decker limps, which he explains. In due time, the two begin having sex in the alley. Mantra, after shoving pizza in Ike's face for not letting her eat in the club's main room, walks outside and sees the couple in their time of intimacy. Decker leaves, and the other dancers playfully mock Shady.

The dancer named Something Else approaches Mantra and asks her for a ride; Mantra suggests she take a bus. She is only kidding, but Something Else furiously storms off. Later, a person walks up to Mantra (she seems to know the person by offering a slight smile) and closes in on her neck. Shady awakes outside, and she goes back to her place and tells Cassandra that she dreamt of Mantra. While Cassandra and Shady are performing on stage, Dazzle gets a call from the police and she gives a note to Ike, who inadvertently reads it over the microphone. An unsettled Shady runs off the stage. Shirl tells Decker that Something Else was once in trouble for assault and Ike had been arrested for peeping. Decker breaks into Ike's apartment later, and he hears Ike's mother leave a message referring to Shady, the woman Ike told her he is going to marry. Seeing pictures of Shady all over the wall, Decker calls in an APB on Ike.

Decker has an encounter with Something Else and Dazzle. The two do not know where the roommates are, and Decker leaves after picking up a pill from the floor. Dazzle is left alone. When Cassandra and Shady return, she tells them she wants to stay with them. When Dazzle sees Cassandra put something in her tea, Cassandra tells her it is something to help Shady "relax." Shady dreams of Dazzle dancing and being grabbed by hands from the wall. Cassandra enters the room to a bloody-lipped Shady and a bloody Dazzle. Ike, who had been watching from the roof, walks in with a razor, saying he is going to protect Shady. Cassandra slowly approaches him, leans over for a kiss and slices his neck with a razor in her mouth. She catches some blood in a cup and pours it on Shady's lip.

Shirl tells Decker about hookers who used to carry razor blades in their mouths for protection, and the cop is told that the pill he found was used in Vietnam for "interrogation." He checks out Cassandra (the only dancer who had no file) and learns that she has a lengthy record, including the murder of her skilled-with-drugs ex–G.I. pimp. Cassandra, speaking to a dazed Shady, "describes" Shady's dream for her. Shady dreams of her dead friends and the masked person. Cassandra cuts Shady's mouth. Decker is there with gun drawn. Cassandra turns around ("You can drop that accent") and attacks with the razor and then with some broken glass. A mannequin from the roof (Cassandra's "decoration") falls through the roof and pins Decker. Cassandra shoves a glass shard into Decker's shoulder as Shady wakes up. Shady grabs Decker's fallen gun, shoots her ex-roommate a few times and helps the wounded cop.

Stripped to Kill II, while not as good as its predecessor, manages to incorporate an intriguing "premonition" bit into the storyline. Actor Bartel, who stars as a coroner, appeared in *Stripped to Kill* as a police officer. Several names in the film (Dazzle, Sonny and Shirl) were used in the first film.

The Surgeon (aka *Exquisite Tenderness*) (1994)

Written by Patrick Cirillo, from a Screenplay by Bernard Sloane; Directed by Carl Schenkel; Capella International/Connexion Film Productions; 100 min.

Cast: Isabel Glasser (Doctor Theresa McCann); James Remar (Doctor Benjamin Hendricks); Sean Haberle (Doctor Julian Matar); Peter Boyle (Lieutenant McEllwaine); Malcolm McDowell (Doctor Stein); Charles Dance (Doctor Ed Mittlesbay); Beverly Todd (Nurse Burns); Charles Bailey-Gates (Sergeant Ross); Walter Olkewicz (Doctor Meade); Mother Love (Milly Putnam); Gregory West (Tommy Beaton); Juliette Jeffers (Lisa Wilson); Nancy Banks (Loreen Ridgeway); Kim Robillard (Doctor Eugene Kaiser); Teryl Rothery (Officer Pierson); Joe-Norman Shaw (Detective Edwards); Don Thompson (Father/1958); Marilyn Norry (Mother/1958); Codie Lucas Wilbee (Older Boy/1958); Jarrett Lennon (Young Matar); Tom Heaton (Doctor/1958); Walter Marsh (Parking Security); Rosanne Hopkins (Mrs. Rodriguez); Debbie Podowski (Doctor Melissa Kyle); Larry Musser, Michael Tiernan (Anesthesiologists); C. Dale Best, MD, Daniel Rubin, MD (Doctors in Operating Theatre); Akiko Morison (Operating Nurse); Rebecca Toolan (Mittlebay's Secretary); Robin Kelly, Sandra P. Grant (ICU Nurses); Bernie Coulsen (Flower Delivery Boy); Veena Sood (Doctor in Dialysis); Frank Cassini (Intern in Dialysis); Curt Willington (Pizza Delivery Boy); Alex Diakun (County General Doctor); Ken Roberts (County General Guard); Zoltan Buday (County General Patrol Guard); Sheelah Megill (Nurse Worley); Dee Jay Jackson (Hospital Orderly); John Destrey (Hospital Superintendent); Andrew Wheeler (Cop in Tunnel); Matt Bennett (Young Cop); Richard Newman (Doctor in O.R.); Sydney Mentiply (Doorman); Christy Lynne (Office White); Walker Bonshor (TV Doctor); Kendra Tucker (TV Nurse)

Crew: David Korda (Executive Producer); Alan Beattie, Chris Chesser, Willi Baer (Producers); Dennis E. Jones (Co-Producer); Christopher Franke (Composer); Thomas Burstyn, C.S.C. (Director of Photography); Jimmy B. Frazier (Editor)

A family rushes to a family physician on a rainy night. Julian waits, as his parents go outside. "Lollipop" plays on the radio, and Julian picks up a lollipop on a desk. He looks in on his brother; as the doctor places a scalpel by his neck, the boy opens his eyes, turns and the scalpel is pushed inside. The doctor tells the parents of the accident, and Julian puts the lollipop in his brother's dead hands.

Doctor Theresa McCann walks into a room where Doctor Stein is talking about his "abdominal implants." After Theresa asks about "serious" complications, the baboon (having received such an implant) goes berserk, runs around the room and dies. Theresa walks around with some med students, and she talks with the "arrogant" Doctor Benjamin Hendricks. Later, she talks to Stein, who is performing another procedure with the implant, and the man tells her that the incident that morning had nothing to do with his implant. Theresa goes to see Doctor Mittlesbay and asks why Stein was approved for another implant; he repeats Stein's assurances. Theresa goes to see Loreen (the patient of Stein's surgery), checks her out and has her moved to dialysis.

A man dressed as a doctor visits Loreen, injecting a syringe into her IV tubes. Blood comes out through her veins, and the man brings out a giant syringe. The nurses find Loreen, and Theresa tries fruitlessly to save the woman. She finds a lollipop nearby and slips it into her pocket. Later, Mittlesbay suspends Theresa for moving the patient to dialysis, and after she leaves, he calls Stein and tells him of the suspension. Theresa calls a hospital and asks to speak to Julian, but it is late, and she says she will call later. The next day, Theresa goes to see Ben, and they talk about Stein's implants. Ben says that either something in the "filtering system" is breaking down or something is being introduced from outside. The two go to the morgue and see Stein working. They hear screaming and find the morgue attendant tied up. Then they hear more noises and run back to find Stein dead and hanging. Ben runs after the mysterious doctor. As Theresa waits, she is grabbed by the man who puts a knife to her throat, and Ben knocks him out. Theresa knows the man (he had called her by her name).

The man, Doctor Julian Matar, is taken away by the police ("Nice to see you again, Doctor McCann"). Mittlesbay tells Lieutenant McEllwaine and Sergeant Ross that Julian was fired three years ago for "unauthorized research." Julian struggles with the police (while cuffed) and is hit by a car. Later, Theresa says Julia cured two terminal patients (they died shortly afterwards), and Theresa found his "thesis," *Exquisite Tenderness* (when pain reaches its "most extreme"), detailing everything. After being fired, Julian jumped out of the window and damaged his spine and was paralyzed from the waist down. Mittlesbay tells Theresa that Stein suspected Julian's meddling, and he only needed Theresa out of the way for a while (explaining the suspension).

Julian is in a hospital bed in prison. He stands and slams his cuffed hand into a metal drawer until he breaks it. A cop comes to see him, and Julian snaps his neck, puts on the doctor's things and gets out by using the man's finger as his identification. At dinner, Ben talks about Julian's thesis, involving "dying tissue regeneration" and "bone regeneration." Julian goes to see the patient, Milly, but leaves when she is uncooperative. Milly tells Doctor Melissa Kyle and they check the room to find no such "crazy doctor." Melissa assures Milly that no one is going to take her liver, and the doctor leaves. Julian comes out from the ceiling as Milly lies in her bed. Another patient, Lisa, is with her boyfriend Tommy. He goes to the bathroom and is attacked and killed by Julian (as Lisa listens with earphones). Julian comes out, knocks out Lisa and ties her hands to the bed. He gases her, brings out his syringe and sticks the needle up her nose to extract a gooey substance. Melissa finds Milly dead in her room.

Theresa and Ben learn of Julian's escape and the dead patients, and based on the gooey substance found on Lisa's body, the two doctors surmise that Julian is collecting pituitary extract. The cops search the hospital. After officers leave the morgue, Julian hooks himself to machines, injects himself and awakens with his broken hand healed. Mittlesbay is down there with a gun, and Julian manages to knock him down. He restrains the man and sews his mouth shut, talks of his serum not being perfected and hooks Mittlesbay to a machine that pumps out his blood. He puts the master switch in the doctor's hand, but Mittlesbay cannot move his hand due to an injection Julian had given him. The cops find the doctor in the trash, and Theresa thinks she is next.

Theresa admits to Ben of her relationship with Julian, and she tells of his brother dying and the "Lollipop" song stuck in his head. Theresa waits in her office as cops are around the hospital. In the kitchen, Julian injects the food on a tray, and a nurse-cop gives the food to cops and Theresa. Sergeant Ross, in the room with Theresa, falls asleep. Julian comes down from the ceiling and makes Melissa scream. Cops rush to Melissa, and Julian walks into Theresa's room, tapes her mouth and takes her away. Julian, stopped in the elevator, crawls through the air vents. As Theresa and Ross sit alone in the lobby, blood drips from the ceiling. Ross stands on a tray of towels and looks inside, and Julian shoves a syringe in his eye. Julian comes down and runs, and Theresa shoots and hits him with Ross' gun. She follows him to the morgue and is grabbed, but she stabs his hand. Out of bullets, Theresa throws a chemical in Julian's face and runs to the elevator, which Julian stops with his foot.

Julian straps Theresa to a chair and prepares for an incision. Julian gets a surgical saw, and Theresa manages to grab a nearby paddle and shock Julian, who falls to the floor. He stands again and is shot multiple times by police officers. On the floor, a bloody Julian injects himself. Julian is thrown unto the table and declared dead. In the morgue, Julian awakes and shoves a syringe into the attendant's head. Theresa awakes in bed. Ben is lying beside her, and she sees a knife in his back. Julian appears, and Theresa grabs the blade and throws it, hitting Julian, who falls back and is impaled by part of her glass coffee table. He reaches for his syringe and Theresa smashes the tubes. Doctor Julian Matar dies.

Although it has a few weak spots (the ending is a bit of a disappointment), *The Surgeon* is a highly enjoyable film, with a great murderous antagonist and a dexterous killing agenda. McDowell might be best known as the charming Alex from Stanley Kubrick's *A Clockwork Orange* (1971).

Sweet 16
(aka *Sweet Sixteen*)
(1981)

Written by Erwin Goldman; Directed by Jim Sotos; 88 min.

Cast: Bo Hopkins (Dan Burke); Susan Strasberg (Joanne Morgan); Patrick Macnee (Doctor Morgan); Don Stroud (Billy T.); Dana Kimmell (Marci Burke); Don Shanks (Jason); Aleisa Shirley (Melissa Morgan); Steve Antin (Hank Burke); Sharon Farrell (Kathy); Logan Clarke (Jimmy); Michael Pataki (George Martin); Henry Wilcoxon (Grayfeather); Larry Storch (Earl); Michael J. Cutt (Frank); Glenn Withrow (Johnny); Tony Perfit (Tommy Jackson); Sandy Charles (Lab Technician)

Crew: Martin and June Perfit (Executive Producers); Sandy Charles (Associate Producer); Tommy Vig (Composer); James L. Carter (Director of Photography); Drake Silliman (Editor)

Marci is reading by the fire on a dark stormy night. She hears a creak, and she goes to the door, where she sees a dirty old man and screams. Marci sits up in bed, with a book, *Murder Mystery*, resting on her. Billy shows up at a bar, and his little brother, Johnny, asks to borrow his truck so he can take Hank home. The elderly Grayfeather walks inside, and Billy tells the man that he is not welcome and throws his hat to the floor. Jason, a younger Native American, walks through the door ("Pick up the hat"), throws Billy's friend, Jimmy, against the wall and pulls a knife on Billy, now armed with a broken bottle. Earl the bartender pulls a gun on them both; Grayfeather calls Jason away. Outside, Melissa hits on Jason, and he tells her to go home. Jason and Grayfeather leave. Melissa asks Johnny if he wants company, and they get in Billy's truck together, leaving Hank behind.

Johnny and Melissa are out kissing, but Melissa wants to leave when Johnny tells her they are on the old Indian burial ground. They go home, and Melissa tells Johnny that her father is an archeologist, and that her family is renting the place for a while. Melissa's father, Doctor Morgan, comes out and tells Johnny that his daughter is only fifteen ("I'll be sixteen next week"). He tells the boy to leave. Later, Johnny runs out of gas, and pulls over to the side of the road. While stumbling around drunk, Johnny is stabbed and killed. The next morning, Hank is having breakfast with his sister, Marci, who is reading her book. Their father, Sheriff Burke, gets a call about Billy's missing brother and truck. They head out to the reservation and find the abandoned truck. A few yards away Marci discovers the murdered Johnny.

The sheriff drops off his children at school, and Hank points out Melissa, the "new girl" that Johnny left with. Sheriff Burke talks with Doctor Morgan and his wife, Joanne, and then speaks with Melissa, who tells him that she and Johnny just drove around. She mentions Jason, who is working at the dig site with Doctor Morgan, and she says he grabbed her. The sheriff and Doctor Morgan go to the reservation and talk to Jason. Sheriff Burke later tells George, the town chairman, to have a town meeting. Joanne, originally from the town, enters the office and recognizes George, who asks how her sister is doing. Joanne then asks the sheriff if it is okay to have a party and invite the town. The sheriff says that, despite the murder, it is fine.

Marci is at school telling some girls about Johnny being stabbed "twenty or thirty times," and she points out Melissa to the others. Football player Tommy Jackson hits on Melissa. She asks what he does (referring to drugs and drink), and he says "a little of everything." The two agree to meet later. The sheriff goes to the town meeting, and he tells Hank and Marci to stay home, but Hank leaves soon after, and Marci hesitantly follows. They are offered a ride by Joanne, and they accept. Tommy is waiting by some steps, and someone approaches him and stabs him. At the meeting, Jimmy is at the microphone, saying the "Indians" murdered Johnny, and the sheriff leads him away. Billy gets in front, the sheriff shuts him up, and Sheriff Burke warns the people of the town not to take the law into their own hands.

Jason is at a bar, and he sees Melissa walk in. Outside, Melissa runs into Grayfeather, who tells her to run. The girl finds Tommy dead. The cops arrive ("Same damn M.O."), and the sheriff is angry to see that his children are there. Melissa blames Grayfeather for the killing, saying he was standing over the body. Billy and Jimmy run out to the truck and leave (for "a little justice"). The sheriff heads out to see the old man, and he finds Grayfeather hanging from a noose. The report cites it as a suicide, but the sheriff disagrees, saying he will find the maniac and then go after the person who killed Grayfeather. At the double funeral for Johnny and Tommy, Marci is very malignant towards Melissa, but then apologizes and the two seem to be on friendly terms.

Doctor Morgan goes to see the sheriff, and says he fired Jason for stealing artifacts (knives) and that he wants the man arrested. Sheriff Burke heads back to the house and discovers the knives hidden in a trunk. The sheriff goes to see his lady friend, Kathy. Hank and Marci go to Melissa's birthday party. The siblings give Melissa her birthday present, and she hugs them both. The sheriff is in the county records with Kathy, and she is telling him about a similar murder involving a drunken driver that killed Jason's mother (the man was let go and was not charged). He is also told blood was found on one of the stolen knives. Cop Frank opens the jail door to give the incarcerated Jason some food, Jason knocks him down, locks him in the jail, and grabs his knife from the desk.

The sheriff is researching some old articles, and Kathy gets a call that the blood found on the knife was squirrel blood. The sheriff finds an article from 1956 that mentions the death of someone named "Joan Platt," and he runs out. Hank and Melissa leave together for a swim, and Jason is following them. They go skinny dipping, and Billy and Jimmy watch. Jason approaches the two friends ("You killed him, didn't you?"). Billy and Jimmy jump the angry man. Melissa sees them. They chase her down and grab her, and during the struggle, Melissa and Hank are knocked out cold.

While Jimmy is at the lake to get some water (to arouse the unconscious Melissa), Billy is stabbed, and Jimmy is killed when he returns. The person walks over to Hank, who is waking up, stabs him in the arm, and Hank jumps up and runs. Marci is out there, finds some dead people, and sees Joannie sitting over Melissa. Hank screams at Marci as Joannie lifts a knife, and the sheriff tackles his daughter to safety. Joannie is trying to wake Melissa (calling her Joannie), and the sheriff tries to calm her and calls her Tricia. The sheriff pulls Melissa away from her mother, and Joannie/Tricia says, "Daddy, don't hurt her anymore!" She then stabs and kills herself. The sheriff later talks about how Tricia's sister, Joan, died, and that Tricia then "became" her sister. Marci goes to offer Melissa solace, but Melissa says she is okay. She walks into her house with a dazed expression, gripping onto the bloody knife and hearing her mother's screaming voice.

Sweet 16 is certainly not an exceptional slasher, but, despite the superfluous opening dream, there are some strong subplots, including the Native Americans and the reservations, and Melissa's desire for attention causing her to perjure her stories. Actor Macnee is perhaps best known as John Steed from the hit television series *The Avengers*.

Tenebrae (aka *Unsane*; *Tenebre*; *Sotto gli occhi dell'assassino*) (1982)

Written by George Kemp and Dario Argento; Directed by Dario Argento; Sigma Cinematografica-Rome; 101 min.

Cast: Anthony Franciosa (Peter Neal); Daria Nicolodi (Anne); John Saxon (Bullmer); Giuliano Gemma (Captain Giermani); Christian Borromeo (Gianni); Mirella D'Angelo (Tilde); Veronica Lario (Jane); Eva Robins (Girl on Beach); Ania Pieroni (Elsa Manni); Carola Stagnaro (Inspector Altieri); John Steiner (Christiano Berti); Lara Wendel (Maria); Isabella Amadeo; Mirella Banti (Marion); Fulvio Mingozzi (Hotel Manager); Gianpaolo Saccarola (Pathologist); Enio Girolami (Store Detective); Ippolita Santarelli; Francesca Viscardi; Monica Maisani; Marino Masé

Crew: Salvatore Argento (Executive Producer); Claudio Argento (Producer); Claudio Simonetti, Fabio Pignatelli, Massimo Morante (Composers); Luciano Tovoli (Director of Photography); Franco Fraticelli (Editor); Lambert Bava (First Assistant Director); Michele Soavi (Second Assisant Director)

Peter Neal, a successful writer of horror novels, is heading to Rome. At the airport, he receives a telephone call from his ex, Jane. Peter apparently argues with her, hangs up the phone and is on his way. Jane, who telephoned from the airport, watches Peter's plane take off. In Rome, a young lady attempts to shoplift a paperback edition of Neal's latest book, *Tenebrae*. She is caught with the book in her purse, but she avoids any trouble by giving out her address. On the way home, she is accosted by a bum, but she manages to escape and get inside her house. Unfortunately, a person in black shows up and shoves pages of *Tenebrae* into the lady's mouth before slashing her with a razor. The killer then snaps a few photographs of the deceased.

Peter's plane lands in Rome; waiting for him at the airport are his agent Bullmer and Tilde, a woman whom Peter has known for ten years. While at a conference, Peter is discussing his writing process to reporters, and Tilde claims his novels are sexist, with violence aimed at women. As Peter and Bullmer are leaving, the writer mentions a man who was at the conference but never said anything. Bullmer tells him it was Christiano Berti, a television book reviewer, with whom Peter is taping a show later.

Peter and Bullmer meet with Peter's assistant Anne and Gianni, an apprentice agent. Peter looks inside his bag for Anne's gift, but the contents of his bag have been destroyed. At the apartment, two police officers are waiting for Peter. They want to discuss the recent murder, which is very similar to the writer's book. Captain Giermani hands Peter a note which had earlier been shoved under the door; it contains a line from *Tenebrae*. While the cops are present, the killer calls Peter but runs away when realizing someone is there with him. Afterwards, a person is shown, groaning in anguish. A flashback presents a lady in white who is acting quite lewdly with a group of boys. One boy, upset, slaps the lady and runs. The other males chase him and hold him down while the lady kicks and beats him.

After a night at a bar, Tilde returns home to her girlfriend, who had earlier left with a man ("No ties" is their apparent agreement). Tilde, angry, stays downstairs while her girlfriend plays loud music above her. The killer drops by and murders them both, then takes some more pictures. Back at the apartment, Peter receives another note under the door. He and Anne are both there, and they see the note a few minutes after it arrives. Peter runs outside but sees no one. At the television station, Christiano Berti expresses his desire to discuss "human perversity" and "deviant behavior," the themes of *Tenebrae*. Peter defends his book, claiming that the killer is simply insane and not singling out "perverts."

Later, from his apartment window, Peter thinks he has seen Jane. He phones New York and gets no response. That night, Maria, the hotel manager's daughter, is left in the middle of nowhere by a jerk biker. She taunts a vicious dog, but it hurdles the fence and chases her. She eventually takes refuge inside the killer's home. After taking some of the photographs of victims with her, Maria tries to call the police. The killer comes home and sees her ("Spy!"), chases and murders her.

Peter, Anne and Gianni are looking through Peter's address book for possible murderers. Peter finally thinks of Berti and the earlier discussion, and he sees that the reviewer lives close to where Maria was found. Peter and Gianni go to investigate, but while at Berti's home, the lights go out and Gianni watches as someone says, "Yes, it was me. I killed them all," and presents Berti with an axe in the head. Gianni finds a recently knocked-in-the-head Peter, and the two men leave.

Another flashback shows the lady in white stabbed by the apparently upset lover; her red shoes are taken. Peter goes to Bullmer's office and discusses leaving Rome. After he is gone, Jane comes out from hiding; she and Bullmer are obviously having an affair. Peter is called over to Berti's place by Giermani, and they discuss the recent death. After Jane receives a package containing red shoes, Bullmer is waiting for someone in the park, and he is stabbed and killed in broad daylight. Later, Peter is dropped off at the airport to go back to the United States. Gianni then realizes what he had actually seen at Berti's place was Christiano saying that he was the one who "killed them all," but Gianni is murdered before he can tell anyone.

Jane calls Anne and says she wants to "explain everything." While Jane is awaiting Anne's arrival with a handgun, an axe crashes through the window and chops off her arm. Now the killer awaits Anne. Someone walks inside and is axed to death. The axe is dropped and it is now clear that the murderer is Peter. Giermani arrives with Anne, and Peter sees that he has killed Inspector Altieri, Giermani's partner. Before he can be taken away, Peter slashes his throat with a razor. Giermani and Anne head to his car, and the captain tells Anne of Peter's murderous rampage from years ago (he was suspected but never tried). Giermani returns to the house and finds Peter missing, with a trick razor resting on the floor. Peter suddenly appears and axes Giermani, who falls and knocks a metal sculpture against the door. When Anne tries to enter the apartment, with Peter waiting and the axe in his hand, she pushes the door open and a sharp piece of the sculpture pierces Peter in the stomach. He is killed and Anne screams.

Tenebrae is another enjoyable film from Argento, inspired by the real-life adversaries of his movies (the arguments against Peter Neal's books were similar to what critics would say about Argento's films). Originally released in America as *Unsane*, the film was missing about ten minutes, including the classic arm-chopping sequence. Composers Simonetti, Pignatelli and Morante, once members of the band Goblin, were not legally allowed to use the Goblin name; without a drummer, they employed a drum machine in the score. The mother of Argento's children (the two were never married), Nicolodi, was originally cast to play the role of the "Girl on Beach," which instead went to Eva Robins, now a popular transsexual in Italy. Look for fellow horror director (and first assistant director of *Tenebrae*) Lamberto Bava as a custodian and for director (and second assistant director) Michele Soavi in the flashback scenes.

Terror Train (1980)

Written by T.Y. Drake; Directed by Roger Spottiswoode; Astral Films; 97 min.

Cast: Ben Johnson (Carne); Jamie Lee Curtis (Alana); Hart Bochner (Doc); David Copperfield (The Magician); Derek MacKinnon (Kenny Hampson); Sandee Currie (Mitchy); Timothy Webber (Mo); Anthony Sherwood (Jackson); Howard Busgang (Ed); Steve Michaels (Brekeman); Greg Swanson (Class President); D.D. Winters (Merry); Joy Boushel (Pet); Victor Knight (Engineer); Don Lamoureux (Shovels); Charles Biddles, Sr. (Chief Porter); Elizabeth Cholette (Dispatcher); Thomas Havertock (Bill Chase); Peter Feingold (Senior); Richard Weinstein, John Busby (Pledges); Roland Nincheri (Bus Driver); Andrea Kenyon (Bunny Girl); Elaine Lakeman (Nurse); Gerald Eastman, Charlies Biddles, Jr. (Porters); Nadia Rona (Corpse); Larry Cohen, Brenda Gagnier, Phil Albery (Crime, the Band)

Crew: Lamar Card (Executive Producer);

The killer kills for revenge and fresh disguises as the party continues on board Roger Spottiswoode's *Terror Train* (1980).

Harold Greenberg (Producer); John Mills-Cockell (Compoer); John Alcott (Director of Photography); Anne Henderson (Editor)

College students are at a bonfire for the New Year's celebration. All of the pledges are wearing beanies, and one pledge, Kenny, is sent upstairs to a room where Alana is waiting in the doorway. Alana walks inside and stands behind the canopy in the dark room. Kenny undresses, sits in the bed and realizes he is sitting by a corpse. Kenny screams in terror and he stands on the bed and is caught up in the canopy. Alana seems repulsed as a group of people rush in and laugh at Kenny.

Three years later, people are exiting a bus at a train station. They have a toast to four great years as they prepare to board the train for their costume party. Everyone laughs at Ed as he walks around with a sword in his stomach (he is a jokester), but he falls down after people walk away, and someone takes his costume and kicks Ed under the train. The train leaves, and the lights at the station are turned off. The killer in Ed's costume is on the train. The magician is talking with his assistant, complaining about the crowd of college kids. Someone asks Doc about the now abolished "hog night," and he mentions something bad that happened, and Alana says they "put a kid in the hospital." Mitchy sees "Ed" later, and he follows her and nearly grabs her until an inebriated Jackson appears and offers Ed a drink. In the bathroom, the killer grabs Jackson, lifts his mask and slams Jackson's head into the mirror.

Alana becomes irate when learning that the train party was Doc's idea (her boyfriend Mo told her it was his). Pet thinks Ed missed the train, and Alana argues with Mo about learning that Doc had set him up again. Carne, the conductor, shows Doc and Mitchy a card trick (it is only a gag), and the couple waits for the occupied bathroom. Later, Doc asks Mo where Jackson and Ed are, and he says he did not hire a magician. Alana tells Carne that someone may have been left behind, but he says the platform was empty. Mitchy hears them and says she saw Ed earlier. Doc and Mo take Merry and Pet to their "consulting room" (they are med students). Carne knocks on the still-occupied bathroom and asks if anyone is inside. He unlocks it and sees blood everywhere with a dead Jackson on the floor. Mitchy motions to Alana on the dance floor that she is leaving, and the magician, after looking at Alana, leaves in the same direction as Mitchy. Carne tells Charlie what he has found ("There's a boy dead back there"). Carne and Walter, the engineer, decide the closest way out is straight ahead.

Charlie is watching the bathroom, and he tells some girls it is out of order. Carne opens the door for Charlie, and the blood is gone and "Jackson" is moving. Carne thinks it was a practical joke ("Damn kids"), and Mitchy shows up and leads Jackson away ("Damn medical students"). Merry points out Kenny in a yearbook, and Pet motions for Doc to keep quiet. Doc and Merry leave Mo alone with Pet. Mitchy is with the killer/Jackson in a bed hiding behind the curtain, and Merry and Doc walk by. Mitchy leans back, the killer takes off a glove and a hand touches Mitchy. She sees that it is a severed hand and gasps, and a hand is put over her mouth. The magician sees Alana, asks her if she liked his show, and tries to woo her with illusions. Doc tells Alana that Mo is waiting to talk to her. Carne finds Mitchy's shoe and then finds her with a slit throat in one of the beds. He runs into Alana and asks her whose shoe he has. She goes with Carne to get Mo, but Mo ignores the knocking (since a rambunctious Pet is with him). Carne finally tells Alana that Mitchy is dead, and he shows her the bed.

Mo wants to talk with Doc, who is skeptical about the magician's show. Doc and Mo are evidently hanging their heads out of boredom, but Mo does not move, and when Doc hits him, Mo falls over. Doc's screams for help are ignored as they people cheer the show. He carries Mo to Alana and Carne, and they discover a large cut in Mo's chest. Carne runs into the engine room and sees that Walter and his partner Shovels are gone (he finds a bloody engineer's cap); he gets the train stopped. People are led out of the train, and Carne has men look around for the killer. Outside, he has everyone take off their masks. Alana suggests to Doc that the killer is Kenny, and she tells him that the hospital would not let him see her because he had possibly killed someone. Doc thinks they will be next, and he leads Alana back onto the train.

Doc throws Alana in a room and locks the doors. He shows her a yearbook and she sees that Kenny was a magician. Doc tries to stop Alana from leaving, but she gets out and runs from a person who turns out to be Charlie. Doc checks every inch of the room and sits, but then realizes he forgot to check under the seat in front. He stands and is grabbed by someone under his seat. He tries to escape, and a hand behind him has painted fingernails and a ring; he settles down, believing it is Mitchy joking with him. A knife comes out and is put to his throat. Alana tells Carne she believes the killer is the magician, and they go to get Doc and find his head detached. Carne and others go to the magician's showroom, lead the assistant and several others outside and lock the door. A man takes Alana to a compartment and says he will be outside the door with an axe. Later, the man is sitting dead in a chair. Carne and the men go to the back of the showroom, and the magician is nowhere to be found.

The killer walks into Alana's room and stabs at the covers, but it is only a doll. Alana jumps out of the closet and stabs the killer with a sword. She runs to the conductor's room and the killer and she struggle. Alana sprays the killer with a fire extinguisher and takes refuge in a caged area with a desk. She locks herself in, and the killer bangs on the gate and knocks out the lights. The killer tries to pry the lock, but Alana stabs him in the face, kicks the door and runs. The killer chases Alana and falls in between train cars. Carne leads Alana away (the killer is holding on the side of the car), and she goes to a room to relax. Later, Alana is in the back of the showroom, and she finds the magician dead. She runs to find Carne and sees Charlie sitting at his desk. She tells him the magician is dead, and he grips her by the wrists and looks up. A mask is taken off, and then Kenny takes off a blonde wig (he was the magician's assistant). Alana tries to apologize to Kenny, he tells her to kiss him and she obeys. Kenny has a similar eerie reaction, and as he is reacting, Carne comes from the engine room and hits him with a shovel. Kenny falls out of the moving train while it is passing on a bridge and lands in the icy and snowy water below.

Terror Train is a great Canadian slasher, preceding the infamous early '80s slasher run in America. The setting is terrific, and the film leads to a bloodcurdling chase sequence. Actor MacKinnon is appropriately bizarre as Kenny. Although most may remember him from *Die Hard* (1988), Bochner also starred in the cult film *Apartment Zero* (1988). Actress Winters, also known as Vanity, was once a protégée of musician Prince. Director Spottiswoode went on to direct bigger American productions, such as *Turner and Hooch* (1988) and *The 6th Day* (2000).

The Texas Chainsaw Massacre (1974)

Written by Kim Henkel and Tobe Hooper; Directed by Tobe Hooper; Vortex, Inc.; 84 min.
Cast: Marilyn Burns (Sally); Allen Danziger (Jerry); Paul A. Partain (Franklin); William Vail (Kirk); Teri McMinn (Pam); Edwin Neal (Hitchiker); Jim Siedow (Old Man); Gunnar Hansen (Leatherface); John Dugan (Grandfather); Robert Courtin (Window Washer); William Creamer (Bearded Man); John Henry Faulk (Storyteller); Jerry Green (Cowboy); Ed Guinn (Cattle Truck Driver); Joe Bill Hogan (Drunk); Perry Lorenz (Pick Up Driver); John Larroquette (Narration).

Crew: Jay Parsley (Executive Producer); Tobe Hooper (Producer); Kim Henkel, Richard Saenz (Associate Producers); Tobe Hooper, Wayne Bell (Composers); Daniel Pearl (Director of Photography); Sallye Richardson, Larry Carroll (Editors)

On August 18, 1973, a corpse is sitting in the cemetery. A man on the radio talks about "grave robbing," with empty crypts being found and sometimes only parts of the bodies being taken. A van stops by the side of the road, and Franklin is rolled out in his wheelchair for a call of nature into a tin can. A semi speeds by, Franklin rolls down a small incline and Kirk runs to his side. The group travels to a graveyard, where Sally, Franklin's sister, asks the locals about her grandfather, who is buried there. In the van, Sally tells Franklin that their grandfather did not look "dug up." Down the road, the group notices a putrid odor, and Franklin tells them they are near the slaughterhouse. He talks about the heads of cattle being bashed in with a sledgehammer and how sometimes they were skinned while still alive.

Jerry stops to pick up a weird looking hitchhiker. The man says his brother and grandfather work at the slaughterhouse, and Franklin asks him if they use the more sanitary air gun to kill the cattle. The hitchhiker says they always use a sledgehammer, and he shows some photographs of chopped meat and talks about what goes into headcheese. Franklin picks his fingernails with his pocket knife, and the hitchhiker takes the knife, slices the palm of his hand and laughs. He shows a razor blade he carries, and Kirk tells him to put it away. The man takes a picture of Franklin, then invites the group for dinner. He shows Franklin the photograph and asks him to pay two dollars for it. Franklin gives the photograph back, and the hitchhiker sets it afire. As the group react, he cuts Franklin's arm with his razor. He is pushed out the door; he kicks the van and wipes blood on it before Jerry speeds away.

The people head to a gas station where an old man tells Jerry that he has no gas. Franklin asks if the old man knows where the old Franklin place is, and the man asks them to stay for some barbeque. Jerry goes inside and comes out with barbeque, and Sally and Pam see the hitchhiker's blood on the van outside. The group reaches the house and look at the blood on the van, which appears to be some kind of symbol. Franklin is left alone while the other four go inside the house and run around. Kirk and Pam come downstairs and ask Franklin where the swimming hole is. He points the way. After they leave, he finds bones and feathers on the porch and bones hanging in the doorway.

Kirk and Pam find a completely dry swimming hole. Kirk hears a motor and thinks someone might have gas. They head to the nearby house and find a generator. Kirk goes to the front door, and Pam waits on the swing in the front yard. Kirk walks inside and trips, and Leatherface suddenly appears and bashes Kirk on the head with a sledgehammer. Kirk convulses, and Leatherface beats him again and slides the steel door shut. Pam calls for Kirk and goes to the door. Inside, she finds a room of feathers and bones, with a couch made of what appear to be human bones. Leatherface jumps up, pulls Pam into a room and throws her onto a hook. As she screams, he revs up a chainsaw and slices into the body of Kirk. Back at the van, Jerry mocks Franklin for being worried about the symbol on the van. Jerry goes alone and calls out to Kirk. On the front porch of the house, Jerry sees the towel that Kirk and Pam had taken with them and walks into the house, calling for his friends. Jerry sees a freezer shaking and finds Pam inside; she sits up and convulses. Leatherface walks in, beats Jerry on the head and pushes Pam back into the freezer.

Night has arrived, and Sally is honking the van's horn for her friends to return. She does not want to leave without Jerry, so she goes looking for them. Franklin refuses to give her the flashlight, until she starts to leave without him. He follows her, and soon Sally is pushing Franklin and they are both calling for Jerry. Franklin thinks he hears something, and Sally stops. Leatherface jumps out and chainsaws Franklin, and Sally screams and runs. She gets to the house and runs through the front door and up the stairs. Leatherface chainsaws through the door. Sally finds corpse-like things in a room and runs out. Leatherface chases her upstairs and she jumps out of a window.

Sally reaches the gas station, and the old man lets her inside. She tries to tell him what has happened, and he settles her down and tells her that he does not have a phone. She waits for him as he gets his truck, and the old man returns with a potato sack and rope. Sally, panicked, gets a knife, which the old man knocks away with a broom. He beats her with the broom until she stops moving, then ties and gags Sally, covers the upper part of her body with the sack and takes her to the truck. The old man returns to the house, where the hitchhiker is waiting, and he scolds the man for going to the graveyard and leaving his brother alone. The hitchhiker carries Sally to the house; the old man is upset about the sawed front door, and he beats a whimpering Leatherface. The hitchhiker takes the sack off of Sally and laughs. He and Leatherface bring their grandfather down the stairs. Leatherface cuts Sally's finger and places it into the mouth of the corpse-esque grandfather, and the decrepit man sucks the blood. Sally passes out.

Sally awakes, tied to a chair with arms for armrests. Realizing where she is, she screams and is mocked by the old man and the two brothers. Sally pleads with the old man to help her, but the hitchhiker says he is just the cook and that he and Leatherface do all the work. The hitchhiker says that they are going to let their grandfather have "this one." The old man assures Sally that it will not hurt because the grandfather is the "best killer there ever was." Sally is untied and held over a bucket while the grandfather struggles just keeping hold of the mallet. Leatherface helps him a bit, and Sally finally flails her arms around, gets free and jumps out of the window. She is chased to the road, where a semi pummels the hitchhiker. The driver stops and helps Sally in the truck, and

Leatherface (Gunnar Hansen), the old man, Drayton (Jim Siedow), the hitchhiker (Edwin Neal) and the crusty grandfather (John Dugan) are waiting for someone to join them for dinner in Tobe Hooper's *The Texas Chainsaw Massacre* (1974).

they both flee from Leatherface and his chainsaw. The driver throws a wrench at Leatherface, who falls and inadvertently slices into his leg. Sally waves down a pick-up truck and jumps in the back; the driver speeds away as Sally laughs hysterically.

Leatherface angrily swings his running saw around.

Tobe Hooper's classic film deserves its cult status, with the unflinching portrayal of a cannibalistic and murderous family. The last part of the film (especially Sally's dinner with the family) is relentless and utterly terrifying.

The Texas Chainsaw Massacre 2 (1986)

Written by L.M. Kit Carson; Directed by Tobe Hooper; Cannon Films; 100 min.

Cast: Dennis Hopper (Leftie); Caroline Williams (Stretch); Jim Siedow (Cook/Drayton Sawyer); Bill Moseley (Chop-Top); Bill Johnson (Leatherface); Ken Evert (Grandpa); Harlan Jordan (Patrolman); Kirk Sisco (Detective); James N. Harrell (Cut-Rite Manager); Lou Perry (L.G. McPeters); Barry Kinyon (Mercedes Driver); Chris Douridas (Gunner); Judy Kelly (Gourmet Yuppette); John Martin Ivey (Yuppie); Kinky Friedman (Sports Anchorman); Wirt Cain (Anchorman); Dan Jenkins (TV Commentator); Joe Bob Briggs (Gonzo Moviegoer)

Crew: Henry Holmes, James Jorgensen (Executive Producers); Menahem Golan, Yoram Globus (Producers); L.M. Kit Carson (Associate Producer); Tobe Hooper (Co-Producer); Tobe Hooper, Jerry Lambert (Composers); Richard Kooris (Director of Photography); Alain Jakubowicz (Editor); Tom Savini (Special Makeup Effects)

After Sally told her tale of the chainsaw massacre, she fell into a catatonic state. A search was conducted, but the family was never found. Two yuppies are driving down the road as the passenger fires shots out of the window. The driver calls Stretch on the radio and requests a song but will not hang up. Later, he calls again, and a truck is blocking the car's way on the bridge. It runs in reverse and is beside the car. Leatherface, with a dead body covering him, stands in the back and runs his chainsaw through the convertible top. Stretch and L.G. hear the two boys screaming. The passenger yuppie shoots and hits the dead body's head, and Leatherface starts sawing the door. Suddenly the driver is missing a chunk of his head. At the radio station, the connection is cut.

Leftie is at the scene, and a detective talks to him about his brother and friends being killed 14 years ago. Leftie knows about the boy with his head sawed off, and he tells the man to get the story out in the newspapers. Stretch visits Leftie in his hotel and says she has the murder on cassette tape and suggests having him on the radio show, but Leftie tells her to leave. Stretch and L.G. cover the story as Drayton is crowned the Texas/Oklahoma Chili Cookoff Grand Champion. A woman asks him for his secret, and Drayton says, "Don't skimp on the meat." Leftie goes to Cut-Rite Chain Saws, buys three chainsaws and practices on a cut tree outside. He goes to the station and asks Stretch to find a way to play the tape on the radio, because he believes the killers are around. Drayton, driving in his truck, gets a call, turns on the radio show and hears the tape being played on the air.

Stretch tries to excuse the playing of the tape by telling L.G. it was a request. They say good night. While alone in the station, Stretch hears a noise. She finds Chop-Top sitting in an outside room, occasionally using a bent coat hanger to scratch his head. He asks for a tour, and Stretch shows him a few things on the desk and tells him to leave. Chop-Top stays and asks about the records in the other room, and Leatherface jumps out and accidentally hits his brother on the metal plate in his head. Stretch slides a door shut and closes the latch.

L.G. comes back, notices the truck outside and walks through the door. He sees Chop-Top going through the records and tells him to get out. Leatherface crashes through the door and knocks L.G. down. Chop-Top pounds on the man's head with a hammer. Leatherface bursts through the wall and is in the room with Stretch. He runs his chainsaw into the tub of ice and soda, and she talks him down by asking how good he is. Leatherface stands and looks at Stretch for a while, then angrily chainsaws the station. He runs out, tells Chop-Top that he got Stretch, and they drag L.G.'s body away. Believing she cannot let the killers get away, Stretch jumps in her Jeep and drives after Leatherface and Chop-Top in their truck.

They arrive at a place, and Stretch gets

out of her Jeep and is chased by a car. The car stops, and it is only Leftie. Stretch falls down a hole, and Leftie tries to help her out, but she slides down. Leftie arms himself with the chainsaws and, while screaming a war cry, goes into the front entrance and chainsaws his way around ("I'm bringin' it down!"). Stretch awakes in a room full of butchered body parts. She hides when Leatherface comes in, and Leatherface strips L.G.'s clothes and skin. He hears Stretch and runs over to her with the cleaver ("No, no good!"). Leatherface settles down, and Stretch asks him to help her. He puts the skin mask of L.G. onto her face and L.G.'s cowboy hat on her head; he "dances" with her until some of the ceiling collapses (from Leftie's rampage). Leatherface ties Stretch's arms and leaves.

The partially skinned L.G. sits up and manages to cut Stretch free before collapsing and finally dying. Stretch gives L.G. his face and hat back, and she walks into the other room, where she sees Drayton arguing with Chop-Top and Leatherface. Stretch crawls through a tunnel and runs past the group as they argue. They see her; Drayton tells Leatherface to check it out. Leftie finds a rotted corpse in a wheelchair ("Franklin"), and he angrily continues sawing everything in sight. Stretch, running in the corridors, sees and hears sawing in front of her (Leftie's work) and runs the other way. Leatherface jumps out. Stretch runs until, due to Leftie's chainsawing, the ceiling collapses, and she is trapped.

Stretch pleads with Leatherface to let her go, and Drayton and Chop-Top show up. Chop-Top says that Stretch is the deejay and that Leatherface likes her ("Bubba's got a girlfriend!"). Drayton tells Leatherface to finish Stretch off, but he refuses to do so. Drayton, upset that Leatherface "turned traitor for a piece of tail," takes the saw from him ("The saw is family"). Chop-Top hits Stretch on the head. The deejay awakes at the table for dinner time, and Grandpa is brought into the room. Leatherface and Chop-Top hold Stretch over the tub while Grandpa tries to swing the hammer. Drayton finally picks up the hammer and hits Stretch on the head.

The group hears a running saw and Leftie singing. Stretch looks up as Leftie enters the room, and Leftie sees Stretch over the tub ("Sister?") and tells her to run. He saws Drayton a bit and cuts Stretch free. Leftie and Leatherface have a chainsaw duel while Drayton hides under the table. Chop-Top chases after Stretch. Leftie and Leatherface duel on the table, and Leftie drives the chainsaw into Leatherface's stomach and brings out his two smaller chainsaws to continue the fight. Drayton takes a grenade from the dead body. Grandpa throws the hammer and hits Leatherface in the head, and Leatherface drops the saw and hits Drayton under the table. The grenade is dropped, and, after another Leftie war cry, it explodes. Chop-Top follows Stretch into the daylight, cutting her with a razor. Chop-Top hangs from a railing. Stretch runs and finds a mummified woman with a chainsaw. Chop-Top follows, Stretch grabs the chainsaw and Chop-Top cuts her in the back until she gets the saw started and cuts into his stomach. Chop-Top falls back and into a tunnel, and Stretch screams as the saw runs.

Rather than try to eclipse, remake or replicate the first film, director Hooper adds much black humor to the sequel, making *The Texas Chainsaw Massacre 2* almost a parody of the original. The majority of the humor works (the chainsaw duel is great, and Drayton as the two-time chili cookoff champion is hilarious), but the film (perhaps intentionally) is not frightening. Joe Bob Briggs is credited as a "Gonzo Moviegoer," but his scenes were cut from the film.

Texas Chainsaw Massacre: The Next Generation (aka *The Return of the Texas Chainsaw Massacre*) (1994)

Written and Directed by Kim Henkel; Ultra Muchos, Inc./River City Films, Inc.; 87 min.

Cast: Renee Zellweger (Jenny); Matthew McConaughey (Vilmer); Robert Jacks (Leatherface); Tonie Perenski (Darla); Joe Stevens (W.E.); Lisa Newmyer (Heather); Tyler Cone (Barry); John Harrison (Sean); James Gale (Rothman); Chris Kilgore (Rothman's Chauffeur); Vince Brock (I'm Not Hurt); Susan Loughran (Jenny's Mother); David Laurence (Jenny's Stepfather); Grayson Victor Schirmacher (Grandfather); Jeanette Wiggins (Woman Eating Chocolates); Carmen Nogales (Girl in Red Dress); Lisa Caraveo (Brenda); Les Martin, Adam White, Bill Wise (Hecklers); Loren Guerra (Bud's Pizza Attendant); Derek Keele, Debra McMichaels (Cops at Bud's Pizza); Geri Wolcott, Axel L. Schiller (Couple in RV); Andy Cockrun (Stuffed DPS Officer); Roger Roe, Angee Huges, Rebecca Rosenberg (Stuffed Family); John Dugan (Cop at Hospital); Paul Partain (Hospital Orderly); Anonymous (Patient on Gurney)

Crew: Robert J. Kuhn (Executive Producer); Robert J. Kuhn, Kim Henkel (Producers); Wayne Bell (Composer); Levie Isaacks (Director of Photography); Sandra Adair (Editor)

No chainsaw family members were apprehended for crimes, and after two "minor reports," the family was silent for five years. On May 22, 1996, Jenny and Sean head for the prom. Heather is already there, looking for Barry, and when she finds him outside kissing another girl, she angrily speeds away in her car. Barry jumps in, and further down the road, Jenny and Sean pop up in the back seat. Heather drives down a deserted road, now looking for a place to turn around, and they are rammed by a car and knocked off the road. The driver of the other car steps out of his vehicle and passes out. Barry's car is stuck, so he, Jenny and Heather go for help while Sean stays with the unconscious boy. They reach Darla's office, where Darla calls Vilmer and tells him about the wreck.

Sean waves down Vilmer in his wrecker, and Vilmer surmises the driver is dead. Sean says that he is only passed out, so Vilmer snaps his neck to make sure he really is dead. Sean runs away, and Vilmer gets back into his wrecker. Vilmer chases Sean, who stops and tries to talk to the man. Vilmer then runs the truck in reverse, hits Sean and rolls over the boy several times. Barry, Heather and Jenny are walking back, and a truck drives by. Barry and Heather run after the moving vehicle, leaving Jenny alone. Jenny walks back to the crash site, but the cars, the driver and Sean are all gone.

Barry and Heather reach a house, and Heather knocks on the door and tells Barry to check in the back. As Heather is sitting on the swing, Leatherface stands behind her. W.E. has a shotgun on Barry. When Heather screams at the sight of Leatherface, W.E. does not let Barry move. Leatherface pulls Heather into the house, but she runs into a room and locks the door. Leatherface breaks through, grabs the girl, puts her in a freezer and puts something heavy on top to weigh the door down. W.E. has Barry go into the house, and Barry shuts the door and locks W.E. out. He goes to the bathroom and sees a rotted corpse in the tub. In the hallway, Leatherface beats him on the head with a sledgehammer. Leatherface drags Barry to the room and prepares to put him in the freezer. When Heather jumps out, Leatherface grabs her and throws her on a hook.

Jenny waves Vilmer down and asks if he moved the cars or if he knows where Sean is. Vilmer eventually makes her look in the back, where the two dead boys are, and Jenny jumps out of the wrecker. Vilmer chases Jenny, who runs into the woods and is chased by Leatherface and his chainsaw. She runs into the house, and Leatherface chainsaws his way inside. Jenny unsuccessfully uses a gun she had taken from a stuffed police officer, jumps out the window and onto the roof. She jumps from the antennae to a line connected to the house, which Leatherface cuts, causing Jenny to fall. She runs to Darla's place and tells Darla what is happening. Darla settles her down and calls W.E. W.E. arrives with a trash bag and cattle prod. He shocks Jenny a few times, puts the trash bag over her head and shoulders and places the girl in Darla's car trunk. Darla drives away.

Darla picks up some pizza, eludes some nosy cops and finds Heather crawling in the road. She reaches the house, and Leatherface carries Jenny inside. Vilmer pulls off the trash bag and mocks Jenny. When Leatherface drags Heather into the room, Vilmer leans in and bites her face. Later, Darla stands by Jenny in the mirror, and Jenny asks her for help. Darla tells her that Vilmer works for people who do things like assassinating Kennedy. Jenny is taken back to the kitchen. While Vilmer and Darla engage in a physical altercation, Jenny points the shotgun at the group. Vilmer tosses a couple of shells at her, implying that the gun is not loaded. Jenny tries to get Heather to stand up and run away, and Vilmer finally points the gun at his mouth, and Jenny only gets a click. Vilmer takes the gun, and the second barrel fires. Jenny runs to Darla's car and drives, but Vilmer jumps on the hood. Jenny stops and Vilmer rolls off, but she must stop the car when the hood pops open. Vilmer grabs her and takes her back inside.

Leatherface puts on make up and a dress, and everyone sits at the dinner table. Vilmer hits Jenny and wakes her up, and Jenny cries and asks Darla for help again. Darla says she cannot help Jenny because Vilmer has put something in her head and can push a button and kill her at any time. Vilmer says his brother wants Jenny's face, and Jenny hits Vilmer back. She tells him to kill her if he is planning to and says that no one believes his stories except his girlfriend. Vilmer, angry, whacks W.E. on the head with a hammer. Jenny says she is leaving, and she tells a whining Leatherface to sit down. Vilmer pours gasoline on a still-living Heather, sitting at the table, and drops a match. Heather screams and burns. Darla puts out the fire with a fire extinguisher as Jenny cries.

Rothman, a man in a business suit, arrives in a limousine and walks in the door. Jenny pleads with him to help, and he settles her down and has her sit. Rothman is upset with Vilmer, saying that he is only there to show people the meaning of horror. Rothman opens his shirt, shows Jenny weird designs and rings on his stomach, licks her face and leaves. Vilmer steps on and crushes Heather's head, and Darla tries to stop him as he cuts himself. Jenny walks to the other room, and Vilmer comes in and grabs her. He holds her head down for Leatherface's chainsaw, but Jenny uses a remote control to operate Vilmer's mechanical leg. She runs out into the breaking day, and a woman helps her into an RV as Leatherface chases her. Vilmer and Leatherface follow the RV in the wrecker, and the RV flips to his side. Jenny jumps out and runs, and a crop dusting plane flies low and whacks Vilmer. Jenny, taken away in the limo, sees Rothman inside. Leatherface furiously spins around with his chainsaw. Rothman asks for Jenny's apology, saying it was meant to be a "spiritual experience." Jenny is taken to a hospital, where a cop talks to her, and she eyes a woman passing on a gurney.

The fourth film of the *Texas Chainsaw Massacre* series has the fourth opening disclaimer and the fourth time the female protagonist is forced to have dinner with the cannibalistic family. By this time, the setting, the murders and even Leatherface are no longer terrifying. Originally completed in 1994 as *The Return of the Texas Chainsaw Massacre*, the film was released in 1997 under the *Next Generation* title (after Zellweger and McConaughey had gained popularity), with some scenes cut, including a subplot of Jenny's abusive stepfather. Paul Partain as a hospital orderly and "Anonymous" (Marilyn Burns) as the patient on the gurney both appeared in *The Texas Chainsaw Massacre* (as, respectively, Frank and Sally).

Theater of Blood (aka *Theatre of Blood*) (1973)

Written by Anthony Greville-Bell; Directed by Douglas Hickox; United Artists/Harbor Productions, Inc./Cineman Films Limited; 104 min.

Cast: Vicent Price (Edward Lionheart); Diana Rigg (Edwina Lionheart); Ian Hendry (Peregrine Devlin); Harry Andrews (Trevor

Edward Lionheart (Vincent Price) lets Meredith Merridew (Robert Morley) know exactly what he had been "chowing" on in Douglas Hickox's *Theater of Blood* (1973).

Dickman); Coral Browne (Chloe Moon); Robert Coote (Oliver Larding); Jack Hawkins (Solomon Psaltery); Michael Hordern (George Maxwell); Arthur Lowe (Horace Sprout); Robert Morley (Meredith Merridew); Dennis Price (Hector Snipe); Milo O'Shea (Inspector Boot); Eric Sykes (Sergeant Dogge); Madeline Smith (Rosemary); Diana Dors (Maisie Psaltery); Joan Hickson (Mrs. Sprout); Renee Asherson (Mrs. Maxwell); Bunny Lemkow, Stanley Bates, Eric Francis, Sally Gilmore, John Gilpin, Joyce Graeme, Jack Maguire, Declan Muholland (The "Meths Drinkers")

Crew: Gustave Berne, Sam Jaffe (Executive Producers); John Kohn, Stanley Mann (Producers); Michael J. Lewis (Composer); Wolfgang Suschitzky (Director of Photography); Malcolm Cooke (Editor)

George Maxwell is sitting with his wife at breakfast when he receives a telephone call about squatters in a building. When George arrives there, two constables lead him to the room of people and George tells them to leave. The squatters approach George with various weapons; as the officers watch, George is attacked and beaten. One constable recites some Shakespeare and removes a disguise for George to see ("It's you!"). Edward Lionheart, "the world's greatest living actor," performs *Julius Caesar* for his squatter-friends.

At the Critics Circle, the critics are irked that George is tardy. As they decide whether to begin, Rosemary walks in and tells the group that George was found "cut to ribbons." Peregrine Devlin, president of the circle, is writing a story on George; at the scene of the murder, he sees a poster of *Julius Caesar,* starring Lionheart. Lionheart's bearded henchman leads critic Hector Snipe to an old theater, telling him that Lionheart is still alive. Under the stage, Lionheart talks to Hector of his belittling review and the Critics Award presentation, and he says that he was about to rehearse a scene of *Troilus and Cressida*. A platform pushes Hector up, the squatters grab him and Lionheart stabs him with a spear.

At George's funeral, a horse rides in, dragging the corpse of Hector. The group of critics are frightened by the realization that someone is killing them for bad reviews. By a memorial for Edward Kendal Sheridan Lionheart, Devlin sees Lionheart's daughter, Edwina. Edwina mentions her father killing himself, but she refers to Devlin as "my father's murderer." When Horace Sprout comes home with his wife, there is a trunk awaiting them in the bedroom. With no tools or key, they leave it for the morning. That night, as the couple sleeps, Lionheart and his assistant step out of the trunk dressed as doctors. Lionheart injects the two with a hypodermic, prepares Horace and saws away. The next morning, the maid screams at a bloody Horace. Horace's wife awakes, and shakes her husband, and his head falls to the floor next to the maid, who screams again. Devlin goes for milk by the door, and Horace's head rests on a bottle.

Edwina, dressed as a blonde, sits by Trevor Dickman at a restaurant talking to him about working with Horace, and asking Trevor to "substitute" at rehearsal. Inspector Boot tells the critics that they are now all protected, but Sergeant Dogge informs the inspector that the cops could not find Trevor at his usual lunch locale. Edwina and Trevor read lines from a slightly revised *Merchant of Venice*, and the group of people hold Trevor down as Lionheart, playing the Shylock, stabs Trevor and cuts out his steaming heart. He weighs it, slices a little and has his "pound of flesh," as he and Edwina bow. Devlin shows the inspector a list of Shakespeare plays in which Lionheart starred, and he says that the first three killings have resembled murders from the plays (the third being *Cymbeline*). He tells the story of two years ago, when Lionheart, upset over losing the Critics Circle Award for Best Actor, entered the room of critics and threw himself over the balcony as Edwina screamed. Devlin believes that Lionheart is alive; he then receives a box with a note from Trevor and the critic's heart inside.

Oliver Larding stops with a police officer, and he walks into a place for some wine tasting (Lionheart's henchman is there). Lionheart reads Oliver's scathing review of the actor's *Richard III* performance, and the group of wine-tasters moves to the cellar (where Lionheart is alone). Lionheart comes out (the other "tasters" are the squatters) and complains of Oliver being drunk and sleeping through his performance. Oliver's body is pushed into a wine barrel, and the lid is sealed. Devlin goes to talk to Edwina, and Inspector Boot arrives and tells them both that Oliver is dead, with his lungs full of Chambertin, 1964. Edwina is taken to the station. Devlin goes to a gym for some fencing, and his sparring partner lifts his mask to reveal himself to be Lionheart. As the two fence, Lionheart tells Devlin of washing ashore and being discovered by the squatters. Lionheart finally gets the better of Devlin (*Romeo and Juliet* is next on the list), but he decides not to kill Devlin, because he would rather make him suffer.

Inspector Boot tells a bed ridden Devlin that Edwina has been released (and will be watched) and that *Othello* is next. Solomon Psaltery gets an anonymous call in reference to his wife and he spies as his wife calls a strange man up to her room. Solomon hears his wife, Maisie, being massaged; the massager (Lionheart) holds her down as Solomon yells at the door. Lionheart tells the critic of his wife's other lovers, and Solomon holds a pillow of Maisie's face. Later, Solomon is taken away to jail. Chloe Moon goes to a beauty salon (with a constable) and is let inside by Lionheart's henchman. Lionheart (as "Butch") leads Chloe away, puts her in a chair and wraps odd rollers in her hair. She is tied as Lionheart talks of Joan of Arc burning at the stake in part one of *Henry VI*. A cord is wrapped around Chloe's mouth and she is electrocuted. Edwina tells Devlin that her father telephoned and admitted to the killings, and Devlin asks to if she would like him to go with her to talk with the Shakespearean actor.

A squatter is put in a "Lionheart mask" as the actor reads a bad review from Meredith Merridew (of *Titus Andronicus*) and mixes an egg in a bowl. The police see "Lionheart" drive by, and a number of cars give chase. Meredith is driven to his home by constables, and he goes inside and calls for his two "doggie woggies" (they are frequently by his side). He is surprised by Lionheart and his pals (as chefs), and Meredith is excited, believing he is on *This is Your Dish*. Meredith eats a pie that he finds "simply delicious," and Lionheart shows Meredith, on a platter, his two dogs, which had been baked into the pie. Lionheart pushes the critic onto a table, then (with a funnel) force-feeds him more until Meredith dies. Devlin drives to meet Edwina, with a homing device and Sergeant Dogge in the trunk. Edwina arrives, and the critic admits that the police are nearby. She asks to drive. Lionheart rides by on a carriage and knocks out Devlin, and he is taken away. Edwina gets rid of the homing device and drives away in Devlin's car. Later, the police get a call from Dogge, who hears a train; this comment is followed by the sound of a crash.

Devlin is strapped to a chair for Lionheart's version of the Critics Circle Awards presentation. Devlin refuses to change his opinion, and Lionheart tells of the character being blinded in *King Lear*. The henchman removes a disguise and reveals herself to be Edwina. As a bag of sand is emptied, two daggers roll slowly down towards the critic's eyes. Sirens are heard outside (the cops had questioned the squatter disguised as Lionheart), and Lionheart begins torching the theater. A squatter hits Edwina on the head with the award, and Lionheart runs to his daughter's side. The cops run inside and free Devlin. The critic, Boot, and Rosemary watch as Lionheart carries Edwina's body on the roof. A burst of flames causes the actor to fall to his presumed death. Devlin tells the others that Lionheart was "madly overacting as usual," and the critic leaves.

Theater of Blood is a terrific slasher, with very creative and innovative murder sequences based on the work of Shakespeare. It is difficult to tell whether the audience was supposed to recognize Dame Diana Rigg as the "henchman" (because her distinctive features are highly evident), but that does not distract from the actress' excellent performance. Vincent Price is wonderful as the critically disdained Edward Lionheart, and it is easy to root for him in the film, since his targets are all stuffy and shallow critics.

To All a Goodnight (1980)

Written by Alex Rebar; Directed by David Hess; Intercontinental Releasing Corporation/I.W.D.C.; 83 min.

Cast: Jennifer Runyon (Nancy); Forrest Swanson (Alex); Linda Gentile (Melody); William Lauer (T.J.); Judith Bridges (Leia); Katherine Herrington (Mrs. Jensen); Buck West (Ralph); Sam Shamshak (Polansky); Angela Bath (Trisha); Denise Stearns (Sam); Solomon Trager (Tom); Jeff Butts (Blake); Bill Martins (Jim); Jay Rasumny (Dan); Judy Hess (Mr. Ronsoni); Carrie Cobb (Mrs. Jensen's Daughter); Lisa Labowskie (Cynthia); Harry Sethe (Irate Father); Vivienne Kove (Sincere Mother); Alain Clenet (Clenet Driver); Dori Tressler (Girl With Cat); Michael George (Pilot); Jamie Nielsen, Lori Eiseman, Jennifer Howard, Cathy Hicky, Mary Hicky, Cathy Fisher, Toby Sternlieb, Mary Wagner, Ann Tucker, Virginia Quiria, Justin Zachary, Robin Theriault, Robin Olsen, Donald Kinn, Linda Mersman, Jane Osborn (School Girls)

Crew: Rick Whitfield, Alex Rebar (Executive Producers); Jay Rasumny (Producer); Sharyon Reis Cobe (Associate Producer); Bil Godsey (Director of Photography); William J. Waters (Editor)

During Christmas vacation at the Calvin Finishing School for Girls, one girl is chased by a group of peers who are yelling about cutting her hair off. The girl runs to a balcony. When the pursuers near her, she falls to her death. The girls scream.

It is two years later, and many females

are leaving for Christmas vacation and saying their good-byes. Nancy, Melody, Leia, Trisha, Cynthia and Sam are all spending their vacations at the school. A person with gloves, alone in a room, gets out a knife and a framed picture of the girl who died two years before. The housemother, Mrs. Jensen, prepares dinner for the girls, and tells them that Mrs. Calvin, the superintendent, cannot make it back until Monday. Leia, seemingly excited, tells the girls that her boyfriend T.J. will be there with some friends. Cynthia, who had gone to bed early, is called to the window by Paul, and she changes clothes. Paul's mouth is covered by a hand, and someone is there with a knife. Cynthia comes outside and is stabbed in the chest.

Leia goes to get some tissue and perfume for Trisha, and she runs into the quaint caretaker, Ralph, who is subsequently mocked by the girls at the dinner table. Mrs. Ronsoni stops by for a visit, and Leia tells Mrs. Jensen that the girls will clean up for her and she can go to bed. Leia returns to the girls in the dining room and tells them that Mrs. Jensen will sleep for hours. Later, Nancy goes to Mrs. Jensen's room and gives the housemother drugged milk (Nancy evidently being the only girl who would not be suspected for something "underhanded"). The girls go to meet the arriving airplane of boys. Ralph sees Nancy, tells her he wants her to be safe and gives her a flashlight. The boys exit the plane dressed as Santa or with Santa's hat. After T.J. tells the pilot to stay with the plane, they are led back to the school by the girls.

A group of people listens to Blake play guitar and sing. Trisha goes to get a beer in the kitchen and thinks she sees Tom dressed as Santa, but Santa grabs her and slits her throat. Nancy sees Ralph in the hallway, and he says he wants her to be safe. ("There's evil here; I can feel it.") Tom goes looking for Trisha, and a bloody trail leads to Trisha's body. The killer Santa chases Tom and tackles him, Tom's head is crushed and Santa buries the new bodies. Leia goes for more beer and runs into Nancy. Leia sees something on the floor near the refrigerator and surmises that someone cut himself while shaving. Nancy gets a glass of milk and pours for Alex before they say good night. Nancy hangs around outside while Blake and Sam are busy inside. The killer approaches the couple (in a knight's armor), shoots an arrow through Blake's neck and chops off Sam's head with an axe. Nancy ignores what she believes are screams of pleasure from Sam. Nancy returns to her room, where Ralph crawls in through the window, says "something is wrong" and tells her to pray. Melody and a nervous Alex spend some time in bed.

The next morning, T.J., Leia, Alex and Melody are eating breakfast as Nancy sits alone at a nearby table. Mrs. Jensen tells the boy that they should not be there, but they say they are leaving soon. T.J. suggests having a picnic, and Nancy looks for the others but finds no one. At the picnic, Alex playfully chases Nancy, who slips and uncovers a dead Ralph. Mr. Polanky is there to investigate, and the group says they don't know where any of the other people are. Polansky tells them he is leaving behind two police officers to watch them. Alex says that the others would not have left without telling them. Leia assures them the people will be back, and Alex consoles an apprehensive Nancy. Alex and Nancy go to see Mrs. Jensen in the kitchen and tell her they believe there is danger, but the housemother says they will be safe with the officers outside.

One officer goes to watch outside while the other decides to get some sleep and is led to a room by Leia. Mrs. Jensen goes to bed, and Nancy suggests to the others that they open their Christmas gifts to lighten the mood. Leia declines and leaves to take a shower. Melody tells T.J. to go get the pilot and let him come inside, but T.J. say he does not like him. T.J. gets a beer and heads upstairs to see Leia and the cop in her room. He goes back to the others and stays with Melody as Alex and Nancy check around the place. The police officer outside gets an axe in the head. T.J. and Melody decide to go outside. Alex and Nancy finish their house checking and sit to talk. Leia finishes up with the police officer and she goes to shower, discovering the decapitated head of Sam behind the curtain. Her cop partner walks in with a knife in his back, and Santa stands in front of Leia as she screams.

T.J. and Melody kiss by a tree, and Alex and Nancy dance inside. T.J. gets a wire around his neck. Melody runs to the door and bangs on it until she is let inside. Melody lets them know the situation ("We're all gonna die!") and they look for the others. They find Sam's head and the dead cop. Alex goes to a phone, but the line is cut. They find Leia in a white dress eerily dancing and singing. Santa appears, and Melody runs outside. "Killed my baby," Santa tells Nancy, and a mask is taken off to reveal Mrs. Jensen. She ignores Nancy's pleas that she did not know her daughter (it is Nancy's first year), and Nancy knocks her down and runs.

Melody wakes the pilot and tells him people are dead. He first must work on the generator (next to the blades). Santa, inside the plane, starts the engine, chopping the pilot and Melody. Mrs. Jensen attacks Nancy again ("Die!"), Nancy runs and hides on a balcony and the housemother finds her but falls over the railing. Nancy sits and cries, as another Santa carries Mrs. Jensen's body to her. "You killed my wife. You killed our daughter." It is Polansky, and he attacks Nancy, but is shot with an arrow by Alex. Alex embraces Nancy and they run outside. Nancy wants to go back for Leia, but Alex says they will send someone later. Leia continues her peculiar dancing and singing atop a balcony outside.

To All a Goodnight is a fairly amateurish production, but a multitude of characters interacting with one another and not one but *two* massive killing sprees keep the film from becoming monotonous. Director Hess is better known as the vicious leader of the lethal punks in Wes Craven's classic *The Last House on the Left* (1972).

The Toolbox Murders (1977)

Written by Neva Friedenn, Robert Easter and Ann Kindberg; Directed by Dennis Donnelly; Tony DiDio Productions; 93 min.

Cast: Cameron Mitchell (Kingsley); Pamelyn Ferdin (Laurie); Wesley Eure (Kent); Nicholas Beauvy (Joey); Tim Donnelly (Detective Jamison); Aneta Corsaut (Joanne Ballard); Faith McSwain (Mrs. Andrews); Marciee Drake (Debbie); Evelyn Guerrero (Maria); Victoria Perry (Woman in Apartment); Robert Bartlett (Man in Apartment); Betty Cole (Middle Aged Woman); John Hawker (Middle Aged Man); Don Diamond (Sergeant Cameron); Alisa Powell (Girlfriend); Marianne Walter (Dee Ann); Robert Forward (Screamer Man); Kathleen O'Malley (Screamer Woman); Gil Galvano (Man); James Nolan (Bartender); George Deaton (Preacher)

Crew: Tony Didio (Producer); Kenneth A. Yates, Jack Kindberg (Associate Producers); George Deaton (Composer); Gary Graver (Director of Photography); Nunzio Darpino (Editor)

A person is driving around at night, and a flashback shows a car wreck, an ambulance and a little girl lying dead on a gurney. The car stops and a person grabs a toolbox from the trunk and heads towards a building. The person walks into an apartment, and Mrs. Andrews walks out of the bathroom, letting the man know that she called a couple of days ago. The man attaches a drill bit and heads for the woman. She breaks a bottle and holds the fractured glass against him, but the man grabs her arm and drills into it. She takes cover in the bathroom, but he drills through the door, gets inside and punches Mrs. Andrews. He carries her to the main room, where he drills her as a record plays. He puts the bloody drill back in the toolbox, puts on a ski mask and leaves the room.

Debbie returns to her apartment and changes clothes. She opens her door to get something in the hall; the killer punches her out and carries her to the top of the stairs, where he beats her with a hammer. He takes the body back into the apartment and places it on the floor. Maria is at the door to ask about the mess outside. When she gets inside, the killer shuts the door, keeps her from leaving and stabs Maria with a screwdriver. In another apartment, the killer sees a woman with a man, and avoids the room. An elderly woman sees the blood at the top of the stairs and calls to a man, and they both knock on Debbie's door. The man opens the door, and the couple sees the two dead women.

The police are at the scene, and they speak with Vance Kingsley, owner of the building. They ask for a list of tenants, and he tells them that he screens all of the applicants. Laurie talks to her brother Joey and leaves for school with one of her friends. Dee Ann is preparing to bathe, and the humming killer is outside with his toolbox. He cuts the chain lock and walks into the bathroom, where he sees the woman in the tub. She sees him and jumps out of the tub; he shoots a nailgun at her and misses. He reloads and misses her again. Dee Ann tries to persuade him to put the tool/weapon down, but after quick flashes of the girl and the accident, the killer shoots and hits her in the stomach. She leans against the wall and fires the nailgun into her head.

Laurie is on the phone with her boyfriend; the killer walks inside behind her as she is hanging up. He grabs her mouth and she struggles, but finally seems to pass out. Joey returns to an empty house, and he gets a drink for his mother when she comes home. They hear screams and run outside, where tenants have crowded around Dee Ann's apartment. Detective Jamison talks to Joey and asks him where he was the last few nights. Joey, anxious to find his sister, heads to Mrs. Andrews' place, where he sees Kent, Vance's nephew, who is there to clean up the bloody mess. The two discuss "that wreck," which resulted in the death of Kent's cousin Cathy. Joey says he wants to know where Laurie is, and the two head over to Dee Ann's apartment. After looking around, Kent sees a bloody nail in the wall (it had gone through the woman's stomach), and he surmises that the murderer used a nailgun to kill Dee Ann. The two boys leave.

Vance Kingsley (Cameron Mitchell) takes a break from working with tools to lovingly embrace his doll, the representation of his lost daughter, in Dennis Donnelly's *The Toolbox Murders* (1977).

Joanne, Laurie and Joey's mom heads to a bar, her place of employment, because she does not want to be at home to think about Laurie. Joey and Kent go to his uncle's place for cleaning equipment. In the garage, they see Vance, who simply hands Kent some money and shuts the door. The boys get some supplies and leave. The murderer's toolbox is sitting in the garage. Vance watches them leave and goes to the bedroom, where Laurie is bound and gagged on a bed. He brushes her hair and talks to her about Cathy and the "evil" world. He says he killed the women because they were evil. ("If you get rid of the evil, then all that's left is good.") Laurie calls him Daddy and, as "Cathy," tries to get him to untie her. Vance says he cannot lose her again, and he gags her and leaves Laurie to cry alone.

Jamison goes to the bar to talk to Joanne but he does not seem to get any useful information from her. Kent goes to his uncle's place, sees Laurie there in bed and gently raps on the window. The next day, Joey goes to Mrs. Andrews' apartment, where Kent is cleaning and Jamison is looking out the window with binoculars. Jamison tells Joey that the killer forced his way into one apartment but may have conned his way into the others. Joey asks if the killer had to con his way in at all, and Kent quickly eyes the two. Joey leaves, gets his mother's car keys and heads over to Vance's place. Inside the garage, he finds the toolbox and a bloody drill bit. Kent enters and tells Joey that he is crazy for believing his uncle is a killer. He then says if anyone believes Joey's claims, there would be much trouble for his uncle. Kent throws some gasoline on Joey and tells him that he has to protect his family. He lights some matches and finally throws one on Joey, who burns and screams.

Kent walks into the bedroom where Vance is with Laurie, and he tells his uncle that he is sick and insane. He agitates his uncle by telling him that Cathy and he made love on several occasions. A chase leads into the kitchen, where Kent arms himself with a knife. Vance grabs the knife and the doll he is holding loses its head. "You killed my Cathy," he tells Kent, and he walks into the knife and falls to the floor. Kent picks up the doll, puts the head back on and cleans the blood off. He returns to the bedroom and cuts Laurie's restraints. Laurie is overjoyed and thanks Kent. Kent tries to kiss Laurie, but he gets on top of her, ignoring her screams. Later, the two are lying in bed together, and Kent is talking about marriage. Laurie asks about her brother, and she knows that Kent murdered Joey. Kent says they will be together, and Laurie turns and eyes a pair of scissors beside the bed. In the dark night, a benumbed Laurie slowly walks home.

The Toolbox Murders has a good beginning, commencing with a few murders and effectively utilizing minimal dialogue, but then the film slows down, with Laurie as hostage and Joey searching for his sister. However, it is fun to watch Mitchell present his maniacal monologues, and Ferdin is very good as Laurie. A disclaimer at the film's conclusion alleges that the events of the movie were based on a true story.

Torso (aka *I corpi presentano tracce li violenzia carnale*) (1973)

Written by Ernesto Castaldi and Sergio Martino; Directed by Sergio Martino; Compagnia Cinematografica Champion; 89 min.

Cast: Suzy Kendall (Jane); Tina Aumont (Dani); Luc Merenda (Roberto); John Richardson (Franz); Roberto Bisacco (Stefano); Angela Covello (Katia); Carla Brait (Ursula); Cristina Airoldi (Carrol); Patricia Adiutori (Flo)

Crew: Antonio Cervi (Executive Producer); Guido De Angelis, Maurizio De Angelis (Composers); Giancarlo Ferrando (Director of Photography); Eugenio Alabiso (Editor)

A man is with two women, all of them nude and on a bed, while a camera is taking photographs. A professor is speaking with his students, and Jane speaks with the professor after class. Stefano offers Jane's friend Dani a ride home, but she turns him down. She later tells Jane that the man is always around her. Later, Flo is with Sean, making out in a car. Sean sees someone in a ski mask watching them, and he runs out of the car and chases the person. Flo gets out of the car, turns on the headlights and looks for Sean. When the headlights are turned off, Flo heads back to the car, where the killer cuts into her chest.

The next day, Dani shows Carrol the news of Flo's death. Classes are canceled for the day, and Jane goes to see the professor, Franz. The two have a drink, and Franz invites Jane to a concert. Stefano later picks up a prostitute, but seems reluctant to do anything with her. When she demands he pay regardless of his actions, Stefano hits and chokes the woman; she leaves behind an unsettled Stefano. Later, Dani watches Carrol being taken away by two bikers. The gloved killer is driving around, passing by Dani, who looks at the driver. At a party, Carrol is kissing the two men, but when one tries to further the interaction, she puts her joint out on his chest. Carrol leaves and ends up in a marshy area. She sees the killer in a fog and runs away, but the killer catches up to her. Carrol is choked with a scarf and her head is pushed underwater. The killer gets a knife and cuts into Carrol.

A police officer shows a room of students the scarf that connects the two murders. Dani tells Jane about the two bikers with Carrol, and she says that the men had no scarfs, but she remembers seeing someone with the scarf. At her house, Dani gets a phone call in which the killer threatens her about her scarf knowledge. Dani's uncle comes home (Jane had seen the man earlier talking to Carrol) and suggests that Dani go to the country house to relax. Inspector Martino interviews a vendor and asks him if he remembers selling a scarf. The man denies any recollection, but after the inspector leaves, he gets on a pay phone and tells someone he wants money to keep quiet about a transaction concerning the scarf in question. Stefano talks to Dani later, saying that she "belongs" to him. Dani remembers Stefano wearing the scarf. She gets away from Stefano, calls Jane and asks her to come over.

After Dani tells Jane about Stefano, his scarf and the threatening phone call, Jane says she will be coming to the country house a little later than the rest. The "scarf seller," walking at night with a healthy chunk of cash, is chased down by a car and crushed against a wall. Jane goes to see Stefano; inside his house, she sees a doll (recalling the doll flashing in the killer's mind during the murders). A woman tells Jane that Stefano was not in his bed last night and that he might be out of town. While Dani and her two friends, Ursula and Katia, are traveling on a train, a doctor, Roberto (having occasionally been around the university), enters their compartment and sits by Dani. Jane arrives at a gas station at night asking for directions and for her car to be worked on. The man says he cannot work on the car until tomorrow, so he drives up to Dani's house with Jane. At the house, Jane tells Dani that Stefano did not commit any murder. Dani remembers that Stefano's scarf design was slightly different, but she knows she saw someone wearing the fatal scarf.

A weird guy, watching through the windows as Ursula and Katia lie on a bed, sees the killer with his knife. He runs and hides, but the killer finds him and finishes him off. The next day, a man comes to deliver some groceries. When Jane runs down the stairs to greet him, she slips and twists her ankle. Roberto visits the house to check on Jane's ankle, and Dani remembers him from the train. Later, when the women are playing in the water, Dani thinks she sees Stefano and she calls out to him, but Ursula and Katia do not see anyone. The women say good night to the bedridden Jane. Downstairs, Dani decides to call Stefano and discovers that the phone is dead. The door buzzes, and Stefano is standing there in his scarf, but he drops dead to reveal the killer behind him (clutching onto Stefano's scarf). Dani and the other two women scream.

The next morning, Jane awakes, limps to the door and calls out to her friends. She slowly walks down the steps and screams when she sees Ursula and Katia dead. Dani's hand grabs Jane, but she collapses to the floor dead. When she sees the door being unlocked, Jane hides. The killer walks in and begins hacksawing a corpse. The man arrives with groceries and leaves when there is no response to his knocking. The killer puts a body in a bag and walks out. Jane heads for the stairs and freezes when the door is opened again, but the killer is only throwing in the bread and milk. Finding the phone dead and the door locked, Jane goes upstairs, resting at the top and not realizing her shoes have come off.

Jane goes to the bedroom window and sees the town below. She tries to signal someone with a mirror reflecting sunlight. Roberto, still in town, looks up at the house, checks the phone book and calls, but receives no answer. Jane, seeing the killer coming back, quickly cleans up the room to give the appearance of no one being there. She sees that her shoes are gone and looks out the door and sees the killer dragging another body away. The gas station man is at the door with Jane's car, but he leaves. Jane goes for the window and knocks over a chair. She hides in the closet when she hears the killer coming up. The killer looks around in the room and leaves. Jane watches the killer walks away with a body.

At night, the grocery man tries to convince a group of men that there are four women up at the house, as opposed to the three the men had seen arrive; the killer is nearby. Roberto sees Jane's car at the gas station; the man tells him that, although no one answered the door, he did not see any of the women leave. Jane, locked inside the bedroom, slides a newspaper under the door and pushes the key through the keyhole. The key misses the paper, but the killer graciously places the key on the paper for her. Jane gets the door open, and Franz grabs her, saying he "had to do it" and that the women "were only dolls." A flashback shows Franz with his brother and a girl, and his brother, wishing to see the girl in an intimate way, goes for her doll at the edge of a cliff and falls to his death. Franz tells Jane that Flo and Carrol seduced and blackmailed him (they were the three from the beginning), and that he had to kill Dani because she would have eventually remembered him and his scarf. Roberto arrives, and he and the professor struggle. Outside, they are fighting near a cliff; Jane hears someone fall. She watches as Roberto returns to her, and the two go to get the police.

Sergio Martino's *Torso* has a few slow spots, but there is enough suspense to keep things interesting. The final third of the film (with Jane hiding from the killer) is particularly impressive. Actress Kendall, having fought off a murderer in Dario Argento's *The Bird with the Crystal Plumage* (1969), appeared with Sidney Poitier in *To Sir, with Love* (1965).

The Town That Dreaded Sundown (1976)

Written by Earl E. Smith; Directed by Charles B. Pierce; Orion Pictures/Charles B. Pierce Film Productions, Inc.; 90 min.

Cast: Ben Johnson (Captain J.D. Morales); Andrew Prine (Deputy Norman Ramsey); Dawn Wells (Helen Reed); Jimmy Clem (Sergeant Mal Griffin); Jim Citty (Police Chief R.J. Sullivan); Charles B. Pierce (Patrolman A.C. Benson); Robert Aquino (Sheriff Otis Barker); Cindy Butler (Peggy Loomis); Christine Ellsworth (Linda Mae Jenkins); Earl E. Smith (Doctor Kress); Steve Lyons (Roy Allen); Joe Catalanatto (Eddie LeDoux); Roy Lee Brown (Rainbow Johnson); Mike Hackworth (Sammy Fuller); Misty West (Emma Lou Cook); Rick Hildreth (Buddy Turner); Jason Darnell (Capt. Gus Wells); Mike Downs, Bill Dietz, Carolyn Moreland (Newspaper Reporters); Michael Brown (Police Officer); Woody Woodman (FBI Agent); James D. McAdams (Sheriff's Deputy); John Stroud (Doctor Preston Hickson); Mason Andres (Rev. Harden); Richard Green (High School Principal); Dorothy Darlene Orr (Dispatcher); Don Adkins (Suspect); Bud Davis (The Phantom Killer); Vern Stierman (Narrator)

Crew: Charles B. Pierce (Producer); Tom Moore (Associate Producer); Jaime Mendosa-Nava (Composer); Jim Roberson (Director of Photography); Tom Boutross (Editor)

It is Sunday, March 3, 1946, in the town of Texarkana, and Sammy and Linda Mae are out parking in a car. The car hood pops open, and a man with a hood over his face takes something from the engine. Sammy fruitlessly tries to start the car as the man breaks the car window with a pipe and pulls Sammy out. Linda Mae screams, and the man goes for her.

Linda Mae is found lying wounded on the side of the road, and she and Sammy are taken to a hospital. A doctor tells Deputy Ramsey and Sheriff Barker that Linda Mae was "bitten" and "literally chewed" on different parts of her body. Police Chief Sullivan asks about the "Lover's Lane Case," and he tells the officers to warn people about "parking on lonely roads." Ramsey states his belief that the mysterious person will strike again. Twenty-one days later, on March 24, Howard and his girlfriend Emma Lou go out driving in the rain. After hearing gunshots, Ramsey finds a parked car but no one around. Ramsey hears more gunshots, and in the woods he finds Howard and Emma Lou dead. The killer gets in the parked car and drives away.

Since the killer, now known as "The Phantom," seems to have no motive, the townspeople begin to "dread sundown." Ramsey goes to the train station to meet Captain Morales, a famous criminal investigator. Morales has the officers set up a curfew. Many people are on the case, including the FBI; a number of criminals are "admitting" to the killings, and a horde of citizens are demanding protection.

Ramsey tells Morales that, on April 14, 21 more days after the second attack, the killer may kill again. Morales sets up "decoys" (cops posing as couples). That night, at the Junior and Senior High School Prom, many people are leaving. Peggy gets her trombone and leaves with Roy. Roy suggests parking at their "favorite spot." The two nod off, and they wake up in the car at 2:40 in the morning. As they drive away, the Phantom jumps on the car, grabs at Roy and causes the both of them to fall out. The Phantom whacks Roy on the head and chases Peggy down, tying her to a tree. A dazed Roy tries to get away, but the killer shoots and kills him. He gets Peggy's trombone, attaches a knife to the end and "plays" the instrument, stabbing Peggy in the back a few times.

Morales is upset that the Phantom was able to kill again with all the law enforcers looking for him. In a restaurant, the group talks to Doctor Kress, who says that the Phantom is motivated by a strong sex drive and will probably not be caught. He says the killings are like a game to the Phantom. Morales asks the doctor if the killer is insane ("Oh, yes!"). At a neighboring table, a man (wearing the Phantom's boots) stands and walks out of the restaurant. Morales talks to a man named Johnson, who says he was held at gunpoint by a man claiming to have killed five people. Morales and Ramsey get a call about an armed man; they spot him speeding away from a store and chase him down. The man, Eddie, is in a stolen car. Johnson identifies him as the man with the gun. Eddie says he is the Phantom, but Morales does not believe him.

On Friday, May 3, Helen drives away and is unknowingly being watched by someone with familiar boots. While she is at home, Floyd, in another room, is shot through the window (the Phantom has a silencer). Helen sees Floyd fall over and die; as she calls the operator she is shot twice by the killer. She manages to crawl away and get outside the door but the Phantom follows with a pickaxe. Helen gets to a house and a concerned citizen, armed with a shotgun, comes out to help her. The killer sees him and flees. The next day, Ramsey and Morales get a call about an abandoned car that fits the description of the car Ramsey saw on the rainy night. They find the car, gets some shotguns and run into the woods. They find the Phantom out there, walking around in his hood, and chase him to railroad tracks; a moving train gets in between them. The killer is hit, but he limps away. Cops and bloodhounds search for him, but the killer is not found. As the narrator says, no one quite knows what happened to the Phantom.

While much of *The Town That Dreaded Sundown* plays like a dreary documentary with the superfluous narrator (and attempts at humor like bumbling Patrolman Benson, played by the director, fall short), the scenes of stalkings and attacks are great, and the train sequence at the end is excellent. Actress Wells might be recognizable to many viewers: She played Mary Ann on the hit television series *Gilligan's Island*.

Trauma (1992)

Written by T. E. D. Klein, Franco Ferrini, Gianni Romoli and Dario Argento; Directed by

Dario Argento; Oversea Filmgroup/ADC Films; 106 min.

Cast: Christopher Rydell (David Parsons); Asia Argento (Aura Petrescu); Piper Laurie (Adriana Petrescu); Brad Dourif (Doctor Lloyd); Frederic Forrest (Doctor Judd); James Russo (Capt. Travis); Laura Johnson (Grace Harrington); Dominique Serrand (Stefan Petrescu); Ira Belgrade (Arnie); Hope Alexander-Willis (Linda Quirk); Sharon Barr (Hilda); Isabell Monn (Georgia Jackson); Cory Garvin (Gabriel Pickering); Terry Pernins (Mrs. Pickering); Tony Saffold (Ben Aldrich); Peter Moore (Mark); Lester Purry (Sergeant Carver); David Chase (Sid Marigold); Jacqui Kim (Alice); Rita Vassallo (Rita); Stephen D'Ambrose (Pale Man); Bonita Parsons (Prima Woman) Gregory Beech (Dead Man); Kevin Dutcher (John Miller); Kathy Quirk (Gare Grayson); E.A. Violet Boor (Mrs. Potter)

Crew: Dario Argento (Producer); Andrea Tinnirello (Executive Producer); Pino Donaggio (Composer); Raffaele Mertes (Director of Photography); Bennett Goldberg (Editor); Tom Savini (Special Make-up Effects)

It is a rainy night, and a chiropractor opens the door to an unseen patient. She says to the person, "You look familiar," but soon a machine-operated wire is brought out and the woman is decapitated. David Parsons is driving over a bridge when he sees a girl standing at the edge, preparing to jump. He stops and helps the seemingly dazed girl back onto the street, where they get into his truck and head to a restaurant. The girl, Aura, eats only a little bit of bread, then leaves for the bathroom. After vomiting, Aura leaves the restaurant, only to be picked up by men taking her back to her parents. Inside, David realizes his wallet has been stolen.

The men drop off Aura with her mother Adriana. Aura's father Stefan locks her in her room. Soon many businesslike people arrive at the house for a seance conducted by Adriana. While trying to summon a soul, Adriana is possessed and mentions a "monster with a noose," and threatens everyone with more murders to come. Adriana eventually becomes more violent and runs out of the room, followed by her husband. Aura goes after her parents, only to stumble upon a headless body and a killer holding up the heads of her mother and father in the pouring rain. Doctor Judd is soon there, and he demands that Aura tell him what she saw.

Captain Travis and other police officers arrive to investigate. Aura gets away from the police, tracks down David (utilizing his ID from the stolen wallet) and tells him she needs help and a place to stay. Gabriel, a young boy, apparently lives next door to the killer, who leaves decapitated heads sitting by the window to stare at the boy. David awakes in the night to find food all over the house and Aura vomiting in the bathroom. He talks to his friend Arnie at work about Aura's problem; Arnie infers that Aura has anorexia.

The next night, Aura sees David and his reporter girlfriend Grace having sex. She leaves, and David runs after her. David and Arnie watch a collection of news stories on the recent murders and realize that they have all occurred when it was raining. David receives a phone call from Aura, who has been taken away. He learns that an apparently covetous Grace had informed Doctor Judd of Aura's whereabouts. Meanwhile, Judd tries to help Aura remember what she may have seen the night of her parents' murders but is unsuccessful at extracting any more details. David visits the Faraday Clinic and helps Aura escape. During that time, the killer has murdered one of the clinic's doctors.

Aura had stolen a set of keys from the deceased doctor, and a keychain has "Marigold" inscribed on it. It is a storage area, and they manage to find a photograph of several doctors before the police arrive. One of the doctors, Linda Quirk, is telling her friend about an accident involving electroconvulsive therapy and "something awful." David telephones her and asks Linda if she knows the other doctors; Linda promptly hangs up. David and Aura go to visit Linda, but the frightened Linda speeds away in her car. David and Aura drive around looking for her, and they finally see her car parked in a hotel parking lot.

Linda's friend, still at the house, receives a call and writes down Linda's hotel room number. The friend is attacked and killed after the murderer learns where Linda is. At the hotel, the killer activates the sprinklers (for the rain effect) and beheads Linda. David arrives in time to hear a headless Linda whisper, "Lloyd." Upon discovering a medical bag displaying the name St. Bartholomew, David visits the hospital and learns that Doctor Lloyd no longer works there. He finally finds Lloyd, now a junkie, and David gives him his phone number. Before long, however, the killer finds Lloyd and murders him. When the cops investigate Lloyd's death, they find David's phone number.

David awakes that night to a Doctor Judd trying to persuade Aura to leave with him. A struggle ensues, but Judd must run to elude the cops. He speeds away, but his car runs off the road. The car's trunk pops open, and inside are all of the missing heads. Before dying, Doctor Judd whispers, "I loved her." David runs back to the house to tell Aura, but she is gone. A note declares, "I've gone to join my mother." David finds her nightgown by the lake. The "Headhunter Murders" are considered solved, and a disheartened David is soon addicted to prescription drugs. He attempts to feign a prescription, but he is found out and is punched when refusing to return the drugs. While sitting on the sidewalk, dazed and moping, David believes he sees someone donning Aura's bracelet. He is eventually led to a house. Gabriel, standing outside, tells David he saw someone in a black coat go into the house next door.

David knocks on the door and says to the unseen person, "I'm sorry. I thought you were someone else." Believing he saw Aura reflected in a rain barrel, David crawls through the window and gets inside the house. He enters a child's room, with the name Nicholas written everywhere, and he is knocked unconscious. He awakes chained up with Aura by his side. David soon learns that Aura's mother is still alive. Many years ago, Adriana was giving birth, and during the procedure, her child was accidentally decapitated. In an effort to make Adriana forget the horrible incident, the doctors electrocuted her. Adriana shows up to kill David, who has used the chains restraining him to lock the door to his cage. When Adriana gets the door open, the pillar tears open the ceiling. Standing above is Gabriel, who had been hiding in the closet. He uses Adriana's portable guillotine to decapitate the murderer.

Trauma was an American production for Argento. The film lacks the quirky and frightful ambiance evident in his other films. Argento's daughter Asia gives a sensational performance as Aura.

Trick or Treats (1982)

Written and Directed by Gary Graver; Lone Star Pictures International; 91 min.

Cast: Jackelyn Giroux (Linda); Peter Jason (Malcolm O'Keefe); Chris Graver (Christopher O'Keefe); David Carradine (Richard Adams); Carrie Snodgress (Joan O'Keefe Adams); Steve Railsback (Bret); Jillian Kresner (Andrea); Dan Pastorini, Tim Rossovich (Attendants); Paul Bartel, Jason Renard (Bums); J.L. Clark (Bert); John Blyth Barrymore (Mad Doctor); Catherine Coulson, Tara Hupp (Nurses); Maria Dillon (TV Reporter); Owen Orr (Actor); Allen Wisch (Man With Scar); Patricia Callahan, Debbie Drissi (Mad Doctor Assistants); Glenn Jacobson (Corpse); Butch Sanders (Cop); Jono Kouzouyan (Crazy Man); Nike Zachmanoglou (Connie); Murray Bolen, Frances Bolen, Thomas Ellison, Wayne Stringer, James E. Johnson, Herb Franklin, Michael Stringer, David Lane (Asylum Inmates); Barron, Annette Dugdale, Glenn Alexakis, Slyvester Stewart, Jason Richards, Angela Uva, David Uva, Lisa Travis, Rashell Travis, Bill Bridges, Alfredo Botello, Har-el Dar-noy, Orin Dar-noy (Trick-or-Treaters).

Crew: Caruth C. Byrd, Lee Thornburg (Executive Producers); Glenn Jacobson (Co-Producer); Hedy Dietz (Associate Producer); Gary Graver (Director of Photography/Editor)

Joan and Malcolm O'Keefe enjoy some quiet time in the backyard by the pool. Joan answers the knocking door and tells men in white to quietly enter. They walk to the back with a straitjacket and chains and cuffs, and they chase Malcolm around the backyard until finally getting him in the jacket and clamping the cuffs onto his ankles. As he is being led away, Malcolm screams for Joan, who almost seems to smile.

Several years later, Linda answers the phone in the shower, and she is asked to do something. Bret calls later, and Linda tells him that she has to miss his opening night (he is playing Othello) so she can babysit someone. She gives him the address and phone number of the place so that they might spend some time together later. Linda arrives at the Adams home, and Joan tells her everything, saying that she and her husband Richard will be home from the Halloween party by tomorrow. At the Western State Hospital, Malcolm plays dominos with Bert and suggests "busting out" to get back home. Richard flirts with Linda a bit (even slightly unzipping her dress), and Joan appears in the doorway. Linda mentions that she has not met Christopher yet, and Joan says that he is around somewhere. The couple leaves.

Linda goes to Christopher's room; he runs a fake guillotine, scaring Linda. Linda answers the door to trick-or-treaters, and Christopher does a tiny explosion and scares Linda again. Then he shakes her hand with a joy buzzer. Meanwhile, Malcolm is formulating his escape, telling Bert that he is going to get "her" and her new husband. Later, a nurse checks the sleeping patients (Bert helps out by snoring loudly); Malcolm grabs her and puts a pillow over her face. Christopher comes down the stairs, feigning pain and near-death, and Linda tells him the story of the boy who cried wolf. Malcolm walks out of the institution dressed as a nurse, knocks out the nightwatch man and drives away in a car.

Bret calls to see how Linda is doing; Malcolm telephones from a pay phone but does not respond when Linda answers. Linda sees Christopher floating in the pool and quickly runs out, pulls him from the water and gives him mouth-to-mouth. Christopher sits up ("Thanks for the kiss, baby!"), and Linda is furious. Malcolm calls again and says nothing, and Linda goes to Christopher's room and tells him to get off the phone. Christopher cuts meat in the kitchen and pretends to accidentally slice off a finger. Malcolm calls once more and this time says, "I'm comin' home to take care of you, darling." Linda goes to Christopher's room and tells the boy to stay off the phone. He says he was not on the phone.

Joan calls and Linda tells her that her son is a "holy terror." Christopher sets up a wire on the door's knocker that allows him to knock on the door while hiding safely behind the fence. He knocks four times, making Linda more enraged each time. Malcolm steals a knife from a diner and puts it in his purse. Malcolm approaches a homeless man and, threatening him with the knife, tells him to take off his clothes. Linda calls Andrea, in an editing room and working on *The Monster Strikes* with Connie, and she asks if she has transferred to video a scene, which her agent needs. Andrea offers to swing by and drop the video off. Linda turns on the television and sees a report of Malcolm's escape.

Linda hears a noise and goes to the shed in back, and Malcolm walks through the front door. In the shed, Christopher drops a rat on Linda and frightens her. She asks the boy to (please) stop. Andrea arrives at the house and walks in, calling for Linda. She reaches the attic, hears a noise and walks up the stairs and turns on the light. Malcolm jumps out and stabs her ("You're not Joan"). Linda goes to the kitchen and pours herself some wine, then answers the ringing phone ("Screw off!"). It is only Bret; after Linda says she is getting obscene phone calls, Bret suggests calling the police. Linda calls the cops and tells of a strange man calling, but she is told nothing can be done about it. Linda goes to Christopher's room and sees the boy lying in the bed with a bloody neck.

She mocks him for his "sore throat" and leaves. Malcolm is in the room, and he wipes his bloody blade clean.

Malcolm goes downstairs and walks into the room where Linda is sitting. ("I'm home, Joan.") As Malcolm talks of "punishment," Linda looks at her make up mirror and sees that it is not Christopher. She pushes Malcolm away and runs to the shed. As he looks around, Linda jumps down and runs to her Jeep. The Jeep will not start, and Linda runs back into the house, finding a dead Andrea. She calls the cops, hears a door slam and runs to the boy's room. Christopher sits up, and he and Linda move the fake guillotine (with a real blade). Linda, with a prop gun, waits for Malcolm. The man tries to get in, and after a few seconds of silence, he bursts in another way, leans over the guillotine (going for Linda) and is cut and killed when Christopher releases the blade. Christopher promises no more tricks, and Linda goes to call the cops. As Linda cries by the phone, Christopher stands behind her with the knife raised.

Trick or Treats is a decent slasher, with a fairly dull killer-maniac and flat characters. Much of the film seems to be building up for something, but nothing comes of it, and the plethora of tricks and pranks from Christopher quickly grow wearisome.

The Untold Story (aka *Ba Xian fan dian zhi ren rou cha shao bao*; *Bunman: The Untold Story*; *Human Meat Pies: The Untold Story*) (1993)

Written by Law Gam Fai; Directed by Herman Yau Lai To; Cinema City Film Productions; 96 min.

Cast: Anthony Wong Chau-Sang (Wong Chi Hang); Danny Lee Sau-Yin (Officer Lee); Emily Kwan Bo Wai (Bo); Shing Fui-On (Cheng Poon); Parkman Wong Pak Man (Bull); Julie Lee Wa-Yuet (Pearl); Yee Ka-Fat; Lam King-Kong; Wong Tin-Fai; Leung Hun-Wah; Cheng Choh-Fai; Lee Yi-Chong; Long Chi; Si Man

Crew: Danny Lee Sau-Yin (Producer); Wong Bong (Composer); Cho Wai Kei (Director of Photography); Choi Hung (Editor)

In Hong Kong, 1978, two men are engaged in an intense argument. One of the men is demanding that the other lend him some money. When he refuses, the man beats him and burns him alive. Eight years later, in Macao, a woman is on the beach with her two sons. While playing, the young boys discover a bag that has apparently washed ashore. Inside the bag are severed human limbs. The police are called out to the beach to investigate. Wong Chi Hang, the murderer from the beginning, is working as a butcher at the Eight Immortals Restaurant. Ah Man shows up for a job (there is a sign posted). After watching him cut some meat, Chi Hang hires him. The postman brings the mail and says he has a letter for someone named Cheng Lam. Chi Hang takes it.

Chi Hang goes to see an attorney, wanting to transfer the deeds to the restaurant. But the attorney tells him the seller, Cheng Lam, must be present for the transaction to be legal. Inside the police station, the cops, Robert, Kong, Bull and Bo (the solitary female officer), are analyzing the murders. The three male cops admire Officer Lee, who is usually present with a prostitute or two under his arm(s). Bo is envious, desiring the attention of Lee. Eventually, Bo must reluctantly retrieve a fingerprint from a mostly rotted arm. Later, the cops receive a letter from Cheng Yi, who is concerned about his missing brother (who owns a restaurant in Macao). The police learn that the fingerprint belonged to a woman named Chan Lai Chun. In the restaurant, Chi Hang overhears Ah Man tell Pearl, the waitress, that Chi Hang cheated at a game of mah-jongg, for which he won money. That night, Chi Hang attacks and kills Ah Man. He cuts and grinds up the body and prepares pork buns with the new meat.

The next day, Chi Hang tells Pearl that Ah Mah went back to China. When the cops continue receiving letters from Cheng Yi, they visit the restaurant to inquire about the previous owner. Before they leave, Chi Hang gives them some pork buns, free of charge. Lee declines a portion, saying, "I don't eat barbeque pork buns. You never know what's in the filling." Wanting to quit her job, Pearl tells Chi Hang that her mother is sick. Chi Hang believes that she has told the police officers something, and he brutally rapes and murders her. After the police question Chi Hang again, they put a surveillance on his restaurant. When he throws out his garbage, they rummage through it and find body parts. Chi Hang tries to leave Macao, but the police stop him and arrest him.

During the interrogation, the cops beat Chi Hang. Several reporters learn of the beating when Chi Hang runs out of the interrogation room, strips off his shirt and yells, "The cops are beating me! Look!" To avoid trouble with the press, but to ensure Chi Hang gets the treatment they believe he deserves, the cops put him in a cell in which Cheng Poon (Cheng Lam's other brother) resides. For several days, Poon and his cellmates continually beat and torture Chi Hang. Chi Hang finally cuts and bites open an artery and is hospitalized. After the prisoner nearly escapes the hospital with a nurse as a hostage, the cops systematically torture Chi Hang until he confesses about the murder of Cheng Lam and his family. (Chan Lan Chun, whose fingerprint was analyzed, was Lam's mother-in-law.)

Chi Hang finally tells a story dealing with an argument over mah-jongg. Chi Hang wanted money he felt he was owed, but Lam refused. Eventually, Chi Hang murdered Lam, his wife, their five children, and Lam's mother-in-law. Then Chi Hang tells the officers what the pork bun mystery meat was, and they all get sick. ("I'm glad I didn't eat any," says Lee.) Although Chi Hang tells the police that they will not be able to charge him with murder, he takes a ring from a can and, while lying in his prison bed, he slits his wrist.

The Untold Story, reportedly based on a true incident, is an exceptionally violent movie with a few truly disturbing scenes (particularly the attack on Pearl). Anthony Wong won a Hong Kong Film Award for Best Actor for his performance as the sanguinary Wong Chi Hang.

Urban Legend (1998)

Written by Silvio Horta; Directed by Jamie Blanks; Phoenix Pictures/Canal + Droits Audiovisuels/Original Films; 99 min.

Cast: Alicia Witt (Natalie); Jared Leto (Paul); Rebecca Gayheart (Brenda); Joshua Jackson (Damon); Tara Reid (Sasha); Natasha Gregson Wagner (Michelle); Loretta Devine (Reese); Danielle Harris (Tosh); Michael Rosenbaum (Parker); John Neville (Dean Adams); Robert Englund (Wexler); Julian Richings (Janitor); Gord Martineau (Newsman); Kay Hawtrey (Library Attendant); Angela Vint (Bitchy Girl); J. C. Kenny (Weather Woman); Vince Corrazza (David Evans); Balazs Koos (Nerdy Guy); Stephanie Miles (Felicia); Danny Comden (Blake); Nancy McAlear (Jenny); Shawn Mathieson (Hippie Girl); Cle Bennett (Dorky Girl); Danielle Brett (Trendy Girl); Roberta Angelica (Swimming Woman); Matt Birman (Killer)

Crew: Brad Luff (Executive Producer); Brian Leslie Parker (Associate Producer); Christopher Young (Composer); Jamie Chressanthis (Director of Photography); Jay Cassidy (Editor)

On a rainy night, a young lady is driving her truck. After nearly colliding with another vehicle, she realizes she is almost out of fuel and pulls into the next gas station. The gas attendant convinces the woman to get out of her truck by saying that her credit card is not working and that someone from the company is on the phone for her. However, when she gets inside the station, she hears no one on the other line. The attendant stutters excitedly, but he cannot say anything clearly. The fearful woman manages to get away from him and back into her truck. She speeds away, with the attendant screaming, "Someone's in the back seat!" Down the road, the lady relaxes, until she sees someone sit up in back, and an axe is swung.

Inside a coffee house-lounge at Pendleton University, college student Parker is telling an urban legend about a crazy professor (the "Stanley Hall Massacre") to his friends Natalie and Brenda. Paul, a pompous college reporter, approaches the storyteller and sneers at Parker's yarn. Brenda is obviously attracted to Paul. Natalie goes home that evening to her gothic roommate Tosh. The next day in class, Professor Wexler is discussing folklore and urban legends. Class goof Damon walks to the front of the class, tries soda and "pop rocks" to prove his stomach will not explode, and feigns convulsions and death to the amusement of his friends. Later in the day, Dean Adams seizes copies of the school newspaper, with an article about the recent murder. Paul protests, claiming students need to know about a possible lunatic. Adams tells Paul, "The only lunatic on this campus is you."

When discussing the murder, Natalie tells her friends she did not know the murdered girl (Michelle), but a yearbook shows that Natalie and Michelle were captains of the cheerleading squad back in high school. Damon arrives at Natalie's dorm room and consoles her. He then takes her somewhere to talk, but it turns out Damon thought Natalie might be "in need of loving." After Natalie becomes angry and expresses her desire to go home, Damon attends to a call of nature and is strung with a rope. When Natalie goes to check on him, the killer attacks her. As she tries to drive away, Damon, tied to the car, is pulled up and choked. His body lands on the car, and Natalie runs away.

After failing to locate Damon's body, Natalie's friends think Damon is playing another joke. Natalie goes to the library to research urban legends (*The Encyclopedia of Urban Legends*). While she is gone, Tosh meets a fellow gothic lover online and they plan to meet. When she returns from the bathroom, the killer is waiting. Natalie walks into the room, assumes the noise she hears is something else and goes to bed with earphones on. The next morning, she awakes and sees her roommate dead. "Aren't you glad you didn't turn on the light?" is written on the wall in blood.

Everyone believes Tosh committed suicide, and the message on the wall was "a very morbid suicide note." Paul and Natalie look for evidence of the Stanley Hall Massacre, which is apparently not just an urban legend; it is the 22nd anniversary of the killing spree. They look in Wexler's office and are caught by the professor. In Dean Adams' office, the dean mentions Natalie having been on probation for "reckless endangerment." Later, Natalie admits to Brenda that she knew Michelle. She tells a story of how she and Michelle were driving with their headlights off, and when they were flashed by another vehicle, they turned around and pursued the car. The other car went off the road, and the driver was killed.

Dean Adams heads for home but is murdered in the parking lot. At a party, Paul finds Natalie and tells her that Wexler was the soul survivor of the Stanley Hall Massacre. During the party, Parker gets a call on his cell phone and is told what has happened to his dog (it has been cooked in the microwave). He runs into the bathroom to meet the caller and is killed. Natalie tries to reach Paul and cannot reach him. On the radio, she hears her deejay friend Sasha being attacked. She runs over to the station but it is too late, and she watches as the murderer kills Sasha. She leaves and runs into Paul. They both find Brenda, and all three head to the gas station. While there, Paul gets on the phone. Natalie and Brenda, in an effort to learn the origin of a wretched odor, open the trunk and find Wexler. They both run into the woods.

After losing Brenda, Natalie is picked up by the eerie janitor. The killer chases them in another vehicle, and the truck runs off the road. Natalie runs away and gets to an emergency phone, but first hears the cries of

Brenda from inside an abandoned building. She runs inside to help her friend, and sees Brenda lying on a bed. But Brenda sits up and manages to restrain Natalie on the bed. The insane Brenda explains that the boy whose death was caused by Natalie and Michelle was Brenda's boyfriend. Eventually both Reese, a campus policewoman, and Paul come to Natalie's rescue and stop Brenda. However, as Paul and Natalie are driving away, Brenda appears in the back seat for another attack. They get out of the car and the vehicle goes over the edge with Brenda still inside. In the end, college students are sitting in a lounge discussing urban legends, when Brenda offers to tell an urban legend that she knows is real.

Although *Urban Legend* devotes too much time explaining well-known urban legends, the film is a fairly good slasher outing. At the film's beginning, when Michelle is driving with the killer in the back seat, she is listening to Bonnie Tyler's song "Total Eclipse of the Heart" (hearing the line "turn around..."). When Damon (played by Joshua Jackson) starts his car, the song playing on the radio is "I Don't Wanna Wait" (by Paula Cole), which is the theme song to a television series (*Dawson's Creek*) on which Jackson starred. At the end of the film, one of the students suggests that Brenda was the "Noxzema girl." Rebecca Gayheart, who portrayed Brenda, appeared in several Noxzema commercials.

Urban Legends: Final Cut (2000)

Written by Paul Harris Boardman and Scott Derrickson; Directed by John Ottman; Phoenix Pictures/Original Films; 99 min.

Cast: Jennifer Morrison (Amy Mayfield); Matthew Davis (Travis/Trevor); Hart Bochner (Professor Solomon); Loretta Davis (Reese); Joseph Lawrence (Graham); Anson Mount (Toby); Anthony Anderson (Stan); Eva Mendes (Vanessa); Michael Bacall (Dirk); Jessica Cauffiel (Sandra); Marco Hofschneider (Simon); Derek Aasland (P.A. Kevin); Jacinda Barrett (Lisa); Peter Millard (Doctor Fain); Chas Lawther (Dean Patterson); Chuck Campbell (Geek in Plane); Yani Gellman (Rob); Jeanette Sousa (Libby); Rory Feore (Killer Flight Attendant); Shauna Black (Blonde Girlfriend); Leland Tildren, Joel Gorson (Jocks on Plane); David Cook, Bianca Muller, Jenny Kim, Nicole Crozier (Student Screamers); Pat Kelly (Crony in Screening Room); Stephanie Moore (Girl in 16mm Film); Kevin Hare, David Sparrow (Police Officers); Clare Martina Preuss (Clapper Girl); Santo (Vicious Dog)

Crew: Nicholas Osborne, Brad Luff (Executive Producers); Neal H. Mortiz, Gina Matthews, Richard Luke Rothschild (Producers); Michael McDonnell (Co-Producer); John Ottman (Composer); Brian Pearson, C.S.C. (Director of Photography); John Ottman, Rob Kobrin (Editors)

A plane is flying through a heavy storm, and a couple head to the bathroom in back to spend some time together. A person is on the plane with a knife. In the bathroom, the girl sees "You're going down" written on the mirror in red. The plane starts a descent, and the girl leaves the bathroom and finds a dead stewardess. The killer is there, and the couple runs to the cockpit of dead pilots, where the girl screams "Mayday!" Toby, the director, appears at the window and yells "Cut!"

Aspiring filmmaker Amy Mayfield is sitting in a room with other film students, listening to talk of the Hitchcock Award and thesis film projects. Walking in the road at night, Amy is given a ride by Reese, campus security, and the two talk of Pam Grier movies. Amy says she has a film due but she does not have a good story. Reese tells her the story of the campus serial killer at Pendleton, which Amy says is only an urban legend. Later, Amy visits Professor Solomon and gives her idea of a killer basing murders on urban legends. The professor thinks it is a great idea.

Travis is in a bar with Lisa, and they talk about his films. Lisa orders two more drinks, and someone puts something in the drinks. Travis leaves to work on a movie, and Toby walks over to Lisa. She leaves, telling him he can pay for the drinks. She stumbles to the room of coats, where a plastic bag is thrown over her face. Lisa awakes in a tub of ice with a wound on her stomach (her kidney is nearby). She sees someone in another room and crawls out and slips, shutting the door on the person. She calls 911, but the operator does not believe her. Lisa tries crawling out of the window. The person pulls her back in, hitting and breaking window. The window is slammed shut, beheading Lisa.

Amy asks Travis if he can look at her approved script. When Amy tells some fellow students about her movie, Toby pulls her aside and accuses her of stealing his genre and says no one will take the Hitchcock Award away from him. Amy goes to see Travis, who is upset about a C– on his film, and asks if he knows an available cinematographer. On the set, Stan, Dirk and Sandra (who was the girl in Toby's film) fake an accident. After Amy describes the scene to Sandra, Simon the cinematographer, shows up with his own camera. People leave for the night, and Sandra returns to the set for her keys. Someone attaches a microphone to the camera and approaches her. In the screening room, the group watches their footage, and the film changes to Sandra being cut, chased and killed. Amy thinks it is real, but the others think it is another Sandra joke.

Amy and the others get the news that Travis has killed himself. Graham talks to Amy, assuring her that Sandra is in L.A., filming a bit part on *ER*. He then says he knows Amy is a Hollywood kid like him (she is the daughter of an Oscar-winning documentary filmmaker) and that she can stop the "girl-next-door crap." Amy goes to the campus tower (she had heard that Travis had killed himself there) and has an encounter with Trevor, Travis' twin brother. He tells Amy he does not think his brother committed suicide, and he asks her not to tell anyone she saw him. Amy films a scene in which students count down to the new year and scream. While Simon is out for a smoke, he is attacked and beaten with his camera lens. Amy, having heard the last part of the killing, goes outside and notices the security camera. She goes to see Reese and asks to borrow tapes of the last hour or so of what the cameras recorded.

Amy watches the tapes in a studio and sees Simon killed. The killer stands nearby in a mask (different from the fencing mask worn earlier). She locks the door but the killer breaks through. Amy is chased out of the building and to the dock. While running in the sewers, she finds Reese. The two go to the room and see the damaged door, but without the tapes (Amy lost them), Reese cannot do anything. Amy tells Trevor she thinks Sandra and Simon are dead, and Trevor says she cannot go to the cops due to his bad relationship with authorities. Amy realizes that the killer might be one of the candidates of the Hitchcock Award.

Amy and Vanessa head to the ride Merry Miners, the location of the "Tunnel of Terror" carnival ride scene. Stan and Dirk arrive to set up dead bodies, and Amy asks Graham why he brought along the odd P.A. Kevin. Graham is upset that Amy is pulling a "power trip" in front of everyone, and he leaves. Amy sees Trevor in the trees, nods to him and tells everyone to get something to eat. The killer appears and hits Stan on the head and electrocutes him with a sliced cable. The killer goes down to see Dirk and pushes him against the control box, electrocuting him. The railcar stops with Amy inside, and she walks the rest of the way. She sees a dead Dirk and is chased by the killer to the entrance, where Reese is waiting. Cops arrive, take the dead boys away and talk to Amy.

Trevor tells Amy that he followed Graham but lost him. They lie down together on the bed, and Amy dreams of intimate moments with Trevor and being stabbed. She awakes in bed alone. She sees a light in the tower and goes there and finds Vanessa, who says she got Amy's note. A dummy falls onto the table, and the two girls run up the tower, followed by the killer. They hide in a room. The door is opened and Vanessa is grabbed. Amy is locked in the room; when she breaks the door open, Vanessa is hanging from the bell. Reese sees Amy run outside. Amy finds

Trevor, who takes her to the library. He says all of the dead people worked on *The Gods of Men*, his brother's film. They watch the bad film, and Amy notices a splice and says that it is not Travis' film. Amy and Trevor stop Toby, the only crew member left. With a gun, they take him to a room and handcuff him to a chair.

When Solomon arrives, Trevor, acting as Travis, says Toby stole his film. Toby reminds "Travis" that Travis did the sound and merely gave the credit to Toby, who had not even seen the film. Solomon pulls a gun and shoots Toby. Trevor goes for the gun, and Amy runs. Solomon has the gun on Trevor. The professor tells Amy that her father cast the deciding vote against him in film school, and he was framing her for the murders so he could steal Travis' film. Graham comes out from hiding and swings a chair at Solomon. The group battles over the gun until Reese arrives. Solomon reminds Reese that she saw Amy running from the tower; she points the gun at the professor, saying she never told anyone. Solomon punches Reese, and she punches him back. After a struggle, prop guns are mixed with real guns. Amy, Trevor and Solomon each have a gun, and Trevor and Solomon both get a click. Amy, with a gold-trimmed gun that Reese had shown her earlier, tries to pass the gun to Reese, and Solomon jumps and is shot. Later, Trevor is accepting the award on behalf of Travis, and Kevin, up high, pulls a rifle and is shot by Reese. He falls into an air bag below, and Amy yells cut. A television is turned off, and a dazed Solomon in a wheelchair is rolled away by a familiar nurse.

With the exception of the violent and grotesque introductory murder, the stalkings and killings of *Urban Legends: Final Cut* are monotonous and uninventive. But while the film fails to deliver scares, it does offer a nice amount of humor (Cauffiel and Anderson have wonderful comedic timing), and it is great to see actress Devine reprise her role as the charming Reese. The little tune at the end is the theme to the television show *Alfred Hitchcock Presents*. The film was the directo-rial debut for Ottman, who is also a film composer and editor (both titles which he also holds in his own movie).

Valentine (2001)

Written by Donna Powers, Wayne Powers, Gretchen J. Berg and Aaron Harberts (from the novel by Tom Savage); Directed by Jamie Blanks; Village Roadshow Pictures/NPV Entertainment; 95 min.

Cast: Denise Richards (Paige); David Boreanaz (Adam); Marley Shelton (Kate); Jessica Capshaw (Dorothy); Jessica Cauffiel (Lily); Katherine Heigl (Shelley); Hedy Burress (Ruthie); Fulvio Cecere (Detective Vaughn); Daniel Cosgrove (Campbell); Johnny Whitworth (Max Raimi); Woody Jeffreys (Brian); Adam Harrington (Jason); Claude Duhamel (Gary); Wyatt Page (Evan Wheeler); Benita Ha (Kim Wheeler); Paul Magel (Lance); Haig Sutherland (Bookish Girl); Adrian Holmes (Banker); Ty Olsson (Jock); Daniel Boileau (Shy Guy); G. Patrick Currie (Religious Guy); Jo-Ann Fernandes (Maid); Alex Diakun (Pastor); Karina Carreck (Gallery Employee); Aaron Dudley, Dalias Blake, Chris Webb (Video Men); Basia Antos, Carla Boudreau, Vanessa Volker (Video Women); Joel Palmer (Jeremy); Sara Mjanes (Young Shelley); Brittany Mayers (Young Kate); Kate Logie (Young Dorothy); Chelcie Burgart (Young Paige); Chelsea Florko (Young Lily); Sterling McKay (Joe Tulga); Kendall Saunders (Waitress); Chad Barager (Chad); Noel Fisher, Cody Serpa, Mark Mullan (Tulga Gang Members); Tammy Pentecost (Waitress); Tyler Vradenburg (Med Student)

Crew: Grant Rosenberg, Bruce Berman (Exective Producers); Dylan Sellers (Producer); Don Davis (Composer); Rick Bota (Director of Photography); Steve Mirkovich, A.C.E. (Editor)

Jeremy Melton, a nerdy young boy, is at a Valentine's dance, asking different girls if they would like to dance. Most of the girls reject him in cruel ways ("I'd rather be boiled alive!"). When Jeremy asks the portly Dorothy to dance, they end up kissing behind the bleachers. Several boys discover the young kissers, and Dorothy tells them Jeremy attacked her. The boys dump a bowl of punch on Jeremy, and his nose begins to bleed. They strip him to his underwear, chase him to the gym, and kick him around while others chant "Fight!"

It is 13 years later, and Shelley (one of the girls who declined Jeremy's dance invitation) is on an unsuccessful blind date. Shelley, a med student, heads over to the lab to work on a cadaver, Chad. She investigates a noise in the locker room and finds a red envelope. ("The journey of love is an arduous trek; My love grows for you as you bleed from your neck.") She returns to slice into Chad, but the stomach moves, and Shelley sees Chad in the closet. The new "cadaver" gone, Shelley heads for the door and is grabbed. A person wearing a cherub mask chases her to a room of body bags and stabs each bag. The killer finds Shelley hiding in the last one, slits her throat (with bleeding nose) and zips the bag up again.

Paige convinces Kate to try "Turbo Dating," where she meets 30 guys with 30 seconds apiece. Kate says she is still more or less with Adam, whom Paige calls a drunk. Kate gets a call about Shelley's death. Later they are at her funeral with Dorothy and Lily. Kate talks to Adam, who says he has been sober for three weeks. He asks her to a possible dinner, and Kate says she will call him. Detective Vaughn talks to the girls and asks if they know Jason Marquette, Shelley's blind date, who the police have not been able to locate. Dorothy gets a red envelope ("Roses are red, violets are blue; They'll need dental records to identify you"), and her new love interest, Campbell, shows up at her door. He says he has been kicked out of his apartment, and he has all his money in a start-up business, so Dorothy has the maid make up the guest room. Kate steps out of the shower and answers the phone. Her door is open and she hears the elevator ringing, trying to shut on a cherub mask. She encounters her neighbor Gary. ("You look great, Kate."/"You're scary, Gary.")

Lily and Paige receive a heart-shaped box with a note signed J.M.: "'Tis a well known fact that beauty is skin deep; Savor the taste… you are what you eat." Lily takes a bite of a chocolate and is repulsed when she sees maggots inside. The two try to figure out who J.M. is, and Paige jokingly says Jeremy Melton. Later, they are at a show for Lily's boyfriend Max. Kate tells the story of what happened at her apartment, and Dorothy refers to the cherub mask at the fateful Valentine's dance. The group split up in a maze of televisions (the art of Max), and Lily is suddenly lost. An arrow is shot into her chest. The cherub killer, with bow in hand and a bloody nose, shoots two more arrows, and Lily falls through a door and into a trash bin.

The other women find Campbell arguing with Ruthie, who says she wants her money back. Kate and Adam are in a bar later, and Adam asks for another chance, telling Kate he has changed. Vaughn visits the group and shows them a remembrance card sent to Shelley's parents that says, "Too bad, so sad," and is signed Jeremy Melton. Dorothy now thinks Jeremy is the murderer, and she admits to Paige and Kate that Jeremy did not attack her at the dance. Adam and Kate have dinner later, and Adam tells her that everything will be all right. The next day, Vaughn suggests that Jeremy may have had plastic surgery, and he asks about any boyfriends. Kate says she has known Adam for a long time, but Dorothy is not even able to say Campbell's last name. Furious, she storms out of the office.

The cherub killer walks into Kate's apartment, finds Scary Gary trying on a few of Kate's clothes and beats him with a hot iron. Kate returns to Adam trying to buzz into her apartment. Adam gives her a little heart sucker and Kate gives him an IOU for TLC. Dorothy gives Campbell a nice watch. Following an unsatisfactory time in bed, he gives Dorothy a necklace. At the pool later, Campbell is trying to transfer some funds over the phone (and providing a false name). Dorothy calls him over the intercom and asks him to relight the pilot light in the base-

A terrified Kate (Marley Shelton) clutches her boyfriend Adam (David Boreanaz), believing that they have killed the cherub killer in Jamie Blanks' *Valentine* (2001).

ment. While down there, the killer axes Campbell in the back.

At Dorothy's party, Adam presents his voucher for TLC, and he and Kate kiss. Ruthie shows up and says Dorothy is wearing her necklace, which was stolen from her. Paige heads to the hot tub for some relaxation, and Kate talks to Max, who tells her that Lily did not make it to L.A. (where she was supposed to be). Ruthie goes through Campbell's bag, finds his watch and takes it. Outside she sees the killer dragging the dead maid. She is chased into the bathroom, where she is eventually thrown through a shower door and killed with the shards of glass. Dorothy and Kate find Adam drinking some champagne, and Kate is upset ("Which one of the 12 steps is this?"). The killer goes to see Paige, throws her into the hot tub and closes the latch. After drilling through the lid several times and hitting Paige once, the killer finally just throws the drill into the water and electrocutes Paige.

Kate and Dorothy argue over who Jeremy could be (Adam or Campbell), and Dorothy walks away from her friend. Kate calls Vaughn. Hearing the phone ring outside, she finds the detective's detached head in the backyard pond next to Adam's IOU TLC paper. Kate runs back inside and is frightened by a somewhat inebriated Adam, who chases her around the house. Kate eventually runs to Dorothy's father's office and gets a handgun. She climbs the stairs and is jumped by the cherub killer; both tumble down the stairs. The killer sits up quickly and is shot repeatedly by Adam. He and Kate embrace, and Adam takes off the cherub mask, revealing Dorothy. Adam calls the police, and he and Kate embrace once more. "I love you, Kate," he says. "I always have." Blood hits Kate's cheek, falling from Adam's nose.

Valentine is a nice fallback to the classic slashers of the '80s, following the overbearing self-reflexivity saturating the slasher run ignited by *Scream* in 1996. Boreanaz's film debut is effective with a nice performance, and he is complemented by very good performances from the whole cast, especially Shelton and Cauffiel. At one point in the film, it is said that Boreanaz's character Adam is "no angel." Boreanaz gained popularity in the TV series *Buffy the Vampire*

Slayer, and moved to the spin-off *Angel* as the title character.

Video Murders (1987)

Written and Directed by Jim McCullough, Jr.; Jim McCullough Productions; 87 min.

Cast: Eric Brown (David Lee Shepherd); Virginia Loridrans (Melissa); John Fertitta (Lieutenant Jerry Delveckio); Frank Baggett (Captain); Tracy Murrell (Lisa); Lee Larrimore (Santini); Deborah Dreher (Blonde Prostitute); Marti Anding Brooks (Miss Webster, the Nurse); Foster Litton (Police Officer); Joy Paradise; Ace Williams; Joe Pipes; Lewis Kalmback; Wendy Westbrook; Sandy Hotrad; Thias Willis; Jan Hubert; Lori Michell Harris; Annette Dyson; Leo Lasana; Allen Berry; Alan Pierce; Joe Prussiano; Clifton Brown; Perry Jones; David Post; Philip Dale; Carly, Mack, and Maggie McCullough; The Insatiables

Crew: Jim McCullough, Sr. (Producer); Richard Mann (Associate Producer); Robert Sprayberry (Composer); Joseph Wilcotts (Director of Photography); David Akin (Editor)

A man walks into a room, turns on the television and sits down to enjoy a video as he eats. A woman is dancing in the video, and a man walks into the frame and dances with her. As the man continues to watch, the sound of gasping can be heard. Later, the video watcher stops at a diner and orders a coffee. When a prostitute, Lisa, leaves the diner, the man quickly finishes his coffee and follows her. Lisa is given a ride by someone on a motorbike; the man trails them in his van. Apparently upset with the bike rider (she gives him the finger), Lisa starts walking; the van driver coaxes her into his van by offering her $100. At his hotel room, there is a video camera, and Lisa (after upping the charge) goes to the bathroom to get ready. The man looks at the camera and introduces himself as David Lee Shepherd. When Lisa comes out, David handcuffs her, shoves her on the bed and chokes and kills her as the camera rolls.

The police are investigating the murder at the hotel. The captain tells Lieutenant Jerry Delveckio of similar murders, and tells him they are already looking for a man named Shepherd. After David cries while watching a family play some football, the lieutenant talks to Leo the pimp to warn him about someone murdering prostitutes. Jerry then talks to a group of streetwalkers; one of them tells him about the Tic Toc Grill, where Lisa used to hang out. He interviews Miss Webster, a midget worker at the diner and a registered nurse, and asks about the night Lisa was at the diner. The nurse says that there was the motorbike guy, who was Santini the TV reporter, and there was a "dirty lookin'" man. David stops a prostitute and asks her if she wants to make a hundred dollars. She asks him if he is the strangler, he does not respond and the woman walks away and gets to a pay phone. Delveckio gets a call, and someone tells him where the woman saw who she thought might be the killer. He drives over there and sees David walking slowly; soon a foot pursuit begins. David evades the lieutenant by jumping onto a moving fire truck.

The lieutenant talks to Santini after he finishes a television report, and he can only remember "some bum" at the diner. Later, Lieutenant Delveckio calls David's mother Ruby, who says that her son is not a murderer and tells the lieutenant to not call her any more. David goes to a club and sits at the bar where Melissa, a receptionist, sits beside him and starts a conversation. She asks him what he does ("I'm between jobs right now"). Melissa is about to leave, believing David does not want company. He stops her and says he would like to keep her company, and they leave together in his van for pie and coffee. At the restaurant, David suddenly becomes impolite and tries to order Melissa around (especially ordering her out the door and into the van when he sees a couple of police officers).

They get back to David's hotel room, and Melissa says they do not need the video camera. On the bed, Melissa tries to relax David, and she asks him if it is his "first time." David, annoyed, stands up. Melissa goes to the bathroom, David sets up the camera and, with cord in hand, he waits for her to come out. Melissa opens the door, but sees David in time to slam the door shut. She climbs out of the window and runs until she finds a sketch of the "strangler," looking very much like David. David sees that Melissa is gone, and he quickly gathers his equipment.

Melissa calls Lieutenant Delveckio and tells him the strangler tried to kill her. She tells him the hotel and the location of the pay phone she is using. She is suddenly grabbed by David, now wielding a razor, and he throws her in his van. The police get to the hotel, where the lieutenant finds numerous videos labeled with female names. The captain tells Delveckio that Melissa was not at the store where the lieutenant told her to wait. David takes Melissa to a house, lights some candles and plays the piano with Melissa tied up. Melissa tells David they can be friends. David tells her to shut up and that he cannot turn himself in because the police will kill him.

The lieutenant and the captain believe David is hiding somewhere. David takes Melissa to another room and tells her to put an ugly dress on. She asks him to leave the room; he finally agrees, leaving the door open "just a crack." Melissa takes the time to find a tiny gun which she points at David when we returns. He gets the gun away from her and handcuffs her to the bed. Then he cleans himself up, sets up the video camera and makes a video for his mother. He talks about how she said everyone was going to love him, and he wants to know if she was lying. He tells his mother he has a new girlfriend, Melissa.

Lieutenant Delveckio and the captain find the house where David is staying (there are several newspapers in the front yard). While the lieutenant checks upstairs and finds Melissa, the captain looks around the kitchen and is shot and killed by David. David jumps in a car, and the lieutenant quickly follows. The chase, which eventually includes many police cars, leads to a bridge, where David gets out and runs on the walkway with Delveckio behind him. Santini and a television crew are in a helicopter; David screams at the camera, telling his mother, "I just wanted you to love me!" He shoots himself in the head and falls to the ground as police officers surround him.

Video Murders is a somewhat amateurish slasher with enough interesting moments to keep the film going (although the car chase at the end goes on a little too long).

Wacko (1981)

Written by Dana Olsen, Michael Spound, M. James Kouf, Jr. and David Greenwalt;l Directed by Greydon Clark; Jensen Farley Pictures, Inc.; 83 min.

Cast: Joe Don Baker (Dick Harbinger); Stella Stevens (Mrs. Doctor Graves); George Kennedy (Mr. Doctor Graves); Julia Duffy (Mary Graves); Scott McGinnis (Norman Bates); Elizabeth Daily (Bambi); Michele Tobin (Rosie); Andrew Clay (Tony Schlongini); Anthony James (Zeke); Sonny Davis (The Weirdo); David Drucker (The Looney); Jeff Altman (Harry Palms); Victor Brandt (Doctor Moreau); Wil Albert (Doctor Denton); Charles Napier (Chief O'Hara); Michael Lee Gogin (Damien); Claudia Lonow (Pam Graves); Tamar Howard (Little Mary); Darby Hinton (Rookie Cop); Jacqulin Cole (Librarian); Ben Hartigan (Doctor); John Avery (Danny); Toni Sawyer (Rosie's Mother); Lou Felder (Rosie's Father); Albert Malbandian (Dale); Laura Dashosh (Wandering Jew); Helen Martin (Harbinger's Mother); Fred D. Scott (Harbinger's Father); Karole Selmon (Harbinger's Sister); Pete Robinson (Harbinger's Brother); Michael R. Starita (Referee); Robert Magnus (Teacher); Steve Wagner (Orderly); Mickey Epps (Plainclothes Cop); David Greenwalt (Uniformed Cop); M. James Kouf, Jr. (Prisoner); Joseph Jay Camen (Boy in Vice); John Bristol (Driver's Education Teacher); Alex Preisman, Paula Jacquard, Shelley Doig (Girls at Prom); Christina Cummings, Larry Wills (Prom Teachers); Michael T. Starita (Boy With Nose); Dan Frischman, Andrew Lederer, Ronald Kennedy (Schlongini Singers); Joshua Daniel (Well-Dressed Student); Janice Davies (Cafeteria Matron); Katina Gardner (Woman in Massage Parlor); Erin Halligon (Gorgeous Young Girl); Suzie Harper (Lola); William Driver, Stephen A. Maginn, Edythe Magnus, Laurie B. McCormick, John Roedell, Mary Ann Roedell, Barbara Starita (Prom Chaperones); Donna Gaff (Nurse); James Gaff (Patient); Chris Coté, Rick Neigher, Simon Teolis, Scott Norman, Mike Mirage (Avalon, Band at Prom)

Crew: Michael R. Starita (Executive Producer); Greydon Clark (Producer); Curtis Burch (Associate Producer); Arthur Kempel (Composer); Nicholas J. von Sternber (Director of Photography); Earl Watson, Curtis Burch (Editors)

A gloved hand carves a pumpkin, and someone puts on a pumpkin head. A cassette tape plays the *Alfred Hitchcock Presents* theme, and the lawnmower is fired up. Mary (via a voice-over) says it is 13 years ago, and her older sister Pam is getting ready for the prom. A man watches her through the window, Pam sees her father and he says he is mowing the lawn. Pam heads to the Halloween Pumpkin Prom with her date, Guy. Mary and her friends Rosie, Bambi and Johnny, are tied and gagged in the backseat, and Pam leaves Mary in charge. Before Guy and Pam leave, the children witness the pumpkin-headed lawnmower killer run the couple down.

Mary, now in high school, wakes up to her father at the window. He falls down a ladder to the ground and tells her he was mowing the lawn. Harbinger gets a phone call in the morning and heads over to the State Mental Facility. A nurse has been killed and a maniac has escaped. Harbinger suggests that it is the lawnmower killer who murdered the woman. A doctor shows him a calendar from the maniac's room, and a date is circled in blood. Harbinger makes note that 31 backwards is 13, that day is Friday, and it is the prom. Norman picks up Mary at her house. Mary mentions making love for the first time that night. Norman is so excited, he makes sounds like a lawnmower.

At the Alfred Hitchcock High School, Mary is talking to Rosie and Bambi, who refer to Johnny running away after the murders. They are in the bathroom, and the maniac is sitting in one of the stalls. Harbinger goes to see the chief, and his superior, tired of the cop believing the killer has returned year after year, refuses to send officers to the school to watch for the lawnmower killer. Outside, guys are mocking Harbinger. A weirdo stops him, says he needs to talk to the cop and "sings" the killer's theme song. Harbinger punches him and knocks him down some steps. In his car, Harbinger recounts some flashbacks, including a pretty girl in need of car assistance and a woman in leather whipping the cop while he is working undercover, before he finally tells the accurate flashback involving the "fateful night." Harbinger, dressed as a clown, goes to tell Pam's parents that she has been murdered. He "eases into it" by trick-or-treating first; he says Mary will probably be screwed up for the rest of her life, and he makes balloon animals to calm the mother.

Harbinger goes to see Zeke, the school gardener; Zeke thinks he is only trying to cast suspicion on the weird gardener. Harry Palms, the sermonizing vice-principal, tells Harbinger that he is sick of the lawnmower killer story. In the library, Mary has (according to an intertitle) an unnecessary dream sequence involving lawnmowers. Later, Norman opens his locker, and Mary screams nearby. Harbinger arrives, fires his six-shooter well over ten times and pulls a "baby lawnmower" from the locker. The maniac shows up and runs away. There is an elaborate chase around the track and field in driver's education cars.

In the locker room, Tony (Rosie's boyfriend) and Norman are frightened by a weird ooze coming from Tony's locker, but it is only his gym socks. Harbinger is on the phone with the chief (ignoring the weirdo standing next to him), and the chief says the nurse was mauled by a werewolf. Doctor Moreau, the science teacher, shoots up the football players with a serum; the players turn into animals and run out to the game (Hitchcock's Birds vs. De Palma's Knifes).

Mary comes home, her mother tells her a message she received ("Your daughter's gonna die tonight!") and Mary surmises it was one of her friends. The maniac chases Bambi around and eventually flashes her; she asks him to the prom. Mary is taking a bath in the steamy bathroom and her father is in there, as he says, mowing the lawn.

Norman and his "mother" (her mummified corpse) have dinner with Mary's family. Harbinger is with his black parents and siblings (he is, inexplicably, white), loads his gun and leaves for the prom. At the school, Bambi walks in with the maniac, and Mary screams when Tony suggests it could be the lawnmower killer. The maniac runs away, and Bambi follows him. Harry Palms is in his officer when the pumpkin-headed lawnmower killer enters and squeezes Palms head in a vise (used on students). Mary's father arrives at the school from his "hospital emergency," and he and his wife meet outside. Bambi is looking for "Looney," she meets the killer in the hallway and the killer swings an axe. Tony and Rosie leave for "kinky sex" (which the chaperones allow so long as it is not drugs or booze), and the killer finds them and murders them both.

Mary is attacked by the killer. At different times, Mary stabs, shoots and uses a tractor to run over the killer, but the murderer keeps coming back. Norman is speaking to the student body (after having been elected prom queen) and Mary runs inside screaming. The killer bursts through the wall on the tractor, jumps off, stumbles and falls to the floor. Zeke and the maniac are there, as is the weirdo riding a talking elephant, who verifies his claim that he is the original lawnmower killer. The pumpkin head is taken off, and it is Harbinger, who says he murdered people "to prove a point." He seems to die, but then keeps on talking.

Harbinger is finally dead, or so it seems. Norman and Mary are together later on a blanket outside, Norman makes lawnmower sounds and a tiny lawnmower comes out of his chest. Mary screams and awakes from her nightmare, and Norman consoles her. They kiss; Mary's father appears with a lawnmower and says he is mowing the lawn.

Wacko, like many slasher parodies, starts off promising and quite amusing, before slipping into a humdrum and sluggish final 30 minutes. The film contains a number of references to other films, and they are enjoyable to look for. The character of Tony is introduced with a small musical number (called "Schlongini Shuffle"), and actor Clay, who played Tony, is credited as the number's writer. After the credits have rolled, Harbinger, the apparently dead killer, awakes one more time. Singer-actress Daily has also starred in *Valley Girl* (1983) and *Pee-Wee's Big Adventure* (1985) and went on to become a voice actress, providing the voice for Tommy of Nickelodeon's *The Rugrats* as well as other things.

Welcome to Spring Break (aka *Nightmare Beach*) (1988)

Written by Vittorio Rambaldi and Harry Kirkpatrick; Directed by Harry Kirkpatrick; Laguna Entertainment/Elpicos S.A.; 92 min.

Cast: Nicholas De Toth (Skip); Sarah Buxton (Gail); Rawley Valverde (Ronnie); Lance Le Gault (Reverend Bates); Michael Parks (Doctor Willet); John Saxon (Strycher); Luis Valderama (Dawg); Fred Buck (Mayor Loomis); Debra Gallagher (Rachael); Turk Harley (Malcolm); Christina Kier (Kimberly); Ben Stotes (Al); Kristy Lachance (Lori); Gregg Todd Davis (Ralph); Yamilet Hidalgo (Trina); John Baldwin (Mad John); Buffy Dee, Greg Gerard Bernet, Frank Logan (Kimberly's Clients); Tony Bolano (Diablo); Shana Rodman, Jennifer Hingel (Hitchhikers); Donna Lee (TV reporter); Theresa Maria Rojas (Hotel Maid); James Di Cuia (Demon Biker); Dan Fitzgerald (Prison Warden); Barry Schreiber (Desk Sergeant); Mitzi Lively (Student); Joe Del Camp (Cop in Cemetery); Earl L. Simpson III (Van Driver); Ferdie Pacheco (Football Jock); Bill Wohrman (Beach Cop); Lisa Vidal (Girl at Pool); Jennifer Coleman (Girl with Al); Tom Boykin (Fratter); Jay Amor (Boy on Beach); Michelle Lee Malm (Girl on Beach)

Crew: William J. Immerman (Producer);

Josi W. Konski (Executive Producer); Valerie Kenny Wolkoff (Associate Producer); Claudio Simonetti (Composer); Antonio Climati (Director of Photography); John Rawson (Editor)

At dusk, a number of bikers are standing together as if in mourning. Inside, Diablo, a prisoner, is led down the mile for his execution. When strapped in, Diablo screams curses at the viewers, in particular the police officer, Strycher. Before he is executed, Diablo says, "I've been framed, but I'll come back to get even." The switch is thrown.

"Welcome to spring break," a cop says, "the annual migration of the idiot." Two boys, Skip and Ronnie, are checking into a hotel. Skip is recognized by the hotel clerk as the quarterback who threw an interception at the Orange Bowl. The cops learn Diablo's body has been taken from the cemetery. Reverend Bates, who was present at the execution, is at the cemetery, and he reminds everyone of Diablo's last words. That night, a girl is hitchhiking, and a biker clad in leather stops. She asks the biker if he is going to Manatee Beach, and he slowly nods his head. After driving at a breakneck speed, the girl complains. The biker stops and lets her off. Then he electocutes her with a system attached to the motorcycle.

Skip and Ronnie almost get into a scuffle with the Demons, Diablo's gang of bikers. Strycher stops the Demons from doing anything, and the boys go inside the bar. Skip meets Gail, the bartender, who earlier had attended Diablo's execution. Skip does not seem to be into the bar scene, and Gail seems impressed by the football player. Skip also turns down a date with the reverend's daughter Rachael. Ronnie is later picked up by Trina, a lady biker. She leads him into an alley, where the Demons proceed to beat him. The mysterious biker is waiting for Ronnie when he finally stands up again. Ronnie swings at him, steadies himself with the motorcycle and is electrocuted and incinerated.

The mayor wants to cover up Ronnie's murder so that no one will suspect a serial killer. While looking for his friend, Skip spots Trina wearing a football medal similar to one Ronnie had. She tells Skip she got it from her "old man," but Skip, who does not believe her, follows Trina to the Demons' hide-out. The bikers prepare for a Skip beating, but Strycher arrives with a warrant; the police officer is looking for Diablo's body. At the hotel, a voyeuristic clerk is murdered while peeping through a hole in the wall of a closet. Kimberly, a student having sex with older men and providing them with sad stories about her parents' lost business (in order to extract pity/pleasure compensation), sees the peephole and an eye looking through it. She runs to check the closet and finds the dead man. Before she can escape in the elevator, the killer murders her.

Gail goes with Skip to the hospital and police station, looking for Ronnie. Later, Skip waits for Doctor Willet in the doctor's car and demands to know where his friend is. Doctor Willet tells him where Ronnie is buried. Strycher finds Skip there, threatens him and tells him to leave town. Meanwhile, Dawg (the Demon leader since Diablo's demise) is arrested for the hotel murders. Skip hides out at Gail's place. Together, they catch Trina alone, and she tells them she does not know who killed Ronnie, and that Diablo did not kill Gail's sister Mary (the murder for which he was blamed and executed). Earlier, Diablo's innocence was verified by Strycher, who told the mayor, "You wanted a patsy," in reference to Mary's death. Skip and Gail suspect Strycher of the killings. They sneak into his place and find photographs of dead girls.

The Demons bust Dawg out of jail. When Skip has a run-in with Strycher, the Demons show up, Dawg shoots Strycher, and the bikers drag the wounded officer around on a chain. Gail finds Diablo's corpse, and soon the murderer arrives and reveals himself to be Reverend Bates, who has been killing people he believes are sinners (and admits to the murder of Mary). Skip shows up in Strycher's car, and he and Gail try to escape the reverend's wrath. Bates wrecks his motorcycle and is electrocuted by wires.

Welcome to Spring Break provides only a few scares, but the assortment of recurring characters (including the jokester and the thief) make for a fun slasher film. Harry Kirkpatrick is a pseudonym for Umberto Lenzi, who directed the popular cannibal film *Cannibal Ferox* (aka *Make Them Die Slowly*) (1981).

What Have They Done to Your Daughters? (aka *La polizio chiede auito*; *Coed Murders*) (1974)

Written by Ettore Sanzò and Massimo Dallamano; Directed by Massimo Dallamano; Primex Italiana; 87 min.

Cast: Giovanna Ralli (Vittoria Stori); Claudio Cassinelli (Silvestri); Mario Adorf (Valentini); Franco Fabrizi (Photographer); Farley Granger (Sylvia's Father); Marina Berti; Paolo Turco; Corrado Gaipa; Michaela Pignatelli; Ferdinando Murolo; Salvatore Puntillo; Eleonora Morana; Cheryl Lee Buchanan; Roberta Paladini; Luigi Antonio Guerra, C.S.C.; Renata Moar; Adriana Falco; Clara Zovianoff; Leonardo Severini; Lorenzo Piani, C.S.C. (Doctor)

Crew: Stelvio Ciprani (Composer); Franco Delli Colli (Director of Photography); Antonio Siciliano (Editor)

Police officers burst into a room where a nude female body is hanging from the ceiling. District Attorney Vittoria Stori arrives; the scene seems like a suicide, with the door bolted from the inside. The following day, Inspector Valentini gives Vittoria the autopsy report, saying that the girl, Sylvia, was 15 and had sexual relations before her death. Valentini talks to Sylvia's maid (the parents are in Africa), who says Sylvia was being frightened by daily telephone calls in which the caller was not responding. Vittoria watches footage of a demonstration and sees Sylvia walk into a building around the time of her death; he is told that no one came out for a long time. Sylvia was found in another building, so Vittoria surmises that she was murdered.

Homicide inspector Silvestri takes over the case. While visiting the scene, a man is spotted photographing from the roof of a nearby building. The man, Mr. Paglia, is questioned; he has many pictures of Sylvia having sex with a man, taken over a three-week period. Silvestri talks to Marcello, the man from the photographs, and he has an alibi (he has been spelunking for days). Marcello tells the inspector that he was not Sylvia's first or only lover. Sylvia's parents return and ID the body. The apartment where Sylvia was murdered is discovered; inside, there are photographers and a tape recorder, and the bathroom walls are covered in blood. Mr. Paglia is set free (the cops have nothing to charge him with). Silvestri tells reporters that they do not know if the blood in the bathroom is human.

Sylvia's mother tells Vittoria that six months ago she found birth control pills in her daughter's coat pocket, and that when she confronted Sylvia about it, her daughter was indifferent. The mother threatened to tell the father, and Sylvia threatened to cut her own throat with a razor. Sylvia's mother hired a detective, but he later dropped the case. Silvestri goes to see Sylvia's doctor, who says she was like any other girl her age. The detective's wife does not know where her husband is, and suggests asking his secretary, Rosa (his "latest lay"), in the clinic for a car accident. When the police find the detective's car, he is in the trunk in many plastic-wrapped pieces.

Rosa, upset about her lover's demise, refuses to answer Silvestri's question (where the detective got the money to pay for her three operations); the inspector suggests blackmail. That night, a cleaver-wielding person in leather and a motorcycle helmet is outside the clinic. Rosa calls Silvestri and says she now wants to help. The person enters Rosa's room and tells her to say where her lover hid everything. Rosa screams, and the person runs out, followed by Silvestri and a fellow cop. The cop gets his hand chopped off when going for a light switch. Silvestri jumps into a car with Georgina. They chase the killer (on a motorbike), but the killer drives into an old train tunnel and gets away.

Back at the clinic, Rosa shows the police the package in the vent, containing tapes. The recordings are of men and sexual encounters with young schoolgirls, one man mentioning payment and in one instance a girl being raped. Vittoria plays some of the tape for Sylvia's mom and the maid, and they agree that it is the voice of Sylvia. The DA says there are six or seven different voices on the recording. Georgina looks for motorcycles with matching bike tracks, and he learns of a butcher (who might have selected a butcher's cleaver as a weapon of choice) purchasing a bike six weeks ago. Later, the cop tells Silvestri that he talked to the butcher's father, and he said that the boy left three months ago and provided Georgina with a photograph.

The following day, Silvestri passes by Valentini and his daughter Patricia; he stops when Patricia says good morning (recognizing her voice from the recordings). The inspector asks Valentini to his office, and Valentini is furious that his daughter is involved with the schoolgirl prostitution ring. Vittoria tries to show Silvestri a threatening note she received the previous night, but he tells her he gets those all the time. She rips up the note. When the DA is dropped off in a parking garage, she is attacked by the killer. She runs and hides behind cars until her driver returns for something she has forgotten. The driver is killed and Vittoria runs to the elevator. The elevator stops on the third floor and the killer crashes through the door, but runs when someone calls out. The building superintendent calms Vittoria as the killer speeds away.

The cops are looking for a butcher named Roberto. Valentini has Patricia talk to Silvestri, but she can tell them only that a fellow student, Julianna, told her about the prostitution. Julianna is picked up, and Silvestri asks her who Bruno is (she had said the name on the tape). She says she has only talked to him on the phone. The police learn that Bruno is the photographer, Mr. Paglia, but the killer has already paid him a visit and stabbed him in the stomach. Bruno dies in the ambulance. The next day, Silvestri misinforms reporters that he survived the attack and has told the police everything. Vittoria is angry about the inspector's fabrication, but he tells her that he is trying to weed out the killer and/or people responsible for the prostitution ring.

After the story of Bruno's reputed incriminating confession, Sylvia's doctor is found dead in the bath tub from an apparent suicide. Vittoria talks to a quiet girl who attended the doctor's funeral, and the girl tells her of how, for her appointments, the doctor would drug her and do certain things to her. She says that once there was another girl there screaming, and another time a man did things to her. Silvestri returns with many files from the doctor's office, incriminating a number of men involved in the ring (the doctor was "recruiting" the girls). Two young girls telephone the police and say they saw the "fellow on TV" ride into a garage. The police surround the area. When the biker tries to shoot his way out, he is gunned down and killed. Silvestri stops a superior and shows him all the files of people to bring down; the superior tells him that it would take too much time, and with the killer dead and his promotion, he should not care about the prostitution ring. Silvestri is upset, but Vittoria is there with him, and Valentini tears up his resignation.

Dallamano's *What Have They Done to Your Daughters?* has some intense and suspenseful scenes, gory moments, good acting, an intricate murder mystery and, for good measure, a great chase sequence.

What Have You Done to Solange? (aka *Cosa avete fatto a Solange?*; *Solange*) (1972)

Written by Bruno Di Geronimo and Massimo Dallamano; Directed by Massimo Dallamano;

Italian International Film/Clodio Cinematografica/Rialto Film Preben Philipsen GmbH & Co. KG; 102 min.

Cast: Fabio Testi (Enrico Rossini); Christine Galbó (Elizabeth); Karin Baal (Herta Rossini); Joachim Fuchsberger (Commissioner Barth); Günther Stoll (Bascombe); Claudia Butenuth (Brenda); Camille Keaton (Solange); Rainer Denkert (Priest); Giancarlo Badessi (Mr. Erickson); Pilar Castel (Janet); Giovanni Di Bernardo (Helene); Emilia Wolkowicz (Ruth Holden)

Crew: Enrico Melonari (Executive Producer); Leonardo Pescarolo (Producer); Ennio Morricone (Composer); Aristide Massaccesi (Director of Photography); Antonio Siciliano (Editor)

Enrico and Elizabeth are making out in a rowboat, and Elizabeth sits up when she thinks she sees a girl running. She interrupts the kissing session again when she sees a knife being swung. Enrico, thinking she just wants an excuse to stop, angrily rows the boat to shore. Enrico and Elizabeth leave, and a pen is dropped. Enrico, at home with his wife Herta, hears a radio report of a murdered girl. On his way to school, Enrico stops by the crime scene. Inspector Barth is at the school with the headmaster Mr. Leach and some teachers when Enrico walks in late. Enrico leaves, passes by a classroom and sees Elizabeth (she is a student). He goes to gym class and tells his students that their classmate Hilda has been killed.

Later, Enrico asks Elizabeth what she saw when they were together. She says she saw a shadow like a man and "something funny." Enrico asks her not to go to the police, for fear that they will ask the girl who she was with. At home, an irate Herta asks Enrico where he was that morning (he had said his car had broken down to explain his tardiness). She shows him the front page of the newspaper, with a photograph of the crime scene and Enrico pictured in the background. Inspector Barth talks to Enrico and asks him how he found such an obscure locale in such a short time. Barth is shown a pen that was found on the victim's dress, and he talks to Hilda's parents, who say that their daughter went to confession the afternoon she was killed.

Enrico calls Elizabeth at home and gives her an address for a place to meet. She tells her uncle she is going to study with Brenda. She rides her bike and is followed by someone in a car. Enrico lets Elizabeth into a flat, and the two lovers kiss. Someone calls from a pay phone and hangs up. Enrico is at home grading papers, and Herta asks him if he had sex with Hilda. The inspector is at the door, and he slyly places Enrico's pen on the table. Enrico sees it. Herta leaves the room, and Barth states his belief that Enrico was a witness. The teacher admits to being there with Elizabeth and says she claims to have seen the killer. Janet is at home with the maid when a man, saying he is Helen's father, calls and says that Helen needs to borrow Janet's Italian book. As she goes to the car outside, tape is slapped over her mouth and she is driven away. Janet is dragged out of the car and stabbed.

Elizabeth wakes up in bed, thinks back to Hilda running and calls Enrico. Elizabeth runs out to the car when Enrico arrives and tells him she remembers that the killer wore a black habit, like a priest. The next day, Elizabeth tells Mr. Bascombe she knows something about Hilda's murder. He leads her to a room of teachers (including Enrico) where she tells of the priest-like pursuer. Afterwards, Enrico thanks the girl for leaving him out of the story. Later, the killer walks into Enrico's flat and takes the needle off of the record. Elizabeth is drowned in the tub. Outside, a bearded man sees the killer run away.

Enrico is arrested, and Barth interrogates the other teachers of the school. The autopsy report comes in. Hair found under Elizabeth's fingernails turns out to be dead hair. The report also says that Elizabeth was not assaulted and was, in fact, a virgin. The bearded man looks at a line-up of priests and says the man he saw had a beard. Barth is told that, because of the dead hair, it was probably a false beard. Barth tells Herta that Enrico did not kill anyone and that Elizabeth was a virgin, and the teacher seems happy.

Enrico says he wants to find out who killed Elizabeth, and Herta offers to help. In Herta's class, Barth asks the girls if they know a bearded priest. Brenda says that Janet confessed to a priest with a beard at Hilda's funeral. Herta talks to the girls and learns of a secret society. She tells Enrico about the society and says that Hilda and Janet once dated university students, and she has a name.

Enrico goes to see Phillip and asks him about Hilda and Janet; he talks about some of the girls hanging out with him and his friends. He says that, after a while, they no longer had sex with boys after what happened to Solange, a girl who went to the high school and suddenly disappeared. At a funeral for Elizabeth and Janet, a man hands something to Helen, who passes it on to Brenda. Enrico talks to the two girls and asks about Solange, whom they claim to not know. Bascombe warns Enrico about "prying" with the girls. Herta calls some schools and learns about one Solange that did not return. Brenda leaves a note in Henry's mail. The next day, Herta goes to school and Enrico goes to the address where Solange once lived; the woman says she does not know the previous owners. Enrico picks up his mail and drops Brenda's note. The killer calls and suggests he take a vacation, or he will not see "her" again. Enrico calls the rental agents, but the offices are closed.

Downstairs, Enrico is handed the fallen note, with the name Ruth Holden written on it. Enrico goes to her place and finds a dead dog, a bloody shovel and Ruth dead from a sickle. Herta asks Helen and Brenda if they know Ruth, and they respond negatively. The inspector stops them and says that Brenda's mother told him Ruth was the girl's maid. Brenda says she forgot the woman's real name. Enrico, lying in the sun with Herta, says he thinks the killings are linked to Ruth Holden and that the killer dressed as a priest and confessed the girls. A quiet girl stands near the couple and runs away, and a woman calls after her ("Solange!").

The killer calls Brenda and tells her to go somewhere, and the cops set up a trap for the killer at the carnival. Brenda sees Solange on the merry-go-round and takes the quiet girl away. A cop dressed as a priest loses sight of the two girls, and they are seen being driven away by another priest. Bascombe comes into the station and says that his daughter Solange is gone, and he shows a picture of her. The inspector tells an inquisitive Enrico that Solange is sick in the head and has experienced "infantile regression." Enrico, Barth and Herta go to Bascombe's place, and the inspector sees a green pin by a photograph of Solange. Solange is in a room with a restrained Brenda, and the killer tells her to explain everything. Brenda recalls the girls going to see Ruth, and Elizabeth and Hilda trying to talk Solange out of going in and letting "nature take its course." But the others lead her inside and hold her down as Ruth gets a needle and performs a painful abortion on the pregnant girl.

Enrico and Herta go to Janet's place, and Enrico looks for her Italian book. He returns to Bascombe's place with Barth and another officer. When the man does not respond, Enrico kicks in the door and shows a second form Italian book (Solange did not get that far in school). Solange is at the door, and Bascombe returns and hugs his daughter. The men talk to him, and Solange pulls Herta away and leads her to a priest's habit. Herta calls Barth, and he and the cop run into the corridor and find the still-living Brenda. In his office, Bascombe pulls out a gun and shoots himself. Barth tells of the girls' society (signified by green pins), their sex parties and Solange's traumatic abortion. Solange sees her father and cries.

What Have You Done to Solange? is a well-made film, with enough twists and intrigue to keep the film entertaining. Actress Keaton is the grand niece of the great silent film star Buster Keaton; she may be best remembered as the vengeful woman in *I Spit on Your Grave!* (1972).

Appendix A: Slasher Directors

Argento, Dario
The Bird with the Crystal Plumage (1969)
The Cat o' Nine Tails (1971)
Four Flies on Grey Velvet (1971)
Deep Red (1975)
Tenebrae (1982)
Phenomena (1984)
Opera (1987)
Trauma (1992)
Sleepless (2001)

Bava, Lamberto
A Blade in the Dark (1983)
Body Puzzle (1991)

Bava, Mario
Blood and Black Lace (1964)
Hatchet for the Honeymoon (1969)
Bay of Blood (1971)

Blanks, Jamie
Urban Legend (1998)
Valentine (2001)

Burr, Jeff
Stepfather II (1989)
Leatherface: Texas Chainsaw Massacre III (1990)

Craven, Wes
Scream (1996)
Scream 2 (1997)
Scream 3 (2000)

Dallamano, Massimo
What Have You Done to Solange? (1972)
What Have They Done to Your Daughters? (1974)

De Palma, Brian
Sisters (1973)
Dressed to Kill (1980)
Body Double (1984)

Franco, Jess
Bloody Moon (1980)
Faceless (1989)

Fulci, Lucio
The New York Ripper (1982)
Murder Rock (1984)

Fuest, Robert
The Abominable Dr. Phibes (1971)
Dr. Phibes Rises Again (1972)

Hitchcock, Alfred
Psycho (1960)
Frenzy (1972)

Hooper, Tobe
The Texas Chainsaw Massacre (1974)
The Funhouse (1981)
The Texas Chainsaw Massacre 2 (1986)

Lenzi, Umberto
Eyeball (1974)
Welcome to Spring Break (1988)

Lustig, William
Maniac (1980)
Maniac Cop (1988)
Maniac Cop 2 (1990)
Maniac Cop 3: Badge of Silence (1992)

Martino, Sergio
Blade of the Ripper (1970)
Torso (1973)

Miner, Steve
Friday the 13th, Part 2 (1981)
Friday the 13th, Part 3 (1982)
Halloween: H20 (1998)

Shea, Katt
Stripped to Kill (1987)
Stripped to Kill II (1989)

Simpson, Michael A.
Sleepaway Camp II: Unhappy Campers (1988)
Sleepaway Camp III: Teenage Wasteland (1988)

Sole, Alfred
Alice, Sweet Alice (1976)
Pandemonium (1982)

Walker, Pete
Frightmare (1974)
Schizo (1977)
The Comeback (1978)

Appendix B: Slasher Actors and Actresses

Airoldi, Cristina
Blade of the Ripper (1970)
Torso (1973)

Arquette, David
Scream (1996)
Scream 2 (1997)
Scream 3 (2000)

Avram, Cristea
Bay of Blood (1971)
The Slasher (1972)

Baker, Kelly
Don't Open Till Christmas (1984)
Slaughter High (1986)

Berger, Helmet
Bloodstained Butterfly (1971)
Faceless (1989)

Bochner, Hart
Terror Train (1980)
Urban Legends: Final Cut (2000)

Borromeo, Cristian
Tenebrae (1982)
Murder Rock (1984)

Campbell, Bruce
Intruder (1988)
Maniac Cop (1988)
Maniac Cop 2 (1990)

Campbell, Neve
Scream (1996)
Scream 2 (1997)
Scream 3 (2000)

Cauffiel, Jessica
Urban Legends: Final Cut (2000)
Valentine (2001)

Cinieri, Cosimo
The New York Ripper (1982)
Murder Rock (1984)

Cornell, Ellie
Halloween 4: The Return of Michael Myers (1988)
Halloween 5: The Revenge of Michael Myers (1989)

Cox-Arquette, Courtney
Scream (1996)
Scream 2 (1997)
Scream 3 (2000)

Cupisti, Barbara
The New York Ripper (1982)
Stage Fright (1987)
Opera (1987)

Curtis, Jamie Lee
Halloween (1978)
Terror Train (1980)
Prom Night (1980)
Halloween II (1981)
Halloween: H20 (1998)

Davi, Robert
Maniac Cop 2 (1990)
Maniac Cop 3: Badge of Silence (1992)

Devine, Loretta
Urban Legend (1998)
Urban Legends: Final Cut (2000)

Donaldson, Lesleh
Happy Birthday to Me (1981)
Curtains (1983)

Dourif, Brad
Eyes of Laura Mars (1978)
Child's Play (1988)
Child's Play 2 (1990)
Child's Play 3 (1991)
Trauma (1992)
Bride of Chucky (1998)
Urban Legend (1998)

Estevez, Renée
Intruder (1988)
Sleepaway Camp II: Unhappy Campers (1988)

Feldman, Corey
Friday the 13th: The Final Chapter (1984)
Friday the 13th: A New Beginning (1985)

Finley, William
Sisters (1973)
The Funhouse (1981)

Ford, Maria
Stripped to Kill II (1989)
Slumber Party Massacre III (1990)

Franz, Dennis
Dressed to Kill (1980)
Psycho II (1983)
Body Double (1984)

Gayheart, Rebecca
Scream 2 (1997)
Urban Legend (1998)
Urban Legends: Final Cut (2000)

Geller, Sarah Michelle
I Know What You Did Last Summer (1997)
Scream 2 (1997)

George, Christopher
Graduation Day (1981)
Pieces (1981)

Gligorov, Robert
Murder Rock (1984)
Stage Fright (1987)

Gorney, Walt
Friday the 13th (1980)
Friday the 13th, Part 2 (1981)

Granger, Farley
The Slasher (1972)
What Have They Done to Your Daughters? (1974)

Harris, Danielle
Halloween 4: The Return of Michael Myers (1988)
Halloween 5: The Revenge of Michael Myers (1989)
Urban Legend (1998)

Heche, Anne
I Know What You Did Last Summer (1997)
Psycho (1998)

Heigl, Katherine
Bride of Chucky (1998)
Valentine (2001)

Henry, Gregg
Just Before Dawn (1980)
Body Double (1984)

Hewitt, Jennifer Love
I Know What You Did Last Summer (1997)
I Still Know What You Did Last Summer (1998)

Hodder, Kane
Friday the 13th, Part VII: The New Blood (1988)
Friday the 13th, Part VIII: Jason Takes Manhattan (1989)

Hoy, Elizabeth
Bloody Birthday (1981)
Hospital Massacre (1981)

Hussey, Olivia
Black Christmas (1974)
Psycho IV: The Beginning (1990)

Jacoby, Billy
Bloody Birthday (1981)
Hospital Massacre (1981)

Johnson, Ben
The Town That Dreaded Sundown (1976)
Terror Train (1980)

Keith, Sheila
Frightmare (1974)
The Comeback (1978)

Kendell, Suzy
The Bird with the Crystal Plumage (1969)
Torso (1973)

Kennedy, George
Just Before Dawn (1980)
Wacko (1981)

Kennedy, Jamie
Scream (1996)
Scream 2 (1997)
Scream 3 (2000)

Kidder, Margot
Sisters (1973)
Black Christmas (1974)

Kimmell, Dana
Sweet 16 (1981)
Friday the 13th, Part 3 (1982)

King, Adrienne
Friday the 13th (1980)
Friday the 13th, Part 2 (1981)

Kinmont, Kathleen
Halloween 4: The Return of Michael Myers (1988)
Rush Week (1989)

Kinski, Klaus
Slaughter Hotel (1971)
Schizoid (1980)
Crawlspace (1986)

Landon, Laurene
Maniac Cop (1988)
Maniac Cop 2 (1990)

Lavia, Gabriele
Deep Red (1975)
Sleepless (2001)

Leto, Jared
Urban Legend (1998)
American Psycho (2000)

Massey, Anna
Peeping Tom (1960)
Frenzy (1972)

Miles, Vera
Psycho (1960)
Psycho II (1983)
The Initiation (1984)

Mitchell, Cameron
Blood and Black Lace (1964)
The Toolbox Murders (1977)

Mortensen, Viggo
Leatherface: Texas Chainsaw Massacre III (1990)
Psycho (1998)

Munro, Caroline
Maniac (1980)
The Last Horror Film (1984)
Don't Open Till Christmas (1984)
Slaughter High (1986)
Faceless (1989)

Nicolodi, Daria
Deep Red (1975)
Tenebrae (1982)
Phenomena (1984)
Opera (1987)

Occhipinti, Andrea
The New York Ripper (1982)
A Blade in the Dark (1983)

O'Quinn, Terry
The Stepfather (1987)
Stepfather II (1989)

Pataki, Michael
Graduation Day (1981)
Sweet 16 (1981)
Halloween 4: The Return of Michael Myers (1988)

Perkins, Anthony
Psycho (1960)
Psycho II (1983)
Psycho III (1986)
Psycho IV: The Beginning (1990)

Pleasence, Donald
Halloween (1978)
Halloween II (1981)
Alone in the Dark (1982)
Phenomena (1984)
Phantom of Death (1988)
Halloween 4: The Return of Michael Myers (1988)
Halloween 5: The Revenge of Michael Myers (1989)
Halloween: The Curse of Michael Myers (1996)

Price, Vincent
The Abominable Dr. Phibes (1971)
Dr. Phibes Rises Again (1972)
Theater of Blood (1973)

Prinze, Jr., Freddie
I Know What You Did Last Summer (1997)
I Still Know What You Did Last Summer (1998)

Purdom, Edmund
Pieces (1981)
Don't Open Till Christmas (1984)

Saxon, John
Black Christmas (1974)
Tenebrae (1982)
Welcome to Spring Break (1988)

Schreiber, Liev
Scream (1996)
Scream 2 (1997)
Scream 3 (2000)

Shafer, Bobby Ray
Psycho Cop (1989)
Psycho Cop 2 (1992)

Schoelen, Jill
The Stepfather (1987)
Cutting Class (1989)
Popcorn (1991)

Siedow, Jim
The Texas Chainsaw Massacre (1974)
The Texas Chainsaw Massacre 2 (1986)

Spinell, Joe
Maniac (1980)
The Last Horror Film (1984)

Springsteen, Pamela
Sleepaway Camp II: Unhappy Campers (1988)
Sleepaway Camp III: Teenage Wasteland (1988)

Steel, Amy
Friday the 13th, Part 2 (1981)
April Fool's Day (1986)

Stephens, Nancy
Halloween (1978)
Halloween II (1982)
Halloween: H20 (1998)

Stoll, Günther
Bloodstained Butterfly (1971)
What Have You Done to Solange? (1972)

Vincent, Alex
Child's Play (1988)
Child's Play 2 (1990)

Ward, Rachel
Night School (1981)
The Final Terror (1983)

Wasson, Craig
Schizoid (1980)
Body Double (1984)

Watson, Muse
I Know What You Did Last Summer (1997)
I Still Know What You Did Last Summer (1998)

Williams, Caroline
The Texas Chainsaw Massacre 2 (1986)
Stepfather II (1989)

Z'Dar, Robert
Maniac Cop (1988)
Maniac Cop 2 (1990)
Maniac Cop 3: Badge of Silence (1992)

Zuniga, Daphne
The Dorm That Dripped Blood (1981)
The Initiation (1984)

Appendix C: Slasher Writers

Argento, Dario
The Bird with the Crystal Plumage (1969)
The Cat o' Nine Tails (1971)
Four Flies on Grey Velvet (1971)
Deep Red (1975)
Tenebrae (1982)
Phenomena (1984)
Opera (1987)
Trauma (1992)
Sleepless (2001)

Bava, Mario
Blood and Black Lace (1964)
Bay of Blood (1971)

Carpenter, John
Halloween (1978)
Eyes of Laura Mars (1978)
Halloween II (1981)

Clerici, Gianfrano
Bloodstained Butterfly (1971)
The New York Ripper (1982)
Murder Rock (1984)
Phantom of Death (1987)

Cohen, Larry
Maniac Cop (1988)
Maniac Cop 2 (1990)
Maniac Cop 3: Badge of Silence (1992)

Dallamano, Massimo
What Have You Done to Solange? (1972)
What Have They Done to Your Daughters? (1974)

De Palma, Brian
Sisters (1973)
Dressed to Kill (1980)
Body Double (1984)

Ferrini, Franco
Phenomena (1984)
Opera (1987)
Trauma (1992)
Sleepless (2001)

Fulci, Lucio
The New York Ripper (1982)
Murder Rock (1984)

Gastaldi, Ernesto
Blade of the Ripper (1970)
Torso (1973)

Gordon, Fritz
Sleepaway Camp II: Unhappy Campers (1988)
Sleepaway Camp III: Teenage Wasteland (1988)

Guza, Jr., Robert
Prom Night (1980)
Curtains (1983)

Henkel, Kim
The Texas Chainsaw Massacre (1974)
Texas Chainsaw Massacre: The Next Generation (1994)

Hill, Debra
Halloween (1978)
Halloween II (1981)

Holland, Tom
Psycho II (1983)
Child's Play (1988)

Kitrosser, Martin
Friday the 13th, Part 3 (1982)
Friday the 13th: A New Beginning (1985)

Lenzi, Umberto
Eyeball (1974)
Welcome to Spring Break (1988)

Mancini, Don
Child's Play (1988)
Child's Play 2 (1990)
Child's Play 3 (1991)
Bride of Chucky (1998)

Mannino, Vincenzo
The New York Ripper (1982)
Murder Rock (1984)
Phantom of Death (1987)

McGillvray, David
Frightmare (1974)
Schizo (1977)

Ray, Marc B.
Scream Bloody Murder (1973)
Stepfather III (1992)

Sacchetti, Dardano
The New York Ripper (1982)
A Blade in the Dark (1983)

Shea, Katt
Stripped to Kill (1987)
Stripped to Kill II (1989)

Stefano, Joseph
Psycho (1960/1998)
Psycho IV: The Beginning (1990)

Williamson, Kevin
Scream (1996)
I Know What You Did Last Summer (1997)
Scream 2 (1997)

Appendix D: Slasher Composers

Bell, Wayne
The Texas Chainsaw Massacre (1974)
Texas Chainsaw Massacre: The Next Generation (1994)

Beltrami, Marco
Scream (1996)
Scream 2 (1997)
Scream 3 (2000)

Boswell, Simon
Phenomena (1984)
Stage Fright (1987)

Carpenter, John
Halloween (1978)
Halloween II (1981)

Chattaway, Jay
Maniac (1980)
Maniac Cop (1988)
Maniac Cop 2 (1990)

Cipriani, Stelvio
Bay of Blood (1971)
What Have They Done to Your Daughters? (1974)

De Angelis, Guido & Maurizio
Torso (1973)
A Blade in the Dark (1983)

Donaggio, Pino
Dressed to Kill (1980)
Body Double (1984)
Crawlspace (1986)
Phantom of Death (1987)
Trauma (1992)

Fiedel, Brad
Just Before Dawn (1980)
Night School (1981)

Gaslini, Giorgio
The Slasher (1972)
Deep Red (1975)

Herrmann, Bernard
Psycho (1960/1998)
Sisters (1973)

Hooper, Tobe
The Texas Chainsaw Massacre (1974)
The Texas Chainsaw Massacre 2 (1986)

Howarth, Alan
Halloween II (1981)
Halloween 4: The Return of Michael Myers (1988)
Halloween 5: The Revenge of Michael Myers (1989)
Halloween: The Curse of Michael Myers (1996)

Kempel, Arthur
Graduation Day (1981)
Wacko (1981)

Manfredini, Harry
Friday the 13th (1980)
Friday the 13th, Part 2 (1981)
Friday the 13th, Part 3 (1982)
Friday the 13th: The Final Chapter (1984)
Friday the 13th: A New Beginning (1985)
Friday the 13th, Part VI: Jason Lives (1986)

Slaughter High (1986)
Friday the 13th, Part VII: The New Blood (1988)

Marangolo, Agostino
Deep Red (1975) (w/Goblin)
Sleepless (2001) (w/Goblin)

Mollin, Fred
Friday the 13th, Part VII: The New Blood (1988)
Friday the 13th, Part VIII: Jason Takes Manhattan (1989)

Morante, Massimo
Deep Red (1975) (w/Goblin)
Tenebrae (1982)
Sleepless (2001) (w/Goblin)

Morricone, Ennio
The Bird with the Crystal Plumage (1969)
The Cat o' Nine Tails (1971)
Four Flies on Grey Velvet (1971)
What Have You Done to Solange? (1972)

Myers, Stanley
Frightmare (1974)
Schizo (1977)
The Comeback (1978)

Ober, Arlon
Bloody Birthday (1981)
Hospital Massacre (1981)

Oliverio, James
Sleepaway Camp II: Unhappy Campers (1988)
Sleepaway Camp III: Teenage Wasteland (1988)

Ottman, John
Halloween: H20 (1998)
Urban Legends: Final Cut (2000)

Pignatelli, Fabio
Deep Red (1975) (w/Goblin)
Tenebrae (1982)
Sleepless (2001) (w/Goblin)

Revell, Graeme
Child's Play 2 (1990)
Psycho IV: The Beginning (1990)
Bride of Chucky (1998)

Simonetti, Claudio
Deep Red (1975) (w/Goblin)
Tenebrae (1982)
Phenomena (1984)
Opera (1987)
Welcome to Spring Break (1988)
Sleepless (2001) (w/Goblin)

Wyman, Bill
Phenomena (1984)
Opera (1987)

Young, Christopher
The Dorm That Dripped Blood (1981)
Urban Legend (1998)

Zaza, Paul
Prom Night (1980)
My Bloody Valentine (1981)
Curtains (1983)
Popcorn (1991)
Prom Night IV: Deliver Us from Evil (1991)

Zittrer, Carl
Black Christmas (1974)
Prom Night (1980)

Index

Numbers in *italics* represent photographs.

A

The A-Team 27
The Abominable Dr. Phibes 2, 6, 9–10, 12, 14, 21
Above the Law 116
The Addiction 102
Airoldi, Cristina 41
Alexander, Jason 66
Alfred Hitchcock Presents 233, 341
Alice, Sweet Alice 8–9, 14, 22, *24*
Alien 8
Ally McBeal 76
Alone in the Dark 25, 66
American Psycho 6, 9, 11, 27, *29*
Anders, Luana 94
Anderson, Anthony 341
Anderson, Melissa Sue *154*, 156
Angel 344
Anguish 4, 6, 12, 29
Anthropophagus 298
Apartment Zero 316
Apocalypse Now 94
April Fool's Day 9, 11, 13, 16, 31, 279
Arana, Tom 60
Argento, Asia 291, 334
Argento, Dario 1–2, 4–6, 8, 17, 36, 68, *91*, 92, 118, *214*, 216, 224, 313, 331, 334
Argento, Fiore 224
Ashes of Time 233
The Avengers 311
Avram, Cristea 277

B

Bad Lieutenant 102
The Bad Seed 196
Bale, Christian 6, *29*, 29
Barbeau, Adrienne 213
Barker, Clive 97, 194
Baron Blood 157
Bartel, J. 307
Bass, Saul 2

Bava, Lamberto 3, 6, 8, 39, 60, 208, 313
Bava, Mario 5–6, 10, 13, 34, 39, 43, 125, 157, 277
Bay of Blood 6, 10, 33, 125
Bender, Lawrence 177
Benton, Barbi 167
Beverly Hills 90210 276
Bianchi, Mario 199
The Bird with the Crystal Plumage 5–6, 17, 35, 92, 331
The Birds 233
Black, Jack 173
Black Christmas 5, 8, 11–12, 15–19, *18*, 36, 37
Black Sabbath 157
A Blade in the Dark 6, 38, 208
Blade of the Ripper 40
Blair, Linda 256
Blees, Robert 99
Bloch, Robert 238
Blood and Black Lace 5, 41, 157
Blood Feast 6
Blood Hook 8–9, 14–16, 43
Blood Rage 9, 45
Bloodmoon 47
Bloodstained Butterfly 10, 49
Bloody Birthday 9, 51
Bloody Moon 5, 52
Bloody Murder 3, 54
Blue Lagoon 24
Bochner, Hart 316
Body Double 4, 14, 56, 251
Body Puzzle 3–5, 12, 58
Boehn, Carl 218
The Bold and the Beautiful 162
Bonsall, Brian 9, 194
Boreanaz, David 343, *343*
The Borrower 160
Bradford, Jesse 73
The Brady Bunch 288
Brennan, Eileen 218
Bride of Chucky 8, 60

The Bride with White Hair 62
Brides of Dracula 8
Briggs, Joe Bob 320
The Brood 38, 86
Bruiser 62
Buffy the Vampire Slayer 343
The Burning 2, 12, 15–16, 64, *65*
Burns, Marilyn 322

C

Campbell, Bruce 107, 177, 188
Campbell, Neve *255*
Cannibal Ferox 349
Cannibal Holocaust 222
Cannibal! The Musical 122
Capobianco, Carmine 243
Carlson, Les 38
Carlton, Hope Marie 293
Carnival of Souls 199
Carpenter, John 1, *3*, 16–17, 143, 145
Carvey, Dana 145
The Cat o' Nine Tails 66
Cauffiel, Jessica 341, 343
Chaney, Lon, Jr. 94
Chateau, René 113
Cheerleader Camp 2, 5, 7, 12–13, 16–17, 68
Cherry Falls 12, 70, *71*, 264
Children Shouldn't Play with Dead Things 38, 227
Child's Play 4, 8–9, 73
Child's Play 2 75
Child's Play 3 8, 76
Christian, Claudia 190
A Christmas Story 38
Chungking Express 233
The Church 8
Cinderella (1977) 142
Cinieri, Cosimo 208
Ciupka, Richard *85*, 86
Clark, Bob 5, 17, *18*, 38, 227
Clay, Andrew 347

363

Clemm, Susanna 100
Clinton, Mildred 24
A Clockwork Orange 94, 310
Coffy 94
Cohen, Larry 188
Color Me Blood Red 78, *79*
The Comeback 80
Conder, Candi *79*
The Conversation 94
Coppola, Francis Ford 5, 94
Corman, Roger 261
Craven, Wes 1, 8, 253, *255*, 256, 327
Crawlspace 4, 82
Crichton, Michael 229
Cronenberg, David 38, 86
Crouching Tiger, Hidden Dragon 62
Cunningham, Sean S. 2, 122
Curtains 84, *85*
Curtis, Jamie Lee 3, 145, *228*
Cutting Class 1, 5, 11, 12, 86

D

Daily, Elizabeth 347
Dallamano, Massimo 350
D'Amato, Joe 225, 298
Dance of the Damned 237
Dane, Lawrence *154*
The Dark Half 64, 97
Davi, Robert 190
David, Lou *65*
Davis, Andrew 116
Dawn of the Dead 184
Dawson's Creek 171, 339
Dead of Night 5, 88
The Dead Zone 38
Dementia 13 5, 92
Demons 8
De Niro, Robert 274
Deodato, Ruggero 222
De Palma, Brian 4–5, 58, 100, 140, 251, *272*, 274
Devine, Loretta 341
DiCaprio, Leonardo 29
Dickinson, Angie 58
Die Hard 316
Dr. Phibes Rises Again 97
Donnelly, Dennis *328*
Don't Open Till Christmas 5, 14, 16, 94
The Dorm That Dripped Blood 10–11, 16–17, 96
Dougal, Miles David 242
Dourif, Brad 74, 78, 111
Doyle, Christopher 233
Dressed to Kill 5, 14, 58, 99
The Driller Killer 12, 15, 101
Drive-In Massacre 6, 10, 17, 102
Dugan, John 318
Dunaway, Faye 111

E

Eating Raoul 268
Edge of the Axe 1, 15, 103

Ellis, Bret Easton 11
Estevez, Emilio 177
Estevez, Renée 177
Evil Dead II: Dead by Dawn 107, 177
Evil Ed 6, 105
The Exorcist 196
Eyeball 4, 107
Eyes of Laura Mars 6, 109

F

Faceless 4, 111
Family Ties 9
Fenech, Edwige 41
Ferdin, Pamelyn 329
Ferrara, Abel 102
Final Exam 11, 14, 113
The Final Terror 9, 114
Finch, Jon *119*
Fincher, David 88
Fine, Billy 206
Finley, William 140, *272*, 274
Fisher, Carrie 261
Five Man Army 36
The Fly 38
For Your Eyes Only 182
Foree, Ken 184
Foreman, Deborah 33
Forster, Robert 192
Foster, Barry *119*
Four Flies on Grey Velvet 4, 116
Franco, Jess 4–5, 54, 113
Frank, Carol 296
Franklin, Richard 235
Fredrick, Lynne 249
Frenzy 6, 118, *119*
Friday the 13th 3, 12–13, 16, 56, 120, 127, 143
Friday the 13th: The Final Chapter 7, 127
Friday the 13th: A New Beginning 5, 7, 129, 134
Friday the 13th, Part 2 7, 12, 34, 122, *124*
Friday the 13th, Part 3 4, 7, 12, 125, 137
Friday the 13th, Part VI: Jason Lives 131, 134
Friday the 13th, Part VII: The New Blood 7, 133, 137
Friday the 13th, Part VIII: Jason Takes Manhattan 5, 135
Frightmare 82, 137
Frogs 99
From Dusk Till Dawn 8
Fuest, Robert 2, 22
The Fugitive 116
Fulci, Lucio 5, 10, 198, 199, 208
The Funhouse 3, 139

G

Garris, Cynthia 238
Garris, Mick 238
Gaslini, Giorgio 92
Gayheart, Rebecca 339

General Hospital 162
George, Christopher 225
George, Linda Day 225
Germann, Greg 76
The Gift 97
Gillette, Warrington *124*
Gilligan's Island 332
Gladiator 60
Gleason, Jackie 24
Goblin 92, 313
The Godfather 94
Graduation Day 2, 11, 13, 15, 17, 140
Griffin, Lynn *18*

H

Haley, Jackie Earle 192
Halloween 1, 3, *3*, 8–9, 13, 16, 17–19, 140, 142
Halloween: The Curse of Michael Myers 149
Halloween: H20 151
Halloween II 3, 5, 143
Halloween III: Season of the Witch 9, 143
Halloween 4: The Return of Michael Myers 145
Halloween 5: The Revenge of Michael Myers 147
Hansen, Gunnar *318*
Happy Birthday to Me 5, 8, 153, *154*
Harris, Danielle 147, 149
Harron, Mary 11, *29*, 29
Hartman, Valerie *285*
Hatchet for the Honeymoon 14–15, 156
Hauer, Rutger 163
Haven, Annette 58
Helfend, Dennis 266
Hellraiser 78, 97, 194
Hemmings, David *91*
Henry: Portrait of a Serial Killer 5, 7, 158, *159*
Herrmann, Bernard 2, 153, 233, 274
Hess, David 327
Hickox, Douglas *323*
Hicks, Danny 177
The Hidden 27, 66
Hide and Go Shriek 1, 15, 145, 160
Hill, Debra 143
Hill, Jack 94
Hindle, Art 38
Hitchcock, Alfred 2–3, 6, *119*, 120, 143, 153, 233, 235, 237
The Hitcher 7–8, 162
Holland, Tom 75
Home Sweet Home 3, 164
Hooper, Tobe 2–3, 140, *318*, 318, 320
Hospital Massacre 3, 16, 52, 165
House of Death 6, 167
Hoy, Elizabeth 52
Hunter, Holly 66

Hunter, Simon 5, 90
Hussey, Olivia 38, 73, 238

I
I Know What You Did Last Summer 5, 153, 169
I Spit on Your Grave! 352
I Still Know What You Did Last Summer 7, 171
The Initiation 3, 10, 173
Interview with the Vampire 88
Intruder 2, 175

J
Jackson, Joshua 339
Jacoby, Billy 52
Jordan, Neil 88
Joseph, Don 79, 80
Just Before Dawn 4, 8–9, 177

K
Kanan, Sean 162
Keaton, Buster 352
Keaton, Camille 352
Keith, Sheila 82
Kendall, Suzy 331
Kennedy, Jamie 14, 256, 258
Kidder, Margot 38, *272*, 274
Kiger, Susan 169
Killer Workout 3, 178
Kinski, Klaus 84, 251
Kirschner, David 74
Knightriders 64
Kubrick, Stanley 94, 310

L
L.A. Confidential 60
Lahaie, Brigitte 113
Landis, John 238
Larrain, Les 212
The Last Horror Film 6, 180
The Last House on the Left 34, 327
Laurence, Ashley
Lavia, Gabriele 291
Leatherface: Texas Chainsaw Massacre III 182
Leigh, Janet 153
Leigh, Jennifer Jason 163
Lemieux, Rachel 196
Lemon, Chris 178
Lemon, Jack 178
Lenzi, Umberto 4, 109, 349
Leone, Sergio 36
Levy, Philip 266
Lewis, Herschell Gordon 6, *79*, 80
Lillard, Matthew 256
Liquid Sky 24
Little House on the Prairie 156
Loomis, Nancy 3
Lustig, William 5, *185*, 188
Lynch, Paul 228

M
MacKinnon, Derek 316
Macnee, Patrick 311

Magee, Patrick 94
Malick-Sánchez, Keram *71*
Mallon, James 8, 45
Maniac 17, 182, 184, *185*
Maniac Cop 5, 186
Maniac Cop 2 188
Maniac Cop 3: Badge of Silence 190
Mansion of the Doomed 142
Mariné, Juan 225
Marsillach, Cristina *214*
Martin 64
Martin, Anne-Marie 229
Martino, Sergio 41, 331
Massey, Anna 218
Mathews, Thom 133
Maylam, Tony 65
McConaughey, Matthew 322
McCormack, Patty 196
McDowell, Malcolm 310
McGowan, Rose *255*
McMaster, Niles 24
McNaughton, John *159*, 160
Melrose Place 97
Mewes, Jason 261
Midnight Cowboy 140
Midnight Express 22
Mihalka, George 1
Mikey 5, 7, 9, 192
Miles, Sylvia 140
Miller, Jason 196
Miller, Linda 24
Miner, Steve 34, *124*, 125
Mitchell, Cameron *328*, 329
Mitchum, Chris 113
Mitchum, Robert 113
Mommy 14, 194
Montefiori, Luigi 298
Moonshine Mountain 80
Moosbrugger, Christoph 54
Morante, Massimo 313
Morley, Robert *323*
Mortensen, Viggo 184
Ms. 45 102
Munro, Caroline 22, 99, 182
Murder Rock 5, 196
The Murder Secret 198
Murphy, Brittany *71*
The Mutilator 2, 9, 199
My Bloody Valentine 1–2, 5, 7, 13, 15–16, 201
Mystery Science Theater 3000 45

N
Nail Gun Massacre 15, 203
Neal, Edwin *318*
New Year's Evil 6, 204
The New York Ripper 10, 206
Nicolodi, Daria 17, 92, 313
Night School 5, 208
Nightmare 210
A Nightmare on Elm Street 8, 256
Niven, Kip 206
North, Virginia 22, 99

O
Occhipinti, Andrea 208
On Her Majesty's Secret Service 22
Once Upon a Time in the West 36
Open House 9, 212
Opera 6, 8, 213, *214*
O'Quinn, Terry 300, 302, 304
Ormsby, Alan 227
Ottman, John 341

P
Palillo, Ron 133
Pandemonium 216
Parker, Trey 122
Partain, Paul 322
Pataki, Michael 142
Patric, Jason 24
Pau, Peter 62
Pee Wee's Big Adventure 347
Peeping Tom 3, 5, 218, *218*
Perkins, Anthony 233, 237
Phantom of Death 220
Phantom of the Paradise 140, 274
Phenomena 1, 7–8, 12, 222
Pieces 3, 224
Pignatelli, Fabio 313
Pigozzi, Luciano 157
Pitt, Brad 88
Pleasence, Donald 27, 149, 151, 222
Poison Ivy 237
Popcorn 15–16, 225
Popeye 225
Porky's 38
Porky's II: The Next Day 38
Posey, Parker 261
Powell, Michael 3, *218*, 220
Praetorius, Scott 212
Predator 8
Pretty Baby 24
Price, Vincent 22, 99, *323*, 325
Prince 316
Prom Night 2–3, 10–13, 227, *228*
Prom Night IV: Deliver Us from Evil 229
Psycho (1960) 2–3, 9, 14, 140, 143, 153, 231, 235, 237
Psycho (1998) 233
Psycho II 7, 17, 75, 233
Psycho III 235
Psycho IV: The Beginning 237
Psycho Cop 238
Psycho Cop 2 5, 240
Psychos in Love 242
Pulp Fiction 177

R
Raimi, Sam 97, 107, 177, 188
Raimi, Ted 177
Reems, Harry 277
The Return of the Living Dead 133
Return of the Living Dead, Part II 133
Reubens, Paul 218

Rifkin, Adam 242
Rigg, Diana 22, 325
Robins, Eva 313
Robinson, Andrew 78
Romero, George A. 63, 97, 184
Rooker, Michael 159, 160
Rosenthal, Rick 145
Rubin, Andy 237
The Rugrats 347
Rush Week 11, 243
Russell, Tina 277

S

Salt, Jennifer 15
Savini, Tom 66, 127, 129, 186, 212
Scary Movie 245
Schizo 247
Schizoid 250
Schmoeller, David 84
Schoelen, Jill 88, 300
Schoolnik, Skip 145
School's Out 5, 251
Scorsese, Martin 220
Scream 1, 7, 9, 10, 12–14, 16, 72, 171, 253, 255, 258, 343
Scream 2 6, 10–11, 153, 256
Scream 3 6, 259
Scream Bloody Murder 261
Scuddamore, Simon 279
Selden, Ken 72
Seven 88
Shafer, Bobby Ray 240, 242
Shea, Katt 237
Sheen, Charlie 177
Sheen, Martin 177
Shelton, Marley 343, *343*
Shepherd, John 134
Sheppard, Paula 24
Sheridan, Dave 247
Shields, Brooke 24
Sholder, Jack 27, 66
Shriek If You Know What I Did Last Friday the Thirteenth 262
Shultz, Dwight 27
Shusett, Ronald 116
Siedow, Jim 318
Silent Madness 7, 10, 264
Silent Night, Bloody Night 9, 266
Silent Night, Deadly Night 16, 96, 268, 271
Silent Night, Deadly Night 2 270
Simonetti, Claudio 313
Simpson, Michael A. 1, *285*
Singin in the Rain 169
Sisters 15, 271, *272*
Sisters of Death 10–11, 274
The 6th Day 316
The Slasher 5, 276
Slaughter High 2, 11, 13, 16, 277
Slaughter Hotel 16, 279
Slaughterhouse 10, 281
Sleepaway Camp 2, 8–9, 282
Sleepaway Camp II: Unhappy Campers 7, 284, *285*

Sleepaway Camp III: Teenage Wasteland 1, 8, 16, 287
Sleepless 289
The Slumber Party Massacre 3, 10, 291, 293
Slumber Party Massacre III 10, 293
Smith, Kevin 261
Smith, Paul 225
Soavi, Michele 5, 8, 40, 60, 216, 224, 298, 313
Sole, Alfred 8, *24*
Sorority House Massacre 11, 295
Spencer, Bud 118
Spider Baby 94
Spiegel, Scott 177
Spinell, Joe 182, *185*, 186
Spottiswoode, Roger *314*, 316
Springsteen, Pamela 286, 288
The Spy Who Loved Me 182
Stage Fright 5, 15–16, 296
Steel, Amy 33, 125
The Stepfather 7, 298
Stepfather II 300
Stepfather III 302
Stevens, Casey 228
Stevens, Fisher 66
Stone, Oliver 29
Stripped to Kill 237, 304
Stripped to Kill II 7, 306
Sunset Beach 162
The Surgeon 14, 307
Suspiria 92
Sweet 16 310
Switchblade Sisters 94

T

Tarantino, Quentin 177
Tata, Joe 276
Taylor, Don 36
Tenebrae 5–6, 10, 12, 17, 311
Terror Train 2, 16, 313, *314*
Tessario, Duccio 10
The Texas Chainsaw Massacre 2, 6, 9–10, 12, 15, 140, 184, 316, *318*, 322
The Texas Chainsaw Massacre 2 319
Texas Chainsaw Massacre: The Next Generation 320
Theater of Blood 322, *323*
They Call Me Trinity 118
Thibeault, Debi 243
The Thing 143
The Thing from Another World 143
Thomas, Henry 238
Thompson, J. Lee *154*
To All a Goodnight 325
To Sir, with Love 331
Tomassi, Vincenzo 199
The Toolbox Murders 14–15, 327, 328
Torso 5, 8, 41, 329
Tourist Trap 84

Towles, Tom 160
The Town That Dreaded Sundown 10, 17, 331
Trauma 6, 8, 14, 332
Trick or Treats 334
Trinity Is Still My Name 118
Turner, Guinevere 29
Turner and Hooch 316
Twin Peaks 76
Twister 229

U

The Untold Story 336
Urban Legend 5, 7, 10–11, 15, 72, 337
Urban Legends: Final Cut 6, 339
The Usual Suspects 247

V

Valentine 341, *343*
Valley Girl 347
Van Sant, Gus 233
Vanity 316
Vaughan, Vince 235
Vernon, Howard 113
Vertigo 237
Video Murders 15, 344
Videodrome 38
von Sydow, Max 291

W

Wacko 15–16, 345
Walker, Pete 82, 249
Wallace, Tommy Lee 143
Wasson, Craig 251
Weigel, Teri 70
Weinstein, Bob 66
Weinstein, Harvey 66
Welcome Back, Kotter 133
Welcome to Spring Break 5, 9, 347
Wells, Dawn 332
West Side Story 288
What Have They Done to Your Daughters? 349
What Have You Done to Solange? 350
Williams, Caroline 184
Williamson, Kevin 153, 171, 256
Wilson, Robert Brian 270
Wilson, Thomas F. 33
Wincott, Jeff 229
Wincott, Michael 229
Wong, Anthony 337
Woronov, Mary 268
Wright, Geoffrey 12, *71*, 72

Y

Yagher, Kevin 75
York, Michael 222
Young, Christopher 97
Yu, Ronny 62

Z

Zabriskie, Grace 76
Zellweger, Renee 322
Zuniga, Daphne 97, 175

www.ingramcontent.com/pod-product-compliance
Lightning Source LLC
Chambersburg PA
CBHW081535300426
44116CB00015B/2639